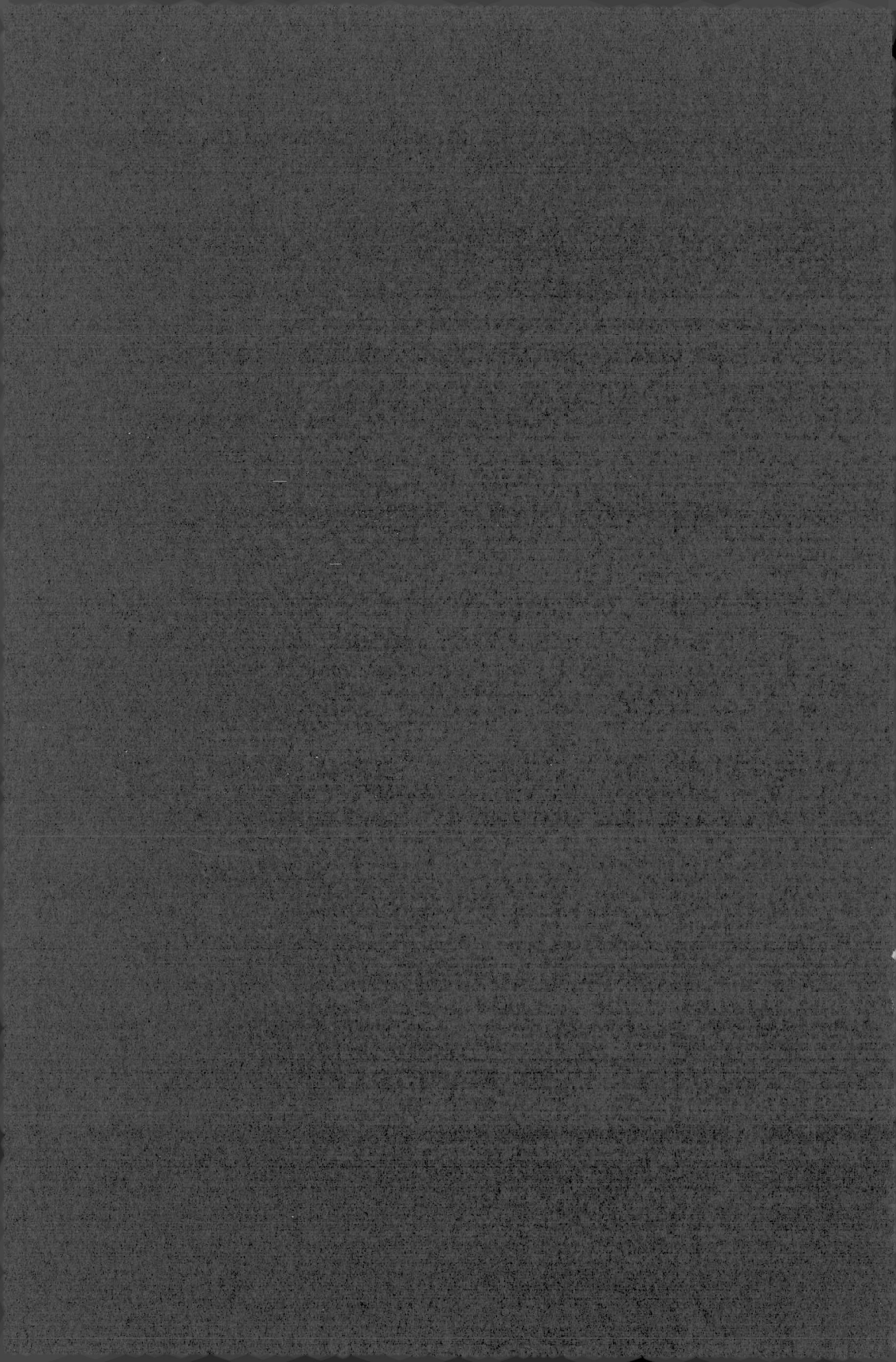

POSTWAR POLITICIAN

POSTWAR

The Life of Former Prime Minister MASAYOSHI ŌHIRA

POLITICIAN

Seizaburō Satō/Ken'ichi Kōyama/Shunpei Kumon

Introduction by Edwin O. Reischauer
Translated by William R. Carter

KODANSHA INTERNATIONAL LTD.
Tokyo and New York

Distributed in the United States by Kodansha Internation-
al/USA Ltd., 114 Fifth Avenue, New York, New York 10011.
Published by Kodansha International Ltd., 17-14 Otowa
1-chome, Bunkyo-ku, Tokyo 112 and Kodansha Internation-
al/USA Ltd., 114 Fifth Avenue, New York, New York 10011.
Copyright © 1990 by the Masayoshi Ōhira Memorial Foundation. All rights reserved. Printed in Japan.
ISBN 4-7700-1499-6 (in Japan)
First edition, 1990

Library of Congress Cataloging-in-Publication Data

Satō, Seizaburō, 1932–
    (Kaisō no Ōhira Masayoshi. English)
    Postwar politician: the life of former Prime Minister
    Masayoshi Ōhira /by Seizaburō Satō, Ken'ichi Kōyama,
    Shunpei Kumon; translated by William R. Carter.
        p.   cm.
    Translation of: Kaisō no Ōhira Masayoshi.
    —ISBN 0-87011-899-0 (USA)
    1. Ōhira, Masayoshi. 1910–. 2. Prime ministers—Japan–
    –Biography. 3. Japan—Politics and government—1945– I.
    Kōyama, Ken'ichi, 1933–. II. Kumon, Shunpei. 1935–. III.
    Title. DS890.0453S28 1990
    952.04'092—dc20
    (B)
                                                        90-4684

CONTENTS

TRANSLATOR'S NOTE

In this English translation, Japanese names are given in the Japanese order, with the family name first. Romanization of Japanese follows the Hepburn system. Chinese proper names are spelled using the *pinyin* system, with the exception of those associated with Taiwan, where the Wade-Giles system is used. Korean personal names are spelled according to the preference of the individuals in question.

The large number of sources, which include Ōhira's 1978 autobiography and interviews with persons who knew him well, are not cited in detail, either in the Japanese or this English edition. Excerpts from Ōhira's UN speeches and policy speeches before the Diet follow translations distributed to the media at the time. Book-format reference materials and Ōhira's own writings are listed in the Bibliography at the end of this volume.

W. R. C.

Introduction

Ōhira Masayoshi and I were both born in 1910, the forty-third year of the Meiji period (1868–1912). In Japan, especially back in those days, people counted their age from the year of their birth, making us both seventy-one the year he died, although actually he had been born seven months before me. He was a mere 217 days older, but he would playfully like to refer to himself as *senpai* ("senior") and me as the *kōhai* ("junior").

Our closeness of age, however, was not the main reason why I felt a special sense of intimacy with Ōhira. He seemed at first a reserved man, not easy to know, but gradually I developed a deep sense of friendship, trust, and respect for him. In fact, I began to see in him a future leader of Japan.

Ōhira was a man who stood out by seeming to hang back. He was a leader by seeming to be a follower. That was because he had a vision of the future, when most Japanese were confused and looking frantically around for guidance. But he realized that there must be broad understanding before progress could be made. He never seemed to push others because he understood that they must first be ready to follow. However, his vision stretched far into the future, when a global world order would be necessary for all nations. He could see that Japan was not ready for this yet, but he bided his time, pushing delicately without angering others.

Ōhira was a natural politician of great skill. He could have tried to push Japan much further than he did during his lifetime, but if he had, he probably would have lost his chance at leadership to some less dynamic or more limited man. Today Japan is one of the great world powers, exercising as much industrial and financial power as any country ever has. But it was not as strong when he was a national leader, and there were deep resentments on the part of the other industrialized nations, many of the countries of Asia, and especially Japan's close neighbors. Ōhira realized that it would

9

take time to achieve his goals, but he clearly had a plan for a strong Japan to take a leading role in creating a global order of peace. He apparently understood that the only road open to Japan and to the world was one of world trade and universal justice. He moved slowly, like Aesop's tortoise, sometimes hardly seeming to move at all. But he had a clear objective and firm principles. He seemed to me a giant in his own unobtrusive way.

Ōhira was a brilliant man of great energy who subtly concealed these attributes. They, together with his outstanding financial abilities and breadth of vision, would have made him a prominent political leader in any case. But what made him truly outstanding were his farsightedness and deeply held principles for a better world.

I have often wished that there was a clear distinction in Japanese between the words "politician" and "statesman." Both are commonly translated as *seijika*, but there is a world of difference between the two. A statesman has a clear sense of principles that govern his life. He has, of course, the skills and qualities with which politicians effectively manipulate people, but he has something more—a set of clear guidelines and the strength to live by them.

Once Ōhira told me that he was a Christian, and later I learned of his work as a street evangelist in his youth and his more mature study of the No Church Movement of Christianity under Yanaihara Tadao. I suspect that it was this Christian background that gave Ōhira the character and principles that made him a statesman and not just a politician. He never discussed with me in detail his religious concepts, nor did he even outline the political principles that underlay his daily maneuvering and his vision of the future world. I gathered some idea of what was in his mind and motivated him from bits and pieces of our conversations together. From the general attitudes he took and many small acts on his part, there emerged not just a picture of a masterful politician, but the figure of a consummate statesman. The more I saw of him, the more convinced I became that he was a potential world leader.

Ōhira and I were not born far apart in space any more than in time. His birthplace was a village near the eastern end of the Inland Sea at the northeast end of Shikoku, the smallest of the three main islands that surround that sea. His village was only about four hundred miles west of Tokyo, where I first saw the light of day. The distance was not great at that time, when railways already skirted the mountainsides of Japan and steamships plied its waters. But it was no short run as from Boston to Philadelphia or Chicago to St. Louis. The distance, in fact, was in a sense immense, covering great differences of culture and perhaps a century of time. Japan still had a lot of catching up to do to equal the West, and

Ōhira's Kagawa Prefecture was still mired in many of its old feudal ways. In 1910, it remained a long, long way from Kagawa to Tokyo.

The cultural gap between an American boy and his Japanese contemporaries was even greater. There were extremely few Westerners in Japan in those days. I doubt that the young Masayoshi ever laid eyes on a *Seiyō-jin*, as we were called at the time, until his late teens. I, of course, saw thousands of Japanese boys all around me, but did not get to mix with them. They mockingly would shout *gudo-bai* (good-bye) at me and a phrase for which I have never been able to find an interpretation—*ijin pappa, neko pappa*—which perhaps suggested that our variously colored eyes and incomprehensible speech were as mystifying as those of cats.

The Japanese boys played baseball with a small hard rubber ball that sailed magnificently when squarely hit, but even though I would hang around their games for hours, hoping that I would be allowed to join in, never once was I invited. The in-group of Japanese boys obviously had no place for an obvious outsider like me.

In my early years, the age of Rudyard Kipling still lingered on. I do not mean to suggest that I accepted the attitudes of Kipling. My parents were educational missionaries, helping to found new schools and accepting without question a position of subordination to their Japanese superiors in the administration of these schools. They had the deepest respect for the Christian leaders with whom they came in contract. My father was somewhat noted for his study of Japanese Buddhism, pointing out, to the irritation of some of his Western colleagues, the absurdity of attempting, without a thorough knowledge of Japanese Buddhism, to discuss such a sophisticated and intellectually advanced religion. My parents lacked the slightest trace of the Raj mentality that most British at that time had in Asia, and they paid full respect to Japanese officials of all types. This, after all, was their country, and they had the right to organize and rule it as they saw fit. Most of the time we had two servants and sometimes three, all of whom we treated as members of the family. They participated in our evening worship and played a large role in raising us children.

I naturally absorbed these attitudes, and as I grew older I took great pride in Japan's economic and military strength and the speed with which it was modernizing itself. We few Western children living in Tokyo were proud of our city as the capital of a great empire. We despised the haughty and supercilious Westerners from Yokohama and Kobe, where more of the obnoxious attitudes of the nineteenth century seemed to linger on. We could understand the resentment of the Japanese to the contempt many Westerners showed them, and their feeling that there was something unfair in Japan being limited to a relatively small slice of empire simply because it had appeared late on the military scene. The insistence of Russia, Germany, and France—that through a clearly racial power play Japan should be forced to disgorge much of what it had managed to pick up in its war with China in 1895—outraged us almost as much as it did the Japanese themselves. That these same three European powers, like a pack of hyenas, then wolfed down what the Japanese had been forced to give up only heightened our indignation. The arrogant dismissal by the Americans, Canadians, and Australians of a proposed clause on racial equality at the Versailles Peace Conference in 1919 seemed to us, as to most Japanese, a needless insult to a country that deserved to be treated as an equal. This act seemed clearly to be just one more way to erect barriers to "Oriental" immigration, designed without the slightest show of tact.

We youngsters, who were known as B.I.J., or "born in Japan," were obviously Asian nationalists. Our attitudes were not limited to Japan, even though we were as blind to Japanese imperialism in Korea and Taiwan as were the Japanese themselves. We disapproved strongly of the European empires that incorporated most of the rest of Asia, and the arrogance and blatant sense of superiority most Westerners exhibited toward Asians. It was not until Japan returned to imperialism in the 1920s, after most other countries had given up empire building, that I began to change my attitude toward its foreign policy and saw the menace to world peace of Japanese imperialism.

I was, of course, not entirely lacking in Japanese friends. I spoke the language well enough to get around with ease. Some of my father's students, in their desire to improve their English, would pal around with us children despite the discrepancy in age. A few Japanese, having been raised partially abroad, attended our small American School In Japan and, in the spirit of the American melting pot, were absorbed fully into our group. Some Japanese of aristocratic background would mix with us from time to time for one reason or another, but I had few Japanese friends before my graduation from high school in 1927 and departure for college in the United States. For the next eight years my contacts with Japanese were minuscule, although it was during these years of study in the United States and Europe that my general historical interests grew into a specialized interest in ancient China and Japan.

What a pity it was that I did not have more contacts with boys like my year-mate, Masayoshi. I could have learned so much from him and he from me. There was a whole world out there—a world in which both he and I would grow up and have our careers—but it might as well have been on a separate planet. Cultural and racial differences were such as to keep us far apart, and social barriers were perhaps even greater. My father was a respected, scholarly educator, Masayoshi's a farmer of middle standing living in a remote village. Class lines have declined since then to an amazing extent in the United States and still more in Japan. Even by the 1930s they had lessened somewhat, but in 1910 they were still very marked, especially in Japan, which was only forty years removed from full feudalism.

It would have been most unlikely that the paths of Masayoshi and I would have ever crossed—except possibly on the battlefield. We were entering a century of tremendous change, but it was up to us to educate ourselves for it. He did it by developing the ambition to achieve a sound education, following the regular steps of Japanese education and the bureaucracy and then progressing up the steep slope of the higher bureaucracy to posts of political influence. I drifted along through college like other middle-class boys, finally developing the scholarly interests that led me to the career of a university professor.

Imagine if, back in our youth, class rigidities had not existed and it had been easy for Japanese and Westerners to mix. How far ahead both Ōhira and I could have been in working for the global ideal we both came to believe in. It is almost unthinkable, but what a wonderful thing it would have been if we could have started to be friends as children and not at the relatively advanced age of fifty-one.

Ōhira grew up at the height of the time known as Taishō Democracy. Actually the period is a vague one stretching over several decades. Within a few years after the official end of the old feudal system, a determined demand for a wider sharing out of the responsibilities of political leadership grew up in many parts of Japan. The feudal system had been destroyed in 1868, and already by the early 1870s political parties were being formed and the demand for a role in government had become common among city merchants and farmers.

By 1890, the new and hitherto authoritarian government was forced to grant some political power and civil rights to the people. To the surprise of the government, however, the people demanded more, and by exploiting certain concessions permitted in the 1890 Constitution came to exercise much more political influence than had ever been planned for it. Elected politicians began to share power with the self-appointed government authorities, until by 1913 it had become quite clear that a Japanese cabinet could not rule effectively without the participation and support of a majority of the elected Parliament, or Diet as it was called. The year 1913 is often marked as the beginning of Taishō Democracy, but four decades of spontaneous democratic development already lay behind it. The years following 1913, which were the most formative for Masayoshi and me, were a time of extraordinary openness and freedom for Japan. The first largely political cabinet took power in 1918. The victory of the three great democracies—Great Britain, France, and the United States—over the German and Austro-Hungarian autocracies and the collapse of Russia, the most backward autocracy of them all, seemed clear signs of the times. Japan's future appeared to lie not in imperial conquest but in free trade and international cooperation, especially with the United States and Britain.

Most social and intellectual trends were strongly liberal. Breezes of intellectual and social freedom seemed to be sweeping not just the great cities but all of Japan, reaching down into such remote corners as where Masayoshi lived. Something of the same sort was happening in the United States but with less of a hurricane force as in long-isolated and feudal Japan. The democratic spirit and open globalism that were to characterize Ōhira's later life undoubtedly drew much of their spirit and vigor from the period of Taishō Democracy that inspired his schoolboy years.

As Ōhira moved up the rungs of education from his native village to the city, he underwent a deep religious experience. Such an episode is so personal and special that it is not easily understood or explained by others, but I have no doubt that he derived much from this special experience that deeply affected the remainder of his life. For almost a year he fell under the influence of an itinerant Christian preacher, and he spent his evenings passing out religious tracts on the city streets. His teacher was an obviously charismatic figure and left a strong impression on his young disciple. For a while, Ōhira's whole life seemed devoted to this new interest. I remember his telling me once of how he had earned his living as a teacher of English. He meant it as a joke, since at the time of our conversation he spoke scarcely a word of English, but it was a good illustration of the strong spirit he devoted to his religious endeavors to attempt on the basis of his trifling knowledge of English to earn enough as a tutor to carry out his work as an evangelist.

In later years, Ōhira spoke very little of his religious experience. No doubt it took on a new character as he became a disciple under Professor Yanaihara of the No Church Movement, which Uchimura Kanzō had started. This was not a movement devoted to open evangelism and charismatic appeal. It was for men who were led by the force of their ideas and ideals and not by emotion. In short, it was for intellectual and political leaders such as Ōhira became. This experience was probably a necessary step on his way to leadership. It may have helped him gain a concept of the world lying beyond Japan, a realization of the fellowship of humanity, and a sense of global law and order—in other words, the basic elements of the one world that mankind must achieve if it is going to survive.

Ōhira was a true product of Taishō Democracy, and as such he was preparing himself to be not just an outstanding bureaucrat, powerful and respected though bureaucrats are in Japan, but a "statesman," who could see beyond the needs of the day and help guide the country across the pass leading from its isolated past, which it had outgrown, into the broad plains of international intercourse and trade, which is the only environment in which Japan can live today.

By the time that Ōhira had graduated from Hitotsubashi University, one of Japan's leading national institutions specializing in economics, the spirit of Taishō Democracy had faded and the military, taking advantage of an ambiguity in the 1890 Constitution, had virtually seized control of the country. In sharp contrast with the Taishō Democracy policy of worldwide trade and close collaboration with the United States and United Kingdom, the army brought Japan into confrontation with these two countries by fresh conquests in China. Japan, which lacked sufficient oil to run either its industry or military machine with only its own resources, had painted itself into a corner from which there was no escape short of war with the great powers or backing down, which the Japanese military was unwilling to do.

One wonders what Ōhira's attitudes were to all this, but here the record remains silent. Very probably his thoughts were like those of myself and many other young men. We watched what was happening with dismay, but it never occurred to us, just starting out in our careers, that there was much we individually could do about it. I continued on my scholarly course, which I did not leave until the American army all but forced me to help out in the breaking and translating of Japanese wireless codes.

When war came, the choice for me was quite simple. I had no doubt that Japan was in the wrong in attempting to conquer China and various other nations and in its sudden "sneak" attack on the United States. Ōhira's thoughts may have been more confused between his belief in democracy and world fellowship and his natural sense of patriotism. On his graduation from university, he acquired one of the few prestigious opening posts in the Ministry of Finance, one of the most important civilian branches of government. His first important position was as the chief civilian representative in the large area of North China the Japanese army had bitten off under the name of Inner Mongolia.

Ōhira's next several years are recorded in great detail as he mounted the steep stairway leading to significant positions for the select few chosen for the higher bureaucracy. He was in a key position because decisions of the Ministry of Finance were vital to the operation of the whole government, particularly in the crucial reconstruction days in the early years after the war.

It was during this time of great transformation after the war that Ōhira made the crucial decision to shift from the powerful and prestigious bureaucracy to the less certain road of politics. According to the new Constitution of 1947, the Diet had become "the highest organ of state power" and was "the sole law-making organ of the State." This put it in control of the bureaucracy and, of course, the symbolic emperor, to say nothing of the military, which had been abolished as an independent force. Japan, in fact, had adopted the fundamentals of the British parliamentary system, toward which it had been drifting already in the time of Taishō Democracy, before the military had seized control of foreign policy and then the whole government in the late 1920s and 1930s.

Accepting the shift in power to the Diet, several ambitious men moved from the bureaucracy to electoral politics as the ultimate way to achieve leadership. Yoshida Shigeru, formerly of the Foreign Ministry, blazed the trail, serving as the prime minister for six of the nine years between October 1945 and December 1954, and the three men who held the post during the fifteen and a half years between February 1957 and July 1972 had all been prewar bureaucrats. Of these, Ikeda Hayato, prime minister between 1960 and 1964, seemed to me to be the most like Ōhira, and unquestionably had the greatest influence on him. He had been Ōhira's senior in the Ministry of Finance, where he had early developed a liking for the younger man and a trust in his judgment. Ikeda seems to me to have shown the same skill and firmness in leadership that Ōhira later displayed, and he had a comparable breadth of political vision and determined optimism. After 1972, political leadership fell increasingly into the hands of elected politicians without previous bureaucratic experience, and men like Ōhira became the exception rather than the rule.

Ikeda, Yoshida, and all the other prime ministers since the end of the war have been strongly pro-American, none more so than Ōhira, and they have cooperated fully with the United States so long as Japan itself was not shoved into a military role or a position of leadership it did not feel ready for. The Japanese public had become almost fiercely pacifistic, and it was uneasy about any role that might involve it in political controversy and, in turn, in military entanglements. Whatever their personal views might be, all the Japanese leaders were tied down by the democratic system of rule to a "low-posture" foreign policy, which would be unlikely to involve Japan in war. The Japanese system of rule, though thoroughly democratic, is quite different from the British, on which it is modeled, and even less like the American system with its tripartite division of power and a strong presidency. The chief reason Japanese democracy operates differently from the British or American is its unusual electoral system.

The House of Representatives, or Lower House, which exercises the bulk of the power, is elected by so-called middle-size electoral districts in which a voter has only a single vote though the district elects three to five seats each, depending on its population. The result is a sort of proportional representation like those in many European countries, though not with quite as much splintering of the parties. A Japanese party that can win around 20 percent of the votes in the district is normally assured one of the seats, but the smaller splinter parties are virtually eliminated.

A two-party system of either the English or American type would almost certainly be a failure in a middle-size electoral district system because no party would be likely to win a majority over a combination of the other parties and independents, some of whom, no doubt, would be elected as single-issue candidates or local heroes. The middle-size system requires that the larger parties win their share of seats by persuading their respective voters to divide their ballots more or less evenly between a suitably limited number of candidates, which is not an easy thing to arrange.

Before World War II, there had been two major parties in Japan, both stemming from the party movements of the 1870s and 1880s. Both were basically conservative in their economic policies but "liberal" in their efforts to win power from the military, the civil bureaucracy, and the court aristocracy. Although they superficially constituted a two-party system like those of England and United States, they were much less ideologically divided than the parties of the British Parliament and were far better organized than the chaotic American Congress.

In the early postwar years, these two traditional parties continued to dominate politics, but by 1955 it had become clear that neither could continue to control a majority in the Diet by itself. The lesser parties, especially the Socialists, Communists, Democratic Socialists, and—a later appearance—the Kōmeitō, were growing so large that neither traditional party could hope to win a majority against them and the other traditional party. Since the two traditional parties shared more with each other than with the newer opposition groups, which leaned more or less to the left, the obvious solution to the problem was to have the two join forces as the Liberal Democratic Party (LDP), a name that reveals much of past party history.

Another way in which Japanese politics differs from the British Parliamentary system is in its composition. Unlike England, Japanese Diet members are the products of their home districts and basically depend for election on their personal contacts and appeal to the local voters—charisma would perhaps be too strong a word. One would think that, as a result, they would be as unruly as American Congressmen, but instead they maintain strong discipline, voting as a bloc for their party's decisions. The major reason for this phenomenon is probably the strong tendency to act as groups, which is ubiquitous in Japanese society. Most Japanese identify themselves as belonging to a group and act accordingly. Junior Dietmen depend on senior members of their group for advancement in party and parliamentary posts, and the leaders depend on their henchmen for support in the struggle to achieve high posts and eventually the prime ministership. Thus, we find in Japan the curious combination of a Parliament elected basically in the American manner by the local personal strength of the individual candidate and reflecting, as a result, strong local interests, together with a parliament displaying the discipline that is more characteristic of London than of Washington.

Most Japanese politicians attach themselves to some faction, or *ha*, under a strong leader who can provide financial backing that will help them defray the costs of their election campaigns. The faction leaders, who are more divided by ambition than by policy, make various coalitions that seek to control the party. The factions give the parties desirable flexibility, making possible easy changes of leadership and policies. Some people describe the LDP not as a single political party but as a congeries of parties embracing such a wide range of personalities and policies as to be able always to attract a majority of voters. It certainly has been successful. All prime ministers since 1955 have belonged to the LDP, and only occasionally has it been necessary to win the support of a few outsiders to maintain a solid majority.

The unbroken dominance of the LDP has naturally given it great strength and a complicated organization. Unlike the American parties, which have virtually no national organization, the LDP has an elaborate structure of officers and committees that are the true decision makers. Proposed legislation undergoes complicated negotiations between the party and the government ministry involved, and is subjected to protracted meetings with various other groups, such as big business, trade groups, concerned interest groups, the opposition parties, and the like. It is then drawn up, usually by the bureaucracy, passes through a complex series of intraparty committee studies and party checks, and is finally accepted by the cabinet. Since the legislation has already been so carefully studied and all interested groups have already had their full say, the final vote in the Diet is usually a lackluster event, the outcome of which is already known. There is little of the bitter debates or eloquent rhetoric that enliven the political process in Washington and London. The three systems are quite different, but the Japanese procedure is every bit as democratic as the other two.

The faction leaders hope to reach the top through the size of their respective factions and their acceptance by other faction leaders in preference to alternative candidates. This situation, together with the normal Japanese style of seeking to achieve agreement through consensus, puts a prime minister in a weak position as a national leader. He must be careful not to step on too many toes. He needs to ingratiate himself with the other faction leaders. It is also vital that he wins and maintains the support of the members of his own faction. It is important that he is able to raise extra campaign funds for them and to get them promoted to posts of influence in the party organization and the Diet. But he must speak with a soft voice even in his own faction, and he must be very cautious about anything he says abroad. Where Western presidents and prime ministers can speak boldly for their countries, Japanese prime ministers must lie low, or else suffer the danger of being misunderstood by other governments and excoriated by the Japanese themselves. The result of this situation has given rise to many embarrassing misunderstandings between Japan and its closest allies. A promise to do one's best is likely to be interpreted as an agreement, whereas it really is only a promise to do one's best by a person who very probably cannot deliver on his well-meant promise.

Ōhira's career as a bureaucrat, politician, and prime minister, which this book sets out in great detail, illustrates clearly the workings of the Japanese political system. He conformed to the basic patterns but also remained true to himself, with a set of firm ideals that made him an unusually strong leader ready to take an untypically firm position when he reached the prime ministership.

Ōhira had the advantage of close bonds with other members of the political leadership. His contacts with fellow graduates of Hitotsubashi University were useful, but far more important was his record as a successful former member of the Ministry of Finance. Experience in this ministry was probably the best bureaucratic background a man could have.

Ōhira was a popular figure in both the ministry and subsequently in the party. He knew how to win support without being domineering or aggressive. His gentle nature, combined with his skills and strong will, made him liked by both his superiors in the party and the rank and file of its members. It is not surprising that eventually it was he who succeeded Ikeda as faction leader and the next member of his faction after Ikeda to become prime minister.

I was always much impressed with how Ōhira was entirely at ease with himself. Japanese of all types tend to be more ill at ease than are other peoples, having greater concern about critical judgments by others, particularly foreigners. Ōhira never showed anything of this, being relaxed at all times. He was not an imposing figure, being short and rotund, and he was often somewhat disheveled, but he never let that bother him, and perhaps it helped put others at ease in his presence. I remember once, after an exhausting trip from Tokyo to Washington, when he stretched himself out on a couch to catch a bit of sleep while he was waiting for an important meeting to begin. His embarrassed comrades roused him almost at once, but he appeared not the least bothered by his possible gaucherie. This incident fits in with his usually sleepy, unalert look. Instead of being put off by his appearance, most Japanese found it somewhat humorous, if not downright appealing—a sort of charisma in reverse.

I first met Ōhira in the spring of 1961, when he was chief cabinet secretary under Ikeda. I did not realize at the time how important this post was, and Ōhira seemed to me a rather unimpressive, retiring person. It was only when Ikeda made him foreign minister that I got to know him better, and my impression changed entirely. Ōhira was not very talkative, but what he said made sense, and he was always direct and reliable. I found that I could have absolute confidence in what he told me and I came to have complete faith in him. This was true of everything he said to the public or told me in private. I might relate one incident to illustrate the point.

In response to inquiries, the United States always stated that it never confirmed or denied the alleged presence of nuclear weapons. For tactical reasons this was a necessary precaution. The Japanese public was understandably sensitive about nuclear weapons and insisted on the Three Non-nuclear Principles: that Japan would not make, emplace, or introduce such weapons. At the time these principles were adopted, it was taken for granted that "introduction" (*mochikomi*) did not include the passage of nuclear weapons through Japanese waters, which was needed for American strategy, including the defense of Japan. But, unfortunately, the Japanese public began to think that the passage of nuclear-armed ships was included, and the opposition parties then used this concept to attack the LDP. To the distress of the American embassy, the Japanese government did not clear up the point but simply evaded it by stating that they had faith in the American government, leaving the impression that the United Stated might indeed be contravening the understanding concerning the "introduction" of nuclear weapons.

Since this was an intolerable situation, I spoke with great caution to Ōhira about it. He replied very simply that he understood the problem and would clear it up, but that I should not talk to anyone else about it. I do not know what he did, but the questions about the matter in the Diet ceased immediately and did not arise again until many years later, by which time I had long departed the American embassy and other people were in charge of the embassy and the Japanese government. The situation, too, had changed by then, and most Japanese took it for granted that American naval vessels transited Japanese waters with nuclear weapons. The whole incident was interesting in itself, but the reason for recounting it here is to illustrate Ōhira's complete reliability, and also the apparent "magic" with which he could get things accomplished in politics.

Early in our friendship, I became persuaded that Ōhira would some day become prime minister, and I never wavered in that conviction. He had an unmatched combination of wise and sincere beliefs, a true sense of internationalism, unchallenged honesty, and pleasant human relations. In his conduct he was modest, almost reticent, but at the same time he was extremely successful in achieving his ends. He had an ideal personality for a politician from the Japanese point of view, and one that would prove impressive to foreigners when they came to know him. Despite his retiring nature, he was extraordinarily talented in many ways. I remember once, when he was already close to the political summit, he did me the honor of attending a reception in my honor, given for a reason I no longer remember. As is customary on such occasions, he was called upon to make a few remarks, and he spontaneously gave a little speech that was as kind, pertinent, and humorous as any I have every heard in any language.

One time after Ōhira had become prime minister and I happened to be on a visit to Japan, I called on him at his office, confessing to him that I had no particular business but that I could not deny myself the pleasure of seeing him in the position he so richly deserved. I, of course, did not realize that his untimely death would remove him from it almost before he could get well started.

When I speculate on what might have been, I am struck by the great loss Japan suffered with Ōhira's death. It is a far greater loss than most Japanese can comprehend. During the succeeding decade, the country established itself as a great industrial power and potential world leader, but it now finds itself beset by doubts and threatened by attitudes of unfriendliness throughout the world. It stands in desperate need of the qualities and concepts that were at the heart of Ōhira's thinking, but no substitute for a man like Ōhira is in sight.

Japan has earned itself a reputation for being a thoroughly egocentric country, interested only in its own welfare, and yet its continued well-being or even existence depends on international cooperation and trust. The Japanese are a part of the human race that will either prosper or perish together, but they have given the rest of the world the feeling that they consider themselves to be distinct from all others. This is indeed a time when

Ōhira's concept of the brotherhood of humanity is desperately needed in Japan. The organization of mankind in larger blocs, as in his Pacific Basin Cooperation Concept, has become an obvious necessity. In fact, he probably would have expanded the concept by now to include the whole world. Global cooperation demands a large contribution of goods and talents by the countries that have the most to give, but the Japanese as a whole, unlike Ōhira, show only a thin intellectual comprehension of this point and very little will to put it into practice. A man like Ōhira could have led Japan in earning a respected position in the world and making a contribution to world peace and prosperity commensurate with its strength. The Japan he could have helped create would have been a much more admired and secure nation than the money-bloated giant it is today. His loss was indeed immense, felt all the more keenly under present conditions of world crisis.

EDWIN O. REISCHAUER

La Jolla, California
January 10, 1990

Part 1

Early Years

Chapter 1
Village Life

Of Japan's four main islands, Shikoku is the smallest. Mainly mountainous, this island of approximately 19,000 square kilometers is only 5 percent of the nation's total and is home to 3.5 percent of Japan's people. Shikoku's southern shores are pounded by the rough waters of the Pacific Ocean, and its northern coast is separated from Japan's largest island, Honshū, by the calm Inland Sea. This sea has long been one of Japan's most important trade routes, and there have been centers of civilization along its shores since ancient times.

Masayoshi Ōhira, whose life we are about to follow, entered this world near the town of Toyohama, which faces the Inland Sea in the Mitoyo District of Shikoku's Kagawa Prefecture. From Toyohama's 496-meter-high Mount Takao, one can look out to the northeast over the whole town and its rural surroundings. Ponds for irrigation dot the mountain slopes. Orchards and fields extend one after the other to the distant water's edge, and are especially picturesque in the golden hues of autumn.

The area of fields and orchards that used to be called Wada Village, before it was administratively annexed to the town of Toyohama in 1955, encompassed several small hamlets, and it was in one of these, called Nagatani, that the Ōhira family made its home. The house still stands in a rather lonely spot, looking not too different from the way it appeared many years ago.

The prosperity one sees today in this farming area reflects centuries of painstaking, often excruciating, labor by its people. First of all, they had to overcome the problems of poor irrigation and drainage systems. The part of Shikoku in which Kagawa Prefecture (called Sanuki in earlier days) is located has relatively few streams and rivers, and with a low annual rainfall neither surface nor underground water is abundant. Thus, from early times the inhabitants of this part of Shikoku have dug ponds to collect water during the winter for use during the summer months. Compared to the 14.4 percent of arable land in the whole of Japan, 28.4 percent of Kagawa Prefecture is arable.

The topography of what was earlier called Wada Village is even hillier than most places in the prefecture, so agricultural development meant cultivation of uneven ground and digging ponds on sloping terrain. But in spite of the difficulties, the people sustained an enthusiasm for agricultural improvements. According to a late nineteenth-century account called *Toyohamachō-shi* (History of Toyohama), ever since the Edo period (1603–1867) agriculture in Wada Village was at a more advanced level than in the other three areas of today's Toyohama. For example, in 1789, Wada Village exceeded the other areas in population, and almost all of its 395 households were engaged in agriculture. Of these, 319 were classified as *honbyakushō* (farming families of relatively high social standing) and 70 were classified as *mōto* (mainly tenant farmers of lower social standing). In the same year, about 100 *chō* (approximately 100 hectares) in Wada Village consisted of "old" paddies and fields, while some 80 *chō* of "new" paddies and fields had been cultivated.

The expansion of cultivated land was matched by continuous improvements in farming technology and the diversification of produce. In addition to high-quality "Sanuki rice," such local crops as sugar and cotton were produced in increasing quantities, together with indigo, sweet potatoes, and rapeseed. Gradually, enterprises to process and market these also developed. Helped by a moderate climate and good transport facilities, the region's agricultural success spurred numerous commercial and manufacturing ventures.

The Meiji period (1868–1912) saw rapid improvements in farm implements and technology, together with more rational use of land and water. Mulberry orchards for the raising of silkworms were introduced around 1884 to 1885, and it was in this period that orchards of citrus fruits, pears, grapes, and persimmons were started. A greater variety of vegetables was also produced.

It was in the forty-third year of Meiji, on March 12, 1910, that Ōhira Masayoshi was born to Rikichi and his wife, Saku, in Wada Village. Though few details of his ancestry are known, in an autobiographical sketch penned in 1978, Ōhira writes of his antecedents as follows: "The genealogy of the Ōhira family is shrouded in the mists of time, but we seem to be descended from Ōhira Kunisuke Iganokami, a local chieftain who moved from southern Tosa to hold sway over this region in the sixteenth century. Traces of stone walls and a spring marking the site of his castle still exist at Shishigahanayama, which is also known as Shiroyama

(Castle Hill). The names of the three hamlets at the foot of Shiroyama also recall these feudal associations.

"Pursued by the Chōsokabe clan during its conquest of Shikoku in the sixteenth century, Kunisuke seems to have sought refuge with one of his retainers, and was never heard from again. His son and heir died in the arms of a nursemaid, who threw herself into a pond called Ubagafutokoro-ike (Pond of the Nurse's Breast), south of Shiroyama. His daughter, too, died tragically by jumping into the sea near Toyohama, at the spot known today as Himehama (Princess Beach). Only Kunisuke's younger son is said to have survived and settled down quietly in the district. The family name Ōhira was used by generations of abbots of Kokuyūji, Kunisuke's family temple."

Masayoshi's grandfather Iwazō—who had been born into a branch household (*bunke*) of the Ōhira "head" family (*sōhonke*)—served on the elected village council during the Meiji years. Because Ōhira Masayoshi's father, Rikichi, was Iwazō's second son, Rikichi, too, set up a branch household, as tradition dictated. A middle-ranking farmer, he cultivated some 1.3 *chō* of paddy fields, part of which was his property and part of which was leased. Like Iwazō, he enjoyed helping others and also served on the village council and as chairman of the local irrigation association.

Irrigation associations took in virtually everybody in a given hamlet who used water from the irrigation ponds, and the chairmanship was not an official post in the village administration but rather an unofficial *kaoyaku* position, undertaken voluntarily by public-spirited individuals. Rikichi was responsible for the management of a pond called Nono-ike that irrigated some fifty *chō*, and was thus a person of considerable local influence.

Ōhira writes of his father as follows: "My father was born in 1870 and had no formal education to speak of, yet he wrote well and was fairly well versed in both Japanese and Chinese classics. Here and there in his books could be found slips of red paper pasted beside passages about which he had queries. Once he had resolved the problem he would carefully remove the slip, taking care not to tear or mark the page. . . .

"Father was fond of saké and never missed his evening drink. He had quite a wide circle of acquaintances and was often invited to parties. I remember how the bills from the village store—which he used to settle before the midsummer Bon Festival and at the end of the year—included almost weekly charges of ¥1.20 to ¥1.30 for *seishu* [a clear saké], along with entries of 3 or 5 *sen* for bean curd and other daily necessities."

As for his mother, Ōhira records, "My mother was the eldest daughter of the Wabima family in the neighboring town of Ōnohara. She was a strong-minded woman and very outgoing. At the time of her marriage, the Wabima family had moved to Korea and ran a general store in the Taesŏng district of Yŏngil County, Kyŏngsang-pukto. My uncle was administrative head of the district. For some reason, only my grandmother remained in Japan to care for the family home."

Masayoshi's elder sister, Muma, remembers her parents in these words: "Father was a scrupulous person, but he never became angry with us or shouted at us. When we were studying he would bring us newly cleaned kerosene lamps, and if one of the boys forgot his cap when he left for school, Father would take it to him, catching up with him by bicycle. These are just a few examples of his kindly disposition. He was well regarded by those around him, and if any kind of argument developed, he would race over at once, saying, 'If I go over, things will be settled.'

"In those days it was unusual for a man to take his wife out with him, but Father would often bring Mother along when he went somewhere. A male cousin used to say it was Mother who was the stricter, but she was nevertheless kind, and if some children happened to be playing nearby, she would fry some *mochi* [rice cakes], sprinkle sugar over them, and call the children in to eat them."

Before Masayoshi, his parents already had five other children, two boys and three girls. Because the oldest daughter, Kiku, died in her first year, and the oldest son, Nobuo, at the age of two and a half, when Masayoshi arrived he shared the household with two elder sisters, Tetsu and Muma, and an elder brother, Kazumitsu. Two and a half years later another brother, Yoshikazu, arrived, and four years after that another sister, Tomie.

What was daily life like in the Ōhira household in Masayoshi's childhood years? As Ōhira himself recalls: "The life of a rice and barley farmer in those days was far from easy, and it was all the harder in my family with six children—three boys and three girls—to feed. My earliest recollections are of wearing straw sandals and clothes with sleeves that were shiny from repeated wipings of a running nose. Meals consisted of soup, a side dish, and *mugimeshi* (barley mixed with rice). Although we lived near the sea, fresh fish was a treat we had only on festival days or special occasions. Once in a while we might be served dried mackerel or dried sardines."

It should be noted that in those days eating *mugimeshi* was not a sign of poverty. According to a local sociological study entitled *Wada-mura no jissō* (A Portrait of Wada Village), "The staple food during the Meiji and early Taishō [1912–26] periods was *mugimeshi*, with rice forming 10 percent to 30 percent and barley the remainder. In later years the proportion of rice increased, so that from the mid-Taishō to early Shōwa [1926–89] periods the proportion of rice ranged between 40 percent and 80 percent. Even up to the early Shōwa period, *mugimeshi* was the staple food for three out of four households."

From such accounts it appears that the Ōhira household lived in a style typical of the middle socio-economic stratum of the village, with a living standard inferior to that of large landowners, known as *danna*. And it was certainly a much lower standard of living than what is usual in farming villages today. To sustain even that relatively low standard, however, all the members of a household, from children to the elderly, had to work hard.

When Ōhira Masayoshi was born, the parceling out of the world into colonies by the "great powers" had more or less come to an end, and movements espousing democratic ideals were arising everywhere. For Japan, the last years of the Meiji period after victory in the Russo-Japanese War (1904–5) were an important turning point. In international affairs, Japan, in imitation of the European powers, pursued colonialist policies by annexing Korea and "managing" parts of Manchuria. It was in this period that Japan succeeded in its long-cherished goal of completely rectifying the so-called unequal treaties concluded with Western powers in the 1850s and 1860s by regaining tariff autonomy in 1911.

In this period, too, the machinery industry—the technological capacity of which had been given a tremendous boost by military procurements during the war with Russia—was spurring Japan's overall industrialization. And with the latter came more acute labor problems, socialist movements, and the heightened social antagonisms that accompanied them.

The life and thinking of the inhabitants of Kagawa Prefecture, especially in its farming villages, still lagged far behind Tokyo and the other major urban centers. Many still clung to the old-fashioned lifestyles that had bound them to the land, and whose patterns of economic production had changed very little since the Edo period. Ōhira has written of his earliest childhood memory in these surroundings as follows: "Right in the center of my forehead is a deep scar almost an inch from left to right. When I was a small boy it was much more conspicuous, and I remember being quite troubled about it. Even in photographs the scar, while not prominent, was still visible, though it became much less so as I grew older.

"I got it when I was three or four years old ... and, funnily enough, I remember clearly how it happened. In those days we had a maid in our house we called Oshige.... One day, she carried me on her back to the edge of the paddy field in front of the gate, and with me still on her back she turned for some reason and I hit my head against the stone wall surrounding the field. Blood poured out of my forehead. My mother, who was just returning from working in the fields, carried me into the house looking almost beside herself and gave me some emergency treatment, perhaps a moxa cauterization [applied to the open wound].

"Oshige worked in our house for two or three more years, and then became a maid at a small inn near the edge of the hamlet. But even then she would often come to take me places, so I was often an uninvited guest at this inn. Then after some time, Oshige became ill and died.

"These are my earliest fleeting memories after I came into the world. The village inn is still there, enclosed in a thicket just like in the old days. I have the impression that as the years pass these fleeting memories are becoming more vivid. It seems as if every time I pass that inn, which is beside a fork in the road at the edge of the village, I am about to be stopped by a call from Oshige." This sketch, titled "The Scar on My Forehead," appeared at the beginning of Ōhira Masayoshi's first book, published in 1953.

A little later Masayoshi's parents toyed with the idea of having him raised as a foster child in another home in the same neighborhood. It was an accepted custom among farming households for families with a large number of offspring to provide foster children (*satogo*) to families with few or no children of their own. In later years Ōhira once tersely recounted to a male cousin, "Because I was so naughty, I was 'relieved of my duties' and brought back home after only a week." Even though the separation had been brief, it was no doubt a bitter experience and Ōhira spoke of it only rarely.

Another method of reducing the number of mouths to feed was to have daughters married off at an early age. At the age of sixteen, Masayoshi's elder sister Tetsu married into the Yamada family in the neighboring town of Ōnohara. Masayoshi remembered this event, which took place the winter before his seventh birthday: "The day my sister got married was a cold wintry day. A procession, with some men carrying a wardrobe and an oblong chest on their shoulders, slowly climbed the long slope at the edge of the hamlet. Men on foot carried the paper lanterns traditionally used on such occasions. It seemed that I desperately wanted to take part in the procession and followed it as far as I could. I remember that while I was obstinately trailing after it, a male cousin from the 'head' house came to bring me back, but I stubbornly resisted his interference."

Within a few years Tetsu fell ill and died, leaving behind two young children. Not long afterward, Masayoshi's second sister, Muma, was married as a second wife into the Yamada family, also at the age of sixteen.

Chapter 2

An Unassuming Boy

In April 1916, Masayoshi entered Taishō Elementary School in Wada Village. His classmates recall him being large and muscular, and also courteous and persevering. However, he did not particularly stand out in a crowd. If a question was asked in class, Masayoshi would never raise his hand to answer it unless he had thought carefully and was sure his answer was correct. Once, when a teacher asked an especially difficult question, no hands were raised, and after some time the teacher picked out Ōhira to respond. Masayoshi thought hard for a while and came up with the right answer. During examinations, most students would try to hide their answer papers from straying eyes, but Masayoshi did not seem to care if surreptitious glances were cast in his direction. Sports were not his strong point, although he liked *sumō* wrestling and often spent recess time practicing *sumō* in the sand pit on the school playground.

For most country children of this era, the hours spent at school seemed a respite from the hardships of life at home. After school, children of most farm families had precious little time for anything except work in the fields, taking care of the animals, and doing side-jobs to supplement the family's income. To quote from Ōhira's autobiography: "A farmer's life was one continuous round of toil with very little to show for it in the end. The new year begins as the barley pushes forth from the frozen earth. In late spring, as the barley begins to ripen, the rice seedlings are waiting to be transplanted. After transplanting and weeding comes the heat of summer. In fall, the rice is harvested, and then the gray days of winter close in upon us once again. A farmer's lot is a repetitive round of hard work in harmony with the majestic rhythms of nature."

Many farm families still had not much more than a subsistence standard of living, and not a few households had to ask the large landowners for help in meeting expenses for medical care, education, marriages, and funerals. In many cases, the large landowners were also fertilizer merchants who distributed fertilizer on credit during the planting and transplanting seasons. At harvest time they would recoup their outlays at high rates of interest, and many families were constantly in debt. Ōhira writes: "My family was no exception, and I recall overhearing many whispered conversations between my parents about debts."

Given these circumstances, families undertook various side-jobs to raise cash. One of the most common in Wada Village was straw weaving. Barley stalks of the kind used for making straw hats were cut into six-inch lengths, avoiding any joints, then bleached with sulfur and split into strips about one-eighth of an inch wide, which were braided by hand into a variety of shapes. Children were taught to do this even before they were old enough to attend school, and their parents gave them daily quotas that had to be met. Ōhira has written about it as follows: "Having these quotas all the time meant that I didn't have enough time for the homework given by the teachers, not to mention time to study lessons in advance. I remember that if I'd gone fishing or played ball until dusk and was then unable to complete my quota, I felt very uncomfortable about facing Mother, like someone who had committed a crime appearing before a judge." Masayoshi's home seems to have been pervaded by tensions caused by the burdens of farm work and side-jobs, the need to support a large number of children and employ some domestic help, and his mother's strictness.

An elementary school classmate recalls that Masayoshi's elder brother, Kazumitsu, and younger brother, Yoshikazu, were rather unruly and often fought with each other, while Masayoshi always played the role of peacemaker. His elder sister, Muma, recalls that, "One day, when Father discovered that a branch had been cut from a pine tree he was fond of, he got angry and, holding up the branch, asked, 'Who did this?' Masayoshi ran up, knelt down with both hands touching the ground, and said, 'I did it without meaning to. Please forgive me.' Father then said, 'I can't be angry with this child.' I wonder, though, who really did it."

With each new school year, Masayoshi acquired a greater fondness for his studies. Family finances did not allow the purchase of books other than the assigned texts, but these were read over and over again. Many people recall seeing Masayoshi reading his books while doing his weaving or while treading the waterwheel that brought water from the well to the fields. These were also years when the youthful urge to play was at its strongest, however, and it sometimes happened that Masayoshi would escape his parents' gaze and be found running about the nearby hills and fields with the neighborhood children.

"I would make the most of every opportunity to hunt for *matsutake* mushrooms and bamboo shoots in the mountains, to swim and fish in the sea, and to catch small fish in the streams. At night I would take part in informal children's gatherings to show off our talents, or would enjoy trials of courage with my friends, testing one another's nerve in the dark by pretending to be ghosts."

The rural areas were not untouched by the wind of change. Electric lights reached the region in 1914, and a telephone service began the following year in neighboring Wadahama. Just when Masayoshi began elementary school in April 1916, the first trains reached the area, and with the railroad came new information and modern ways, some of which raised persistent doubts in Masayoshi's young mind. One of these was the recruiting of workers for the burgeoning textile industry in the cities. Tempted by the blandishments of recruiters, a steady flow of young men and women left their homes to work in and around Osaka. As Ōhira wrote in later years, "This, however, resulted in many unfortunate people. We began to see people coming back to the countryside to recuperate, their faces pale from illness (mainly respiratory ailments). Household budgets would be strained as parents, intent on curing their children's illnesses, sought to improve their nutrition. Some young people even became infected with diseases like tuberculosis, or succumbed to dissipation in the cities and met pitiable ends."

When Masayoshi was a second-year university student in 1934, the theme "Lancashire and Osaka" was given for an examination in economic history. At the time, Osaka's textile industry was outproducing that of Lancashire, in the north of England, and was laying claim to world supremacy. Ōhira got an "Excellent" for his essay, which made the point that Japan's textile industry had developed thanks to the diligence and low wages of the country's female mill workers, who were made available through the "irrational structure" of Japan's farming villages. It may be surmised that this view had been influenced by what he had seen or heard about in his boyhood.

Advances in transportation also facilitated the movement of itinerant traders, who would come to the villages to deal in a variety of products. These traders' glib tongues had been trained in the cities, while the farming folk were skilled at neither buying nor selling; consequently, the farmers were frequently taken advantage of. Ōhira describes one such episode: "About the time the cold winds of late fall began to blow after the rice had been harvested and the barley planted, we would dig up the sugar cane stalks, which would be about five or six feet high, strip off the outer bark, and make brown sugar from the squeezed, boiled, and hardened sap. We would line up several 4-*to* [1 *to* = 18 liters] buckets of sugar, each more or less full, in the yard, and a trader with a balancing rod would come along to weigh the sugar together with the sacks into which it was transferred. A little before the copper counterweight hanging from one end of the balance had risen and settled into a balanced position, the trader would deftly grab the counterweight and announce that the sugar weighed so many *kan*, so many *monme*.

"There were so many times when, even as a small child, I wanted this copper counterweight to go up a little further and to see the up-and-down movement subside of its own accord, so that the sugar was weighed fairly. I thought these traders were dishonest fellows, but the farmers made no protest. Even in my own village several men amassed huge fortunes in a few years from sugar trading."

Standing in the crowd, young Masayoshi watched the changes around him and filed them away in his young, sensitive mind. In the world at large, World War I had ended and a new era was about to begin. Japan had taken part in the war, and, even though it had not fought on the main battlegrounds of Europe, it took its seat as one of the five powers drawing up the Treaty of Versailles. Japan's economy had progressed greatly during the time the European powers and the United States were busy with the war. As a result, Japan's industrial production grew by leaps and bounds, and its international balance of payments, which had hitherto suffered a deficit, suddenly registered a hefty surplus.

World War I was a major turning point not only politically but also in the areas of thought and culture. Although Japanese political parties had maintained a lively agenda ever since the establishment of the National Diet in 1890, the small suprapartisan group of elder statesmen known as the *genrō* (many of Meiji Restoration vintage) had dominated the government, depriving any majority faction in the Diet from forming a party cabinet. But the Rice Riots of 1918 gave rise to the *Rikken Seiyūkai* (Friends of Constitutional Government Party) cabinet under Prime Minister Hara Takashi (also known as Hara Kei), the first real party cabinet in Japan. The movement for universal male suffrage displayed new vigor, labor unions and agricultural cooperatives were organized, and several political parties with a socialist orientation were formed, among them the Japan Communist Party, clandestinely organized by a small group of intellectuals.

The Hara Cabinet emphasized the development of education, and during its tenure opportunities for higher and vocational education were greatly expanded. In the three years of the Hara Administration, the total number of the country's so-called higher schools (in effect, preparatory courses for entering a university), higher commercial schools, and higher industrial schools increased by twenty-nine to almost double the previous number. The Hara Cabinet's education program increased the number of faculties in government universities and elevated certain vocational schools to the status of junior colleges (*tanka daigaku*). A new bill was promulgated that facilitated the establishment of other prefectural and municipal universities in addition to the so-called imperial universities. Intellectuals and students, more numerous than ever before, were quickly introduced to new European and American currents of thinking. American-style democracy and Russian-style communism had particular influence. Ōhira recalls, "On the underside of farm people's lives, the burdens and struggles that went with making a living remained, of course, but all in all we can say it was a liberal and tranquil era."

In March 1922, Masayoshi graduated from the sixth and final year of the general course of his elementary school and entered the first year of its two-year upper course. His brother Kazumitsu, one year his senior, had entered this course the previous year and was expected to take over the management of the family finances upon graduation. Masayoshi had hoped that immediately upon graduation from the general course, he could enter a five-year middle school, but the family budget and other circumstances dictated against it.

At that time, on completing the six years of compulsory general education or the optional two years of an elementary school's upper course, children of most farming families would either take up the family occupation or a job. At the most they would continue their formal education no further than a vocational course in a commercial, industrial, or agricultural school. To enter a middle school meant that one was expected to continue on to a higher school and then, very likely, to a university. In Masayoshi's school, in a class of over forty pupils, only two or three at the most would go on to middle school, mainly the children of well-to-do landowners.

According to recollections of family members, several factors contributed to Masayoshi's desire to go to middle school. His father seems to have felt that although he did not have enough property for it to be shared with his second and third sons, he would at least like to encourage one or both to embark on an academic career. Masayoshi's high marks at school were also in his favor. But perhaps the most important factor was Kazumitsu's goodwill and recognition of his younger brother's promising qualities. Masayoshi's wish to go to middle school was fulfilled a year later, when Kazumitsu graduated from the advanced course of the village school and began to devote himself full-time to the family's livelihood.

The immediate object of Masayoshi's aspirations was Kagawa Prefectural Mitoyo Middle School in the town (now city) of Kan'onji, known today as Kan'onji No. 1 High School. In preparing for the entrance exam,

Masayoshi was tutored by a female instructor from the public elementary
school in neighboring Toyohama. She recalls: "On April 3, just as the new
school year was beginning, a boy neatly dressed in a navy blue splashed-
pattern kimono came to see me. His first words were, 'Please teach me.'
After asking a number of questions, I learned that he was the second son of
Ōhira Rikichi, that he was in the first year of the upper course at the
elementary school, and that he hoped to enter Mitoyo Middle School the
following spring.

"Ōhira Rikichi's home was in the hamlet of Nagatani, only a little over
a kilometer from my house, so we knew each other, but I knew nothing
whatsoever about his having this rosy-cheeked, gentle-mannered son. Two
or three days earlier, another boy from the neighborhood had started coming for lessons, so I agreed to teach the Ōhira boy at the same time.

"From the next day, the two boys came for their lessons at my house at
about the time the evening meal was over. And this continued for 365 days
of the year, without a single day off. Now that I think about it, they really
did well to keep it up. On evenings when it was snowing, Masayoshi would
come with a red blanket over his head. One fall evening when there was a
strong typhoon, no sooner had my husband said, 'It seems that even
Masayoshi has decided to take the evening off,' than the door opened.
Before we recovered from our surprise he started to apologize for being
late, saying, 'The river was overflowing, so I came the long way around
through Kajitani.' "

Masayoshi's companion during these lessons later recalled that, when
Masayoshi was given a question he was unable to answer, "Perhaps
because this was so painful for him, tears would start to roll down his
cheeks. I feel this was a sign of an unusually strong spirit of not wanting to
be defeated."

Masayoshi passed the entrance exams and entered Mitoyo Middle
School in April 1923. The school's registration book records his marks for
courses taken during his final semester in elementary school as follows:
Ethics 10, Reading 10, Calligraphy 10, Composition 10, Arithmetic 10,
History 10, Geography 10, Natural Sciences 8, Physical Education 10, and
Singing 9. His ranking was second out of forty-eight pupils in his
graduating class. A notation under "Family Particulars" lists as living
under the same roof one elder brother, one younger brother, one younger
sister, one male servant, and one female servant.

It is interesting to note that in the column titled "Aspirations," there is
no entry in the space for expectations held by "parents and family," but
"public official" (kanri) is given as the occupational goal of "the student
himself." What Masayoshi's image of public officials was at that time we

cannot really say. Whether they were clerks in local government offices or public servants he encountered in everyday life, such as teachers, policemen, or railroad workers, or whether he had in mind the elite bureaucrats of government agencies, the fact remains that in an era when everyone with a government post was looked up to, young Masayoshi recorded this as his personal aspiration and then advanced along an appropriate path.

Mitoyo Middle School had been founded in March 1900, initially a branch of Kagawa Prefectural Marugame Middle School. It became an independent prefectural middle school three years later, in 1903, and Kagawa Prefectural Kan'onji No. 1 High School in the education reforms following World War II. Throughout its history, it has produced numerous capable graduates who have subsequently been active on the local and national scene.

Masayoshi spent all five middle-school years at Kan'onji, surrounded by friends and supportive teachers. At the time Kan'onji's population was less than 15,000, but it was nonetheless a town, and thus a quite different sort of place from Wada Village. The stimulation of associating with new friends away from home could not help but make Masayoshi happy, and he contributed some of his recollections of this period to a collection of essays commemorating the eightieth anniversary of Mitoyo Middle School. One excerpt reads: "Every day I'd commute to school by train from Toyohama Station. At first it was an old-style passenger train, and it was only when I was in the senior years that smoother-running 'bogie-type' rail cars came into service. I don't recall exactly when it was, but once, when a touring group of *sumō* wrestlers from Tokyo were boarding the train, I remember seeing them having to turn sideways to get to their seats since the entrance to each compartment was so narrow. It was an unwritten custom that male students boarded the front half of the train and female students boarded the rear half.

"Around that time, the Ikkandō bakery near Kan'onji Station had begun to enjoy brisk business, and we would frequently buy sweet-smelling, freshly steamed buns from its rear kitchen, ignoring school rules against spending money on snacks. . . . The bustle of early spring at graduation time and the beginning of the new school year, the fresh feel of the new textbooks, the many faces and figures of friends who brought color to the outdoor sports events, the famous swimming parties on the beach, the joyous attraction of box lunches with different kinds of fish paste and pickled side dishes with a strong aroma of rice bran, the tension surrounding the hazing that would sometimes take place at the hands of upperclassmen in a corner of the schoolyard, the excitement of sports competitions against Marugame Middle School and Saijō Middle School. These school-associated memories are endless."

The year Masayoshi entered Mitoyo Middle School was the last in which the school accepted only 100 entering pupils, divided into two classes of 50. (From 1924, the school took 150 pupils every year.) During these years at the end of the Taishō period (1912–26), there were still only five middle schools, both tax-supported and private, in Kagawa Prefecture. Ōhira recalls: "In my middle school . . . there were an unusual number of very bright pupils, and needless to say my marks were by no means at the top. Of the 80 who graduated, a record was made in that 12 or 13 went on to the old [prewar] higher schools and 14 or 15 to the old higher technical schools." According to Ministry of Education statistics (1929), the average proportion of middle school graduates who at that time went on to higher schools or higher technical schools was 18 percent, representing 3 percent of their age group nationwide.

That Masayoshi seems not to stand out in the recollections of his classmates was no doubt due in part to his temperate character and careful behavior, but it should also be seen as influenced by the circumstances of his daily life. During the years Masayoshi was commuting to middle school, he still had to help with work at home and, unlike the majority of students, did not have time to spend with friends after class. As his sister Muma remembers it: "At harvest time, Masayoshi would be woken at three o'clock every morning. He would cut about one *tan* (992 square meters) of paddy with the other boys and men, and would then have breakfast, prepare his own box lunch, and run along the back road to the station.

"Quite early on, though I can't say exactly when, he was cutting rice at night by the light of a gas lantern. He never complained, but I think he felt he wanted a little more time to study. As for his weaving, even though Father took Masayoshi's studies seriously and asked Masayoshi to be excused from this task, Mother used to insist he did his weaving even if it meant failing at school."

Even though most of his friends remember Masayoshi as an "unassuming boy," this comment offers a more perplexing nuance: "As a child he was of the pure and innocent type, bashful and shy. Yet at times he had a surprising capacity to show his opposition to something. If you said anything he didn't agree with, he would right away and in no uncertain terms disagree. Occasionally, he would bellow out a song or recite in a loud voice some English passage he had taken a liking to. I don't know if I'd call it rambuctiousness or what, but he had a strong core of self-confidence. He was not very good at judo, but in his strength of spirit there was something indomitable about him, ever since he was a boy."

By their fourth year, which was over halfway through their middle school, students needed to start thinking about what they would do after graduating. It was in the summer after Masayoshi started his fourth year that he contracted typhoid fever, and for four months lingered on the border of life and death. Thanks in large part to the unstinting care given by his parents, his life was saved, but he lagged behind in his school work and his marks fell below average. With the family's finances being what they were, it was necessary to choose a higher school that did not require fees.

From early childhood Masayoshi had had a favorite cousin from the "head" family, Hideo, whom he affectionately called *Nii-chan* (Elder Brother). As Hideo graduated from the Military Academy and became an officer (later a major general), Masayoshi decided on a career in the navy. As soon as his health had recovered, he began studying for the entrance examination for the Naval Academy, which he took the following spring, but just before the examination he suffered an acute inner-ear infection and failed the physical examination. One of the possible avenues to higher schooling had been blocked, which no doubt left Masayoshi deeply frustrated.

A greater misfortune, however, was soon to come. On August 29, 1927, when Masayoshi was in his fifth and final year of middle school, his father died of a stomach ulcer at the relatively youthful age of fifty-six. It was supposed that his malady might have been caused, or exacerbated, by worry over Masayoshi's illness of the previous year, and by the fatigue of the intensive care given to Masayoshi at the time.

"This sudden misfortune was a mortal blow to our family. My mother's health was poor and my elder brother was still too young to take on all my father's responsibilities. My mother and brother must have felt utterly bereft, but they never lost courage. I shall always be grateful for the tender, loving care they gave my younger brother and sister and me."

A classmate has the following recollection from this difficult period: "I'm sure it was in the fifth year of middle school that the two of us were walking on the grounds during recess. Ōhira looked up at the sky and said, in English, 'We must be vivacious.' I didn't understand the meaning of 'vivacious,' but when I got home I learned from the dictionary that it meant lively or cheerful. I was startled. He had pointed out a negative trait of mine that had secretly bothered me and, moreover, he had known a word that I didn't." Most likely, Masayoshi had voiced the need to be vivacious at least as much for himself as for his friend.

As for the impression held by many that Masayoshi was "unassuming," another middle school classmate states, "It's not that he was unassuming in a simple sort of way. Rather, I think there was something in his basic character that allowed him to apply a brake on himself." In other words, his was a conscious effort to be unpretentious. No doubt the strong capacity for self-restraint that Ōhira displayed in later years was already forming.

Masayoshi would have to overcome the misfortunes and disappointments encountered during his final two years in middle school and to chart his own future course. For the Ōhira household, which had just lost the head of the family, sending Masayoshi for higher education posed a formidable economic problem. After his failure to enter a military school, the only completely tuition-free alternative was the night class of a school for the training of teachers.

Ōhira writes: "One of my aunts happened to be married to a police officer and lived not far from Takamatsu. She suggested that I live with her and attend the Takamatsu Higher School of Commerce, saying that I could commute to school from her house. In the end, that's the way it worked out, so upon my graduation from middle school I entered Takamatsu Higher School of Commerce." Of the 932 applicants that year, 161 successfully passed the entrance examinations.

When Masayoshi began his studies at the Mitoyo Middle School, his scholastic rank was forty-first among a class of one hundred, and in his graduating class of seventy-three he was fifteenth. The difference in numbers of entering and graduating students was due to some students dropping out during the five-year period because of illness or family circumstances, and to the fact that, in the prevailing system, some outstanding students were allowed to enter higher institutions upon successfully passing an entrance examination in their fourth year. Masayoshi's middle school class ranking might be characterized as "middle" to "upper middle." On his graduation, his composite marks were highest in Japanese (90), Chinese Classics (88), and English Composition (87). His poorest marks were in Chemistry (65), English Translation (68), and Algebra (69).

Chapter 3

The Awakening of Faith

Takamatsu Higher School of Commerce (now the Economics Department of Kagawa University), was founded in 1924 as a result of the Hara Cabinet policy of increasing opportunities for higher education. With a capable teaching staff, the school made rapid progress in its mission of preparing future businessmen both honorable in spirit and talented in commerce. It gradually became the equal in prestige of other higher commercial schools in the western part of the country, such as those in Kōbe, Hikone, Yamaguchi, and Nagasaki. It was still rather new when Masayoshi entered it, having just graduated its first class the previous year.

Ōhira once wrote: "When I entered the school in 1928, the expansive mood of Taishō Democracy had already begun to fade. Due partly to the aftereffects of the 1927 financial crisis [Japan's most extensive banking system crisis, when thirty-seven banks closed], there was an impalpable heaviness in the air, with no bright prospects in sight. But the heady campus atmosphere had not disappeared, and we were able to enjoy a free and easy campus life combined with the bright and charming natural attractions of our southern region."

For eighteen-year-old Masayoshi, entering Takamatsu Higher School of Commerce was, in a sense, a release from the strictures of home. His new lodging in the home of his aunt Yoshi, his mother's younger sister, was in the seaside town of Tsuda, in Ōkawa District, a full hour's commute by train, but he nevertheless had time to concentrate on his studies and thoughts. Before, almost all his time outside class had been occupied by farm work and side-jobs.

At this juncture, in April 1928, just after Masayoshi had entered Takamatsu Higher School of Commerce, a professor at Tōhoku Imperial University in Sendai and a man of great religious conviction by the name of Satō Sadakichi visited the city to lecture on the theme of "Science and

41

Religion." Satō had been born in the city of Tokushima in neighboring Tokushima Prefecture. In his youth he had attended the Third Higher School in Kyoto, where he majored in natural sciences. Influenced by friends he made there, including Katayama Tetsu (later chairman of the Japan Socialist Party and a postwar prime minister), he had become interested in Christianity and had joined the YMCA. He then entered Tokyo Imperial University, where he majored in applied chemistry. His academic achievements won him, as a special honor at his graduation ceremony, a silver pocket watch donated by the emperor. He continued his studies in the United States, and in 1919, while employed at Tōhoku Imperial University, he established the Satō Industrial Research Center in the Shimo-ochiai district of Yodobashi (now Shinjuku) Ward, Tokyo. There he invented a synthetic resin, made from soybean protein, which he named Satōlite. He was thus one of the pioneers of the modern age of plastics.

Around 1921, Satō began working with Yamamuro Gunpei, head of the Japan Salvation Army, to propagate the Christian faith. After his fifth daughter died of dysentery, he seems to have felt a personal calling to spread Christianity among students in higher schools and universities throughout the country. In 1927, an association inspired by Satō called "Servants of Jesus" (*Iesu no Shimobekai*) was founded, with branches in Tokyo and many other parts of the country. In August of that year, its first training camp was held at the foot of Mount Asama in Nagano Prefecture.

The year 1928, when Masayoshi met Satō Sadakichi, was a critical period for the politics and economy of Japan. In February, the first general elections under the new Universal Manhood Suffrage Law were held. Although democracy and party politics appeared to have made great advances, the business boom that had accompanied World War I had long since ended, and Japan's economy was still suffering from postwar depression and the effects of the Great Kantō Earthquake of 1923. The financial crisis of 1927 had brought the economy to its knees, and Japanese society was pervaded with gloom. Marxism was gaining popularity among students, but those associated with the Japan Communist Party were severely persecuted, as in the mass arrests of March and April 1928.

The temper of the times was certainly one factor behind the support many young students showed for movements of the sort started by Satō Sadakichi. Indeed, a number of young people had been frustrated by the reverses suffered by Marxism at the hands of governmental restrictions, as well as by the lack of clear direction in the movement. They therefore sought to resolve these and other dissatisfactions through associations espousing moral or religious training.

Satō's lectures addressed to such young people covered a wide range of topics, but they fell roughly into two categories. One warned against the trend of emphasizing materialism, advocating instead the unity of religion and science on a more elevated plane. The other recommended personal experience of God through Jesus. A characteristic of Satō's lectures of the first type was a focus on specific aspects of contemporary Japanese civilization. His lectures were both lively and intense. When one ended, students would rush to the podium to shake Satō's hand, some even moved to tears as they requested to be counted among his disciples. Satō's charismatic powers were beyond doubt, and, indeed, in some of his ideas we catch a glimpse of Ōhira Masayoshi's thinking in later years.

Satō advised his young sympathizers to try to become one with God in a spirit of selflessness. He taught that the "ideal Japan" would be realized as the number and strength of sympathizers grew. He needed disciples to carry forth his message, and he requested them to make their own appeal to the masses. The youthful Masayoshi, who had lost his father a year earlier and had only just left a restrictive environment for the stimulating city of Takamatsu, had earlier had little time or occasion to ponder philosophy or religion. Genuinely fascinated, he was caught up by Satō's eloquence. Like many other students, he resolved to answer Satō's call and become a disciple.

As part of the street evangelical activities that were known among initiates as "field operations," he carried a paper lantern inscribed with the sign of the cross and appealed to passers-by to accept the guidance of Jesus. On days without classes, members of the Servants of Jesus would assemble in one or another's lodgings to talk about life and God, to pray, and to profess their faith. A companion of this time recalls: "Prayer meetings were a way of talking freely about one's spiritual or family troubles and asking for God's help. Ōhira was the most zealous of us, and would shed tears while confessing. At the time we thought the most important thing was to be modest before God and to humble oneself like a child. Thus, to shed tears of gratitude was natural."

The degree to which Masayoshi immersed himself in the movement is seen in his taking part in the second Servants of Jesus training camp held at the Sengataki Mountain Lodge at Mount Asama the summer after he had first heard Satō speak. In order to partake in a large evangelical meeting held for the public at Aoyama Kaikan in Tokyo on December 28, 1928, Masayoshi made the long trip to the capital, where, dressed in a formal *haori-hakama*, he made an ardent speech.

Unlike a number of other students, Masayoshi's contact with Christianity appears not to have been in any way political. Having lost his father and experienced other difficulties at home, Masayoshi seems to have grown more introspective. Thus, his encounter with Christianity appears to have been a genuine revelatory experience in both a philosophical and a religious sense. This probably explains why he devoted himself to the movement with such ardor.

In the summer of 1929, during his second year at Takamatsu Higher School of Commerce, Masayoshi suffered a bout of pleurisy and for some time ran a slight fever. He recalls that: "For some reason, around this time I lost almost all interest in my social science studies. Although my health did not actually necessitate it, I decided to take a leave of absence to recuperate and to reconsider whether or not I should continue in school. Fortunately, neither my mother nor my brother objected. During this time, I made it a habit to walk daily in the hills surrounding our hamlet, and luckily my health began to improve. In the meantime, I enjoyed reading novels by Natsume Sōseki and the works of Uchimura Kanzō [a noted Christian philosopher]."

From this passage alone it is hard to judge the nature or depth of Masayoshi's anxieties. However, it should not be surprising that a young man who had rather suddenly and unexpectedly become a fervent Christian activist entertained some wide-ranging doubts about his course in life and his earlier values. According to the recollections of friends, Masayoshi was an avid reader not only of books on Christianity but also of philosophy, poetry, and essays. With a few special friends he exchanged letters in which they communicated their innermost thoughts and ideas. In these letters much was written about philosophy, and a good deal of English was used.

Members of the Servants of Jesus were called "commitment makers" (kesshinsha) meaning those who shared the purposes of the organization and had made a personal commitment to serve it. In essence, being a member meant being an activist in a sort of mass movement, not necessarily the same thing as being a believer in the ordinary sense. "Although Professor Satō's theories helped instill in us a reverence for God, they failed to persuade me why this same God was Love. To attain this insight, I had to receive further instruction in Christianity. Many of these Servants of Jesus later followed the path of Christ, and the teachings of Professor Satō on the relation between science and religion had played a prime role in attracting them to Christianity. My own faith later deepened as I read the Bible." At the end of 1929 Masayoshi was baptized. Baptismal records show that he submitted a letter of intent to Mitoyo Church on December 22, and was baptized by a Reverend Buchanan at Kan'onji Church a few days later.

In the spring of 1930, Masayoshi returned to school, "still unable to make up my mind about either quitting or changing schools." He enrolled again as a second-year student. A friend who was at that time in the same class writes: "During his student years he was a class secretary, and if others didn't carry out his instructions he was liable to burst into tears, convinced that he lacked sincerity. That's how pure his motivations were. He was like the very embodiment of honesty and dedication. . . . Although his character and mine did not conflict, they were rather different, and this may be the reason our relationship has continued for such a long time without ever getting stale. . . . In our youth, we exchanged a number of letters, which were rather sentimental and full of youthful ardor. Unfortunately, the letters I got from him were all burned in the war."

The letters are said to have been full of pedantic references to Kant, Schopenhauer, and Nietzsche, suggesting barely digested new concepts. It is surprising, however, that to this intimate friend Masayoshi never mentioned anything at all about his activities with the Servants of Jesus. This friend hypothesizes that "because I was an atheist, he probably thought there would be no point in talking to me about God." Yet is it really possible that a sensitive youth who shed tears while confessing his faith and who almost every night did evangelical work on the streets could not have let slip any mention of his faith or evangelical work when conversing with an intimate friend with whom he often shared thoughts on philosophy and love, even if he considered this friend to be an atheist? If this was, in fact, the case, it must surely be attributed either to extreme shyness or else to a powerful will. In either case, it was probably related to Masayoshi's capacity for self-restraint that was mentioned in the previous chapter.

It is interesting to note that at this time Masayoshi's family, too, knew absolutely nothing about his participation in religious activities. It is also worth mentioning that while Masayoshi was still a middle school student, he is said to have acted as go-between in the arranged marriage of an older member of the Servants of Jesus. Thanks to Masayoshi's efforts, the marriage took place two years after the initial introduction. The friend for whom Masayoshi performed this service recalls, "During that time, Ōhira was always in the background, like a dependable shadow, and he was always a source of strength for us." Masayoshi's mother, Saku, was quite a social person and is known to have volunteered on numerous occasions to assist in match-making, so perhaps Masayoshi inherited a good part of his obliging nature from his mother. In any case, most of his friends at Takamatsu Higher School of Commerce knew nothing about Masayoshi's extracurricular activities, and within the school he continued, as before, not to draw any particular attention to himself.

On returning to Takamatsu Higher School of Commerce as a second year student, Masayoshi moved from his aunt's home in Tsuda to lodgings in Takamatsu itself. At the beginning of his third year, he took up residence with a Christian family who helped with the activities of the Servants of Jesus off-campus.

When Masayoshi entered his third year in 1931, Japan's economy was in great difficulties. A year and a half before, on October 24, 1929, the "Black Thursday" Wall Street stock market crash had occurred in New York, spreading waves of financial panic throughout the world. Japan had tried to regulate its international debt payments (which had ballooned during the process of industrialization) and to stabilize its exchange rate through budgetary retrenchment and a lifting of the gold embargo to prepare for a return to the gold standard. Now, with the worldwide economic downturn, Japan was in the throes of a severe crisis later known as the Shōwa Depression (1930–35). Gold specie flowed abroad virtually without any end in sight. In 1930, prices had fallen by 18 percent and exports by over 34 percent compared with the previous year. In 1931, the situation was no better, and prices fell by a further 16 percent and exports by 20 percent. As economic conditions worsened, businesses went bankrupt in rapid succession, and the state of the country's farming villages truly beggared description.

It was in this environment that students of Masayoshi's generation were obliged to choose their future careers. As for his own decisions, Ōhira recalls: "I had long ago made up my mind to go on to university, and without telling my family had already applied for admission to Hitotsubashi University [then called Tokyo University of Commerce]. My mother, however, never dreaming that I had any such plans, had gone to see Tanaka Takashi, a former resident of our village and a managing director of Shikoku Hydraulic Company, to ask him to hire me, but on the eve of my graduation the company announced it was not hiring any new employees because of the depression. I hesitated in letting my family know that I wished to continue my studies, and as a result I lost both opportunities of going on to university and of getting a job.

"Just at that moment I received an encouraging offer from Momotani Kanzaburō of Osaka, whom I had met through the Servants of Jesus. Momotani was planning to raise funds for evangelical work by the production of a medicament developed by Professor Satō, who had first aroused my interest in the Christian faith. He asked me to help with the project, and I readily accepted. Upon graduation I set off for Osaka."

Momotani Kanzaburō was a businessman who ran the cosmetics firm Momotani Juntenkan in Osaka. He was a Christian and an invaluable patron of Satō Sadakichi, whom he assisted with funds and in other ways.

In the summer of 1931, Momotani attended the fifth Servants of Jesus training camp at Mount Asama. He had received from Satō the proposition of mass-producing an ointment to be called Silver-zoll, whose main ingredient was a silver colloid first produced by Satō, and then marketing it through Momotani Juntenkan and using the profits for student evangelical work. Momotani had accepted this proposal and wanted to hire one or two employees, if possible from among the students gathered at the training camp, to work on this new endeavor.

It was on this occasion that Momotani first met Masayoshi. During the four or five days the training camp lasted, Momotani looked over some forty students, many of them from national higher schools and imperial universities. In the end he decided on Masayoshi. As he recalled in later years: "Ōhira at first had not said much and did not make much of an impression on me. But when the time came for him to speak, he did so readily, and what he said was quite to the point, if not particularly eloquent. When I mentioned to him the plan for marketing the new pharmaceutical and invited him to join Momotani Company, he readily accepted. So upon graduation in the spring of the following year, he came to Osaka and began to commute to Momotani Juntenkan from my home in Tezukayama."

Masayoshi graduated from Takamatsu Higher School of Commerce in March 1932. Details of his scholastic record there are unknown because all records were lost in a fire that gutted the school after a bombing raid in July 1945. All that remains in the way of school records is a personal report submitted by Takamatsu Higher School of Commerce to Tokyo University of Commerce at the latter's request when Masayoshi took the university entrance examination in the early spring of 1933. It noted that Masayoshi had "strong religious faith."

Masayoshi set to work at his new job, using the Momotani residence as a temporary office. Satō's silver colloid ointment, however, did not sell—it was found to turn the hands and faces of users completely black—and Satō promised to develop a new product using a gold colloid. Ōhira recalls, "I spent two or three months as a hanger-on in the Momotanis' home and made use of my free time during this period to translate Nash's *The Golden Rule [in Business]*." Arthur Nash was an American garment merchant who claimed to have met success through the Golden Rule, that is, the Biblical injunction from the seventh chapter of Matthew (v. 12) to "always treat others as you would like them to treat you." What Masayoshi translated was Nash's autobiography (published in 1920), which was often recommended by the Salvation Army's Yamamuro Gunpei. Very likely Masayoshi also felt that the experiences of this Christian businessman would be helpful now that he himself was entering the business world.

The promised new pharmaceutical seemed to elude commercialization, and Masayoshi, who wanted to do his utmost to further evangelical work, was disappointed. He moved from the Momotani home to a dormitory near the company premises and began working in the advertising section, translating foreign magazine articles and advertisements. While awaiting the manufacture of the new pharmaceutical, he also served as the convener of a monthly Bible study meeting.

Some of Masayoshi's feelings at the time are shown in the following excerpts from a letter written in the summer of 1932 to a Servants of Jesus colleague he had known in Takamatsu: "As you know, by a wholly unanticipated and abrupt turn of fate, I find myself in a corner of the 'Smokestack City,' sweating away over detailed figures and statistics. . . . I am embarrassed by your laudatory words about 'always viewing human life seriously. . . .' Unable to be really serious, I am only pursuing selfish things and so *am constantly* [original emphasis] in turmoil. I very much wish, and hope and pray, that I might have some pulse of life in this lukewarm blood flowing through me. In any case, I have been banished forever from the world of cold, four-square, four-sided logic and from the ivory-tower flower garden. Whether or not we would go so far as to accept Mephistopheles' words about 'all logic being gray,' we ought to have no use for the gray sort of logic or for rigid quibbling. So I am trying to go forward, and at the same time to give substance to the logic of truth, while keeping my ears pressed to the silent, solemn progress of our great earth, loyal insofar as possible to the truth."

Granted that the turn of phrase leans toward sentimentality, the mention of being "banished forever from the world of cold, four-square, four-sided logic and from the ivory-tower flower garden" suggests that Masayoshi had totally abandoned the idea of going on to university. However, the gloominess of the letter clearly indicates that he recognized his decision of the previous summer had been a mistake. Masayoshi would have to pass the fall months with no prospect of the promised new medical product ever being developed.

While working in Osaka, Masayoshi's thoughts turned homeward. According to his younger sister, Tomie: "When he first went to Osaka to take employment with Momotani, he gave me presents several times a year. He'd ask me what I'd like him to buy with his new salary, asking if I'd prefer something to wear, extra spending money, or some cosmetic. I wrote saying that I'd like some clothing, and he wrote back saying he'd send a serge kimono. I was so happy to know it would be coming that several times, just at the hour the postman was expected, I'd run out to the road to look."

The work in Osaka did not last long and the plan for commercializing the new ointment was finally abandoned. Masayoshi resolved to make a fresh start by returning once again to school: "Since my family could not afford to send me to university, the Kamata Mutual Aid Society of Sakaide City and the Kagawa Prefectural Scholarship Society of Takamatsu City loaned me the necessary funds. These two foundations, established through the generosity of the Kamata family of Sakaide and the family of Count Matsudaira, respectively, enabled many young people from Kagawa Prefecture to pursue their studies, and I was most grateful to have been one of them."

Momotani recalls: "I offered to provide Masayoshi's school expenses if he didn't have enough to cover them. However, Masayoshi's clear answer was, 'I'll be able to manage.' I thought that to be too insistent might seem as if I was trying to gain his gratitude, so no funds were disbursed. He had received his salary for working at Juntenkan, and because I hadn't taken any payment for his meals and the like, he had a certain amount saved up. He seems to have felt that there was a way of getting a loan from a scholarship foundation and that, if necessary, he could work as a home tutor." In this way, Masayoshi's life in Osaka came to an end.

How, then, did Masayoshi evaluate the five-year period between the time he left his village to enter Takamatsu Higher School of Commerce and the time he left Osaka? Not long after he started his career in Tokyo, he contributed these thoughts to the journal of the Alumni Association of Takamatsu Higher School of Commerce: "Those of you who were in our school from 1928 until 1931 or 1932 will probably remember the intrepid activities of a group called the Servants of Jesus. This was a society made up of students fascinated by the views on natural science and religion expressed by Doctor of Engineering Satō Sadakichi, who at the time was lecturing to higher schools, colleges, and universities throughout the country and had gained many followers. Helped in part by people's reaction to a decline in the activities of the YMCA, this group developed and demonstrated its own special and very spirited activities both on the campus and on the streets. Of course, in its early period the movement was not well focused, and its program had many points that needed revision, with the result that it perhaps seemed bizarre, as if it somehow did not have its feet on the ground. Or it may have been generally perceived as a sort of *spiritual writhing* [original emphasis] through which some students sought to disperse some of the general anxiety that affected the student population at that time. In any case, this group caused an indescribable sensation both on and off campus and attracted a large number of rather gifted students. Through a process of difficult-to-suppress inner struggle and revision, they ended up either following Christian orthodoxy or else abandoning it."

These remarks do not make it clear whether Ōhira himself was among those following orthodoxy or those abandoning it. From his subsequent life, while we do find indications of an intimate regard for the Bible, he never particularly tried to highlight his identity as a Christian, to say nothing of engaging in further evangelical work. Seen in this context, the quotation may well have been intended as words of parting from an earlier self and the youthful days when he had so fervently immersed himself in the Servants of Jesus.

Chapter 4

Learning and Ambition

In those days, for a young man from a rural part of Shikoku to go to Tokyo to study seemed even more fantastic than going to the United States for students today. Tokyo was the city everyone dreamed about, Japan's window onto the world. After entering Takamatsu Higher School of Commerce, Masayoshi became fascinated with Tokyo's liveliness and its possibilities during his several visits there, and he once told a close friend, "Tokyo is a city worth living in." Now, in the spring of 1933, at the age of twenty-three, Masayoshi's dream would be realized and he would become a resident of Tokyo.

After entering Tokyo University of Commerce (now Hitotsubashi University), Masayoshi found lodgings in the suburb of Kokubunji, which, like the adjacent suburb of Kunitachi in which the university was located, was a part of the greater Tokyo metropolis. As the result of an introduction, he tutored a middle school student from the same neighborhood in English. Besides the income from this job, he had financial help from the two scholarship funds mentioned in the previous chapter and also occasionally received money from his elder brother back home. Although his financial situation could not be called easy, as a student his daily expenses were fairly well provided for.

Masayoshi writes: "Tokyo University of Commerce had by then already moved from Kanda in the center of Tokyo to Kunitachi, and the preparatory course had been transferred from Shakujii to Kodaira. The Musashino Plain [which extended across the western suburbs] still retained the rural appearance so vividly described in the stories of Kunikida Doppo, and a university of commerce seemed rather anomalous in this rustic setting. We often went out to dig sweet potatoes in the middle of classes, and the leaf-strewn campus was a desolate and melancholy place in fall and winter. We had to go all the way to Shinjuku to see a movie, to Kanda to find secondhand book stores, and to the Sumida River for boating. The round-trip train fare alone made a serious dent in our student billfolds."

Tokyo University of Commerce had grown out of the Commercial Law Lecture Institute (*Shōhō Kōshūjo*), founded in 1875 by Mori Arinori, and had played a continuous and important role in Japan's modernization. Its history, however, had by no means been uncheckered. Prior to becoming a national university administered by the Ministry of Education in 1885, it had undergone several changes of administration, and, due to financial difficulties, had at one point been on the verge of being disbanded. Even after becoming a national university several crises occurred, but the faculty and students had always worked successfully to overcome them. One of these crises took place two years before Masayoshi entered the school. In response to the fiscal retrenchment policies of the *Rikken Minseitō* (Constitutional Democratic Party) cabinet under Wakatsuki Reijirō, plans were laid to abolish the school's traditional preparatory course as well as its specialized short-term vocational courses. The students strongly protested and as a last resort occupied campus buildings. There was some fighting between students and the police who had been sent to suppress them, resulting in a number of injuries. Appeals and stratagems on the part of former graduates finally persuaded the government to withdraw its plan.

In January 1933, just before Masayoshi entered the school, a professor who was an authority on Marxist economics was arrested by the Special Secret Service Section of the Metropolitan Police Department. Students who had been no more than sympathizers were also arrested and punished by being expelled from university. Arrested, too, were some of the up-and-coming young professors who belonged to the Study Group on Materialism.

In the later recollection of one of Masayoshi's university friends: "The period from 1933 to 1936 was one of great excitement and confusion. The students were split into two groups, one that studied as hard as possible and the other that mainly played around." Masayoshi presumably belonged to the former. Ōhira writes: "In addition to the compulsory courses, I took advantage of the opportunity to attend lectures by Professor Sugimura Hirozō on economic philosophy, Professor Yamanouchi Tokuryū on the history of philosophy, Professor Miura Shinshichi on the history of civilization, and Professor Makino Eiichi on the history of legal thought. These were all difficult courses, but they aroused my interest in the history of thought and in that of economic thought in particular."

The following is an excerpt from an essay Ōhira contributed in 1963 to a book in memory of Professor Sugimura: "It was a great awakening to be able to come closer to understanding Professor Sugimura's views on capitalism and socialism, his thinking about currency, the functions and limitations of production, savings, and investment, the ramifications of the concept of economic efficiency, and ultimately the spirit and structure of such things as underlying cultural values. It was also a great joy to be exposed to his views on history and his reflections on human motives. He often said that, for a university, methodology is its very life, and therefore if a university student did not acquire a methodology there was no *value* [original emphasis], in studying at a university. For my university training in *Denken* [how to think] this served as a great stimulus and guiding principle." Even in his later years, Ōhira always kept Professor Sugimura's writings close at hand.

One other course made a particularly strong impression on Masayoshi: "A teacher who rivaled Professor Sugimura in popularity was Assistant Professor Nakayama Ichirō. He was an up-and-coming young scholar of the Schumpeter school, and had once studied under the Austrian-born economist. He lectured us on the principles of economics, and his position was that economic phenomena are in a state of constant flux, that examination of such phenomena show their outstanding characteristic is mutual dependence, and that what we call economics is permeated by equilibrium theory since the basis of economic theory derives from the various forms that equilibrium theory may assume. Such an approach was crystallized in the theory of pure economics."

On entering his second year at university, Masayoshi attended seminars with Professor Ueda Tatsunosuke. "Professor Ueda was more a sociologist than an economist and really a philologist more than a sociologist. His studies of St. Thomas Aquinas and other works would have been inconceivable without his considerable linguistic accomplishments. His seminars were usually held at his home in Kichijōji. For our text we used R. H. Tawney's *The Acquisitive Society*, though less emphasis was given to Tawney's economic thinking than to a socio-linguistic interpretation of the English text. . . . Under Professor Ueda's strict tutelage, I was taught the value of words." Later, Ōhira would command a rich vocabulary and write prose with an original rhythm and power of persuasion, an unusual accomplishment for a politician. These abilities were no doubt considerably polished in the course of the Ueda seminar.

In this way, Masayoshi studied the methodologies of history and philosophy with Professor Sugimura and the fundamentals of economic science with Professor Nakayama, and studied with Professor Ueda the words upon which these depend to support their structures of thought. All were vital elements in the formation of Ōhira's character and abilities.

In the more than one hundred years of its history, Hitotsubashi University sity has not only provided the business world and industry with many talented people but has also produced graduates who have made important contributions in the fields of politics, government, scholarship, and education. Due to its relatively small student body, and perhaps also because of the repeated instances of successfully withstanding outside pressures ever since the Meiji period, tight bonds have always existed among the students and between the students and alumni. Indeed, it became a university tradition for persons associated with it to extend help to one another, even if they did not belong to the same graduating class. Ōhira has written, "It certainly helped me incalculably just to have been admitted as a member of the Hitotsubashi family." Certainly in later years in the world of politics, he received much support through these Hitotsubashi connections.

One important person in this regard was Katō Tōtarō, who had graduated in 1910. Katō had earlier been in the second graduating class of Kagawa Prefectural Mitoyo Middle School, so he was a *senpai*, or senior colleague, of Masayoshi twice over. After graduation Katō entered the Ōji Paper Company, where later, at the end of World War II, he became vice-president. He then left the company, purged from his position by the General Headquarters of the Allied Powers. When the purge order was lifted, he rebuilt the Ōji Paper Company's bombed-out Kanzaki plant and founded Kanzaki Paper Company, becoming its first president.

In his university years, Masayoshi had numerous opportunities to talk with Katō and often visited him at the Ōji Paper Company's offices in Sanshin Building in Tokyo's central Hibiya district to ask for contributions to the Tokyo Association of Students from Kagawa Prefecture. Such visits deepened his feelings of respect and affection for Katō, and for his part Katō took a special liking to Masayoshi.

After entering university, Masayoshi did not lose interest in Christianity and now directed this interest largely to acquiring a deeper understanding of the Bible. From the time he lived in Osaka he had been drawn particularly to the writings of Yanaihara Tadao, who was at the time an intellectual leader of the No Church (*Mukyōkai*) Movement of Japanese Christians and after the war became president of the University of Tokyo. In the capital, Masayoshi often went to the Yanaihara home in the Jiyūgaoka district of Setagaya Ward to attend meetings of a Bible study group. He also occasionally visited the home of Christian social reformer Kagawa Toyohiko for lectures on the Bible.

A friend who was at the time a fellow member of the Hitotsubashi YMCA remembers: "Not long after we met, I introduced Ōhira to Kagawa Toyohiko, whose church was in Matsubara along the Keiō rail line, but that day he was giving a lecture at a kindergarten in Fuchū. The topic was 'The Sermon on the Mount.' After the lecture I introduced Ōhira, and the two of us saw Kagawa-*sensei* off at the station. After *sensei* had gone through the wicket and onto the platform, in a loud voice he called back in the dark, 'Ohira-*kun!*' adding the suffix to show a sense of affection. He then added, 'Come over during New Year and eat some *zōni* (rice cakes in vegetable soup).' It is strange how *sensei*'s voice still rings clearly in my ears. Perhaps it's because I felt some jealousy about his not having called my name but Masayoshi's, even though he had just met him for the first time."

During this period, Masayoshi displayed considerable talent for recruiting people and raising funds. In regard to the plan, approved in April 1934, for building the Hitotsubashi YMCA dormitory, Ōhira has written: "I traveled with a prospectus for it throughout the Kantō and Kansai regions, visiting alumni to ask for funds. We succeeded in obtaining ¥15,000 in contributions, which enabled us to construct a two-storied building in a well-wooded area of Kunitachi, with a kind and devout Christian housemother named Mrs. Ōhori."

When Professor Minobe Tatsukichi of Tokyo Imperial University, who also gave lectures on administrative law at Tokyo University of Commerce, was attacked by ultranationalists over his "Emperor-as-organ-of-the-state theory" in 1934 and was forced to step down from his academic posts, Masayoshi felt that a farewell party of only the five students who had attended his lecture would be a waste, so he put up posters on the university's notice boards inviting the student body at large to a "Lunch Meeting with Dr. Minobe." It is said that so many students came they could not all fit into the university dining hall.

The mid-1930s, when Masayoshi was at the university, were a time when the Japanese army was steadily gaining control of more and more territory on the Chinese mainland, leading toward all-out war between China and Japan. Domestically, there was a corresponding growth of militarism, and the country was being put increasingly on a wartime footing. The economy, however, which had been in a disastrous state in the first years of the Shōwa era, was beginning to recover, helped by growing investments and the military procurements that came in the wake of the Manchurian Incident of 1931. Exports were increasing, and the economic outlook, helped largely by the growth of the heavy and chemical industries, was generally improving. Along another dimension, urbanization and the trend toward mass culture were proceeding apace as vital aspects of the "new Shōwa culture."

During their university years, Masayoshi and his companions had a certain amount of leisure to enjoy some of the new cultural trends, but such time was brief, and as they approached the end of their studies university students had to be concerned with the most difficult of hurdles, that of securing employment. Ōhira writes: "I had always been strongly attracted to Sumitomo and had hoped to join that company. As a boy on my way to school, I had watched the smoke rising from the smokestacks of the Sumitomo Mining Company's copper smelter on Shisaka Island, and many men from my village had gone to work there in the Besshi Copper Mine, where the Sumitomo family had first made its fortune. Many of the books on Christianity that I had read were by Yanaihara Tadao, Kurosaki Kōkichi, and Ebara Banri, all of whom had some connection with Sumitomo. I was then particularly fond of Kawada Jun's waka [classical poems of thirty-one syllables] and essays, particularly on historical subjects, and had read most of the more than twenty books he had written. Kawada was a director of Sumitomo and often wrote about the company, and this may have influenced me psychologically as well."

In hiring university graduates for responsible posts in the central government, there was a move toward giving more consideration to graduates of economics faculties rather than to graduates of the law faculty of Tokyo Imperial University as had been done previously. Because of this, many students at Tokyo University of Commerce, which was particularly strong in the field of economics, began to set their sights on becoming government officials, and prepared for the challenge of taking the difficult Higher Civil Service Examination. Probably Masayoshi, who on entering middle school had recorded his ambition of becoming an official, could not fail to be influenced by seeing university classmates preparing to take this state examination. He, too, decided to take it and began to study intensely in preparation.

In the spring of 1935, when Masayoshi entered his third year at the university, his cousin Hideo, who had been living in Tokyo and thus provided a family connection there, went to the Republic of China as a military attaché. His wife and children were left at home, and in the spring of that year Masayoshi moved from his lodgings in Kokubunji to Hideo's home in Nakano Ward, where he studied until graduation. When tired of studying, he would play ball with Hideo's oldest son, who was in primary school, or might join him to sing some popular song.

In May of that year, Professor Yonetani Ryūzō returned to Japan after studying commercial law in Europe, and Masayoshi began taking a course with him. A classmate recalls that: "Yonetani was a scholar of firm character and Ōhira was very fond of him. I have forgotten the occasion, but I remember one day hearing Yonetani say about Ōhira, 'He is indeed

promising.' " Masayoshi took the Higher Civil Service Examination in
September 1935, and the results were announced in October. Masayoshi's
score was among the top one hundred in the administrative division.

All of the classmates and junior students who had graduated from
Takamatsu Higher School of Commerce gathered for a party to congratulate Masayoshi on his success. In a short speech, he said, "The
answers to the exam should be modest, like a woman with light makeup."
By this he meant that it was risky to write too elaborately, "as if one knows
everything," like the risk of having bare skin exposed should the heavy
makeup get smeared. Everyone burst into laughter when someone asked,
"Are you really acquainted with so many women, either heavily made-up
or only lightly made-up?" When Masayoshi graduated, he invited the same
people to his Nakano lodgings where, in his small room, they prepared
sukiyaki in two big cooking pots.

The August 1936 issue of the journal of the alumni association of
Takamatsu Higher School of Commerce published a short essay contributed by Masayoshi, titled "Random Thoughts on the Higher Civil Service Examination." Addressed to younger students interested in taking the
examination, he emphasized, first, the need to have a definite awareness
that one wants to become an official; second, choosing courses in
economics and developing whatever areas one is particularly strong in; and
third, carrying out "living studies" (*ikita gakumon*), in other words, thinking about everyday experiences in such a way that they are related to the
principles of economics.

After successfully passing the examination, Masayoshi consulted
Kamata Katsutarō (then a member of the House of Peers), who had established the Kamata Mutual Aid Society, one of the two foundations that
had assisted him with his expenses. Carrying a letter of introduction from
Kamata, he then paid a call, probably in October of 1935, on Tsushima
Juichi, the vice-minister of finance. Tsushima was a native of Sakaide in
Kagawa Prefecture. A member of the elite, he had distinguished himself at
an early age in the Ministry of Finance, which he had joined after attending the First Higher School and Tokyo Imperial University. He had been
active as a financial official stationed abroad, and had been head of the Financial Bureau. As vice-minister, he was the right-hand man to Finance
Minister Takahashi Korekiyo.

Together with other students from Kagawa Prefecture, Masayoshi had
earlier met Tsushima at a garden party in Tokyo, at the spacious home of
Count Matsudaira Yorihisa (a member of the House of Peers and eldest
son of the former head of the Takamatsu domain in Shikoku, Matsudaira
Yorifusa). On another occasion Masayoshi had had his photo taken with

Tsushima and several students from Kagawa Prefecture when Tsushima, still a financial official, had come to the university to deliver a lecture. However, the relationship was not so intimate that Masayoshi could make a request concerning employment with no introduction at all, and so it was that he received from Kamata Katsutarō a proper introduction.

According to Ōhira's later recollection, his meeting went like this: "Seeing that I had come hoping to get an introduction to a suitable place of work, Tsushima promptly and unexpectedly said, 'Come to the Ministry of Finance.' Flustered and surprised, I said, 'You say to come, but will they hire me?' Without further ado, Tsushima declared, 'I am hiring you here and now. There is no need to bother looking elsewhere.'

"I continued, 'But since I'm from Tokyo University of Commerce, isn't it possible that I won't be suitable for the Ministry of Finance?' Tsushima's answer was, 'Don't be silly. Up till now the Ministry of Finance has had people only from Tokyo Imperial University, and occasionally from Kyoto Imperial University. You ask any official a question and their answers are all the same. This won't do, and we need new blood. Come to the Ministry of Finance.'"

Although it used to be common enough for successful people to help young men who were born and grew up in the same village, or even in the same prefecture, find employment, if this account of how Ōhira Masayoshi entered the Ministry of Finance is accurate, Tsushima's handling of the matter seems rather unusual. It could only have come about because of Tsushima's widespread influence within the ministry, or else because he knew beforehand about Masayoshi's visit and had already undertaken the appropriate personal investigations and other procedures. In any case, it was decided that Masayoshi would enter the Ministry of Finance. He was the first recruit in seven years to enter the ministry from Tokyo University of Commerce. Masayoshi immediately sent a letter to inform his family. In it, he is said to have written: "Tsushima spoke with me, and when I was ready to leave he accompanied me home by car. I was as happy as if I was going to Heaven."

Presumably, it was shortly after his talk with Vice-Minister Tsushima that Masayoshi filled out the personal report that the university requested students to submit to help in the search for a job. In this survey, Masayoshi wrote, under the heading "desired place of employment," the following: "First choice: government agency; second choice: chartered bank." In other words, if he had not been able to enter the Ministry of Finance, he would have preferred a semigovernmental financial institution, such as the Bank of Japan. We see that he was clearly aiming to become an official. We may also note that in this personal report he gave his height as 169 centimeters, his weight as 69 kilograms, his hobbies and pastimes as "cinema and Japanese music," and his favorite sports as "tennis, track and field events, and table tennis." He specified his strong points as being "cheerful, easy to get along with, and unpretentious," and his weak point as being "liable to flounder in sentiment rather than make intelligent judgments." Given our earlier observations about Masayoshi's sentimental side, it is interesting that upon graduation from the university he saw this propensity for sentimentality in a somewhat negative light.

Masayoshi did not commence writing his graduation thesis, titled "The Vocational Society and Trade Associations," until some time after he had taken the Higher Civil Service Examination and had been informally designated to join the Ministry of Finance. In a note at the end of his dissertation he wrote: "After completing the state examination, in October and November I was affected by a slackness and had some difficulty in choosing a theme, with the result that I continued, to no avail, at a low level of activity and made not the slightest preparation. I finally wrote this very hurriedly after the beginning of December."

The dissertation evaluated Tawney's *The Acquisitive Society* as a contemporary version of St. Thomas Aquinas's writings on politics, economics, and philosophy. In it Masayoshi stated: "At present, when both free competition and the class struggle are pushing society into confusion, it is historically inevitable for a demand for wholeness to transcend opposition, for unity to overcome division, and for harmony to go beyond struggle." At the same time he drew attention to what was at the time a very immediate concern—the trend toward industrial controls in countries throughout the world. Professional trade associations were seen as "organizations mediating between the state and the individual." For the courses taken during his three years at the university, Masayoshi received twenty-six marks of "Excellent," seven marks of "Good," and no mark lower than that. His dissertation was graded "Excellent."

Masayoshi was no longer the same person as three years earlier, when he was employed by Momotani Juntenkan in Osaka and had sent an agonized letter to his friend. Though he had deepened his understanding of Christianity through the Bible, he was no longer the person once sent around the streets as part of an evangelical movement. He had come to know excellent instructors and had learned to appreciate some of the deeper realms of knowledge. He had come in contact with colleagues of diverse background and upbringing, and had cultivated their friendship. At the same time, amid the vitality as well as the seedier aspects of big city living, he had enriched his personality and had surely expanded his field of vision vis-à-vis the greater society.

Part 2

A Career in Government

Chapter 5

Life as a Young Bureaucrat

Although Japan's party-led administrations, which began with the Hara Cabinet in 1918, basically upheld the parliamentary ideal and, in the international arena, cooperation with Great Britain and the United States, on several occasions in the early Shōwa era (1926–89), dissatisfied groups within the military masterminded acts of terrorism that were motivated by opposition to both. Especially destructive was the February 26 Incident of 1936, when junior officers of the so-called Imperial Way Faction within the military attempted a predawn coup d'état aimed at restructuring the state. During a heavy snowstorm, they stormed the Prime Minister's Official Residence and the private homes of several other important persons. Although Prime Minister Okada Keisuke barely escaped with his life, many high government officials, including Finance Minister Takahashi Korekiyo, were murdered. The rebellious military units were suppressed in a few days, but this incident no doubt marked a key point in Japan's subsequent plunge into full-fledged militarism.

When a new cabinet led by Hirota Kōki replaced the Okada Cabinet after the February 26 Incident, the murdered Finance Minister Takahashi was succeeded by Baba Eiichi. Baba, a member of the House of Peers and an assistant to Prince Konoe Fumimaro, occupied a key position in the financial and banking world, having been president of the Nippon Kangyō Bank since 1927. As finance minister, Baba discarded the circumspect policies of his predecessor and, to accommodate the budgetary demands of the military, promoted his own financial policy, which involved lower interest rates and higher taxes and abandoned earlier attempts to reduce the national debt. By dismissing or moving to less influential posts people such as Vice-Minister Tsushima Juichi, who had supported Takahashi's policies, Baba's personnel policies underlined the transition within the Ministry of Finance to a quasi-wartime footing.

As soon as he learned that Vice-Minister Tsushima would be resigning, Ōhira hurried to the Ministry of Finance to see him, and said, "I hear you are going to resign, but will my position be all right?" Tsushima's reply was, "Don't talk nonsense! Just study hard so you can graduate."

Ōhira officially began his employment on April 10. He writes: "In newly tailored suits and bursting with expectations, the ten university graduates who were new recruits gathered at the ministry and then proceeded to the Finance Minister's Official Residence. . . .The minister at that time was Baba Eiichi, who with a misanthropic expression gave us all an admonitory speech along the following lines: 'You mustn't think that just because you have graduated from the university your studies are at an end. You must be ready and willing to begin your real studies from now onward. In English, graduation is called 'commencement,' and this is certainly a splendid way of putting it.' "

Ōhira in later years wrote many words of praise for Takahashi Korekiyo but never had good feelings about Baba Eiichi, who had rejected Takahashi's policies. Ōhira's general feeling about Baba surfaces in the remark about his "misanthropic expression." Nevertheless, Baba's mention of graduation being called "commencement" seems to have made a positive impression, and in later years Ōhira himself often explained the meaning of this English expression at gatherings of recent university graduates.

At the Ministry of Finance, there was a certain urgency to establish policies for Japan's changeover to a quasi-wartime regime. Research was begun on foreign governments' spending policies, and in particular on the policies of the recently established Nazi (National Socialist) government in Germany. Ōhira was in the Financial Bureau, whose chief, Kaya Okinori, had been "demoted" under the Baba regime from being chief of the Budget Bureau. Directly under Kaya was Sakomizu Hisatsune, who had been secretary to Prime Minister Okada Keisuke (and later became head of the Economic Planning Agency). Under Sakomizu were Morinaga Teiichirō (later president of the Bank of Japan) and Ihara Takashi (later president of the Bank of Yokohama). Ōhira was attached to a group working under Morinaga and Ihara. Morinaga recalls: "Under special orders from Kaya, we set up various plans and also studied Germany's policies. Ōhira and I were a team that mainly took up German resources policy. Ōhira would read the German materials and then make very solid reports."

The Baba financial regime acknowledged as a *fait accompli* Japan's policies on the Asian continent in the wake of the Manchurian Incident, and approved government expenses thought necessary for a corresponding growth of "national defense." Sympathetic to the national defense concept being touted by the military, Baba resolved to accept those expenditures thought necessary for expanding the nation's military power and for fostering economic strength. This, of course, meant issuing more government bonds and increasing tax revenues, for which purpose Baba drafted a Plan for Revising the Central and Local Tax Systems. The entire ministry set to work on this plan and soon became known as the "Electric Bureau" because the lights were usually on until 11 P.M. or midnight as work on the plan progressed. Nevertheless, Ōhira has written that life for his group of new recruits, as they prepared for their future managerial roles, was "half-study, half-play."

"After finishing lunch, we would walk along the edge of the moat around the Imperial Palace . . . or would play billiards in a billiard hall. We had lunch together once a week." However, "Each year in July there occurred a great migration at the Ministry of Finance. University graduates serving their second year left their nests at this time to be appointed heads of district tax offices or vice-councillors in the Monopoly Bureau, and the responsibilities of the first-year recruits immediately became heavier. They could no longer spend so much time playing billiards or mahjongg. Some acquired girlfriends, others got married. And some began neglecting the Book Club whose sessions they had faithfully attended. We gradually became more worldly."

Each year, the new Finance Ministry recruits would appear. From 1937, the number of yearly recruits increased from ten, the number through 1936, when Ōhira joined, to sixteen. Among those who joined in 1937 were Murayama Tatsuo (later minister of finance) and Satō Ichirō (later minister of international trade and industry), both accomplished drinkers. Ōhira and his companions from the group of 1936 were responsible for looking after the next year's recruits and initiating them into such activities as the Book Club.

Texts studied by the Book Club included Marx's *Zur Kritik der politischen Ökonomie*, Hilferding's *Das Finanzkapital*, Yamada Moritarō's *Nihon shihonshugi bunseki* (Analysis of Japanese Capitalism), and Keynes's *Treatise on Money*. But the Book Club meetings were more than just study. Murayama Tatsuo recalls: "What we called the Book Club meeting was actually an occasion for drinking and eating, and a fund was provided by the senior members. We were linked through this Book Club in a hierarchical fashion, and the senior members took turns guiding us around the ministry. They held welcoming parties and took us drinking afterward. In our year, it was at a small place in the Ginza, rather fashionable, with an eight-mat and two two-mat rooms upstairs and tables and chairs downstairs. The guests included people from the *Asahi* newspaper and from the ministries of Finance, Justice, and Foreign Affairs. At any rate, the liquor was good and the waitresses were all pretty, so all us heavy drinkers took a great liking to the place, and from the very next day began frequenting it daily. Even though Ōhira could not hold much liquor, he always accompanied us."

Satō Ichirō has the following recollection: "Because we used to have to work only half a day in the summer, we rented the second floor of a fish shop in Zushi [on Sagami Bay near Kamakura], and when work was over at noon we would go there every day to swim, play, read, and spend the night, in effect commuting from there to the ministry. So it was a sort of shared life in a common lodging. Ōhira would sometimes join us. At that time he was more of a listener than a talker. And he was a formidable reader. More than economics, he read philosophy and literature. I think as a young man he made a great effort to store things inside rather than release them to the surface."

In April 1937, one year after entering the ministry, Ōhira married Shigeko, the second daughter of Suzuki Mikinosuke. "Our marriage was arranged by go-betweens, like most others at the time," he has written. This match was helped by the fact that a relative of the Suzuki family lived next door to Ōhira Hideo, the cousin in whose home Ōhira was living in Tokyo. This relative of the future bride used to meet Ōhira at the public bath and, having taken a liking to him, became a go-between in the marriage.

Suzuki Mikinosuke was from the village of Usuginu (now Kawasaki Village) in southern Iwate Prefecture, where his family ran a soy sauce factory. On coming to Tokyo, he became a member of the Tokyo Rice Exchange, and after working for Nakahara Stock Brokerage Company, which had ties with his family in Usuginu, he established his own stock brokerage firm under the name Miki Shōken. Having looked into Ōhira's credentials and character, Mikinosuke grew fond of him, and after an initial meeting between his daughter and Ōhira in early March, things proceeded quickly up to the wedding ceremony in the Tōkyō Kaikan on April 15. The ceremony was presided over by Professor Ueda Tatsunosuke, Ōhira's former teacher at Tokyo University of Commerce.

Shigeko was born on November 20, 1916, in the Tamachi district of Tokyo's Hongō (now Bunkyō) Ward. She had attended the private Minami-takanawa Elementary School (now the elementary school of Morimura Gakuen) in Tokyo's Shiba Ward and then Ōin Women's High School (now Ōin Gakuen) in Hongō Ward. When she first met Ōhira, some months after her graduation, she was taking lessons to polish her social and household skills in preparation for marriage.

When Ōhira told Katō Tōtarō of Ōji Paper Company that he was to be married, Katō replied, "You don't look as though you can afford it, but try to pay at least half of the wedding expenses yourself," and then took his billfold from his pocket and handed Ōhira ¥800. It was a substantial sum, since Ōhira's starting salary was ¥75 per month and in those days a new house could be built for only ¥1,000.

Following his marriage, Ōhira first set up house in the Wada-honchō district of Tokyo's Suginami Ward. Before he could really settle in, however, his one year and three months as a junior official came to an end, and in the personnel transfers on July 1, 1937, he was appointed head of the Yokohama Tax Office, a Grade 7 higher official. In those days there was a sharp line between higher and junior officials, who had different dining rooms and even different lavatories.

The difference was not limited to status, for there was also a large disparity in salary. Ōhira's salary almost doubled from the ¥75 he had received as a junior official to ¥137. In those days, the starting salary of a company employee who had graduated from a private university was around ¥50, while the monthly wage of a live-in factory worker was only ¥5. Ōhira frequently treated junior officials to meals, and managing the household budget within his salary was not easy for Shigeko, who had had a comfortable upbringing. But if funds ran a bit short, her father Mikinosuke was willing to help out.

Ōhira took up his new post in Yokohama on July 7, 1937, the day of the Marco Polo Bridge Incident, which would develop into full-scale war between Japan and China. Ōhira has described Yokohama at that time as follows: "Yokohama still had scars of the Great Kantō Earthquake of 1923. Control of foreign trade had gradually been usurped by the large trading firms located in Nihonbashi and Marunouchi in Tokyo, and Yokohama, having lost its old identity, was now slipping into the status of just another entrepôt. Yokohama was usually mentioned along with the other port cities of Kōbe and Nagoya, but from my vantage point at the tax office, it was only too clear that Yokohama had fallen far behind these two rivals economically. Nevertheless, its citizens, known as "Hamakko," continued to display their typical town spirit and pride, and the large number of Americans, Chinese, Indians, and Europeans who lived there lent an air of exoticism to the Kannai area of town. The British Consulate-General often held formal parties to which I was invited."

The Yokohama Tax Office was just one of sixty-four district tax offices under the Tokyo Tax Supervision Bureau, whose purview encompassed Tokyo and the seven nearby prefectures of Kanagawa, Chiba, Yamanashi, Saitama, Ibaragi, Tochigi, and Gunma. In Yokohama, there had traditionally been only one office, but just when Ōhira assumed his post, a new

Kanagawa Tax Office was established in the city, with the result that the Yokohama Tax Office was reduced in size and its personnel trimmed to about eighty persons. Ōhira writes that from the very first day, "I sat in the director's chair and, while watching rather absentmindedly the goings-on in the office, kept rubber-stamping tall piles of documents on the designated spot."

An employee of the Yokohama Tax Office at that time recalls that Ōhira often accompanied the office staff on trips—something that office chiefs almost never did in those days. He would exchange cups of saké with them and, if they went to the beach, he would swim and do *sumō* wrestling with them, stripped to a loincloth like everyone else. Others remember Ōhira seeing officially stamped attachment notices pasted on the display windows of shops that had not been able to keep up with their tax payments and tearing them off because he felt sorry about their owners' plight. Appointed head of the Direct Taxation Department of the Tokyo Tax Supervision Bureau on October 25 of that year was Ikeda Hayato, who later served as minister of finance, minister of international trade and industry, and prime minister. The links between Ikeda and Ōhira, which were to grow in significance, dated from this time.

Ikeda had been born into a wealthy family in Yoshina Village, Toyota District, Hiroshima Prefecture, in 1899. After finishing the Fifth Higher School in Kumamoto and Kyoto Imperial University, he entered the Ministry of Finance in 1925. In his sixth year there, he caught a rare disease and was granted a five-year leave of absence to recuperate. He rejoined the ministry in 1934. Before being appointed to his post in the Direct Taxation Department of the Tokyo Tax Supervision Bureau, Ikeda served as head of the Tamatsukuri Tax Office in Osaka, head of the Direct Taxation Department of the Kumamoto Tax Supervision Bureau in Kyūshū, and as an official in the Tax Bureau of the ministry.

A head of a direct taxation department of a tax supervision bureau was expected to keep track of all the heads of tax offices under his jurisdiction and to deal with any problems the latter could not handle. At that time Ikeda had a reputation of being a heavy drinker in the best Ministry of Finance tradition and also a somewhat clouded reputation as a man who showed little mercy in the business of collecting taxes. He was intent on climbing the ladder of success as fast as possible to make up for the delay occasioned by his illness. Ōhira was frequently obliged to call on Ikeda, and Ikeda from time to time came to the Yokohama Tax Office to provide guidance on tax collection matters. Ōhira recalls Ikeda telling him, "Since you're in Yokohama, I hope you'll take advantage of the opportunity to thoroughly study conditions there." Ikeda also criticized him for "not having a sufficient specific grasp of matters concerning the area's single biggest taxpayer, the Yokohama Specie Bank." Ōhira's wife, Shigeko, remembers Ōhira would sometimes leave home in the morning with a strained expression on his face, saying, "Ikeda is coming to the office today."

Despite being in his mid-twenties, as head of a tax office Ōhira had to fulfill the role of a leader, responsible for the work and livelihood of over eighty individuals. This was indeed what the Ministry of Finance expected of its young higher officials. At the New Year's ceremony, Ōhira addressed the employees of the Yokohama Tax Office as follows: "Administration, like an ellipse, has two centers, and administration may be said to be good when the two centers are in a relationship of tension with each other but still maintain a balance.... Even in the controlled economy that has begun to develop with the outbreak of the China [Marco Polo Bridge] Incident, one center is the controls, and the other center is what we call freedom. When controls and freedom are in a tight, yet balanced, relationship, only then will the controls work well. We must not lean too much in either direction." Ōhira might have here been recalling Schumpeter's equilibrium theory, which he had studied at the university with Professor Nakayama Ichirō. His speech continued: "Tax work is also like this: one center is the superior authority to levy taxes and the other is the taxpayers. Neither a levying of taxes that pretends to have omnipotent authority nor a levying of taxes that too easily compromises with taxpayers will do. A reasonable way of imposing taxes is one that maintains an unbiased standpoint throughout, leaning to neither side." About this speech Ōhira has written, "I think what I said was at the time rather too sophisticated." Nevertheless, the "ellipse theory" became an important element in the philosophy that subsequently underlay his behavior throughout his life.

Immediately after assuming his post in Yokohama, Ōhira had moved into government employees' lodgings. However, because the building was already old and falling into disrepair, it was razed about two months after his arrival, and he then moved to a quiet rented house in Isogo Ward near Ashinabashi, only a block from the beach. Shigeko had become pregnant not long after their marriage, and gave birth here to their first son, Masaki, on February 6, 1938.

On June 25, 1938, Ōhira was appointed head of the Indirect Taxation Department of the Sendai Tax Supervision Bureau (now called the Sendai Regional Tax Administration Bureau), and left Yokohama for Sendai about a week after his appointment. On the day set for his northward departure, the Tokyo–Yokohama region was flooded from heavy rains, with transportation routes between the two cities temporarily severed. Ōhira had to be at his new post immediately, in advance of his family, and so managed to wade across the Rokugō River, stripped to his underwear and carrying his trunk on his head.

"My work in Sendai had to do with indirect taxation, that is, duty on liquor, textiles, benzine, sugar, official documents, and other things. However, the Tōhoku region had no large factories and the standard of living was low, so the sources of indirect taxes were not so numerous. But because Akita, Iwate, Miyagi and Yamagata prefectures had saké breweries that were well known beyond their borders, the single largest source was the tax imposed on saké." Linked to the saké tax was the difficult task of trying to eliminate home brewing.

In the farming villages of the Tōhoku region of northern Japan, the custom of brewing for home consumption began in the feudal period and became deeply rooted in the life of each feudal domain throughout the region, among commoners and the samurai class alike. Brewing for home consumption was in theory completely abolished by the Brewery Tax Law of 1899, but in subsequent years it was still customary in rural areas for every household, throughout the four seasons, to make its own saké, and for all household members, even women and young children, to drink it with each meal, during work breaks, and in the evenings. It was also homemade saké that was usually consumed at weddings and funerals, at large and small parties of all kinds, and in welcoming guests.

The authorities, in their zeal to protect sources of revenue by eradicating the "pernicious custom" of home brewing, had launched ambitious campaigns to deal with offenders, but to eliminate such an entrenched practice was far from easy. The "crime" was one which whole families engaged in, and any sense of impropriety among the perpetrators was slight. Often whole villages would band together against the authorities, and there had been frequent incidents in the region, some involving bloodshed. Until the early years of the Shōwa era, the Indirect Taxation Department's policy on illegal brewing was centered on strict law enforcement, in accordance with the oft-quoted slogan: "No better correction than arrest."

However, in 1932, much publicity was given to an incident in which an elderly woman fell and died while trying to escape during a raid on an illegal brewer in Akita Prefecture. In the wake of this, emphasis came to be placed not only on "arrest" but also on "guidance." Against this background, in Akita and Iwate prefectures the Ministry of Finance organized Societies to Eliminate the Illicit Manufacture of Liquor, which embarked on a campaign of education. They held general meetings once a year, were headed by prefectural governors, and included within their ranks many local notables.

In spite of these efforts, according to statistics of the Sendai Regional Tax Administration Bureau, during fiscal 1938—the year Ōhira assumed his post there—in the six prefectures of the Tōhoku region there were 2,463 arrests for the illegal manufacture of liquor, or 70.4 percent of the national total of arrests in this category. Regarding this attempt to rid Tōhoku of home brewing, Ōhira has written: "To exaggerate a bit, this was an activity that lay outside the purview of those matters properly administered by the tax authorities. It was more properly speaking a political activity, and whether from the point of view of public hygiene, social education, or social policy, it was a strange sort of work that entailed all kinds of problems."

Because of the nature of the work, the Ministry of Finance paid considerable attention to selecting persons to head the Sendai Bureau's Indirect Taxation Department. Having observed Ōhira's work style at the Yokohama Tax Office, it was Ikeda Hayato who decided to recommend him as the most appropriate person for the Sendai post. No doubt Ikeda already intuitively recognized the political talents that Ōhira would display in later years.

In Sendai, Ōhira organized Societies to Eliminate the Illicit Manufacture of Liquor in the four other prefectures in his jurisdiction (in addition to Akita and Iwate), and he sought out persons from all walks of life to attend their general meetings. His public relations activities extended to the editing of a 200-page book titled *Shurui mitsuzō kyosei shisetsu ippan* (Overview of Means for Eliminating the Illicit Manufacture of Liquor). However, despite the authorities' repeated attempts at control and the efforts of these societies, illegal brewing did not diminish. Each time a case was revealed, a cut-and-dried investigative report was filed, a fine was imposed, and in especially serious cases corporal punishment was inflicted. One even heard stories about fathers selling their daughters to pay the fines, and in cases of corporal punishment it was often elderly people who were the victims. Having been born into a farming family, it was only natural that Ōhira could not stand to see farming people being treated in this way. He later wrote down his thoughts on the matter: "These poverty-stricken farmers in the Tōhoku region not only receive practically no benefits from the state, but under the name of taxation [policy] they are suffering in these shackles. How sad is their fate of having to suffer like this just because they happen to be living in this area. I felt a sort of revulsion against the cold and stern conventions attached to 'the state' and to 'national law.' "

In those days, the work of the head of an indirect taxation department included not only efforts to eliminate home-made saké but also, influenced by the escalating war in the wake of the Marco Polo Bridge Incident, the issue of enforcing wartime controls over legitimate liquor manufacturing facilities and the related problems of liquor retailers who were being ordered to either abandon their businesses or convert to other lines of activity. Here, too, Ōhira showed his understanding of the standpoint of private entrepreneurs, and assisted them in drawing up various types of petitions to the Ministry of Finance in Tokyo.

Ōhira's life had thus changed greatly in the more than three years since he had graduated from the university. After serving his apprenticeship as a junior official in Tokyo, he was now, as a higher official, associating as the social equal of the local notables in the prefectures to which his work had taken him. His salary was nearly three times that of university classmates who had taken jobs in the private sector, and in restaurants that he frequented he was accorded the utmost respect and addressed by his formal titles. These were the realities of an elite bureaucrat's life in the society of the time. He continued to find time for Bible study and other serious reading, but at the same time he did not refuse to enjoy his elite status. He did not try to avoid saké parties (even if these were not very frequent), and indeed found much satisfaction in his contacts with local people.

In this interval, a certain inner quality, which neither he nor others had particularly noticed during his student years or his rather strained childhood on the family farm, began to grow and flower. This was the quality of being able to adapt flexibly to various types of situations and structures in Japan's society; in other words, what we might call a "political" capacity. Compared to others who joined the Ministry of Finance at the same time, the fact that Ōhira had extended his pre-university life by three years—one extra year spent in elementary school, a year's leave of absence in his higher school years, and a year of hardship and uncertainty in the workaday world in Osaka—probably helped him develop a tolerant and multifaceted character.

One day in May 1939, after living in Sendai almost a year, Ōhira unexpectedly received a cryptic telegram from Vice-Minister of Finance Ōno Ryūta, asking him to come to Tokyo urgently. "On arriving in Tokyo the next day, I visited Ōno in the vice-minister's office with some trepidation. Vice-Minister Ōno was together with Secretarial Section Chief Yamagiwa Masamichi (later president of the Bank of Japan), and said, 'First, let's all go out and have something to eat.' I didn't know what might be going on, but I obediently accompanied them, still feeling thoroughly puzzled. I was taken to a certain restaurant near the entrance to Shiba Park, and when we had just about finished lunch, Vice-Minister Ōno said, 'Won't you go to China for us? It has been decided in the government that we will set up

Asia Development Board liaison offices in four places: Beijing, Shanghai, Zhangjiakou, and Xiamen (Amoy). People will be sent by the Ministry of Finance to each liaison office, and I'd like you to go to Zhangjiakou. The summers are cool and the winters are warm there, and all in all it's a good place to live. And if you go, you will be something like a finance minister for Inner Mongolia and can do any work you want. It will be like drawing pictures on a blank sheet of paper. The time to travel around and see things is while you are young. How about it? Can we ask you to do this?'

"I thought I was being flattered, but since I'd been treated to lunch I couldn't immediately refuse so I said, 'Let me think about it. I'll talk to my family and give you an answer in a few days,' and I took my leave. On the way home I bought a big map of China, found out the whereabouts of Zhangjiakou, and let my imagination go to work in regard to the Chinese continent I had never seen. In the end I changed my mind, realizing that indeed 'the time to travel around and see things is while you are young.' I already had friends working in Beijing and Tianjin, and decided that if I became lonely I could always make a trip to Beijing to see them. So the next day, without even consulting my family in Sendai, I gave Vice-Minister Ōno my reply of acceptance."

Chapter 6

Continental Management

As a result of the Marco Polo Bridge Incident near Beijing on July 7, 1937, full-scale war broke out between Japan and China. After the Hirota Cabinet and the short-lived Hayashi Cabinet, Prince Konoe Fumimaro left the House of Peers to organize the First Konoe Cabinet, which many hoped would keep the military under control. However, in spite of the government's "non-expansionist policy," military engagements spread across China. In November, the military established an Imperial Head-quarters (*Daihon'ei*), with jurisdiction over both the army and the navy, to coordinate all important decisions in the prosecution of the war. A con-trolled wartime economy was promoted by the Planning Board (*Kikakuin*), which was set up in October directly subordinate to the cabinet. This board elaborated an annual Plan for Materials Mobilization and, in fact, usurped from the Ministry of Finance much of its authority for coor-dinating financial and budgetary policies.

After occupying large sections of Chinese territory, Japan faced the problem of how to administer them. From the beginning of 1938, the con-cept of establishing a centralized body revolving around the military to standardize policy toward China was discussed, but the Ministry of Foreign Affairs, which saw the military as intent not only on controlling the occupied territories but also on taking over the prerogative of conducting diplomacy with China, was strongly opposed. After much argument, the decision to establish such a new body was officially announced on December 16, 1938. It was to be named the Asia Development Board (*Kōain*) and given jurisdiction over the making and execution of all China-related policies, with the exception of top-level diplomacy. It was charged with the management of China-related administrative work from all the various ministries, as well as supervision of the "special corporations" set up in China with Japanese capital. The president of the Asia Development

Board was the prime minister, and the four vice-presidents we ministers of foreign affairs, the army, the navy, and finance.

Ōhira left his wife (now pregnant for the second time) and son Masaki at his wife's family home in the Wakamiyachō district of Tokyo's Ushigome (now Shinjuku) Ward, and left Tokyo Station on June 15, 1939, to assume his post in China. He took the ferry between Shimonoseki and Pusan, spent a night in the Korean capital of Seoul (then known as Keijō in Japanese), and after passing by train through P'yŏngyang in northern Korea, Fengtian (Mukden) in Manchuria, and Beijing, he finally arrived in Zhangjiakou on the evening of June 20.

"Zhangjiakou was, in a word, a city of earth. It was a country town completely the color of earth, with hardly a tree to be seen. Although I stayed at a Japanese inn that had been recently remodeled, I felt that I had come to a pretty awful place and had been deceived by the sweet words of the vice-minister. In brief, I felt somewhat bitter about having come all the way to this desolate northern place. Water was scarce, and what water there was had a hardness of twenty to thirty degrees, like mineral water. The Lipton tea I had brought along completely lost its flavor, and I was frequently bothered by stomach upsets."

Zhangjiakou, located 150 kilometers northwest of Beijing, was a key transportation center for traffic between China and Inner Mongolia, and the Asia Development Board's Mongolian Border Region Liaison Department (*Mōkyō Renrakubu*) to be located there would operate in a far more complex political environment than the other liaison departments in the Asia Development Board system. At the time, Zhangjiakou was already the headquarters for all Japanese armies stationed in Inner Mongolia. Under the control of Japanese forces, the so-called Chanan Autonomous Government had been established there in September 1937, and when the Japanese military subsequently entered Datong, to the southwest, a similar so-called Jinbei Autonomous Government was established in the latter city. In November 1937, a so-called Inner Mongolia Federation Committee (*Mōkyō Rengō Iinkai*) had been set up in Zhangjiakou to deal with political and economic development throughout Inner Mongolia under the guidance of the Kantō Army and the Manchukuo government headquartered in Changchun.

The Japanese government felt that the methods used by the Kantō Army and the Manchukuo government were excessive and that, for the time being, the Mongolian Border Region should be administered as a part of "North China" (*Kahoku*), but Japanese on the spot tended to think it should be administered as if it was a part of Manchuria. It was in this situation that bureaucrats began coming from Tokyo to staff the new Zhangjiakou offices of the unfamiliar and still loosely organized Asia Development Board. Not surprisingly, many local Japanese, first and foremost the military, regarded the arriving bureaucrats with suspicion.

In September 1939, not long after Ōhira arrived at his Zhangjiakou post, the Inner Mongolia Federation Committee was abolished and the so-called Mongolian, Chanan, and Jinbei governments were amalgamated with the Mongolian Autonomous Government of Allied Leagues to form the Federated Autonomous Government of Mongolia (*Mōko Rengō Jichi Seifu*) with the Mongolian De Wang (whose Mongolian name was Demchugdongrub) as chairman. However, in Ōhira's words, "In Inner Mongolia as a whole, there were said to be 7 to 8 million people, but most were Han people and Mongolians numbered only 200,000 to 300,000. So the fact that De Wang was made chairman of its autonomous government was rather unnatural."

Economic policy toward the Inner Mongolia region emphasized investment and resource utilization projects. Particularly important were Longyan Iron Mining Company and Datong Coal Mining Company, both established as Japan–Inner Mongolia joint ventures. In Ōhira's opinion: "Due to the abnormal nature of this Inner Mongolian political entity, some of the items agreed upon in the management of these two companies were quite strange, and matters concerning personnel were never fully settled, always being caught in a tug of war between Tokyo and Shinkyō [the Japanese name for Changchun, the new capital of Manchukuo]." The production of both companies far exceeded that of similar mining enterprises in Japan. Allocations of capital goods and other materials to increase the two companies' production were proposed by the Liaison Department in accordance with each year's Plan for Materials Mobilization (the first of which was announced in January 1938), and then had to be reviewed by the Asia Development Board headquarters in Tokyo and given final approval by the Planning Board.

It was Ōhira's job to analyze the business and management of these and similar companies, establish policy guidelines, and present them to the Asia Development Board headquarters and to the Planning Board. Ōhira's efforts were generally effective, and since the military and local government people knew that work plans had to go through the Asia Development Board's Mongolian Border Region Liaison Department in line with its investment guidelines and the directives of the resources mobilization plan, and that it was Ōhira who would fight for approval in Tokyo if the plans made sense, they came to treat him with respect. From these sorts of planning activities Ōhira went on to tackle some of the broader management problems of the economy of the Mongolian Border Region.

One of the first things he learned was that the Mongolian Border Region, as distinct from the stereotyped image of deserts, nomads, and underground resources, was also an agricultural area. The majority of its population were ethnically Han, mostly descendants of people who had crossed the Great Wall from China proper during the famines of the late Ming Dynasty (1368–1644) and had converted much of the desert into arable land. The major crops were wheat and other grains, and opium poppies. Yet, while any discussion of the region's economy should have taken account of the important role played by agriculture, this was generally not understood by the Japanese either in Tokyo or locally, partly because of the circumstance that in this region the Japanese only had control of scattered pockets, unlike the situation in Manchuria, where control extended over the whole countryside. Ōhira recalls: "[Tokyo], unaware of local conditions, stuck stubbornly to its hard-and-fast rules and refused to budge from its 'low-price policy.' In effect, this policy applied only to goods and services under Japanese control such as coal, salt, railway fares, electricity and telegraph rates, and did not filter down to the local economy. . . . Consequently, the prices of local agricultural produce were generally high." Ōhira tried to enlighten those around him by contributing an article titled "Mōkyō keizai o hadaka ni suru" (Baring the Facts about the Mongolian Border Region Economy) to the local Japanese newspaper, the Mōkyō Shinbun. He aired similar views toward Inner Mongolia in articles submitted to the continental editions of the Asahi and the Mainichi newspapers.

Albeit in an occupied territory, the Federated Autonomous Government of Inner Mongolia was nevertheless a government. It had enjoyed a good measure of independence with respect to public security, budget, prices, and exchange rates, and both its own currency and Japanese bank notes were legal tender. Business transactions with Japan and other parts of China fell within the category of foreign trade. Coal and iron were exported to Japan, and opium to Shanghai and Tianjin, and the money thus earned was used to import needed commodities.

Even if the year and a half Ōhira spent in Zhangjiakou did not quite enable him to "draw pictures on a blank sheet of paper," it was nonetheless a fine opportunity to study the workings of what he called a "prototype state." In Zhangjiakou, Ōhira had ample occasion to distinguish between persons he liked and those he did not. Especially in occupied areas, with their clear distinctions between the controller and the controlled, cases of improper conduct by the military under the guise of authority were frequent, and in Ōhira such behavior evoked strong disgust. He has written, however, that "these were not matters for which we should criticize only the military. Equally responsible, I felt, were those officials and civilians who blindly followed the military, cowering at the mere sight of military epaulettes, the visible symbols of authority, and making no independent judgments as to the rightness and wrongness or the relative importance of a matter, or else who tried to divert the military's authority for their own selfish ends." Whether it was among the military, officialdom, or civilians, there must have been many with whom Ōhira felt little patience.

After a few months, Ōhira came to understand more about the region, its people, and its natural environment. As one of the top-ranking representatives of the Japanese government, Ōhira frequently shared banquet tables with De Wang, who once invited Ōhira to West Sönid Banner, the district where his court was. Ōhira has described this visit as follows: "Traveling from Zhangjiakou in a small five-passenger airplane, I was shown around by De Wang and was a guest at his court, where we were served an alcoholic beverage made from the milk of sheep and cows. De Wang and his son gave me quite a reception, and I discovered for the first time that he was a formidable drinker, because at banquets held in Zhangjiakou he almost invariably drank very little. A person familiar with the situation later told me that princes among the minority peoples abstained from indulging in alcohol when away from home because they felt their lives were constantly in danger. I realized that the minority peoples certainly had many difficulties we were unable to fathom."

On another occasion, Ōhira traveled far into the interior during a census of Mongolian households. "After riding in a truck for two or three hours across an endless plateau, we would come to a small settlement. Wolves sometimes ran after us along the way. On reaching a settlement, we would leave the vehicle and visit each yurt to survey the family situation and the particulars of its property, for example, how many sheep, cows, and horses it had. When night came we would either put up our own tent or be the guests of Mongolians. On visiting a Lamaist temple, we met a Living Buddha and observed the temple ceremonies. For nine days we journeyed around the grass-covered plains, and though it was only November, it was already bitterly cold. When the survey was over, we returned via Zhangbei to Zhangjiakou, and when I first caught sight of Zhangjiakou's twinkling lights I felt the same happy sense of homecoming that I would have felt at seeing the lights of Tokyo. From that time on, Zhangjiakou, which I had considered a remote outpost in the northern wilderness, curiously began to seem like a town within the bounds of civilization, and I no longer had any special difficulty working there."

Most of the other members of the Ministry of Finance "entering class of 1936" had, like Ōhira, been transferred to jobs with the Asia Development Board. But most of them were working in cities like Shanghai,

Qingdao, or Xiamen, where conditions were far better than in the mud-brick town of Zhangjiakou. Indeed, initially, it seemed that Ōhira had gotten the raw end of the deal. He had first felt "deceived by the sweet words of the vice-minister" and, confronted with the arrogance of the military, spent some "cheerless days in a state of trepidation." On the other hand, in the other cities with better living conditions, section heads in the Asia Development Board liaison departments had begun their government careers in 1932 or 1933, while those who, like Ōhira, began their careers in 1936 were no more than assistants. In Zhangjiakou, however, Ōhira was in charge of his liaison group's Economic Section and thus responsible for resolving, in an unfavorable environment, major problems in a brand-new organization. Unlike the work of heading a tax office or an indirect taxation department, in keeping with the long-established traditions of the Ministry of Finance, this work in Inner Mongolia had no precedent and required a definite creativity.

On balance, this was for Ōhira a good experience. No longer the same lonely person who had boarded the Shimonoseki–Pusan ferry, he had grown into a tough and self-assured administrator amid the biting northern winds. A colleague who was sent to the Asia Development Board's Zhangjiakou liaison group from the Ministry of Commerce and Industry and who worked at a desk next to Ōhira's, recalls: "I was greatly impressed by the way Ōhira negotiated, sometimes flexibly and sometimes taking a hard line, with the military headquarters in Inner Mongolia, the Autonomous Government of Mongolia, the Tokyo headquarters of the Asia Development Board, and the neighboring Asia Development Board liaison group for North China and achieved results. I was fascinated by his ability to handle matters quickly and efficiently and by the persistence with which he patiently explained his opinions to superiors and got his way without modifying his own views."

Colleagues who had assumed posts in other Asia Development Board liaison groups in other areas of China were similarly impressed. One recalls: "Ōhira would always stop at the North China liaison office in Beijing on his way to and from Tokyo. On these occasions several of us would meet to exchange reports on the current situation, and I remember we were always astounded at how complete and well-rounded Ōhira's reports were. It wasn't merely that they were different from the ordinary; he approached matters, made judgments, and guided discussions in a way quite apart from that of the ordinary official, as if from a different dimension."

While Ōhira was in Zhangjiakou, his second son, Hiroshi, was born on October 17, 1939. By the summer of 1940, the end of Ōhira's term was approaching, even though a successor had not yet been found. One of the problems in finding a replacement was that many officials had been taken from the Ministry of Finance to serve in the military, so the number of possible candidates had declined. But it also appears that just about everyone, on hearing Zhangjiakou's reputation, refused to be stationed there. During a visit to Tokyo in the early autumn of 1940, Ōhira asked the chief of the ministry's secretarial section, Yamagiwa Masamichi, "What are you going to do about me?" and Yamagiwa replied, "If you can find your own successor, I'll bring you back." Ōhira then remembered that Satō Ichirō, who was one year his junior in the ministry, was working at the Planning Board. He invited him to a meal and persuaded him to take the Zhangjiakou post.

Consequently, in October 1940 Ōhira received a cabinet order to return to Japan. He arrived in Tokyo at the end of the month, after traveling through parts of Inner Mongolia and Manchuria. His new work was in the Second Section of the Economic Department at the Asia Development Board headquarters. This section had three tasks: (1) the supervision of the state-supported Japanese "special corporations" in China; (2) the regulation of other enterprises in China; and (3) land development work in China. Ōhira dealt with the first of these.

In Ōhira's words: "Japanese governmental authority extended to the two Japanese special corporations, the North China Development Company and the Central China Promotion Company, but did not extend to their locally incorporated subsidiary companies in China. However, the government indirectly extended guidance and supervision to these subsidiary companies insofar as the two parent corporations invested in them. There were several tens of such subsidiary companies in such fields as mining, railroads, harbors, transport, salt production, electricity, and telecommunications."

Through his experience in Zhangjiakou with managing the economic affairs of a government, even if a small one, Ōhira had gained self-confidence and become adept at getting his own way. These traits are reflected in the following episode. When he assumed his new post in Tokyo, the president of the North China Development Company was Kaya Okinori (later minister of finance), who had been his superior when Ōhira first joined the Ministry of Finance. Kaya liked large projects and wished to establish a research bureau to carry out large-scale surveys of resources throughout North China, along the lines of the South Manchuria Railway's Research Institute. When he presented his proposed budget for this, Ōhira severely revised it. Kaya was furious, and there was a face-to-face confrontation. When the research bureau finally came into being, however, it was considerably smaller than Kaya had hoped.

The Asia Development Board headquarters consisted of a financial department, an economic department, a cultural department, and a technical department. The section heads and most other staff members in each department were on loan, according to their specialties, from the various ministries, as well as from the army and navy, which were not administratively treated as ministries. The army and navy were on extremely bad terms with each other and were constantly embroiled in jurisdictional quarrels. Personnel from the ministries often suffered inconveniences due to these army–navy quarrels, but among themselves they generally cooperated and did not try to force parochial interests.

Isozaki Satoshi (later president of the Japanese National Railways), who was at the time on loan to the Asia Development Board from the National Railways and also worked in the Economic Department, recalls: "The Asia Development Board, which was located in Hayabusachō, between Miyakezaka and Hanzōmon in the area now occupied by the National Theater, was concerned not only with current policy toward China but also with China-related management problems foreseen for the period after the war's end. It was a very broad-minded place, completely different in atmosphere from the overly serious Planning Board, the body entrusted with making the detailed plans for prosecuting the war.

"The Asia Development Board was an anomaly among Japanese government offices, and we were always looking at maps of China and entertaining vague notions of 'East Asia management,' here proposing to establish a steel mill, there to develop agriculture. Many of the persons gathered there tended to be not so hard-headed and rather nontraditional."

Within this free-wheeling organization, the Nine Wise Men's Group was formed by nine younger officials, including Ōhira. The meetings of this group, whose members came from different universities, regions of Japan, and parent agencies within the government, doubtless did much to expand Ōhira's field of vision. Among his friends from this period were Itō Masayoshi (later minister of foreign affairs) and Sasaki Yoshitake (later minister of international trade and industry), both of whom would later be valued political allies. However, dreams of "East Asia management" were destroyed with the outbreak of the Pacific War and subsequent world events.

Despite all their vicissitudes, Ōhira's three years with the Asia Development Board (including the one and a half years in Zhangjiakou), made him quite knowledgeable about China. His work was directly concerned with China's economy, society, traditions, and national character, and he also had to be conversant with a wide range of matters relating to Chinese industry, from natural resources to finished products, consumption, and trade. Considering the fact that twenty-seven years after Japan's defeat in World War II—a defeat that was, in effect, a declaration of bankruptcy for what was often called Japan's "continental management" (*tairiku keiei*)— Ōhira staked his political career on the reopening of Japan–China diplomatic relations, it is of interest to know what he may have thought of Japan's "continental management" methods.

Eight years after the end of the war, he wrote that he considered there were aspects in which Japanese enterprises had contributed to expanding China's economic base and developing its economic strength, and that, in comparison with the English or the French, the Japanese had been far less self-centered. Yet at the same time he wrote: "I must say that the planning and establishment of the China policy was, on the whole, myopic. Although it was supposed to be a 'people's policy' for the benefit of the Han people, it was also tinged with the regrettable aspect of the Japanese competing among themselves. Also, from the world view, the opinions and expectations of the United States, Britain, and the Soviet Union ought to have been fully taken into account. On this point, although the Ministry of Foreign Affairs did try to make some objections, its views unfortunately lacked sufficient strength and courage.

"Questions about the way the Manchurian Incident, which triggered the Greater East Asia War, was handled later tended to become overshadowed by World War II. I cannot divide the two and separately discuss the pros and cons of each, but the very tenor of the thinking underlying Japanese handling of this incident was, I think, part of the basic cause of failure in the Greater East Asia War. That said, it cannot be denied that the China policies were for the Japanese a valuable national test, even if one for which a very high tuition fee was paid."

During the years Ōhira was employed by the Asia Development Board, Japan took on more and more of a wartime coloring as the civilian government found it could no longer control the military in any way. The First Konoe Cabinet was replaced after January 1939 with a series of three short-lived cabinets, after which Prince Konoe again assumed the reins of government with the Second and Third Konoe cabinets. Contrary to expectations, not even Prince Konoe could improve the situation, and in October 1941 he finally yielded the prime ministership to General Tōjō Hideki. In the meantime, Japanese party politics continued to decline, and in October 1940 all the political parties were dissolved and absorbed into the Imperial Rule Assistance Association (*Taisei Yokusankai*).

At the time the Pacific War began on December 8, 1941, Ōhira was living in a two-story home overlooking Sankei Gardens in Yokohama. When he first returned from Zhangjiakou, he rented a house near his wife's family in Tokyo, but he still had a fondness for Yokohama, where he had lived when heading the tax office there. So in early 1941 the Ōhiras, with their two sons, Masaki and Hiroshi, acquired a home of their own in this city, which was not too distant for commuting to the Asia Development Board headquarters in central Tokyo. On December 30, 1941, Shigeko gave birth to a daughter, Yoshiko.

Chapter 7

The Ministry of Finance in Wartime

It was the summer of 1942, six months after the beginning of the war between Japan and the United States, when thirty-two-year-old Ōhira returned to the Ministry of Finance after three years with the Asia Development Board. With Japan's defeat in the naval Battle of Midway, the mood of intoxication that had followed earlier military victories was dampened and the war would soon turn to Japan's disadvantage.

Ōhira was appointed chief budget reviewer within the Budget Bureau of the Ministry of Finance for the operating budgets of the Ministry of Education and the South Seas Agency. When he assumed this job, his immediate task was compiling the budget for fiscal 1943. The budget of the previous year had had an emergency, stop-gap nature—since the Pacific War had begun not long after its initial compilation and the greater part of the war expenses had to depend on *ad hoc* approvals of additional military expenditures—but it had been decided that the fiscal 1943 budget by contrast would be a full-scale war budget from the start.

In the educational administration field, for which Ōhira was responsible within the Budget Bureau, such matters were taken up as the promotion of science and technology, raising the level of teachers' training colleges, aid for education for the specially gifted, and the development of "Oriental culture," reflecting strong demands from a number of quarters under the rubric of "educational reform" (*bunkyō sasshin*). In regard to the question of establishing new schools, the Ministry of Education asked for funding to establish, at a single stroke, fifteen new technological institutes, eleven medical schools, and four higher teachers' training institutes.

"On hearing of these enormous demands," Ōhira writes, "I was frankly stupefied. . . . To set up a school was something to be done only with the utmost care. Being told in this way to build so many schools at once, I wondered what on earth was up, and could not hold back a feeling of indignation over these bold and seemingly incautious demands."

Upon requesting relevant materials from the Ministry of Education, Ōhira found that the ministry "wanted Japan's various branches of industry to benefit optimally from persons with technical and leadership abilities and wanted to see the ratio of technical personnel to ordinary workers returned to the same high benchmark that had been reached in 1939." His own preliminary calculations showed that, for technological institutes, existing facilities could more than meet the 1939 ratio without any new ones being established or the number of years a student would spend in a given institution being extended. Similar results were obtained with respect to medical schools and higher teachers' training institutes. As a result, the plan to establish new schools was wholly shelved for the time being—or so it appeared.

However, let us see what Ōhira has written of his experience on New Year's Eve, just as 1942 was drawing to a close: "Just as I had cleared up my desk and was getting ready to return home after finishing computations for the fiscal 1943 budget and putting together the documents to be submitted to the first cabinet meeting of the new year, to be held on January 4, I was called in to see Budget Bureau Director Ueki Kōshirō. Wondering what on earth could be the matter at this time, I entered his office feeling out of sorts and thinking he lacked compassion as I had intended to go home early on New Year's Eve, take a hot bath, and enjoy waiting for the New Year. The director immediately said, 'Revise the budget to allow for building a technological institute in Nagano and a medical school in Maebashi.' I protested, in terms that bordered on the rebellious: 'How can that be, when it has already been decided between me and the Ministry of Education authorities not to build a single school?' With a dour face, the director said, 'Sorry, but this has been decided at a level we can't influence. It can't be helped. Anyway, make your revised calculations.' " So he had to spend the entire night at work in his office. Later he learned that the decision had been made as a result of talks at the ministerial level.

An important project, dating from the spring of 1941, was that of establishing the Japan Scholarship Foundation (*Dai-Nippon Ikueikai*). One underlying issue had been whether this government-run foundation should provide grants or loans. At the end of 1941, a prototype plan of impressive scale was put together by Lower House Dietman Miyake Shōichi, one of the leaders of the National Parliamentarians' League for Education, based on a loan system. Miyake's plan aimed to provide assistance to 200,000 middle school students, 10,000 students in technological institutes, and 10,000 students in colleges and universities. In February 1942, the National Parliamentarians' League for Education presented to the Diet a Bill to Establish a Greater East Asia Educational System (*Daitōa kyōiku taisei*), featuring "a fund to nurture excellence for Asian development."

In the publication commemorating the Japan Scholarship Foundation's twentieth anniversary in 1963, Koyama Ryō, who had been a leading member of the parliamentarians' league, writes, "The stated objective of this bill was twofold: first, to train leaders for an enormous number of persons who were to be sent out all over Asia; and second, to provide equitable educational opportunities for Japanese citizens who had ability but lacked economic means. The real motive of the parliamentarians' league was the latter. However, the trend toward militarism had become so pronounced that it was, in effect, impossible to go against it, so it was necessary to accept the former in the project's statement of purpose."

The project was unanimously approved in the Diet. Since Ōhira was at the time chief reviewer for the Ministry of Education budget, he was instructed by Finance Minister Kaya Okinori to handle this issue. Ōhira knew from personal experience how welcome was the provision of funds to support one's studies. We have seen how he was helped by the Kagawa Prefectural Scholarship Society and the Kamata Mutual Aid Society to get his university education. He even offered, upon completing the repayment of these student loans to contribute a small monthly amount for a year or two "as a token of gratitude." But even if he had been able to go to a university thanks to these sorts of loans from private funds that might assist even students like himself who were not at the top of their class, he seems to have felt that the encouragement of academic excellence through public funding should operate under a different concept and system.

The tentative plan Ōhira drew up sharply limited the number of students who would benefit, reflecting a standpoint that public assistance should only be in the form of grants and only to the relatively few who had proven themselves to be the cream of academic talent. The Ministry of Education's plan, which claimed to take account of "current conditions," would benefit 30,000 middle school students yearly (as opposed to 200,000 in the Dietmen's original proposal), but the Ōhira draft pared down this number even further and could not but provoke opposition from the parliamentarians' league.

Various arguments were advanced within the Ministry of Finance, and finally Budget Bureau Director Ueki (later a minister of finance) expressed the following opinion: "I was born into a poor family and had little hope of getting a higher education. So I had no choice but to change my surname and become an adopted child. It was my adoptive family that sent me to the First Higher School and then to Tokyo Imperial University. It is painful to have to change one's family name; yet there are many people with a love of learning who, because of poverty, are forced to choose this path. I cannot bear seeing the younger generation go through this sort of anguish. This is why I am so passionately pushing to institute this system. Ōhira, please understand my feelings. I'd like to have you reconsider so that the largest possible number of persons can benefit equally from its provisions." Tears welled up in Ueki's eyes as he sought Ōhira's cooperation. Ōhira writes: "Up until then I had stuck to figures and logic, but on hearing these words my stubborn stance melted as if in the sun. I took Budget Bureau Director Ueki's words to heart, greatly revised my original draft plan, changed the grants to loans, and submitted my plan to the Diet."

The Dai-Nippon Ikueikai formally commenced its activities on October 18, 1943. The history of the organization mentions "difficulties in negotiations with the Ministry of Finance," an apparent reference to Ōhira's original hard line. Ōhira writes of his role at that time: "Bureaucrats in the Ministry of Finance were wedded to their profession, and whatever they did, their instinct was to spend as little money as possible. On the one hand, that was certainly a good thing, but, on the other, it often resulted in things being only half-done, and there were certainly cases that left regrets in later years. To make good use of money is almost always difficult. In particular, to handle public funds is the most difficult thing of all. Because I was brought up in far-from-prosperous circumstances, it was perhaps second nature to me to squeeze as much as I could, so very often my budget revisions were rather severe. The Dai-Nippon Ikueikai was unfortunately one of the cases where I, with my severe attitude, happened to be around in the role of midwife."

After Japan's defeat, the Japan Scholarship Foundation (renamed Nihon Ikueikai), which had resulted from the efforts of many persons amidst tightening budgetary restrictions in a deteriorating war situation, continued to play a vital role, supporting students whose lives were often on the verge of collapse in the postwar confusion. As of 1989, 4,210,000 persons had received student loans from the organization, totaling ¥1.65 trillion. It is a rare example of a public body begun during the war years that has both continued to the present and maintained its importance.

In August 1943, when the plan for inaugurating the Japan Scholarship Foundation was nearly complete, Ōhira moved to the General Affairs Section of the Foreign Funds Bureau (*Gaishikyoku*). This bureau was established as a result of organizational reforms of November 1942 aimed at simplifying fiscal administration. It both replaced the Foreign Exchange Bureau (*Kawasekyoku*) and signaled the organization of a new body that could better respond to the nation's overseas financial and economic policies, which had greatly changed with the outbreak of the Pacific War in December 1941.

It is probable that Ōhira was appointed to this post because of his work in an overseas branch of the Asia Development Board and his experience there with foreign exchange and overseas investment. However, just as he was beginning to learn the ropes of international finance in the Foreign Funds Bureau, Ikeda Hayato, head of the National Tax Section of the Budget Bureau, invited him to move, together with him, to the Tokyo Local Finance Bureau (formerly the Tokyo Tax Supervision Bureau, renamed in July 1941), where Ikeda was to work as director. Ōhira would head the office's Indirect Taxation Department. Thus, Ōhira left the Foreign Funds Bureau after only three months, and Ikeda, who had long been interested in Ōhira, began to work together with him for the first time.

"On the day I assumed the post, Ikeda summoned me and, smiling cheerfully, said, 'You have not really studied tax law in any detail, but while I am head of the office, be prepared for me to give you some thorough training.' To this I responded flatly, 'Your kindness is appreciated, but I'll have to decline. I have a lot of capable and trained subordinates who are well versed in tax law, and I'd hope to consult them on any tax law questions. I am not well versed in tax law, but I think that effective administration does not come from the texts of law statutes. I'd like to try an indirect tax administration that relies on common sense and is not bound by conventional procedures.' Ikeda did not force the matter."

One example of what Ōhira meant by an "indirect tax administration not bound by conventional procedures" were the so-called People's Taverns (*Kokumin sakaba*). As the war intensified, all types of commodities became scarce, and liquor was no exception. Production of alcoholic beverages throughout the nation dropped from 4.4 million *koku* (1 *koku* = 180 liters) in 1936 to 1.86 million *koku* in 1941. Through the Regulation on the Control of Alcoholic Beverages and the like, bodies to control distribution were set up, with authority vested in the hands of the tax authorities.

For distribution purposes, alcohol was classified into three categories: for "home use," "commercial use," and "special commercial use." For "home use" around two *gō* [1 *gō* = 180 milliliters] per household per month was allowed, and for "commercial use" around two to three *shō* [1 *shō* = 1.8 liters] per enterprise. It was commonly rumored that restaurants serving alcohol did not actually sell the allotted amounts to their customers but rather diverted much of it to the black market to be consumed in private homes.

As the head of the Tokyo Local Finance Bureau's Indirect Taxation Department, Ōhira racked his brains over appropriate alcohol-related countermeasures. In the meantime, the Tōjō Cabinet promulgated the so-called Entertainment Stoppage Order (*Kyōraku teishirei*) under which all eating and drinking establishments were closed except those with a "mass character," like public dining halls. Establishments that had up to then received allotments of alcoholic beverages in accordance with past business records no longer received these allotments, and a glut of commercial-use alcohol arose. In response, Ōhira drew up a draft Outline for the Efficient Distribution of Commercial-Use Alcohol, according to which some of the establishments closed by the Entertainment Stoppage Order would be reopened as People's Taverns, employing those who had lost their jobs and making surplus commercial-use alcohol available for consumption by the general public. The former eating and drinking establishments were happy to maintain sales records in preparation for the time they might be reopened in their former guise. Ōhira's proposal was thus designed to kill two or three birds with one stone.

The official body charged with the supervision of eating and drinking establishments was the Tokyo Metropolitan Police Department, and to open so-called People's Taverns its permission was necessary. Here Ōhira gave ample play to his negotiating talent. The cooperation of liquor shops also had to be requested. Within metropolitan Tokyo there were approximately 5,000 liquor retailers, which comprised an association whose director was Kawashima Shōjirō (later vice-president of the Liberal Democratic Party) and whose vice-director was Hirokawa Kōzen (later minister of agriculture and forestry). Ōhira's acquaintance with both these men dates from this time, when their influence was already growing in the political world.

As oases for the common people, the People's Taverns were formally opened on May 5, 1944, when the war situation was worsening daily. The May 1 issue of *Asahi Shinbun*, in an article titled "Business Policy of People's Taverns is Saké 1 gō, Beer 1 glass," reported as follows: "From around May 5, People's Taverns will be opened in 104 locations in the 35 wards of the metropolis. Operating particulars were made public on the thirtieth by the Police Agency as follows: (1) the number of People's Taverns serving saké will be 65, the number serving beer will be 39; one gō of 3rd-class saké, one bottle of beer, or one mug holding a half-liter will be sold at officially set prices, and, at the customer's request, simple snacks costing less than 15 sen will also be served; (2) operating hours will depend on the locality, but will, as a rule, be during a two-hour period from 6 P.M., 26 days per month; (3) management will follow an accounting system worked out jointly by committee members elected by the Caterers' Association; (4) most establishments will accommodate around 250 to 260 people." The success of this Tokyo Local Finance Bureau scheme for the efficient distribution of commercial-use alcohol brought a positive response from other revenue offices, as outlets similar to People's Taverns in the capital opened one after another in cities throughout the country to succor a thirsty citizenry.

We have already seen that Ōhira, as a budget reviewer, tended to be even stricter than most of his colleagues and always tried to match "figures and logic," which sometimes meant opposing his superiors. On the other hand, his attitude toward the public as head of the Indirect Taxation Department in Tokyo was kindly, even compassionate. The surplus alcohol resulting from the Entertainment Stoppage Order would have been diverted to military industries had Ōhira not channeled it to the general populace. His basic thinking was that alcoholic beverages should be equitably provided to all who had a fondness for them, irrespective of class or occupation. The success of the effort reflected the fact that Ōhira had also tried to understand the difficult position of the owners and employees of liquor shops, restaurants, and pubs, and had adopted methods that took their interests into account.

Ikeda Hayato's wife, Mitsue, recalls Ōhira at around this time as follows: "The war was almost over, and because it was a time when there was almost nothing resembling a restaurant, Ikeda often brought members of the office staff home with him for small parties. Ōhira seemed to be very happy over the success of the People's Taverns, and when he came to the house he'd say, 'Everyone is happily lining up and drinking.' He was well-built, and, thinking he was probably a good drinker, at first I tried to offer him something to drink, but he said, 'To tell the truth, I'm no good when it comes to alcohol.' I thought it ironic that a person who didn't drink should head the department dealing with alcoholic beverages."

As 1944 progressed, the war situation was finally showing terminal symptoms. The Tōjō Cabinet fell in July. Beginning in the fall, American B-29 bombers appeared over Japan and their bombs began to rain down. On February 23, 1945, the buildings of the Tokyo Local Finance Bureau in Ōtemachi were hit by incendiary bombs and burned to the ground. Writing in 1978, Ōhira recalls this day as follows: "The flames even reached the steel-reinforced basement where stationery, printing presses, and important documents were kept, and they were all enveloped in the fire. If the basement burned, our work would virtually come to a standstill. I happened to be working that day, which was a Sunday, and encouraged the other employees on duty to do their best to extinguish the fire with a bucket relay from the Kanda River, but we were no match for the conflagration. We ran to a fire hydrant that happened to be at the edge of the Imperial Palace moat and asked some fire station employees for help, but they were exhausted and showed no sign of responding to our entreaties.

"At that moment I remembered that a short time previously one of the finance bureau guards had hidden a bottle of saké in a manhole. On the spur of the moment I said, 'It's only a little but I have some saké. If you'll help with the fire, it's yours.' The firemen unrolled the hoses they had rolled up, let them down into the Imperial Palace Outer Moat, and finally started to try to deal with the fire. Fortunately, we succeeded in putting out the fire in the basement. As a result, I was presented with a letter of commendation (together with ¥50) by Director Ikeda. Here, then, was one unexpected example of the beneficial effects of saké."

Since Tokyo and its environs had become so dangerous, Ōhira finally sent his wife and children to his father-in-law's home in Usuginu Village, Higashi-iwai District, Iwate Prefecture. "Relatives managed a soy sauce shop, a grocery store, a pharmacy, and a dry goods store, so my family managed to pass the final stage of the war without any inconvenience."

Chapter 8

War's End

The Tōjō Cabinet was replaced in July 1944 by the cabinet headed by Koiso Kuniaki. Its minister of finance was at first Ishiwata Sōtarō, a holdover from the Tōjō Cabinet, but in February 1945 Ishiwata became Lord Keeper of the Privy Seal (the official name still given to the chief cabinet secretary) and was replaced as minister of finance by Tsushima Juichi, who until then had been president of the North China Development Company.

Tsushima, believing it necessary to vastly increase the budget to counter the disastrous effects of the air raids, immediately drafted a supplementary budget of ¥2 billion. His first major personnel change was the appointment of Ikeda Hayato (until then director of the Tokyo Local Finance Bureau) as director of the Tax Bureau at ministry headquarters. Ikeda's reputation as a "tax ogre" was a decisive consideration. Kurogane Yasumi (later chief cabinet secretary), who was by one year Ōhira's senior in the ministry, was appointed one of Tsushima's two secretaries, and about a month later, on March 19, 1945, Ōhira was appointed to share the secretarial duties as a replacement for Tanimura Hiroshi, who was two years his junior in the ministry and, as secretary to Finance Minister Ishiwata, had initially been appointed to continue in the same post under Tsushima but, in fact, was to serve Tsushima only until the end of March. Ōhira recalls: "Never in my life had I dreamed of being a private secretary to a top official. Even after leaving university and becoming an official, I had always considered it unlikely that I would have any personal dealings with ministers or their private secretaries." Tanimura (later head of the Tokyo Stock Exchange) recalls: "Even now I remember vividly how Ōhira would be at the minister's residence, which was only dimly lit at night because of the wartime blackout policy, and would endure with commendable calm the minister's outbursts of patriotic lamentation until a late hour."

Alarmed over the increasingly bleak war situation, the Koiso Cabinet devised a plan for concluding peace with Chiang Kai-shek's government in Chongqing, and presented this plan on March 21 to the Supreme Council for the Direction of the War. However, Foreign Minister Shigemitsu Mamoru was strongly opposed to it, and consequently the cabinet resigned en masse.

Tsushima served as finance minister for only forty-five days and accomplished little other than the successful passage of the above-mentioned supplementary budget. Despite its brevity, the period gave Ōhira, working for the first time as a secretary to a top official, the opportunity to observe things from a broad perspective, even if he experienced some difficulty in trying to cater to the wishes of the aristocratic and egotistical Tsushima. One of Ōhira's old friends wrote after Ōhira's death: "He used to say that he had already decided that, while it would be regrettable for Japan to lose the war, we could only expect a frightful situation if Japan, with its uncontrolled military, should win. He said he expected that the day Japan would be defeated was soon to come." Through his work for Finance Minister Tsushima, Ōhira must surely have gained a better understanding of Japan's prospects for the future. After the fall of the Koiso Cabinet, a new cabinet—and, as it turned out, the last wartime cabinet—was formed with Suzuki Kantarō as prime minister. Tsushima retired from his ministerial post, and Ōhira returned to the Budget Bureau.

On the evening of May 25, 1945, it so happened that the Finance Ministry staff members who had served Tsushima were gathered in the garden of his residence having drinks when endless formations of B-29 bombers appeared in Tokyo's skies and dropped a rain of incendiary bombs, the most extensive air raid—covering a much wider area than the Great Tokyo Air Raid of March 10 that left 100,000 dead—carried out over the city. Ōhira recalls: "I was fleeing with Mrs. Tsushima and a maid when she suddenly asked me to rescue an image of Kannon, the Goddess of Mercy, from the family altar. I went back and got the statue but in the process became separated from the rest of the group. As I was carrying the heavy metal statue toward Yotsuya Station, a large steel ring used to hold a cluster of incendiary bombs fell a meter or two in front of me. I was unhurt but decided it was safer to leave the statue in the stationmaster's office and fled unencumbered toward Ichigaya Station, near which I found a tunnel where I spent the night. The next morning I retrieved the statue, and, at the Shimo-nibanchō air warden's station, was reunited with the Tsushimas, who had survived the bombing unharmed. Their house, however, had burned to the ground.

"I then returned home to Ushigome only to discover that my own house and that of my parents-in-law had also been completely destroyed. A light drizzle was falling as I surveyed the ruins. What remains in my mind are the piano wires that were twisted like strands of candy. I had already evacuated my family, so I rented a house in Karasuyama in Setagaya Ward, not far from Sakurajōsui where the [relocated] Budget Bureau was situated, and commuted from there until the end of the war."

On August 15, 1945, the day the war ended, many Japanese were in tears as they listened to the emperor's broadcast announcing the surrender. Yet Ōhira recalls: "Somehow, I did not feel any great emotion. On the contrary, a sense of relief swept over me as I realized that the inevitable had finally come." With the end of the war, the Suzuki Cabinet resigned and a new cabinet under Prince Higashikuni Naruhiko was formed on August 17. In the Higashikuni Cabinet, Tsushima Juichi once again became finance minister, and Ōhira was again his private secretary, together with his junior ministry colleague, Miyazawa Kiichi.

Broadly speaking, this aristocrat-led cabinet had three missions. The first was to persuade the military and the general populace to accept the emperor's "sacred decision to end the war" (shūsen no seidan) and to avoid letting the shock of defeat bring chaos to Japanese society. In spite of a very few desperate attempts at resistance within the military establishment, the Higashikuni Cabinet succeeded in gaining the cooperation of the imperial family and of the military authorities. The second mission was to adopt necessary measures so that the first army of occupation ever experienced would be received without undue friction or resistance. The Higashikuni Cabinet generally succeeded in paving the way for this transition and signed the surrender document. The third mission was to carry out the provisions of the Potsdam Declaration, which were a condition of the surrender.

There were difficulties foreseen in this task since the Higashikuni Cabinet and the Occupation authorities were far apart in their thinking as to how Japanese society should be reformed. On October 4, 1945, the Occupation authorities, delivering a Memorandum on Removal of Restriction on Political, Civil and Religious Liberties, demanded the release of political prisoners and the complete abolition of the "thought police." The Higashikuni Cabinet was unable to put these demands into effect and resigned after fifty-one days. During the term of the Higashikuni Cabinet, Finance Minister Tsushima's top priority was preventing Japan's banking and government finance system from falling into chaos because of the defeat. He was particularly concerned that runs on savings accounts might force many banks to close and thus paralyze economic transactions.

At the time of the Great Kantō Earthquake in 1923, Tsushima had had the difficult experience of setting up emergency measures limiting withdrawals from savings deposits and imposing a moratorium on debt payments; then, in the financial crisis of 1927, he had seen runs on banks lead to shutdowns and financial chaos. Determined that a similar situation should be avoided, on his first day in office Tsushima officially announced: "Whatever else may happen, there will be no moratorium."

The next target of Finance Minister Tsushima's concern was whether the Occupation forces would use military scrip as currency. He felt that if the United States army began to use military scrip in Japan, confidence in Japan's currency, already weakened by the defeat, would slip drastically. He also believed that with two types of currency in circulation the postwar economy was likely fall into utter confusion. Through American radio broadcasts, there had already been clear hints that the Occupation forces were considering the use of military scrip. In a direct communication from Foreign Minister Shigemitsu to General MacArthur while the latter was still in Manila, the government requested that Japanese bank notes be honored, but no reply was received.

Tsushima recollects: "The advance party of the Occupation forces arrived at Atsugi [air base near Tokyo] on August 28, followed by Supreme Commander MacArthur and his staff on the thirtieth. After consultation with Bank of Japan President Shibusawa Keizō, I had the Bank of Japan pay out, for the time being, a maximum of ¥1 billion in Bank of Japan notes from its suspense account, and designed an emergency measure whereby this would be handed over to the Occupation forces for their use. I made arrangements for a part of these funds to be taken first by truck to Atsugi airport (and also to Yokosuka and to Kanoya in Kagoshima Prefecture), to be handed to the American military."

The government prepared to receive the Occupation forces by setting up the Atsugi Liaison Committee, headed by Lieutenant General Arisue Seizō. It turned out, however, that the Occupation forces were primarily interested in the military port of Yokosuka; thus, arriving American personnel did not remain long in Atsugi but proceeded to Yokohama, not far from Yokosuka. Accordingly, the Bank of Japan notes that Finance Minister Tsushima had prepared were not handed over to the American military at the time originally intended. The issue of using military scrip became a matter for negotiation with General Headquarters of the Allied Powers (GHQ) in Yokohama, and Kubo Bunzō, head of the Foreign Funds Bureau, was sent to Yokohama to try to prevent the adoption of a military scrip system.

The day American forces first set foot on Japanese soil (August 28) was a day of deep personal sadness for Ōhira, for on that day his mother, Saku, who had been bedridden, passed away in his home village at the age of seventy-two. As secretary to a minister who was working almost round the clock to deal with the issues posed by the end of the war, Ōhira was unable to return home to attend her funeral. His father-in-law, Suzuki Miki-nosuke, went in his stead.

During the short period he served as private secretary to Japan's first postwar finance minister, Ōhira kept a diary titled "*Higashikuni no miya naikaku ōkura daijin nisshi*" (Diary of the Finance Minister in Prince Higashikuni's Cabinet). It has the following entry for the day the surrender document was signed:

> 7 o'clock, September 2 (Sunday)
> Prime Minister's Residence
> Today on the *Missouri* in Yokohama harbor, the agreement to end the war was signed by the Allied nations and plenipoten-tiaries Shigemitsu and Umezu. After sending off plenipoten-tiaries and party at 5 A.M. early morning, Official Residence quiet, without a voice.

On the evening of the same day, September 2, 1945, a draft announce-ment planned for public release the next day was delivered by GHQ to the government. It consisted of three items. The first stated the intention of establishing a military government; the second concerned public security and punishments for disobeying orders; and the third stated the intention of using military scrip. Surprised at this, Foreign Minister Shigemitsu visited MacArthur at GHQ in Yokohama the next day, expressed his views on a military government, and requested that the plan be canceled. MacAr-thur conceded to the foreign minister's arguments and plans to enforce a military regime were abandoned.

Foreign Minister Shigemitsu's direct appeal to MacArthur also resulted in an agreement that, at least for the time being, there would be no use of military scrip, even though GHQ insisted that they formally maintained the right to issue such scrip at any time. As a result of further negotiations, the Occupation forces agreed to use Bank of Japan notes, and on September 7 were provided with "funds necessary for their stay in Japan," namely the earlier-mentioned ¥100 million. The plan to prevent the use of military scrip had thereby succeeded, and Japan was spared currency disorder during the Occupation.

Soon afterwards, the Occupation forces requisitioned the Ministry of Finance headquarters. According to Ōhira's diary: "September 10, cloudy, occasional drizzle. 7:20, Narita, head of the First Division of the Foreign Ministry's Central Liaison Office, pays visit, [says] GHQ requests 'the handing over of Finance Ministry office buildings,' everyone astounded; after various consultations it is decided to do what we can in the situation as best we can."

On the next day, September 11, it was formally decided to hand over the Ministry of Finance buildings to the Occupation forces at noon on September 15. Finance Minister Tsushima moved his office to the office of the president of the South Manchuria Railway Company in Mamiana, Minato Ward. The various departments and bureaus became geographically separated in such structures as the headquarters of the Nippon Kangyō Bank, the Ministry of the Interior, the Tōtaku Building, the Tokyo Stock Exchange, and Yotsuya Elementary School. It was not until over ten years later, in March 1956, that all the departments and bureaus were again housed in their old Kasumigaseki headquarters. According to Ōhira's diary: "September 14 (Friday), cloudy, 10 o'clock cabinet meeting, 1 o'clock arrive at headquarters, last time in Kasumigaseki, meeting of bureau directors held, just before evacuation, minister's office extremely quiet. All bureaus in feverish preparation for headquarters evacuation. Transport congestion."

On September 23, Finance Minister Tsushima paid a call on General MacArthur. The following account is based on Ōhira's written recollections. Finance Minister Tsushima had for some time sought a meeting with General MacArthur through the intermediary of the Central Liaison Office, and in due course a reply came from GHQ saying a meeting would be arranged for September 23. When Secretary Ōhira relayed this to Tsushima, the finance minister repeated to himself, "That's strange, that's really strange." When Ōhira asked him why it was so strange, he answered: "That day is an important holiday in Japan, the Autumn Festival of Imperial Spirits. It is the height of impropriety to schedule work meetings for Sundays or holidays. Though we may be a defeated nation, I am a minister of state personally appointed by the emperor. Therefore, I think this shows a lack of respect toward Japan. Let us decline the appointment."

Ōhira was taken aback. After all, MacArthur was in those days superior to the emperor. There was no telling what might happen if Japan's finance minister should decline an appointment so hard to come by. He tried to persuade Tsushima as follows: "What you say is quite understandable, but a peace treaty between Japan and the United States has not yet been achieved. Technically, we are still in a state of war. It is, so to speak, an invitation to meet in camp on the field of battle. In this case, I think there is no reason for censure even if etiquette is not being strictly observed. I feel it will be reasonable to accept."

Reluctantly, Finance Minister Tsushima accepted his secretary's advice, and after attending the ceremonies of the Autumn Festival of Imperial Spirits held in the Imperial Palace, he went to MacArthur's office on the seventh floor of the Daiichi Sōgō Building at 11 A.M. MacArthur's aide-de-camp, Colonel Laurence E. Bunker, was there to greet him and said, "Actually the general was expecting you at 11 A.M. *yesterday* and was sorry you couldn't make it. Just now he is in a staff meeting, but will meet with you shortly."

The misunderstanding may have stemmed from an erroneous communication between GHQ and the Central Liaison Office, or Bunker's words may have been the result of advice communicated by Japanese and American authorities who had been forewarned of Tsushima's displeasure; it is now impossible to know for sure. In any case, Finance Minister Tsushima's face visibly brightened, and he apologized for the discourtesy of a failure in communications. He was led into the general's room, where the two men conferred without an interpreter for nearly an hour, presumably about means of overcoming the food shortage that was causing the utmost concern.

"After the meeting, Finance Minister Tsushima emerged with a very cheerful countenance and was in top spirits. In the car he told me, 'The general's aide-de-camp is indeed a polished and courteous secretary. A really fine person.' I took this as something of an indirect hint and somewhat peevishly replied, 'You, on the other hand, must be considerably inconvenienced by having such a boorish secretary.' The minister burst into laughter as the car sped along the streets of the capital under the noonday sun."

On September 30, despite it being a Sunday, Finance Minister Tsushima came to his office for two morning conferences, returning home at four P.M. According to Ōhira's diary entry for that day: "I then went to the minister's Official Residence and continued consultations about orders to close banks, development companies, and special wartime bodies in colonies and foreign countries, which lasted until 5 o'clock the next morning, October 1; back again to the residence at 5:30."

Ōhira elsewhere describes that day in greater detail as follows: "Supreme Commander MacArthur gave the Japanese government a memorandum ordering the closure of the Bank of Korea and the Bank of Taiwan. The Ministry of Finance, which received this memorandum, was extremely perplexed and shocked and immediately held an intraministry conference to discuss remedial measures. At this conference the minister spoke extremely harshly to the director of the Financial Bureau as follows: 'Did you tamely accept this memorandum and say you would go along with it? As you must know, banks have many depositors. These depositors in-

clude widows and orphans. If those persons are prohibited from withdraw-
ing their savings they will be wondering how they can manage to live, and I
think they will not be able to sleep soundly. If I had been you, at the time I
was given that memorandum I would have immediately told the official in
GHQ that I could not accept it until due attention had been given to how,
and by what date, to take care of these deposits. What if you had thought a
little about these hapless depositors?'

"To these words nobody voiced the slightest objection or tried to vin-
dicate the course already taken. Intraministry meetings continued to
devise remedial measures. It must have been around 2:30 A.M. that the
Financial Bureau chief and his colleagues began to show signs of fatigue. I
couldn't bear seeing this and so slipped in a word to the minister, from the
side, suggesting, 'How about stopping here for tonight and continuing
tomorrow morning? The vice-minister and some of the bureau directors
are not as healthy as you are and some have children to look after at home
(Tsushima had no children), so although it might seem like interfering, I'd
like to have the meeting stop here and resume tomorrow morning.'

"The minister's face immediately went red and he flung back, 'What do
you mean by that sort of attitude when the country is in an emergency? I
have observed that there are several misguided persons who have been
looking first at those next to them and then at the clock. Are they really
missing their wives so much? If it's a matter of being hungry, Tsushima
here will get you some rice-balls to eat. Do you (pointing at me) also really
want to see your wife's face so much?' For a while there didn't seem to be
any way of settling the matter, but finally the meeting adjourned around 3
A.M., and it was decided that Vice-Minister Yamagiwa Masamichi and Archives and Documents Section Chief Aichi Kiichi would work out proposed countermeasures by 8 A.M. and then report to the finance minister's
residence.

"As scheduled, the next morning Yamagiwa and Aichi knocked on the
door of the Ishikawa-tei in Tokyo's Himonya district (where Tsushima
resided), bringing with them, as promised, a long written petition (in
English) and the main points of a proposal for alternative countermeasures. Negotiations on the matter subsequently got on the right track."
In his 1978 autobiography, Ōhira notes: "I will never forget the emotion
that welled up in me when I went to announce their [Yamagiwa's and
Aichi's] arrival and saw Finance Minister Tsushima already hard at work at
his desk, dressed in formal kimono."

Everyone who worked closely with Tsushima at that time has
memories of being scolded by him. Fukuda Takeo (later prime minister),
who was at the time chief ministry secretary, has written about how the

ministry staff, from the vice-minister down, were once subjected, starting around 8 P.M., to "an admonitory speech lasting eight hours." He recalls: "Steadfast Yamagiwa stood straight and listened without batting an eyelash. Fukuda and Miyazawa sat and made appropriate indications of response and agreement, while Ōhira, with head bowed throughout, was not reverentially listening but had apparently fallen asleep."

Ōhira goes on to write about the night in question as follows: "Generally speaking, bureaucrats resemble one another in liking to avoid tackling issues and come out wanting in enthusiasm for pursuing an objective without flagging. They tend to be insensitive to people's interests and feelings. This temperament is inseparable from the very nature of official work. It was these ingrown evils that Finance Minister Tsushima sought to correct through his strong words. Having been forced by my work to rise very early that morning while still tired and sleepy, I felt very tense, as if I'd been hit on the cheek." On October 15, 1945, the Higashikuni Cabinet resigned en masse and power passed to a new cabinet headed by Shidehara Kijūrō.

Ōhira's home, it will be recalled, had burned down in one of the air raids toward the end of the war; thus, he was living alone in a temporary residence in the Karasuyama district of Setagaya Ward. Soon after the end of hostilities, his family, who had evacuated to Iwate Prefecture, rejoined him, and in late September his father-in-law, Suzuki Mikinosuke, bought a house in the Komagome-hayashichō district of Hongō (now Bunkyō) Ward, where they all took up residence.

This house was formerly owned by Viscount Ogyū Wataru, a descendant of the Edo-period scholar Ogyū Sorai, and it was situated on a large lot of 1,200 tsubo (1 tsubo = 3.3 square meters) that had some 500-year-old ginkgo trees on it. The house had several large Japanese-style rooms with traditional alcoves and tatami-matted corridors. A sitting room had been destroyed in the bombing, but the house was otherwise intact. It resembled the mansions of feudal lords seen in period films, complete with wide sliding wall panels, an old-fashioned doorway to the entrance hall, a roofed area for parking horse-drawn coaches, a room originally designed for receiving coachmen, and a bronze-roofed outer gate.

The Tokyo of those days was largely an expanse of burned-out desolation, and most people wishing to return from outlying areas they had evacuated to could find no place to live. Because of this housing dilemma, a number of different families with some special relationship to the Suzukis or the Ōhiras came to share the same large house in Komagome-hayashichō. At one point it was home to as many as seven other households in addition to Ōhira's own family and his parents-in-law.

Among these families was that of Itō Masayoshi, who had once worked with Ōhira at the Asia Development Board headquarters. At the war's end he was in Jinan, China, but returned to Japan in the early spring of 1946. Learning that Itō was in need of a place to live, Ōhira offered him one of the rooms that his own family had been using. Itō, who remained a lifelong friend, lived there for the next two years.

On September 9, 1946, the Ōhiras saw the birth at home of their third son, Akira.

Chapter 9
Reconstruction

The words *yake-ato* (burned-out ruins) and *yami-ichi* (black market) symbolize the depths Japan found itself in just after its defeat in the war. Many people with no homes and no jobs fell into a state of semitorpor and whiled away the hours staring at a sky no longer visited by B-29 bombers. Production stopped, consumer items disappeared, and prices rose steadily. The food situation was dire, and the calories in daily food rations barely reached subsistence level. Even so, the deliveries of food rations were often delayed or incomplete.

Based upon the "United States Initial Post-Surrender Policy for Japan," which had been put together during the final stages of the war, GHQ enforced a policy of complete demilitarization and democratization. The aforementioned Memorandum on Removal of Restriction on Political, Civil and Religious Liberties, which had brought the downfall of the Higashikuni Cabinet, was announced on October 4, 1945, to be followed on October 11 by the demand for five reforms to insure human rights, namely, women's liberation, encouragement of the formation of labor unions, the democratization of education, the abolition of secret interrogation in judicial processes, and the democratization of economic bodies. Through such measures as the dissolution of the *zaibatsu* (industrial and financial conglomerates) on November 6 and the agricultural reforms decreed on December 9, progressives at GHQ pushed ahead in rapid succession with idealistic programs of demilitarization and democratic reform that they could not carry out in their own country. They intended to top off these reforms with the establishment of a new constitution.

In an article in *Encyclopaedia Britannica* on the century since the beginning of the Meiji era, Yoshida Shigeru, who was foreign minister soon after the end of the war and later became prime minister, claimed that the sweeping postwar reforms were, without doubt, a great change that could be called a "bloodless revolution." The objects of authority that had been built up since the Meiji Restoration had failed, and people vied with one another in the search for new values. However, it must be remembered that the Occupation forces adopted means of indirect rule rather than a directly imposed military government, and the functions of the emperor, the Diet, and the government were preserved.

On October 20, 1945, the now legal Japan Communist Party (chaired by Tokuda Kyūichi) began to republish its official organ, *Akahata* (Red Flag). This was followed on November 2 by the official start of the Japan Socialist Party (*Nihon Shakaitō*), which had links to various prewar proletarian parties, under the chairmanship of Katayama Tetsu. On November 9, the Japan Liberal Party (*Nihon Jiyūtō*, with Hatoyama Ichirō as president) was formed as a sort of continuation of the prewar *Seiyūkai*. Then, on November 16, the Japan Progressive Party (*Nihon Shinpotō*, with Tsurumi Yūsuke as secretary-general and later Machida Chūji as president) was set up as an extension of the prewar Rikken Minseitō. Shortly after, on December 18, the Japan Cooperative Party (*Nihon Kyōdōtō*), which espoused cooperatism, was established with Yamamoto Sanehiko as chairman.

All the elements of Japan's postwar party politics had now appeared in anticipation of the general election to decide which party or parties would be entrusted with political power. In preparation for this election, the House of Representatives (*Shūgiin*, hereafter called the Lower House) was dissolved on December 18. However, immediately after this, the Occupation forces ordered that the election be postponed, that all former militarists be purged from public office, and that any group favoring renewed ultranationalism be dissolved.

In the meantime, Japan's economic situation stood obstinately still. Enterprises were reluctant to improve productivity, and because government restrictions set low prices for most commodities, it was far more profitable to divert any available raw materials to the black market than use them to produce goods. The abandonment of wartime subsidies and the breaking up of the *zaibatsu* had also dampened enthusiasm for attaining former production levels. As to how the Japanese economy ought to be managed, the Occupation forces provided no clear goals. In fact, the American government had instructed General MacArthur that he bore no responsibility for the recovery or strengthening of Japan's economy. And the Japanese government itself showed no sign of establishing a framework for economic reconstruction.

With the collapse of the Higashikuni Cabinet, Tsushima left his post as finance minister, and Ōhira, no longer private secretary to the minister, once more returned to the ministry's Budget Bureau. The work of this bureau was to draft the budget and also to plan emergency measures to deal with postwar government finances. The compilation of the fiscal 1946 budget (covering the period between April 1, 1946, and March 31, 1947) was extremely tough, since it was the first following the military defeat, and neither revenue nor expenditures could be accurately forecast. Moreover, there was a vast accumulation of matters requiring financial countermeasures that remained in a policy limbo. It was estimated that the total liabilities for unpaid wartime subsidies and currency adjustments in areas that had been under Japanese occupation amounted to over ¥400 billion, or more than three times the size of the ¥120 billion ordinary account budget for fiscal 1946.

The fact that industrial production, which ought properly to sustain the nation's livelihood, had come to a standstill only compounded the problem. Industrial production at the end of 1945 was in fact only one-sixth the average for the period from 1934 to 1936. Available commodities could not nearly meet demand, and the amount of currency in circulation swelled, jumping from ¥32 billion at the end of the war to ¥55.4 billion at the end of December 1945, with no end to the surge in sight. Retail prices between September and December approximately doubled, and black market prices jumped to some forty times official prices. Unable to cope with this inflation, in February 1946 the Shidehara Cabinet put into effect an emergency financial and banking moratorium by which savings were frozen and a switchover was made from "old yen" to "new yen." For a time this drastically cut back purchasing power, but within a short period the money in circulation began to increase again and spiraling inflation resumed.

The twenty-second general election for the Lower House, which had been postponed by the Occupation, was finally held on April 10, 1946. The prior execution of the strict public office purge order, together with the recognition of women's right to vote and stand for election, favored the election of first-time candidates, and indeed a great number were successful, giving the Diet a new look. By party break down, the election results were as follows:

Japan Liberal Party	140
Japan Progressive Party	94
Japan Socialist Party	92
Japan Cooperative Party	14
Japan Communist Party	5
Other affiliations	38
Unaffiliated (Independent)	81
Total	464

Japan Liberal Party President Hatoyama Ichirō started to organize a Liberal–Progressive coalition cabinet, but just at that point he was barred from holding public office by GHQ, and was replaced in this task by Foreign Minister Yoshida Shigeru. It is said that one of the promises made at that juncture between Yoshida and Hatoyama was that Yoshida would return the party presidency to Hatoyama whenever the ban on Hatoyama was lifted, but another view holds that no such commitment was made. The repeated schisms and realignments that later occurred in the Japan Liberal Party were related to the question of how the matter was to be interpreted.

The First Yoshida Cabinet finally came into being on May 22, 1946, over a month after the election. Ishibashi Tanzan, who had run for a Diet seat on the Japan Liberal Party ticket but had lost, was made finance minister. Ishibashi, who had long been editor-in-chief of the economic journal *Tōyō Keizai Shinpō*, was a strong believer in Keynesian ideas and was convinced that the greatest danger came from deflation and unemployment rather than from inflation. To get idle facilities producing again, Ishibashi drew up a so-called positive financial policy, which far from merely deterring deflation turned out to fuel inflation, all the more difficult to control because of GHQ restrictions on imports and the continuing shortages of raw materials.

Around this time, Ōhira received a long letter from the elected mayor of his native Wada Village. It read, in part: "Looking at recent developments, we see that despite the nation's hardships from losing the war, compulsory education has been extended under the 'six-three system' from six to nine years. The number of salaried public officials is increasing. We do not see the decisive will to dispose of national property. Will it not, in this way, be difficult to establish goals for reconstruction? When soil lacks the necessary nutrients to support an oak, the tree is certain to wither unless most of the branches and leaves are cut off to produce a 'stick oak.' If, after the life of the tree has been saved, the nutrients in the soil are increased, the tree will put out more branches and leaves and grow into a great tree providing abundant shade. Looking carefully at present conditions, I can't help but feel deep apprehension. Thus, I have taken the liberty of composing this humble letter to present my ideas through you to the minister of finance." Ōhira soon afterward delivered this village leader's suggestions to Ishibashi at the minister's Official Residence, but recalls, "I did not have time to hear Ishibashi's comments on these views." Most likely Ishibashi, as a Keynesian, would not have shown much interest in such types of minimalist policy.

The basic reason for the rampant inflation over the first four postwar years was the widening gap between supply and demand caused, on the one hand, by the near-cessation of productive activities and, on the other, by the continuous growth of government expenditure dependent on increased currency issues. Furthermore, a large part of government expenditure was backward-looking, in as much as it was directed at fulfilling obligations contracted in connection with the war and its termination, rather than achieving the positive goals of economic reconstruction and social reform. Prime examples were the profligate and unjustified expenditures from the Special Account for Emergency Military Expenses made just after the defeat (¥10 billion was disbursed from this account between August 15, 1945, and the end of that month), the "war termination adjustment expenses" (shūsen shorihi) covering expenditures of the Occupation forces, and the "subsidies to reconstruct financial institutions," by which the national treasury picked up the bill for losses suffered by banks as a result of the termination of wartime subsidies. We may imagine that Ōhira felt uncomfortable about the ongoing government financial inflation, and the letter from the village mayor may have expressed Ōhira's own feelings.

Around this time, Ōhira presented his superiors with several policy recommendations of his own, two or three of which remain in the Ministry of Finance archives and are of interest for what they reveal of his thinking. A summary of the main points follows.

First, Ōhira made a proposal on the matter of selling government enterprises. At the time, there was much discussion about whether the huge amounts of government bonds issued during the war should be redeemed or, using the defeat as justification, should be abandoned and no attempt at redemption made. The Ministry of Finance took the attitude that although Japan had lost the war, the state's credit must not be compromised, so it established a policy of redeeming these bonds. Ōhira agreed with this view, arguing that government enterprises should be sold or auctioned off to raise revenues to redeem the bonds. As he stated in his formal proposal, "Rather, the crux of this matter is that unless the government balance of accounts is made progressively more equitable, and unless we can halt inflation or slow its progress, we cannot expect either a stabilization of the people's livelihood or economic reconstruction."

Going on to discuss the issue "from the standpoint of postwar industrial policy," he suggested that, first, government enterprises should be released from existing accounting regulations and restrictions imposed by other administrative practices. If they could be transformed into places for engaging the spirit of private enterprise, he predicted that "these undertakings will be able to develop fresh and vigorous activities." He wrote, "I feel all the more the need for this as a way of hastening the process of postwar reconstruction."

Referring to the issue of public employees, he considered that, while it was a good thing for the state to have a small number of first-class administrative personnel, to maintain large numbers of public employees in the industrial sector would not only encourage a lowering of abilities and sense of complacency but would also complicate the process of improving the treatment given to bureaucrats in general. The fact that failures in one area spread to other areas was "by no means in the interest of public servants." His third point was that because the scope of private capital and privately developed technology, together with the private labor market, had become very restricted in post-defeat Japan, government enterprises should open their markets to the private sector. "Since it has been made clear that the Allied countries are intent on democratizing the Japanese economy through the dissolution of the *zaibatsu*, to boldly resolve also to free government enterprises along the same lines should contribute to overcoming the stagnation of the Japanese economy and to Japan's democratization." For Ōhira, this became a cherished article of faith. Already, alongside the "stick oak" perspective on fiscal policy, he was clearly advocating a "small government" stance and an economy led by the vitality of the private sector.

A second proposal by Ōhira bore the title, Memorandum on Policy for Postwar Fiscal Reconstruction. Its contents show that it was written after Ishibashi Tanzan had replaced Shibusawa Keizō as finance minister. "With respect to handling the national debt," Ōhira wrote, "there is the need to seek, as the most efficacious means, material help from the Allied countries, especially the United States. To do so, Japan's international credit must be restored. To this end, we should, in full view of the world, work hard at reconstructing Japan's economy and the other remedial measures in which the government is so intently engaged. In particular, we must earn a favorable opinion from the world by swiftly and resolutely breaking with past conventions and proceeding with political democratization. The basic direction for our industrial reconstruction must be sought in planning to participate in international trade, and this should also have the effect of attracting material assistance."

Although any prospect of balancing government accounts over the next two or three years seemed impossible, no matter how much effort might be expended, Ōhira went on to state, in regard to budgetary adjustments beginning from the following fiscal year, the need "to establish a fiscal plan that would restore a balance of revenue and expenditure over the next five years or so, and that would provide guidelines for the free management of the private-sector economy and contribute to the stability of public sentiment and to a restoration of faith in the government." At the same time he stressed the need to "give substance to the finance minister's 'production fiscal policy' and to put the utmost effort into suppressing a 'consumption fiscal policy.'"

The First Yoshida Cabinet was formed on May 22, 1946, and Ōhira served in the Budget Bureau until June 25; thus, his work on compiling the budget under the new finance minister, Ishibashi Tanzan, lasted barely more than a month. The above proposal appears to have been written during this period. Most likely, Ōhira, while favorable toward Ishibashi's "production fiscal policy," felt uncomfortable with his views on inflation.

Based on his own opinions, Ōhira submitted a more comprehensive Memorandum on Financial Crisis Countermeasures. Although its contents are arranged in an abbreviated, itemized way, they reveal aspects of Ōhira's thinking that continued into his later years. The first item, titled "Assumptions," pointed to the danger that the increasing tendency for production to be resumed only on a much diminished scale, if at all, coupled with the stubborn advance of inflation, could bring a general crisis. The second item, titled "Countermeasures," took as its premise the need for an accurate grasp of realities and the abandonment of existing policy concepts. In particular, it argued that "controls from above" should be halted, that plans should be made for "giving the government a businessman's mentality," and that the courage must be found to abandon "entrenched low-price policies." Noteworthy among the proposed fiscal measures were "a radical restructuring of the tax system . . . shifting emphasis from direct to indirect taxes," as well as "carrying through policies that promote public subscriptions to government bonds" and "encouraging self-reliance in local government financial policies." Labor-related measures emphasized "union participation in management" and, in particular, special incentives (such as a stock-sharing plan) to be offered to union members. Prices and rationing policy were also dealt with. Of note under the third item, "Matters to Heed," is Ōhira's assertion of the need "to create a new philosophy for rebuilding the country—not an anemic, abstract philosophy but a fresh and vital life philosophy—and to devise skillful ways of propagating it that make use of new concepts unfettered by convention."

Amid the hardships occasioned by inflation and food shortages, labor unions, with MacArthur's blessing and encouragement, were organized throughout the country from the autumn of 1945 through 1946, and many keenly fought labor disputes ensued. Government offices proved no exception as unions of laborers and staff were formed, first among nonclerical government workers and then among clerical workers. These unions began to negotiate for improved salaries and living conditions. In this period, it was becoming clear that two political currents divided the postwar world, and this schism was also felt within Japan, where the conflict between "left" and "right" was becoming ever more palpable, giving added intensity to the labor unions' struggles.

As an integral part of the democratization program, the Occupation authorities had begun demanding a fundamental revision of the salaries of public employees, and the Japanese government was under pressure to respond. On March 17, 1946, labor and staff unions representing the post and telegraph services, the Japanese National Railways, the Ministry of Agriculture and Forestry, the Ministry of Education, and other government agencies merged to form the All-Japan Public Employees Labor Union Council (with the Japanese abbreviation *Zenkankōrō*) and immediately presented the government with unified demands for salary hikes.

"At first, the government entrusted a conference of vice-ministers with responsibility for carrying out negotiations, but it became apparent that there was a need for a unified office or agency to do this. For this purpose, the Compensation Bureau was established within the Ministry of Finance on June 25, 1946. Headed by Imai Kazuo, this bureau had three sections, the first dealing with studies and plans for revising the government personnel system, the second and third with the salaries of clerical (white-collar) and nonclerical (blue-collar) government employees, respectively."

With the inauguration of the Compensation Bureau, Ōhira was put in charge of the Third Section and asked to pay particular attention to welfare systems (especially mutual benefit societies), retirement benefits, overtime pay, and other types of monetary compensation. Ōhira has written: "In the prewar system of public service, there was a strict rank system in which the so-called emperor's public servants were either officials directly appointed by the emperor (*shinninkan*), officials appointed with the emperor's approval (*sōninkan*), junior officials (*hanninkan*), or junior clerks (*koin*). Salaries were established according to rank and were generally unrelated to the importance of the job. To correct these premodern and irrational elements, we used as a reference the report of the American Hoover Commission (named after Blaine Hoover, the head of the personnel administration consultant team that came to Japan in October 1946 and produced in June 1947 draft recommendations for a National Public Employees Law) and set up a classification of government jobs, in accordance with the degree of complexity and responsibility, with salaries determined accordingly. Also in the area of miscellaneous payments, we pushed for a more democratic and rational system, eliminating former opportunities for abuse."

Problems of compensation had to do with more than just money, and various kinds of welfare measures also had to be considered. Ōhira felt it was quite irrational that although the basic salaries for blue- and white-collar workers were approximately the same, there was a noticeable gap in other welfare measures, and he thought there must be a way of correcting this imbalance. In the immediate postwar period, marked by hardships in the material and other aspects of life, the welfare measures that had been established by mutual benefit societies were extremely important to the livelihoods of public employees. However, while the mutual benefit societies in such predominantly blue-collar organizations as the Japanese National Railways and the postal and telecommunications agencies had generally excellent facilities for providing daily necessities as well as well-developed networks of hospitals, sanatoriums, health resorts, clubs, and public housing, the facilities available to white-collar government workers, especially to those working in various agency headquarters, were quite meager by comparison.

In the meanwhile, workers' movements were becoming more intense by the day. In September 1946, there were struggles opposing layoffs of seamen and Japanese National Railways workers, and the following month there were the "October struggles," mainly by nongovernmental labor unions under the leadership of the Congress of Industrial Organizations of Japan (*Sanbetsu Kaigi*). From November through the end of the year and into 1947, there were numerous disputes spearheaded by public employees' and teachers' unions.

At first, workers' demands were largely economic; for example, demands for higher salaries (with which workers might even so be on the verge of hunger), for introducing a system of minimum wages, for abolishing income tax on workers' salaries, and for restoring production. However, after Prime Minister Yoshida referred to labor leaders as "unruly gangs" (*futei no yakara*) at the beginning of 1947, political demands suddenly came to the fore.

In an attempt to overcome current problems, Prime Minister Yoshida secretly maneuvered for a coalition with the "right-leaning" factions of the Japan Socialist Party, but this ended in failure when talks among the heads of the Liberal, Progressive, and Socialist parties broke down on January 17, 1947. The next day, a Joint Struggle Committee of All Government and Public Workers adopted a resolution to seek the cabinet's downfall by staging a general strike from February 1. Nongovernmental labor unions gave a sympathetic response. The All-Japan Labor Union Joint Struggle Committee (abbreviated to Zentō in Japanese) was formed, and a general strike appeared unavoidable.

Ōhira has written of this period as follows: "Compensation Bureau Director Imai, First Section Chief Sakata [Taiji], and other members of our Compensation Bureau staff joined with such persons as Personnel Bureau Director Kagayama [Yukio] of the Ministry of Railroads and Personnel Division Chief Abiko [Tōkichi] of the same ministry to form a Strike Countermeasures Headquarters. Every day we carried on talks with the labor side, headed by Committee Chairman Ii Yashirō . . . . Whenever we entered one of the labor side's meeting places, we would be treated to ample white rice, beef, and vegetables, a curious contrast to the unattractive box lunches consisting mainly of rice mixed with maize that we 'employers' were used to eating."

On the afternoon of January 31, the day before the general strike was scheduled, MacArthur issued an order to stop it, and thus a massive disruption was averted. Even if the February 1 strike was finally avoided, the fact that it was planned at all had a tremendous influence on many aspects of life. Labor disputes were themselves by no means at an end, and in the public sphere the Compensation Bureau continued to devise appropriate means of resolving problems. During this period, Ōhira made a special effort to expand the scope of mutual benefit society activities.

Investigation of actual conditions in each of the government employees' mutual benefit societies revealed many shortcomings, and Ōhira first considered amalgamating these societies and creating a new system to correct such faults. At first, he suggested uniting all the ministries' mutual benefit societies into a single association that would manage the disbursement of long-term pension funds, and welfare facilities such as hospitals and health resorts. However, this plan met strong opposition from authorities in the various ministries concerned.

Meanwhile, he heard that the Army Mutual Benefit Society had been disbanded and that the state was being asked to buy some of its assets, such as hospitals and health resorts. Ōhira wanted somehow to acquire these facilities, but under current conditions there was no suitable body to handle their acquisition and management. Yet if one waited until a law regulating mutual benefit associations for public employees might be drawn up and approved before creating such a body, a rare chance would be missed. He thus prevailed upon the mutual benefit societies in the different ministries to make contributions to a fund that was speedily used to organize a foundation known as the Government Employees Mutual Benefit Societies Federation, which was to manage the facilities purchased by the government.

Now that the project was under way, it proceeded rapidly. Imai Kazuo, the Compensation Bureau director, wrote twenty-five years later: "First of all, Ōhira got a conference of vice-ministers to decide on the principle of expanding and upgrading welfare facilities. At the same time, he assembled concerned section heads in the ministries and explained the plan to establish a foundation to serve as a liaison body. In each of the other ministries, the person responsible for the mutual benefit societies was either the director of the personnel division or of the budget and accounts division, in either case an individual of considerable standing. On the other hand, Ōhira was still only a brand-new section head.

"However, it was not clear what benefits would accrue for the new organization. The plan, impeccably presented, was that each mutual benefit society member would contribute ¥3 toward the creation of a basic fund of ¥1 million. As joint sponsors, the relevant section heads in the various ministries affixed their seals, and Ōhira lost no time in submitting the plan for final approval. The new body began to function on April 1. For an inexperienced section head this demonstrated truly extraordinary political skills similar to those we see [in Ōhira] today." The new federation had Imai as chairman and Ōhira as managing director. The assets of the former Army Mutual Benefit Society were purchased with ¥57 million from the national treasury, and were then managed by the federation, which commenced operating many of the same hospitals and clinics. Toranomon Hospital, where Ōhira spent his last days, was later built with funds managed by the federation.

Ōhira also set about acquiring housing for public employees. At the time, large numbers of people were still living in air raid shelters and makeshift huts roofed with scraps of tin sheeting. By the end of the war, personnel employed in the central offices of ministries and government agencies in Tokyo had decreased by more than half, and there was now a definite need to increase their number (as well as to include among them persons who had returned to Japan from overseas or were returning to Tokyo from places of wartime evacuation), but existing government housing could not accommodate the projected increase. On surveying the razed areas of Tokyo for possible sites for new housing, Ōhira became interested in the Toyamagahara Drill Grounds formerly used by the army. The Occupation forces had already designated this area to be used to increase food production. Ōhira thus paid a visit to the Tokyo branch of the Military Government Section of the Occupation GHQ and made a fervent plea for the land to be returned to Japanese government control to build housing for government employees.

Imai writes: "I know absolutely nothing about what turns of speech the future foreign minister used at this time or how he won the other side around, but in any case he received control of several tens of thousands of *tsubo* of land. He switched to studying what sorts of structures should be built, although this was of course still premature because of lack of funds. He then looked to the [GHQ's] Fiscal Section for the necessary money. However, unless an organization was directly a part of the government, there was no way to borrow from this source. As nothing could be done along those lines, the Tokyo metropolitan government borrowed the money, which was then be transferred in its entirety to us. The Tokyo Metropolitan Assembly gave its approval for repayment of principal and interest on a long-term basis, half from the general budget account and half from rent paid by residents. This artful maneuver took some doing, but everything proceeded smoothly." After Ōhira had left the Compensation Bureau, this project was temporarily abandoned with the enforcement of the austere Dodge Plan during the drafting of the budget for fiscal 1949. The project was later revived, and Toyamagahara became a large housing complex open to both government and nongovernment employees.

The main objectives of the mutual benefit societies were not limited to the acquisition and management of welfare facilities. Ōhira was soon at work also on plans to revamp and systematize under the provisions of a single law the separate mutual benefit societies that had been established by imperial decree in the various ministries, with the aim of creating a system that would provide retirement pensions not only to blue-collar employees (as before) but also to white-collar government employees. Ōhira writes: "This law constituted a complicated system in which legal elements of the civil service system, the social welfare system, and the budget-making system overlapped. I dedicated myself to its enactment over a period of several months. I worked on it part of the time while confining myself to a hotel in Tokyo and sometimes in retreat at a mountain or seaside health resort."

This law was promulgated on June 30, 1948, as the Government Employees Mutual Aid Association Law and entered into force the next day. Based on its provisions, the above-mentioned federation became a "special corporation" known as the White-Collar Mutual Aid Association (*Higengyō Kyōsai Kumiai*), which later developed into today's National Public Employees Mutual Aid Association (*Kokka Kōmuin Kyōsai Kumiai*). This organization has not only provided long-term pension payments and other monetary benefits but has also given rise to various welfare facilities throughout Japan, thus contributing greatly to improving the lives of public employees.

During Ōhira's time with the Compensation Bureau, the world around him continued to produce momentous changes. Most important of all was the drawing up of the new Constitution of Japan, presented by imperial decree to the Diet as a revision of the Meiji Constitution. After Diet consideration and passage, the new Constitution was promulgated on November 3, 1946, and entered into effect six months later, on May 3, 1947. In spite of many problems in drafting it, which involved the direct intervention of GHQ, Japan and its people were thereby covenanted as a nation espousing peace and popular sovereignty, where the respect for fundamental human rights was guaranteed. The Constitution stated that "the National Diet is the highest organ of state power." The House of Peers was abolished and a new Upper House, called the House of Councillors (*Sangiin*), was established, all of whose members were to be elected by popular vote.

As mentioned earlier, the effects of the preparations for the planned February 1, 1947, strike were far-reaching on all levels. On February 7, less than a week after the strike had been halted by GHQ order, a letter from MacArthur to Prime Minister Yoshida was made public that recommended holding a general election under the provisions of the new Constitution as soon as possible after the closing of the 92nd (and last) Imperial Diet. It was hoped that these elections would crystallize political forces strong enough to dissolve some of the general social unrest manifest in the labor unions' struggles.

In the twenty-third general election for the Lower House on April 25, 1947, the Japan Socialist Party became the leading party with 143 elected members, and the Japan Liberal Party fell to second place with 131 members. Likewise, in the first Upper House (House of Councillors) election, which had preceded the Lower House election, the Japan Socialist Party became the majority party, with its 47 successful candidates, elected from both prefectural constituencies and by the country at large, considerably outnumbering either the 39 elected on the Japan Liberal Party ticket or the 29 on the Democratic Party ticket.

Honoring the principle of the alternation of political power, Prime Minister Yoshida stepped down and Katayama Tetsu of the Japan Socialist Party, now the party with the largest representation in the first Diet convened under the new Constitution, became head of state. A coalition cabinet emerged through cooperation among the Japan Socialist Party, the third-ranking Democratic Party (*Minshutō*, formed from the Japan Progressive Party with Ashida Hitoshi, who had broken away from the Japan Liberal Party, as president), and the fourth-ranking National Cooperative Party (*Kokumin Kyōdōtō*, resulting from a merger of the Japan Cooperative Party, the Cooperative Democratic Party [*Kyōdō Minshutō*], and the National People's Party [*Kokumintō*] and headed by Miki Takeo).

The new Katayama Cabinet continued to carry out the Yoshida

Cabinet's "priority production system" (devised by a group of economists around Tokyo University Professor Arisawa Hiromi), by which production was to be rapidly increased in such basic industrial sectors as coal and steel and used as a lever for raising production in general. However, the price differential subsidies set up under this plan grew so large that they spurred further inflation, and the expected stabilization in living conditions did not materialize. The rift between the "right" and "left" in the Japan Socialist Party intensified, and in the 2nd Ordinary Diet the government's draft budget was rejected in the Lower House Budget Committee, even though it was chaired by a member of the governing Japan Socialist Party, Suzuki Mosaburō (leader of the party's left wing). This was a fatal blow to the Katayama Cabinet, which resigned after only a little over eight months in power.

In choosing the next prime minister in February 1948, the Japan Socialist, Democratic, and National Cooperative parties again formed a coalition, and Ashida Hitoshi, president of the Democratic Party, was appointed to head the new cabinet. The opposition Japan Liberal Party joined the Comrades' Club (*Dōshi Kurabu*), made up of persons who had defected from the Democratic Party, to form the Democratic Liberal Party (*Minshu Jiyūtō*) as the leading opposition party.

Oh July 10, 1948, four months after the start of the Ashida Cabinet, Ōhira was sent on loan from the Compensation Bureau to the Economic Stabilization Board where he took up the post of chief of the Public Works Section. The Economic Stabilization Board (abbreviated to *Anpon* in Japanese) was the predecessor of today's Economic Planning Agency. It was founded in August 1946 as "a government agency to establish basic economic policy to overcome the economic crisis and to make comprehensive studies of economic policy from a supraministerial standpoint." In May 1947, the Economic Stabilization Board Ordinance was completely revised, and the board extended its functions to virtually all fields of economic administration. This was the beginning of the "Anpon that can even silence a crying child," as a popular phrase of the time described the powerful organ. This structural reorganization took place during the period of transition from the First Yoshida Cabinet to the Katayama Cabinet. The organization's Construction Bureau, in which Ōhira was to head the Public Works Section, was established at this time. Ōhira writes: "The Public Works Section was to oversee all public construction projects undertaken by the central and local governments under both general and special accounts. The Ministry of Finance allotted a lump sum for public works expenses to be handled by the Economic Stabilization Board, which would then devise a public works plan for the given fiscal year, and would take charge of making allocations in response to the requests of the various ministries. In this way, the Public Works Section had far-reaching powers beyond those of today's Ministry of Construction. Its greatest difficulty lay in negotiating with the Occupation authorities, who were poorly acquainted with Japanese realities."

Differences in thinking between the Japanese and GHQ in regard to public works had become a problem. In the immediate postwar period, the majority of GHQ staff were liberals of the stripe known as "New Dealers." To them, the term "public works" was synonymous with projects to deal with unemployment that were part of the New Deal policies of President Roosevelt to invigorate the American economy in the wake of the worldwide financial panic of the 1930s. Thus, when the Economic Stabilization Board was first begun, the Labor Division of GHQ's Economic and Scientific Section had instructed that the ¥6 billion in the public works budget mandated by GHQ should be used to generate productive activities for Japan's 2 million unemployed. At the same time, GHQ requested that the ¥3 billion being considered as a budget allocation for "people's livelihood stabilization expenses" be permitted to be used instead for "public works projects expenses." This meant that when public works projects could not be undertaken because of insufficient materials or some other reason, expenses allocated for public works were to be transferred from "the people's livelihood stabilization expenses." The Labor Division of the Economic and Scientific Section thus had a powerful voice in the public works field, and public works, which ought basically to be considered in long-range terms, became subject to methods that could not be called entirely rational, whereby most projects were approved only piecemeal, on a quarterly basis, after referring to current employment statistics.

Ōhira continues: "However, the reality of our country was the continuing occurrence of disasters stemming from the wartime devastation, and from the mountains to the coasts this situation was absolutely not being addressed. Japanese public works had to begin, first of all, with repairing this devastation, and the places and extent of the ruin had absolutely no relation to the places where the unemployed were concentrated. Herein lay a basic difference in thinking between the GHQ and the Japanese government on public works."

Almost immediately after assuming his new post as chief of the Public Works Section, Ōhira had to begin coping with this conflict, and he presented several written suggestions, of which two are extant. The first of these, titled "Statement of Views on Improving the Method of Deciding Public Works Priorities," bears his signature and is dated September 7,

1948. The second, titled "On Improving the Public Works System," does not indicate the date it was drafted, although the date of what appears to be the stamp of a filing clerk is November 12, 1948.

The former begins by pointing out the discrepancy in the two views of public works, stating that "there are two aspects to methods for deciding priorities," of which "one is economic importance and the other is subsidies given to the project." The document continues: "In the past it was thought that priority projects should be given large subsidies. However, the subsidy should be proportionate to the potential of the beneficiary. When the project beneficiary is the general public, the project is eligible for a large subsidy. If, on the other hand, the beneficiaries are limited to certain designated people, there is no eligibility for large subsidies, which represent a burden on taxpayers, yet some such projects may nevertheless be given priority treatment. If the above view is correct, then we should judge that the preparation of new agricultural land, irrigation projects, land improvement, and the construction of fishing ports and housing should not receive big subsidies, since the beneficiaries of such projects are only a small number of people, some of whom have been liberated by the end of the war and whose economic conditions have improved. Pursuing this line of reasoning still further, projects for the construction of production facilities (coal, petroleum, and so on) ought to be excluded from public works." In other words, this method of deciding followed the so-called benefit principle of having the burden borne by the beneficiary.

The same document considered that although the current priority system was limited to short-term judgments of economic effectiveness, there was a need to study plans from the long-term viewpoint. It further stressed that cost–profit ratios should be more strictly considered and that when various projects were mutually related, they should be considered in their overall relationship. The other extant document composed by Ōhira at this time also adopts this viewpoint and deals in detail with specific proposals for improvements in the system of approving projects, transferring project funds, and calculating overhead costs.

In both documents, Ōhira's thinking on public works centered on how to restore and generally improve a desolated land and public facilities that were on the verge of collapse. A few years later, in 1953, he recollected this period in the following words: "I felt that the mainstay of Japan's public works projects definitely had to be water conservancy. And more than building dikes along rivers, water conservancy depended on sand arrestation in mountain streams; even more, it depended on sand arrestation on mountainous land; and more than sand arrestation on mountainous land, it depended on afforestation. In this way I felt it was important and logical to grasp the basic causes of things. Accordingly, we more than doubled sand arrestation work over the previous year and we significantly increased expenditures for afforestation. Next, it was only natural that we placed emphasis on road-building, which meant solid public works projects in the true sense of the word, since roads lie at the very core of goods distribution and have the greatest economic effects. Because large agricultural civil engineering projects with limited numbers of beneficiaries did not basically have the requisites to qualify as public works projects and because their benefits would be reaped by only a few individuals, I was relatively reluctant to accept them as such. (Later the government removed such agricultural civil engineering projects from public works and included them with expenditures for increasing food production.) My idea was, in fact, to remove government subsidies from small-scale land improvement projects, leaving them to rely instead on bank loans or various other means of financing."

While chief of Anpon's Public Works Section, Ōhira's days were typically spent negotiating persistently with persons in GHQ who were not well acquainted with Japan's realities. He recalls: "In negotiating with the Occupation forces, the projects I had the most trouble with were ports, city planning, and construction of school buildings under the [new] 'six-three' educational system. For harbor projects, it seemed that some official from the Occupation forces would inspect the harbor and then take a very cold attitude [toward including it in our budget] with the excuse that other means of finance existed outside the normal channels of approval. . . . [The Occupation forces] had absolutely no understanding of urban planning. . . . Urban planning can be very fruitful for hygiene, efficiency, and preventing disasters, and in the Japan of that time, when city after city had been reduced to a burned-out wasteland, we had a golden opportunity to revamp city plans. Looking back, it was really a pity that I had to sweat this way in dealing with these types of officials who did not understand the situation. As for the 'six-three' system, in spite of the fact that it was a system they had somewhat rashly pushed on Japan without considering the financial position in which Japan found itself, they were extremely cold-hearted when it came to constructing the required school buildings. They refused to yield, claiming that even in the United States some classes met in tents and some schools operated on a two-shift system, and so people in Japan should be patient and impart education making use of temples, churches, and public auditoriums."

Another recollection of day-to-day work is given by Satō Ichirō, at the time the budget officer at the Ministry of Finance in charge of reviewing the budget of the Ministry of Construction (newly created through an ordinance of July 8, 1948): "I was to decide the general size [of the budget] from the standpoint of the Finance Ministry's Budget Bureau. The Ministry of Construction was mainly concerned with the actual execution of projects, while decisions on what was to be done at which place was the work of Ōhira's Public Works Section of the Economic Stabilization Board. At the time, such work was known as kasho-zuke ("place-fixing"), and for this purpose there were in this section a large number of engineers from the Ministry of Construction. There must have been a hundred and twenty or thirty of them. . . . To guide this collective and do the "place-fixing" was the job of the chief of the Public Works Section, so Ōhira was at the time quite powerful. He constantly received petitions, traveled throughout the country, and was engaged in a lot of activity."

Ōhira himself recounts: "On January 1, 1949, when I was chief of the Public Works Section, I was surprised to get several thousand New Year cards from the men and women of a certain fishing village in Niigata Prefecture. Together with a New Year's greeting, the cards bore earnest requests for the renovation of their fishing port. I was impressed by how such a large number of persons of both sexes and all ages had been mobilized." Ōhira had earlier experience with receiving large numbers of petitions as private secretary to Finance Minister Tsushima, but now he was the one directly responsible for making decisions. Most petitions were urgent pleas for help in postwar reconstruction, and they came from all parts of Japan. During this period he no doubt had the opportunity to gain a wider and deeper understanding of local conditions and to ponder the basic issues of nation-building.

The Ashida Cabinet, which inherited a so-called conservative-reformist coalition government from the previous Katayama Cabinet, experienced an even more unfortunate fate than its predecessor. Nishio Suehiro, of the right wing of the Japan Socialist Party, had been chief cabinet secretary in the Katayama Cabinet and now assumed the post of deputy prime minister in the Ashida Cabinet and was expected to work to enhance cooperation among the three governing parties. The fact that he had received a contribution of ¥500,000 in political funds from a certain civil engineering and building contractor became an issue, and this led to accusations of violating a government ordinance and committing perjury in court, forcing him to resign. (He was later acquitted in both a first trial, and a second one undertaken on an appeal by the public prosecutor.)

Already shaken by the Nishio Affair, the Ashida Cabinet received a fatal blow from the Shōwa Denkō Incident at the end of June 1948. In late September, the head of the Economic Stabilization Board, a former finance minister in the Katayama Cabinet, was arrested on suspicion of accepting a bribe from Shōwa Denkō, the largest fertilizer manufacturer, followed in October by Nishio Suehiro's arrest on suspicion of trying to hush up the incident. This sealed the fate of the cabinet, which resigned en masse on October 7.

With the Ashida Cabinet's resignation, it was the turn of the top opposition party, the Democratic Liberal Party led by Yoshida Shigeru, to take power. At this juncture, a curious incident occurred, known as the Yamazaki Premiership Affair. In it, elements of both the Democratic and the Democratic Liberal parties colluded with staff members of the Government Section of GHQ, who disliked Yoshida since they judged him to be an ultraconservative, to push for making the Democratic Liberal Party's secretary-general, Yamazaki Takeshi, the next prime minister. Needless to say, GHQ had the ultimate power under the Occupation, but although the majority of Democratic Liberal Party members had at one point favored Yamazaki to be prime minister, he was finally persuaded by party elders to resign his Diet seat, and so that alternative automatically became irrelevant, regardless of GHQ opinion. Yoshida thus became premier.

Nevertheless, this incident showed that Yoshida's position as party president was by no means stable. Within the party there were many who considered Yoshida only a temporary president so long as Hatoyama remained inactive through the purge order, and who were generally angry at the way Yoshida ignored party members loyal to Hatoyama and instead brought scholars and bureaucrats into cabinet positions. To keep these divisive tendencies under control, Yoshida had to maintain a group of loyal followers within the party to form, so to speak, a protective barrier around his own fiefdom. Yoshida's efforts to strengthen his own political position were similarly responsible for the appearance of the group of ex-bureaucrat politicians who would come to be known as the "Yoshida school."

In any event, Yoshida easily won the premiership in the voting at the session of the 3rd Extraordinary Diet convened on October 14, 1948. He then immediately formed a cabinet, even though it was clear that this minority-party cabinet would be largely limited to "caretaker" functions pending new elections. The various opposition parties and factions out of power schemed to postpone the dissolution of the Diet and tried to influence the government in various ways, but Yoshida insistently countered that, under Article 7 of the Constitution, the sole authority to dissolve the Diet rested with the cabinet. MacArthur thereupon presented a compromise plan whereby the Diet would be dissolved after passage of a supplementary budget and the revised Salaries Law being pushed by the Socialist Party, and after passage of a motion of no-confidence brought by the parties not represented in the cabinet. Matters proceeded accordingly, and on the evening of December 23 the Lower House was dissolved after passage of the motion of no-confidence. Newspapers at the time called it a "dissolution by agreement" (*hanashiai kaisan*).

The twenty-fourth general election for the Lower House was held on January 23, 1949. Among successful candidates officially endorsed by the Democratic Liberal Party were Satō Eisaku, Ikeda Hayato, Okazaki Katsuo, and Yoshitake Eiichi, who had previously served as vice-ministers in the ministries of Transport, Finance, Foreign Affairs, and Labor, respectively. Among those elected on the party slate were as many as forty powerful members who had been former bureaucrats, including Maeo Shigesaburō, Hashimoto Ryōgo, Nishimura Eiichi, and Fukunaga Kenji.

When the ballot boxes were opened, many were astounded to find that the Democratic Liberal Party, which had thought that it would be doing well if it won only 200 seats, had at a single stroke increased its seats by more than 80 to a total of 264. Reflecting the recent uproar over alleged corruption, the Democratic and Socialist parties suffered a sharp drop in Lower House seats, to 68 and 49, respectively. On the other hand, the Japan Communist Party made a striking advance, seating 35 members.

Having won an overwhelming majority of Lower House seats, the Democratic Liberal Party could have gone it alone with an exclusive party cabinet, but Yoshida honored his preelection commitment to the Democratic Party for a conservative coalition and admitted two Democratic Party members to the new cabinet formed on February 16. Other factors favoring this coalition were probably Yoshida's interest in dealing with the economic crisis and his strong concern with halting the Communist Party advance.

The Democratic Party became split between a pro-coalition faction and one favoring "opposition party" status. In March 1950, pro-coalition members, including Hori Shigeru, Kosaka Zentarō, and Tsubokawa Shinzō, joined the Democratic Liberal Party to form the Liberal Party (*Jiyūtō*). The opposition faction, which included Tomabechi Gizō, Kitamura Tokutarō, Nakasone Yasuhiro, Sonoda Sunao, Kawasaki Hideji, and Inaba Osamu, joined the National Cooperative Party, whose Diet membership included Miki Takeo, Hayakawa Takashi, and Ide Ichitarō, to form the National Democratic Party (*Kokumin Minshutō*) the following month.

In setting up the Third Yoshida Cabinet, Yoshida ignored a number of veteran politicians and had the courage to introduce new faces. The choice for minister of finance was Ikeda Hayato, who had just been elected to the Diet for the first time. There exist various written accounts detailing how Ikeda came to acquire this post. The following is an excerpt from a book by an *Asahi* journalist: "Yoshida, who was troubled over how to choose a finance minister for the Third Yoshida Cabinet in 1949, paid a call on Miyajima Seijirō, the president of Nisshin Textile Company [and a member of the Bank of Japan's Policy Committee], and asked if he knew of any suitable candidates. Mukai Tadaharu was first mentioned, but he was still affected by the purge order. Yoshida was impatient, saying he could not wait more than two or three days. As they were about to give up, Sakurada Takeshi, who was something like Miyajima's right-hand man, asked Miyajima, 'How about Ikeda?' Sakurada and Ikeda were from the same home town and had known each other for a long time. Miyajima had once consulted Ikeda, then head of the Tokyo Local Finance Bureau, when there had been a lengthy dispute about the payment of ¥5 million in inheritance taxes—an enormous sum at that time—that had been levied in 1940 on the estate of Nezu Kaichirō, founder of Tōbu Railway Company.... Miyajima had been involved in setting up, with backing from the Nezu Foundation, a museum to house the Nezu Collection and had asked Ikeda to relent on the taxes as the project was to be undertaken by a legally recognized public interest organization. Ikeda had shown his understanding of the matter, saying, 'As long as it is a public undertaking. . . .'

"One day in the early afternoon, Miyajima invited newly elected Ikeda to the sixth-floor offices of Nisshin Textile Company overlooking the shops in Tokyo's Nihonbashi Yokoyamachō that specialized in the wholesale textile trade. Miyajima put one question after another to him: 'What should be done about the issuance of government bonds? What about greater expenditures for public works? What about tax reductions? What about GHQ's economic policies? What about overseas assistance?' Ikeda responded thoughtfully, and included relevant statistics. After about two hours of this, Miyajima telephoned Yoshida and said, 'Ikeda knows what he's doing. He can be finance minister.' Then he announced to Ikeda, 'You are minister of finance.'

"Sakurada, who was present during this interview, said, 'Ikeda was dumbfounded with surprise. I recall that he several times lowered his head and said, "Thank you." He had of course not been aware that he had been taking an oral examination to be [finance] minister.' "

Around that time, Ōhira heard that Ikeda was ill with a cold and went to see him at his residence in Tokyo's Shinanomachi district. He recalls that: "Ikeda was in bed in a back room and said in a casual way, 'Ōhira-kun, I may become finance minister in the new cabinet.' It was a big surprise to me. I gave some worldly-wise counsel to the effect that, 'Wouldn't it rather be preferable to stay put? Without being familiar with the trials and tribulations of the actors' common room, to suddenly become finance minister might not benefit either the governing party or yourself.' Ikeda listened in silence, but in the end did not take my advice and entered the cabinet as finance minister, as planned."

On assuming his post, Ikeda made Kurogane Yasumi and Miyazawa Kiichi his two private secretaries. Within three months, however, Kurogane was transferred to head the Sendai Regional Tax Administration Bureau and began to prepare to run in the next general election as a candidate from Yamagata Prefecture. Ōhira has written: "[In May of that year] as chief of the Public Works Section I happened to be on an official trip to southern Kyūshū. While I was having supper with Governor Shigenari [Kaku] at the Iwasakidani estate in Kagoshima, I received a telegram from Finance Minister Ikeda: WISH TO EMPLOY YOU AS SECRETARY, PLEASE RETURN TOKYO QUICKLY, IKEDA." Ōhira had thus been chosen to succeed Kurogane as Ikeda's secretary.

"Because it was so unexpected (in fact, I had already reconciled myself to not becoming a secretary), my thoughts were torn between feelings of obligation and pride, and I could not sleep a wink all night. The next morning I sent a telegram in reply: 'WHILE HEARTILY GRATEFUL YOUR PATRONAGE, IN GREAT QUANDARY AND CANNOT DECIDE, REQUEST DELAY UNTIL RETURN TOKYO.' Helped by the expectation that, with this done, colleagues in the Ministry of Finance might somehow have second thoughts about me, I calmly proceeded with the rest of my journey. From Kirishima I passed through Miyakonojō, Miyazaki, and Nobeoka to Beppu, where for two days I quietly enjoyed the thermal baths before returning to the capital in a way that would escape people's notice. After my return, I called on Finance Minister Ikeda in his office at the ministry, merely intending to pay my respects in acknowledgment of his having contacted me. Then I said, 'You have been so kind as to want me for your secretary, but in the ministry there are countless persons who would be more appropriate than me. I will select and recommend someone who is best qualified, and so I wish to ask your forbearance in my regard.' Finance Minister Ikeda listened with a smile, and then stated: 'Well, it has already been officially announced for a whole week that you are to be my secretary. With me as minister, isn't it natural that you should be secretary? It will be all right if you do nothing at all, just so long as you sit quietly in the next room.' I had no reply, and so became master of the secretary's office."

Part 3

An Upward Current

Part 3

An Upward Current

Chapter 10

The Road to Politics

It is not clear exactly when Ōhira began to consider a career in politics. However, let us examine briefly some of the conditions in the political world of the time, together with what a switch to a political career might signify for a middle-ranking bureaucrat.

As we have seen, as a result of the twenty-fourth Lower House general election of January 1949, Yoshida Shigeru brought into the political arena a large number of bureaucrats who served as a sort of personal support group. For bureaucrats, too, conditions were such as to make a changeover to a political career appealing. First and foremost, with democratization and the new Constitution, the position of the Diet as "the highest organ of state power" had been sharply elevated.

Moreover, as a result of the purge order, not only former military personnel and members of the nobility but most former politicians had been excluded from running for seats in either house; thus, the work of drawing up plans for the nation was entrusted to politicians of a new vintage. Also noteworthy is the fact that, particularly after 1949, Japan was beginning to emerge from its postwar condition of collapse as reconstruction efforts began to bear fruit. The policies of the Allied Occupation also changed in response to the escalation of the Cold War, and there was growing readiness to actively support Japan's economic recovery. This meant that able persons with technocratic backgrounds in government administration could expect to make even better use of their talents if elected to the Diet. Furthermore, due to inflation the salaries of high-ranking bureaucrats had become relatively smaller, and they could not look forward to the same sort of leisured post-retirement lives as in prewar days, or the same chances of rising further up the social pyramid.

As a secretary to the minister of finance, Ōhira had already been able to learn a good deal about the political world and politicians, and he had a first-hand view of the activities of politicians who had been former bureaucrats. A typical and close example was Ikeda Hayato. Ōhira must also have been encouraged by the fact that Kurogane Yasumi, who was one year his senior in the ministry and likewise a protégé of Ikeda, had made a successful entry into politics. However, Ōhira had not yet completely tired of the bureaucratic life, and he once recounted how he continued to feel "interest and pride and nostalgia" in regard to his former job as chief of the Public Works Section at the Economic Stabilization Board. We have already seen how, when he was appointed secretary to Finance Minister Ikeda, he was unable to sleep all night and sent a telegram informing Ikeda of his quandary. Already at that time he seems to have had some inkling of what might lie in store for him in the semipolitical position of a minister's secretary.

About this, however, he gives us no further details. It is worth noting that the last place he visited in Kyūshū was Beppu and that he returned to the capital "in a way that would escape people's notice." From Beppu, it would have been only a very short boat trip to Ōhira's home prefecture of Kagawa. And we may suppose that, at this time of important decisions at the age of thirty-nine, he may have been interested in stopping by his native place. From the Second Electoral District of Kagawa Prefecture to which he belonged, there were at that time three Lower House members, two from the Democratic Party and one from the Japan Socialist Party. No Diet member had yet been elected from the Democratic Liberal Party (later renamed the Liberal Party as previously mentioned). The runner-up in the previous election had been the candidate of the National Cooperative Party, and the candidate of the Democratic Liberal Party had gained even fewer votes than the Japan Communist Party candidate.

Ikeda's first task as finance minister was to cooperate with U.S. special envoy Joseph M. Dodge, who arrived in Japan just before Ikeda took up his new post, in laying the foundations for rebuilding the Japanese economy. GHQ had in December 1948 issued nine principles for economic stabilization, aimed at stabilizing the currency and balancing the budget.

The following recollections of the period are taken from Ikeda's book *Kinkō zaisei* (Balanced Government Finance), published in August 1952: "Dodge thought, first of all, that the scope of government-financed projects should be cut and that revenues should meet expenditures. On this point I was in agreement, and I agreed also that the only way to effect this goal was to direct attention to the existing system of price differential subsidies. In the last election the Democratic Liberal Party had used slogans calling for a relaxation of troublesome controls, respect for self-determination by enterprises, and lighter tax burdens on the people. The provision of subsidies by the government necessarily meant interference in the internal affairs of businesses, and since the combined volume of these subsidies was ¥200 billion, or one-third of the total budget, any hope of reducing taxes seemed remote so long as these were in place. Therefore, to cut these subsidies was a way of killing two birds with one stone. But the argument of most of the so-called scholars of the time was that taking away the subsidies would not only bring confusion to enterprise accounts but would also cause production to decrease. It was said that prices would rise by an amount equivalent to the discontinued subsidies, making people's livelihoods all the more difficult and causing great confusion throughout the country. In GHQ there were also a large number of young theorists who had been influenced by the New Deal, so both from within and without there was furious opposition to the conclusions shared by Dodge and myself."

The budget for fiscal 1949 that Dodge and Ikeda worked out, rejecting opposition from the Occupation forces and the Diet, indeed eliminated most price differential subsidies, but it also stopped the issuance of new bonds to finance reconstruction and included enormous sums for repayments of past obligations to be dispensed from the regular budget. Thus, a large-scale increase in revenues was still needed to balance the budget. The average per capita tax burden (including national and local taxes and profits earned by government monopolies) grew by roughly 50 percent to ¥9,942, compared with ¥6,140 in the preceding fiscal year. The total tax burden, in fact, came to represent 26.7 percent of the national income, the latter being ¥2.94 trillion. This was the reality of the fiscal 1949 "overbalanced" budget.

Only a few days after the passage of this budget, a United Press dispatch from Washington announced the decision to set the exchange rate of the yen at ¥360 to the dollar. This rate was put into effect on April 25, 1949, and was then thought to value the yen too highly. By keeping down the prices of imports, however, it was effective in curbing inflation. To have a single fixed rate, rather than dual or multiple exchange rates, contributed in a very important way to linking Japan's domestic economy with the world economy. The strong medicine that Dodge had prescribed in the form of the "overbalanced" budget later gave rise to various side effects, but it succeeded admirably in overcoming the fever of inflation and in saving the patient's life.

Ōhira was appointed secretary to the minister of finance a little over a month after passage of this budget. He has written: "The minister's office was assaulted by an unending barrage of complaints about high taxes and credit difficulties.... One way in which I responded to these complaints was to try to put myself in the position of the complainant and indicate sympathy for his point of view while trying to explain that Ikeda was limited in what he could do. I tried not to forget to explain that Ikeda was by no means a cruel-hearted individual, but was a gentle and kindly disposed person, even if his appearance and manner sometimes invited unintended misunderstanding or antagonism. I tried to instruct the complainants accurately on such matters and to seek their understanding.

"A second method was to counsel taxation offices to take greater pains to avoid, or to promptly rectify, mistakes. There is no denying the fact that the Dodge policies, known in Japan as the 'Dodge Line,' forced an unprecedentedly heavy tax burden on the populace. And it was only natural that overextended taxation offices committed errors. There were everywhere cases of careless handling in which taxpayers were twice issued the same tax assessments. Each time I came across such a complaint, I would telephone the head of the appropriate taxation office and request that he promptly apologize to the taxpayer in question and correct the error.

"A third sort of response had to do with banks. Of course, decisions on the granting of credit to applicants and the conditions and sizes of loans had basically to be carried out under the responsibility, and at the discretion, of the various banks. Given the extremely tight conditions on credit, I would show understanding and sympathy for the complaints of credit applicants, but I could not, and should not, apply pressure on any particular bank. What I could do at most was to provide some sort of advice on which financial institutions might be approached and what sorts of requests might be made. With this sort of consultation my hands were quite full."

According to a number of people who knew Ōhira at this time, his attitude toward his job as Ikeda's secretary was somewhat leisurely. Ikeda's wife, Mitsue, once remarked, "Ōhira had not been showing up at our place, and Ikeda would sometimes say to me, 'You tell him to be sure to come tomorrow morning.'"

One of Ikeda's close associates recalls: "Ōhira would often say, 'I don't know anything about the details; you'll have to ask the minister about them. I take care of things in broad outline.' He would usually appear in the secretary's office once each morning, but then would move around outside as he wished. Ōhira was especially good at managing relations between Ikeda and the ministry, the political world, and the financial world. Ikeda was the sort of person who would entrust you with his life if he was confident of you, and Ōhira had a certain amount of leisure and a good time acting as his representative."

The daily details were in the hands of the finance minister's junior secretary, and Ōhira felt that it was enough if he was in control of the most important matters. To know which were the most important was not, however, easy. To make correct judgments for someone like Ikeda, who was still a newcomer to politics and not yet familiar with the political environment, could often mean that one had to be more in contact than Ikeda himself with behind-the-scenes political, financial, and bureaucratic maneuvers and to have an accurate grasp of these. In any case, willingly or not, one would have to think, as well as be motivated, politically.

One of the places where these kinds of contacts took place was a Japanese inn called the Sakaeya in Tokyo's waterfront Tsukiji district. This inn's proprietress, Oei-*san* (whose full name was Wada Eiko), was from Hiroshima, and perhaps partly for this reason Ikeda took a special liking to her and held numerous get-togethers at her establishment. For Ōhira, the Sakaeya was thus a key place for building personal connections. Ōhira often used to be called by the nickname "*Otō-chan*," meaning "Daddy," influenced no doubt by his appearance and unflappable demeanor, and many people suspect that this affectionate name was coined by Oei-*san*.

Writing in the year following his first election to the Diet, Ōhira gives two motives behind his entry into the political world. One is that, while carrying out his work as a private secretary, he came to feel psychologically unsuited to returning in the future to the work of a Ministry of Finance bureaucrat: "I tried to tell myself that even supposing I went back from the work of being a political affairs officer as a private secretary to work as an ordinary administrative officer, I could surely discover something good in it. I thought about it, but in my case I frankly didn't have any enthusiasm about going back to administrative work. I was rather more interested in trying my hand at some extraordinary adventure in which a man might give full rein to his vitality as an individual. I wanted to break through the boredom of the present and let life burn to its natural limit." The other reason was his future prospects in a bureaucratic career. "Generally speaking, administrative officers give up early. In Japan, it is rare for one to still be an administrative officer at the age of fifty, so one will be thrown into another occupation only half-prepared."

It is noteworthy that even today a similar pattern persists. While so-called higher officials often do not really reach maturity in their jobs until their forties, it is common for almost everyone in a given class entering a ministry to have resigned by the time one classmate has been made a vice-minister in his mid-fifties. In earlier times there was no compulsory retirement age, but most government employees today have to retire by the age of sixty.

In any case, Ōhira was feeling the pressures of time, and saw that it would not be easy to switch to another career on retirement from the government bureaucracy. He decided that he lacked the confidence to succeed in business. Around this time he wrote: "Carefully scanning the faces of the bureau chiefs and even the vice-ministers who attended our ministerial meetings, I wondered how many of them could succeed by their own efforts if they left their official posts and were thrown naked onto the streets of the Ginza. A writing career is very difficult to get started in, and in any case I still have too much worldly ambition to become the sort of ascetic who could live in seclusion on a tiny income."

For these two reasons, then, Ōhira began to think seriously about running for a seat in the Diet: "So I asked myself, how would it be if I entered politics? That would certainly be one road, though it would have to be remembered that, first of all, there is no work as gruelling or difficult as politics. It would mean a hard struggle every day. It would be something like walking a tightrope or stepping onto thin ice. One would be more often reviled than praised. One would have to be ready to sacrifice one's home life. It is by no means the best-paying job, and yet one would have to bear being criticized and go about kowtowing to everybody. And then one would rather not have to be always going through the difficulties and expense of elections. . . . I tried to analyze my own character to see if I was really confident I could pursue the usual course followed by party politicians, and found that a solid core of confidence would be hard to come by.

"But this said, the profession of politics is very basic to human society. Human beings are said to be political animals. At the beginning of everything there is politics, and politics forms the core of all social endeavors. Consequently, this public profession is necessary, and somebody has to take it on. . . . So reconsidering all this and comparing myself with former politicians, I came to feel—though this may sound conceited—some confidence that there was no reason why I shouldn't be able to do as well as they."

Nevertheless, his days were filled with a curious mixture of assurance and unease. "As I turned things over in my mind, the days and months kept flying by, and I was put in the position of having to make a decision."

One of those whose reminiscences shed light on the psychological nuances of Ōhira's thinking about whether to run for elected office is Ikeda's wife, Mitsue: "One day, Ōhira, who had not been to see us for quite a while, suddenly appeared . . . at the partition between the hallway and the tea room and said, with a sincere look on his face, 'I have finally reached forty, the age when one should be free of vacillation. Thus, I feel it is not proper to vacillate, but I wonder if I'm not now beginning to do so.' "

Ōhira had turned forty on March 12, 1950, a year after becoming

Ikeda's senior private secretary. Ikeda's wife further recalls: "On the way back by train from Hiroshima, where Ikeda had gone to lend his support to the candidate he wished to win in what seemed a losing battle for election as governor of Hiroshima Prefecture, Ōhira said, 'I really feel it's an awful thing to be a politician. It makes me feel all the more like changing to become a businessman and earning lots of money. Then I'd give you a lot in campaign contributions.'" This remark was made in April 1951, not long after Ōhira's forty-first birthday, at the time of the second postwar unified local elections.

The following recollection of the summer of the same year is from Ikeda's junior secretary, Tosaka Jūjirō (later a member of the Lower House): "When Ikeda was minister of finance, Ikeda, Ōhira, Miyazawa, and I had a drink at Yanagibashi and then took a boat ride on the Sumida River. Ōhira suddenly said to Ikeda, 'I think I'd like to become a politician. How about it?' Ikeda replied, 'I think it would be fine. For a politician you have just the right character. But I wonder how much money you can get together.' When Ōhira mentioned a figure, Ikeda responded, 'Well, I'll take care of the rest.'"

Ever since a U.S. State Department spokesman announced on November 1, 1949, that a peace treaty with Japan was being actively studied, there had been all manner of lively discussion and speculation as to what form the treaty might take. First and foremost was the question of whether it would be an all-encompassing treaty with all wartime opponents or whether there would be a number of separate peace arrangements with different nations or groups of nations. The so-called progressive elements, who liked to speak of "absolute pacifism," favored an overall peace treaty with all former belligerents, while Prime Minister Yoshida stated in the Upper House on November 11, 1949, that he would gladly accept separate peace treaties if that was a means to an eventual overall peace agreement. In February 1950, Yoshida met General MacArthur and expressed his desire to dispatch appropriate persons to the United States to sound out the American government concerning the peace treaty issue. Between the two men a general understanding on this issue was reached. The person chosen to head this secret mission was Yoshida's favorite, Ikeda, who thus left on April 25, 1950, to become the first postwar cabinet minister to visit the United States. For the sake of outward appearances, his mission was said to be for the purpose of "observing government finance and economic conditions in the United States."

Ikeda's American visit was an extremely unassuming affair, and he was accompanied only by one of his secretaries, Miyazawa Kiichi, who was fluent in English. Through the intermediary Joseph Dodge, Ikeda informed the U.S. State Department that Yoshida was willing to accept the continued presence of the American military forces after the conclusion of a peace treaty. As for economic matters, he was able to exact a promise that the stringent Dodge Line would be considerably softened. As a result of this visit, the American government sent John Foster Dulles to Japan on June 21, 1950, to exchange views with General MacArthur on the early conclusion of a peace treaty.

On June 25, 1950, only four days after Dulles arrived in Japan, war suddenly broke out in Korea. Because of this unexpected turn of events, the peace settlement with Japan was postponed until the following year. On the other hand, the war caused a sudden and sharp increase in the demand for services and supplies that the United States forces could procure in Japan. As a result, the Japanese economy, which had been running in very low gear under the Dodge Line, was given a powerful stimulant. Idle funds were suddenly idle no longer, and soon every factory in the country was in operation. This was the beginning of what was commonly dubbed the "special procurements boom."

The war in Korea also had an enormous political effect on Japan. MacArthur's statement that "The Japanese National Constitution does not negate the right to self-defense against aggression" contributed to the birth of the National Police Reserve that developed into today's Self Defense Forces. The National Police Reserve Ordinance was promulgated on August 10, one and a half months after the war broke out in Korea.

With the arrival on the front lines of volunteer "righteous hero" troops from China, the war became increasingly a quagmire. General MacArthur requested permission to bomb Chinese military bases in northeast China across the Korean border, but the American government refused, and in April 1951 appointed General Matthew B. Ridgway to replace MacArthur in command of all U.S. forces in the Far East and as head of the Allied Occupation in Japan. An end to the fighting seemed finally in sight when the North Korean and Chinese forces accepted the United Nations offer for cease-fire negotiations, and armistice talks were begun on July 19, 1951. Negotiations for a peace treaty with Japan also developed rapidly, and the long-awaited treaty was signed on September 8.

Soon after assuming his new post, General Ridgway allowed a reappraisal of various regulations and practices, including the purge order, that had been operative during the Occupation period, which was soon to end. Some 69,000 names were on the first list (announced on June 29 and July 2) of those to be freed from the prohibition against holding public office, among them a large number of prewar and wartime politicians. Some, notably Liberal Party supporters Miki Bukichi and Ishibashi Tanzan, intended, upon ratification of the peace treaty, to back Hatoyama Ichirō's bid for the premiership. Hatoyama suffered an incapacitating stroke ten days before the purge was lifted, but his supporters were undaunted as they closed ranks to plan for a political change of guard.

In the summer of 1951, just prior to the peace conference, Ikeda suddenly ordered Ōhira to undertake an "inspection trip" in the United States. Writing in 1956, Ōhira recalls: "In August 1951, it was decided, at Finance Minister Ikeda's instigation, that I would make a trip to the United States for about three months. Determined not to be bothered by the inconvenience of not having me nearby, Ikeda strongly urged me to make the trip and personally undertook all the arrangements. But as to why exactly he wanted me to go abroad—in other words, his purpose—nothing was made clear. All he said was, 'Go because it will be a good opportunity and also the peace conference will be taking place.' I asked him when I should leave and was told, 'How about within the week?' So I quickly packed my things and left for the United States from Haneda airport on August 13. On arriving back in Japan toward the end of October, Ikeda insistently advised, 'You don't need to worry about your work at the Ministry of Finance. You should return as often as possible to your home town and become acquainted with the people there. There's no telling when the Lower House may be dissolved.' It was only then that I understood Ikeda's true intention in arranging for me to go to the United States. Earlier on, Ikeda had always been fond of saying things like, 'You should not become a politician. There are not enough people like you in administration, and it is my hope that you'll stay in the Ministry of Finance. You should not even dream of going into politics.' So I was surprised at the way he had changed his tune."

According to the above reminiscences, it was only in late October, after Ōhira's return from the United States, that Ikeda encouraged him to run for political office. How, then, should we interpret Tosaka's recollection that Ōhira had already in the summer of 1951 expressed to Ikeda his interest in a political career? In his 1978 autobiography, Ōhira simply wrote: "The reason Finance Minister Ikeda went out of his way to have me, his personal secretary, participate in this group was that he wanted me to run in the next election. For this purpose he wanted me to have the experience of seeing something of the United States." In any case, Ikeda appears to have been thinking along the lines of wanting to have a group of Dietmen personally loyal to him, in much the same way as Yoshida in 1949 had encouraged the candidacy and election of a large number of his friends from the bureaucracy.

Ōhira's visit to the United States was made under the auspices of the

National Leaders Program administered by the U.S. Department of Defense. In Ōhira's words, "This was a program of sending to the United States parliamentarians, scholars, officials, and so on, from occupied territories for a given period of time (in my case, ninety days) to observe, study, and undergo training on particular themes." The official objective of this visit was defined as investigating budgetary aspects of research and development projects.

When Ōhira left Haneda on August 13, 1951, he was part of a group that included Lower House Dietman Takase Sōtarō and Upper House member Maeda Masao. He arrived in San Francisco the next day, after refuelling stops at Wake Island and Hawaii, and on August 15, he boarded a transcontinental train to arrive in Washington, D.C., on the nineteenth. He stayed in Washington for nearly forty days, until September 26, before going to New York via Baltimore, Wilmington, and Philadelphia. The originally planned ninety days were cut to seventy-two, and he returned to Japan, via San Francisco, on October 21. Ōhira thus met leaders in both government and private enterprise, learning first-hand about policies to stimulate science and technology and visiting universities, factories, research institutes, and experimental stations in various parts of the country. It was not only Ōhira's first trip to the United States but also one of the earliest educational visits there by a Japanese after the war. Not surprisingly, everything he saw and heard had a sense of freshness.

Ōhira recorded his travel impressions in a seventeen-article newspaper series titled *"Amerika o yuku"* (Traveling in America), published every few days in the *Shikoku Shinbun* between September 8 and October 26. At the end of the thirteenth article in the series, he writes: "My stay in Washington was longer than expected, but because of a request from Tokyo to shorten my trip by one month, I intend to leave this city on September 26 and arrive in New York on the evening of the twenty-eighth. After a week in New York, I plan to visit the South, where not many Japanese have been, and to arrive at the West Coast in mid-October. I hope to send further reports from various places en route."

In the seventeenth and last article published, he writes: "Already a week has passed since I arrived in New York, and I will have to leave tomorrow night for Montgomery [capital of Alabama]." Unfortunately, the reports end here and we do not know exactly which regions of the South Ōhira visited or what impressions he received. In an eighteenth report, which still remains although it was not published, Ōhira states some overall impressions that may be considered a summary of his American travels: "The culture that flourishes in today's United States seems to be of a somehow distinct sort, hard to assess by the culture-history methodologies we have had until now. It is an empirical culture, which links heaven and earth, and which specifically aims at being a bridge between the limitless and the limited. . . .

"From another perspective, it can be called a culture of diligence and thrift. Granted that the land that stretched before one's eyes was exceedingly rich, from any perspective it was surely no mean feat to have built up so much and to have fostered the strength of a nation to this extent in a period of only 200 years. . . . Then, too, it is a dynamic culture, always in motion, which knows no rest or stagnation. One can even say that, through the motive force of competition, the diligence and thrift, which express themselves in a range of practical applications, are, by a process of self-motivation and self-evolution, following a limitless course in the midst of abundance, almost like an automated machine. . . .

"Thus, today's United States, which may have the visage of a strange, gigantic creature never before seen in history, is displaying an enormous, boundless productivity. . . . Perhaps in all my reports I have praised the United States too much, but it strikes a visitor basically as I have described. These reports have been, in other words, a bright scroll of many colors that I shall now quietly roll up. (October 16, San Francisco)"

During Ōhira's visit to the United States, the San Francisco Peace Conference was held between September 4 and 8. Japan's signing of the peace treaty permitted it to return to the international fold, while the U.S.–Japan Security Treaty, signed on the same day, envisioned a system for guaranteeing Japan's future security. Ōhira recalls: "Descriptions of the conference and photographs of the delegation head, Yoshida Shigeru, and the other Japanese plenipotentiaries appeared daily in the American newspapers. Reading these articles, I was overcome with joy at the realization that the day when Japan would regain its independence was about to come." The series of seventeen articles published in the *Shikoku Shinbun* no doubt had an important public relations impact on voters in Kagawa Prefecture, since they became acquainted in this way with Ōhira's name.

The 12th Extraordinary Diet was convened on October 10, 1951, for the purpose of ratifying the peace and security treaties. Opposition party attitudes were far from simple. Left and right opposition within the Japan Socialist Party resulted in an emergency party convention on October 24 and a formal division into two parties: the Right-wing Socialist Party (headed by General Secretary Asanuma Inejirō), which favored only the peace treaty, and the Left-wing Socialist Party (headed by Chairman Suzuki Mosaburō), which opposed both treaties. The Japan Communist Party also opposed both treaties. There was also opposition from some members of the National Democratic Party, which had been formed in

April 1950, in a merger of the National Cooperative Party and opposition groups within the Democratic Party. Despite this opposition, however, the vote by a plenary session of the Lower House on October 26 gave overwhelming approval to both the peace treaty (307 votes to 47) and the security treaty (289 votes to 71).

With the conclusion of the peace treaty, it seemed likely that the political situation would veer in a new direction, and the fact that Ōhira had been requested (probably by Ikeda) to return to Japan a month earlier was probably related. Many thought that Yoshida—for whom conclusion of the peace treaty had been a self-avowed personal mission—would be willing to leave the premiership once this goal was achieved. However, Yoshida intended to personally direct the posttreaty adjustments that would accompany its full enforcement (beginning on April 28, 1952), and he became ever more determined to keep his position. The so-called Christmas reorganization of the cabinet on December 25, 1951, was a concrete indication of this. Its personnel changes, which aimed to strengthen Yoshida's influence in the public security and defense spheres, involved the appointment of prewar Justice Minister Kimura Tokutarō to the post of justice minister, and the transfer of Okazaki Katsuo from the post of chief cabinet secretary to that of state minister, later changed to that of foreign minister. In his place, Yoshida appointed his old friend Hori Shigeru to the post of chief cabinet secretary, a move he had long intended to make. Thus, the Third Yoshida Cabinet came into being in the last days of 1951.

Hoping to one day inherit political power from the Yoshida Liberal Party cabinet, the Reform Party (*Kaishintō*) was formed in February 1952 through the merger of the National Democratic Party, the small Shinsei Club (*Shinsei Kurabu*), and a number of purged but reinstated politicians (notably Matsumura Kenzō) who had belonged to the prewar Minseitō. Miki Takeo served as party secretary and Shigemitsu Mamoru, now free of purge restrictions, was elected party president in June.

Although the political scene seemed to call for dissolution of the Diet, Prime Minister Yoshida continued in his post until January 22, 1953, with no call for elections or any indication that they would be desirable. Matters involving independence and the peace treaty continued to accumulate as the 13th Ordinary Diet, first convened on December 10, 1951, was extended five times to last a total of 235 days. Among the legislation to which Yoshida paid special attention were the Subversive Activities Prevention Law (commonly called by its abbreviated form, *Habōhō*) and the Public Security Agency Law (*Hoanchōhō*). The former was a public security law designed to cope with the end of Occupation restrictions on certain organizations, while the latter aimed at reorganizing the National Police Reserve, established in 1950, into the National Safety Forces (*Hoantai*) as part of the new dispensation envisaged for the period following establishment of the U.S.–Japan Security Treaty.

As might be expected, these laws invited opposition from various elements. The Diet was in frequent turmoil, and demonstrations outside the Diet building intensified. The Japan Communist Party had for a considerable time after the end of the war considered the Occupation forces an "army of liberation" and envisioned a peaceful transition from a democratic to a socialist revolution. With the intensification of the Cold War, however, its pacifist stance was criticized by the Comintern and, stimulated by the success of China's revolution, the outbreak of the Korean War, and a peace treaty that entailed continued military cooperation with the United States, the party opted for an ideology of violence-condoning struggle. Although the majority of the Japanese people supported the San Francisco Peace Treaty and the security arrangements with the United States, a mood of disenchantment finally built up with the already long-entrenched Yoshida regime.

While keeping his post as senior secretary to Finance Minister Ikeda, Ōhira began to prepare for the next general election well in advance. At first, he sought supporters mainly among those in the cities and villages of his electoral district with whom he had family ties or geographical, school, or work connections. Because of contacts made in the course of his work in the Ministry of Finance, he was quickly able to gain numerous supporters among those engaged in the manufacture and sale of salt and saké, as well as among producers of leaf tobacco. It had been twenty years since he had actually lived and studied in Shikoku, however, and many of his elementary and middle school classmates had little recollection of him—he had been, after all, a boy who did not stand out from the crowd—and it was no simple matter to organize a local group of supporters and campaign workers (*kōenkai*).

Ōhira has described his feelings at this time as follows: "Although I had finally decided to run for public office, there were still no signs of a Diet dissolution. Prime Minister Yoshida appeared to be determined to continue without a break until he had straightened out the remaining problems in connection with enforcement of the peace treaty. But, of course, politics is unpredictable, and you never know when there may be a call for elections. They may first seem to be near at hand, and then quite far off. It is by no means easy for us to be always in such an uncertain position. My feeling at the time, that I wanted an early Diet dissolution, was somewhat similar to the feeling of a new army recruit wanting to take part in a real battle as soon as possible. Ikeda advised me to spend as much time as I could back home, but that was more easily said than done. There were piles of work to be taken care of in Tokyo. And if I traveled around for a week in my home district, it took at least a month to attend to the various chores and favors I'd be asked for. And again, considerable expense is involved each time one returns home. I began to realize the burden that it would be to have to do this sort of thing throughout the year."

In the meantime, a problem arose that seemed to threaten Yoshida Shigeru's ambition of putting off elections until he had served a full term. It arose from Yoshida's attempt to appoint first-year Dietman Fukunaga Kenji to replace Liberal Party Secretary-General Masuda Kaneshichi, whose term in that post was to expire in July. As a result, a general meeting of Liberal Party Diet members fell into serious disarray, and Yoshida finally backed off and appointed instead a party veteran, Hayashi Jōji. The incident was nevertheless a sign of the waning of the authority that "one-man Yoshida" (as he had come to be called because of his success in getting his way with things) could muster.

Following this incident, intraparty conflict deepened, and it soon became clear that the only way to straighten things out would be a dissolution of the Diet and new elections. On August 28, 1952, the third day of the 14th Ordinary Diet, Yoshida carried out a "surprise dissolution," invoking Article 7 of the Constitution. Campaigning for the twenty-fifth general election was officially begun on September 5, with the voting day set for October 1. It was the first general election after the end of the Occupation, and the list of candidates included more than 300 who had been barred during the Occupation from participating in political activities.

A central figure in Ōhira's election campaign was his elder brother, Kazumitsu. After his father's death, Kazumitsu had taken charge of managing the household and had selflessly provided the funds to help meet his brother's expenses at Takamatsu Higher School of Commerce and at Tokyo University of Commerce. He was perfectly cut out to be an election campaign leader and had even acquired the nickname "MacArthur" because of his spirited demeanor and his clear and decisive way of saying things. Ōhira's wife, Shigeko, began a busy schedule of visits to towns, islands, and mountainous regions all over the electoral district. Her modern looks and refined eye for fashion were a big plus for Ōhira's image. His cousin Ōhira Hideo, who had formerly been an army major general, helped all the way from planning board to actual engagement, serving as both staff officer and foot soldier. He became famous for paying close attention to his watch, making sure that Shigeko would not be late for the next appointment. Ōhira's elder sister, Muma, and his younger sister, Tomie, served beyond the call of duty, preparing meals and helping with other necessary chores. Throughout the campaign, they were in charge of all food and supplies, and got no more than three or four hours of sleep each night. Ōhira's father-in-law, Suzuki Mikinosuke, mortgaged his home in Komagome-hayashichō to raise funds for the campaign. All these efforts by Ōhira's family began to produce results.

A group of forty who had been in the same Wada Village Elementary School graduating class got together at the Yorozuya inn in Toyohama in February 1952, and in high spirits determined to canvass the town by bicycle to win votes for Ōhira. Former schoolmates at Mitoyo Middle School also pitched in. Very important support also came from Katō Tōtarō. Although Katō had only recently founded Kanzaki Paper Company and was extremely busy trying to keep the firm in a healthy financial state, he gave unstinting material and moral assistance to Ōhira, toward whom he felt a fatherly affection. Another person who helped from the beginning was Uemori Tsuyoshi, one year Ōhira's junior. He later headed Ōhira's election campaign headquarters, a position he maintained until Ōhira's death. Uemori recalls being impressed when Ōhira explained, "Campaigning for the sake of an election and campaigning for the sake of politics are two different things."

Most of Ōhira's classmates at Takamatsu Higher School of Commerce had gone to live and work in Osaka, but many of them, on hearing of Ōhira's candidacy, tried to garner votes in their home towns and villages. When the election was over and the votes counted, it was discovered that several hundred votes had come from areas that Ōhira's campaign trail had not managed to cover. It was supposed that many of these votes reflected the unpublicized efforts of these former classmates.

Ōhira soon afterward recorded some of his feelings about this election as follows: "Because it was my first experience of an election, I let others take care of all the campaign logistics and tried as far as possible to avoid giving advice of my own. In any case, I still lacked both the experience and the knowledge to give such advice. The only exception was that I asked everybody involved to refrain absolutely from saying anything against an opponent. And I feel that everyone did very well to observe this etiquette throughout the campaign. In my speeches I tried to say only what I could be confident of saying. All of us, as human beings, cannot avoid some exaggeration and ostentation in our words and actions, but I tried my best to avoid this sort of thing."

Ōhira was not overly concerned with all the details of the platform of the Liberal Party to which he belonged. A mainstay of his speeches was: "To control inflation and maintain the value of the currency is the basis for economic development, a cornerstone for upholding moral principles, and a necessary condition for maintaining social order." Another favorite theme was: "We must resolutely carry out a budget retrenchment and go forward with the building of a 'cheap government.' " Wherever he spoke— even in the most remote island and mountain area—he voiced the same conviction. "I felt there was something ignoble about trying to win voters' allegiance by propagandizing in an exaggerated way about immediate miraculous benefits. I felt that the people's common sense would surely one day pronounce judgment on speech and conduct of this type. Democracy is supposed to be grounded in the conscience of the citizens, and I told myself, with considerable conviction, that I would even be ready to part ways with democracy if the time ever came when irresponsible propaganda might appear to be permanently successful among the people at large."

From this first election, Ōhira displayed the same attitude he later showed in the first election campaign after becoming prime minister, when he candidly appealed to the people to support an unpopular policy, involving increased taxes, to restructure government finances. Recalling his first campaign experience, Ōhira has also written: "There was very little spirit of fighting against opponents. Rather I came to feel that the election campaign was more of a struggle with myself than a struggle against others. If I could win over myself, I could surely win in the election. To win the election, I had first to win out over arrogance and cowardice hiding deep within me. And I had to get rid of the shyness and retiring disposition that always seemed so much a part of me, and I had to eliminate my short temper and my tendency to be impatient about seeing things to a successful conclusion. I was constantly doing battle with this enemy within." Indeed, the election was an occasion for training the spirit.

Needless to say, for a local campaign organization to promote a candidate like Ōhira was not without problems. In particular, Ōhira's speech-making was (in his own words) "completely unskilled." According to his nephew, Kaji Kazunori, "At that time, my uncle's speeches were often likened to an old motor that worked at a very slow speed, and you had to wait for a while between one 'putt' and the next. Everyone was a little uneasy about whether with speeches like that he would get elected." This shortcoming was, however, compensated for by the dedicated voluntary efforts of Ōhira's family and friends.

Writing in 1978, Ōhira recalls: "I am still not very good at making speeches, but in those days my speeches were totally poor and very flat, so much so that my supporters began to worry about how the election would turn out. But the world is a funny place and friends can be found in the most unexpected places. More than one woman came up to me and said, 'Anyway I'm going to give you my vote because of your nice smile.' On another occasion, a man in a horse-drawn cart called out to me as he drove by, 'There are five of us with votes at our house and we're all casting them for you. Keep up the good work!' "

In Ōhira's three-representative electoral district, the top winner (with 47,356 votes) was a member of the Liberal Party's Hatoyama faction who had previously served in the Upper House. Ōhira gained second place with 43,093 votes, and a Socialist candidate was third with 36,137 votes. Another Liberal Party candidate was unsuccessful in fourth place.

Chapter 11

Toward a Conservative Coalition

In the campaign for the Lower House general election of October 1, 1952, which followed Yoshida Shigeru's surprise dissolution, the Yoshida and Hatoyama factions of the Liberal Party engaged in a mighty internecine struggle. Partly as a result, the party's 285 Lower House seats before dissolution dropped by 45 to 240. While the Liberal Party still commanded a majority, its poor showing indicated that many people were happy to see an end to Yoshida's long term in power. The opposition Reform Party raised its representation from 67 to 85 seats. The Right-wing Socialist Party advanced from 30 to 57 seats, and the Left-wing Socialist Party advanced from 16 to 54 seats. The Japan Communist Party (JCP), which had alienated most people with its rhetoric and tactics of armed struggle, fell from 22 seats to zero. Of the 329 candidates who had formerly been barred by the Occupation forces from holding office, 139 were elected, among them such well-known figures as Hatoyama Ichirō and Ogata Taketora (Liberal Party), Shigemitsu Mamoru (Reform Party), Kawakami Jōtarō (Right-wing Socialist Party), and Kuhara Fusanosuke (unaffiliated). This was a major turning point in postwar democratic politics.

Following the election, the first priority was to decide who should be prime minister. From Hatoyama's point of view, he had handed over the party presidency to Yoshida only for the duration of the purge and naturally expected the post to be returned to him on his return to politics. When he saw that Yoshida had no such intention, he was indignant, and for a time there were fears of a head-on clash, but talks between Yoshida and Hatoyama were finally arranged that resulted in a continuation of the Yoshida premiership.

However, when Yoshida failed to appoint a single member of the Hatoyama faction to a cabinet position, it was outraged as it considered Yoshida to be breaking a promise and organized a Democratic League within the party. This grouping, abbreviated as *Mindō* in Japanese, was headed by Miki Bukichi and brought together a large number of party members who were dissatisfied with Yoshida and those in prominent positions around him. For the party leadership, it was a disquieting movement.

In the new cabinet, Ikeda changed from finance minister to head the Ministry of International Trade and Industry. Soon afterward, he came in for public criticism because of some remarks he made about small enterprises. In reply to questioning by a Right-wing Socialist Party Dietman during a Lower House plenary session on November 27, 1952, Ikeda stated: "In this transition period, it can't be helped if five or ten people who conduct business dealings according to their own ideas, or contrary to the usual rules, go bankrupt. I feel sorry for them, but I have to say plainly that it can't be helped." While this may logically have been true, the words did not befit a leading politician. To further questions he responded again with characteristic candor that bordered on indiscretion. This would obviously become an issue in the Diet, and, indeed, the very next day, the opposition parties presented a joint motion of no-confidence against Ikeda. Because twenty-five members of the Liberal Party's Mindō faction were absent during the vote, the motion carried 208 to 201. Suddenly, Ikeda, who had held key cabinet posts throughout the four years since he was first elected to the Diet, found himself out in the cold.

At the Liberal Party general convention held on January 25, 1953, pressure from the Mindō faction forced Yoshida to postpone appointing his protégé Satō Eisaku to the party post of secretary-general. At the same time, Miki Bukichi, an unabashed lobbyist for a Hatoyama cabinet, was made chairman of the party's General Council, which would have to give its stamp of approval to all Yoshida's appointments and policy proposals. On February 28, another misfortune befell the Yoshida Cabinet. In a session of the Lower House Budget Committee, Nishimura Eiichi of the Right-wing Socialist Party, intent on learning Yoshida's views on the current international situation, kept insisting that he wanted to hear not a "translation" of the opinions of American and British leaders but "the opinion of the prime minister of Japan." Yoshida could not hide his annoyance and finally, staring fixing at Nishimura, muttered, *"Burei da* (That's impolite)," followed by, *"Bakayarō* (Idiot)."

This verbal indiscretion gave the opposition parties a perfect opportunity to react, and during the March 2 plenary session of the Lower House, before a vote was taken on the budget, an unprecedented motion was presented to discipline the prime minister. Due to the premeditated absence of the Liberal Party's Mindō and Hirokawa factions, the motion passed 191 votes to 63. This incident led to Yoshida's immediate firing of

Agriculture and Forestry Minister Hirokawa Kōzen, once a faithful supporter. On March 14, the opposition parties presented a motion of no-confidence in the Yoshida Cabinet, which passed 229 votes to 218. Yoshida then ordered what has been remembered as the *"bakayarō* dissolution."

Miki Bukichi, the central Mindō organizer, had not really expected Yoshida to dissolve the Diet as only six months elapsed since the last election but had trusted that the strategy of inducing the Hirokawa faction to cooperate in the vote of no-confidence would result in Yoshida's resignation and a new Hatoyama administration. This proved to be a major miscalculation. Following the dissolution, both Miki and Hirokawa were officially ousted from the Liberal Party, whereupon they formed a new party, headed by Hatoyama, which stubbornly kept the same Liberal Party name. Because of the confusion, the general public called the new party the "Hatoyama Liberal Party," or the "Separatists' Liberal Party" (*Buntōha Jiyūtō,* or *Bunjitō* for short).

This *"bakayarō* dissolution" was the second postwar dissolution through a motion of no-confidence in the cabinet, the first having been the "dissolution by agreement" carried out with backing from GHQ in December 1948. The third would take place at the end of the tenure of the Second Ōhira Cabinet in May 1980. It just so happened that Ōhira's first direct experience with this infrequent type of dissolution came during his first year in an elective post. He recalls: "That same evening, an imperial edict was read by Speaker Ōno Banboku: 'In accordance with Article 7 of the Constitution, I hereby dissolve the House of Representatives [Lower House]. Signed and sealed by me this day: Hirohito.' At that moment all representatives were stripped of their seats in the Diet. To me, this was a bolt from the blue and a cruel turn of events. I was in an awkward position because, in deference to an informal Diet agreement [on ways to cut expenses and promote fair campaign practices], I had refrained from sending New Year's cards and was thus out of touch with my constituency. I was made painfully aware how heartless and brutal politics can be."

Everyone who has any personal knowledge of Ōhira's second election campaign agrees that it was the most difficult of his political career. Although Kagawa Prefecture's Second Electoral District sent only three representatives to the Lower House, nine candidates entered the contest: three from the Liberal Party, three from the two socialist parties, one from the Reform Party, one from the JCP, and one without party affiliation.

The campaign for the twenty-sixth Lower House general election was officially begun on March 24, 1953, with voting set for April 19. Ōhira's campaign workers had literally worn themselves out in the previous election, and many had not yet completely recovered from it. Ōhira had yet to hold any public meetings to report on Diet matters (*Kokkai hōkokukai*) in his home district, even though this was considered obligatory for a Diet member, and he had made no preparations for funding a second campaign.

In early April, toward the end of the campaign, Hashimoto Ryōgo, a former minister of health and welfare, came to Ōhira's district to speak in his support, but because of a communications slip-up nobody was at the station to welcome him. Hashimoto became genuinely concerned about Ōhira's prospects, and at his instigation it was decided that Ōhira's wife, Shigeko, would go to Kōchi—where Prime Minister Yoshida was to make a stop on a Liberal Party campaign tour—to request that Yoshida include Kan'onji in his itinerary and give a short speech supporting Ōhira's candidacy. Shigeko recalls: "Preparations to receive Prime Minister Yoshida were a big worry, and when I telephoned from Kōchi to the campaign headquarters in Kan'onji, I was told that they didn't have an appropriate meeting place, that they weren't ready to receive him, and that one thing after another was still not done. I felt this was a really serious matter, and because I'd heard that Yoshida was the sort of person who might just up and return home if he wasn't pleased with something, I was at a complete loss." When the hasty preparations for Yoshida's speech at Kamitakano Elementary School were completed, a capacity crowd filled the school grounds beneath blossoming cherry trees. All the members of the local fire department enthusiastically lined both sides of a red carpet rolled out to welcome the prime minister. Yoshida seemed very pleased and spoke eloquently for forty-five minutes, much longer than the fifteen minutes originally scheduled. Even today, people still joke about how Prime Minister Yoshida, in his speech supporting Ōhira, kept calling him "Ōdaira," mispronouncing the second Chinese character of his surname.

A memo made at the time at Ōhira's campaign headquarters reads: "Now confident of definitely winning 40,000 votes. . . . Ōhira, a completely honest candidate, for whom personal character is a fundamental concern; Ōhira, who can be trusted; Ōhira, who is well versed in government finance and economics. The great trust placed in him by the Liberal Party, which wants to see him elected, is clearly proved by the visit of our outstanding Prime Minister Yoshida, giving further impetus to his election. . . ."

When the votes began to be counted the day following the April 19 election, the first tallies were not favorable for Ōhira. Throughout the day, his campaign headquarters was a cheerless place. Toward evening, supporters of another Liberal Party candidate, who had lost in the previous election but hoped to come in third in the current polling, began to raise victory cheers. However, on the next day the tally for Ōhira swung up, and he finally came in among the three winners by a margin of 1,143 votes.

In this election, the Yoshida Liberal Party won only 199 seats, or considerably less than half the total of 466 at stake. The splinter Hatoyama Liberal Party won 35 seats, the Reform Party 76, the Left-wing Socialist Party 72, the Right-wing Socialist Party 66; 5 seats were won by the Worker-Peasant Party (*Rōdōsha Nōmintō*), 1 seat by another minor group, 1 seat by the JCP, and 11 seats by unaffiliated candidates. Both the Left-wing and Right-wing Socialist parties increased their representation, while each of the conservative parties suffered a decline. Of 56 Liberal Party Dietmen who had been elected for the first time in October 1952, 28 failed to be reelected in what had been a truly difficult contest. Because the Yoshida Liberal Party had failed to win a majority, it sounded out the possibilities of a coalition with the Reform Party, but the latter declined, preferring the freedom to develop its own independent policies. Thus, Yoshida had no choice but to form a minority cabinet. The Fifth Yoshida Cabinet, the last in the Yoshida-led Administration, was established on May 21, 1953.

Ōhira switched from being a member of the Lower House Committee on Agriculture and Forestry to become a member of the Finance Committee. He gradually became more at home with a Dietman's life and began to serve as a Liberal Party secretary and as vice-director of the party's Youth Division. But these were still more or less honorary positions, and his time was mainly occupied with special favors for his constituents.

Around this time he described a Dietman's life: "When it comes to money, there is no business that requires as much money as this one. Whether it is a happy event or a misfortune, if you are in any way involved with those affected, a wreath must be sent. For events involving large numbers of people, it may be necessary to send congratulatory telegrams and perhaps victory banners or cups, or two or three bottles of liquor. . . . When you go back to your constituency, bills are waiting to be paid: office rent, telephone, taxi fares, to say nothing of fees for rented halls for public addresses. . . . In Tokyo, visitors will average more than a dozen a day, most of them people who have come from your constituency with some request. When it is time to eat, it is expected that you will provide at least a simple meal. And everyone must be treated more or less alike. To take care of the work that piles up, telephone calls alone are not sufficient and you must go out and take care of things in person. . . . A single secretary is unable to manage things, and you need two or three persons to help with communications both in Tokyo and the home district. . . .

"A constituent's son is going to Tokyo, and can you help him get into a school there? Fortunately, he got into a school, but are there lodgings for him? He will soon be graduating, and could you help him find a suitable job?... Other constituents ask for consideration in getting licenses to sell liquor or cigarettes. You have to do your best in every case, but for each success it is possible that you will make several times that many enemies.

"Certainly one feels both responsibility and pride in being engaged, as a Dietman, in such public work as arranging subsidies and loans needed for projects such as the improvement and repair of river banks, streets, and roads, commercial and fishing ports, irrigation ponds and waterworks; or the construction or remodeling of school buildings, the establishment of new nursery schools and sewerage projects, the purchase or construction of tobacco leaf warehouses and electric power projects, the planting of forests, and the designation of national parks. However, to do all this within the limitations of one's budget is by no means easy.

"While it is still all right to be told by the public that taxes are too high, or to be asked for help in obtaining a license for the sale of government-monopoly products, or in getting a certain loan, you may be a little taken aback when asked to cooperate in selling a certain product or mediating a quarrel. The telephone starts ringing around seven in the morning, and you are likely to be called to the phone even after midnight. In any case, a Dietman is expected to provide services that far exceed the capabilities of a single individual."

Around this time, Ōhira rented a 300-*tsubo* plot of land in the Nakachō district (present-day Nishiki 1-chōme) of Nerima Ward, with three buildings that he converted into a dormitory for students from his constituency who had come to study in Tokyo. It was named Seisanryō, meaning "West Sanuki [Kagawa] Dormitory," with a superintendent and a lady who prepared meals, and it was managed by the students themselves. Ōhira bore all the expenses, excluding the cost of meals. After some years he decided that the aging buildings needed to be torn down and rebuilt, but when the owner refused to permit this, the dormitory was discontinued in 1960.

The summer of 1953, the year of Ōhira's second election, was the hottest on record since the Central Meteorological Observatory was founded in 1887, and on August 21 the temperature in Tokyo reached an unprecedented 38.4 degrees Centigrade. At the height of the heat wave, Ōhira made time in his busy schedule to write a book titled *Zaisei tsurezuregusa* (Random Notes on Financial Administration), which was published on October 20 in commemoration of having completed one year in elected office. In the preface to this autobiographical work, he writes: "I hope this will be a sort of carrier pigeon that will communicate to my many *senpai* [senior friends], acquaintances, and colleagues something of my inner self. At the same time, I am looking forward to hearing readers' criticisms of my comments and views on financial policy, and hope that these will serve to improve my judgment and knowledge." The book is divided into five chapters: "Anecdotes of a Farm Village," "Reminiscences of a Bureaucrat," "Some Comments on Financial Policy," "The Road to the Diet," and "Some Descriptions of the United States." About two years later, this work was expanded and revised and combined with a new essay titled "Comments on Well-known Persons" in a publication that appeared in January 1956 under the title *Sugao no daigishi* (A Dietman as He Really Is).

In the meantime, the political world was becoming ever more complex. The Yoshida Liberal Party, without a majority in the Diet, worked hard to get the Hatoyama Liberal Party to rejoin it, and on November 29 Hatoyama himself and twenty-three others rejoined. Miki Bukichi, Kōno Ichirō, and six others who stayed away renamed their group the Japan Liberal Party. Yoshida was happy that the Liberal Party now finally held almost a majority, but the party was soon to be hounded by the so-called Shipbuilding Scandal, which made headlines just after the New Year. A January 7, 1954, investigation of Yamashita Steamship Company by the Ministry of Justice authorities revealed that those involved in the bribery for contracts included the Shipowners Association, the shipbuilding industry, the Ministry of Transport, and finally other government agencies and certain Diet members.

Suspicions were even cast on Liberal Party Secretary-General Satō Eisaku and Policy Research Council Chairman Ikeda Hayato. The Supreme Public Prosecutor's Office was about to request permission from the Lower House to take Satō into police custody, but on April 21 Justice Minister Inukai Takeshi, having conferred with Prime Minister Yoshida and Deputy Prime Minister Ogata, cited the prerogative of administrative control vis-à-vis the chief public prosecutor and instructed him not to have Satō arrested. Further investigation was made only at the discretion of the minister of justice, and the incident was subsequently hushed up with no definitive proof of wrongdoing.

Although Ōhira believed Ikeda to be innocent, when he heard that Ikeda was being investigated by the judicial authorities he rushed to Ikeda's Shinanomachi residence and tearfully begged, "Please quit being a politician. I, too, am going to quit." According to Ikeda's wife, Mitsue, "Ōhira had a sentimental streak somewhere in him." We may recall that Ōhira himself had written, on graduating from the university, that he was "liable to flounder in sentiment," regarding this as one of his weak points.

In any event, the Yoshida Cabinet's activation of the prerogative of administrative control of the prosecutors became a target of public censure, and, like a candle flickering in the wind, the cabinet's fortunes seemed uncertain. On April 28, just after the prerogative had been invoked, a

Council to Promote the Establishment of a New Party was set up by factions within the Liberal and Reform parties that were groping toward cooperation. Unhappy with this development, in July Yoshida appointed Ikeda as the Liberal Party's secretary-general in the hope that Ikeda's shrewdness could help keep things under control. The Japanese people, however, was coming to feel it was time for a change, and there was little that Ikeda could do about it. At the end of September, while Yoshida was traveling outside the country, a Preparatory Group for the Establishment of a New Party was inaugurated, with Hatoyama at its helm. Two leading members of this group, Ishibashi Tanzan and Kishi Nobusuke, an influential prewar and wartime bureaucrat and politician, met strong disapproval from Ikeda, who dismissed them from the Liberal Party by authority of his position as secretary-general. The preparatory group proceeded to sponsor a meeting of a New Party Founding Committee on November 15, two days before Yoshida's return to Japan. Shortly thereafter, thirty-five Hatoyama supporters in the Lower House and two in the Upper House announced that they were leaving the Liberal Party on their own initiative. Under the banner of opposition to Yoshida, the Japan Democratic Party (*Nihon Minshutō*) was formed on November 24 through a coming together of the Reform Party, the former Kishi faction of the Liberal Party (which had been expelled from the party), and the Japan Liberal Party that had grown out of the so-called Hatoyama Liberal Party. The new party president was, to nobody's surprise, Hatoyama.

The distribution of seats in the 20th Extraordinary Diet convened on November 30 was 185 for the Liberal Party, 120 for the Japan Democratic Party, 72 for the Left-wing Socialist Party, and 61 for the Right-wing Socialist Party. Together, the three opposition parties commanded a large majority, and the passage of an opposition-sponsored motion of no-confidence in the cabinet was virtually inevitable. The only choice for Yoshida was to dissolve the Diet or for the cabinet to resign en masse. Yoshida was stubbornly determined to pursue the former way, but voices opposed to dissolution were strong within the Liberal Party itself, and the situation was definitely not in Yoshida's favor. Faced with the threat from a majority within the party that he would likely be removed from the post of party president if he actually carried through a dissolution of the Diet, Yoshida finally agreed to resign early on the morning of December 7. The resignation of the cabinet was announced before any motion of no-confidence was proposed before the Diet. Yoshida relinquished the party presidency to Vice-President Ogata Taketora, prewar editor-in-chief of the *Asahi Shinbun*; and Ikeda followed Yoshida by stepping down from his post as secretary-general. A new prime minister was to be designated three days later on

December 9, 1954, and it was to be a contest between Ogata and Hatoyama. Together, the two socialist parties held a casting vote. Because neither wanted to see political power pass to a successor of Yoshida, Hatoyama was elected prime minister.

The Japanese people, already weary of Yoshida's long term in office, were favorably disposed toward the new Hatoyama Cabinet. In the twenty-seventh Lower House general election of February 27, 1955, the Japan Democratic Party ran on a platform that favored revision of the Constitution, building an independent defense capability, and restoration of diplomatic relations with China and the Soviet Union. Although it failed to win a majority (that is, at least 234 seats) in the Lower House, it increased its representation by over 50 percent, to 185 seats. The Liberal Party, on the other hand, declined to second place with only 120 seats. The two socialist parties, which just before the election had jointly resolved to be unified, increased their combined representation by 21 seats to 156, thus insuring the necessary one-third of Lower House votes to prevent any revision of the Constitution. In his home electoral district, Ōhira came in third as in the previous election, even though he won approximately 10,000 more votes, or a total of 48,851.

Hatoyama's Japan Democratic Party, while now the largest, still failed to command a majority, and the cabinet it formed did not enjoy an easy relationship with the Diet. As prime minister, Hatoyama always took a rough beating in both plenary sessions and Diet committee meetings, and most of the bills put forward by members of his party were stillborn. Things reached such a point that on April 12, 1955, Miki Bukichi, who had avidly worked for the formation of a Hatoyama Cabinet, declared that a conservative coalition was needed for the sake of political stability and that if it could be achieved he would not be a stickler as to who served as prime minister. Soon afterward, this idea was promoted by Japan Democratic Party members Kishi Nobusuke (secretary-general) and Miki Bukichi (chairman of the General Council) and by Liberal Party members Ishii Mitsujirō (secretary-general) and Ōno Banboku (chairman of the General Council). In June, Hatoyama and Ogata held talks, which brought to a new stage the willingness to effect a conservative coalition. However, the Yoshida faction of the Liberal Party, now led by Ikeda and Satō, was not pleased with this development and did not commit itself, in deference to opinion that favored the adherence to certain positions and keeping a distinct identity, even if it had to be as a small group.

In later years, Ōhira described the situation as follows: "Miki [Bukichi] came from Takamatsu and felt close to me because of the proximity of our home towns. Aware that I was a close associate of Ikeda Hayato, he started to increase the frequency of his contacts with me. At his request, I called at his home in Ushigome-yamabushichō. . . . He told me: 'A coalition of conservative forces will assure us two-thirds of the seats in both houses of the Diet, and we will be in a position to revise the existing Occupation Constitution. I won't be able to die in peace until we do so.'

". . . The conversations between Miki and Ikeda that took place several times that summer and early autumn were held through my mediation. They used to meet at the Sakaeya in Tsukiji. However, their points of view failed to mesh. . . . One morning, I was asked by Miki to deliver a message to Ikeda to the effect that, at Miki's request, he should refrain from saying anything at that day's session of the standing committee of the Council to Promote the Establishment of a New Party. I delivered this message to Ikeda as instructed, but he did not seem to pay much attention to it. The meeting of the committee that day was brief. When I met Miki just outside the Diet restaurant, he thanked me and said all had gone as planned."

At a public meeting held in October in his home electoral district to report on Diet affairs, Ōhira spoke of Miki Bukichi as follows: "Miki, who has recently been working for a conservative coalition, is, I believe, serious and doing everything he possibly can. It has, indeed, become a habit for Miki to say, 'I don't have much longer to live, and I have no intention of becoming prime minister, but I do want to accomplish something good before I die.' We are talking about the same Miki who has almost become a skeleton and whose shoulders shake with each breath he takes while sipping his rice gruel. I don't think there is anything feigned or put on about his saying he doesn't have long to live. And I think his wish to die having done something good for the country and its people is Miki's natural feeling as a human being. . . . And isn't a proof of it the fact that while the flame of a conservative coalition may often have seemed on the verge of dying, it has not done so but keeps on burning? Frankly, I must respect Miki's unselfish concern for the country."

Talk about forming a new party gradually became more concrete, but when it came to the question of who would be the next prime minister, there was still no meeting of minds as the Japan Democratic Party factions wanted to have Hatoyama chosen in behind-the-scenes negotiations, while the Liberal Party people insisted on an election by all conservative Lower House members. On October 13, the Left-wing and Right-wing Socialist parties, which had similarly been holding talks aimed at a formal coalition, finally held a Socialist Unity Conference, which resulted in a single Japan Socialist Party. This served as a further stimulus to the Japan Democratic and Liberal parties, and it was resolved in consultations among the secretaries-general and chairmen of the general councils of the two parties that a similar conference to inaugurate a new party would be held, that elections for the party president would be held the following April, and that in the meantime the rather awkward policy of a "presidential proxy committee system" would be adopted, comprising four members, namely, Hatoyama, Ogata, Miki, and Ōno. Yoshida faction members tended to keep a guarded attitude until the very end, but most, with the exception of Yoshida Shigeru himself, Satō Eisaku, and a few others, did not go against the general trend and finally agreed to participate in the new party.

The new conservative party, to be known as the Liberal Democratic Party (*Jiyū Minshutō*), was officially inaugurated on November 15. Kishi Nobusuke was secretary-general, Ishii Mitsujirō was chairman of the General Council, and Mizuta Mikio was chairman of the Policy Research Council. The new conservative coalition changed the map of Japan's political world. The Second Hatoyama Cabinet resigned en masse, and the Third Hatoyama Cabinet was formed on November 22. It had become clear that the election for party president would be fought between Hatoyama and Ogata in the spring of the following year, 1956, and there was no predicting who would win. But with Ogata's sudden death on January 28, 1956, it became virtually certain that Hatoyama would be the party's first president, and this was formally confirmed at a party convention held on April 5, when he won 394 of the 489 votes cast. All members of the former Yoshida faction cast blank votes.

The three years between the time Ōhira first entered politics in 1952 and the founding of the Liberal Democratic Party in 1955 were a decisive period that set the direction for Japan's future political development. To get an idea of how Ōhira viewed the state of parliamentary politics at the time, we may refer to an essay that he wrote in October 1955, one month before the conservative coalition was finalized: "On April 28, 1952, Japan finally regained its independence and our country's politics reverted to the hands of the people, who exercise sovereign rights. However, in regard to the behavior of the Diet after regaining independence, there have been many incidents that have invited a loss of faith among a great many people. . . . Violence has been perpetrated openly, and some parties have tried to carry out serious discussions to the effect that parliamentary democracy is not worth preserving, or have only thought of trying to use the Diet as a place to advance their tactical interests.

". . . Our country's National Diet has on occasion been the site of a new McCarthyism, where political enemies have been mercilessly badgered from morning to night as if before a public prosecutor, and even the slightest and most mundane details of government administration have been interfered with.

"The white stone edifice and the red carpets are surely feeling at least halfway disappointed, together with our countrymen who have a conscience, over such behavior in the Diet. This is the reason for the lamentations about a crisis in parliamentary democracy. However, I have certainly not lost faith. There is the saying, 'Rome was not built in a day.' Parliaments must necessarily, with the passage of the years, grow and we must necessarily help them grow.

"There is nothing more pitiable than a people living under dictatorial feudal rule of the type that tries to claim that those who have power 'ought to leave the people uninformed and to make them obey blindly.' It is in open and public remonstration, where even the rocks at the roadside can appeal, that the truth can be dug out and corruption be prevented. It is not permissible that a country's fate or that the life or property of an individual be deprecated, at the hands of anybody, as if they were of no more substance than the morning mist. Through parliamentary politics, matters affecting life and property are handled in a way that meets with public consent. However one may evaluate parliamentary politics, it at least has the function of avoiding the very worst situations. And there is a unique reason why safety, freedom, and honesty will always remain alive. It is because a parliament is a mirror reflecting the hearts of the people."

The conservative coalition and the unification of the two socialist parties meant that Japanese politics had reached a certain plateau separating it from the confusion of the first postwar decade, and it appeared that parliamentary politics would become established on the basis of a system of two major parties. In terms of numbers of Diet seats, it was not yet a system of two parties of approximately equal strength but a "one-and-a-half party" system. Nevertheless, the rapid growth of the Japan Socialist Party in those days appeared to indicate that it would be possible for the party eventually to gain political power. Thus, people expected that a time would come when, as in the British Parliament, there would be an alternation between conservative and progressive administrations. These expectations were held not only by the Japan Socialist Party but also by many of the leaders of the new conservative party. The mass media shared in this expectation and labeled the expected new dispensation the "system of 1955," after the year when the new system was put together.

Chapter 12

A Burning Ideal

In the little more than three years since he was first elected, Ōhira had undergone three elections and could now be considered well experienced in Diet affairs. In the new Liberal Democratic Party (LDP) that grew out of the conservative coalition, he was appointed Prime Minister's Office division chief of the Policy Research Council on December 3, 1955. This division was charged with keeping track, for the party, of all affairs administered by the Prime Minister's Office. In his new post, Ōhira was primarily occupied with the problem of compensation for property abroad lost by people returning to Japan after the war, and also the issue of increasing retirement benefits for former military men.

Hatoyama's LDP cabinet considered that it was obligated to reevaluate and revise various practices that had been initiated during the Occupation and continued after it had ended. For instance, it addressed the issues of amending the Constitution, rearmament, and compensating former landowners for land redistributed during the agricultural reform. The two issues to which Ōhira first devoted his attention were similar.

The problem of whether or not the Japanese government was obliged to compensate returnees (*hikiagesha*) for overseas property lost with the end of the war was not susceptible to easy judgment, and the special commission set up within the Ministry of Finance to study such matters was long unable to reach any conclusions. Ōhira held the view that Japan's economic resurgence had made such compensation possible and took a political stand that favored solving the problem by conciliatory means. He conferred numerous times with Secretary-General Kishi and other party leaders and submitted a report to the government that counseled handling the matter "with earnestness and sincerity," and resulted in the establishment, by law, of an Investigative Commission on Problems of Overseas Property (*Zaigai Zaisan Mondai Chōsakai*). Ōhira has written: "It was not

156

proper for a solution to the problem to depend only on cold legal principles and fossilized administrative practices; rather it had to be sought on a higher plane of political morality. In common-sense terms, these various troubles that affected the relationship between the defeated state and the people of the defeated state needed to be approached with a bold conciliatory stance based on political harmony and overall political morality. And, in fact, these problems were approached and resolved in that spirit."

As to retirement benefits for former military personnel, these had been abolished under the Occupation but restored after the peace treaty. There were complaints, however, that the conditions of eligibility for pensions were much stricter than in the case of former civilian government employees, and that the number of persons receiving such benefits was too limited. For this reason it was a continuing political issue. On May 15, 1956, Ōhira led the Diet members concerned in presenting a draft law on special cases concerning benefits for the surviving families of former military men. This draft, which among other things attempted to extend the definition of "death in government service" (kōmushi), was studied and then approved unanimously by the cabinet committees of both houses. The new law was officially promulgated on December 20, 1956. Through its provisions, approximately 36,000 people became eligible to receive "public service allowances" or pensions for bereaved family members.

Strident voices questioned why only former military men and their families were being given such treatment. If it was a question of being victims of the war, there were also survivors of the atomic bombings and persons who suffered in earlier air raids, and shouldn't they also receive compensation? Narita Tomomi, secretary of the Policy Board of the Japan Socialist Party (JSP), asserted, "The Liberal Democratic Party's system for military pensions will lead to rearmament." The government and the governing party were being pressed to make their actions more acceptable to the public. Ōhira took on this task, arguing that the new system of military-related pensions should not be seen merely in terms of increases over former pensions but most importantly as a rectification of the former imbalance vis-à-vis civilian pensions. He criticized as rash and ill-considered the argument that the existing system of military-related benefits should be scrapped or that other social welfare programs would be adequate.

Demonstrating its great interest in this issue, the government in May 1957 established an Emergency Pension Study Council, headed by Hara Yasusaburō and with Ōhira as one of its principal members. A newspaper reporter at the time commented: "Despite the opposition of the mass media, Ōhira remained firm. Whenever we would say something, he would explain his views to us in a logical and well-formulated way. Hearing his arguments, you would come around to agree that they were reasonable. For that reason people began to say, 'Ōhira may be young but he's quite an able fellow.' " While Ōhira was building up his reputation for policy skills in this way, the reins of administration passed from Hatoyama to Ishibashi and then, hardly before one knew it, from Ishibashi to Kishi.

After being elected LDP president at the April 1956 party convention, Hatoyama launched into the long-awaited negotiations to restore diplomatic relations with the Soviet Union. Japan's most important diplomatic task at this time was to return to the international fold by becoming a member of the United Nations, but this step was being barred by the Soviet Union, which still had no diplomatic relations with Japan. In October 1956, Hatoyama traveled to Moscow, where he and Premier Bulganin signed a Joint Declaration on the Reestablishment of Diplomatic Relations between Japan and the Soviet Union. Members of the former Yoshida faction were critical of these hasty negotiations for not resolving the Northern Territories issue, and Ikeda even went so far as to declare that he was going to vote against ratification of the joint declaration even if it meant being dismissed from the LDP. However, Yoshida persuaded him not to do so, and when the vote on ratification came up, all members of the former Yoshida faction adopted the more passive measure of absenting themselves from the Diet when the vote was taken.

Hatoyama resigned with the satisfaction of having presided over the restoration of diplomatic relations with the Soviet Union and over Japan's becoming a member of the United Nations. Miki Bukichi, upon whom Hatoyama had especially relied for support, had died in July 1956. Besides the Yoshida faction, which supported Ikeda Hayato and Satō Eisaku, the party had numerous other factions around such personalities as Kishi Nobusuke, Ishibashi Tanzan, Ishii Mitsujirō, Ōno Banboku, Matsumura Kenzō, and Miki Takeo. Accordingly, the LDP still lacked a unified leadership, and there was no mutually acceptable candidate for the next party president. An election among LDP Diet members seemed to be the only way of choosing the next president, and three candidates ran for the post: Kishi, Ishii, and Ishibashi.

In those days, factions were not so clearly defined as today, but Kishi tended to represent those who had belonged to the now defunct Japan Democratic Party, and Ishii those who had belonged to the Liberal Party. On the other hand, there were also some who had tired of the existing political alignments and sought new directions in thought and action. These persons, who tended to have friendly ties with Ōno, Matsumura, and Miki Takeo, generally lent their support to Ishibashi. Ikeda Hayato adopted the official stance of supporting Ishii, although his personal preference was, in fact, Ishibashi. Satō Eisaku supported his elder brother, Kishi Nobusuke. It was from this time that Ikeda and Satō, two of the star pupils of the "Yoshida school," began to part ways.

The election for party president was held on December 14, 1956. In the initial vote, first, second, and third place went to Kishi, Ishibashi, and Ishii, respectively. Because Kishi failed to win a majority, a runoff election was held in which Ishibashi and Ishii supporters cooperated to defeat Kishi by seven votes, 258 to 251. Thus, Ishibashi became the new party president. Miki Takeo was installed in the post of secretary-general and Kishi was picked as minister of foreign affairs. After a hiatus of two years, Ikeda again headed the Ministry of Finance, chosen by Ishibashi whom he, as the former Liberal Party's secretary-general, had once expelled from that party.

Japan's economy was now indisputably in a period of rapid growth, moving from the "quantity boom" of 1955 (helped by an abundant harvest and an upsurge in exports) to the "Jinmu boom" of 1956–57, led by new investments in plant and equipment. This transition was noted in the government's Economic White Paper of 1956, which stated: "The postwar period has ended, and we are facing an entirely new situation. Growth as a result of postwar reconstruction has finished and from now on will be supported by modernization." It was during this period that the production of transistor radios and TV sets began. However, Japan's economic strength was still slight in international terms, and national income in 1955 was a mere US$18.3 billion, while that of the United States was US$324 billion. Furthermore, Japan suffered from a chronic trade deficit. As a result of the economic boom, imports increased further and the deficit widened, bringing about a lack of foreign currency. Around this time, a sort of fatalism took hold, to the effect that Japanese economic growth was subject to a certain ceiling imposed by the international balance of payments.

In these circumstances, Finance Minister Ikeda, now serving under a self-proclaimed Keynesian in the person of Prime Minister Ishibashi, put together a budget that was larger than the ¥1 trillion budgets prevailing since 1954. The budget for fiscal 1957, which sought to lead Japan's economy to a new stage of development, was promoted under the slogan "¥100 billion fewer taxes and ¥100 billion more services." However, from around the autumn of 1956, the economic boom showed signs of overheating, and this coincided with a sudden speculation-motivated increase in imports related to unstable (and generally rising) international commodity prices following the Suez Canal crisis in October. Foreign currency reserves fell from US$1.4 billion at the end of 1956 to US$0.5 billion during the summer of 1957. Indeed, the theory of a ceiling to growth imposed by the international balance of payments seemed to be borne out.

In February 1957, only two months after he had formed his cabinet, Ishibashi fell gravely ill and was succeeded as prime minister by Kishi, who initially kept the same cabinet members. At first, its policy was also identical, but, as the government became more apprehensive lest an overheated economy bring about a foreign currency crisis, in June 1957 it switched to a policy of credit retrenchment. Thus, the "Jinmu boom" ended, and during the rest of 1957 and into 1958 the economy moved into a gradual and lingering recession. Thereafter, over approximately one year, the economy would show a "V-shaped recovery," leading to the "Iwato boom" that lasted for forty-two months. There were many people, however, who interpreted the economic slump as the failure of Ikeda's financial policy, and those who understood the Japanese economy's underlying growth potential were all too few.

In July 1957, when the effects of the economic retrenchment policy were rapidly making themselves felt, Kishi changed all members of the cabinet (with the exception of Ishii Mitsujirō) with a view to making it his own rather than one inherited from the previous Ishibashi Administration. It was, in effect, the equivalent of organizing a new cabinet at the outset of a new administration. It was suggested that Ikeda assume the post of direc-tor-general of the Defense Agency or else head the Economic Planning Agency, but he preferred to leave the government, insisting that the only way he could cooperate would be to continue as finance minister, and he pushed for a cabinet post for his protégé Maeo Shigesaburō. For the post of foreign minister, Kishi, who planned to revise the sensitive U.S.–Japan Security Treaty, picked Japan Chamber of Commerce and Industry Presi-dent Fujiyama Aiichirō. Kōno Ichirō was appointed head of the Economic Planning Agency and Maeo Shigesaburō as minister of international trade and industry.

Ikeda's decision to leave the cabinet would turn out to be to his future benefit. Former Prime Minister Yoshida, who was living in retirement at his home in Ōiso, praised Ikeda's unyielding attitude by sending him a package of fresh sea breams with the note, "A mark of 150 [that is, A+]. Congratulations." From this time on, important political and financial figures began to visit Ikeda's Shinanomachi home even more frequently.

After the demise of the Yoshida Administration in late 1954, the Yoshida faction had adopted the name *Heishinkai*, and, as a base for its ac-tivities, had rented an office in the Machine Trade Promotion Society Building (later the Japan Shortwave Broadcasting Society Building) in the Akasaka district in Minato Ward. Some of Ikeda's supporters in the Heishinkai and outside the Diet who wanted him to become party president and prime minister came out in favor of establishing a broader, supraparliamentary political association to support this goal. Thus, the *Kōchikai* was inaugurated in April 1957. The name literally means "Wide Pond Society," and is said to have been taken by Yasuoka Masahiro, a prominent Orientalist, from a couplet of the Later Han–Dynasty scholar Ma Rong: "Reclining in a high and shining tower, I gaze out over a wide pond." This Kōchikai association was the beginning of what became, within the LDP, a clearly distinguishable Ikeda faction. It initially included the two political elders Hayashi Jōji and Masutani Shūji, as well as such top-level supporters as Sutō Hideo, Kosaka Zentarō, Maeo Shigesaburō, and Ōhashi Takeo. Younger supporters included Ōhira Masayoshi, Suzuki Zenkō, Uchida Tsuneo, Kurogane Yasumi, and Miyazawa Kiichi.

The budget for fiscal 1958 was finally passed before the deadline of March 31, 1958 (last day of fiscal 1957). A Diet dissolution was in the offing, and agreement on a negotiated dissolution was reached in talks between Kishi and Suzuki Mosaburō, heads of the LDP and JSP. It is here worth noting that although the statutory term of office for Lower House members is four years (set by the Constitution), in all the postwar years the only election to be held at the end of a full term of office was the thirty-fourth general election during the Miki Administration in the autumn of 1976. Elections have otherwise always been called prematurely because prime ministers, who have the power to dissolve the Diet, have tried to schedule elections at times deemed favorable to the governing party. By the spring of 1958, over three years had passed since the previous election, and a possible dissolution of the Diet was not seen as anything strange or unexpected.

On May 1, the campaign for the twenty-eighth Lower House general election (set for May 22, 1958) was officially began. The first general election with a unified conservative and a unified socialist party, it was to be a tough contest reflecting ideological opposition on such issues as the Sunagawa Case, which involved efforts to stop the expansion of a United States military base, the issue of "lethal rain" from American nuclear tests in the Pacific, and the so-called *kinpyō* issue, involving widespread criticism of the system of "efficiency ratings" applied to instructors in public schools. The proportions of conservative and socialist voters turned out to be about the same as in the previous general election, with the difference that the votes were divided almost entirely between only two parties. The final tally was 287 seats for the LDP, 166 seats for the JSP, 1 seat for the JCP, and 13 seats for minor parties and unaffiliated candidates.

In the election campaign, Ikeda made an all-out effort to at least double the size of his Diet faction from its preelection strength of around thirty, and thus to advance along the road to the prime ministership. Throughout the country he busily raised campaign funds and gave speeches in support of candidates who shared his ideals. Fifty Ikeda faction members were elected, making it the second-largest faction in the Lower House after the Kishi faction, which had fifty-seven members.

Following the election, Prime Minister Kishi consolidated his strength by appointing Ōno Banboku as deputy prime minister, Kawashima Shōjirō as secretary-general, Kōno Ichirō as chairman of the General Council, and Fukuda Takeo as chairman of the Policy Research Council. He completely revamped the cabinet, with the sole exception of Fujiyama Aiichirō, who was retained as foreign minister. Satō Eisaku assumed the post of finance minister, and Ikeda finally agreed, with encouragement from Deputy Prime Minister Ōno, to enter the cabinet as state minister without portfolio. Ikeda grumbled, "It's being a minister only on Tuesdays and Fridays," meaning there was nothing to do except attending the cabinet meetings.

This election was the fourth for Ōhira, who now had a strong political base and this time won the largest block of votes in his electoral district. After the election, a local newspaper ran an article titled "A Man Who Thinks Things Through—Hope of the Diet Conservatives," which evaluated Ōhira as follows: "It is rare to find someone like him about whom people have so little bad to say. Because he is so well thought of, I thought I'd play devil's advocate and keep my ears open for some unfavorable criticism, but I never heard any. His unpretentious manner is an asset, as is the fact that he trained and disciplined himself for many years as an administrator in the Ministry of Finance. . . . His membership on the Diet Budget Committee fits him perfectly. He is known as a man who proceeds in a down-to-earth way and who is incapable of telling a lie. But at the same time one who knows him well says, 'It may also be true that he is at a disadvantage in lacking the politician's characteristic bluff.'. . . He is never flustered. Whatever might suddenly come up, he doesn't take any action until he has carefully thought things through. He has the reputation of being slow to start a job but being the fastest in finishing it."

Ōhira became vice-chairman of the LDP's Policy Research Council in June, 1958, an expert member of the party's Extraordinary Research Commission on the Tax System in July, vice-chairman of the party's Subcommittee on Policy Toward the Forestry Industry in November, and chairman of the Expert Committee on Policy Toward the Tobacco Industry in December. This experience as a policy maker and in the field of policy issues brought him into an ever closer working relationship with Ikeda, and in this way he was becoming a central figure in the leadership of the Ikeda faction.

In the interests of political stability, the Kishi Cabinet had included non-mainstream Ikeda and Miki Takeo, but this stability was suddenly destroyed by an incident connected with the revision of the Police Duties Execution Law, usually abbreviated in Japanese as the *Keishokuhō*. To elucidate this issue, we have to review the background to plans for revisions in the U.S.–Japan Security Treaty, considered by Prime Minister Kishi to be his cabinet's paramount task.

The U.S.–Japan Security Treaty, which had been concluded at the same time as the peace treaty in 1951, contained various points that were considered to be inequitable or one-sided, and its revision had become an important pending issue for subsequent cabinets. Prime Minister Kishi talked this over with President Eisenhower during his visit to the United States in June 1957, and, on sounding out American views on treaty revision, it appeared that the Americans might be willing to compromise in directions desired by Japan. Thus, informal negotiations on the issue were begun in the first days of 1958, and in September of that year negotiations were formally commenced at a meeting between Foreign Minister Fujiyama and Secretary of State Dulles.

Both the People's Republic of China and the Soviet Union were fearful that Japan, once on a more equal footing vis-à-vis the United States, would follow the road toward becoming a strong military power, and consequently they were opposed to any treaty revision. At the same time, the opposition camp within Japan unanimously pronounced itself against the U.S.–Japan Security Treaty in any form, whether newly formulated or not, saying that the proposed revision would only perpetuate the system of U.S.–Japan mutual defense. Labor unions were frequently engaged in all kinds of illegal strikes inspired by the strong opposition being shown by the Japan Teachers Union to the *kinpyō* system of official evaluations of teaching performance, and it was expected that such strikes would intensify, spurred by opposition to the security treaty. The proposed revision of the Police Duties Execution Law would supposedly help prevent this by strengthening the jurisdiction of police officers to carry out *ex officio* questioning or enter premises of suspect persons or organizations.

On October 8, the government presented its proposed revision of the Police Duties Execution Law to the 30th Extraordinary Diet, which had been convened on September 29. In an attempt to prevent consideration of the draft revision, opposition Diet members and their secretaries and office staff forcibly occupied the committee meeting rooms, which led to violence. For the time being, the revised Police Duties Execution Law and more than forty other pieces of legislation put forward by the government had to be shelved.

At the height of the disturbances surrounding the proposed revision of the Police Duties Execution Law, Ikeda was in Seattle to attend a conference of representatives of the nations that had set up the Colombo Plan, but each day he received several telephone calls from Ōhira informing him of the situation in Japan. By the time Ikeda was back in Tokyo, consideration of the controversial bill had already been shelved, and the political abilities of the prime minister and the party leadership were being sharply questioned by the LDP non-mainstream factions.

Responding to non-mainstream maneuvers, the mainstream factions of Kishi, Satō, Ōno, and Kōno arranged for a party convention to be held in January 1959, before the party president's term in office (then two years) expired in February. They intended that Kishi would be reelected as party president at this, but the non-mainstream factions of Ikeda, Ishibashi, Ishii, Matsumura, and Miki countered by forming a Party Renovation Round Table Conference (Tō Sasshin Kondankai). Then, on December 27, 1958, three cabinet members, namely, Minister of State without Portfolio Ikeda, Economic Planning Agency Director-General Miki, and Education Minister Nadao, tendered their resignations.

In the election for party president held on January 24, 1959, the non-mainstream factions supported the candidacy of Matsumura Kenzō, but he trailed Kishi 166 votes to 320. Prior to this election, the Ikeda faction held frequent meetings to discuss strategy for weakening Kishi's chances for success. Ōhira, however, did not often attend these meetings. For the most part he kept to himself, sometimes going out of town for a leisurely game of golf. When a newspaper reporter questioned him about the propriety of staying away from these Ikeda faction meetings, Ōhira only made the wry reply, "Mochiya wa mochiya da yo," meaning something like "Every man to his trade." He did not look favorably on the practice of making cabinet positions—which ought to carry an overriding responsibility—tools for factional infighting. In fact, despite numerous entreaties by colleagues in the course of his political career, he never once agreed to support a cabinet resignation as a means of factional manipulation.

Ten or more years later, Ōhira once remarked on the situation at that time: "After all, for three cabinet members to resign was really crazy. . . . At the time of his resignation, Ikeda was pronouncing high-minded sentiments—something unusual for him—like 'your political ideology and mine are different.' I did not understand it." Indeed, Ōhira's close relationship to Ikeda did not necessarily mean that he always agreed with Ikeda's behavior.

Around this time Ōhira wrote an essay titled "Ketten no bi" (The Beauty of Shortcomings), which throws additional light on their relationship:

"For many years, Ikeda Hayato has been for me like an elder brother. Thus, it is no exaggeration to say that I am well aware of his virtues and shortcomings in both public and private life. If I were to describe Ikeda briefly, I'd probably say that while he has a simple and virtuous character quite separate from the intricacies of ruse and deception, this is balanced by all kinds of shortcomings and a certain lack of refinement. This is proved by the fact that things he thinks nothing of are considered outlandish by people in general, and things he feels it is quite natural to say are taken as irresponsible. As regards 'Ikeda financial management' or 'indiscrete Ikeda utterances,' people might well have a different reaction if they were carried out or said by someone other than Ikeda himself. Anyway, Ikeda is to this extent a difficult human being. And we could probably say this is because of his shortcomings rather than his virtues.

"In any case, he is an unusual presence on Japan's political scene. If we examine him closely, he is unendingly fascinating. Whenever I reflect upon individuals, upon history, or upon politics, I am forever surprised at the mysterious ways in which God's will is manifest through shortcomings. And there is also much I have become aware of by the way Ikeda's life in particular has been bound up with the vagaries of God's will."

Soon after the completion of the new party and cabinet appointments, the time was approaching for the fourth unified local elections in April and the fifth Upper House elections in May. In the speeches he made in support of Upper House candidates, Ikeda elaborated on his "salary-doubling plan," which may be called the prototype of the National Income-Doubling Plan he would later emphasize as prime minister. In an article by Ikeda titled *"Watakushi no gekkyū nibairon"* (My Scheme for Doubling Monthly Salaries), which appeared in the March 9, 1959, issue of the *Nihon Keizai Shinbun*, he focused on the following three points: "(1) Japan's economy has in recent years become stronger than ever before; (2) although Japan's economy today has great productive power, it lacks corresponding demand, with the result that the economy is suffering from the pressures of so-called oversupply; thus (3) we must stimulate demand and put our productive power (labor force, together with plant and equipment) fully to work to develop further Japan's already robust economic strength. This is both necessary and possible.

". . . If these points are correctly understood, and the earnest efforts of the people can be brought into play via wise political leadership, it will by no means be impossible in the coming five to ten years to double or even triple incomes, that is, monthly salaries. In the next few years, I hope to see us catch up with Western Europe in national income. The means to do this are, first of all, to refrain from uselessly or inappropriately restraining economic growth and to make the most of the Japanese people's creativity and resourcefulness by eliminating, so far as possible, various types of controls and restrictions. We must work to improve roads and harbors, water supplies for industry, sanitation, science and technology, as well as housing and other facilities. This is my dream as a politician."

Toward the end of the Upper House election campaign, these ideas of Ikeda's were adopted as party policy, and the government's long-term economic policy was changed from the previous goal of 6.5 percent average yearly growth to 7.2 percent, as envisaged in the new National Income-Doubling Plan.

On the occasion of the new cabinet and party appointments following the Upper House elections, Kōno hoped to gain the post of party secretary-general, but his bid was rejected by Kishi, who was instrumental in arranging for the post to go to Kawashima instead. In public appearances in Kansai, Kōno peevishly began suggesting that the Kishi Cabinet should step down once success was achieved in revising the security treaty. Given this deepening rift between the mainstream factions, Kishi became increasingly intent on securing Ikeda's loyalty for the sake of political stability. Kishi finally asked Ikeda to rejoin the cabinet, but general sentiment in the Ikeda faction was opposed to this. It had been only six months since Ikeda and the other two cabinet members had submitted their resignations, and too many people, including Ikeda himself, were of the opinion that there were still too many incompatibilities standing in the way of cabinet cooperation.

In 1959, Ōhira wrote an essay titled "Omowaku to gūzen" (Intention and Chance) on some of his own activities during this period. It is quite detailed but may be summarized as follows: On the evening of June 6, a meeting of the Kayōkai (Tuesday Club), which was organized largely around Ikeda and industrial magnate Matsunaga Yasuzaemon, produced some outspoken discussion in regard to a possible cabinet reshuffle. When Ōhira entered the meeting, Matsunaga told him: "If Kishi makes mistakes in this cabinet reorganization, the political situation might go in an undesirable direction. However much you may dwell on circumstances or compatibility of standpoint, what you people are doing is not right. It looks as if we can't treat Ikeda as a real politician. And what business do you have being so close to him?"

Feeling rather like a defendant in court, Ōhira retorted: "I can't simply ignore what you have just said. The political situation has become unstable due to the difficulties in carrying out the cabinet reorganization that the prime minister proposed and is involved with. You are saying that responsibility to resolve this issue lies with Ikeda and the rest of us, but aren't you and your friends being too easy on Kishi and too hard on Ikeda?" Softening a little, Matsunaga admitted, "Perhaps I went too far." Throughout the meeting Ikeda stuck to his position of refusing a cabinet appointment. Ōhira was unable to sleep that night, and after due consideration telephoned Ikeda at his Shinanomachi residence before dawn, counseling: "Try not to make refusal to participate in the cabinet anything definite." Ikeda gave his laconic assent.

It was on that day that the political situation seemed to reach its nadir, and rumor had it that the Kishi Cabinet was about to resign en masse. Around 3 P.M., Ōhira called on Ikeda, saying: "In our human world there is something about the turn of Fortune's wheel that exceeds our wisdom and understanding. I do not think the standpoint we have taken up to now was incorrect, but, faced with the present political situation, you have literally become the central figure in the proposed cabinet reorganization, even though you did not seek this. In several events, such as the forming of the Democratic Party, the birth of the Hatoyama Cabinet, and the end of the Yoshida Cabinet, Kishi has always been a political rival of yours. Be that as it may, today you hold the key to saving Kishi's position and to showing a way out of the current political mess. And you often say that as politicians we must not look at things solely within the confines of the world of politics but must go out and 'dance before the people.' At this stage, is it not a priority for you to want to give the people a sense of security by getting the present confused situation back on track? Whether you should move forward or backward, I honestly don't know. . . . This is what being in a dilemma must mean, but there is only one way out, not two. And now a decision is being required of you. I ask you to make a courageous choice. It will be a difficult and thorny path, but please decide on a course of action that will tidy up the political situation. Leave questions of praise or censure to the critics and historians and, with your awareness and responsibility as a leader in politics, please have a frank talk with the prime minister and decide to enter the cabinet if you can be satisfied with his true motives." In the end, Kishi's cabinet reorganization was successfully accomplished with Ikeda's cooperation. And subsequent developments showed that Ikeda's entry into the cabinet at this time paved the way for him to become Kishi's successor as prime minister.

It is said that during the Upper House elections, when Kishi adopted Ikeda's income-doubling proposal as part of the party platform, Kishi had already informed Ikeda that in the interests of realizing this policy he wanted to make him minister of international trade and industry. Now that this had come about and the National Income-Doubling Plan was formally approved by the Kishi Administration, the mainstream in the reorganized Kishi Cabinet switched from the Ōno and Kōno factions (who generally had no experience as bureaucrats before becoming party politicians) to the two major factions from the former Yoshida faction centering around Satō, who continued as finance minister, and Ikeda.

On June 30, less than two weeks after the June 18 cabinet reorganization, Ōhira was selected chairman of the Lower House Education Committee. Among the various bills this committee was considering, Ōhira was putting particular effort into plans to promote scientific research. At a session of the Education Committee on March 18, 1960, he pleaded for higher salaries for university professors, making the point that they were responsible not only for educating students but also for upholding the country's overall standards of scholarship: "With respect to university professors, who have an important role in maintaining and improving standards of scholarship and research, we should not think merely about such interim matters as research allowances but rather—taking due cognizance of the nature of their work and reevaluating the very important functions they perform—it is my hope that we will make efforts to have these considerations reflected in their basic salary structure."

While serving as chairman of the Lower House Education Committee, Ōhira also became involved in the establishment of the Assistance Society for Frequent School Non-attenders (*Chōketsu Jidō Seito Engokai*)—today little known to the general public—aimed at educating 200,000 to 300,000 truant children. Having heard about this movement, Ōhira consulted with Miyazawa Kiichi, who was then an Upper House Dietman and the parliamentary vice-minister of education, and also talked with Ikeda, who gladly agreed to be head of the new society. Ōhira and Miyazawa were vice-presidents.

The founding prospectus for this society stated that its aim was not to give welfare to the children in question but to provide them with a basic education, and its activities consisted mainly of members volunteering to give instruction in reading, writing, and arithmetic. The first efforts began in the Asakusa San'ya district of Tokyo for the benefit of children living in that area's slums. Ōhira not only provided financial assistance but made time to be with the children at year-end parties and summer camps. The wives of Ikeda, Ōhira, and Miyazawa also cooperated with the society's activities by canvassing for funds and organizing donations of clothing and educational materials.

As to why he took on this voluntary activity, Ōhira some years later wrote a pamphlet titled *"Watakushi wa naze chōketsu jidō ni kanshin o motsu ka"* (Why Do I Take an Interest in Truant Children?) in which he states: "In my work as chairman of the Education Committee, I came to feel that education is politics, or rather the *Kern* [core] of politics, or even something superior to politics. And I recognized anew that the driving force behind Japan's progress in the past had been public education, which by the fifth decade after the Meiji Restoration [that is, the decade beginning in 1908] had caught up with and surpassed levels in other major countries of the world. Deep within, I decided that I was likely never to separate myself from educational issues for the rest of my life.

"This favorable psychological timing was without doubt the reason why, in spite of my reputation as a slow mover, I found it easier than expected to respond to this issue of assisting truant children. Although I am more timid than most when it comes to money matters, I made telephone calls and sent letters to various senior acquaintances in the financial world requesting funds for the society. And it was I who made requests for people to continue to work with the society as directors or board members."

After Ikeda's death, Ōhira became the society's president and continued to serve in that position. Unlike some presidents or vice-presidents of voluntary organizations who more or less exist in name only, Ōhira well understood the organization's purposes and was an active participant in its management. Although certain acquaintances reproached him for spending time looking after such a group in spite of his busy schedule in public office, he allotted time to soliciting funds to support it. After Ikeda's death, Ōhira became the society's president and continued to serve in that position. The society was disbanded in 1971, its purposes having been for the most part achieved. Part of the society's work was continued thereafter by NHK, Japan's public broadcasting network.

With his position as chairman of the Lower House Education Committee and with the backing that came from being Ikeda's favorite protégé, Ōhira, now a vigorous fifty, was gradually becoming better known to the mass media and to members of other factions within his party.

Chapter 13

A Storm of Protest

At this time, the revision of the U.S.–Japan Security Treaty, which the Kishi Cabinet considered its most important task, was running aground amidst angry protest demonstrations and even incidents of violence. In the 33rd Extraordinary Diet held after the 1959 Upper House election, Foreign Minister Fujiyama explained that negotiations with the United States were now approaching a dénouement. However, the opposition parties remained adamantly opposed to revision and encouraged demonstrations outside the Diet building. On November 27, a crowd of nearly 10,000 demonstrators, led by the general secretary of the Japan Socialist Party (JSP), Asanuma Inejirō, forced its way into the Diet precincts and clashed with police, resulting in nearly 300 wounded on both sides.

In January 1960, a security treaty negotiating team headed by Prime Minister Kishi left for the United States, and on January 19 a new Treaty of Mutual Cooperation and Security between Japan and the United States was concluded, and an improved Status of Forces Agreement replaced the former U.S.–Japan Administrative Agreement. The 34th Diet, which was expected to ratify these, was inaugurated on January 30, and discussion there focused on interpretation of two aspects of the treaty, namely, the scope of the "Far East" and the right of treaty revision. There was inadequate agreement even within the LDP itself, and the battle of words, in which the opposition parties took a major part, was heated.

At the JSP convention held in September 1959, former General Secretary Nishio Suehiro, who had been in favor of a revised treaty, was ousted from the party, and four months later, in January 1960, Nishio, together with Kawakami Jōtarō and others who had also left the party, formed the Democratic Socialist Party (DSP; *Minshu Shakaitō*).

As the opposition parties, which could not hope to put together a parliamentary majority, concentrated on extraparliamentary activities, and with the All-Japan Federation of Student Self-Governing Associations (*Zengakuren*) expanding its own spirited demonstrations, the general atmosphere could only be called highly charged. Demonstrations intensified in April, and the frequent clashes between Zengakuren students and riot police gave rise to some bloody incidents.

Because of opposition party recalcitrance, Diet deliberation on the new treaty was delayed. The Kishi Cabinet's plans were further undermined when the LDP non-mainstream Miki, Matsumura, Ishibashi, and Kōno factions adopted the position that the Diet session should be extended, that deliberations should proceed cautiously, and that any forced means of ratification or police involvement should be avoided.

A visit to Japan by President Eisenhower had been set for June 19 in commemoration of the centenary of the United States–Japan Treaty of Amity and Commerce ratified in 1860. The government wanted to have the new treaty ratified before then and on May 19 forced approval by the Lower House Special Committee on the Security Treaty. If approved by a plenary session of the Lower House, the treaty would automatically become ratified thirty days later, even if the Upper House had not approved it. Lower House Speaker Kiyose Ichirō mobilized 500 policemen to eject the enraged JSP Dietmen and staff members who had been occupying the Lower House chamber and adjacent areas of the Diet building. A plenary session of the Lower House was then convened—despite the absence of opposition members—and a resolution passed to extend the Diet by fifty days. Then, in the early pre-dawn hours of May 20, those present ratified the new treaty. However, twenty-six members of LDP non-mainstream factions joined the opposition Diet members in absenting themselves from the voting. Nearby, angry members of the Zengakuren climbed over a cordon of armored cars and forced their way into the Prime Minister's Official Residence.

These events signaled a turning point in the anti-American, anti-treaty struggle to an appeal for the overthrow of the Kishi Cabinet and cancellation of Eisenhower's visit. Supported by the mass media, the opposition parties claimed as invalid the extension of the Diet period and the one-sided adoption of the security treaty. The political battle now moved completely outside the Diet, and the main issue changed from the security treaty to democracy itself. The area around the Diet building was clogged with demonstrators, and an uneasy atmosphere pervaded the city center. Although Ikeda was critical of Kishi's political methods, he supported Kishi in the difficult month leading up to the treaty's ratification because he considered the new treaty to form the core of Japan's diplomacy.

On June 12, 1960, President Eisenhower left Washington on his Far

Eastern tour, but it was still uncertain whether the Japanese would be able to receive him. In this tense period, on the evening of June 15, Zengakuren students forced their way onto the Diet grounds, where they clashed with police, and a large number were injured on both sides. The demonstrators were no longer under the control of the Socialist and Communist parties, and there was a threat of more violence. In the confusion of clashes with the police that continued that night, a female student was badly hurt and died a few hours later. Cabinet meetings agonized over how to handle the situation, and when, on the afternoon of June 16, Prime Minister Kishi proposed requesting a postponement of the American president's visit, this was accepted by the cabinet, although two members withheld their agreement. At this juncture, Prime Minister Kishi had already decided to resign.

The new treaty was automatically ratified on June 19 and implemented on June 23, when ratification papers were exchanged at the Ministry of Foreign Affairs. That same morning, Kishi tendered his resignation before a government-party liaison meeting (*seifu-yotō kaigi*) of the members of the cabinet and the top three LDP officers next to the president.

The new treaty, which in reality improved Japan's position and brought greater equality to Japanese–American relations, was nevertheless branded by the so-called progressive camp as a "change for the worse" (*kaiaku*), and gave rise to huge demonstrations of up to 300,000 people that ultimately brought down the Kishi Cabinet. Writing in 1966, Ōhira summarized contributing domestic and international factors: "Before we knew it, these disturbances departed radically from being a dispute over the pros and cons of revising the U.S.–Japan Security Treaty and took on the character of a great political struggle between conservatism and progressivism that brought into question the relationship between rulers and the ruled. The Japanese people, who had finally recovered from the material deprivations caused by a long war and defeat, had become aware of a certain dryness and emptiness in their spirit. Toward the Occupation policies and the conservative policies that followed, the people were coming to feel a dissatisfaction that was hard to define simply as either a will to resist or fatigue.

"There was no reason to expect that the left-wing forces would silently overlook this charged atmosphere. It so happened that just at that time the Kishi Administration was planning a revision of the security treaty—which actually was well intentioned and gave a certain degree of self-determination to Japan under the joint security system, and thus aimed at eliminating a bit of the Japanese people's spiritual emptiness—and the left-wing forces craftily represented this change for the better as one for the worse, using the issue to inflame the people's feelings of spiritual craving and encouraging them to overthrow the joint security system and the conservative government. And this attempt was carried out on a large scale in coordination with the steady development of policies toward Japan by China and the Soviet Union. Behind these security treaty disturbances, such maneuvers were constantly going on, even half openly."

After Prime Minister Kishi announced his intention to resign, the next prime minister had to be chosen from among the likely candidates: Ikeda, Ōno, and Ishii. Satō was expected to refrain from running at this time, given that he was the younger brother of the outgoing party president. As mentioned earlier, Ōhira had counseled Ikeda against accepting Finance Minister Ishibashi Tanzan's bid to have him switch from his post as head of the Tax Bureau to serve as vice-minister of finance. Later, when Ikeda was serving his first year in the Diet, Ōhira had counseled against accepting the appointment of finance minister. However, Ikeda had become vice-minister and minister of finance, ignoring Ōhira's advice. Ōhira recalls: "The final goal for Ikeda as a politician was the post of prime minister. When he ran for the LDP presidency in the summer of 1960, I did not try to counsel caution and have him give up the idea. Rather . . . I prayed for his success and even tried to be of some help."

All the members of the Ikeda faction worked to support Ikeda's candidacy. However, the method to be used in selecting the party president was still undecided. The mainstream Kishi and Satō factions were against including the Miki or Kōno factions in a new cabinet as their members had criticized the Kishi Cabinet's handling of the security treaty issue. They envisioned a five-faction coalition of the Kishi, Satō, Ikeda, Ōno, and Ishii factions, and wanted the prime minister to be chosen through consultations among the faction leaders rather than through a party election, which they feared would leave bad feelings within the party. But the three candidates—Ikeda, Ōno, and Ishii—all insisted on a vote and showed no intention of backing down. Then the Ōno and Ishii factions, offended at the Ikeda faction's supercilious attitude, and at former Prime Minister Yoshida's support for Ikeda, decided to work out their own coalition strategy. Prime Minister Kishi took a wait-and-see attitude, although he did ask that the intraparty personnel choices be made as quickly as possible.

A meeting was held of eight LDP leaders (Ōno, Masutani, Kawashima, Matsuno, Shigemune, Satō, Ikeda, and Ishii), which decided to hold an extraordinary Diet session on July 13, but there were still no definite indications as to whether the new president would be chosen by a vote or by consultation among faction leaders. However, the view eventually prevailed that the latter way would be difficult, and all the factions began to prepare for a party election. On July 8, Secretary-General Kawashima told Kishi there was no way except by an election, and received Kishi's approval.

Although the Ikeda faction had wanted an election from the beginning, nobody in the faction had direct experience in organizing a presidential candidate's election campaign. Feeling in need of advice, Ōhira sought the counsel of Tanaka Kakuei, who before the last party presidential election in December 1956 had been a key adviser to the Satō faction in the Kishi camp. Tanaka was a distant relative of Ikeda and often visited Ikeda's office and residence. Partly because of this, he was already on friendly terms with Ōhira. Ōhira recalls: "Two or three days later I received a long memorandum from Tanaka containing not only a broad outline of what policies to pursue in the election but also detailed instructions on how to conduct the campaign and even a budget. Most of this was written in blue ink, but the important passages were carefully written in red. I was most grateful to Tanaka for going to all this trouble for me.

"Armed with this memo, I visited Ikeda and went over its contents. He was extremely displeased and told me that under no circumstances was I to spend a single cent on his behalf. 'Very well,' I replied. 'I don't know how well we can comply with your wishes, but we shall do our best. However, I would like to ask you to let me and my colleagues run this campaign and for you to stay out of it as much as possible.' And that, in fact, is how the campaign was waged." Ikeda, Ōno, Ishii, and Matsumura announced their candidacies on July 9, and Fujiyama announced his on the tenth. Finance Minister Satō came out in support of Ikeda, while the Kishi faction allowed each member to vote for whomever he wished.

According to the July 10, 1960, issue of the *Asahi Shinbun*, Ikeda announced his candidacy in these words: "I am deeply concerned about how the confused situation that has prevailed since mid-May has weakened the nation's social order and harmed Japan's credibility internationally. To correct this situation quickly and to build a free and prosperous Japan is, I think, the urgent task before us. I believe that for the building of a self-reliant and growth-oriented Japan, we must put into practice the following six points:

> (1) Rebuilding parliamentary politics: We must recover faith in politicians and our compromised parliamentary politics and, more than anything else, bear in mind the need for tolerance and patience toward opposing political parties.
> (2) Establishment of social order: I believe the basis of public peace and order lies in people's hearts, and is a sense of mutual trust and mental composure. To attain this, I believe a necessary condition is for politics to be pursued in ways that will win public trust.

(3) Improvement of the people's livelihood and expansion of social security measures: I propose as a policy goal to more than double our gross national product within ten years from now. I hope to take energetic and constructive measures to raise the income levels of all strata of society and especially to eliminate—in the process of the growth of the national economy—income gaps among the sectors of agriculture, commerce, and industry, between large and small enterprises, and among regions, as well as to improve the overall living standards of all people to levels that are comparable with those of advanced countries. Also, I will work to expand social security measures so that the benefits of a prospering society may be also shared by the unfortunate and the disadvantaged.

(4) Educational renewal: A major focus of my policies will be education. I intend to carry out educational renewal and expansion with the unstinting provision of adequate financial backing. I hope most especially to work for the unprecedented promotion of science and technology and the sound training of the young people who will be responsible for Japan in the future.

(5) The establishment of peaceful, free, and cooperative international relations: Genuine international peace can only be achieved on the basis of mutual understanding, trust, and cooperation. Thus, our country can maintain a base for peaceful and free international cooperation only by being trusted in the free world and respected by the Communist world. I deeply regret the fact that the U.S.–Japan Security Treaty, which has this purpose, is not only looked on with suspicion by one or two of our neighboring countries but has also engendered suspicion and opposition within Japan.

(6) Renovation of party spirit: I consider it our immediate mission to inject a fresh spirit into the LDP by first of all establishing democracy within the party and by sticking scrupulously to a policy of giving party posts to the most appropriate people.

Judging from both style and content, the above statement was without any doubt drafted by Ōhira. The same issue of the *Asahi Shinbun* also carried declarations by the other four candidates for the LDP presidency, but none dealt head-on with policy issues as Ikeda's did.

A point in Ikeda's announcement that merits special attention is the mention of "tolerance and patience" (*kan'yo to nintai*) toward other parties. Various opinions have been voiced as to the origins of this phrase, but few knew of Ōhira's frequent use of the word "tolerance" in his first election campaign in 1952. For example, in the June 4, 1952, issue of the Kagawa edition of *Asahi Shinbun*, Ōhira was quoted as saying, "To live in a small and crowded country, a spirit of tolerance is necessary." The same article went on, in Ōhira's words, to elaborate on what he meant by a "spirit of tolerance." We may suppose that from this period Ōhira had always regarded tolerance as an important element in politics.

Five days before the date set for the party election, the Ikeda faction set up an election campaign office in the Akasaka Prince Hotel and charged its members with winning supporters among those still uncommitted. Ōhira has written: "Information gathering by reporters and the like took place all hours of the day and night, and the war of nerves was intensifying as true and false reports got mixed up. However, for the most part it was pretty certain in advance who was supported by each LDP Dietman or other voting delegate. So the object of all the maneuvering was a relatively small number of persons. And for all camps the object appeared, curiously, to be almost the same. The world had to be in this big turmoil, so to speak, over this small number of people. How to persuade this small number was, after all, the price that had to be paid for democracy and couldn't be helped."

For Ōhira, who had been entrusted with management of the Ikeda faction and in effect played the role of campaign manager, the basic strategy was, on the one hand, to win support for Ikeda from the Satō faction through the endorsement of former Prime Minister Yoshida in Ōiso and to use Satō's endorsement as a lever to influence the Kishi faction, and, on the other hand, to try to absorb votes from members of the Fujiyama, Ishii, and Miki factions, which might expect to participate in an Ikeda-led government.

Within the Satō faction, many felt initially that, rather than support Ikeda, the quickest route to an eventual Satō administration was to support the more flexible Ishii, who had led one of the main factions in the old Liberal Party. It was here that Ōhira met the greatest difficulties in his approaches to the Satō faction. But through the help of Tanaka Kakuei, who was an influential adviser to the Satō faction, he ultimately succeeded in obtaining Satō's support for Ikeda. Indeed, it has often been said that there was a tacit understanding that after Ikeda had served two terms the reins of administration would be passed to Satō. In any case, the Satō faction unanimously moved behind Ikeda, and Satō himself began to frequent Ikeda's campaign office at the Akasaka Prince Hotel.

Sensing the growing support for Ikeda, the Ōno and Ishii factions met on the twelfth, the day prior to the election, to analyze the situation and to compare prospective votes. It was concluded that if Ōno were to remain a candidate against Ikeda in a runoff election, a substantial number of those who had supported Ishii would likely then cast their votes for Ikeda. It was concluded that there was no choice but to concentrate on Ishii's candidacy alone, and Ōno agreed to withdraw from the ballot. This led to a meeting at the Marunouchi Hotel on the afternoon of the thirteenth among Ōno, Ishii, Matsumura, and non-candidates Kawashima (the party secretary-general), Kōno Ichirō, Miki Takeo, and Ishibashi Tanzan.

As Ōhira noted in his last volume of memoirs, "The election campaign had unexpectedly begun to shape up into a struggle between factions behind 'former bureaucrats' and factions behind 'long-time party politicians.'" This distinction between the two types of factions had been evident ever since the founding of the LDP, but the distinction did not necessarily mean that an absolute majority of bureaucrat-faction members had served as bureaucrats; only in the case of the Kōchikai, the political grouping around Ikeda, did the majority of members come from bureaucratic backgrounds. (After the 1970s, differences along these lines in the makeup of factions lost any real meaning.) As it turned out, the long-time party politicians factions did not attend the party convention in Sankei Hall on the thirteenth, which was to have elected the new party president. Lacking a quorum, the meeting adjourned after choosing a convention chairman.

After discussing this new situation, the Kishi faction, which had never made its views clear, seemed irritated by this latest maneuver, seen as originating with the Kōno and Miki factions. It was thus decided that the Kishi faction members would vote as a bloc for Ikeda. The Kawashima subgroup within the Kishi faction had earlier supported Ōno, but with Ōno's withdrawal it felt no particular obligation toward Ishii and so agreed to support Ikeda. Fujiyama, whose main purpose in running for the party presidency was the symbolic one of providing a tighter identity for his own faction, agreed to support Ikeda in a runoff vote.

After the vote by the party convention had been postponed, all factions continued their maneuvers. Ōhira recalls: "I was called into a room in Sankei Hall by Ikeda and Satō and instructed to see Miki Takeo immediately to ask for his support. I soon found out that Miki was in a room on the seventh floor of the Marunouchi Hotel. I went there right away and found the whole building jammed with people and the atmosphere heavy with humidity and the smell of sweat.

"Panting up the stairs to the seventh floor, I came face to face with Tsukada Jūichirō, Nadao Hirokichi, and Inaba Osamu, who were barring the entrance to Miki's room. They refused to let me in because Miki,

Kōno, Matsumura, and others had gotten together with Ishii and Ōno and an important conference was going on inside. The formation of an Ishii cabinet was already taken for granted, and people had even begun to congratulate one another. Yet I recalled what Tsukada had said to me in a conversation broadcast on NHK [Japan Broadcasting Corporation] a few days earlier: 'In a battle it's the last five minutes that count.'

"Unable to meet with Miki, upon whom we had pinned our hopes, I descended the dusty emergency stairs and returned to Sankei Hall. By now the auditorium where the party vote was to have been taken was deserted." Arriving at Sankei Hall, Ōhira happened to run into Shiina Etsusaburō of the Kishi faction on the wide steps leading up to the building. In greeting him, Shiina mumbled: "I don't understand what's going on. . . . They may talk about a coalition of party factions, but how can Beijing supporters and Taiwan supporters ever get together?"

On his way back to the campaign office in his car, Ōhira pondered the meaning of Shiina's words. Most likely, it was an indication that the Matsumura and Miki factions, which were friendly toward Beijing, had made some agreement with the Ishii and Ōno factions, which favored Taiwan, but that under the surface there were policy conflicts that would not yield to such an easy resolution. In any case, Ōhira felt that the voting should be held quickly since the anti-Ikeda factions were likely to consolidate if they had more time.

One of Ikeda's secretaries at the time has described the evening of July 13 at Ikeda's residence: "After we returned to Shinanomachi on the evening after the election had been postponed for a day, Ōhira arrived, and then a telephone call came for him from Yasuoka Masahiro. He said something like, 'Ikeda will probably become party president tomorrow, but he must not seem high-handed. As for his having been responsible for bringing about this situation, I think he must take as low-keyed an attitude as possible.' Ōhira then said to Ikeda, '*Daijin* [Minister], please adopt a low posture tomorrow.' Ikeda said, 'Yes, I understand.' We felt we had already won."

The party convention was opened at 10 A.M., July 14, in Hibiya Public Hall, and the election for party president resulted in the following votes:

First Vote

Ikeda Hayato	246
Ishii Mitsujirō	199
Fujiyama Aiichirō	49

Runoff Vote

Ikeda Hayato	302
Ishii Mitsujirō	194

Consequently, Ikeda Hayato became the new LDP president.

Ōhira has written: "On the evening of July 14, I remarked to Ikeda, 'So you have finally become party president.' Obviously moved, Ikeda said 'Yes,' and then there was a considerable silence. Then I asked, 'When you first came to Tokyo, did you ever think that some day you would reach this position?' Naturally, Ikeda answered in the negative. I continued: 'Since you have attained a position that you never originally expected, however short your tenure you should have no reason to complain. To take an extreme example, even if your cabinet is organized in the morning and falls the same evening, it may be a turn of fate that you can do nothing about. As for how long you will be allowed to hold the reins of administration, this is something for the people to decide and not, I think, something you can decide. At this time I'd like you to make me one promise: I want you and those around you to make the words 'long-term administration' an absolutely taboo phrase.' With no hesitation, Ikeda replied, 'I will.'

"I then counseled: 'Whoever is prime minister and president of the ruling party must be thoroughly at one with the general populace. Policies that the general public will accept and to which they will lend their cooperation cannot, I think, come from thinking or behavior that is divorced from that of people in general. It is surely hypocritical to be greedy for a life of ease and a full stomach and at the same time ask the people to economize on their spending. Now there are two other promises I'd like you to make: first, while serving as prime minister, please give up golf, and, second, please refrain from visiting geisha houses. Do you promise?' Ikeda answered immediately, 'I do.'"

Accompanied only by his wife, Mitsue, Ikeda traveled the next day to the newly completed Hakone Kankō Hotel in Hakone Sengokubara, where he was joined by Ōhira and some secretaries the following morning. By the time they returned from the mountains on the seventeenth, the outline for the new cabinet had been completed. Ōhira was to be the new chief cabinet secretary. In the train on the way back from Hakone to Tokyo, Ōhira joked with newspaper reporters, "I'd like to have a marvelous romance," and further repeated in English the words of Edward VIII when he renounced the British throne for Mrs. Simpson: "I cannot endure the heavy duty of a king without the woman I love." Ōhira no doubt felt that he, too, now had a heavy duty, that of helping Ikeda to shoulder Japan's destiny.

The most problematic personnel issue was the choice of party secretary-general. On his way to Hakone, Ikeda had stopped in Ōiso to pay his respects to former Prime Minister Yoshida, at which time Yoshida recommended a former bureaucrat in the Ministry of Home Affairs,

Yamazaki Iwao, for the post. However, this met with fierce opposition from other members of Ikeda's faction, and as a result the post of secretary-general was conferred upon respected veteran politician Masutani Shūji. Hori Shigeru of the Satō faction was made chairman of the General Council, and Shiina Etsusaburō of the Kishi faction became chairman of the Policy Research Council. Thus, in these three top posts each of the LDP's three main factions was represented.

Ikeda was officially appointed prime minister on July 18, and he immediately formed his cabinet. The original draft of candidates for cabinet appointments was made by Ōhira and revised by Ikeda. In any event, because the First Ikeda Cabinet was formed with unusual speed, it was nicknamed the "Speed Cabinet." Its appointees included Kosaka Zentarō (Foreign Affairs), Kojima Tetsuzō (Justice), Mizuta Mikio (Finance), Araki Masuo (Education), Nanjō Tokuo (Agriculture), Ishii Mitsujirō (International Trade and Industry), Minami Yoshio (Transport), Suzuki Zenkō (Posts and Telecommunications), Ishida Hirohide (Labor), and Hashimoto Tomisaburō (Construction). In response to Ōhira's idea of having a woman in the cabinet, Nakayama Masa was made minister of health and welfare.

The most noteworthy feature of the new cabinet was surely that it was headed by a prime minister who had entered politics after the war and thus represented a change of generations. Partly as a reflection of this, a number of the other cabinet members were relatively young. None, except for Ishii, was a leader of a Diet faction. And the appointment of a woman to the cabinet was the first in Japan's modern political history. As the new chief cabinet secretary, Ōhira—a previously inconspicuous right-hand man of Ikeda who had never served as a minister or even vice-minister—was finally moving onto the center stage of Japanese politics at the age of fifty.

Chapter 14

Tolerance and Patience

The priority of the Ikeda Cabinet was to cope with the unease in society and public opinion brought on by the new security treaty and to facilitate movement in constructive directions. It was necessary, for example, to produce quickly some concrete policies to expedite the plan for doubling incomes promised in the election campaign. But for the moment the government faced a still more urgent problem, namely, the labor dispute at the Mitsui Mining Corporation's Miike coal mines.

Due to the change from coal to petroleum for energy, the coal industry had fallen on hard times, and the managers of the Miike mines announced their intention to lay off over 2,000 workers. This dispute had continued since early 1959 and had resulted in violence and even loss of life, but the Kishi Cabinet, preoccupied with the security treaty, had made little progress in settling it. The question of how to resolve this dispute, which had grown from a labor–management dispute in a single enterprise to a political and social issue that many saw as an across-the-board confrontation between capital and labor, evolved into the touchstone for judging the new cabinet. Ikeda had a strong interest in these problems, and prior to his official appointment as prime minister he had decided, on Ōhira's recommendation, to appoint Ishida Hirohide, who was well versed in labor problems, as labor minister.

In one of the first actions taken by the new Ikeda Cabinet, Labor Minister Ishida asked the two sides to submit to compulsory arbitration by the Central Labor Relations Board, whose chairman was Professor Nakayama Ichirō, Ōhira's former teacher at Hitotsubashi University. Because of the hardened attitudes of both labor and management, these attempts proved difficult, but Ishida's insistence that "respect for human life is a matter that transcends all controversy" produced results, and representatives from labor and management finally agreed to sit down and talk. In the meantime Chief Cabinet Secretary Ōhira chaired a conciliation commission that included the prime minister, the labor minister, the head of the General Council of Trade Unions of Japan (Sōhyō), Ōta Kaoru, and the head of the Japan Coal Miners Union, Hara Shigeru. In this capacity, Ōhira engaged in a variety of activities and enjoyed some success in obtaining the understanding of influential persons in financial circles. These were bold steps at a time when the gulf between the conservative and progressive camps often seemed unbridgeable. The final conciliation plan presented by the Central Labor Relations Board was accepted by the Mitsui side on August 12, 1960, and by the coal workers on August 18, concluding the long Miike mines dispute only a month after the formation of the new cabinet. In Ōhira's words, "The first task of the new cabinet was tackled with a certain amount of success."

Reports of violent and sometimes bloody incidents that had appeared in the press ever since the security treaty disturbances had now almost disappeared, and the new era was one of formulating new policies. To give more specific substance to the income-doubling policy, Ōhira worked on policy formulation with Kōchikai secretary-general Tamura Toshio, Shimomura Osamu from the Finance Ministry, and a small number of persons from the other ministries. A problem area was what the economic growth rate should be, but this was more or less settled when Prime Minister Ikeda announced at a government-party liaison meeting on September 1 that it was to be 9 percent over the next three years.

The new policies announced on September 5 were an elaboration of the six points outlined during the election for party president, and were presented under the following nine items:

> (1) Support for democratic politics and administrative renovation;
> (2) Promotion of peace diplomacy and establishment of a [joint] security system;
> (3) Promotion of economic growth policies and achievement of full employment;
> (4) A tax reduction of more than ¥100 billion;
> (5) Increased social security;
> (6) Establishment of basic policies for agriculture, forestry, and fisheries;
> (7) Modernization of small and medium-sized enterprises;
> (8) Renovation and expansion of education and promotion of science and technology;
> (9) Promotion of measures to benefit youth and women.

Ōhira later wrote: "These new policies had, I think, in ways both good and bad, several features worthy of serious discussion. First, they brought a spirit of tolerance and patience into political management, which became the keynote in the management of the Diet; and they specifically made the establishment of a system of personnel management the central axis for administrative reform. Second, they emphasized the coordination of diplomacy and domestic politics as a basic concept of political management. Third, they adopted the plan for doubling income over the next ten years as the goal for economic policy management. And fourth, they specified the growth-related duties of government as a strengthening of the economic base, an elevation of the industrial structure, the development of human potential, and the expansion of social security measures. As in the long-term plans for highways, forest and water conservancy, and ports and harbors or in the draft Agriculture Basic Law, these policies clearly indicated a will to make important policies with a long-term vision."

An important part of the job of chief cabinet secretary is speaking to the media. Outside certain circles, Ōhira was still unknown to most of the populace, and few newspaper reporters had yet made his acquaintance, except for those who had specialized in covering the activities of the Ikeda faction. The day after the Ikeda Cabinet was formed, the *Asahi Shinbun* published this portrait of Ōhira: "His outward appearance is stolid, unusual for persons from the Finance Ministry, who usually at least appear to possess a superior intellect. . . . Many say they are quite unable to guess what he is thinking. Be that as it may, he has the deep trust of his patron, Prime Minister Ikeda, and even wrote the prime minister's declarations during his campaign for the party presidency. Even before the prime minister was confirmed in the post, it was rumored that Ōhira was sure to be his chief cabinet secretary. He was highly thought of by the heads of other factions as well, such as those of Kōno Ichirō and former Prime Minister Kishi, even if one is at times puzzled over just where this charm lies. There is the view that his outward nonchalance is a political pose, and that one must not be fooled by appearances, since, in fact, he is a very clever operator."

As their contracts with Ōhira deepened, the reporters' impressions began to change. One belonging to the group covering the Prime Minister's Official Residence recalls: "For those of us sending stories by telephone, Ōhira's way of speaking was very convenient. There would always be an introduction and then the main text. Then there were a lot of English words. For instance, I'd call saying, 'Tomorrow is Sunday, but do you have any special plan,' and he'd answer, 'No, tomorrow there's no schedule. It's a *non-political holiday* [original English].' I think it was this

Ōhira English that went a long way toward making him famous."

When the Diet was in session, interviews with the chief cabinet secretary were conducted in a small room on the way to the ministers' offices in the Diet. When the Diet was not in session they were held in a small room beside the entrance hall of the Prime Minister's Official Residence. Construction of the present-day Official Residence Annex (also called the Press Center), with its rooms for reporters from the various newspapers or news agencies, its interview rooms, dining room, and special rooms for taking photographs and delivering cabinet news reports, began during the Ikeda Administration in January 1962, and was completed in July of that year. Reporters hailed this as a prime example of Ikeda-Ōhira "good administration."

For a chief cabinet secretary to make time in his busy schedule for six daily meetings with reporters—some who came to his home first thing in the morning, others who came for the thrice-daily official interviews, those who would come around 10:30 P.M., followed by those reporters who were on closest terms with Ōhira—was by no means easy, either physically or mentally. After the last reporter left around one o'clock in the morning, Ōhira would go to Ikeda's private residence in Shinanomachi—where Ikeda preferred to live instead of in the Prime Minister's Official Residence—to report on the day's activities. If the gate was already locked, he would ask a policeman on duty to help him climb over the wall, after which he would go directly to Ikeda's bedroom to discuss important matters of the day. By the time he got home there would often be scarcely time for a brief doze before he would be wakened by the early morning group of reporters. With characteristic patience, Ōhira always received reporters cordially and never showed any sign of displeasure. This was no doubt because, in the wake of the security treaty turmoil, he had come to view public opinion trends as extremely important. He tried not only to relay opinions and information accurately to reporters but also to learn from them in turn.

Of course, the work of a chief cabinet secretary was more than just receiving media representatives. Ōhira has written: "Being chief cabinet secretary is an exhausting job. You have to have your wits about you at all times and keep close and constant watch over both domestic and foreign affairs. Should any important matter arise either at home or abroad, day or night, you have to act as the government's spokesman and deal with it immediately. Furthermore, you must obtain the full cooperation of the various governmental agencies and the party in power, and maintain good relations not only with the opposition parties, the media and labor but also with academic, educational, entertainment, and sports circles. This requires a flexible attitude capable of handling any change that might take place. Rigidity must be avoided at all costs. The chief cabinet secretary must disregard himself; otherwise, he will not be able to make prompt and proper responses.

"My first act in office was to clear the top of my desk and drawers of all pending files. When a problem arose, I wasted no time in deciding who in what agency should handle the matter and sending it on for immediate action. I made it a point not to give any advice on how the matter should be handled, but to respect the way it was settled even though I might not be fully satisfied."

Very soon after the new policies centering around the National Income-Doubling Plan were formulated in September 1960, Prime Minister Ikeda began a nationwide speaking tour. This was related, needless to say, to his expectation that there would soon be a Diet dissolution and new elections. One of his speaking engagements was at Hibiya Public Hall in Tokyo on October 12, sponsored by the suprapartisan *Kōmei Senkyo Renmei* (Clean Elections League, unconnected to the later Kōmeitō political party) and featuring a tripartite debate by Ikeda and the heads of the JSP and DSP. While speaking at the podium during this debate, JSP Chairman Asanuma Inejirō was suddenly attacked and killed by a demented youth.

The General Council of Trade Unions of Japan immediately held a meeting that attempted to place the blame on insufficient security measures, and resolved to carry out daily demonstrations around the Diet building. Ōhira felt that in order to calm the situation there was no choice but to have Yamazaki Iwao, chairman of the National Public Safety Commission, resign immediately. He insisted to Prime Minister Ikeda, who wanted more time to consider, that a decision on the matter should be taken that very night. At the next morning's emergency cabinet meeting, Yamazaki's resignation was announced.Thus, the 36th Extraordinary Diet, the first Diet of the Ikeda Administration, began on October 18 with a memorial oration for Asanuma delivered by Ikeda.

On October 21, Ikeda gave his first policy speech in the Diet, outlining the aims of his administration, which centered around the already announced new policies. The speech was drafted by Ōhira, who commented on this type of work: "Responsibility for putting together a policy speech (*shisei hōshin enzetsu*) on administration goals belongs to the chief cabinet secretary, who is expected to make judicious use of printed information from the various government ministries and agencies. Of course, the prime minister makes revisions of important points after hearing views from the governing party, and the speech is finally approved in a cabinet meeting. If one tries to include all aspects of every important topic, the text may become too long and wordy, and if one tries to focus on eloquence and high-brow philosophy, the fact that certain topics are not covered is likely to become a problem. It is difficult to craft a speech that is neither too general nor too lengthy and tedious, and that communicates a certain philosophy at the same time. If one chooses too simple a style, the speech will be called unprofessional, and if the style is too ponderous, it will be criticized for lacking content. However you try to do it, you run into problems." The Diet was dissolved on October 24, following a session of rather stereotyped questions presented by the various parties.

In the campaign for the twenty-ninth Lower House general election, public attention focused on televised debates among party leaders. At that time, such debates between presidential candidates Kennedy and Nixon were being held in the United States, and NHK appeared intent on providing Japanese viewers with a similar broadcast.

On November 12, just after John F. Kennedy was elected president of the United States, an unprecedented TV debate in Japan, sponsored by NHK and hosted by commentator Karashima Kichizō brought together LDP President Ikeda Hayato, Acting JSP Chairman Eda Saburō, and DSP Chairman Nishio Suehiro. This was well received and a second debate was organized, this time with Chief Cabinet Secretary Ōhira Masayoshi, the JSP's Policy Board Secretary Narita Tomomi, and DSP Secretary-General Sone Eki. From this time on, Ōhira became a familiar figure to the general public.

When the votes cast in the November 20 election were counted, LDP candidates won 296 seats, up from 283 before the dissolution. This number soon rose to 300 when four of the five independent candidates joined the party. The JSP, which probably won some sympathy votes because of Asanuma's violent death, also made a good showing, with 145 seats, or 23 more than in the previous election. But in view of the overwhelming LDP majority, there was in the JSP something less than a real feeling of success. DSP seats dropped steeply from 40 to 17.

Because of his duties as chief cabinet secretary, Ōhira had almost no time to return to his electoral district. His eldest son, Masaki, now twenty-two years old, stood in for him and gave campaign speeches, often sharing the podium with other candidates. He would usually carry the text of his speech on a board suspended around his neck by a string, and would read each page. Some of his audience were visibly moved and made such remarks as, "But he's so young!" In backstage waiting rooms, he was likely to be told by other speakers, "It must be difficult to have a dad who is so famous." In the election, Ōhira came in top, 22,000 votes ahead of the second winner in his three-representative electoral district. Now, beyond any doubt, he was a leading politician and had gained his constituents' trust.

As chief cabinet secretary, Ōhira was constantly vexed by intraparty problems. In particular, he had to make a great effort to try to keep Kōno Ichirō, who had been excluded from the First Ikeda Cabinet, from resorting to such rash action as forming a separate party, as he had threatened. Around this time, Ōhira expounded on his long-held "ellipse theory" to a reporter friend: "In order to maintain a stable Ikeda Cabinet, it is necessary to keep a balanced ellipse, whose focal points are the two opposing party forces of Kōno and Satō." Kōno Ichirō had been an *Asahi Shinbun* journalist before becoming a Dietman representing the prewar Rikken Seiyūkai Party. After the war, he had helped Hatoyama Ichirō establish the Japan Liberal Party (becoming its secretary-general) and subsequently held numerous cabinet posts.

However, Satō Eisaku, whose help had been invaluable in Ikeda's election to the party presidency, was displeased with the Ikeda–Ōhira strategy regarding Kōno. Although Ōhira's respect for Satō remained and he felt that Satō was in any case in line to inherit Ikeda's mantle—which he also judged to be the mainstream conservative view—Satō was definitely coming to hold some unfavorable feelings toward Ōhira.

The Second Ikeda Cabinet had the backing of 300 Diet seats, but from the very start it ran into problems over the choice of the Lower House speaker. Ikeda had wanted Ishii Mitsujirō in this position, but Ishii, dissatisfied because his faction was not represented in the cabinet, refused. Ikeda then asked former speaker Kiyose Ichirō to assume the post, although this choice was strongly criticized by the opposition parties, who held Kiyose responsible for the behavior of the "Security Treaty Diet." The resulting confusion and behind-the-scenes negotiations meant a two-and-a-half-day delay in Diet proceedings. As for party appointments, Fukuda Takeo became chairman of the Policy Research Council while Masutani and Hori retained their posts as secretary-general and chairman of the General Council, respectively. As new cabinet members were chosen from the Kōno and Miki factions, the cabinet could be both praised as reflecting party unity and criticized as a cabinet of factional balances. Foreign Minister Kosaka, Finance Minister Mizuta, and Labor Minister Ishida retained their posts, while other portfolios changed hands: Justice went to Ueki Kōshirō, Welfare to Furui Yoshimi, International Trade and Industry to Shiina Etsusaburō, and Construction to the Kōno faction's Nakamura Umekichi. Ōhira continued as chief cabinet secretary.

During the First Ikeda Cabinet, a report on the National Income-Doubling Plan elaborated mainly by the Economic Planning Agency in preparation for expected new legislation had been presented on November 1,

1960, by Ishikawa Ichirō, head of the Economic Council, an advisory body to the prime minister. The recommendations of this report were approved almost unchanged by the cabinet on December 27 and taken into consideration in compiling the budget for fiscal 1961.

Ōhira seems to have had misgivings about this becoming an official plan. He once said: "The concept of doubling incomes was simply that in Japan's current situation, provided the wisdom, labor, technology, and savings potential of the Japanese people were put to good use, there was no reason why real income should not double over a ten-year period. But when the Ikeda Cabinet was formed it made this into an official plan. I am not a believer in a planned economy, so I argued that it was a mistake to make it a government plan and that it would be better to hold it up as a model, as a guideline in carrying out government policies to reveal the relative merits of various governmental measures. Ikeda insisted, however, on making the National Income-Doubling Plan an official government plan." Ōhira considered that policies should be skillfully attuned to the flow of events, and that it was a mistake to try to manipulate reality. His thinking on income-doubling policy was undoubtedly grounded in this point of view.

Before long, Ōhira was busy preparing the prime minister's second policy speech to be delivered before the 38th Ordinary Diet. He has written about it as follows: "The policy speech before the newly opened Diet in January 1961 formally indicated the direction to be taken by the Ikeda Administration. As for foreign policy, it emphasized the inseparability of foreign relations and domestic politics, pointing out that political developments at home influence our nation's international credibility, and also arguing forcefully that so-called neutrality was only illusory. In other words, neutrality was, to quote from the speech, 'an illusion that neglects a concrete examination of the environment surrounding our country, that overlooks the fact that our country's national strength has a great influence on the East–West balance of power, and that fails to perceive adequately that the economic prosperity of Japan is the basis for cooperation with the community of free nations.' This argument about neutrality being an illusion soon gave rise to fierce disputes in the Diet.

"In regard to economic policy, the speech was grounded in the awareness that faith in our country's great potential for economic growth, together with its underlying strengths, was beginning to see a historic period of flowering. It then explained in some detail the complex of measures envisioned in the long-term perspective of the National Income-Doubling Plan. However, this speech carefully explained that it would only be possible through the creativity and efforts of the people as a whole and that Ikeda had absolutely no intention of pushing such developments onto the people against their will. It was further explained that measures to assist the free movement of the labor force and the upgrading of employment opportunities must also be taken into consideration in present-day economic policy. New recruits into the labor market were expected to number 5 million during the three-year period from 1961, and so places of work would have to be prepared for them. Another barrier that would have to be crossed on the economy's road to modernization was the modernization of agriculture, forestry, and fishing, and of those small and medium-sized enterprises whose development had slowed or which were negatively affected by less than full employment. The speech went on to announce Ikeda's sense of personal mission in tackling these difficult issues, saying, 'At some point, it is necessary for somebody to explore solutions for these problems as if with a surgical knife.' This, too, later led to lively discussion both in and out of the Diet."

Although the Ikeda Administration was at first relatively smooth, during the six months or so between the commencement of the 38th Ordinary Diet in January 1961 and Ikeda's visit to the United States in June, its luck turned. First of all, in response to questioning by the JSP, Prime Minister Ikeda was on January 31 considered to have used "indiscreet language" by saying, "Whatever the case with small or weak countries, Japan will not adopt neutrality." He later retracted the statement because of the criticism it aroused. Then, on February 1, a rightist youth attacked the home of Shimanaka Hōji, president of Chūōkōronsha Publishing Co., killing and wounding household members in reaction to what he felt to be a defamation of the imperial family in a novel, *Fūryū mutan* (A Humorous Dream-Story), by Fukazawa Shichirō carried in the widely read monthly journal *Chūōkōron*. The incident led to the resignation of the superintendent-general of the Metropolitan Police. Chief Cabinet Secretary Ōhira immediately visited the Shimanaka residence with condolences, but the incident turned out to encourage the view that Fukazawa Shichirō and Chūō-kōronsha Publishing Co. should be indicted in court on defamation charges, with the result that both Ōhira and Prime Minister Ikeda were constantly pestered with demands to that effect. Ōhira was deeply troubled over this: "When, where, and what will happen, one never knows. But whatever occurs, the government must decide its own views and respond from its own standpoint. The chief cabinet secretary has to be the government's eyes, ears, brain, and mouth.

"In coping with this incident I really had to rack my brains, although perhaps few knew it. To elucidate the incident further was of course important, but that was something that ought to be delegated to the judicial authorities. Feeling that the government should stay calm and collected and await a political dénouement, I began in a way that would not attract too much attention to seek the opinions of knowledgeable persons in various positions.... The prime minister and I had already decided that we did not want to exercise the right to initiate legal proceedings. That was because bringing this matter to the law courts would mean subjecting the relationship between the Imperial Household and the Japanese people to cold laws and legal logic. To have this matter made into grist for dry disputation in law courts would have been, for both the prime minister and myself, extremely hard to endure."

On April 1, the Diet passed an ambitious budget that was 24.4 percent larger than the year before and was intended to be coordinated with the National Income-Doubling Plan. However, around that time Diet affairs were becoming highly unpredictable. Draft bills that had been presented included two on defense, two on medical care, an Agriculture Basic Law, a Welfare Pension Insurance Law, and a law on relations with the International Labour Organisation (ILO). Although the two defense-related laws managed to pass the Lower House in April, the Agriculture Basic Law promised by Prime Minister Ikeda had a rough passage. It was meant to set new directions for agriculture in the process of Japan's economic modernization and could rightly be called an "Agricultural Constitution." However, both the JSP and DSP opposed it and were busy preparing their own bill incorporating their points of view.

On April 29, Lower House Speaker Kiyose used his prerogative to convene a plenary session of the Diet at which the Agriculture Basic Law was approved by majority vote even though the session was attended by only LDP and DSP members—the JSP preferring to stay away. The turmoil-ridden Diet remained tense for some time. On May 13, the LDP and DSP jointly presented a Bill for the Prevention of Political Acts of Violence (abbreviated in Japanese as Seibō Hōan). This had among its objectives the prevention of right-wing terrorist attacks like the assassination of Asanuma and the attack on the home of Shimanaka, but because it also aimed at regulating left-wing demonstrations, it was labeled the "New Police Law" by the Socialist and Communist parties.

Those close to the prime minister, including Ōhira and Miyazawa, were opposed to presenting this bill, but Ikeda obstinately pushed forward, dismissing their objections. In his handling of this matter, Ikeda revealed an imperiousness that seems to have been part of his character. As discussion of the bill progressed, the Diet became more agitated and even within the LDP more voices surfaced calling for a cautious approach. When Prime Minister Ikeda forced a majority vote of approval in the Lower

House, the controversial bill was sent to the Upper House, where opposition from Upper House President Matsuno Tsuruhei and other LDP leaders meant that it would again have to be subjected to a period of scrutiny.

On June 19, as if to get away from the troubles around him, Prime Minister Ikeda left for a trip to the United States, a visit judged essential to promote friendly relations with the Kennedy Administration. Ōhira advised Ikeda's wife, Mitsue, to accompany him, and she has written: "At the time of Ikeda's first trip to the United States, it was none other than Ōhira who enthusiastically told me, 'You don't have to speak a foreign language, so please, go along by all means.' Prime Minister Kishi's wife could not go abroad because of her health, and I had thought that it would be best if I looked after things at home, but I finally gave in to Ōhira's persistence and, still somewhat reluctantly, went to the United States. With this, a precedent was established for wives of prime ministers to accompany their husbands on foreign trips. I have remained impressed with Ōhira's foresight as a politician and his resourcefulness in coming up with new ideas."

Ikeda's journey to the United States was a success. President Kennedy entertained the prime minister and his wife on two yachts, and in the course of the official talks it was proposed by the Americans and accepted by the Japanese that there should be regular meetings of two newly established Japanese–American joint cabinet committees, one dealing with trade and the economy and the other with science and technology. It was from this time that the phrase "Japanese–American partnership" evolved.

Ōhira, holding the fort back home, was pleased with these results but also anxious lest Ikeda let his high spirits get the better of him and say too much on returning home (as had sometimes happened). In a letter sent to the hotel in Hawaii where Ikeda would be stopping on the way back, Ōhira wrote at length about how, on reaching Haneda airport, he should avoid waving and giving the impression of a general returning in triumph or suggest that he had achieved any great results in the United States. "Anti-Japanese sentiment," he wrote, was stronger in Japan than anywhere else. On reading this letter in Hawaii, Ikeda remarked to Miyazawa Kiichi, "Ōhira is saying a lot of silly things, like an overanxious wife. The Ikeda–Kennedy talks seem to have been regarded in Tokyo, too, as a big success." Nevertheless, on his return to Japan on the evening of June 30, Ikeda did not wave as he descended from the plane.

Buoyed by the success of his American trip, Ikeda set to work on a cabinet reorganization. On July 13, he held a meeting with the most influential LDP members, followed by three days of one-to-one consultations that determined, first of all, the main party posts, whose time for reappointment was drawing near. Ōno remained as party vice-president, while the top three appointive party posts after the president (the so-called *san'yaku*, hereafter called "the top three party posts") went to Maeo (secretary-general), Akagi (chairman of the General Council), and Tanaka (chairman of the Policy Research Council). Suzuki Zenkō was named to assist Maeo as senior deputy secretary-general. Ikeda proceeded to make some cabinet changes, and several influential LDP members entered the cabinet at this time: Kōno (Agriculture), Satō (International Trade and Industry), Fujiyama (Economic Planning Agency), Kawashima (Administrative Management Agency), and Miki (Science and Technology Agency). Ōhira remained chief cabinet secretary. By this arrangement the heads of six of the seven major factions—excluding the Ishii faction—were represented in the cabinet.

At that time the chief cabinet secretary was not yet a minister of state, since the post was only so designated after the end of the Ikeda Administration, when Hashimoto Tomisaburō served in that position in the Satō Administration. On hearing this, Ōhira remarked, "It's really better for the chief cabinet secretary not to be a state minister, you know." When a newspaper reporter asked why, he continued: "When I was chief cabinet secretary, there were heavyweights like Kōno and Satō in the cabinet. And a 'heavyweight cabinet' (*jitsuryokusha naikaku*) is, if you'll excuse the expression, like a circus full of wild animals. The chief cabinet secretary is, so to speak, a sort of animal trainer, so he can't be on the same level as the wild animals. If he is one notch below, he can get away with saying, 'I'm sorry,' even if the wild animals are angry."

Although party posts were considered somewhat less weighty than cabinet posts in their executive importance, Ikeda was happy to be able to install his trusted friend Maeo in the post of party secretary-general. And now that almost all the faction leaders and other influential party members were in the cabinet, there seemed little cause for anxiety over the stability of the political situation, and conditions seemed favorable for concentrating on governing the nation. No longer playing golf or visiting geisha houses, Ikeda would relax on weekends at his relatives' country house in Hakone, where he became an assiduous gardener. He became particularly interested in rocks and arranged all shapes and sizes of them in the front of his garden. Ōhira once joked to Ikeda's wife, "As people get older they become fond of rocks, but I'm still more interested in living things."

As if to celebrate the debut of the Second Ikeda Cabinet, the Tokyo Stock Exchange Dow average reached a record high of ¥1,829. It was not long, however, before red lights began to flash, warning of the dangers of an overheated economy. During the January–March 1961 quarter, private sector investment in plant and equipment was being carried out at a yearly rate of some ¥3.67 trillion, which, if continued, already exceeded the ¥3 trillion of investment envisioned for the final year of the decade-long National Income-Doubling Plan. Real GNP growth was proceeding at a pace that would top 10 percent per year. The international balance of payments fell into a deficit after May. In the early autumn, even bullish-minded Ikeda indicated he would approve of measures to restrict economic expansion, and at the end of September the official discount rate was lowered. The Tokyo Dow index steadily declined and in October fell below ¥1,300. Signs of dissatisfaction surfaced within the party, exacerbated by the rivalry between Agriculture and Forestry Minister Kōno and International Trade and Industry Minister Satō.

A "heavyweight cabinet" could, indeed, generate a healthy competitive spirit, as shown by Kōno's performance as minister of agriculture and forestry, for although he had opposed Ikeda in the party presidential election, he now tried his best to promote Ikeda's policies. He energetically set to reorganizing personnel within his ministry, expediting the free sale of surplus rice and trying to stabilize prices for perishable foods. Ikeda would from time to time praise him with words like, "Kōno is an able man and we can use him." Consequently, relations between Ikeda and Kōno's rival Satō became less cordial.

For three days from November 2, 1961, the first meeting of the U.S.-Japan Joint Committee on Trade and Economic Affairs, established by an agreement between Foreign Minister Kosaka and Secretary of State Dean Rusk at the time of Ikeda's United States visit, was held in Hakone. Regarding the significance of these conferences, Ōhira has written: "Basically this joint committee is not a place for negotiations and decisions on specific issues. It was established to strengthen friendly ties between Japan and the United States through the mutual and free exchange of views, and to contribute to closer economic relationships between the two countries. Thus, by having each country's representatives say what they want to say and deepening their mutual understanding of each other's standpoints, whenever concrete problems arise it should be possible to make accurate and prompt evaluations and responses. And at various international economic conferences United States–Japan cooperation can be expected to play an effective role since basic issues have already been discussed between the two countries. Moreover, the very fact that cabinet members dealing with economic matters in the two countries devote themselves for a period of two or three days to discussions on economic issues and other matters of mutual concern is an important diplomatic breakthrough for both Japan and the United States. Its influence is by no means small, either on the people of the two countries or on the world as a whole." Ōhira once enlarged on the same theme to a reporter: "Although Japan has to think about the United States at all hours of the day and night, the United States has to think about many countries, and it is extremely significant if, for even two or three days a year, the Americans think about Japan."

On October 30, three days before the U.S.–Japan Joint Committee on Trade and Economic Affairs opened its Hakone meeting, Ōhira's eldest daughter, Yoshiko, was married to Morita Hajime, a promising young official in the Ministry of Finance, at the Palace Hotel in Tokyo. Ōhira had always told Yoshiko, "For a girl, it's quite all right if she doesn't want to continue with her studies. It's quite acceptable for her to be attractive and to become a good wife while young." Assistance with the matchmaking had been provided by Ōhira's prewar patron in the Ministry of Finance, Tsushima Juichi, and his wife. Morita was a native of the city of Sakaide in Kagawa Prefecture and had graduated from Takamatsu High School and the University of Tokyo before entering the ministry in 1957. At the time of his marriage, he was working in the General Affairs Section of the Budget Bureau.

For the new year, 1962, both an Upper House election and an LDP presidential election were scheduled. A relatively restrained economic climate continued into the new year, and rising consumer prices were causing ever greater concern. As might be expected, spirited exchanges took place between those who emphasized economic growth and those who stressed stability. On April 8, Prime Minister Ikeda, on a speaking tour during the Upper House election campaign, was criticized by the media when he stated, "The rise in prices is the responsibility not just of the government but of the people as a whole." On April 13, Economic Planning Agency Director-General Fujiyama Aiichirō, in a talk before a general meeting of the Japan Committee for Economic Development (*Keizai Dōyūkai*) emphasized that balance in the economy as a whole was more important than economic growth and claimed, "Low-interest policies have [overly] stimulated investment in plant and equipment and have created conditions that are inviting a crisis." This criticism of Ikeda's economic policies had important reverberations in both political and financial circles.

The 40th Ordinary Diet remained in considerable disarray throughout the session. Although it did pass an electoral reform bill and approved six treaties, including one concerning the repayment of the GARIOA-EROA (Government and Relief in Occupied Areas–Economic Rehabilitation in Occupied Areas) loans, and an agreement with Thailand on the special disposal of yen currency, the draft law on industrial investment special accounts required for the settlement of the GARIOA-EROA loans was still being discussed, pending a definitive vote in the Upper House at the time the Diet session ended. As a result, Upper House President Shigemune Yūzō took responsibility and tendered his resignation to Ikeda. A bill on medical care also failed to materialize, leading to tenders of resignation from Finance Minister Mizuta and Health and Welfare Minister Nadao. The three men were later persuaded to stay on, but these episodes were symptomatic of the unsettled atmosphere that was beginning to undermine the Ikeda Administration.

Although the Diet session somehow managed to end on schedule on May 7, the Fujiyama statement remained a divisive issue. To discuss this, the government held four so-called economic ministerial conferences attended by those cabinet members most concerned with economic matters. These discussions finally closed with the announcement of a unified opinion under the title Fundamental Attitudes Toward Future Economic Management. This report, which incorporated Fujiyama's views, was largely compiled by Ōhira.

As it was the year of a LDP presidential election, the political situation was particularly sensitive. Fujiyama's non-mainstream statement had stimulated Satō in the same direction, and Fukuda Takeo, who was seen as an eventual leader of the Kishi faction, became explicitly critical of the Ikeda Administration and created a League for the Reformation of Party Behavior. Given these maneuvers by Fujiyama, Satō, and Fukuda, rumors were rife that soon after the end of the Diet session there might be a sort of coup to establish a Satō Administration.

Ikeda was fortunate that he now had the strong support of both Ōno and Kōno, who at the outset of his administration had headed non-mainstream factions. He was also helped by the fact that the sixth Upper House election was in the offing, which helped to prevent a deepening of factional rivalries. In this election, the LDP won sixty-nine seats, adding five additional seats to its total representation.

Immediately after the Upper House election, Ōhira tried unsuccessfully to dissuade Fujiyama from resigning. Fujiyama later recalled: "I had already privately decided to resign from the cabinet, but the question was the timing. I agreed with Kōno it would not be good to quit just before an election. Yet it would also be awkward after the election results were known, so on the day of the election, July 1, after the polls had closed at about 7:30 P.M., I telephoned Chief Cabinet Secretary Ōhira at his home and told him I'd like to see him that evening at the Prime Minister's Official Residence. Because it was such a sudden request, Ōhira hesitated, saying, 'I've already sent the car back, so today have pity. Tomorrow will do, won't it?' But the only opportunity was that evening, so I insisted on seeing him, and when I did so I tendered my resignation with the words, 'There are differences of opinion on economic policy and I want you to allow me to resign.' " On July 6, Fujiyama resigned. On July 4, Fukuda Takeo's League for the Reformation of Party Behavior adopted a resolution recommending that all party factions be discontinued, and this was communicated to all the influential party members.

The presidential election was set for July 14, 1962, and in the days leading up to the election everyone was interested in what course of action Satō and presidential candidate Fujiyama would take. As it turned out, Satō opted for friendship with Ikeda, while Fujiyama was persuaded by Ōno and others to relinquish his candidacy. In the election, Ikeda received 391 votes, while 75 blank or invalid votes were cast in opposition.

Ikeda went alone to Hakone to work out a plan for cabinet reorganization but returned with nothing definite. Tanaka Kakuei has written about the period following Ikeda's return from Hakone as follows: "On the night before the Ikeda Cabinet's reorganization, Secretary-General Maeo Shigesaburō, General Council Chairman Akagi Munenori, Ōhira (who was chief cabinet secretary) and I (who was chairman of the Policy Research Council) were summoned to Ikeda's residence in Shinanomachi. (Akagi was convalescing in the Defense Agency Hospital and could not be present.) Right away, Ikeda told us, 'For tomorrow's cabinet reorganization, first of all decide on the three posts of party secretary-general, minister of foreign affairs, and minister of finance.' Because of Prime Minister Ikeda's own background in the Finance Ministry, I knew he preferred not to have someone in that post who might play too prominent a role there, so I became finance minister. It was most appropriate that Maeo remain in his important post of party secretary-general, and it was likewise very naturally decided that Ōhira would be minister of foreign affairs. Once this central framework was settled, the rest of the cabinet appointments easily fell into place. Yet the following day there was one troubling gust of wind.

"A meeting was held at the Prime Minister's Official Residence with the top three party officers and the party vice-president as advisers on the cabinet reorganization. Ikeda showed Vice-President Ōno Banboku his list, saying, 'I'd like to settle on this plan.' It was then that Ōno thundered, 'But this looks like a plan for a Tanaka–Ōhira coalition cabinet!'

"Ōhira and I silently left our seats and went into the chief cabinet secretary's office. We locked the door, lined up some chairs and lay down to rest. I was feeling a bit upset, but before long Ōhira was snoring lightly. I was surprised but also couldn't help smiling over the fact that Ōhira, whom I had thought of as sensitive and strictly proper, had such nerves. After an hour or so there was a knock at the door, and when we went into the prime minister's office Ōno was grinning broadly. I supposed that Ōno had probably made some revisions in the original draft, but when I looked at the list handed me by the prime minister, I saw that the posts allotted to Maeo, Ōhira, and Tanaka were unchanged. What Ōhira's expression was at the time, I don't remember."

The party positions of vice-president, secretary-general, and General Council chairman stayed with Ōno, Maeo, and Akagi, respectively, while the chairmanship of the Policy Research Council went to Kaya Okinori. Besides Tanaka as finance minister and Ōhira as foreign minister, the cabinet included Fukuda Hajime as minister of international trade and industry, and Kōno Ichirō as minister of construction. Ōhira's successor as chief cabinet secretary was Kurogane Yasumi. The official date of the cabinet reorganization was July 18, 1962.

Chapter 15

Ventures in Diplomacy

When Ōhira became foreign minister in 1962, it had already been ten years since Japan regained its independence, and the major hurdles of entering the United Nations (in 1956) and revising the security treaty with the United States (1960) had been passed. However, no prospect was yet in sight for restoring diplomatic relations with China and Korea or for the return by the United States of administrative rights over Okinawa and the Ogasawara Archipelago. And in relations with Southeast Asian countries much remained unfinished in regard to postwar settlements. Partly as a result of the Ikeda Administration's policies of rapid growth, the world was beginning to show great interest in Japan's new economic prowess, but Japan had not yet been made a member of the OECD (Organization for Economic Cooperation and Development), which would make it a member of the club of advanced nations.

Ōhira's task as foreign minister was to settle as soon as possible issues remaining from the end of the war, to start negotiations with those countries with which diplomatic relations had not yet been restored, and to win acceptance for Japan as a trustworthy and influential member of the international family of nations. He was somewhat tense at the outset if only because the vice-minister, deputy ministers, and bureau chiefs were for the most part his seniors. Soon after his appointment, Ōhira broke the ice at a press conference with the remark, "Please treat me kindly as I am new to foreign affairs." Of course, he was really no novice. As chief cabinet secretary, he had set aside a good part of each Monday afternoon to listen to lectures on foreign affairs given by the vice-minister of foreign affairs among others.

The cornerstone of Ōhira's emerging diplomacy was, not surprisingly, cooperation with the United States, which he had long shared with one of its foremost advocates, former Prime Minister Yoshida. Living in retirement in Ōiso, fifty kilometers southwest of Tokyo, Yoshida continued to exert a great influence on Foreign Ministry personnel, and it had become customary for each foreign minister appointee to go to Ōiso to pay his respects as soon as he assumed his post. Ōhira was no exception. He has written: "When I became minister of foreign affairs, I, too, would pay frequent visits to Yoshida and always looked forward to hearing him talk. There was something artless and endearing about this easygoing man, and his conversations were full of humor. Once, when Ohira called on Yoshida with a package of fruits as a present and said with a humble attitude that Yoshida might not like such a simple thing, Yoshida replied, "No, I'll take anything, even if it's cash."

To maintain a policy of cooperation with the United States it was necessary to promote continual mutual understanding between the two countries. In Ōhira's words: "As foreign minister my most important work, needless to say, dealt with cooperating with the defense authorities in faithfully carrying out the provisions of the U.S.–Japan Security Treaty. The basis for this was mutual understanding and trust between the two countries. I tried my best to prevent sowing any seeds of mistrust, however tiny, between Japan and the United States."

Foreign Minister Ōhira's most trusted partner at the personal level was Edwin O. Reischauer, the United States ambassador to Japan. They were by chance born in the same year, 1910, but because Ōhira was born in March and Reischauer in October, Reischauer often informally addressed Ōhira in Japanese as *senpai,* a term used for one older than oneself. They cultivated their friendship by breakfasting together at the Kayū Kaikan once a month, accompanied only by their secretaries. The fact that Reischauer was proficient in Japanese aided communication. Reischauer has written:

> Before I came to Japan in 1961 as the American ambassador, I had never known any prominent Japanese politicians. At first I was aware of Mr. Ōhira, then the chief cabinet secretary, only as a background figure behind Prime Minister Ikeda, but when he was appointed in 1962 for a two-year stint as foreign minister, our contacts became much closer and our friendship developed. . . .
>
> The chief thing I remember Mr. Ōhira for was his strong, steady hand in helping to build up a relationship of friendship and equality between Japan and the United States. The political attitudes of the 1960s were quite different from what they are today, and Japanese–American relations were far more

delicate and explosive then. One example may suffice to illustrate Mr. Ōhira's skill in conducting relations with America. The United States wished Japan to purchase more of its wheat imports from the United States in order to help America in its balance of payments problems. When I explained the situation to Mr. Ōhira in a conversation at the American Embassy Residence, he simply said, "I understand. But please do not say anything about this to anyone." I accordingly kept silent, and within a very short time the matter was solved satisfactorily with no undesirable publicity. Seeing then how understanding and politically skillful Mr. Ōhira was, I came to the conclusion that he was certain to become prime minister one day.

With this basis of a growing United States–Japan relationship, it was also necessary for Japan to establish and promote close and friendly relations with other countries. Helped by Japan's growing economic strength, Ōhira set out to put in order, one at a time, a number of yet unresolved problems involving Japan's war responsibility, and at the same time he strove to give greater overall visibility to Japan's role in the world.

The address that Ōhira gave before the 17th United Nations General Assembly on September 21, 1962, two months after assuming the office of foreign minister, showed a willingness to deal positively with important world issues and draw people's attention in many countries. In this address he spoke of the need to eliminate the vestiges of colonialism and racial discrimination, advocated strengthening the United Nations Organization, and spoke in favor of a nuclear test ban, greater attention to disarmament issues, and assistance to developing countries. It was a time when the problems of the Third World were beginning to be accorded much greater importance.

Following his United Nations speech, Ōhira had talks with U.S. Secretary of State Dean Rusk on bilateral economic issues, which provided the occasion for Ōhira to request that the Americans seriously consider the issue of returning Okinawa. Ōhira then flew to Europe to visit England, France, West Germany, Italy, Belgium, and the Netherlands, where he held talks with President de Gaulle and other heads of state.

Early in the morning of October 22, 1962, not long after Ōhira's return, Ambassador Reischauer unexpectedly visited Ikeda's residence in Shinanomachi and handed him a personal letter from President Kennedy. It explained that the United States was going to carry out a naval blockade of Cuba because of the construction of Soviet missile bases there, and requested Japan's support for this. When informed of this situation, where a false step could lead to a third world war, many of Japan's government officials felt extremely uneasy. However, Prime Minister Ikeda's stance of cooperation with the United States was unchanged, as was that of Ōhira. Fortunately, the Cuban crisis was resolved in accordance with President Kennedy's objective and without war.

Following Ōhira's pace-setting European trip, Prime Minister Ikeda visited a number of European countries between November 4 and 20. Prior to this, the influential British journal *The Economist* ran a feature article titled "Consider Japan," which reported on the achievements of Japan's economic growth. And in countries around the world Ikeda's European visit was seen as an important step in Japan's return to the international community. Soon after Ikeda's European trip, Japan applied for OECD membership in February 1963, and following negotiations and consideration by the Diet, it formally became a member in April. After the difficult period of postwar reconstruction and having entered a period of rapid economic growth, Japan had at last gained international recognition as a member of the advanced industrial nations.

While Prime Minister Ikeda was in Europe, Ōhira, as foreign minister, was responsible for making one important decision. In the process of negotiations begun in Japan on November 12, 1962, with Kim Jong Pil, head of the South Korean Central Intelligence Agency (later prime minister), he had to answer Korean requests for Japanese economic aid. Already in June 1962, in a speech supporting LDP candidates in the Upper House election campaign, Prime Minister Ikeda, who judged that the time was ripe for normalizing relations with South Korea, had declared, "I definitely want to do this after the election." As if in response, South Korea's military junta leader, Park Chung Hee, declared in September, "Even if I am criticized by a part of the people, I intend to bring about a normalization of Japanese–South Korean relations." In October, there were preliminary talks in Tokyo between Prime Minister Ikeda and Kim Jong Pil.

At the preliminary negotiation stage, a major problem was how to deal with the problem of claims for compensation that South Korea might make following normalization. Originally, the South Korean claim was for US$600 million, while Japan's policy was to offer only US$300 million in total as compensated and non-compensated financial assistance. During the prime minister's absence, it was up to Ōhira to handle this wide gap in the two countries' negotiating positions. Ōhira expressed his feelings to a close associate as follows: "Chang Tu Yong [former head of the South Korean Ministry of National Defense] and Park Chung Hee are military men, so perhaps it can't be helped, but it doesn't seem necessary for even a military regime to go that far. I understand the threat from the north, but isn't it all right not to play it up quite so much?" Japan and South Korea not only had different evaluations of the threat from the north, but had persistent feelings of mistrust conditioned by their past relations. How, then, should talks proceed with South Korea's representative?

According to Ōhira's secretary, Ōhira told him afterward that the first thing Kim Jong Pil said was, "Our country's defense is Japan's shield." This opening assertion implied that, given the tacit understanding that Japan could have only limited defense forces because of its "Peace Constitution," South Korea was in fact playing a proxy defense role that should be recognized in fixing the sum of money to be requested of Japan. Ōhira answered: 'What you are asking is quite strange. Does not South Korea's defense strength exist for the purpose of safeguarding South Korea? I'd think the pride of the South Korean people would not allow you to say such things." In response, Kim is said to have remained silent for some time.

According to a speech made by Ōhira three years later, in April 1965, Ōhira said to Kim: "I can well understand the feelings of your people toward Japan. However, I don't think there is any benefit for your country in saying only resentful things about Japan. . . . Even if you want to move because you don't like Japan, there is nowhere the 26 million South Koreans can move to, and the same is true for the Japanese. . . . Our two countries are perpetual neighbors, so shouldn't we make up our minds to discard, like ash in an ashtray, everything that is past and have some vision for the future? If there is such a sentiment on your side, Japan, too, will be sensible enough to behave accordingly. Now that you have become independent and are faced with the difficult task of building up your nation, Japan, as your country's perpetual neighbor, will be willing to assist your future progress with substantial economic cooperation. . . ."

Kim Jong Pil, in an interview with a Japanese newspaper twenty-six years later, in August 1988, stated that Ōhira had originally said the ceiling for economic aid given him by Prime Minister Ikeda was US$80 million. According to this interview, Kim then stood up and claimed that he had come to the negotiations at the risk of being called a traitor and that Japan's cooperation was essential to build South Korea into a country with an export-based economy. Ōhira continued to look grave and soon nearly three hours had passed. Eventually, Ōhira asked Kim to state what he truly had in mind, and Kim replied, "US$300 million as a non-compensated grant, US$200 million as compensated aid, and US$100 million plus alpha in private economic cooperation." Ōhira thought for a while and said, "How about US$100 million non-compensated and US$200 million or US$300 million compensated?" After thinking a further forty minutes, he said, "It should be all right. I'll take responsibility," and wrote down on two pieces of paper the points agreed upon. This was the so-called Ōhira–Kim Memorandum. According to Ōhira' recollection, "Kim agreed in principle to my proposal, which took a heap of courage. I felt that this man was a commendable statesman." In any case, the request for monetary transfers was eventually agreed at US$300 million in non-compensated grants, US$200 million in government assistance to be paid back later, and US$100 million to be made available as private banks loans.

As mentioned, these negotiations were concluded on Foreign Minister Ōhira's own judgment during Prime Minister Ikeda's absence from Japan and showed, as it were, a resolve to go it alone. Ōhira has written: "Prime Minister Ikeda was away on his trip at the time. I was really extremely worried about whether or not he would give his blessing to the items upon which we had reached an understanding. To the extent that Ikeda was at least a financier, he later gave detailed advice on the handling of uncollectible loans and on schedules and other conditions for economic cooperation, but on the whole he good-naturedly accepted the items in question. Thus, in the Japanese–South Korean negotiations both parties came onto the same *sumō* ring, and this opened the way for negotiations on other pending issues."

This candid recollection hints at the concern which Ōhira and those around him had for Prime Minister Ikeda's possible reaction, a concern that was conditioned by the tradition of payoffs and unwholesome collusion that had earlier accompanied Japanese–South Korean political and economic relations. Ikeda and Ōhira intended to discontinue such practices, and this was an additional reason why caution was called for in planning the normalization of diplomatic relations.

Although Ōhira had originally been expected to continue with the final stage of negotiations arising from his talks with Kim, on the instructions of Ikeda, who took into consideration party opinion, this task was given to party Vice-President Ōno Banboku, although Ōhira directed all essential matters from behind the scenes.

A month later, in December, Special Envoy Ōno visited Korea and formally presented the Japanese draft plan by which Korea's claims would be met in the form of economic cooperation. The South Korean side was amenable, and the negotiations were at a point of effective agreement, with only a few specific procedural matters left unsettled. However, due to unstable political conditions in South Korea, ultimate official agreement on the economic cooperation plan and the initial signing of the Treaty on Basic Relations Between Japan and the Republic of Korea had to wait another two and a half years, until the visit to South Korea in February 1965 by Foreign Minister Shiina Etsusaburō during the Satō Administration. (The formal signing of the treaty took place on June 22, 1965.)

Immediately after the official normalization of relations between the two countries, Ōhira gave a speech in his capacity as former foreign minister, in which he stated: "This treaty does not try to represent any elaborate new diplomatic policy. It resembles instead a letter of reconciliation between Japan and the Republic of Korea. It has accomplished something extremely natural and reasonable, an agreement that it is better for us, once and for all, to get rid of a past of mutual feelings of distrust, and even feelings of hatred or jealousy, and that we should instead have tranquil relations with one another."

The post of foreign minister was and is a busy one. Not long after his talks with Kim Jong Pil, Ōhira was on his way to the United States to attend the second meeting of the U.S.-Japan Joint Committee on Trade and Economic Affairs, which opened on November 30, 1962, in the State Department in Washington. At the first meeting of the joint committee in Hakone, the American delegates had brought their wives, and now it was the turn of the Japanese to take their wives across the Pacific. Ōhira's wife, Shigeko, recalls: "This was my first trip abroad. Ōhira was chief of delegation, and Finance Minister Tanaka, Labor Minister Ōhashi, International Trade and Industry Minister Fukuda [Hajime] and Economic Planning Agency Director-General Miyazawa were also present with their wives. In the airplane, the 'ladies first' rule was observed, so we wives got to sit next to the windows. In Washington, we were invited to the home of Secretary of State Rusk. It was a simple home and we were entertained simply, with tea and homemade cookies. We were also invited to the home of Vice President Johnson. It was quite a splendid mansion and we were entertained there by singers from the New York Metropolitan Opera."

After the turn of the new year, 1963, the Ikeda Cabinet welcomed its third spring. The 42nd Extraordinary Diet that met for two weeks in December 1962 had been nicknamed the "Coal Diet" because of a major bill introduced to establish measures for dealing with the declining coal industry. The opposition parties, aiming to move matters in directions favoring labor, obstructed Diet consideration of this bill, and as a result other matters on the Diet agenda were blocked as well, with more than 80 percent of the proposed bills not acted upon. Some people close to the prime minister considered a dissolution, but nobody was really very enthusiastic about it, and the prevailing mood among cabinet ministers was more one of fatigue after more than two years of responsibility for administering the country.

It was with this heavy feeling that the New Year was ushered in, and not long afterwards, on January 9, United States Ambassador Reischauer told Foreign Minister Ōhira that he "would like to have ordinary nuclear-driven submarines, though not those of the [nuclear missile carrying] Polaris type, stop at Japanese ports to take on provisions and give rest opportunities to the crews." Although this was a troublesome issue, Foreign Minister Ōhira's judgment from the very beginning was, "Because the submarines that the United States wants to have make port calls use nuclear power only for propulsion, and because they are part of the United States fleet that contributes to international peace in the Far East and to our country's security, so long as they do not carry nuclear weapons it should be only natural and in accordance with the principles of the security treaty that they should be able to call at ports in our country. In other words, this does not become a subject for the prior consultation mentioned in the treaty." Nonetheless, due attention had to be given to the complex sentiments of unease in Japan with respect to atomic energy. Foreign Minister Ōhira responded by asking Japan's Atomic Energy Commission and Science and Technology Agency to investigate the safety issue, and through diplomatic channels he strove to verify matters with the United States that needed to be checked.

After the budget passed the Lower House in the 43rd Ordinary Diet in March 1963, the focus of domestic politics moved to the upcoming unified local elections. In the campaign for governor of Tokyo, the LDP, with support from the new Kōmei Political League (which was affiliated with the Buddhist *Sōka Gakkai* organization), promoted the candidacy of Azuma Ryūtarō, while the JSP, DSP, and JCP put up a spirited fight in support of former Hyōgo Prefectural Governor Sakamoto Masaru. Azuma won, but there were disturbing revelations in regard to corruption in the Tokyo Metropolitan Assembly. Elsewhere, the conservative forces lost out to opposition parties in the campaigns for the governorship of Fukuoka, Iwate, and Ōita prefectures and in mayoral races in the important cities of Osaka and Yokohama. This was a harbinger of further advances by "progressive forces" that would be made in local governments over the next decade.

Soon after these local elections were over, there began the now customary summer reorganization of the Ikeda Cabinet. The reorganized cabinet was officially announced on July 17, as well as the top three party posts: Maeo continued as secretary-general, Fujiyama became General Council chairman, and Miki became Policy Research Council chairman. Continuing in the same cabinet posts were Ōhira (Foreign Affairs), Tanaka (Finance), Fukuda Hajime (International Trade and Industry), Ōhashi (Labor), Kōno (Construction), Ayabe Kentarō (Transport), Economic Planning Agency Director-General Miyazawa, and Chief Cabinet Secretary Kurogane. Satō Eisaku, ever more noticeably anti-Ikeda, was made concurrently director-general of the Science and Technology Agency and director of the Hokkaidō Development Agency. The media dubbed it a "regime of new leaders" (*shin jitsuryokusha taisei*).

On July 18, the first working day of the reorganized cabinet, President Kennedy appeared before the United States Congress with a special presidential message on the international balance of payments, which set forth a "Buy American" policy aimed at defense of the dollar, and also advocated the establishment of an "interest equalization tax" which would be a 10 percent levy by the U.S. federal government on interest from American investments abroad. In Japan, there was anxiety that such a tax would not only make it difficult to attract capital investment from the United States but might also endanger the international balance of payments and the successful management of Japan's economy in a period of growth.

Prime Minister Ikeda had originally intended to send Economic Planning Agency Director-General Miyazawa to the United States to discuss this matter, but Miyazawa had an attack of appendicitis just before his scheduled departure, so Foreign Minister Ōhira went in his stead. Prime Minister Ikeda instructed him, "Try to persuade the United States to give up this tax, but if that is impossible, negotiate to have Japan excluded from its provisions as in the case of Canada."

On leaving for the United States, Ōhira confided to close associates, "I will go, but even if this sort of thing occurs [that is, imposition of the tax] I doubt that U.S.–Japan relations would really be much changed." He later recalled: "I departed on July 31 aboard a Japan Air Lines jet. . . . [My discussions with the Americans] included, most importantly, talks with Treasury Secretary Douglas Dillon. Ambassador Reischauer, who happened to be back in his country on vacation, kindly introduced me to a number of people and helped in other ways.

"I explained at some length the effects that the interest equalization tax was expected to have on our country's economy and requested that Japan be given the same exemption as was given Canada. Dillon emphasized the special nature of the U.S.–Canada relationship and, with respect to what I had said about effects of the tax on the Japanese economy, he expressed the opinion that because of the difference in interest rates between the two countries and the strength of Japan's demand for capital, necessary American capital would surely be attracted in spite of such a tax.

"However, he did come around to recognizing that the Japanese interest in, and anxiety over, this problem far exceeded the cool-headed assessments of the Americans, and helped by the standpoint that friendship with Japan must definitely be maintained, the American attitude softened somewhat. In the U.S.–Japan joint statement made public on August 2, it was agreed that. . . . if serious difficulties should arise in Japan due to the interest equalization tax, there was a mutual readiness to undertake discussions on remedial measures, including possible exemptions from the tax."

On the way home from Washington, Ōhira stopped in New York, where at a luncheon hosted by business and banking leaders he remarked, "During the past hundred years the Pacific Ocean has seen both calm weather and stormy seas. However, during these years your country has had confidence in Japan and invested large sums of money there, and Japan has been able to achieve modernization. Now it happens that some dark clouds in the form of the interest equalization tax have appeared in one corner of the clear sky, but surely they will not stay very long."

A prominent banker who was seated next to Ōhira whispered in his ear, "There is no need to worry. If your country's international balance of payments should be in a pinch, my bank alone is ready to make available immediately US$70 million or US$80 million." Ōhira instinctively felt that his visit to the United States had gone well. The interest equalization tax did not, in fact, materialize until September 2, 1964, considerably later than originally planned. In keeping with a promise made to Ōhira, US$100 million per year in Japanese government-related loans were exempted from the tax.

Two weeks after returning to Japan from the United States, Ōhira departed for his second trip to Europe. It was a goodwill trip in response to invitations from Norway, Sweden, and Denmark, three countries he had not visited on his previous trip. This second European journey spanned the period from August 25 to September 10, and also took in England, France, and Iran, six countries in all. Appropriately enough for a goodwill trip, in Norway Ōhira visited fjords along the North Sea coast and met with the king; in Sweden he visited a nuclear power plant and the Museum of Far Eastern Antiquities; and in Denmark he enjoyed visiting farms and old castles, where he felt "as if I were in a fairyland." In France he was deeply impressed by President de Gaulle: "His famous clear blue eyes and long legs were most impressive. The general has been introduced to the Japanese public by Furukaki Tetsurō in a book that reflects the author's great friendship and respect for de Gaulle, and I, too, felt that this man was no mere soldier, nor just a rather unique politician, but a philosopher and thinker on a grand scale." On his visit to Great Britain, he and Ambassador Ōno Katsumi were invited by Foreign Secretary (later Prime Minister) Sir

Alec Douglas-Home to spend the night at his estate near Glasgow, where they enjoyed grouse shooting with the foreign secretary.

Scarcely had he time to get settled after his return to Japan before he left Haneda airport on September 15 to attend the 18th United Nations General Assembly in New York. It was a quiet assembly, reflecting the changed mood following the conclusion of the Partial Nuclear Test Ban Treaty. In a speech that was the keynote for a general discussion, Ōhira expounded some of his ideas on peace:

> Mr. President, at no time has the problem of peace been so intensely discussed as it is being done today. We are now giving our most sober thoughts to this problem, because of the increasing danger of nuclear war which, should it ever come, would mean the total destruction of mankind. Still fresh in our minds is the Cuban crisis of less than a year ago which made the whole world shudder with fear. . . .
>
> But it is not only in such a negative sense that we share this common fate. Developments in science and technology have so dramatically increased intercourse in all aspects of human life that the people of one nation are now closely linked with the people of all other nations politically, economically, culturally. As no individual can live in isolation in his own country, no nation can exist in isolation from the rest of the world. In life, and indeed in death too, mankind is linked together by a fate that is one and inseparable. World peace, therefore, is not merely an abstract concept; it is something real and tangible which we ourselves must secure with our own hands. To win it is the duty and the responsibility of all of us now living.

As shown in this excerpt, this speech, like the one he gave at the United Nations a year earlier, was grounded in the concept of interdependence in international relations. During the year he had served as minister of foreign affairs, Ōhira had come directly to grips with many problems facing the world and had learned to talk about them in his own words and in relation to his own ideas. For one aspiring to become an international political figure, this was an essential and necessary process of growth. It was at the same time important to the development of Japan's diplomacy and integration into the world at large.

The 44th Extraordinary Diet began on October 15, 1963, and was dissolved eight days later on October 23 on completion of the period of interpellation by each party. The coming general election was to be called a "mood election," since neither the reasons for the dissolution nor the points of conflict between the government and the opposition parties had been clearly specified.

Polling day for the thirtieth Lower House election was November 21. The vote resulted in 283 seats for the LDP, 144 for the JSP, 23 for the DSP, 5 for the JCP, and 12 for unaffiliated candidates. The number of LDP seats was 3 less than at the time of the dissolution, but because 11 of the 12 unaffiliated candidates later joined the party, the number of its seats rose to 294, which was considered to be a respectable showing. The JSP lost one seat, giving an impression of stagnation in the progressive camp.

In his constituency, which was represented by three members, Ōhira relinquished the leading position he had enjoyed in the 1958 and 1960 elections to another LDP candidate by a margin of 3,201 votes. Considerably shocked, his campaign staff immediately set to work to rejuvenate and strengthen his local support organization. They also set up an Ōhira Political Forum (Ōhira Seiji Kyōshitsu), a study group on public affairs aimed mainly at young people, who in turn formed a club called the Hōyūkai. Public relations activities were further stepped up with the publication of Tōkyō-dayori (Tokyo Newsletter) and the Hōyūkaishi (Hō-yūkai Magazine).

Two days after the election, in the early morning of November 23 in Japan, an earthshaking event occurred on the other side of the world—the assassination of President Kennedy. This tragedy coincided with the scheduled third meeting, in Japan, of the U.S.-Japan Joint Committee on Trade and Economic Affairs. The airplane carrying Secretary of State Dean Rusk and his party to Japan for this meeting turned back midway over the Pacific.

In Japan, there was the question of who would attend the funeral. Prime Minister Ikeda, who was resting in Hakone, telephoned Ōhira to say that while Ōhira should of course go, he felt it desirable if Ōhira went in the company of a member of the imperial family, who could represent the emperor. Eventually, the Imperial Household Agency rejected the idea on the grounds that no precedent existed, and it was then decided, at the last moment, that Ōhira would attend the funeral in the company of Ikeda himself. Because of this confusion, a typical attack by journalists unfamiliar with all the ins and outs of the situation was, "All along Ikeda has had a wavering attitude and lacked assertiveness, waiting to see how other countries behave."

The date for the official designation of the prime minister following the general election was set for December 9, following the return of Ikeda and Ōhira from the Kennedy funeral. Initially, the Third Ikeda Cabinet witnessed no changes in cabinet personnel, largely due to the fact that a reorganization had taken place in July, only five months previously. The next cabinet reorganization did not take place until July 1964, following Ikeda's third election as party president. Thus, Ōhira remained minister of foreign affairs until the summer of 1964.

One important and difficult area of concern for Ōhira during his two years as foreign minister under the Ikeda Administration was Japan–China negotiations. The efforts he made at this time would bear more fruit when he was minister of foreign affairs a second time after the summer of 1972. Before considering Ōhira's approach to Chinese issues, let us first briefly review postwar Japan–China relations. With American encouragement, Japan had concluded a peace treaty with Taiwan in April 1952, six months after the San Francisco Peace Treaty. Although this action had brought strong condemnation from the Beijing government, nongovernmental economic and cultural exchanges between Japan and mainland China went forward in spite of intergovernmental antagonisms. In 1955, a non-governmental fisheries agreement was concluded and an exhibition of Chinese products opened in Tokyo. In spite of these signs of a gradual thaw in Japan–China relations, this mood was suddenly shattered by the so-called Nagasaki National Flag Incident in May 1958. At an exhibit of Chinese folkcrafts held in a department store in Nagasaki, an anti-Communist Japanese youth tore down the five-star flag of the People's Republic. This incident hardened the attitude of the Beijing government, and the problem became further complicated when virtually all Japan–China trade was halted.

However, at the outset of the Ikeda Administration, the prime minister decided to change the preceding policy of confrontation toward Beijing and to actively promote friendly relations through economic exchanges. He judged that historical and geographical factors made such an approach almost inevitable. China, for its part, was indicating a more flexible posture toward Japan. Perhaps reflecting in part growing disaffection with the Soviet Union, it was developing policies that encouraged the conclusion of private contracts with Japanese companies even in the absence of inter-governmental agreements.

In his talks with President Kennedy in June 1961, Prime Minister Ikeda indicated his view that it was natural for Japan, which had a special historical relationship with China, to carry out trade on the same level as European countries with China, and he sought American understanding on this point. Ōhira likewise emphasized the need to develop Japan–China trade whenever he spoke with President Kennedy or Secretary of State Rusk. The Americans, however, who had adopted a containment policy out of fear of an expanding Chinese military potential, were extremely cautious. When Foreign Minister Ōhira explained that "the Japanese government neither particularly encourages trade with Communist China, nor does it discourage it," the American response was, in Ōhira's words, "of a sort that they neither agreed nor disagreed, but were able to *understand* [original English]."

As the desire for a Japan–China rapprochement was strong in both countries, in October 1962, four months after Ōhira assumed the Foreign Ministry portfolio, a Memorandum on Comprehensive Trade Between Japan and China was signed by Liao Chengzhi, secretary-general of the China–Japan Friendship Association, and Takasaki Tatsunosuke, an LDP Dietman influential in business circles. The resulting trade was often called LT Trade after the initials of the surnames of the two signatories.

This rapprochement could not help but irritate Taiwan as well as Taiwan supporters within the LDP, and their dissatisfaction reached boiling point in the summer of 1963, when the Japanese government approved the export to mainland China of a vinylon plant by the Kurashiki Rayon Company under a financing arrangement with the Export-Import Bank of Japan. Foreign Minister Ōhira had a number of talks with Taiwan's ambassador in Tokyo, Chang Li-shêng, in an attempt to win his understanding. He recalls: "I repeatedly tried to explain . . . that the leading form of world trade today is changing from the buying and selling of goods to that of whole manufacturing plants, and that payment is coming to be more in the form of long-term deferrals rather than immediate cash settlements. Insofar as one is engaged in trade, one can hardly ignore this trend of the times. I also explained to him on repeated occasions that I wanted him to understand that I felt it would be difficult to convince the Japanese people that their country should not engage in levels of trade with Communist China commensurate with trade between China and Western Europe."

However, the Taiwanese showed unremitting opposition. It was feared that if this sort of trade were recognized, it would expand and eventually lead to a normalization of Japan–China diplomatic ties. There was also considerable opposition to this plant export scheme within the ranks of the LDP, which had its pro-Taiwan factions, and even within the cabinet. All in all, most voices were calling for caution toward the China problem.

Fukuda Hajime, then minister of international trade and industry, who grappled with this problem together with Ōhira, later recalled: "It was still a long way from diplomatic normalization, and the voices of caution on China tended to dominate in both the government and the ruling party. It once happened that in the course of some random conversation before a cabinet meeting, Ōhira remarked to me that he thought Japan and China had a relationship something like that of *ōmisoka* (the last day of the year) and *gantan* (the first day of the new year). It was an off-the-cuff and rather peculiar comparison, but I continued to listen with interest as he continued: 'People talk about the two countries having the same script and being of the same race, but in our overall approaches to culture and in people's way of life there are far more points of difference than of similarity. For this reason I see China as an important neighboring country with which we must, through a corresponding degree of patience and effort, get along peacefully. You are indeed trying hard and I want you to do your best.' "

It is not easy to confirm the thoughts Ōhira had on the China question. His foreign affairs speeches before the Diet during his tenure as foreign minister rarely mentioned China, and this is true also of his writings. Even his closest associates were rarely appraised of his real feelings. He had no doubt adopted this attitude in line with his customary caution. It is of interest, however, that at a session of the Foreign Affairs Committee of the Lower House on February 12, 1964, he referred to the issue of China's representation in the United Nations in response to questioning from JSP Dietman Hozumi Shichirō:

> **Hozumi**: As to the issue of recognizing a changeover in China's representation, in the event that this should be approved by a majority in the United Nations, would it be possible to make the decision to recognize China?
>
> **Ōhira**: If ... such a situation should come about that the government of Communist China became a member of the United Nations with the world's blessing, then naturally I think it would stand to reason that our country would have to make an important decision.
>
> **Hozumi**: Then you are saying that diplomatic normalization is a matter that you would promote in a concrete way at the time when China recovers its right of representation in the United Nations?
>
> **Ōhira**: The basic concept is one that you have understood. In other words, if the situation should come about whereby China was given the blessing of being a regular member of the United Nations, it would be only natural to have to think about the normalization of diplomatic relations.

Curiously, because of these few words uttered by the foreign minister, the opposition camp relaxed its pursuit. Perhaps they were caught off-balance by Ōhira's word "blessing," which was somehow of a different dimension from the vocabulary ordinarily used in Diet discussions. On examination, these remarks by Ōhira did not depart in the least from Japan's consistent diplomatic policy of paying great attention to the United Nations and respecting the results of its deliberations. Ōhira was only voicing a general principle, and by the magic of words he had skillfully avoided committing himself on the troublesome China issue.

Yet we may ask what Ōhira's true feelings on Japan–China relations were. In a speech titled "The Coordinates of Japanese Diplomacy" that he gave at the LDP-managed institute for the training of party organizers known as the Central Institute of Politics (*Chūō Seiji Daigakuin*) on April 5, 1966, almost two years after finishing his first stint as foreign minister, Ōhira referred to the China problem in some detail. After discussing the various aspects of politics, economics, defense, and the recognition of favors rendered in the past, he explained that "our seniors (*senpai*) anyhow chose Taiwan" and that "insofar as they chose Taiwan, Beijing could not be recognized." (It is almost certain that in using the word *senpai* he had in mind, first of all, former Prime Minister Yoshida.) He continued: "Consequently, we maintain official relations with Taiwan. With Beijing, although . . . we are unable to have intergovernmental relations, there is the willingness to associate at the people-to-people level. In other words, we are observing something like a principle of separating politics and economics." However, he added: "Nowhere in the world is a separation of politics and economics really valid. Politics and economics have a persistent way of being one and undivided." (The same sentiment had, of course, been repeatedly stressed by Premier Zhou Enlai.) According to Ōhira, in order to normalize "these abnormal relations," China would have to modify the view it had hitherto taken that "China is one," but this was something Japan could do nothing about.

Another approach acknowledged by Ōhira was that "a way toward resolving the problem would seem to be if world public opinion on this should crystallize, though this might be very difficult." He then asked himself: "But what kind of situation would come about if the United Nations should conclude, after taking a vote, that China's representation rightfully belongs to Beijing?" His answer was: "I think it would probably develop into a situation more difficult than we might imagine."

Why more difficult? The gist of Ōhira's explanation was the following. First of all, it was unclear whether Beijing would, in fact, so easily agree to become a member of the United Nations. And what would happen to the authority of United Nations resolutions that had condemned Beijing as a belligerent government? Then, too, what would be the attitude taken in Taiwan? These could be expected to be extremely difficult problems both for the United Nations and for Japan.

Granted that the difficulties were there, what did he expect if international opinion definitively held that the right to represent China belonged to Beijing? Ōhira did not go beyond stating: "I think that our country's United Nations and China policies would face a great turning point, and the only thing certain is that domestic public debate would become increasingly lively." Exactly what Ōhira meant to say here remains a matter of conjecture even today. Although we must admit that Ōhira was thinking about possible responses in the eventuality, it is too hasty to conclude that he was from this time expecting China to change its international status, or win diplomatic recognition by Japan, in the very near future.

As mentioned before, the Ikeda Cabinet had in the summer of 1963 approved the export to China, on a deferred payment basis, of a vinylon plant. Commenting on the Taiwanese reaction, Ōhira later wrote: "Ambassador Chang seemed to be greatly shocked, and not long afterward he resigned his post and returned home. A former secretary-general of the Nationalist Party, he was not only an outstanding statesman but, due to his charm and kindly personality, had earned the deep respect of many persons at home and abroad. I, too, was disappointed by his departure." The irate Taiwanese government adopted such hard-hitting measures as the limiting of trade with Japan and a complete embargo on government purchases of Japanese products and services. In Ōhira's view, "Japan–Taiwan relations appear to be falling into a dark chasm."

In October 1963, the Zhou Hongqing Incident further aggravated relations between Japan and Taiwan. Zhou Hongqing, an interpreter with a delegation from mainland China who came to Tokyo to participate in an international exhibit of hydraulic equipment, went to the Soviet embassy on the day he was supposed to return to China (October 7) to ask for asylum. When the Soviet embassy refused his request, the Japanese police arrested him for violating immigration regulations. While being held in police custody he kept changing his mind as to whether he wanted to stay in Japan, go to Taiwan, or return to the mainland. The Taiwanese authorities were strongly opposed to Zhou's being returned to the mainland and delivered a message, saying, "In view of the report that Zhou originally intended to seek asylum in Taiwan, we are ready to honor his wishes and accept him." The pro-Taiwan factions in the LDP were sympathetic and began trying to bring about such an outcome.

One of Ōhira's secretaries at the time recalls: "For the Ministry of Foreign Affairs this was the biggest incident of the two years Ōhira was foreign minister. If mishandled, it could have led to both a cutting of the fine economic thread linking us with China and a break with Taiwan. There were huddled meetings in a heavy atmosphere, and I say 'heavy' because of the way this could affect the country's fortunes. Within the Foreign Ministry itself there were both views: send him to Taiwan and return him to Beijing. At the time, I would carefully study Foreign Minister Ōhira's face, but it was not that easy for him to form a definite judgment. As the arguments became more heated, he decided that it would be best to handle the matter in accordance with Japanese law and asked the Ministry of Justice to determine what Zhou was really saying. With such an approach, even a really big political problem can be brought down to a technical level, or to the level of a legal detail. I think that Ōhira certainly was aiming at such an approach. It was a method of having matters judged by the testimony of facts and figures, and it permitted what in German is called a *sachlich* way of seeing things. This was ultimately, I think, successful."

On October 24, during a final examination at the Justice Ministry's Immigration Bureau, Zhou Hongqing definitely expressed his wish to return to the mainland, and consequently was allowed to return to the mainland of his own free will any time after January 1, 1964. He left Osaka by ship for Dairen on January 9. Regarding the resolution of this problem, Ōhira has written as follows: "In handling this problem, I tried to reach a resolution through the routine and impartial application of domestic regulations, taking the same measures as had consistently been taken in the past with respect to persons who had illegally remained in Japan without a proper visa. . . . I acted while keeping in mind both the impartial application of the relevant laws, which is the natural responsibility of a nation with a legal framework, as well as respect for fundamental human rights, which is recognized the world over and is a major principle of Japan's Constitution."

With the export to China of the vinylon plant and then the return to the mainland of Zhou Hongqing, dissatisfaction in Taiwan continued to grow and its relations with Japan could only be called strained. To defuse this tension, former Prime Minister Yoshida, who had headed the government in 1952, at the time of the conclusion of the Japan–Republic of China peace treaty with Taiwan, and who was an old friend of President Chiang Kai-shek, visited Taiwan in a personal capacity in May 1964, met with President Chiang, and delivered to Taiwanese authorities the famous "Yoshida letter." This letter, dated May 7 and sent to the chief secretary of the president's office, Chang Chun, has never been made public. However, it is believed to have promised, in effect, that funding from the Export-Import Bank of Japan, which had raised such a controversy in connection with the vinylon plant, would not, for the time being, be made available for other deferred-payment exports to mainland China. In drafting the letter, Ōhira is known to have conferred several times with Yoshida.

As a result, Taiwan finally relaxed its stance, including the various retaliatory measures it had taken following the vinylon plant controversy. The Taiwanese authorities asked Foreign Minister Ōhira to visit Taipei as a symbol of government-level peacemaking. For Ōhira, who genuinely felt that it would one day be necessary to face up to the problem of normalizing diplomatic relations with mainland China, it was a "heavy-hearted" trip. He left on July 3, influenced in part by the fact that Prime Minister Ikeda, who hoped to be reelected party president on July 10, was concerned about the behavior of the pro-Taiwan Ōno and other factions within the party. In Taiwan, Ōhira met with President Chiang Kai-shek and other government leaders, and during his stay the embargo on Taiwanese government purchases from Japan was officially lifted. This was the first and last trip Ōhira ever made to Taiwan.

Part 4

A Period of Winter

Part 4

A Period of Winter

Chapter 16

An Unexpected Turn

$\mathbf{A}$s the Ikeda Administration greeted its fourth new year, 1964, Prime Minister Ikeda's Income-Doubling Plan was making steady progress, and the Olympic Games, which would show the results of the rapid-growth policies to the world, were scheduled for the autumn of that year. Nevertheless, the prime minister and many of his close associates were showing definite signs of fatigue. Stamina seemed to have eroded under the burdens of government. First, LDP Secretary-General Maeo's health had suffered in his efforts to clear up intraparty problems. A native of Kyoto Prefecture, Maeo had entered the Ministry of Finance four years after Ikeda and, like Ikeda, had a background in tax administration. Also like Ikeda, he had in his youth been forced by illness to give up working for a considerable period; after his recovery, as head of the Wakayama Tax Office, he befriended Ikeda, who was at the time director of the nearby Osaka Tamatsukuri Tax Office. Curiously, the contrast in their personalities—Ikeda was stubborn while Maeo was more accommodating—may even have helped cement their friendship. The fact that Maeo, well regarded as a mediator, had fallen ill, however, seems to have brought a situation where party and intrafactional frictions were left unattended.

Another development was a coolness in what had been the close relationship between Ikeda and Ōhira. Preoccupied with his work as foreign minister, Ōhira no longer visited the Prime Minister's Official Residence or his home in Shinanomachi as often as before, and this seems to have contributed to a lack of understanding and coordination between the two. Within the party and the Kōchikai, there had occasionally been some jealousy toward Ōhira, who had rapidly risen in prominence, and this was now surfacing in a feeling of dissatisfaction. In the general elections of 1960 and 1963, several old friends of Ōhira's, such as Sasaki Yoshitake and Itō Masayoshi, had made their debuts in political office and appeared to be forming their own subgroup under Ōhira's aegis within the Ikeda faction of the LDP.

In the meantime, Ikeda somehow got word of a rumor that Ōhira was about to encourage a revolt against his leadership, a story that grew from a fanciful interpretation of the fact that Ōhira had personally donated some funds for the activities of some of the younger Dietmen in the Kōchikai. Ikeda summoned Ōhira and complained, "I haven't said anything about it before, but is it true that you are building a new faction?" Ōhira replied, "I am not thinking of any such thing. They asked to be given some spending money, and all I did was to give them a little in your stead. Haven't I done similar things in the past? I don't think I have to ask your judgment on every matter." Ikeda was nonetheless indignant, saying, "It won't do, it won't do," and for some time Ōhira was forbidden access to Ikeda's Shinanomachi residence.

In the background was the circumstance that, although only six months remained until the end of Ikeda's second two-year term as party president, no plan for dealing with this had been drawn up by the Kōchikai top echelons or by Ikeda himself. Ikeda wished to round off his administration by inspiring confidence in the policies of rapid growth that he had promoted, at the same time correcting the more evident strains that accompanied this growth and expediting his "people-building policy" (*hitozukuri seisaku*) focusing on better education. Ōhira had not forgotten the cooperation received from Satō Eisaku at the time the Ikeda Administration came into being and shared much of Satō's apprehensions about what seemed at times like an almost reckless desire on Ikeda's part to push ahead oblivious to possible consequences. He would often confide to people around him, "The prime minister is so much of a go-getter that it's a real problem."

As foreign minister, Ōhira met frequently with former Prime Minister Yoshida in Ōiso and was well aware that Yoshida expected Satō Eisaku to be prime minister after Ikeda had served two terms. Ikeda was aware of this, too, and although he had been accustomed to stopping in Ōiso on his way to or from weekends in Hakone, he now gave up doing so. It was his way of showing that any intervention by Yoshida regarding the party presidency would not be welcome. On the other hand, Satō's rival Kōno Ichirō, hoping to thwart Satō's chances, became closer to Ikeda and indicated a willingness to cooperate in electing him for a third term.

On May 18, Satō asked Ikeda if he could visit him in Hakone, but Ikeda refused. On May 19, Vice-President Ōno, who had supported Ikeda, died. When Satō resigned his cabinet post immediately after the end of the ordinary Diet session, it was a foregone conclusion that there would be a showdown between Satō and Ikeda in the election for party president to be held at the extraordinary party convention scheduled for July 10. General Council Chairman Fujiyama also tendered his resignation and announced his own candidacy.

After Ikeda had made clear his intention with the words, "I'm certainly going ahead with it," Ōhira lamented to a reporter friend, "I am not in favor of a third term, but so long as he says he'll do it, we'll have to go along with it. But it's an expensive ticket." In fact, Ōhira helped at this crucial stage to garner support for Ikeda from financial circles. But he was no longer the chief campaign organizer as he had been four years before.

Besides Ikeda's own faction, his other supporters in the election for party president tended to belong to the factions led by career party politicians (Kōno, Miki, Kawashima, and the late Ōno) rather than those led by former bureaucrats. Strangely enough, Ikeda's former political rivals were now his allies, and he was being opposed by Satō, who had been his greatest ally at the start of his administration. On the surface, Ikeda was ahead, but complacency was unwarranted as there was known to be a secret "*ninja* (spy) corps" of Satō supporters among the factions supporting Ikeda.

Ikeda felt sure that he would "settle things at one stroke," and, in fact, expected to win a twenty-vote absolute majority in the first vote. The Satō strategy was to prevent a majority vote for Ikeda on the first ballot, in which case Satō hoped to win by as much as a ten-vote majority in the runoff vote. As it turned out, of the total 478 votes cast (3 of which were invalid), 242 went to Ikeda Hayato, 160 to Satō Eisaku, 72 to Fujiyama Aiichirō, and 1 to non-candidate Nadao Hirokichi. The votes for Ikeda were only 4 more than an absolute majority and only 10 more than the votes for Satō and Fujiyama combined. Ikeda was heard to grumble that it was "a close call" and sensed that his time at the nation's helm was coming to an end. Political veteran Matsumura Kenzō, one of his supporters, tried to cheer him with the old Japanese saying, "Though just a single flower is in bloom, it is a flower all the same."

Immediately after being elected to a third term as party president, Ikeda set to work on personnel changes. The task was made especially difficult because of the sharp lines that had been drawn between friend and foe in the election. A central role in planning this reorganization was played by Maeo. Although for health reasons he had made it clear that he did not personally want to continue in a party or cabinet post, he tried, in consultation with Ikeda, to bring about a stable administration, arguing that it would not be wise to lean too far in favor of Kōno Ichirō (who had given important support in the election) and thus push the Satō camp, which had support from nearly a majority of the Dietmen, into a non-mainstream posture. He advocated, in other words, a balance between the Kōno and Satō forces.

Thus, he established a scheme for giving preference to the Satō faction in cabinet posts, while favoring career politicians for party posts. As his own successor as secretary-general, Maeo proposed Policy Research Council Chairman Miki Takeo, who had not long before submitted a proposal on party modernization and the dissolution of factions. Prime Minister Ikeda followed Maeo's suggestion, with the following proviso: "I'll be party president for the next two years, but it will be enough if Miki serves just one year." As a mainstay of the Ikeda Administration, Ōhira hoped that he might himself later have the post of secretary-general, which had been filled at the outset of the Ikeda Administration by Masutani Shūji and then by Maeo, both members of the Ikeda faction. In this, however, Ōhira was disappointed.

The major party posts were finally designated as follows: Kawashima as vice-president, Miki as secretary-general, Nakamura Umekichi as General Council chairman, and Sutō Hideo as Policy Research Council chairman. In the new cabinet, Tanaka Kakuei and Akagi Munenori were kept as finance and agriculture ministers, respectively, while Construction Minister Kōno Ichirō was switched to the post of deputy prime minister, carrying the rank of a minister of state. Otherwise the cabinet was one of new faces. For a while it had seemed fairly certain that Maeo, who had served three years as party secretary-general, would, in spite of his poor health, be brought into the cabinet as finance minister. However, Maeo at the last minute declined the position, and thus it continued to be filled by Tanaka, who belonged to the Satō faction. Another Satō faction member, Aichi Kiichi, was made minister of international trade and industry, the appointment being symbolic of a restoration of relations with the Satō faction.

About thirty minutes after the decision had been made to appoint Aichi, Satō telephoned Ikeda at the Prime Minister's Official Residence thanking him for his consideration. It was during this reorganization that Suzuki Zenkō, until then the party's senior deputy secretary-general, was chosen as chief cabinet secretary, replacing Kurogane, who was left out of the new cabinet. Also left out were Ikeda's two other former secretaries, namely, Foreign Minister Ōhira and Economic Planning Agency Director-General Miyazawa. Ōhira was given the party post of senior deputy secretary-general, in which capacity he was to assist Secretary-General Miki Takeo.

When asked at a press conference about his aspirations upon being appointed senior deputy secretary-general, Ōhira stated, "It is my first party post, which is all the more reason to have some sort of new feeling. Unlike government administration, a party job means searching for possibilities and, as such, is a real art." Kaya Okinori, who had been one of Ōhira's mentors in the Finance Ministry and was a former finance minister himself, offered some tongue-in-cheek praise: "You are really to be admired. It's truly something the way you quietly accepted this post and are working without complaint." However, the fact that Ōhira was not given the post of secretary-general greatly affected his subsequent political life and contributed to his having to follow a roundabout path. His career, which had been borne on an upward current ever since his entry into politics, had now entered a long winter.

At this juncture, Ōhira's misfortune was compounded by the tragic death of his eldest son, Masaki, on August 6, 1964, less than a month after the formation of the Third Ikeda Cabinet. Masaki had been born in Yokohama on February 6, 1938, when his father was head of the Yokohama Tax Office. In 1960, he had graduated from Keiō University and began working for Kanzaki Paper Company. As he explained it, two years later his father, "giving his own reasons, arranged to have them release me from this employment." Ōhira was thinking of Masaki one day beginning a career in politics and so had encouraged him to give up his job before getting too set in the routine of company life, and hoped to work closely with him as he continued to develop his talents and abilities.

Masaki made a plan to travel to forty-two countries beginning in July 1962, and first went to Hawaii and then traveled for two months in North and South America. He met his father in New York in September when Ōhira, as foreign minister, was there to address the United Nations General Assembly. He then accompanied his father on his European tour and, on parting in Amsterdam, continued by himself. His health problem was first noticed in Vienna, Austria, where he felt difficulty in walking.

After returning to Japan in the spring of 1963, Masaki was visiting the home of his relatives, the Moritas, in Sakaide, Shikoku, when Mrs. Morita, who was an ophthalmologist, discovered some bleeding inside one eye. He later entered the Tokyo University Hospital, where he was diagnosed as suffering from a difficult illness known as Behcet's Disease. He was given all sorts of treatment, including *shiatsu* massage, but before long he lost the sight of his right eye and suffered nerve impairment in his arms and legs. The disease continued its relentless attack until midsummer, 1964, when on the evening of August 6 Masaki said to his younger brother, Akira, who was at his bedside, "I am going on a trip, so please get my shoes ready." Without saying anything else, his twenty-six-year life came to close. Ordinarily known for staying calm and collected and never appearing distraught, Ōhira did not try to hide his grief. Many came to offer condolences, including Prime Minister Ikeda and former Secretary-General Maeo, and each time Ōhira only said, "Thank you," in a choked voice.

Masaki's cremated remains were deposited in Tama Reien Cemetery. Because he had adopted the Christian name of Paulo Miki, a young boy who had been killed in the early seventeenth century for refusing to recant his Christian faith, Ōhira inscribed on the memorial stone, "PAULO MIKI ŌHIRA MASAKI," together with his signature: "Father and friend, Ōhira Masayoshi."

Hardly had Ōhira recovered from the grief of losing his eldest son than he had to face the illness of Prime Minister Ikeda. Ikeda himself had been aware of an unusual hoarseness in his voice ever since the general election in the autumn of 1963. His voice had always been rather husky, however, and if it had become strained while making campaign speeches, neither he nor those around him paid it any particular attention. He had tried to mitigate the hoarseness by gargling and taking medicines, yet there was a certain pain that never seemed to go away.

One day, after election to his third term as party president, Ikeda was eating *kanten*, a gelatinlike dessert made from seaweed, during a luncheon meeting. He remarked to his secretaries, "This has a nice feeling because it slides so easily down the throat." Taking the advice of a number of people who felt that this remark might be more significant than intended, he agreed to undergo a thorough physical examination. A specialist from the Tokyo University Hospital's Ear, Nose and Throat Department, a specialist from the Jikei Medical College, and Dr. Hiki Yoshisato, president of the National Cancer Center, all came to the same conclusion: the prime minister had unmistakable symptoms of cancer of the larynx. Dr. Hiki, who was the physician in charge and happened to be a relative of Ōhira's wife, telephoned Ōhira at home the evening after the examination, saying that the condition appeared cancerous and that the prime minister would have to be admitted to a hospital for treatment as quickly as possible.

For Ōhira, this was an enormous shock, and he was sure that the diagnosis should not be communicated either to Ikeda, his family, or to the world at large. After consulting with Maeo, Ōhira decided for the time being to tell Ikeda that because there was a danger the malady could destroy the throat cartilage he should undergo radiation therapy, and that he should have these treatments at the Cancer Center because the needed facilities were not available at the Tokyo University Hospital. Ikeda waited until he had given a speech before the 19th Annual Meeting of the International Monetary Fund at the Hotel Ōkura on September 7 before beginning treatment at the Cancer Center on September 9. Ōhira recollects: "It was the genuine feeling of myself and others near him that we were in a serious situation. And at that moment, although we didn't put it into words, we were aware of the great problems that would be caused by any end of the current administration. While there was no way to know Ikeda's innermost thoughts, on the surface he was quite calm and readily consented to enter the center for treatment."

From this time on, various persons close to Ikeda were engaged in difficult decisions, the details of which could not be openly acknowledged. Maeo and Ōhira were most concerned over how to explain the prime minister's hospitalization and malady to the general public. If it were plainly stated that the illness was cancer, it would get into the newspapers, and if it were in the newspapers, Ikeda himself would know. The political situation would become unsettled and would most likely cast a shadow over the Tokyo Olympic Games, which were just about to get under way. Thus Maeo and Ōhira inconspicuously met with the National Cancer Center's president, Dr. Hiki, and its hospital director, Dr. Kuru Masaru, requesting: "We want you to keep the fact that it is cancer absolutely secret and to say something different. Although this will surely go against a physician's conscience, we will later make a full apology to the nation." On September 25, it was announced that the prime minister had a "precancerous condition."

The announcement of this condition—which was said to be not cancer though it might develop in that direction—was a delicate matter, but was accepted within the party with relative calm as it seemed to mean that there was little likelihood of a change in administration. However, Deputy Secretary-General Ōhira's premonition of a change in administration was making him increasingly preoccupied with the question of how to handle this eventuality. Among other moves, he telephoned Secretary-General Miki Takeo, then resting in the mountain resort of Karuizawa, requesting that he return to Tokyo.

As the radiation therapy progressed and the pain subsided, Prime Minister Ikeda wanted to get back to his full-time schedule. However, his condition had not truly made a turn for the better. Although it was fortunate that public attention was focused on the Olympic Games that were to open on October 10, Ōhira expected that sooner or later attention would be directed to the question of whether the prime minister would remain in office or step down. He has written: "At first glance, the situation seemed to be progressing smoothly. . . . However, the grave fact that a prime minister in office was in the hospital undergoing treatment was a reality that could not be hidden. The heavy responsibilities borne by the prime minister at home and abroad could not be laid aside, and it was only natural that there should be a limit to the public's sympathy and generosity. The anxiety of those close to him increased daily in a sort of inverse ratio to the calmness of the outer environment. An important decision was going to be necessary."

Nothing could be more difficult than to request the resignation of a prime minister who was still unaware he was afflicted with cancer. Concentrating on what would seem to be the optimum strategy, Maeo and Ōhira decided to have the prime minister's resignation announced on Sunday, October 25, the day following the close of the Olympic Games. Thus, between October 16 and October 20, they would need to secure the prime minister's agreement to give up his post.

Prime Minister Ikeda and his wife, Mitsue, had been present at the opening ceremonies for the Olympic Games on October 10, but a few days later Dr. Hiki advised the prime minister that it would be impossible for him to attend the extraordinary Diet session in November or the ordinary Diet session the following year and that he might best consider resigning immediately after the Olympics. When Ikeda asked if it would not be all right to stay in office if he "were willing to die on the job," Dr. Hiki replied, "As a doctor, I cannot recommend that." Ikeda then asked, "Who, after all, put you up to this?" The doctor answered, "Maeo and Ōhira. I don't think anyone else has been informed about it." Ikeda then said straightforwardly, "I see. Since it is they who are involved, I'll let them take care of it." On October 20, he made the definite decision to resign.

A memo remains that was written by Ōhira around this time. Next to the main entries for October 25 (the day the resignation was to be announced) and October 26 are additional notations that are underlined and accompanied by circles and "X" marks, suggesting the hurried circumstances in which they were written. The draft of Ikeda's announcement for October 25 is concisely stated in five sections in Ōhira's handwriting. As for the proposed order of procedure, the memo reads:

> October 25: Announcement of general diagnosis of illness. Call in Kawashima, Miki, Kōno, Suzuki (make decision clear; question of whether to install deputy prime minister; discussion of prime minister's speech to the people), announcement of prime minister's speech to the people.
> October 26: 10 o'clock, party officers meeting: four officers, secretary-general, directives for handling, noon emergency officers meeting.

A line is drawn from "10 o'clock" to the notation "extraordinary cabinet meeting—until succeeding prime minister decided upon, no interruption of government activities. Cooperation of all in handling situation." At the side of "directives for handling" is the notation: "(1) Succeeding party president through negotiations; (2) for negotiations, Kawashima and Miki play leading roles; (3) for time being, keep present setup; (4) with main emphasis on established bodies, proceed with discussion by main party officers, General Council, advisory board made up of members of both houses of Diet, and meetings with other advisers, then final approval by all party members of both houses." In front of Kawashima's name under item (1), the two Chinese characters for "Kōno" had been written in but later crossed out. Next to item (2) were two circular marks and the two Chinese characters meaning "to be appointed," probably indicating appointment by Prime Minister Ikeda.

The five-part draft of Ikeda's statement on his decision to step down was as follows: "(1) Since entering the hospital I have been doing my best to have my illness treated, and up to now things have been going smoothly; however, it will still take five months before I will be able to endure hard work; (2) the international situation is witnessing rapid change, and at home we will have the extraordinary Diet session, the drawing up of the budget, and the next ordinary Diet session, and it is not possible for me to attend to my government responsibilities in this state of health; (3) thus, at this time I shall resign and wish to have a new party president chosen and to have domestic and foreign matters handled in a forthright way with party unity under his leadership; (4) I should like to ask approval of my wish to resign and should like to ask the particular assistance of the vice-president and the secretary-general in choosing the new party president; and (5) it is desirable that, if possible, the new party president be chosen through negotiations and that there be a brisk, harmonious, and considerate handling of the situation, with the utmost effort made to avoid a reorganization of the present party and governmental setup."

In the prime minister's speech on October 25, points (4) and (5) above were not touched upon because they concerned intraparty affairs and might appear to make the statement as a whole overladen with demands by the prime minister in the choice of his successor. In its final form, Ikeda's speech announcing his decision began with: "Over one month has passed since I entered the hospital, but doctors are requesting that I undergo treatment for a much longer time. I have decided to resign my position as prime minister." It ended with the words: "I express my gratitude to every one of the nation's people, who have been unstinting in their support and encouragement in spite of my many shortcomings."

Ōhira has recalled that day as follows: "At two o'clock, Ikeda had summoned to the hospital, from the government side, State Minister Kōno and Chief Cabinet Secretary Suzuki and, from the party side, Vice-President Kawashima, Secretary-General Miki, and myself. He expressed appreciation for what he called sincere cooperation in spite of inconveniences caused by his hospitalization. He stated calmly that he had decided to step down for the purpose of avoiding an interregnum vacuum or political turmoil. Then he asked that his successor be selected smoothly at the earliest possible date through negotiations under the guidance of the party leadership, in particular, Kawashima and Miki. At the same time, he requested the representatives from the government side to lend their full support to this work of the party leadership, to which everyone readily assented."

Thus, the Ikeda Administration, which had begun in July 1960, when it had to restore order to politics in the wake of the security treaty turmoil, in effect drew to a close in October 1964. What role in Japan's postwar history had these four years and three months played? Needless to say, its greatest role was in building the foundations of Japan's present-day prosperity through the National Income-Doubling Plan, which quickly brought calm and stability to sensitivities badly bruised during the security treaty crisis and provided a focus for people's energies. Seen in the long-term perspective, its importance could be said to lie in having led the Japanese people through a cathartic period of frustrated nationalism, during which there was still a widespread feeling of subordination to the United States, to a stage where they set new goals of their own. After the announcement of the Income-Doubling Plan, the real economic growth rate in fiscal 1962 was only 5.7 percent, or less than anticipated; but the growth rates for fiscal 1961 and 1963 were higher than planned, at 14.4 percent and 12.9 percent, respectively, and the goals of the ten-year plan would be attained in only seven years. This pace of growth greatly encouraged the Japanese people, most of whom had at first been doubtful about the plan, and nurtured a widespread willingness to put unstinting effort into improving their standard of living. This, in turn, greatly helped to establish firm grounds for entry into the international family of nations.

Of course, such unprecedented economic growth was not brought about by any single statesman or any single policy. In particular, we must not forget the activities of the new stratum of business managers and entrepreneurs who had appeared after the war, helped by the temporary purge of many veteran business and financial leaders from their former positions. These new business leaders in many cases had more than ten years of experience before the beginning of the Ikeda Administration and were thus approaching a period of maturity. They were of the same generation as the group of bureaucrats and politicians around Ikeda, which bound them all the more closely together. And together they were willing to look beyond old ways of thinking and behavior and to embrace the rising wave of worldwide technological innovation. The Japanese people were strongly attracted by this dynamism that could change ideals into realities and became gradually estranged from the arid theoretical formulations still being advocated by the opposition parties.

This was the period that saw the widespread adoption of the so-called Japanese style of management, coordinating for common purposes the worlds of politics, administration, finance, and labor. It meant that a new type of community was being created among the Japanese people as they became divorced from old ties based on kinship or geography. Indeed, this new type of community was beginning to exercise a strong centripetal force. However, it was only natural that all these rapid changes would have various side effects. In particular, there were the growing problems of pollution, and, in a society that gave precedence to economic prosperity, the concentration of industry and population in the cities and the resulting trend toward smaller, nuclear families brought many changes in values, seen throughout society, that came to be widely discussed under the name of "the phenomena of alienation" (*sogaika genshō*).

Ikeda seems to have felt that, just as economic growth was helped by the National Income-Doubling Plan, these problems of alienation should be solved through some sort of policy. He had made his "people-building policy" a key slogan in his campaign for election to a third term as party president, and set up a large advisory council to make preparatory recommendations. However, his vision of what "people-building" consisted of was not as clear as his plan for income-doubling, and it was unable to attract the same degree of public enthusiasm.

Prime Minister Ikeda's announcement of his intention to step down suddenly brought political circles into frenzied preoccupation with choosing a new party president. Both inside and outside the LDP, three candidates were considered likely: Satō Eisaku, Kōno Ichirō, and Fujiyama Aiichirō. If this situation was unresolved, there was the danger that the LDP might split into three streams, making things even more confused than during the party presidential election three months earlier.

At the time he publicly announced his decision to step down, Ikeda told LDP Vice-President Kawashima and Secretary-General Miki, "I want the next party president chosen smoothly, at the earliest possible date, and through negotiations." Miki suggested: "As in the recent change of administration within the British Conservative Party—in other words, the transition from Harold Macmillan, who resigned because of illness, to Sir Alec Douglas-Home—it would be appropriate for you, as party president, to make the nomination." Kawashima expressed agreement, and the idea thus took shape that ultimately Prime Minister Ikeda should choose his own successor.

October 25, 1964, the day of the public announcement of Ikeda's intention to step down, was the beginning of two very tense weeks before November 9, the date set for a final decision on Ikeda's successor. Ōhira writes as follows: "The main actors were Kawashima Shōjirō and Miki Takeo. My task was liaison and communication between Ikeda and these two. . . . To assure that the work [of choosing the next president] would be carried out by this leadership team and it alone . . . was the way to preserve party unity and to respond to people's faith in politics. . . . If this should fail, I feared that the ailing prime minister in the Cancer Center would himself be put in the forefront of negotiations, which could imperil his very life."

Satō, Kōno, and Fujiyama each felt himself to be the strongest candidate; each was sure he would be nominated by Prime Minister Ikeda. Beginning October 26, supporters of all three began to make spirited overtures to the mainstream Ikeda faction and to the appointed negotiators Kawashima and Miki. Each group of supporters had a set of claims. First, the Satō camp expected considerable influence to be exercised by former Prime Minister Yoshida, mentor of both Satō and Ikeda. Also the long personal acquaintance between Satō and Ikeda, dating back to their days as students at the Fifth Higher School in Kumamoto, Kyūshū, could not be ignored. Then, too, there was the undeniable fact that Satō had come second in the party presidential election three months previously. These points were recognized by a great many persons in business and financial circles, who tended to support Satō. Second, the Kōno camp had given its full support to Ikeda during the latter half of his administration and had contributed greatly to the success of his policies and to Ikeda's success in the third presidential election. Ikeda himself thought highly of this cooperation and had expressed his appreciation. The fact that both Kawashima and Miki were party men was also seen by Kōno's supporters as favoring their candidate. Kawashima, in particular, disliked Satō but had a good opinion of Kōno. Third, the Fujiyama camp had not given its all-out cooperation in the Ikeda Administration, but nevertheless was banking on a good possibility of benefiting from the others' lack of accord, given the deeply opposing views on certain issues between Satō and Kōno and the still unforgiven resentments between Satō and Ikeda in the wake of the party presidential election.

In the meantime, apart from the maneuvers of these three camps, four in-between factions without candidates of their own—namely, the Kawashima, Miki, Ikeda, and former Ōno factions—got together to advocate supporting one or another of the three candidates. The Ikeda faction at one point seemed especially restless as Maeo and other members made anti-Satō moves and indicated that they might seriously consider an administration led by Fujiyama.

Various feelers were put out by the Satō camp to try to influence Ikeda and those around him, like Kawashima and Miki. Ikeda's mentor, former Prime Minister Yoshida, made frequent trips from Ōiso to Tokyo to promote, before the two negotiators and the leadership of the Ikeda faction, the concept of a Satō succession. Mutual friends of Ikeda and Satō, some going back to their Fifth Higher School days, went back and forth between the two. Many members of business and financial circles made assertions to the effect that "the only way to assure the stable continuation of a conservative administration is the smooth transition of power from Ikeda to Satō."

Tanaka Kakuei, who was then one of the leaders of the Satō faction and had also been for many years a close friend of Ōhira's, came to the prime minister's hospital room for discussions immediately after Ikeda's announcement of his impending resignation, and also, on repeated occasions, approached Ōhira on the matter of realizing a Satō succession. Tanaka has written: "When I entered Ikeda's room at the Cancer Center, he looked me closely in the face and said somewhat unexpectedly, 'Just a while ago Kōno Ichirō was here to see me and has just left.'. . . Again he asked tartly, 'Who are we going to make my successor?'. . . Looking directly into Prime Minister Ikeda's eyes, I said clearly and simply, 'It is going to be Satō Eisaku.'. . . Looking straight at me, Prime Minister Ikeda gave only a grunt that he had understood what I'd said, and lay down. . . . I said, 'Tell this only to Ōhira,' and left."

Ōhira later acknowledged having been approached by Tanaka: "It is true that there was talk from Tanaka about putting Satō in power and strong requests that this be realized. I responded by telling him, 'Leave this question alone, and please don't make any awkward moves. Things in this world must be allowed to settle as they will, and so while I understand the Satō faction's desire to put Satō in power, please keep a lid on any ostentatious behavior.'. . . Tanaka said he understood, and thereafter, so far as I could tell, the activities of the Satō faction became very circumspect." Ōhira's thinking was that so long as no great intraparty turmoil was caused by the various factional rivalries, the overall situation would be settled in the most natural way—in other words, there would be a smooth closing of the Ikeda Administration and, with agreement on permitting Ikeda to name his own successor, Satō would be named for the post.

In contrast with the Satō camp, the Kōno and Fujiyama factions were active in very obvious ways. When confronted with information from persons close to Ikeda that it seemed most likely Satō would be nominated by the prime minister, Kōno and Fujiyama rapidly closed ranks and on November 4 concluded a Kōno–Fujiyama covenant according to which, if either were selected as party president, the other would cooperate fully in the new administration.

Fujiyama had been encouraged by the fact that Ikeda had grasped his hand and told him, "I want you to think seriously about what is to come." But more than anything else he had been encouraged by the fact that former Secretary-General Maeo, who was one of Prime Minister Ikeda's closest friends, had indicated that he was favorable to Fujiyama's candidacy. In an interview for a book of Fujiyama's memoirs, Maeo stated: "Within the party there was the danger that with either Satō or Kōno the party might split. Prime Minister Ikeda called Secretary-General Miki and Deputy Secretary-General Ōhira to his hospital room and told them, 'I want you to think about Fujiyama, too.' This was my thinking as well. I felt that we should propose Fujiyama and then back him up in every way we could. Kōno was disliked, had a rather officious air about him, and was not very well thought of in business and financial circles. A plan to unite behind Fujiyama was never very specific, but it seems that those outside the Kōno faction felt that if Kōno was going to persist, they would be more comfortable with Fujiyama."

For Ōhira, who had been working behind the scenes for Satō's nomination in the process of the negotiations being carried on by Kawashima and Miki and had strongly advised the Satō faction to be circumspect, the above-mentioned Kōno–Fujiyama agreement was quite unexpected. And it was now evident that within the Ikeda faction were two separate currents, represented by Maeo and Ōhira.

As soon as he was informed of the Kōno–Fujiyama agreement, Ōhira called on former Secretary-General Maeo and demanded, "Ikeda has asked Kawashima and Miki from the party leadership [to act as mediators], and so I want the Ikeda faction to stick scrupulously to an attitude of waiting calmly for their mediation. Therefore, please break off all other action." At the same time, Ōhira visited the Kōno faction's office and berated the Kōno–Fujiyama scheme to faction leaders Sonoda Sunao and Shigemasa Seishi: "Japan's politics depend on a stable arrangement between the two forces around Kōno and Satō. It is important that there be two clearly defined centers of an ellipse. What is all this that I've been hearing about your considering, in talks with Fujiyama, the possibility of stepping down from your position [at one of these two centers]? Wouldn't it be a bit too naive?" In Ōhira's view, talk of a Kōno–Fujiyama coalition was a maneuver that tended to split the party, and, just as he had criticized actions by the Satō faction that might highlight intraparty rivalries, he probably felt that any such tendency was undesirable in light of ongoing efforts at mediation.

During this period, only two persons could freely enter Prime Minister Ikeda's room at the Cancer Center: Chief Cabinet Secretary Suzuki Zenkō from the government side and Deputy Secretary-General Ōhira from the party side. Ōhira spent two or three hours a day in Ikeda's room and kept the prime minister company, chatting about various, mainly nonpolitical, subjects. Ōhira recalls: "Every day I first of all looked at the prime minister's face and then checked on other aspects of his situation, such as whether his physical and mental condition was stable, who had visited him, and who had telephoned him. Then I reported on what mediators Kawashima and Miki were doing. Thus, I kept a very objective position, and therefore no proper names ever came up between me and Ikeda. This I can vow before God."

Although Ōhira testifies that he never tried to win Ikeda's support for any particular candidate as successor, Tanaka Kakuei of the Satō camp anxiously approached Ōhira on several occasions after Ōhira had advised him to play down overt campaigning. Tanaka recollects: "[When I went to Satō's office in Tameike], Satō was waiting alone. The door was closed and he wore a rather severe expression. At first, he said only, 'It's definite, isn't it?' I replied, 'There's no reason it shouldn't be.' He then said, 'Call Ōhira just to make sure,' and I picked up the telephone and called the Sakaeya, where I expected Ōhira to be, and had him brought to the phone. When I said, 'I know it's impolite, but Satō has just asked me to phone to check with you about whether there might have been any changes,' his voice answered clearly, 'There has been absolutely no change.' When I checked with Satō about whether he wanted to talk on the phone, he said, 'No, it's all right,' and began walking over to the window. So I said, 'Thank you. See you soon,' and hung up."

The two mediators Kawashima and Miki became very actively involved, first of all in hearing the opinions of Lower House Speaker Funada Naka, Upper House President Shigemune Yūzō, the chairmen and vice-chairmen of the various party organs, and other party veterans, as well as junior Dietmen who had been elected only once or twice, and then in holding separate talks with the three aspirants, Satō, Kōno, and Fujiyama. Most of the party veterans told the mediators they wished Ikeda to appoint his successor. Former Prime Minister Ishibashi was an exception in that he explicitly said he felt "Satō to be the most appropriate."

November 9 was fast approaching. On the evening of November 8, the two mediators invited the three candidates to the Palace Hotel, where they informed them: "We want you to leave it up to us. And whoever is chosen as the next party president, we want to have the matter handled in a way consistent with party unity." To this the three aspirants gave their consent. On November 8, Ōhira also told Prime Minister Ikeda in his room: "Tomorrow is the day to name your successor. Tomorrow morning Kawashima, Miki, and the two of us [Ōhira and Suzuki] will come here. You will have to make your nomination." When Ōhira said that Kawashima and Miki would probably make such-and-such a report, Ikeda complained: "Then doesn't that mean there is no unified opinion? That's a bad sign. I told you to come back with a unified opinion." Ōhira replied: "No, we are totally unified. Don't you see that we've reached agreement that ultimately the matter should be decided by the party president? Because we've agreed on this, we're quite unified. There is nothing to be anxious about." Having said this, Ōhira left the hospital room. That evening, Ōhira wrote out a statement, leaving blank only a space for Ikeda to fill in the appropriate name the next morning.

At 7 A.M. on the day of the nomination, November 9, Kawashima and Miki entered the hospital room. With Deputy Secretary-General Ōhira and Chief Cabinet Secretary Suzuki in attendance, they made a concise report to Ikeda on the progress of their mediation efforts. After both Kawashima and Miki reported that the majority supported Satō, they ended by saying, "We await the party president's nomination." Ikeda said, "It's too bad for Kōno, but Satō will do best as my successor." Then, with thick strokes, he wrote in the four characters for Satō Eisaku on the statement prepared in advance by Ōhira. It was a little after 7:20 A.M.

As the LDP Joint Plenary Meeting of Party Members of Both Houses of the Diet, which would formally approve Satō as the new party president, was to start at 10 A.M., Kawashima, Miki, Ōhira, and Suzuki had planned to leave Ikeda's hospital room at 9 A.M. They whiled away the time chatting with Ikeda, deliberately avoiding politics. Ōhira was most worried about the possible reaction of members of the Kōno and Fujiyama camps at the morning meeting and at the plenary session of the Lower House, scheduled for 1 P.M., which was to formally name the next prime minister. However, he was relieved when he happened to encounter Mori Kiyoshi, a leader of the Kōno faction, in the entrance hall of the party headquarters a little before 10 A.M. Mori, who had already learned of Ikeda's decision, told Ōhira, "Well, we lost out. But we will gladly cooperate. All of us will attend the plenary session and cast our votes for the nominee for prime minister." At the meeting of all LDP members from both houses Satō was uneventfully elected as the new president of the party.

In the afternoon plenary session, soon after Kōno had taken his seat, Ōhira came up to him and lowered his head, saying, "Really, we caused you much trouble." Kōno replied, "Oh well, it's all right. Today the Kōno faction members are all in attendance, you know. And we are all going to write 'Satō Eisaku,' so you may put your mind at ease."

After Satō had been duly named prime minister by both houses, Ōhira returned to Ikeda's room at the Cancer Center. Although Ikeda, now a former prime minister, had already heard most of the news on television, Ōhira told him: "I am happy to report that the closing ceremony for your administration was completed smoothly. Today's *highlight* [original English] was Kōno. If Kōno and the Kōno faction had not acted as they did, this closing ceremony could have been a nasty affair. So I think we should be grateful to Kōno and his faction. In politics, it's, of course, nice to take over an administration, yet Kōno's behavior today is surely something to be admired." Ikeda listened with tears in his eyes and then nodded silently when Ōhira said, "This November 9 has been for you, and also for me, the best day in our lives, I think."

Two years later, Ōhira wrote: "The two weeks between October 25 and November 9 were like being in a tub of very hot water. It was a historic period, full of tension and seeming longer than it was in reality." In 1978, he described it thus: "It had truly been a very, very long two weeks. The elusive genie of political power wandered disconsolately between the Cancer Center in Tsukiji and LDP headquarters in Hirakawachō, seeking a resting place." It was a genie from whose grasp Ikeda had now managed to escape.

The new Satō Administration started off with the same party leadership and cabinet members as its predecessor. However, Chief Cabinet Secretary Suzuki Zenkō soon tendered his resignation, explaining, "A prime minister and his chief cabinet secretary must be of one mind." Prime Minister Satō consented and named Hashimoto Tomisaburō to replace him. Then, for a rather similar reason, Ōhira gave up his post of senior deputy secretary-general to Setoyama Mitsuo of the Satō faction, and for a time became free of all responsibilities of party or government positions other than those of being a member of the Lower House.

Chapter 17

A Time for Contemplation

At New Year 1965, in an essay with the classical sounding title *"Wazawai wa tokui ni umare, fuku wa inbi ni sodatsu"* (Misfortune is born in times of pride, while fortune is nurtured in adversity) published in the newsletter that was sent to readers in the Second Electoral District of Kagawa, Ōhira wrote: "All in all, last year was a momentous year for me. It was a dark year, but it was also an important year. My eldest son, Masaki, died on August 6, and then, in rapid succession, such unexpected events followed as former Prime Minister Ikeda's hospitalization on September 9, his resignation on October 25, the end of the Ikeda Administration, and the beginning of the Satō Administration on November 9. It was a year when I was constantly trying to keep up with the changing scene."

In the same essay he referred to the type of mental attitude one should maintain in such circumstances: "What we call 'time' is curiously structured. If there are times when it flows smoothly, without faltering, like a river, there are also times when it goes berserk in a fierce, turbulent rush. One who poles in the currents at such a time must try to make no error, to be completely alert, and to act as if he had faith in divine guidance. In any case, we must keep in mind that misfortune mostly occurs when we are prideful or complacent, while good fortune, almost without exception, grows and is nurtured in periods of adversity."

On August 13, 1965, approximately one year after Masaki's death, former Prime Minister Ikeda Hayato died. After leaving the hospital on December 2 of the previous year, Ikeda had continued to convalesce at home. His progress had been good, to the extent that the Cancer Center's director, Dr. Kuru, issued a report of "complete recovery" in March 1965. Greatly relieved, Ikeda attended a party to celebrate this hosted by business and financial leaders, and at one point planned to make a trip to his birthplace in Hiroshima Prefecture.

In July, Ikeda attended the funeral of Kōno Ichirō (once Ikeda's ablest rival but also at times a source of cooperation), who suddenly died of a dissecting aneurysm. Ikeda seemed genuinely saddened and was heard to say, "It is surely a great pity." Soon after Kōno's funeral, during a periodic check-up on July 16, it was discovered that the laryngeal cancer had reappeared. The diagnosis made by his doctors was: "If the patient leaves things as they are, it will be very painful. If he undergoes an operation now, while he has the physical and mental stamina, he should be able to live for a year." Thus, on July 29, Ikeda entered the Tokyo University Hospital, where he underwent an operation on August 4.

The doctors' pronouncement was: "The operation was successful. Now we have only to wait for the recovery of physical strength." Ikeda's condition worsened, however, and he remained comatose until his death at 12:25 P.M. on August 13. For Ōhira, the death of Ikeda, who had acted as a father and elder brother throughout his career in the Ministry of Finance and in the world of politics, brought an indescribable desolation. He made no attempt to hide his sense of loss and dismay: "Anything and everything was distasteful. I had lost my desire for living."

Already in November 1964, after the succession to political power had been completed, Ikeda had summoned Maeo, telling him he wanted him to take over the chairmanship of the Kōchikai whenever Ikeda might leave the scene. Maeo was himself in poor health and was unsure of his ability to attract funds, so he had at first hesitated to accept, but since it was a personal request, he told Ikeda he would comply. To head the Kōchikai meant having a good chance of becoming party president and prime minister. Maeo, feeling that the recovery of his health was his first priority, underwent a successful operation in February 1965 that cured his chronic pleuritis.

On Ikeda's death, the Kōchikai came to have Maeo as its leader, with party veteran Sutō Hideo in the auxiliary post of "representative manager" (*daihyō sewanin*). Before his operation, Ikeda had called Maeo, Ōhira, and Suzuki to his bedside to pass on his wishes in the event he did not survive. It had always been customary for party factions to be formed around individual political figures and to be dissolved or reorganized if that individual should die or otherwise leave the political world. In this sense, the continuation of the Kōchikai after Ikeda's death was the first example in the LDP's history of inheriting a faction, and as such there were naturally many difficulties. Rifts in the Kōchikai, already evident in the last days of the Ikeda Administration, were becoming more noticeable, and the old unity between Maeo and Ōhira no longer existed. This was an unfortunate start for the post-Ikeda Kōchikai, and was so felt by both Ōhira, who had earlier been very fond of Maeo, whom he had always regarded as an elder brother, and by Maeo, who had always been fond of Ōhira, treating him as a younger brother. This situation might be regarded as a stroke of luck for Prime Minister Satō, as schisms in the most powerful opposing faction could only insure the stability of his own faction. A difficult time lay ahead for both Maeo and Ōhira, and the Kōchikai as a whole.

Ōhira recorded some of his feelings at this time in a publication put out by his local support group in Kagawa Prefecture: "In a person's life there is both joy and sadness. If there are mornings of pride in one's accomplishments, there are evenings of gloom about disappointed expectations. If there are times for basking in glory, there are also situations where one must endure insult." Around this time Ōhira was often heard to remark, "Life is sunny days and days that are overcast," borrowing the phrase from the title of an Osaragi Jirō novel, *Teru hi, kumoru hi* (Sunny Days, Cloudy Days).

In the meantime, in June 1965, already eight months into his administration, Prime Minister Satō put together his own cabinet for the first time. He decided against including Kōno Ichirō, who then had the greatest influence in the party, but gave consideration, for example, to the former Ikeda faction by appointing two of its members, Maeo Shigesaburō as LDP General Council chairman and Suzuki Zenkō as minister of health and welfare. The deaths in the summer of 1965 of Kōno and Ikeda had meant the splintering of the factions they had headed, with the result that forces within the LDP that might raise a banner of opposition to Satō were disappearing. Therefore, a key to Satō's control of the party was a skillful balance between forces that had once been aligned with the former Kishi and Yoshida factions.

In the reorganization on July 29, 1966, Ōhira was appointed vice-chairman of the party's Research Commission on Foreign Policy, which was a position without any well-defined responsibilities. Compared to Ōhira's weakened political position, Tanaka Kakuei's career was advancing by leaps and bounds. He was becoming a pillar of the Satō Administration, and in the cabinet reorganization of July 1966 he was switched from the post of finance minister to party secretary-general. At the time of this reorganization, Tanaka, who had been given a mandate by Prime Minister Satō to take charge of party matters, had asked Ōhira to accept the post of Policy Research Council chairman. Ōhira replied with some surprise, "I am grateful for your consideration, but is it really all right with the fellow upstairs?"

Quite as Ōhira had suspected, the prime minister vetoed the idea, and Ōhira remained outside the top political arena. In spite of his usually cool way of reacting to things, Ōhira seems to have been at least inwardly upset over this incident. Immediately afterward, with no effort to hide his displeasure, he told a newspaper reporter who called at his home, "I'm now playing the role of letting Satō balance his accounts."

In this same reorganization, Maeo was replaced as party General Council chairman by Fukunaga Kenji and received the leisurely cabinet post of director-general of the Hokkaidō Development Agency. As for other members of the former Ikeda faction, Suzuki Zenkō was retained as health and welfare minister, and Shiomi Shunji from the Upper House entered the cabinet as minister of home affairs.

In December 1966 came the scheduled election of the LDP president. In the absence of any strong rivals, Satō was sure to be reelected; yet the Kōchikai members remained preoccupied with the question of how they would ultimately vote. In spite of the fact that many, both in and out of the LDP, had expected the Satō Administration to consciously continue Ikeda's relatively accommodating stance, especially with regard to interfactional and interparty relations, its personnel policies tended to split the former Ikeda faction, and there were differing attitudes on management of the Diet, reflected, for example, in the "forced ratification" of the ILO Treaty and the treaty normalizing relations between Japan and South Korea during the 48th Ordinary Diet in 1965 (the first of the new administration). A harder line began to be apparent in such actions as the passing of a bill, by the 51st Ordinary Diet in 1966, to establish National Foundation Day on February 11 as a national holiday, to which the opposition parties were strongly opposed.

With the approach of the party presidential election, many members—especially junior members—of the former Ikeda faction were beginning to show opposition to Satō Administration attitudes, and voices were heard calling for Maeo's formal candidacy. However, a certain group within the faction felt that since Satō had come from the same former Yoshida faction, it was unseemly to oppose him. As a result of repeated consultations orchestrated by the faction leadership—in this case mainly by Sutō and Ōhira—it was decided that in principle faction members were to vote individually for the person of their choice; yet, in fact, there had appeared a definite agreement among most members that they would vote for Maeo even if he was not running as a candidate. It was not until 1972 that a system was adopted in party presidential elections that required votes to be cast for formally registered candidates.

In the December 1 vote at the party convention, Satō was reelected with 289 votes out of a total of 459 votes cast (9 of which were invalid). Maeo, even though he had not announced his candidacy, won 47 votes, or less than the 89 votes won by Fujiyama Aiichirō. Another 25 votes went to other individuals. The total of 161 "opposition votes" represented more than one-third of the total votes cast and was thus a considerable embarrassment to the Satō Administration. In post-election personnel changes, Satō appointed Fukuda Takeo as party secretary-general, Shiina Etsusaburō as General Council chairman, and Nishimura Naomi as Policy Research Council chairman. Under this arrangement, the top three party posts outside the presidency itself were monopolized by members of the Satō and former Kishi factions.

Shortly prior to this reorganization, on November 15, 1966, Ōhira moved from the house he had lived in for many years near Dangozaka in the Komagome-hayashichō district of Tokyo's Bunkyō Ward. He no longer wished to live in the same house he had shared with Masaki and where Masaki had died. The Ōhiras' new home was on a hill in the Seta district of Setagaya Ward. Where one lives is said to influence the way one feels, and in Ōhira's case he found more time at his new home for reading and writing. These literary pursuits were facilitated, too, no doubt, by the fact that he did not hold any cabinet or top party posts. It was, so to speak, a time for recharging the batteries. Although he had long had the custom of visiting Toranomon bookstores two or three times a month, he now found himself dropping in much more often. He recalls: "In bookstores I am attracted not so much by the sections on politics, economics, or law as by the sections on essays, history, and sociology. The fresh smell and soft feel of the new books stocked each week spark a certain indescribable satisfaction. These are moments when I can truly taste the joy of living."

Here we catch a glimpse of Ōhira, in the midst of multiple disappointments, finding solace in reading. Although he once commented that the uses of reading lay, rather than in "honing and polishing one's writing style, finding illumination in the course of one's daily living," his own enthusiasm for reading extended also to writing. In October 1966, he published a volume of reminiscences of his son, as well as a collection of essays recalling the years of the Ikeda Administration, under the title *Shunpū shūu* (Spring Wind and Autumn Rain), his first large publishing venture since *Sugao no daigishi* (A Dietman as He Really Is) appeared ten years earlier in 1956.

Just at this time Ōhira's second son, Hiroshi, married, bringing some brightness to the Ōhira household. Hiroshi, who had been hired by the Overseas Operations Division of Furukawa Electric Company after his graduation from Keiō University, had fallen in love with a Seishin Women's University student, Endō Kimiko (the second daughter of Endō Fukuo, later president of Kanzaki Paper Company), and became engaged to her in the spring following her graduation. The wedding ceremony was held at the Hotel Ōkura the following October 14, 1966. Ōhira's new book was published to commemorate Hiroshi's and Kimiko's marriage and bears the dedication: "This small volume I dedicate to the spirits of Ikeda Hayato *sensei* and my eldest son, Masaki."

Prime Minister Satō continued with an ambitious political program but at the same time was put in a painful situation by the Black Mist (*kuroi kiri*) Affair, sparked by allegations that a group of sugar manufacturers had improperly received financing from government agencies. This led to a year-end Lower House dissolution on December 27, 1966, and a campaign, straddling the New Year holidays, leading up to the thirty-first general election on January 29, 1967. LDP members, caught in a sense of crisis, campaigned energetically, and the number of seats won by the party did not decline as precipitously as many had feared. Nevertheless, only 48.8 percent of the total number of votes cast went to LDP candidates, the first time it had fallen below 50 percent since the party's founding.

Owing to the efforts to reinvigorate his local support organization after the unpleasant experience of losing the position of top vote-winner in the last general election three years previously, Ōhira was this time elected (for the seventh consecutive time) with 75,000 votes, the greatest number of votes ever won by any candidate from the Kagawa Second Electoral District and 25,000 more than the second-place winner. The Second Satō Cabinet, formed after the election, brought in from the Kōchikai Fukunaga Kenji as chief cabinet secretary and Miyazawa Kiichi as director-general of the Economic Planning Agency.

On February 7, 1967, former Finance Minister Tsushima Juichi, whose native place was near Ōhira's and who had helped Ōhira get started in his career in the Ministry of Finance, passed away, and later the same year, on October 20, former Prime Minister Yoshida Shigeru left this world at the age of eighty-nine. Thus, a number of people who meant much to Ōhira were no longer there, and he no doubt sensed keenly the world's impermanence. Now leading a life removed from cabinet and high party positions, he confided to a close friend: "Only when he has a fairly easy job is a human being able to study; then he can have close contacts with others, and there is much that he will learn in the process. To be in an exalted position may seem splendid, but in fact there is not so much to be gained from it."

Ōhira wrote in the summer of 1967: "To climb a mountain peak one must endure steep trails. And one cannot taste the great pleasure of seeing snow [in the deep mountains] unless one crosses some dangerous bridges. . . . There are indeed many such occasions that recall themselves. . . . Even though I was not suited for it, I worked in the government for four full years. It was a period of continual stress, being pressed by tight schedules day after day. There was no time to think deeply about things, and with every situation it was necessary to make snap judgments. . . .But even to-day, when I am away from the government, I do not really have the time to enjoy 'the leisurely clouds and the wild cranes' [extolled in a Chinese poem]. Nevertheless, I am able to watch, from a certain distance, the psychology and performance of people with major roles on the stage of politics. I am able to stay away from places that burn with abusive language and jealousy. Rather, I am able to take an objective view, in relatively balanced circumstances, of the world about me, but most importantly of myself."

The Satō Administration, now entering its third year and having weathered, in the general election, the Black Mist Affair that had endangered its survival, finally decided to come squarely to grips with the issue of regaining full sovereignty over Okinawa and the Ogasawara Archipelago—an issue that the Satō Administration had pushed as a key part of its political agenda. In talks between Prime Minister Satō and President Johnson held in Washington on November 14 and 16, 1967, it was decided that agreement should be reached "within the next two or three years" (ryōsannen in the Japanese text was rather loosely made "in a few years" in the English version) on the date for the return of Okinawa, and that the islands of the Ogasawara Archipelago would be returned within one year.

At a press conference held in Honolulu, on his way back to Japan, Prime Minister Satō hinted that soon after his return to Tokyo he would begin a reorganization of the cabinet and party apparatus, establishing a new basis for party unity. He had in mind not only increasing his chances for a successful third bid for the party presidency in LDP presidential elections scheduled for the end of 1968 but also his desire to carry out negotiations for the return of Okinawa from as strong a position as possible. Picking up on this hint of a probable reorganization, Tanaka Kakuei and other mainstream party figures made a point of telling reporters that to be successful such a reorganization should include the appointment of Ōhira Masayoshi and Nakasone Yasuhiro to important posts.

The only party members thought likely to contest Satō's bid for a third term were Miki Takeo and Maeo Shigesaburō. Although it turned out that Miki preferred to remain as foreign minister, Maeo decided to consolidate his own plans for the presidential election and not fill any posts under the reorganized Satō Administration. Meanwhile, Prime Minister Satō asked Ōhira, who had been "neglected" for three years, to assume one of the top three party posts.

Ōhira's feelings on the matter were complex. It was in part a reaction to what seemed a certain deviousness in Satō's handling of personnel matters. After all, at the time of the reorganization one and a half years before, Satō had vetoed former Secretary-General Tanaka's suggestion that Ōhira be made Policy Research Council chairman, and yet he now appeared to think that Ōhira's appointment to this post would be acceptable in combination with Fukuda Takeo, Satō's protégé, as secretary-general. To now give Ōhira one of the top three party posts also appeared to be a move aimed at making it more difficult for him to engage in actions that might support Maeo's expected bid to oppose Satō in the elections next year. After several discussions with Tanaka (who was encouraging) and Maeo, Ōhira finally agreed to chair the Policy Research Council, in response to the view that "the Maeo faction of the conservative mainstream should be represented in one of the top three party posts."

In the reorganization of November 25, 1967, Fukuda Takeo remained in his post as party secretary-general and Hashimoto Tomisaburō became chairman of the General Council. As Tanaka and others had hoped, both Ōhira and Nakasone received appointments, as chairman of the Policy Research Council and transport minister, respectively. However, Tanaka remained without any appointment to a major post. The mass media tended to see this as a very deliberate decision by Prime Minister Satō, who was thought to be wary of the emergence of a joint "Ōhira–Tanaka line" if Tanaka were appointed to a key post. From the Kōchikai, Ogawa Heiji entered the cabinet as labor minister, while Miyazawa Kiichi was kept as director-general of the Economic Planning Agency.

In this way, Ōhira again appeared on the main political stage as one of the top three party officials, three years after the Ikeda Administration had ended in November 1964. Immediately after his appointment, Ōhira answered in an interview regarding his intentions as Policy Research Council chairman: "First, to be modest. Given the extremely complex domestic and international environment in which Japan finds itself, and the fact that the economy has become almost unrecognizably large-scale, I hope to deal with matters flexibly. Second, I hope to approach things in a long-term and straightforward way, free of preconceived notions. Third, to proceed only in a forward direction is not always the wisest course. Reconsideration is also necessary, which means looking back over what we have already done and trying to eliminate any harmful aspects. Fourth, it is essential to discuss things fully. I want to have an adequate dialogue not only between the government and members of the ruling party, but also with the opposition parties and with the people as a whole. We must lay the groundwork for realizing policies in a liberal atmosphere. I do not find myself sympathizing with things that are advertised under too showy a banner."

One of the interviewer's questions was: "Given your position in the Satō Administration, which is a more difficult one than in the Ikeda Administration, do you feel you will be able to exercise your abilities as you would like?" Ōhira replied, "Of course, I would like my ideas to go through without any hitches, but that would be counting on too much when it comes down to real business. I intend to try my best, and not to mind if I encounter some hurdles."

The biggest issue Ōhira had to deal with as Policy Research Council chairman was how to overcome wasteful structural rigidities in government-financed enterprises and programs. At the time, the Finance Ministry was headed by Mizuta Mikio and Vice-Minister Murakami Kōtarō (later a member of the Upper House), and Murakami came almost every other day to Ōhira's new office to complain: "Unless we do something right away about government finances we'll be in deep trouble. Starting with rice subsidies, and the Japanese National Railways and National Health Insurance, both of which are going ever deeper in the red, we need to do something immediately to get rid of the main factors causing these wasteful policies." Ōhira gave his opinion as follows: "We must seriously grapple with the problem. A first step is to consider carefully the figures for "natural increase in expenditure" given by the ministry. Second, there is the problem of deciding what should be the approximate size of the budget for the next fiscal year. And a definite prerequisite for dealing with the problem of structural rigidities is to evaluate accurately the future growth of the Japanese economy and, based on that, to clarify a long-range vision on how government finance fits into the overall scheme."

Representing the LDP in making an interpellation of the government in a plenary session of the Lower House of the 58th Ordinary Diet on January 30, 1968, Ōhira said: "When we examine in detail the major factors causing these rigidities, we find that the root of the evil is not limited to the field of government finance but is deeply rooted in the wider [economic and social] system and in traditional practices. . . . I admit that the functions of government tend to become more diversified with the passage of time. However, the overall system and various practices need to respond flexibly to the demands of the times, within the limits of government financial capabilities. I definitely think that today's government is burdened with more agencies and personnel and functions than it is able to nourish. . . . The key to a true solution is, needless to say, courageous government decisions and wisdom on the part of the people, who must be expected to understand and accept them. I think that the people are already turning against political postures of indulgent opportunism. I should ask that the government adopt a straightforward attitude of communicating to the people the truth as it really is and to appeal to them to recognize difficult matters for what they are." These comments on the need for administrative reforms showed foresight and were surely to the point.

If an essential issue in domestic politics was persistent and inefficient rigidities in government funding (*zaisei kōchokuka*), serious issues in foreign relations were the problem of Vietnam, negotiations for the return of Okinawa, and the related issue of American nuclear strategy. The Ikeda Administration had over the years tried to feel its way toward resolving the issue of Okinawa's return, which was assumed to require time and to evolve through the building of closer cooperative relations between the United States and Japan, and also as a result of a process of changes in nuclear strategy and in the overall situation in Asia. In comparison, the Satō Administration was, so to speak, more linear in its approach, as suggested, for example, in Prime Minister Satō's well-known statement, "Japan's postwar period will not end without the return of Okinawa."

Ōhira's basic conviction was that the United States would return Okinawa in due time. Regarding demands that the United States return the archipelago "at an early date," he once wrote: "Aside from the possibility that places like Okinawa may eventually not be needed as nuclear bases, given the gradual transition of nuclear systems toward ICBMs and Polaris submarines, the idea of negotiating a return of Okinawa with the nuclear bases intact is surely something that must be very carefully considered." If demands were made for a quick return before conditions had matured, it was possible that the United States might insist on returning Okinawa with nuclear bases intact, or might return it as part of a bargain that would compromise some other important Japanese interest, and that this could, in turn, backfire in the form of fierce disputes on the domestic political scene. Ōhira harbored such apprehensions. Ultimately, after four years of negotiations, the United States returned Okinawa, free of nuclear weapons, on May 15, 1972. Ōhira's apprehensions turned out to be, in one sense, unfounded but, in another sense, not without some raison d'être.

During the above-mentioned Lower House questioning of January 1968, Ōhira asked Satō about nuclear policy. Ōhira stated, first of all, "Whether we like it or not, nuclear problems will no doubt be one of the biggest political issues to be dealt with in the future." He then went on, "There is no good reason why Japan should be allergic to having accurate knowledge on nuclear matters." This suggests that Ōhira continued to hold doubts about the government's know-nothing attitude in connection with the U.S.–Japan Security Treaty when it came to the interpretation and application of the third of Japan's Three Non-nuclear Principles—namely, nuclear weapons would not be introduced into Japan.

While Ōhira was chairman of the LDP's Policy Research Council, Tanaka Kakuei was chairman of the party's Research Commission on Municipal Policy, during which time he laid the groundwork for his Plan for the Remodeling of the Japanese Archipelago (which he later used as a slogan when seeking the party presidency), and also chairman of the Research Commission on Rice Prices. Tanaka has left an account of how in July 1968, during the period of deciding the year's rice subsidies, Ōhira helped resolve an intraparty feud over producers' rice prices.

There had been much animated discussion around a suggested rise in prices to be paid to producers for the 1968 crop, and strong demands for a price hike were repeatedly made by the members of the LDP General Council who represented farming districts. One day, in a meeting where Ōhira was present, two of these members rose and took turns to complain: "It is because our party does not have a good enough understanding of agriculture that such a low rice price is being talked about. Policy Research Council Chairman Ōhira and others like him are former elite bureaucrats from the Ministry of Finance and don't know how farming people live, and that's what has brought on this sort of situation. So resign right away, leave your post!"

Ōhira listened silently to this outburst and then, no doubt totally fed up with such talk, started to get up to leave the room. Tanaka, who was sitting next to him, caught him by the arm and quietly reprimanded him: "If you leave, you won't be able to come back, you know." For some time Ōhira stared fixedly in silence and finally spoke: "You have both said to me that Ōhira does not know the life of farmers. Both of you come from well-known families, both your fathers were Diet members in earlier days, and you were raised in wealthy homes. To compare, I am the son of a poor farmer in Sanuki. When I was a boy, my daily schedule was to leave the house at dawn to tend to paddy fields halfway up the mountain where there was little water, and then take the first morning train to school. Because my family was poor and had little to spend for schooling, I studied as a subsidized student and finally completed a university course. It is regrettable to be told that this Ōhira Masayoshi is someone who is ignorant of farming." Tanaka goes on to write, "This was the first time I had ever heard Ōhira say something that seemed to reverberate from the innermost depths of his being." After Ōhira had finished, the General Council decided to entrust the matter of rice prices to the top three party officers (of which Ōhira was one) and the chairman (that is, Tanaka) of the Research Commission on Rice Prices.

Chapter 18

Industrial Policy at a Crossroads

The year 1968 marked the centennial of the Meiji Restoration. It was also notable for the achievement, two years ahead of schedule, of the goals set forth in the Ikeda Administration's ten-year National Income-Doubling Plan. In GNP, Japan now stood second to the United States in the free world, and other aspects of the so-called Japanese miracle (full employment, for instance) had also caught the world's attention. Nonetheless, with the approach of the November 1968 LDP presidential election, the Satō Administration was coming to be looked at unfavorably by a large segment of the population.

First, there was displeasure and irritation over economic distortions and other imbalances that had come with rapid economic growth. Although the rate of wage increases was accelerating, consumer prices were also beginning to rise fast. Problems with pollution were cropping up in many industries and problems of overcrowding, rural depopulation, and lack of social capital for improving the living environment were becoming acute. The rebellion of the younger generation, a problem shared by prosperous industrial nations throughout the world, was becoming common in Japan, too, as evidenced in the spread of "campus struggles" (gakuen tōsō). The government's policies toward China and Vietnam were causing discontent and unease, not only among the opposition parties but even within the LDP itself.

In these circumstances, opinions critical of Satō's policies were smoldering in the non-mainstream factions headed by Miki, Maeo, Fujiyama, and Nakasone, and there was no lack of anti-Satō feeling even among the so-called middle-of-the-road factions and Dietmen unaffiliated with any particular faction. Thus, if all these individuals and groups opposed to him could cooperate, it seemed possible to prevent Satō's election to a third term as party president. Nevertheless, within the Kōchikai, which might be expected to be a strong center of opposition, there was a tendency, influenced by the feeling that the old Yoshida Liberal Party should be the legitimate conservative mainstream, to think it improper to join with Miki and Nakasone forces descended from the old Reform Party; and there was a group that was, in fact, friendly to Satō. In addition to this, Kōchikai Chairman Maeo, who was a prime focus of attention, was not himself overly eager to carry through a fight to the finish to wrest control of the administration.

However, as the election approached, the mood encouraging a standoff intensified, and Maeo finally announced his candidacy on November 1, following the announcement of Miki's candidacy on October 30. In a press conference on November 8, Prime Minister Satō made quite clear his own intention to run for a third term as party president, with the goals of "achieving full independence through the early return of Okinawa" and "maintaining lawful order." With a view to supporting both Miki and Maeo, Fujiyama Aiichirō (who did not himself run in the election) set up a Headquarters for Promoting a Renewal of Public Conscience (*Jinshin Isshin Suishin Honbu*), which he headed. Thus, regarding Satō's policies, the party became divided into those supporting Satō and those opposing him.

Although it was clear that Satō would win more votes than either of the other two candidates, attention was focused on whether he would win an absolute majority on the first ballot. If not, and if the anti-Satō forces should then group around the runner-up, he could possibly be defeated in a runoff. In that case, the crucial point was whether the second position went to Maeo or to Miki. Most tended to think that it would go to Maeo since he was the leader of the party's second-largest faction. However, the prospect that things might happen in just this way was feared not so much by Satō as by Maeo himself. Maeo was, in fact, quite unprepared, psychologically and practically, to take control of the government. Moreover, the Kōchikai had been affected by considerable hidden discord since Ikeda's death and lacked unity, and, as Satō must have calculated, Ōhira, as chairman of the party's Policy Research Council, could not easily throw his weight behind the chairman of his own faction.

The three candidates agreed among themselves that the election would be carried out openly and fairly, with no irregularities. However, on the evening before the election, information was brought to Kōchikai members that Maeo faced an uphill battle to come in second, as pressure tactics were being resorted to in other quarters. Hearing this, Ōhira counseled Maeo, "Even starting now, if we really get down to work, we can change the score." But Maeo, in strict observance of the agreement, refrained from taking any action.

The results of the November 27 vote were:

Satō Eisaku	249
Miki Takeo	107
Maeo Shigesaburō	95
Others	3
Total	454

Thus, despite the fact that 45 percent of the votes were opposed to him, Satō was elected on the first ballot to a third term as party president.

The Kōchikai saw that it had problems. In response to the fact that Maeo had come third, voices of such junior faction members as Sasaki Yoshitake, Itō Masayoshi, Hattori Yasushi, and Tanaka Rokusuke, were saying, for example, "We have a conclusion of sorts on Maeo, so how about having him retire now and hand on the leader's seat to Ōhira?" Intrafaction schisms widened as certain persons close to Maeo went so far as to claim that Ōhira must share blame for the defeat by not having been active enough on Maeo's behalf.

While steering clear of any sort of defensive stance, Ōhira told reporters: "Now that the results of the election are in, I think there's nothing we can do but accept them. There is no use grumbling forever about something that is already past. What to do about the Maeo faction and what Maeo himself will do are surely things for him to think over carefully and decide."

In the November 30, 1968, cabinet reorganization that followed the election, Fukuda Takeo was switched from party secretary-general to minister of finance, being replaced as secretary-general by Tanaka Kakuei. The appointment of Hori Shigeru as chief cabinet secretary helped consolidate what appeared to be a fairly stable regime based around the Satō-led mainstream. In this same reorganization, Ōhira was appointed minister of international trade and industry, four years after stepping down from his last cabinet post as foreign minister under the Ikeda Administration.

At the start of the 61st Ordinary Diet on January 27, 1969, Prime Minister Satō made this point: "Now that our country has completed one hundred years since the beginning of the Meiji era and is beginning a new century, it is in a period of transition in a great number of areas." When he then went on to advocate the "early restitution" of administrative rights in Okinawa, the opposition parties reacted vehemently to any scheme by which Okinawa might be returned with American nuclear bases and showed that they were ready to mount a unified attack on such a notion. Speaking again before the Diet on March 10, Prime Minister Satō, who had not previously made very clear what conditions, if any, for Okinawa's return he had in mind, said, "The Three Non-nuclear Principles should not be applied to Okinawa in a way differently than to the rest of Japan." Thus, it was made clear that the basis for negotiations with the United States was to be Okinawa's return under the same status as the rest of Japan, free of nuclear weapons.

Reflecting the turbulence in society as a whole, the Diet had very rough going. After the budget for fiscal 1969 was passed, discussion on almost every important bill ran into obstructive tactics by the opposition parties, and altogether over fifty legislative proposals were left unapproved. International Trade and Industry Minister Ōhira adopted a fairly distant attitude to all this and tried to concentrate on his ministerial duties. The biggest issue facing him in his new post was how to respond to sudden strident demands from other nations, resulting from Japan's economic growth, for trade and capital liberalization, and how Japan's industries should adapt themselves.

The Outline on Liberalizing Trade and Exchange (Bōeki kawase jiyūka taikō), drawn up at the end of the Kishi Administration in 1960, had set forth Japan's basic policies and the ideal of equitable treatment, and had aimed at the same time to raise Japan's rate of tariff-free imports from the current 40 percent or so of product items to 80–90 percent three years later. This goal had been for the most part achieved, and by 1968 the rate of tariff-free imports was 97 percent, with only 120 items left on the negative list. However, due to the rapid increase in exports, demands from overseas for market liberalization continued. In December 1968, just after Ōhira had become minister of international trade and industry, the government approved new guidelines for promoting further liberalization. On July 18, 1969, just prior to the seventh U.S.–Japan Joint Committee on Trade and Economic Affairs, it was decided that by the end of December 1971, two years hence, residual import restriction items would be reduced to less than 60.

Ōhira recognized that liberalization could have positive effects on the competitive strength of Japanese products. Within Japan's industrial circles there was a view that liberalization was a "second coming of Commodore Perry's black ships," coupled with a hope that the government would do its best to retain protective measures. Yet Ōhira felt that competitive conditions in which the hurdles were somewhat raised would ultimately benefit Japan's industries. Privately a strong enthusiast for liberalization, he would listen politely to the petitions of business circles but make determined efforts to win them over. Japan had now begun to register a chronic trade surplus, and Ōhira sensed that if further liberalization was not rapidly pushed through, criticism from other countries would mount and trade frictions might become serious.

Since the first half of 1968, the United States had been considering an import surcharge as a part of its policies for defending the U.S. dollar, but the major industrial countries, fearing the decrease in world trade that would result, managed to get the United States to abandon this idea by agreeing, among other things, to put into effect the measures agreed upon in the Kennedy Round of GATT negotiations earlier than originally envisioned. Conscious of its responsibilities as a nation with a trade surplus, Japan in April 1970 finalized its new schedule for a hastening of across-the-board tariff reductions. In response to developing countries' dissatisfaction with the Kennedy Round provisions, various schemes for granting these nations preferential status were discussed between July and November 1969. On November 14, these proposals were presented to the developing countries through the intermediary of the United Nations Conference on Trade and Development (UNCTAD).

Japan's first series of measures for capital liberalization had been put into effect in 1967, three years after Japan joined the OECD; a second series was agreed upon in 1969 during Ōhira's tenure as minister of international trade and industry. These measures, which in principle aimed at eventual 100 percent capital liberalization in keeping with OECD decisions, greatly expanded the number and types of industries to be affected by a freer international flow of capital. It was during Ōhira's tenure that agreement was reached on the early capital liberalization of the automotive industry, a matter that was of the greatest interest domestically and internationally. This was put into effect in April 1971.

As to how Japanese industry should adapt to changing circumstances, Ōhira made his basic stance clear: "From now on, the economy should be managed with the initiative coming from the private sector." This was stated in his first public speech as minister of international trade and industry and caused consternation among large sections of the ministry's bureaucracy trained to believe that domestic industries should be guided by the bureaucracy, and that as far as possible liberalization should be delayed until the industries were sufficiently competitive.

In this regard, Ōhira concisely stated his thinking about private-sector leadership: "We want to hasten a clear awareness on the part of private industries that from now on they will have to overcome stiff international competition by their own efforts. Needless to say, in a free economic system private enterprise is responsible for economic development, and it is private know-how, vitality, and creativity that are the basic forces behind this development. In the past, we saw the attitude among Japanese enterprises that if they encountered a difficult situation there was always the possibility of relying on the government. Unless we change such lax attitudes, we cannot hope for robust development in the future." As we have seen, even in his proposals for reviving the Japanese economy written when he worked at the Budget Bureau immediately after the war, Ōhira had emphasized the need to pay due attention to the vitality of the private sector and the need to integrate Japan's economy into the international economy. His thinking on these lines had become even better defined during the Ikeda Administration.

An important issue relating to policies to cope with trade liberalization was the merger of Yawata Iron and Steel Corporation and Fuji Iron and Steel Corporation. These two companies had developed out of the same Japan Iron and Steel Corporation, established as a semigovernmental, semiprivate enterprise through the merger of the government-run Yawata Iron and Steel Works (founded in 1896) and four private companies. After the war, Japan Iron and Steel was split into Fuji and Yawata by the Law for the Elimination of Excessive Concentrations of Economic Power, but later these two companies, eager to invest in new technologies, looked for the opportunity to reunite, and on April 17, 1967, they announced their intention of forming a new company to be called Nippon Steel Corporation (*Shin-Nippon Seitetsu*, or *Shin-nittetsu* for short). The Ministry of International Trade and Industry set up a Special Committee on Basic Problems within its Industrial Structure Research Council, which recognized the new company's necessity and legality; however, the government's Fair Trade Commission was cautious in its attitude, fearing the new company would violate the Antimonopoly Law.

Ōhira, as minister of international trade and industry, felt that "from the viewpoint of industrial policy, the merger is something that should be realized." He explained: "As industrial policy, the improvement of technology and management that would come from the unification of the two companies' marketing and R&D was very attractive. With nothing but weak industries, an industrial policy that inspires confidence is impossible. Moreover, effective industrial policy cannot be promoted solely through the power of the government. Whatever the government's industrial policy, it must depend on the cooperation of well-run enterprises that have ability and judgment. In that sense, I was one of those who entertained positive hopes for the creation of Nippon Steel Corporation." Ōhira worked energetically behind the scenes to effect the merger, which was formally approved on October 13. He has written: "I have thus a certain amount of sentimental feeling over having played the role of midwife in Shin-nittetsu's birth."

Another issue Ōhira encountered was how to harmonize growing industrial prowess with people's daily lives. In May 1969, he expressed himself as follows before a convention of the Young Presidents' Organization, a group of young top managers from Japan and the United States: "Because economic growth has been so rapid, in all sectors of the economy and society there have emerged imbalances, contradictions, and what may be called frictions. I think it can be said that the fact that income levels have risen has brought greater interest in improving our living environment. Things like shortcomings and delays in providing public services, pollution problems, and urban overcrowding are examples of bad adaptation to economic growth, and appropriate and effective measures on the part of the government are, I think, definitely needed. Until now the greatest emphasis in industrial policy has been to protect Japanese industries from well-run industries in other countries, and to spur their development in terms of both quantity and quality. But from now on we must think about putting emphasis on policies that also directly address the interests of consumers and residents: for example, policy on industrial siting, pollution policy, and price policy." Ōhira seems to have felt that even though Japan's industrial economy involved many kinds of problems, the Japanese people could surely overcome them, although "for this purpose a change in thinking will be necessary."

At around the time of the above address, he wrote in an essay published in a small journal: "I can't help but feel that, among the Japanese people, there is a certain passive type of thinking—one could even call it a feeling of victimization—that lies at the core of discussions [on public issues]. As long as this persists, not only will the Japanese be ultimately unable to become a great people, but they may become divorced from the fundamental conditions for enjoying balanced everyday lives, supported by a wholesome common sense.

"... We have, for example, the way [many] Japanese respond to the liberalization of imports and capital. It is a fear that if the door to liberalization is opened, foreign goods and capital will suddenly flood in, their wonderful technology and financial power dominating the Japanese market in the twinkling of an eye and totally crushing Japan's small-scale local industries. ... This feeling of victimization is not only seen with respect to foreign countries. ... We can also see it, for example, in the pollution issue that has recently raised so much clamor. ... Not only the general populace but also government administrators and leaders have become prisoner to a sense of victimization by pollution, and there are many who are reacting cynically or with wounded feelings regarding the modernization of our economy and culture. In fact, we now have a situation where many are thoughtlessly emotional and combative, considering business enterprises their enemy. . . . Is it not evident that the best way to proceed is for us, on the one hand, to properly appreciate the material basis of the life we enjoy, and, on the other, to coolly consider ways of eliminating pollution and methods of helping those suffering from pollution? The same may be said about commodity prices. It certainly seems one-sided, while enjoying the benefits of economic growth and full employment, to forget about these and talk only about rising prices, again revealing a feeling of victimization." The text from which these remarks are quoted was written before the decade of intense change of the 1970s. It is of great interest for its accurate assessment of the times and even, some might say, for seeing a decade or so into the future.

Although Japan was steadily advancing toward greater liberalization and a sophistication of its industrial structure, around this time the Nixon Administration's demand for voluntary restraints on the export of Japanese textiles to the United States was perceived by many as working at cross-purposes with trade liberalization. Due to the political framework from which it evolved, this issue cannot be dismissed as a merely economic one. In the 1968 American presidential campaign, Nixon had promised comprehensive import restrictions on textiles as a way of gaining the support of the Southern states, where a large segment of the ailing textile industry was located. Even before Ōhira became minister of international trade and industry, the United States had been suggesting such restrictions. Then, in May 1969, about six months after Ōhira assumed his post, United States Secretary of Commerce Maurice Stans visited Japan, where he simultaneously called for greater Japanese liberalization and Japan's voluntary participation in international accords on trade in woolen and synthetic fiber products.

The Ōhira–Stans talks were held on May 12 and 13. While Stans strongly asked for import restrictions, Ōhira contended: "Restrictive measures would ignore the rules of GATT (General Agreement on Tariffs and Trade), which evolved largely as the result of U.S. advocacy, and would serve neither Japan–U.S. relations nor the U.S. textile industry." Immediately after the talks, Ōhira confided to Ministry of International Trade and Industry associates: "The U.S. has begun to say many troubling things, and doesn't maintain the pride it used to. I said a lot of things, too, but I wonder if they were understood."

Although these Ōhira–Stans talks in effect failed to reach agreement, approximately two months later, from July 29 to 31, 1969, the seventh U.S.-Japan Joint Committee on Trade and Economic Affairs was held in Tokyo, with Secretary of State William Rogers, Secretary of Commerce

Stans, and Chairman of the Council of Economic Advisors Paul Mc-Cracken attending from the United States. Despite such important issues on the agenda as the removal of many remaining negative-list items, capital liberalization, and a lowering of tariff rates, the biggest topic at the meeting was the textile issue. One-to-one talks between Ōhira and Stans tended to be a repeat of the frustrated earlier talks in May.

Stans insisted that the Ministry of International Trade and Industry should carry out an on-the-spot survey to determine the extent of the harm suffered by the American textile industry due to imports. Ōhira finally agreed, and after he had persuaded some unenthusiastic Ministry of International Trade and Industry officials, it was decided to send to the United States a study team whose objective was limited to making a "factual survey." This team stayed in the United States from September 16 to 19, 1969, talked with persons in the government, Congress, the textile industry, and labor unions. The conclusion reached in its report to the Ministry of International Trade and Industry was: "The United States textile industry is, on the whole, healthy and has suffered no harm."

In mid-October, after basic agreement had been reached on the Yawata–Fuji merger but before there were any prospects of agreement in the U.S.–Japan textile negotiations, Ōhira visited four Eastern European countries from which he had received invitations, and also visited several Western European countries to promote friendly relations. Changing planes in Rome, he first went to Bulgaria, Hungary, Poland, and Czechoslovakia, and then to Austria, West Germany, England, and France. His trip took eighteen days, from October 17 to November 3.

He has described some of his impressions of this trip as follows: "The atmosphere in Eastern Europe was not necessarily bright, and little vitality was seen either in politics or the economy. These countries' dependence on the Soviet Union was extremely high not only in the security field but also in the economic field. But at the same time I felt they had a rather deep-rooted inclination toward Western Europe, both psychologically and economically.... Situated between East and West, they seemed to be trying not to lose a sense of balance. Their interest in and expectations of Japan were gradually rising."

If the situation in Eastern Europe was no better than expected, it was conditions in Germany that seemed to draw Ōhira's closest attention. Willy Brandt of the Social Democratic Party had just been elected as the new chancellor of the Federal Republic of Germany, and as part of his new policies the deutsche mark had just been revalued. While staying at the Hôtel de Crillon in Paris, Ōhira wrote the following remarks on hotel notepaper for a certain newspaper: "The recent appreciation of the deutsche mark was somewhat higher than anticipated. . . . A major factor in world currency machinations and instability has been removed by this, and now, and for some time in the future, the fixed exchange rate system will be firmly in place thanks to this new value for the deutsche mark. This must be called a big plus for the world economy.

". . . Traveling from Eastern to Western Europe, I keenly sensed the growth in Germany's prowess and the strength of its underlying energy. The European economy, including that of Eastern Europe, is coming to rely more heavily on Germany, and the incident in Czechoslovakia [in August 1968] is probably not unrelated to this new German prominence. . . . East Germany is making good progress as the star pupil of the Comecon [Council for Mutual Economic Assistance] bloc. Moreover, between East Germans and West Germans we do not see the sort of antagonism visible in other divided nations. It should be said that quietly, between East and West, the German people are steadily consolidating their position both economically and diplomatically."

After referring to current conditions in France and the United Kingdom, Ōhira went on to express some worries about Japan: "Although the Japanese economy has on the surface indeed made some eye-catching leaps forward, an in-depth physical examination will certainly show it to be neither strong nor balanced. The level of indigenously developed technology remains low, and financial and organizational capacities are not strong. I keenly feel there remains much to be done toward a sense of trust between labor and management. At the same time, pressures from abroad are daily becoming more intense. They are becoming something other than what we imagined, and in some quarters even the 'yellow peril' argument is starting to make the rounds. The situation after the revaluation of the deutsche mark will probably heighten these tendencies."

Ōhira's European trip in one sense gave some time for his emotions and mind to rest, away from his usual strenuous duties. There were no particular diplomatic issues that required his attention, and only four persons were traveling with him: his wife, Shigeko, his eldest daughter, Yoshiko, and two persons from the Ministry of International Trade and Industry. Even if the atmosphere in the Eastern European countries was not bright, Ōhira nonetheless was able to experience the profundity of their culture. He savored the streets of Budapest, pearl of the Danube, and in Warsaw he visited the birthplace of Chopin.

November 3, the day Ōhira got back to Japan was Culture Day, a national holiday. It was not culture, however, but the U.S.–Japan textile negotiations that were again to claim his attention. The Japanese study team's report that the United States textile industry had suffered no harm had not been acceptable to the American negotiators, and on October 2, shortly before Ōhira's departure for Europe, they had suddenly made a formal proposal for concluding a bilateral agreement that would establish textile import restrictions in a three-tier scheme, comprising overall, group, and individual-item categories.

The negotiations were considered pending while Ōhira was in Europe, but on November 7, soon after his return, the Japanese government gave a formal reply that negotiations should be based on multilateral discussion and presented a counterproposal. In response to the American proposal, which it was feared could open the way to a protectionism that would go against the world's free trading system, Ōhira considered that it was important to stick to free-trade principles, but at the same time he worried that U.S.–Japan relations could be badly damaged by the continuing dispute. Thus, he personally worked to promote a compromise proposal. On receiving the Japanese reply, the American side proposed another round of bilateral discussions. Although the Japanese side at first rejected this request on the grounds that it went against the principle of multilateral trade agreements, it was finally decided that, considering the upcoming U.S.–Japan summit talks, bilateral talks on the textile issue would be held in Geneva between November 17 and 22 under the name of "preparatory talks."

Apart from the textile issue, it had been decided that Prime Minister Satō, who was determined to finalize negotiations on the early return of Okinawa, would travel to the United States for talks with President Nixon. On November 16, the day before his departure, Satō telephoned Ōhira briefly. According to Ōhira, the purport of the call was to "make absolutely sure the textile negotiations keep going so as not to bring any bad influence on the U.S.–Japan summit talks." In Washington, Satō spoke with Nixon three times from November 19, and on November 21 (November 22 in Japan) a U.S.–Japan joint communiqué addressing the Okinawa issue promised the return of Okinawa in 1972, application of the security treaty on the same basis as in the rest of Japan, and no introduction of nuclear weapons. No mention was made of the textile negotiations.

The Geneva negotiations went anything but smoothly. The American team again proposed the "trigger method," famous throughout the course of U.S.–Japan textile negotiations. According to this method, whenever imports into the United States of any given item exceeded a certain ratio with respect to the previous year, the exporting country would automatically stop exports of the item in question, after which there would be discussions on appropriate measures. The Japanese side rejected this, and the talks came to an end with the two sides still in disagreement.

On November 26, following a cabinet meeting at which Prime Minister Satō was congratulated for his success on the return of Okinawa, Ōhira asked him, "Apart from what you have told us, is there not anything else we should hear from you?" The prime minister's curt reply was, "Not a thing." However, Ōhira's uneasiness did not disappear, and he confided to persons close to him, "I wonder what Satō promised. If for the return of Okinawa it was necessary to resolve the textile problem, there would have been some way to go about it. He might have frankly told me if he'd made such a promise."

Later, answering questions before the Diet, Satō stuck to the position that he would "try to resolve the textile issue in a spirit of mutual compromise." In spite of official government pronouncements, it was being openly rumored in the mass media and business circles that a secret agreement between Satō and Nixon might have involved a trade-off between textiles and Okinawa. Today, the truth of the matter is still unclear.

The 62nd Extraordinary Diet was convened on November 29, and after Prime Minister Satō's policy speech on the return of Okinawa and the subsequent interpellations from spokesmen for the various parties, the Lower House was dissolved on December 2 and an election campaign was begun, as a result of which the LDP hoped to be favored on election day (set for December 27) because of public approval of the agreement on Okinawa. In the midst of the election campaign, on December 19 the United States delivered another memorandum calling for a reopening of textile negotiations, later to be known as the "first formal proposal." It was a shock to Japan that in these textile negotiations the American side seemed to adopt an obstinate attitude of paying no attention whatsoever to what the Japanese side said. Returning to Tokyo in the midst of a campaign tour for consultations on the textile issue with Ministry of International Trade and Industry officials concerned, Ōhira sighed, "It's a depressing, dark road." In the thirty-second Lower House general election held on December 27, 1969, the LDP won 288 seats in a resounding victory. Ōhira was elected for the eighth consecutive time in his Kagawa district, with the highest number of votes among the three successful candidates.

The year 1970 started with the textile problem still unresolved. On January 2, the American side, as if to further press the matter, produced a second proposal. Because it was only a slightly revised version of the first, the Japanese side rejected it through diplomatic channels and requested the provision of material to substantiate the claims that the American textile industry was being hurt. The assertions of the two sides were completely at odds.

Following the general election, the 63rd Special Diet was convened on

January 14, 1970, and Satō Eisaku was chosen prime minister for the third time. On the evening before the new cabinet was to be formed, Ōhira received a telephone call from LDP Secretary-General Tanaka asking him to remain as minister of international trade and industry. The formal process of assigning cabinet posts began around 4 P.M. on January 14, and a little after 6 P.M. Chief Cabinet Secretary Hori announced the list. While the key posts of foreign minister, finance minister, and chief cabinet secretary remained with Aichi Kiichi, Fukuda Takeo, and Hori Shigeru, respectively, the post of minister of international trade and industry was listed as going to Miyazawa Kiichi instead of to Ōhira. Learning this from the television in his office in the Sannō Grand Building, Ōhira's face tensed, and he told his office staff, "I guess I caused everyone a lot of trouble."

Ōhira had been confident that in the U.S.-Japan textile negotiations he would ultimately be able to deal successfully with American pushiness by adhering to principle. He was no doubt under the impression that he could accomplish this in part with the help of the network of personal acquaintances he had built up in the United States since his days as foreign minister. With the cabinet reorganization, however, this dream vanished.

Miyazawa Kiichi, who replaced Ōhira as minister of international trade and industry, was also enthusiastic about bringing an end to the textile negotiations, but the two sides remained at odds, and his efforts were not immediately successful in finding a way to agreement. After the beginning of 1971, there were growing indications that the United States Congress might legislate import restrictions. As a result, the Japanese government in October of that year decided to handle the U.S.-Japan textile problem through a bilateral agreement between the two governments. The problem was finally resolved when this agreement was formally signed at the end of January, 1972.

Having suddenly returned to a situation of not holding any cabinet or party posts, Ōhira at first made no effort to hide expressions of displeasure and was heard to say, "What is Satō thinking of?" After some time, however, he revealed to those around him a fresher attitude and was even heard to remark, "In this way, I can really act more decisively than I might otherwise be able." One day, not long after the January 1970 cabinet reorganization, while Ōhira was visiting Ikeda's wife, Mitsue, in Shinano-machi, she happened to ask him why he had been replaced. He ruefully answered: "You see, behind my face there is Ikeda's face, in a sort of double exposure. That's probably the reason Satō doesn't like anything I do."

On March 12, 1970, Ōhira celebrated his sixtieth birthday, known as *kanreki* in Japanese, which marks the beginning of a new sixty-year cycle in the traditional Chinese calendrical system. To commemorate the day, he wrote a short composition titled "*Kanreki to jikai*" (The Age of Sixty and Self-Instruction), from which the following is an excerpt: "While not young, I don't feel myself to be old. . . . My sixty years of life have not been anything so very splendid, but they have fortunately not met any terrible headwinds or waves. . . . The task with which I am assigned from now on is, needless to say, to try my best to balance the figures I have up to now entered on the debit side of the ledger. In the West, there is the saying, 'Life begins at seventy.' To have ambitions at sixty is by no means too late for them." After stating this attitude for the future, he went on: "I believe the question of whether one advances or retreats must depend on Heaven, while being praised or censured must follow the dictates of destiny. From now on, this will be my signpost for self-instruction."

Chapter 19

The Drama of a Changeover

Prime Minister Satō Eisaku's third term as LDP president, to which he had been elected in November 1968, was to end after two years. Thus, after the beginning of 1970, a major point of interest in the political world was whether Satō, now satisfied with his success in realizing his long-held desire to see the reversion of Okinawa without nuclear weapons, would try to keep power over a longer period. Prime Minister Satō had hinted during his November 1969 trip to the United States that he would not run for a fourth term, saying, "If I've done it three times, that is enough. After all, within the LDP there is a whole series [of possible successors]."

Prime Minister Satō's elder brother, former Prime Minister Kishi, considered that Finance Minister Fukuda was the most appropriate candidate to succeed to the nation's top political post, and that Satō should not run for a fourth term, even though he should have the right to name his successor and thus leave his stamp on the following administration. Chief Cabinet Secretary Hori had similar feelings. On the other hand, LDP Secretary-General Tanaka and Vice-President Kawashima backed the idea of a fourth term for Satō because they were looking forward to a Tanaka administration and thus felt it was necessary to consolidate their strength during his time in office. Ōhira considered that if a fourth term for Satō could be prevented, he might work with Tanaka to roll back the Fukuda alternative so that the Kōchikai might emerge as a serious contender on the political scene. Consistent with past pronouncements, Miki Takeo hoped for an early face-off with Satō.

As these various ambitions developed, it was the striking success of the negotiations over Okinawa that increased Satō's self-confidence, to the point where he definitely decided to run for a fourth term in the hope of seeing Okinawa's return with the support from all factions but under the aegis of his own cabinet. Maneuvers for the election of Satō to a fourth

261

term proceeded steadily, orchestrated by Kawashima and Tanaka, and such "middle-ground" influential figures as Funada Naka, Mizuta Mikio, and Ishii Mitsujirō were quick to express their support. Nakasone Yasuhiro began to work for the same goal.

The party convention to elect the party president was scheduled for October 29, 1970. While the majority in the party seemed to be fairly consolidated behind a fourth term for Satō, from the summer interest focused on what Miki Takeo and Maeo Shigesaburō, both of whom had challenged Satō in the presidential election two years previously, would do in the current circumstances. Miki's standpoint was clear. In a press conference in July he stated: "The prime minister is tired both mentally and physically. In thinking about the 1970s, it is in the prime minister's own interest to retire." Then, in a September meeting of the Miki Faction Study Group, he expressed his intention of putting up a fight to prevent a fourth term for Satō: "Although there is a tendency within the party to believe that speaking out puts one at a disadvantage, now is the time to return to the fundamental principles of party politics and recover fresh vigor through free discussion."

For the Kōchikai, which had always held the attitude that it should put up a candidate in party presidential elections, the question of a fourth term for Satō was not easy. After all, in the previous election two years before, Kōchikai Chairman Maeo had come in last with only ninety-five votes, giving rise to serious controversy within the faction. Within the party as a whole and outside it as well, there was a growing mood in favor of letting Satō preside over the happy event of the return of Okinawa. Thus, with the exception of Miki and his faction, there remained no noticeable opposition to a Satō fourth term.

At the same time, active approaches were being made to some of the non-mainstream factions by the "fourth-term factions." Especially persistent were those made to the Kōchikai and its chairman, Maeo Shigesaburō. Maeo was contacted by party Vice-President Kawashima personally and by Secretary-General Tanaka through Suzuki Zenkō and asked to cooperate in Satō's election to a fourth term. In a speech before a meeting of the Kōchikai's Young Men's Study Group in Hakone on July 6, Maeo had criticized the government's economic and fiscal policies, stating: "The emergence of pollution problems and other social imbalances reflects the fact that public investment has not kept pace with private economic growth. To make up for the lag, we will have to adopt more energetic policies on public borrowing." He emphasized overhauling and improving the party's organic capacities: "New wine must be poured into new skins." At first glance, these pronouncements by Maeo might have seemed like criticism of Satō, but there was also the view that they were, in fact, meant primarily as an attack on Fukuda's financial policies.

Two days after his speech in Hakone, Maeo made the following reply to questions from a group of reporters: "As to whether I will run in the presidential election, I can't say. A number of factors are presently under consideration." What Maeo was considering were the proposals made by Kawashima, Tanaka, and others promoting a fourth term for Satō. These are said to have been as follows: first, a cabinet reorganization would take place after Satō's fourth-term election; second, Maeo would thereupon be given an important cabinet post; third, the ideas of the Maeo faction would be reflected in the next Satō administration. This plan corresponded close-ly with the strategy already favored by some of Maeo's close associates and veteran Kōchikai members, to the effect that even though Satō might be elected a fourth time, he would not be elected a fifth. In the meantime, Maeo would enter the cabinet as a sort of alternate prime minister who could later expect the cooperation of the Satō faction in effecting a Maeo administration.

Ōhira had for a long time refrained from making public statements about Maeo, whom Ikeda had always treated fondly like a younger brother and who was his own "senior" in both his early career in the Ministry of Finance and later in the Diet. However, during the summer of 1970, Ōhira broke with tradition and stated some of his views on Maeo in a press inter-view: "He is a great man of considerable depth of character, a man without greed, a fine person as far as character is concerned. However, in terms of health, nature, and inclination, he is not well suited to public acclaim or to schemes to win majority support within the party. So it seems he may be unable to become the ruler of the country. That is not, though, to belittle his character." This evaluation was, no doubt, made quite honestly by Ōhira, but, of course, Maeo would not feel happy to read it. On the other hand, this type of interaction between Maeo and Ōhira naturally suited Prime Minister Satō.

On September 22, a little over a month before the election day, a discus-sion took place between Satō and Maeo. When Maeo asked Satō—just to make sure—if he was determined to go ahead with a fourth-term election, Satō stated: "To make a definite decision on that I will have to ask for your cooperation. Insofar as I have a say in things, I will not work aimlessly. I in-tend to have you in the cabinet, but is your health up to it?" Satō thus hinted at a cabinet reorganization immediately following his reelection and indicated he wanted Maeo to be part of it. Following this, Maeo gave up the idea of running for party president, and Miki Takeo was the sole con-tender against Satō. Some of the junior Dietmen in the Kōchikai expressed opinions such as: "We have never written the name 'Satō Eisaku' on a ballot. Having been opposed to his election for a third term, it is illogical—however strategic it might be—to support him for a fourth term." Yet they could hardly support a Maeo candidacy when Maeo himself was not willing to run. Ultimately, things moved in the direction of supporting Satō's bid for a fourth term.

In October, Prime Minister Satō went to New York to speak at the United Nations General Assembly and then held talks with President Nixon in Washington before returning to Japan prior to the October 29 party presidential election. Interest focused on how many votes would be cast against his candidacy. In the election results, 353 votes out of a total 481 went to Satō Eisaku, 111 to Miki Takeo, and 3 to non-candidates, while 14 were blank or otherwise invalid. Considerable attention was given the fact that Miki had put up such a good fight, collecting 111 votes that were considered votes of opposition to Satō. As this October 29 party convention was ending, Satō surprised party Vice-President Kawashima by saying to him softly, "Let's call off the cabinet reorganization." This remark was not heard by others in the room because of the general confusion as people were leaving, getting ready to go to the party habitually hosted by the new party president on such occasions, this time held at the Prime Minister's Official Residence.

Returning immediately to this residence, Prime Minister Satō instructed his secretaries to direct Maeo to the prime minister's office as soon as he arrived. When this was done, a conversation between Satō and Maeo began, and Satō announced a cancellation of the cabinet reorganization. After a few exchanges, the conversation ended within ten minutes. Getting wind of the fact that a talk was going on between Satō and Maeo, a group of reporters immediately surrounded Maeo at the party. Maeo gulped down a glass of whisky and water but said nothing. Before long, as if from nowhere, the rumor began to spread that the expected reorganization had been called off. Maeo then retired to the Kōchikai office, where for the first time he referred to the outcome of his talk with Satō, saying simply, "The reorganization has been called off." This prompted an enraged reaction, especially from the Kōchikai's junior members.

These junior Dietmen were all persons who had begun their political careers during the Ikeda Administration. After Ikeda's death, the Kōchikai, perhaps because its energies were absorbed in coping with Prime Minister Satō's stratagems, allowed seniority within the faction to play an inordinately large role, with the result that while the faction's leadership, which was friendly to Satō, continued to fill prominent positions in Diet committees and the like, junior members failed to get such posts or even to be given adequate opportunities to express their opinions. In the six years after Ikeda's retirement, only three of these junior Dietmen had been selected for ministerial posts. At this rate, not only they personally but the Kōchikai itself would be driven into an obscure corner of the political scene: this was the conviction behind their impatience.

Immediately after Maeo's revelation, an emergency meeting of Kōchikai Diet members was held at which the first speaker was Tanaka Rokusuke, who stood looking at a photograph on the wall of the late former Prime Minister Ikeda as he spoke: "I had intended that, so long as the Ikeda faction continued to exist, I would bury my bones with it. But this very day, my patience has run out. When Satō made his promise as worthless as a scrap of paper, why did Maeo not say, 'Wait until I have consulted with all my colleagues'? Maeo's role is to serve as a check on Satō's selfishness. Yet he allowed himself to be tricked into thinking a cabinet reorganization was in the air, and was then taken complete advantage of. I can no longer tolerate it. I am parting ways with Maeo and will surely never enter this place again." Tanaka Rokusuke then opened the door and left, wiping tears from his eyes.

At the same meeting, others, including Tazawa Kichirō, Hattori Yasushi, Sasaki Yoshitake, and Itō Masayoshi also rose to speak. One opinion was: "In the September 22 conversation between Satō and Maeo, what amounted to a policy agreement was concluded, and although we all agreed to it and voted for Prime Minister Satō, we have only been betrayed by the prime minister. Our faction should withdraw all its members from cabinet and party posts." Another opinion was: "Since Maeo has been duped by the prime minister, should he not take responsibility for it? The faction has been weakened, and it is necessary to quickly renovate its organization and strength."

Members of the *Mokuyōkai* (Thursday Club), a grouping of junior Kōchikai adherents, met in a room at the back of the Kōchikai office known as the "chairman's room" to discuss Chairman Maeo's responsibility and the option of demanding his resignation. It was soon announced that a covenant "demanding the resignation of Maeo" had been signed by seventeen members. On the other hand, voices were raised among many of the senior members, asking if this did not constitute "a sort of coup d'état, a rebellion by persons associated with Ōhira." Maeo announced in an unusual speech, "Because the matter is so serious, I will within a month make some decisions, including whether to continue or to resign."

The dissatisfaction felt by the junior members came to be directed also at Ōhira: "However you may think about the matter, this is something we cannot tolerate. We intend to bring it to a clear-cut conclusion." They also asked Ōhira to make up his mind. Ōhira searched for a way to break the deadlock and urged circumspection: "It's not that I cannot understand your feelings, but Maeo must surely have his reasons, so don't be in such a hurry."

Seen from Ōhira's perspective, during the Satō years Tanaka Kakuei, who had at the time of the Ikeda Administration been on a par with, or even a little behind, Ōhira, had continued to hold the important posts of LDP secretary-general and minister of finance, greatly increasing his stature within the party. At the same time, Kishi's protégé Fukuda Takeo was also rapidly rising. Nakasone was also gaining strength, and Miki had shown he was no political lightweight, having won 111 votes in the last election for LDP president. By comparison, although Ōhira had held the posts of LDP Policy Research Council chairman and minister of international trade and industry during the middle years of the Satō Administration, he was still just one of the leading members of the Maeo faction. If Ikeda and Satō were considered as belonging to the first postwar generation of statesmen, the time for the second generation was now beginning. It was only natural that Ōhira might feel somewhat in a hurry, but it seemed quite necessary to avoid a situation whereby Maeo, who still remained in a position of "elder brother," would be unceremoniously pulled down and his position as faction chairman taken by forcible methods. Ōhira's feeling was rather this: "In the Kōchikai office, in which there hangs a photograph of Ikeda Hayato, transfers of leadership must be done in a proper way."

From around November 3, Maeo and Ōhira began having discussions on the matter, and both were agreed on the importance of keeping the organization together. Maeo sought some face-saving compromise. Ōhira suggested that if there could be a written agreement making clear that Ōhira was to succeed Maeo as faction leader, Ōhira would not ask for an immediate transfer of leadership. However, to Maeo it was clear that the moment such a succession was clearly designated he would already have lost his authority as faction leader. The discussions did not go smoothly, but finally, as an interim measure, a compromise was reached on building up a system of collective leadership. And although it was not put in writing, Ōhira was informed of Maeo's willingness to step down as Kōchikai chairman sometime following the August 1971 observance of the seventh anniversary—which has a special significance in the Buddhist tradition—of Ikeda's death.

The collective leadership system was announced on November 18. Its five members were Ōhira Masayoshi (in the central position), Suzuki Zenkō, Kodaira Hisao, Ogawa Heiji, and Shiomi Shunji, all of whom were to assist Maeo. This system was very much the product of compromise, and so it could not be expected that all problems would thereby be settled. First and foremost was the problem of how to administer the faction's finances. The end of the year was approaching, and it was necessary to distribute to faction members extra money for year-end expenses, known as *mochidai*. However, since it was evident that Maeo was retiring as faction head, it became difficult for him to get contributions from business circles. By borrowing the needed funds in a private, individual capacity, Maeo managed, though only barely, to fulfil his function as faction chairman. Dissatisfaction continued to mount around Maeo, however, especially among the junior group who looked to Ōhira for leadership. At issue for them was the fact that, although it had been for all practical purposes decided that Ōhira was to be the next faction chairman, Maeo had not made clear exactly when he would retire. They feared that at this rate their political positions, together with the entire Kōchikai, could collapse. This feeling was particularly acute when they returned to their home districts at the end of the year and the beginning of the New Year. Unified local elections were coming up in the spring of 1971, and in the various electoral districts questions were being asked as to whether the Kōchikai was prepared for electoral battle. Some of the junior Dietmen, influenced by this sort of atmosphere back home, seemed increasingly willing, in the absence of clear directions from Maeo and other leading members, to form their own new political grouping around Ōhira, which they hoped would allow them to devote themselves wholeheartedly to politics without being constrained by what others might think or do. Almost every day they would gather in the office Ōhira had set up in Aoyama to discuss strategy and try to win Ōhira's cooperation.

Meanwhile, Suzuki Zenkō, who acted as a sort of bridge between the faction leaders and some of the junior Kōchikai members, visited Maeo at his residence on three occasions—twice in mid-January and once in early February—to explain that Satō would undoubtedly retire the following year and press Maeo for some indication of whether he planned to fight to succeed Satō as party president. On one pretext or another, Maeo never gave a clear answer. In exasperation, Suzuki finally complained, "I'm sorry, but I'm tired of trying to wrestle with a shop curtain" (meaning his attempts to get a clear answer were as ineffectual as beating the air), and he gave up his attempts to get Maeo to commit himself.

Around this time the number of persons within the Kōchikai who sympathized with the more impatient junior members increased to make a group of twenty-six or twenty-seven Dietmen from both houses. If one included sympathizers from other factions and those who belonged to no faction, the group came to about forty. Together they tried to convince Ōhira that "It's no longer a time to cling to the Kōchikai. To realize our own aspirations we should cast off old restraints." Ōhira, however, found himself unwilling to break with the Kōchikai that Ikeda had founded and he and the other members had so painstakingly maintained and protected. Even if he and the more impatient junior members did leave and cooperated, for example, with Tanaka, they would become subordinate to Tanaka. There was apprehension also that, in the very worst case, they might be unable, in fact, to win a vote over Fukuda supporters for the LDP presidency.

The junior group set March 1, prior to the unified local elections, as the day to raise a separatist banner and asked Ōhira to pledge cooperation. Ōhira was thus faced with the most difficult decision in his political career. The matter could not wait for the time Maeo had suggested, namely, after the seventh anniversary of Ikeda's death, which was not until August. Was there no way in which, by talking with Maeo, a changeover in the faction's leadership could be smoothly effected? Nearly every day, intensive talks were carried out between Maeo's close associates and Ōhira's, and between Ōhira and the "young rebel" group.

The latter tried their very best to win Ōhira over. A typical argument was: "By procrastinating, you are the same as the present leader. Doesn't the problem really boil down to whether you really want to take on the job?" Finally, Ōhira said, "If the time comes when there is no way out of the deadlock, I will act together with you fellows." In the meantime, Maeo summoned Itō and other younger members individually, asking them to be prudent and avoid rash action; yet he could no longer stop the momentum for change.

One of those who exerted himself to the utmost in this situation was Suzuki Zenkō, who urged restraint on Ōhira's part and tried to convince the rebel group to be a little more patient. He summoned several hard-liners and told them: "In July 1965, Ikeda's illness reappeared and the morning of July 29, when it was decided that he would be readmitted to the hospital for surgery, Maeo, Ōhira, and I were called to his home in Shinanomachi. Ikeda said, 'It's possible that I may not be able to speak later. Because this may be the last thing you'll hear from me, please all three of you listen carefully. The Kōchikai is the *backbone* [original English] of the conservative party, so in the future stick together and carry out political activities befitting this backbone. If anything should happen to me, have Maeo in a central position, with Ōhira and Suzuki assisting.' These 'last words' of Ikeda have always stuck in my mind, so as persons belonging to the Kōchikai that Ikeda created, I think we must quickly remedy the present situation.

"From this perspective, Ōhira is the most important person in the Kōchikai next to Maeo. Whether we help Ōhira or hinder him depends on the manner in which we colleagues in the Kōchikai help him. But what you fellows are doing is making Ōhira into a Saigō Takamori [leader of the defeated Satsuma Rebellion of 1877] dying from arrow wounds at Kagoshima's Shiroyama. Now the most important thing is for Maeo and Ōhira to talk candidly, but unfortunately they have become the persons immediately concerned. Fortunately, I am a third party, and I intend to talk carefully with them and to find a way out of this situation, so please do not act rashly but leave it up to me." The hard-liners were persuaded and agreed to allow more time for resolving the problem.

In this way, the March 1 date that had been set for raising the separatist banner of revolt was temporarily postponed, but direct talks between Maeo and Ōhira took on a more serious slant. The situation reached a point where, in early March, Maeo was heard to say, "Ōhira is really something, having managed to stab me in the side." After the first ten days of March, Maeo finally agreed to a leadership changeover four months earlier than anticipated. The last talk between Maeo and Ōhira took place on March 14 and basic agreement was reached, which included the provision that, to avoid influencing the local elections, the change of leadership would be kept secret for one month. For all practical purposes, however, the drama of changing the chairmanship of the Kōchikai, which had been on the verge of splitting up, had come to an end.

On March 9, 1971, an essay by Ōhira appeared in the Nihon Keizai Shinbun titled "Shin kenryoku ron" (A New Look at Authority), which is of particular interest because it reflects Ōhira's state of mind at the time. It begins with the question, "For what purpose is authority necessary?" and then elaborates as follows: "When we think about authority, it is necessary not only to investigate the structure and functions of authority as such, but to be aware that something on a higher dimension is also involved that makes it necessary. Authority is not something that stands alone, and there should be certain purposes served by it. Authority should be allowed to exist to the extent that it is needed to serve these purposes and only to the limited extent that it is so needed."

What, then, are these purposes? Ōhira puts forth "peace" and "welfare" as possible answers, even though "their definition is not necessarily clear." A major purpose, more easy to grasp, "must be whatever can most actively bring us a feeling of purpose in living." But such things are, in fact, hard to define. Therefore, "What authority should strive for is surely, more than to seek understanding and sympathy for its own ideology, to form its own raison d'être by finding ways to make the broad

stratum [of the population]—which is unconcerned with ideology—
something that is advantageous, or at least not harmful, to its existence."

Ōhira admits, however, that such work is certainly not easy and that
schemes and expedients have their limits: "There must be in authority
something that is still deeper and more fundamental. In the Orient, people
have sought the basis for the exercise of political power not in expedients
but in personal character as the inherent embodiment of authority. They
have sought the moral influence of these personal embodiments of authority more than they have nursed expectations of any complex network of
systems and laws. It has been considered that the basis for the exercise of
political power is, first of all, to know oneself, to overcome oneself, to exert
oneself. This concept is by no means a monopoly of the East and can also
be found in the political thought of the West. . . . We must remember that
the basic qualities of authority . . . lie in ideals about what those who exercise authority should be. More than any number of stratagems or the relative skill with which they might be combined, what brings true confidence
in authority and gives it dignity is the degree of confidence attained by
those individuals who represent the authority. André Maurois has said,
'The secret to controlling others is to learn from experience how to control
oneself,' and I believe this precisely hits the mark in relation to those in
whom authority is represented."

This should not be seen merely as a sort of criticism of Maeo. Ōhira was
no doubt aiming the scourge of admonition very much at himself. In any
case, these were thoughts he wrote at a time when he was about to reach
hailing distance of the top political power in the nation, yet was still in a
situation hemmed in by jealousies and outbursts of calumny or anger.
Because he gave serious thought to the sorts of things expressed in this
essay, Ōhira must surely be rated a very "unusual" or "different" sort of
politician in a political environment where it was customary to act without
giving much thought to the phenomenon known as "authority," which all
too often expresses itself in a diabolical manner.

The latter half of the drama of the Kōchikai's change in leadership took
place wholly in behind-the-scenes negotiations. After the changeover decision had been made, Maeo summoned each Kōchikai member individually
to hear his ideas and to communicate to him his own intentions. This was
done with a view to prevent the lingering of any bad feelings. Some of the
leading members were strongly opposed to the change of chairmanship on
the grounds that it was so sudden, but Maeo managed to win them over.
After intrafaction persuasion was completed, the change in leadership was
formally realized at a plenary meeting of Kōchikai members on April 17,
1971. By moving from what had been the problematic second seat in the

Kōchikai to the chairmanship, Ōhira had passed the crucial first stage on the road to running for party president.

At the April 17 plenary meeting, Maeo prefaced the announcement of his resignation with these words: "Our faction, which has the mission of being the traditional conservative mainstream, must make further strides and become a body actually in control of political power. I want you to decide on a new leader, to build up a new system, and to go forward to achieve those goals that I was not able to realize." Ōhira was then unanimously selected as the Kōchikai's new chairman, after which veteran politician Kosaka Zentarō quoted a favorite phrase of former Prime Minister Yoshida from the Chinese classic *Liezi* by Lie Yukou: "Big fish capable of swallowing a boat do not swim in small streams." He then elaborated: "From now on, the Kōchikai must be in the main current of the basic conservative stream." Then another faction stalwart, Fukunaga Kenji, added his words of encouragement for the new chairman and represented the feelings of all present as he expressed his hopes for a Kōchikai renewal: "On the occasion of this change, we must do all we can to return to the Kōchikai of the early days."

By comparison with the complicated twists and turns that had preceded his selection as the new chairman, Ōhira's first remarks to the assembled members were clear and easily understood. First of all, he expressed thanks for the guidance that Chairman Maeo had up till then provided and then, after proposing that Maeo be named Kōchikai chairman emeritus, he continued: "This change of chairmanship involved the possibility of the biggest crisis for the Kōchikai since its founding. Faced with this grave situation, Fukunaga, Kosaka, and the other leading members exercised to the fullest their wisdom and reason, communicating back and forth between our colleagues. And, fortunately, we have been able not only to resolve the situation but have also succeeded in elevating a difficult situation into an occasion for stronger unity. The most important thing is to strengthen, with a deep-seated confidence, our mutual trust and to develop active and lively communication among our colleagues, and in this way to advance along a straight road toward those goals [shown to us by Maeo]."

Part 5

Rising Waves

Chapter 20

Turning the Tide

The year 1970, in October of which Prime Minister Satō was elected to his fourth term as party president, was something of a turning point for Japan. The Osaka Expo '70, which had opened in March, drew more than 64 million visitors before it closed in September and was a proud showcase of what Japan had achieved through its rapid economic growth. Domestic demand, however, was beginning to lack its former vigor. Such leading industrial sectors as automobiles and home electric appliances, which had been pillars of the country's economic growth, were tending to stagnate, while consumer prices showed a disquieting rise. To make matters worse, a number of severe cases of environmental pollution caused by industrial wastes were emerging. Although campus struggles were subsiding in the wake of the Law on Emergency Measures for University Administration, passed in 1969, certain ultraradical student elements were forming terrorist groups, such as the Red Army group that hijacked a Japan Air Lines airplane. A number of residents' movements arose in response to pollution, rising prices, and the fact that the Japanese, although they accepted the necessity for a certain degree of sacrifice to achieve economic growth, were, with full employment and rising wages, showing greater interest in raising their quality of life. On November 9, 1970, just eleven days after Satō's election to a fourth term as LDP president, Kawashima Shōjirō, who with Tanaka Kakuei had played a central role in Satō's election, died. His death somehow seemed to presage an end in the not too distant future to Satō's long tenure as prime minister.

The same year saw important changes in the international situation with regard to China. The Japanese government had not changed its position, held consistently until that time, that the Nationalist regime in Taiwan was the legitimate government of China, but on November 20 the resolution put forward by Albania at the United Nations to expel the Na-

275

tionalist government and replace it with the People's Republic of China won majority approval. Although the inclusion of the mainland government was subsequently delayed by the two-thirds majority vote required for substantive issues ("important questions"), the ultimate outcome was understood as being just a matter of time. This was a blow to the foreign policy of the Satō Administration, which had always supported Taiwan. In the 64th Extraordinary Diet convened on November 24, the government was on the defensive in discussions on China, no less than on issues of trade frictions (such as the U.S.–Japan textile negotiations), pollution, prices, and the state of the economy.

In April 1971, in the seventh unified local elections held every four years, the LDP suffered a heavy defeat in Tokyo, where its candidate, Hatano Akira, lost in his bid for the governorship to progressive candidate Minobe Ryōkichi, one of whose slogans was "Stop Satō." Progressive candidates were also elected as governor of Osaka and mayor of Kawasaki. This was an indication that following the rapid economic growth of the 1960s, the values of the Japanese people were changing and the traditional policies of the conservative party were no longer able to meet the new expectations.

The transfer of the chairmanship of the Kōchikai from Maeo to Ōhira had taken place at just this time. It was a period when the political world, always quick to perceive new trends, was adopting the view that Prime Minister Satō's days in office were numbered. Interest was already shifting to the coming battle to choose Satō's successor. There were expected to be four candidates for the party presidency, namely, Finance Minister Fukuda Takeo (a firm supporter of the Satō Administration), LDP Secretary-General Tanaka Kakuei (who had served five terms as secretary-general), Miki Takeo (who had already twice run for the party presidency), and Ōhira. This four-man race became one of consuming interest for Japanese journalists.

Ōhira's biggest headache was the lingering dissension that had affected the Kōchikai for so long. In particular, the attitude toward Ōhira of some old-timers, who would have preferred to see Maeo continue as faction chairman, could only be called uncooperative, and it was still often mentioned that Ikeda had allegedly entrusted Maeo, not Ōhira, with the faction leadership. Concerning this problem, Ōhira later recalled: "This transfer [of the chairmanship from Maeo] may have appeared quite natural on the surface, but people's psychology is not quite so mechanical. Due partly to my own shortcomings, Maeo's attitude toward me, consciously or not, had become rather hard, and the Kōchikai as a whole failed to show cohesion. Such were the circumstances surrounding the announcement of my candidacy for the party presidency; but, in any case, the majority wanted to go ahead and have me represent them in the election."

Disappointed in the results of the unified local elections held in the spring, the government and the LDP looked forward to Prime Minister Satō's signing of the document finalizing the return of Okinawa, which was to take place just prior to the June 27 ninth Upper House election, considering it likely to help regain strength for the ruling party. The signing ceremonies were held simultaneously in Tokyo and Washington on June 17, 1971, promising the return of Okinawa on April 1, 1972.

However, in spite of these efforts of the LDP, the opposition parties made important inroads in the election, aided by a cooperative strategy among the JSP, Kōmeitō, and DSP. The LDP won only 62 seats, or just half the 125 seats up for election. This was 7 seats less than those won by the LDP in the Upper House election six years previously, and 9 seats less than in the election three years previously. Many predicted that before long the LDP would be unable to maintain a majority in the Upper House. Perhaps due in part to the fact that this Upper House election was held so soon after the unified local elections, voter turnout was low at 59.2 percent for both local and nationwide constituency votes, or some ten percentage points less than in the previous Upper House election. The election's most important aspect was the rapid increase in what public opinion polls called persons "without any particular party preference." This phenomenon suggested not merely a crisis in conservative politics but the transformation of postwar Japanese party politics as a whole.

In the cabinet reorganization that took place on July 5 following the election, the top three party posts went to Hori Shigeru (secretary-general), Nakasone Yasuhiro (General Council chairman), and Kosaka Zentarō (Policy Research Council chairman). The fact that Hori, who was close to Fukuda Takeo, was made secretary-general was seen as establishing a balance between Fukuda and his rival Tanaka Kakuei. Cabinet appointments included Maeo Shigesaburō as minister of ustice, Fukuda Takeo as minister of foreign affairs, Mizuta Mikio as minister of finance, Tanaka Kakuei as minister of international trade and industry, and Takeshita Noboru as chief cabinet secretary.

The practice of allotting given numbers of cabinet posts to certain factions in proportion to faction size began during the Satō years. This has been sometimes maligned as "imposing" a factional balance, yet it has proved to be an important means, still applied today, for maintaining stability. It has been a necessary prerogative and responsibility of each faction leader to determine which faction member or members would be proposed. As of 1971, the Kōchikai was allotted three cabinet seats. This was the first cabinet reorganization Ōhira had to deal with since becoming Kōchikai chairman. Given their former relations, this meeting between Satō and Ōhira was delicate, and Ōhira felt rather tense beforehand. In talks with Satō at the Prime Minister's Official Residence, he requested cabinet posts for former Kōchikai Chairman Maeo and for Maeo's close associate Niwa Kyōshirō. The remaining allotment could, he presumed, go to one of his own close associates. Their talk proceeded more easily than expected, and Satō quickly agreed to bring Maeo into the cabinet as minister of justice and to make Niwa minister of transport. However, the third post allotted to the Kōchikai went to Maeo's associate Takami Saburō, who was made minister of education, somewhat disappointing Ōhira.

It was clear to everybody that this was to be the last cabinet reorganization of the Satō Administration. Thus, each of the factions that hoped to put up a candidate for the party presidency began to prepare for the presidential election that was expected to come perhaps as early as the end of the year. The Kōchikai needed some sort of an announcement that Ōhira would, in fact, be a candidate for the party presidency. Important issues were when and how such an announcement would be made, as well as how to consolidate factional unity beforehand. And the wording of the announcement would have to be suitable for a Kōchikai leader like Ōhira, who emphasized policy issues.

It was decided that the best time would be during the study meeting for Kōchikai Diet members held, as in other years, at the end of the summer. In preparation for this meeting, a Kōchikai Policy Committee was set up in May. Headed by Ōkubo Takeo, it commenced a sort of crash program of studying important public issues. Other members were Kaneko Ippei, Sasaki Yoshitake, Urano Sachio, Tanigaki Sen'ichi, Furuuchi Hiroo, and Itō Masayoshi, all Dietmen close to Ōhira. This committee tried to study issues in depth and often exchanged opinions with scholars and intellectuals from outside political circles. Ōhira attended almost all of the committee's meetings, assuming the role of an opinion leader and often expressing his views.

On July 15 (July 16 in Japan), just a month after the signing of the agreement for the return of Okinawa, the American government suddenly announced that President Nixon would visit China sometime before May 1972. This was the "Nixon shock," which meant "going over the heads of the Japanese," as the journalists put it, and was exactly the sort of American–Chinese diplomacy that the Satō Administration, which had always followed in America's wake and supported the Nationalist Taiwan government, had wanted to avoid. There was no hiding the consternation of Japanese government leaders. Then, on August 15 (August 16 in Japan), came the second "Nixon shock," when the United States announced measures to protect the dollar whereby the convertibility of gold and dollars was halted and a 10 percent surcharge, aimed primarily at Japan, was applied to imports from all countries.

All the opposition parties made use of this occasion to attack the government, and critical voices could be heard even in the ranks of the LDP. The mass media, too, stepped up the call for an early end to the Satō Administration and a new departure in public morale. There were lively discussions by the Kōchikai's Policy Committee as to how these trends should be reflected in its draft statement and how the faction's own views should be formulated. Special attention was given to the question of the People's Republic of China's representation in the United Nations. On this matter Ōhira was extremely cautious. In a press interview soon after assuming the Kōchikai chairmanship, he had stated that it was necessary to deal with the question of China's representation with a forward-looking viewpoint, and stressed the importance of policy toward Taiwan, saying, "With respect to the Taiwan question, first of all we must clarify what is possible and what is not possible." But he avoided specifying any concrete methods or expectations.

On July 22, the day after the opening of the 26th United Nations General Assembly, Prime Minister Satō announced his support for a dual recognition whereby Japan "would invite the Beijing government to the United Nations but recognizes the existence of the Nationalist government," at the same time stating that Japan would jointly sponsor with the United States an inverse substantive issue resolution to make exclusion of the Nationalist government subject to a two-thirds majority. However, since neither Beijing nor Taiwan was willing to recognize "two Chinas," it seemed doubtful that either resolution could win approval.

This attitude on the part of the government invited protest not only from the opposition parties but also from the Miki and Nakasone factions of the LDP. The reactions of the Ōhira faction were also interesting. Many of the junior members insisted that, so as not to lag behind world trends, the draft of the speech to be presented at the faction's study meeting—which would, in effect, be an announcement of Ōhira's candidacy for the party presidency—include an expression of recognition for the Beijing government. Yet for some time Ōhira did not change his stance of caution. It was only after virtually all of the junior faction members adopted a statement that "there is no point in making a speech unless it reveals a clear attitude on the China question," that Ōhira finally made up his mind.

The completed speech draft was handed to Ōhira, and after he had made several revisions it was finalized under the provisional title *"Ushio no nagare o kaeyō"* (Let Us Turn the Tide). While not disapproving of this title, Ōhira wrote beside it, *"Shin seiki no kaimaku"* (Commencement of a New Century). This title may be said to have accurately expressed his perception that both internationally and domestically Japan was at an important turning point. The proposals began with a concise statement on the current era as follows:

> Our country is just now at a turning point that might be called the end of the postwar era. Until now we have worked intently in the quest for more material wealth, but we have not necessarily been able to find true happiness or purpose of life in the wealth we have attained. We have run full speed ahead, without pause, along the path of economic growth, but because of the very speed with which this growth has taken place we now have no choice but to aim again at stability. With considerable nonchalance we have attempted economic advances abroad, but because of the intensity of these advances we have sometimes become the object of jealousy and resistance in other countries. Our keynote has been cooperation with the United States and we have avoided [full] participation in international politics, but certainly with the present weakening of the dollar system we must embark on the difficult path of a self-reliant diplomacy. Our nation has concentrated on economic reconstruction, but precisely because of the scale of our economic growth, as "global insiders" we now have no choice but to support an internationalization of the economy.
>
> This must surely be called an important turning point. In response to this turning point, it is the mission of politics to avoid mistakes in our future course. The people of our nation certainly have the energy to meet this test. To promote the most effective development of this energy, we must correct some political postures and carry out some bold revisions in policy approaches.

This assessment of the times was unusual for its foresight in a political milieu where most still placed high expectations on continued rapid economic growth and seemed unable to grasp the significance of the end of gold–dollar convertibility. The proposals continued with a call for "ridding politics of mistrust." Politicians were warned against "lightly taking on tasks that are unlikely to be accomplished" and a plea was made for returning "discretion and solidarity" to human relations that were beginning to show "rift and rivalry."

With respect to foreign relations, under the subheading "Vigorous Development of a Self-Reliant and Peaceful Diplomacy," the need was emphasized, first of all, for improving relations with the United States; second, for normalizing relations with the People's Republic of China; and third, for global economic and cultural cooperation. The China issue, which was attracting so much attention, was discussed as follows:

> In the Diet in 1964, I made a statement to the effect that if Beijing should receive the world's blessing and become a member of the United Nations, Japan, too, should work for a normalization of relations with Beijing.
>
> After that, discussion of China's representation at the United Nations took place on several occasions, and since last autumn the majority opinion at the United Nations has rapidly inclined toward recognizing the right of Beijing to represent China. Since then, not only have the number of countries with diplomatic relations with Beijing continued to grow, but public opinion in our country has also been moving noticeably in this direction.
>
> I judge that the time is now ripe for the government to correctly assess this situation and to make, as it were, an ultimate decision on the China issue. Therefore, I believe that the government, in keeping with the spirit and principle of Japan–China friendship, would be faithful to public opinion at home and abroad by opening, as quickly as possible, negotiations with the government in Beijing. And until such a decision is reached, I should ask the government to refrain from actions, such as supporting the scheme for inverse substantive issue designation in the United Nations, which run counter to the mainstream of public opinion.

On the China issue, Ōhira had finally crossed the Rubicon. The final part of the speech, quoted in part below, was a proposal for Japan to aim at transforming itself into "a nation of garden-cities" (den'en toshi kokka).

> The Japanese people now want, more than the boundless pursuit of material wealth, a stable life with ample room for the spirit. . . . To respond to these hopes, we must build on our four islands a human society in harmonious balance with nature. I have in mind a society that would have automatic means of reconstituting itself so as to stop the more ruthless trends of urbanization, and one that would combine the merits of both

cities and rural villages. In other words, we should provide employment opportunities and good living environments in farming and mountain villages, making them into prosperous areas of fields and gardens; and such fields and gardens should also be brought into the cities to make a new nation of garden-cities. This nation of garden-cities would by no means deny future economic growth; it would be a society in which industry and agriculture, with mutually complementary high productivity, would be combined—as would cities and villages—on a higher dimension. . . .

A nation of garden-cities would be composed of innumerable local societies, each with its own special character, functioning together as an organic whole. Depending on the region, specific needs and demands would be diverse, and no single-pattern imposition [of solutions or activities] would be allowed. . . .

To realize this sort of a nation is by no means impossible. To do this on our four islands with their one hundred million people is our challenge for the new century.

At the time this proposal was being drawn up, various suggestions were made as to what title should be given to the concept. It was around the same time that Minister of International Trade and Industry Tanaka Kakuei was elaborating his Plan for the Remodeling of the Japanese Archipelago (Nihon rettō kaizōron), a name that sounded rather austere. The Kōchikai members wanted something more down-to-earth and in keeping with Ōhira's ability to appeal to the popular mind. When the nation of garden-cities proposal was first made, some members of the drafting committee were rather perplexed—no doubt because the words seemed unusual in the arena of politics—but Ōhira did not hesitate to choose this as the title he liked best.

On the morning when advance notices of the plan were being prepared for the press, Ōhira turned up at the Kōchikai office and simply remarked to those who happened to be present: "This is my debut, you know. Up to now, I have really felt I am still just small fry. Thinking about all these things last night, I didn't sleep at all."

The above-quoted "Commencement of a New Century" speech, which encapsulated Ōhira's political philosophy and understanding of the times and looked boldly to the future of Japanese society, was not at the time sufficiently understood in its entirety by either the political world or the mass media, perhaps because it was in so many ways ahead of its time. It would take nearly ten years for it to be understood within the LDP.

Nevertheless, on the question of China's representation in the United Nations, which was at the time the greatest political issue, Ōhira's statement did have an important effect.

Following this speech's delivery before the study meeting of Kōchikai Dietmen held at Hakone on September 1, 1971, the morning editions of the next day's papers gave it such front-page headlines as "Ōhira in Anti-Satō Declaration, Urges Quick Change of China Policy" (*Asahi*); "Government in Tight Spot over LDP Opposition to China Representation as Inverse Substantive Issue; Ōhira Also Opposed" (*Yomiuri*); and "Beijing Is Legitimate Government, Says Ōhira in Statement Eyeing LDP Presidency" (*Sankei*).

As a follow-up to these policy proposals, the Kōchikai Policy Committee announced further proposals on September 28, under the title "Revising the Course of the Economy and the Role of Government Finance"; on November 17, under the title "A Law on Special Measures for Emergency Government Finance"; and on December 16, under the title "Policy on Public Borrowing."

These various proposals, even if somewhat uneven in content, served to inform the public about Ōhira's policy package, his policy methods, and some of his political ideals that had not been widely known. Because of the requested participation of nearly all Kōchikai members in their formulation, these proposals also served to strengthen Kōchikai cooperation and to provide a vehicle for Ōhira's leadership. The series of proposals continued into 1972, with the last two titled "Principles of Behavior for a Peaceful Nation" (May 8) and "New Directions for Education and Social Welfare" (June 14).

On October 24, 1971, the United Nations General Assembly voted against the resolution to make the ouster of the Nationalist Chinese government a substantive issue requiring a two-thirds majority and at the same time approved seating the Beijing government to replace the Nationalists. Prior to this, when Japan cosponsored the motion to designate the ouster of the Nationalists a substantive issue, Ōhira had criticized the Satō Cabinet's position: "I certainly cannot think of it as a praiseworthy measure," and, in a less partisan vein, said: "We are not so irresponsible as to make the China issue a tool for political infighting. It is no time for a cabinet or any group within the party to sulk or to walk on tiptoe; what we must seriously think about is how to catch the big whale that is the China issue. . . . The Japan–China problem, like ice melting in spring, has taken quite a long time, but domestic public opinion is approaching a well-founded consensus."

The struggle between Fukuda Takeo (aged sixty-five) and Tanaka

Kakuei (aged fifty-four) to take over the mantle of leadership within the Satō mainstream faction was already heating up. Prime Minister Satō hoped to see a Fukuda administration and thought highly of Fukuda's abilities to formulate and direct policies. Fukuda also enjoyed the support of Satō's brother, Kishi Nobusuke. However, Tanaka's efforts to expand his influence within the Satō faction were paying off, to the extent that the greater part of the Satō faction's funding was now being raised by Tanaka. Tanaka had established his influence not only in the Satō faction but in the party as a whole, and this influence could not be easily overridden, even by the considerable power wielded by Satō.

To determine the final details for the return of Okinawa, Prime Minister Satō attended the U.S.–Japan summit at San Clemente, California, on January 6 and 7, 1972, and indeed one of his motives in running for a fourth term as party president had been to attend this meeting. Because he was accompanied by both Foreign Minister Fukuda and International Trade and Industry Minister Tanaka, many in the political world expected that he would use this opportunity to somehow resolve the problem of who should be the next party president. When Satō made no move to do so, the situation soon developed into what journalists dubbed the "Tanaka–Fukuda war" (*Kakufuku sensō*).

After seeing on television the announcement of the U.S.–Japan joint statement and Prime Minister Satō's press conference on January 8, Miki Takeo made clear his own intention to run for the party presidency and said of Satō: "The prime minister's mission has now ended. He should step down for the sake of refreshing public confidence." Miki, who had won 111 votes in the previous presidential election, seems to have decided that his future political destiny might lie in the extent to which he could eat into the strength of the front-runner, even if he could not this time win.

Ōhira had to be a candidate because one of the reasons Maeo had been replaced as faction chairman was that he had not run for the position in the previous election. For Ōhira it was also important that he should win more than the ninety-five votes won by Maeo at the time Satō was elected to his third term. If he failed in this, his ability to lead the Kōchikai could be questioned. In this sense, regardless of who the front-runner might be, Ōhira's future political career depended on the next presidential election.

It should not be forgotten that ever since the Ikeda Administration Tanaka and Ōhira had developed a close friendship, which Ōhira once described as "superseding politics." The basic strategy of both men for the next presidential election was, first of all, to make a firm coalition between their two factions and then to get the cooperation of the Miki, Nakasone, and middle-of-the-road factions to form an anti-Fukuda front. But even supposing that this plan might succeed, there would still be the problem of which of the two would become party president. To questioning by a newspaper reporter, Ōhira replied, "Leave this problem up to me and Tanaka." He probably meant that the two had agreed to support, in a run-off vote, whoever had the larger number of votes on the first ballot. But already at this point their relative strengths were no secret. It was not expected to be easy for Ōhira to win even the number of votes that Maeo had won, so the Ōhira camp, wanting to leave no stone unturned, resolved to do its best to cultivate the support of the middle-of-the-road factions.

Okinawa's return, which had been Satō's long-cherished goal, became a reality on May 15, 1972. Throughout the ceremony held at the Nihon Budōkan hall, the prime minister was visibly moved. One saw not just a statesman who had achieved a major goal but also a man whose days in office were approaching an end. Always quick to exploit a situation, Tanaka had upstaged the Nihon Budōkan ceremony by announcing on May 9 the formation of the Tanaka faction, which, with the help of Kimura Takeo, a Satō faction veteran, brought in 80 percent of the Satō faction members plus several who had been associated with middle-of-the-road factions, over eighty Dietmen in all. From this moment the Satō faction became, in effect, the Tanaka faction. A small group associated with Hori Shigeru that supported Fukuda stayed behind as the Shūzan Club. It is of interest to note that in 1987 Takeshita Noboru brought together 80 percent of the Tanaka faction to form his own faction. It is thus tempting to say it is usual, in leadership transfers within very large factions, for about 20 percent of the faction's members to become dissatisfied outsiders.

On June 17, 1972, the day after the adjournment of the 68th Ordinary Diet session, Prime Minister Satō formally announced his retirement before an LDP Joint Plenary Meeting of Party Members of Both Houses of the Diet held in the Diet building. Two days later, on June 19, he summoned Fukuda and Tanaka to the Prime Minister's Official Residence and asked them both to promise that whoever came in second on the first ballot would, in the runoff, support the first-ballot winner of the most votes. Fukuda, confident that he would be in first position, agreed, and Tanaka did so, too, though he is said to have attached the following condition: "If this leaks out it will be difficult, so I want you to keep it a secret." Ōhira had already been the first to formally announce his candidacy for the party presidency on the afternoon of June 17. Fukuda announced his candidacy on June 20, and Miki and Tanaka announced theirs the next day. Nakasone, who had earlier shown interest in becoming a candidate, decided to give up the idea for the time being and to support Tanaka.

This election campaign, popularly known as the *"Sankaku-daifuku"* campaign (taking one Chinese character from each of the four candidates' family or first names), differed from previous campaigns in that for the first time in many years no current LDP president was among the candidates. It also differed in the number of candidates—there had never before been more than three—and in the fact that the campaign gave prominence to certain policy issues, such as the China question. At the party convention of January 1971, following Satō's election to a fourth term, the party rules had been revised so that the party president's term of office was now three years instead of two, and all candidates had to register a certain number of written recommendations.

Among the policy principles Ōhira put forth in this first bid for the party presidency were "heart-to-heart politics" (*kokoro no fureau seiji*), "politics that doesn't shun hard work" (*ase o oshimanai seiji*), and "politics without lies" (*uso no nai seiji*). He also pointed out that the LDP had to think seriously about how it would respond to changes in the times and in popular awareness. In this regard he spoke to a newspaper reporter as follows: "There has been the vague expectation [among LDP members] that people will continue to think that so long as you leave things up to the LDP there will be no great mistake. But people's thinking is changing. It is becoming more goal-oriented, and they are not satisfied with the idea that they will somehow get by if they just rely on the system; rather, they want to know when and how problems will be dealt with. . . . This is a warning for parliamentary politics. Because it is a parliamentary party, the LDP must energetically carry out party activities of a sort that have some meaningful connection with the lives of ordinary citizens, and within the party this sort of awareness is growing."

As for the usefulness of the current campaign, "The presidential campaign itself is one sort of politics; it is a good opportunity for expressing in a concise way what one is thinking every day." Yet compared to Tanaka Kakuei's Plan for the Remodeling of the Japanese Archipelago and the way in which the other two candidates were also fairly specific in expressing policy ideas and positions, Ōhira's approach seemed to place more weight on general principles than on specific suggestions.

In another of the many interviews he gave at this time, Ōhira elaborated on the reasons for this approach: "Up until now we have proceeded in a Satō-like fashion, that is to say, by steadily promoting the administrative aspect. However, in thinking about the Japan of the future, to the extent that realities have changed we will have to change our approach. The emphasis must change from administration (*gyōsei*) to statesmanship (*seiji*)." As for the normalization of relations with China, Ōhira had adopted a positive stance ever since his statement at Hakone the previous summer, and he welcomed subsequent positive expressions from Tanaka, Miki, and their supporters. In this regard he felt a certain pride in having played the role of a pace-setter.

Ōhira's views on the China question were now quite clear: "The China policy of today's government no longer fits the proper measurements, and I think the time has come to recognize China diplomatically. For this purpose, what we need more than anything else is a more unified opinion within Japan. We are now at the stage for forming a consensus."

The key to restoring diplomatic relations was whether or not Japan would recognize the "three principles" for restoring relations. When a delegation of the suprapartisan Parliamentarians' League for the Normalization of Japan–China Relations, led by Fujiyama Aiichirō, visited China in the autumn of 1971, it had signed a joint declaration calling for the observation of "four principles" for restoring relations. These were: (1) the People's Republic of China is the only government representing the Chinese people; (2) Taiwan is a province and an inseparable part of the People's Republic of China; (3) the so-called Japan–Taiwan treaty lacks legality and should be abrogated; and (4) all legal rights should be restored to the People's Republic of China in the United Nations, including its seat as a permanent member of the Security Council, and the representation of the Chiang Kai-shek group should be expelled. As a result of China's admission into the United Nations in the late autumn of 1971, the "four principles" became "three principles." In any event, the focus remained on how to deal with Taiwan.

Anticipating the way in which the matter was eventually to be handled, Ōhira addressed the China issue as follows: "If diplomatic relations between Japan and China are normalized, the Japan–Taiwan treaty will no longer exist. To pursue a normalization of Japanese–Chinese diplomatic relations is to attempt a new covenant with Beijing, and so the problem is, I think, extremely clear. Politically, if Japanese–Chinese relations are normalized, Japanese–Taiwanese relations come to an end. However, between Japan and Taiwan there have been exchanges of people and goods in the past, and these will continue in the future. I have no right to say anything about the details of Taiwan's future, but a normalization of Japanese–Chinese diplomatic relations must be made in a way that puts these exchanges of people and goods on a stable basis."

Normalization of Japanese–Chinese relations was a policy shared by the Ōhira and Tanaka camps, which had promised to assist each other regardless of who might win the LDP presidential race. And because the Miki camp, too, put forth the same sort of slogans, there was a beginning of concrete talks on policy agreements among three of the four camps (that is, with the exception of the Fukuda camp) contesting the election. After a series of talks among top members of the staffs of the respective factions—namely, Suzuki Zenkō (Ōhira faction), Nikaidō Susumu (Tanaka faction), and Ide Ichitarō (Miki faction)—direct talks among the faction leaders were held on July 2 at the Hotel Ōkura just before the election. Centering around normalization of relations with China, an agreement on policy matters was established among the three camps.

During these talks, leading to what became known as the "three-faction agreement," it was Miki who expressed himself most precisely on the issue of normalization. Having had long discussions with Premier Zhou Enlai during a visit to China in the spring of that year, Miki requested that the three parties to the agreement make clear their desire for the conclusion of a peace treaty that would specifically call for abandonment of diplomatic relations between Japan and Taiwan.

In response to Miki's suggestion, Ōhira and Tanaka showed caution, saying that normalization would entail very important diplomatic negotiations and that it should be sufficient for the "three-faction agreement" to put forth the overall goal of "working for the normalization of diplomatic relations between the two countries," but to leave the specifics to diplomatic channels. In the scheme for cooperation among the three factions that ultimately emerged, however, Miki's assertions were largely respected in words of support for "carrying out negotiations aimed at the conclusion of a peace treaty with the People's Republic of China."

The twenty-seventh LDP convention was convened at Hibiya Public Hall at 10 A.M. on July 5, 1972, for the purpose of choosing a party president. Following Satō's final speech as outgoing president, the 476 voting delegates cast their ballots. The first vote was as follows:

Tanaka Kakuei 156
Fukuda Takeo 150
Ōhira Masayoshi 101
Miki Takeo 69

In the leading position by six votes, Tanaka was ebullient, his face flushed. Fukuda, by contrast, was glum. Ōhira, in this first bid for the party's top post, appeared relieved to have passed the one-hundred mark. Miki looked definitely disappointed over his less-than-expected showing. Almost immediately, the runoff vote was taken, with the following result:

Tanaka Kakuei 282
Fukuda Takeo 190
(Invalid) 4

It was thus Tanaka Kakuei who would be the party's new president. As seen in the first vote, despite the main contest between Tanaka and Fukuda, Ōhira had succeeded in his approaches to the Nakasone and middle-of-the-road factions and had received over a hundred votes, outstripping Miki, who had been widely expected to be in third place. This could not help but bring an appreciation inside and outside the party that Ōhira had definite capabilities and was likely to be a strong candidate in the future.

Just before the election, Ōhira and Tanaka had exchanged opinions on post-Satō personnel matters, and it had been decided that if Tanaka should win, Ōhira would assume the post of foreign minister, which meant he would be responsible for handling the Foreign Ministry's outstanding problem—normalization of relations with China. It seems that Ōhira's wish to become foreign minister reflected some misgivings about Tanaka's approach to diplomatic affairs. He had, for example, once advised Tanaka: "Quit coming to hasty conclusions when negotiating with foreign countries. At home I'd like to have you say yes or no only after getting some consensus, first of all among the LDP, and also among the various government ministries, opposition parties, financial and labor circles, and so on. In saying yes or no a lot of responsibility is involved, so I want to hear you say yes or no after making preparations that will leave a clean aftermath at home. Your mind works fast and so you often do things only halfway along, when you think you've already understood everything, and that's why I'm a little worried."

Some within the Ōhira faction felt rather strongly that their leader should have asked for the post of LDP secretary-general, but even before the election that ushered in the new Tanaka Administration, Ōhira had once said rather cryptically, "It has been decided that I will be making the outside rounds," which suggested it was already decided that he would be responsible for foreign affairs in a Tanaka regime. Thus, a division of labor between Tanaka and Ōhira was established whereby Tanaka was in charge of domestic and party affairs while Ōhira dealt with international relations. Journalists soon popularized the phrase *"Uchimawari wa Tanaka, sotomawari wa Ōhira"* (Tanaka on the inner beat, Ōhira on the outer).

On the afternoon of July 5, immediately after the presidential election, Ōhira returned to his campaign headquarters at Tokyo's Hilton Hotel (now the Capitol Tōkyū Hotel) and instructed Kōchikai associates, "There will be a Tanaka Cabinet, and I want all of us in the Kōchikai, through each division or committee we belong to, to cooperate with it." He thus made clear that cooperation between Tanaka and himself was not merely on a personal level but was to involve the entire faction.

The party's top three party posts went to Hashimoto Tomisaburō (secretary-general, from the Tanaka faction), Suzuki Zenkō (chairman of the General Council, Ōhira faction), and Sakurauchi Yoshio (chairman of the Policy Research Council, Nakasone faction). Cabinet members included Miki Takeo as director-general of the Environment Agency (with the additional rank of deputy prime minister), Ōhira Masayoshi as foreign minister, Ueki Kōshirō as finance minister, Inaba Osamu as education minister, Shiomi Shunji as health and welfare minister, Nakasone Yasuhiro as international trade and industry minister and director-general of the Science and Technology Agency, Kimura Takeo as construction minister, Fukuda Hajime as home affairs minister, and Nikaidō Susumu as chief cabinet secretary. After an eight-year absence, Ōhira was again to be one of "the masters of Kasumigaseki," the section of central Tokyo where the main ministries are located.

Chapter 21

A Bridge to China

During the campaign for party presidency, the major policies proposed by Tanaka Kakuei were, externally, the normalization of Japan–China relations and, domestically, the remodeling of the Japanese archipelago. In keeping with his slogan *ketsudan to jikkō* (decision and execution), on the very day his cabinet was formed, July 7, 1972, Tanaka spoke to the nation, affirming his intention "to carry out normalization of relations with the People's Republic of China quickly and, given the turbulent world situation, to firmly promote a peaceful diplomacy." China's response was quick in coming. Two days later, on July 9, Premier Zhou Enlai announced that China "welcomes Prime Minister Tanaka's speech expressing his desire to strive for the early normalization of Japan–China relations."

The opposition parties also made a quick response. On July 10, Narita Tomomi, chairman of the JSP, stated that his party would "give its support if the Tanaka Cabinet recognizes the 'three principles' for restoring relations." On July 12, the DSP announced that it would "cooperate if the topics for discussion are handled seriously and clearly," and the Kōmeitō expressed its position of "sparing no efforts for cooperation so long as Prime Minister Tanaka has the determination to open a new chapter in Japan–China relations." The LDP, in order to harmonize views within the party, reorganized the party's Research Commission on Chinese Affairs as the Council on the Normalization of Japan–China Relations (chaired by Kosaka Zentarō). This body was placed under the direct supervision of the prime minister.

Despite the quickening mood, cutting across all the parties, in favor of normalizing Japan–China relations, Foreign Minister Ōhira, true to his cautious nature, expressed himself in a press conference on July 14 as follows: "In the Foreign Ministry there is a group of people who from dawn to dusk are thinking only about this problem. I am now listening and digesting what they have to say. Two things are essential: this and creating a consensus in the party. If we say we can do things that can't be done, and then try and don't succeed, it becomes a serious problem. The matters at hand are big ones, so I prefer that we go slowly."

Ōhira had his reasons for such a stance. In the first place, it was impossible to ascertain precisely to what extent unofficial contacts with China, as reported by Dietmen friendly to China and others concerned with relations between the two countries, represented China's "real sentiments"; second, although with Tanaka as the new party president normalization had definitely become the leading trend, there were many within the party who still advocated caution, and it was uncertain how a consensus might be reached; and third, even though Nixon had visited China, it was unclear how the United States, which had yet to establish diplomatic relations with China, would react to normalization of relations between China and Japan. On the other hand, movements in China had been extremely swift. For example, on July 3, just before the LDP presidential election, China sent Xiao Xiangqian, who was known for his friendly attitude toward Japan, as its top representative to the Tokyo Liaison Office for the Japan–China Memorandum Trade. On July 11, a former top representative at the same office, Sun Pinghua (at the time vice secretary-general of the China–Japan Friendship Association), was sent to Japan to head a delegation accompanying the Shanghai Dance Drama Troupe.

Soon after Sun Pinghua's arrival in Japan, Chen Kang, head of the Japan division of the Chinese Foreign Ministry's Asia Bureau, conveyed to Sun instructions from Premier Zhou that are said to have been the following: "One reason I called the Tanaka Cabinet's efforts to realize normalization a welcome development is that Chairman Mao has said we should adopt a positive attitude. . . . Whether the talks come to a conclusion or not, now is the right time for them. . . . Sun Pinghua must build a sturdy palace on the plain [a classical metaphor for laying a firm groundwork], and Xiao Xiangqian must continue to advance."

Japan's Ministry of Foreign Affairs, which under the Satō Administration had placed a low priority on Chinese diplomatic representation, could not discard its former way of thinking just because of a change of administration and a new foreign minister. Foreign Minister Ōhira, after careful consideration, instructed officials in charge of Chinese affairs to report directly to him on the developing situation. As another unusual example of diplomatic practice, he sought face-to-face contact with China's representatives by arranging personal meetings with Sun Pinghua and Xiao Xiangqian.

All this time, the mood for restoring relations quickened. On July 16,

Zhou Enlai met with former JSP Chairman Sasaki Kōzō and told him that "We would welcome Prime Minister Tanaka's visit to Beijing." Then, on July 19, in Tanaka's first meeting with a group of foreign journalists, he showed his enthusiasm for normalization by saying, "It's all summed up in saying that the time is ripe." On the previous day, Ōhira had announced his intention of establishing official routes for Japan–China contacts such as the Tokyo Liaison Office for the Japan–China Memorandum Trade. Since previous contact routes had been on the private level or through the opposition parties, this was a new departure.

The talks between Ōhira and Chinese representatives Sun Pinghua and Xiao Xiangqian were arranged by Fujiyama Aiichirō, chairman of the suprapartisan Parliamentarians' League for the Normalization of Japan–China Relations. On July 20, Fujiyama hosted a "Welcome Party for Mr. Sun and Mr. Xiao" at the Hotel New Japan, and asked Ōhira to attend. Following Fujiyama's introduction to Sun and Xiao, Ōhira said to them in a low voice, "Let's see each other again soon." Sun Pinghua replied, "I am hopeful that normalization of Japan–China relations will not remain just a mood but will flower and bear fruit."

The next day, July 21, it was decided that the Shanghai Dance Drama Troupe delegation led by Sun Pinghua would fly directly to Shanghai on specially routed Japan Air Lines (JAL) and All Nippon Airways (ANA) planes leaving Japan on August 16. These flights were also practice runs for the Tanaka-Ōhira visit to Beijing. Sun Pinghua was said to be critical of the direct flights as being too much of a luxury until Premier Zhou informed him of their special character.

On July 22, there was a preliminary meeting between Sun, Xiao, and members of the Japanese Ministry of Foreign Affairs, followed by a meeting just between Sun, Xiao, and Ōhira. Sun Pinghua later recalled that on that day Ōhira stated: "Prime Minister Tanaka and I are sworn friends with the same thinking. The prime minister has entrusted me with responsibility for diplomatic affairs, with full jurisdiction over how to handle them. The present time is ripe for Japan's head of state to visit China and achieve the normalization of diplomatic relations."

During this period, Foreign Minister Ōhira consulted with Dietman Furui Yoshimi, his most trusted adviser on Chinese affairs who had been a close friend since prewar times. He had long played the role of a bridge between Japan and China, and after the death of Matsumura Kenzō he was the person most trusted by the Chinese. Furui and Ōhira held numerous discussions at the Sakaeya on many problems. First, would China accept normalization of diplomatic relations while the U.S.-Japan Security Treaty remained in force? Second, following normalization, would it be possible for Japan to maintain economic and cultural links with Taiwan? Third, would China consent to an interpretation of the Japan–Taiwan peace treaty whereby it would become invalid only in the future, and not retroactively? And fourth, would China abandon the enormous reparations payments it had demanded of Japan?

To tackle these problems Ōhira set up within the Ministry of Foreign Affairs a China Policy Council with fifteen members (heads of bureaus, departments, and sections dealing with Chinese affairs), which was chaired by Vice-Minister Hōgen Shinsaku and entrusted with studying Japan's basic positions for negotiations on normalization. An explicitly stated point of departure for the China Policy Council was that "when Japan–China normalization is realized, it will no longer be possible to maintain diplomatic relations with Taiwan." This matter, which would be taken for granted from today's vantage point, caused considerable difficulty then for Ministry of Foreign Affairs officials, who had been trying to move toward normalization with Beijing while maintaining diplomatic relations with Taiwan. At the inaugural meeting of the China Policy Council on August 2, Ōhira instructed: "Because this is a matter of deciding on national policies for a hundred years and more, we can't afford to be negligent in any way. And because these matters require our urgent attention, I want you to give up your summer vacations."

The following day, at a meeting of the vice-ministers of all ministries and agencies, the Ministry of Foreign Affairs revealed the government's basic views on furthering normalization: (1) the first objective of normalization was to end the unnatural relationship between the two countries and to strengthen Japan's diplomacy of peace; a related objective was that normalization should contribute to peace and security in Asia and the world, and not, therefore, be directed against any third party; (2) the Japanese government, as a matter of fundamental approach, fully understood the People's Republic of China's "three principles" for restoring diplomatic relations and wished to seek concrete points of agreement through talks between the two countries; (3) if diplomatic relations were reestablished, diplomatic relations between Taiwan and Japan could, as a natural consequence, no longer continue; in that event, trade, economic, and all other "practical relationships" between Taiwan and Japan would be solved "in a realistic way." This was the first time that the government had announced its intention of breaking off diplomatic relations with Taiwan.

Ōhira presented the above government positions at a meeting of the standing committee of the LDP's Council on the Normalization of Japan–China Relations. The council had become a large assembly of 316 members (212 from the Lower House, 99 from the Upper House, and 5

former Dietmen) and included both those in favor of and those wary of normalization. From August 2 onward, animated discussions took place
almost daily. When Ōhira explained the government position, pro-Taiwan
Dietmen such as Kaya Okinori, Fujio Masayuki, and Watanabe Michio produced counterarguments saying that Taiwan was extremely important and
diplomatic relations could not be severed lightly, and that it was unnatural
for China alone to put forth principles and for "there to be none on our
side." Countering these arguments, Foreign Minister Ōhira spent hours explaining basic policy: "Diplomacy should, of course, be carried out on an
equal basis to protect national interests, and it's enough that Japan
operates with this kind of overriding principle." This only increased opposition from the pro-Taiwan faction. However, an increasingly prevailing view
among junior Dietmen was, "I've changed my opinion of Ōhira. It takes
guts to do what he's doing."

Ōhira was not yet sure what conditions China would ultimately put forward. Various intermediaries, some of them self-appointed, had from time
to time brought reports that Zhou Enlai had said such-and-such or some
other person thought this or that, but such reports were often self-serving
and could not be entirely trusted. Just at this juncture, Kōmeitō Chairman Takeiri Yoshikatsu returned from a visit to China that began on July
25 and included a total of ten hours of talks, on three occasions, with
Zhou Enlai. Takeiri conveyed, as best he could, China's most recent views
to Tanaka and Ōhira. He recalls the scene as follows: "Having returned to
Japan late on the night of August 3, I visited the prime minister and foreign
minister at the Prime Minister's Official Residence the next day and gave
him the memo on which I had written down Premier Zhou's suggestions with regard to drafting a joint communiqué on normalization. Smiling broadly, Ōhira's famous small eyes (quite the opposite of mine) became
even smaller, and he put my memo in his pocket. Afterward, he said to me,
'Takeiri, all that's left is the prime minster's decision. Once that's made, as
foreign minister I'll overcome any difficulties, I promise.' "

Takeiri's memorandum contained eight detailed items, including the
following: (1) during Tanaka's visit to China for the purpose of effecting
normalization, it would be desirable that the two countries make a joint
communiqué or a joint statement; (2) the U.S.-Japan Security Treaty
would pose no obstacle to normalization, and neither would the "Taiwan
clause" in the Satō-Nixon talks be an obstacle; (3) the territorial issue of
the Senkaku Islands was not thought to be an obstacle; (4) considering
future Japan-China friendship, China intended to abandon its claim for
reparations for Japanese aggression; (5) with respect to concluding a
Japan-China peace treaty, it was suggested that Japan conclude a new trea-

ty of peace and friendship to replace the Japan–Republic of China peace treaty between Japan and Taiwan.

The LDP's Council on the Normalization of Japan–China Relations held a general meeting on August 10 to approve a visit to China by Prime Minister Tanaka. The next day, Ōhira had a second formal meeting with Sun and Xiao, in which he relayed the prime minister's hope of visiting China and promised to arrange a meeting with Tanaka. Four days later, on August 15, a meeting was held at the Imperial Hotel between Tanaka, Chief Cabinet Secretary Nikaidō Susumu, Sun, and Xiao. At this meeting, Sun expressed China's heartfelt wish to welcome Prime Minister Tanaka, and Tanaka, in turn, expressed the hope that talks with Premier Zhou would be fruitful. When Chinese representatives requested that Prime Minister Tanaka visit China at the earliest possible date, Tanaka asked when the Beijing weather was at its best, to which the reply was, "late September or early October." Thus, this period was in effect designated for Tanaka's visit.

The meeting ended smoothly, and since Tanaka himself had indicated his desire to visit China, Ōhira asked Tanaka to make the final decision to do so, judging that the agenda for the China visit had virtually been settled except for some adjustments of outlook within the LDP and a comparison of views with the United States. Ōhira told Tanaka, "I have almost understood now what the real intentions of the Chinese are. All that remains is to take action. I think you, too, have always done what you wanted. Isn't it just a matter of both sides having the will to go ahead?" Tanaka immediately replied, "I understand. In any case a person has only one life to live. So I guess I'll go." He then added, "I leave the specific negotiations to you. I'll take responsibility for matters within the party."

Although the preparations were progressing steadily, Ōhira needed to feel out Beijing further, as well as to gauge trends in Washington and Taipei. Especially, given China's long opposition to the U.S.–Japan Security Treaty, he felt he needed to learn what China's attitude toward this would be in the forthcoming talks, and to explore any American concerns in regard to the Japan–China negotiations. Not long after the establishment of the Tanaka Administration, a summit meeting between Japan and the United States had been proposed by Japan, and on July 24, 1972, an announcement was made that such a meeting would be held in Honolulu in early September. At the time of the announcement, the United States had not foreseen that Japan–China normalization would proceed so quickly, and it had been assumed that the summit talks would focus mainly on correcting the U.S.–Japan trade imbalance, with a view to securing support from American financial circles to help reelect Nixon in November. In-

deed, such problems formed the gist of the discussions at the U.S.–Japan
trade talks held in Hakone in late July. Dissatisfied with the results of the
Hakone talks, the Americans were hoping that Tanaka would bring some
appropriate "gift" to the forthcoming summit.

On August 18, Assistant to the President for National Security Affairs
Henry Kissinger stopped off in Japan on his way home from Vietnam-
related peace negotiations in Paris and Saigon. He conferred with Tanaka
and Ōhira but, in spite of explanations of the Japanese attitudes toward
normalization, he failed to make the American standpoint clear. According
to one of Ōhira's secretaries, Ōhira talked about "not going straight to Beijing, but needing to go there via Hawaii." This, no doubt, expressed his
wish to first meet directly with President Nixon and to achieve Japan–
China normalization with Nixon's understanding and in a way that would
not harm U.S.–Japan relations.

On August 20, Ōhira met with Tanaka to discuss specific measures aiming at normalization. It was decided that in September, before the prime
minister's visit to China, a large delegation of LDP members would be sent
to Beijing and a special government envoy would be sent to Taiwan. On
August 22, the prime minister appointed former Foreign Minister Shiina
Etsusaburō to the post of LDP vice-president, and at the same time requested that he serve as the special envoy to Taiwan, and Shiina accepted.

Taiwan was, of course, interested in what was happening, and it was
natural that Shiina's mission would be burdensome, given the fact that he
had to explain what was for the Taiwanese government a very unpleasant
situation. One evening, soon after Shiina's mission to Taiwan was decided
upon, he talked with Ōhira in a Roppongi restaurant. During this conversation he sought some sort of apology he could offer Taiwan, saying in effect:
"It's fine to normalize Japan–China relations, but isn't it a little strange to
break off all relations with Taipei just because we are now normalizing
them with Beijing? Isn't there some way whereby we don't have to suddenly tell the Taiwanese we won't be associating with them any more?"

Ōhira replied: "If we choose one side, we have to give up the other side.
In dealing with divided countries, like the Korean Peninsula, Germany,
and Vietnam, there is no other alternative." This left Shiina disappointed.
The two men had often in the past alternated in important posts. For example, when the First Ikeda Cabinet was formed after the dissolution of the
Kishi Cabinet, Ōhira had replaced Shiina as chief cabinet secretary; later,
still during the Ikeda years, Shiina had replaced Ōhira as foreign minister.
So far their personal relations had been relatively smooth, but this night
they were on different wavelengths and a definite shadow fell over their
relationship.

The reason for the difference in wavelength was clear enough. From Shiina's perspective, he was going to Taiwan as a special envoy, and it would be good if he got from the foreign minister a clear idea of the latter's intentions as to how Japan would treat Taiwan in the future. After all, he had himself been foreign minister and well understood the formal argument about dealings with divided countries, without needing to have it repeated to him. On the other hand, Ōhira took the stance that how to treat Taiwan was a major issue in negotiations with China. If anything specific was said on how to maintain working relations with Taiwan, the normalization of relations with China would become impossible. This was the position he wanted Shiina to be aware of. In the meantime, within the LDP's Council on the Normalization of Japan–China Relations, spirited debates continued between pro-normalization Dietmen and those who wanted to protect Taiwan.

Meanwhile, with the summit in Hawaii approaching, Tanaka and Ōhira left Haneda airport on August 31 for Honolulu. The main U.S. participants were President Nixon and Secretary of State William P. Rogers. As anticipated, the American side raised the issue of how to redress the trade imbalance, and the Japanese side presented the issue of Japan–China normalization. With respect to Tanaka's China visit, the September 1 joint statement following the U.S.–Japan talks said both countries hoped this would "further the trend for the relaxation of tension in Asia." As for the trade imbalance, it noted that the Japanese government "has indicated its intention to reduce the imbalance to a reasonable level within a reasonable period of time." Apart from the joint statement, the Japanese side announced that Japan would make emergency imports from the United States worth approximately US$710 million, at which the American side expressed satisfaction.

These talks may be said to have also ended quite satisfactorily with respect to the normalization question, in which Japan had such great interest. The United States, which had not yet normalized relations with China in spite of Nixon's China visit, did not show a negative response to Japan's being first to proceed with full normalization. And from China there came no specific reaction to the policy, specified in the Hawaii talks, of maintaining the U.S.–Japan Security Treaty, and thus another of Ōhira's main concerns was obviated. The foreign minister, greatly relieved that the talks had gone so well, felt he now had at least a one-way ticket to Beijing. In the car back to Honolulu from Kuilima Hotel on the north side of Oahu, where the meetings had been held, he began humming a favorite tune, and at Waikiki Beach he enjoyed a few moments of swimming under blue skies.

Following the U.S.-Japan summit, the LDP's Council on the Normalization of Japan–China Relations held a plenary meeting at party headquarters on September 8 to determine still unresolved questions of basic policy, and the government adopted, in preparation for the upcoming negotiations, a Basic Policy on Normalization of Japan–China Diplomatic Relations. This document stated: "Considering the deep relations between our country and the Republic of China, we should negotiate giving due consideration to having these traditional relations continued." This statement was followed by five principles for normalization: (1) normalization should be carried out in accordance with the United Nations Charter and the ten-point declaration of principles on the promotion of world peace and cooperation made at the 1955 Bandung Conference; (2) without interference in internal politics, respect will be given to mutually differing systems and relationships with friendly countries; (3) neither country will use force or the threat of force; (4) both countries will try to promote equitable economic and cultural exchanges and neither will give discriminatory treatment; (5) both countries will cooperate for Asian peace and prosperity.

The pro-Taiwan faction insisted that "traditional relations" should be interpreted as including diplomatic relations, but the council's chairman, Kosaka Zentarō, did not indicate any clear interpretation on this point and considered that for the time being intraparty agreement had been reached through this basic policy statement. Then, on September 14, a delegation of representatives from the LDP Council on the Normalization of Japan–China Relations (known as the "Kosaka Delegation") left for a one-week visit to Beijing.

Three days later, on September 17, Special Envoy Shiina and his entourage left for Taiwan, where they talked with Taiwan officials on September 18 and 19. As expected, they were met by demonstrating students at the airport. Their car was pelted with eggs on Taipei's streets, and President Chiang Kai-shek refused to meet them, thereby showing that he did not welcome their mission. Nevertheless, Special Envoy Shiina met with lesser officials and explained that negotiations for Japan–China normalization were supposed to be carried out on the basis of LDP party decisions, which aimed at maintaining all existing relations, including diplomatic relations with Taiwan. Even though this was quite removed from the Beijing government's line on normalization, there was no change in Taiwan's chilly response. Shiina returned home looking disheartened.

In Beijing, Zhou Enlai, who was hosting the Kosaka Delegation, was angered by Shiina's pronouncements in Taiwan. Some of those making up the Kosaka Delegation favored normalization, but others advocated caution and some of these irritated Beijing by referring to the "Republic of China" and "President Chiang Kai-shek." Nevertheless, Premier Zhou Enlai and other Chinese leaders refrained from breaking off contacts, partly because they realized that any negotiations would inevitably be disturbed by pro-Taiwan Dietmen in the LDP, and partly because of ongoing negotiations in Beijing with a Memorandum Trade delegation led by Furui Yoshimi and Tagawa Seiichi, who, under Ōhira's instructions, had left Japan one day before the Kosaka Delegation and, while shunning contact with the Kosaka group, had discussed a joint communiqué to be announced during the Tanaka visit.

Furui and Tagawa were, in fact, able to carry out intensive discussions with Premier Zhou concerning China's "three principles" for restoring diplomatic relations and such points as the termination of the state of war to be covered in negotiations during Tanaka's visit. Regarding the latter point, Japan considered that the state of war with China had ended with the Japan–Taiwan peace treaty, while China insisted that it would end only with normalization of relations. Japan and China were also at odds over the handling of the "three principles," with China insisting they be kept in a nearly unadulterated form in any joint communiqué, and Japan in favor of expressing them in a more paraphrased and scattered way in the joint communiqué or by other means. All these points were to be deliberated and settled at the forthcoming meeting. It was decided by mutual consultation that details of Furui's and Tagawa's preliminary contacts with the Chinese were to remain secret until after Tanaka's visit had ended.

In this way, the ground was prepared for the Tanaka visit within two months of the beginning of his administration. On September 21, the Japanese and Chinese governments simultaneously announced that "Prime Minister Tanaka has accepted with pleasure Premier Zhou's invitation, and will visit China from September 25 to 30 to negotiate and resolve the normalization of relations between Japan and China." At this point, the visit to China by Prime Minister Tanaka and Foreign Minister Ōhira was a certainty. While the Japan–China negotiations were advancing at unexpected speed, activities by those opposed to these negotiations were increasing daily. Threatening letters were frequently thrown into the yard of Ōhira's home, and those close to him began to worry about their personal safety.

Around this time, Ōhira went to Yamagata Prefecture to lend support to the candidacy of his colleague Kurogane Yasumi, who was running in an election to fill a vacated Lower House seat. A reporter who accompanied Ōhira on this trip recalls that soon after the train had left Fukushima and was nearing the Itaya Pass, Ōhira suddenly said with a serious expression, "This may be the last time I'll travel with you. I don't know when I might be killed [by some extremist]. If Heaven helps me, these negotiations will be successful." He then again gazed out at the passing scenery. Ōhira had, in fact, drawn up a will after having decided to visit China. Just as he was about to leave Haneda airport for China, Ōhira told one of his secretaries, "If by some chance these negotiations don't go as intended, I may not be able to come back to Japan. Because of them, there may be some danger. Please take care of things while I'm gone."

The special JAL plane carrying Prime Minister Tanaka, Foreign Minister Ōhira, Chief Cabinet Secretary Nikaidō, and the rest of their entourage left Haneda airport on the morning of September 25. Both Tanaka and Ōhira looked tense but seemed to have accepted that the die was cast. At 11:30 A.M. (12:30 P.M. in Japan) their plane landed under clear autumn skies at Beijing airport. On the main flagstaff at the airport fluttered Japan's red sun flag next to China's five-star flag. Premier Zhou Enlai greeted the entourage at the airport and shook hands with Prime Minister Tanaka and Foreign Minister Ōhira. The national anthems of both countries were played and there was a review of honor guards. In the city proper, negotiations and various welcoming events were carried out simultaneously. The negotiations, begun on the day of the Japanese guests' arrival, took place mainly between Foreign Minister Ōhira and Premier Zhou Enlai, although Ōhira also conferred with Foreign Minister Ji Peng-fei about points needing clarification. Tanaka seemed relaxed as he composed Chinese poems in the State Guest House. Whenever his advisers asked his opinion, he minced no words: "Everything's all right, you know, because Ōhira is in charge. If things don't come together, we'll extend our stay a few days. We won't go back unless there's agreement."

However, from the very start, negotiations ran into difficulties. At the first meeting, when the Japanese side stated its basic thinking on normalization and the Ministry of Foreign Affairs Treaty Bureau Director-General Takashima Masuo gave detailed explanations, Premier Zhou, as a truly skilled negotiator, reacted strongly: "Today I was really surprised. Indeed I can't believe that what Director-General Takashima said conveys Prime Minister Tanaka's and Foreign Minister Ōhira's real intent. From what he said one can't tell whether he has come to pick a fight or to bring about normalization." Tanaka and Ōhira countered with the question, "What, then, are China's views?" and the conversation was stalemated as Zhou and his aides restated their stance, which called for including in the text of the joint communiqué a sequential rendering of the "three principles." After the meetings, it was to this atmosphere that Chief Cabinet Secretary

Nikaidō was referring when he said, "The leaders of the two countries carried out their discussions with surprising frankness."

As for pending matters affecting normalization, in spite of the fact that, to a certain degree, the respective positions had already been sounded out through Ōhira's contacts with important Chinese personages in Tokyo and through unofficial contacts mediated by LDP and opposition party Diet members, when it came down to actual negotiations some unexpected points became difficult. During the negotiations, Ōhira was heard to complain, "It doesn't help to have soldiers in ambush. Suddenly, things that we had not expected become problems." The points in question all had to do with Taiwan. How should one bring up again the interpretation, according to the peace treaty between Japan and Taiwan, whereby the state of war between Japan and China was considered terminated and the problem of reparations already resolved? Or how should one express the differing positions of China, which claimed territorial rights on Taiwan, and of Japan, which had abandoned territorial rights there? Or again, in what form could Japan–Taiwan working relations, which had been operative over a long period in the economic sphere, be continued?

The Chinese also took exception to Prime Minister Tanaka's formal remarks on the first evening. These were delivered in response to a statement by Premier Zhou at a banquet in the Great Hall of the People in honor of the Japanese delegation. Premier Zhou had said, "The Chinese people suffered great harm due to Japan's military aggression in China for half a century after 1894 [the Sino-Japanese War], and the Japanese people, too, received much damage." Prime Minister Tanaka said in response, "My country again expresses a feeling of profound regret (*fukai hansei*) over the great inconveniences (*tadai no gomeiwaku*) that it caused the Chinese people." The Chinese had expected a rather stronger apology, and were far from satisfied by the reference to the past with such a lightweight expression as "inconveniences."

China took an extremely hard stance in the negotiations, which by the second day were already deadlocked. Ōhira said to Tanaka, who had been waiting at the State Guest House, "What shall we do? At this rate we can't go home." The Prime Minister answered, "At times like this, intellectuals who have graduated from universities are really of no use." Ōhira again asked, "Well, what should we do?" To this, Tanaka was heard to say— which caused some laughter among those present—"You university graduates will have to come up with some ideas." At the same time, however, the Prime Minister offered this encouragement to Ōhira and his colleagues: "Since we've come this far, there's no need to step back. Even if it turns out to be a failure, we can always go home. We can just pretend we came for sightseeing. I'll take responsibility for whatever comes afterward. Once again, stick to your positions."

From the evening of the second day, Foreign Minister Ji replaced Premier Zhou as the chief negotiator. In response to a Chinese request, Ōhira went through each clause of the Japanese proposal, and Foreign Minister Ji carefully made notes. As the explanation of each clause was completed, a man presumed to be a secretary for the Chinese negotiators took the notes into another room. Some twenty minutes later, a Chinese memo was delivered from the other room, upon which Foreign Minister Ji stated his country's views. It is still not clear why the Chinese worked in this way, but it seems likely that Premier Zhou was studying the Japanese proposals in the other room. At the time, the influence of the "Gang of Four" was quite strong, and Zhou was in a difficult position. It may be supposed that Zhou sat in the other room so as to appear, as far as possible, not to be in the forefront of the negotiations, while, in effect, directing them via reports on the general situation made to Chairman Mao and trying to adjust views within the Chinese Communist Party.

On their third day in China, the Japanese negotiators toured the Great Wall and the Ming Tombs, as arranged by their hosts. During the four-hour round trip, foreign ministers Ōhira and Ji continued their negotiations in the car. Prime Minister Tanaka climbed carefully up the Great Wall, but Ōhira's steps were heavy and he made few remarks, although he was overheard to say, "Long ago I crossed this Badaling [Pass] on the way to Zhangjiakou. There were lots of night trains." Otherwise his mind seemed preoccupied with the negotiations in Beijing.

In due course, the negotiations began to be held directly between Foreign Minister Ōhira and Premier Zhou, who suggested rephrasing the termination of the state of war between Japan and China with the words "putting an end to the abnormal state of affairs that has hitherto existed between the two countries." The problem of Taiwan fell into place by including in the joint communiqué the words: "The Government of the People's Republic of China reiterates that Taiwan is an inalienable part of the territory of the People's Republic of China. The Government of Japan fully understands and respects this stand." For the joint communiqué, Ōhira rephrased Tanaka's earlier expression about "great inconveniences" and agreement was reached on the following words: "The Japanese side is keenly conscious of the responsibility for the serious damage that Japan in the past caused to the Chinese people through war, and deeply reproaches itself. Further, the Japanese side reaffirms its position that it intends to realize the normalization of relations between the two countries from the stand of fully understanding 'the three principles for the restoration of relations' put foward by the Government of the People's Republic of China." Although the joint communiqué made no mention of maintaining working relations with Taiwan in such fields as economy and culture, the Chinese indicated that they would tacitly accept such arrangements. One problem remained until the very last, namely, the problem of when and how Japan would break off diplomatic ties with Taiwan.

On the evening of the third day, the Chinese unexpectedly announced that Chairman Mao would meet Prime Minister Tanaka and Foreign Minister Ōhira. Ōhira immediately asked that Nikaidō also be included, and this request was accepted. This meeting, which took place in Mao Zedong's Zhongnanhai residence, lasted an hour. Chairman Mao began the meeting by saying, "Have the arguments finished? It's no good if you don't quarrel." To speak about "arguments being finished" was Mao's way of indicating that the Japan–China negotiations were for the most part wrapped up. Sitting in his library crammed with volumes of classical literature, Chairman Mao puffed on a small cigar and, pointing to Liao Chengzhi, secretary-general of the China–Japan Friendship Association, joked with his three Japanese guests, "Since he was born in Japan, please take him back with you." But with respect to the problematic phrase Tanaka had used earlier, he remarked trenchantly, "Our young people say the expression about causing inconveniences was not enough and don't accept it. In China, that's an expression you use when you spill water on a woman's skirt."

The meeting with Mao had, in effect, brought the negotiations over the hump. As for the remaining problem of what to do about Japan–Taiwan diplomatic ties, although the Japanese signaled that they would announce "the termination of diplomatic ties with Taiwan," Premier Zhou persisted in demanding, "When will you announce it? Indicate a specific time." Foreign Minister Ōhira replied, "Even though one may truly believe that questions of diplomacy are settled beyond the shadow of a doubt, if a time is specifically indicated, cracks may enter the relations of trust between two countries in the unlikely event that the timing is delayed by an hour or a day. I want you to trust us to take care of it." The matter was laid to rest when Zhou then said, "Let us trust Mr. Ōhira." Toward the end of the summit meeting on the fourth day, Premier Zhou wrote his expectations of Ōhira on a square piece of paper and passed it to the Japanese guests. The meaning of the six Chinese characters was "What is said must definitely be believed, what is done must definitely be completed." This was one of the three necessary attributes of a virtuous man, as explained by Kongzi (Confucius) to a questioner, according to The Analects.

September 29, the fifth day, saw the signing ceremony in the east wing of the Great Hall of the People, under just the sort of cloudless sky suggested in the popular expression "a Beijing autumn day." Prime Minister Tanaka, Foreign Minister Ōhira, Premier Zhou, and Foreign Minister Ji sat at a table decorated with the flags of both countries. Amid the dazzle of flashlights, the four men exchanged greetings, took pens from their respective trays, affixed their signatures to the joint communiqué, exchanged official copies, and shook hands repeatedly.

After the ceremony, Ōhira gave a press interview in the vestibule of the Nationalities Culture Palace, which was serving as a press center. He stated: "The fact that an end has been brought to the abnormal relationship between Japan and China is an important contribution to peace in Asia and the world." He then immediately referred to Japan's ties with Taiwan, declaring bluntly, "As a result of the normalization of Japan–China relations, the Japan–Taiwan peace treaty has lost its raison d'être, and in the Japanese government's view it is recognized that this treaty has come to an end." This problem, about which Zhou had many times asked, "When will you make it clear?" had now been decisively handled by the Japanese foreign minister on the same day the joint communiqué was made public. Premier Zhou, referring to Ōhira's attitude and handling of matters in this series of negotiations, later told close associates, "Ōhira is honest and does not tell lies. He is not so skilled at speaking but is very learned and has an inner excellence. He assisted Tanaka with the utmost faithfulness; Tanaka could be as he was because of Ōhira, and it was because of Ōhira that we have a restoration of relations between China and Japan."

On their return to the State Guest House, Tanaka, Ōhira, and Nikaidō toasted their efforts. Prime Minister Tanaka told Ōhira, "You did a really good job. Let's continue working together in the future." Ōhira wrote down his feelings in the form of a poem, which he handed to Nikaidō:

> The Great Wall extends six thousand leagues,
> Exhausting people to the bitter end.
> The first emperor believed all within was calm,
> Not knowing the opposition in people's hearts.
> The mountains and the wall are silent,
> And the ups and downs of fortune like a dream.

With the negotiations concluded, Tanaka indicated his intention to return home immediately to report to the party and help along any necessary adjustment of views. However, it had already been arranged for the Japanese guests to visit Shanghai before going home. Feeling it would be a major calamity to have to call off the visit to Shanghai, the main rallying point of Zhang Chunqiao and others of the then powerful "Gang of Four," the Chinese hosts would not be dissuaded, and in the end Premier Zhou himself accompanied his Japanese guests to Shanghai in a small plane. As the plane was about to depart, Liao Chengzhi approached the boarding ladder and called out, "Tanaka-*san*, Ōhira-*san*, please take good care of yourselves." The feelings of these two Japanese leaders, who had visited China at the risk of their lives, had been recognized by their hosts. It is said that in complete secret two divisions of People's Liberation Army troops had been mobilized both to protect the State Guest House and to discourage any domestic elements that might have opposed the normalization of relations between the two countries.

Tanaka and Ōhira sat facing Zhou, and before long Tanaka fell asleep, snoring loudly. Ōhira adroitly tried to keep Zhou company, but Tanaka did not awake till the plane approached Shanghai. At the welcome party in Shanghai, both Tanaka and Ōhira joined in repeated toasts. In making his rounds of the tables, Ōhira, who ordinarily refrained from alcohol, drank twenty or more small cups of strong *maotai* spirit in toasts. In the end, quite inebriated, he plopped into bed as soon as he reached his hotel and fell asleep. The next day, September 30, Tanaka and Ōhira left Shanghai for home. Premier Zhou and other Chinese leaders saw them off at the airport, as did a large group of children dressed in ethnic costumes who danced and sang some touching words of farewell.

The normalization of relations between Japan and China meant a definite repudiation of the aggressions against China that Japan had perpetrated in the past. It was a truly historic achievement that not only established a new relationship of trust between the two countries but also contributed to building the foundations of peace in Asia. At the same time, it was a difficult undertaking that involved considerable problems at home and abroad related to abandoning recognition of the Taiwanese government, which had earlier restored diplomatic relations with Japan without any demands for reparations in spite of the economic damage and loss of human life suffered before the end of World War II. And it also represented the difficult choice of moving away from a diplomacy of always letting the United States take new initiatives toward a diplomacy of self-reliance.

Ōhira later commented on the process of normalization and the making of the joint communiqué: "At that time we were wholly engrossed in our job and really did well to overcome the obstacles we encountered along the way. . . . I am happy that this diplomatic task, which was similar in importance to the conclusion of the San Francisco Peace Treaty, could be smoothly concluded." Having always shown a prudent attitude toward

Chinese problems, which he was all the more familiar with by having worked in China before World War II, the fact that Ōhira achieved Japan–China normalization on virtually his own responsibility—even if this meant a decisive break in relations with Taiwan—had great significance for his political career. He had made the leap to become a statesman and political leader of the first rank.

Chapter 22

A Troubled Foreign Minister

By the early autumn of 1972, in the less than two months since it had been formed, the Tanaka Cabinet had seen normalization of relations with China and the beginning of a business boom accompanying the Plan for the Remodeling of the Japanese Archipelago. Its popularity was thus still on the ascendant, with no great enemies in the offing. However, after this first surge of popularity, the Tanaka Administration began to tread a troubled path against a backdrop of developments that indicated the changing times. Ōhira, as a key cabinet member and a close friend of the prime minister, found himself almost constantly beset with difficulties.

First of all, there were negative responses from some countries to the Japan–China normalization of relations, and not surprisingly the sharpest one came from the Soviet Union. Its ambassador in Tokyo, Oleg Troyanovsky, who immediately after the establishment of the Tanaka Administration had proposed preliminary negotiations on a Japanese–Soviet peace treaty, returned to Moscow as soon as he saw that there was to be no change in the Tanaka Cabinet's policies regarding China. After Troyanovsky's departure, which was intended to convey displeasure with Japan, however much the Ministry of Foreign Affairs might have wished to commence preliminary negotiations with the Soviet Union, these did not get off the ground.

The reactions of the Asian countries were various, with some even foreseeing with anxiety a sort of Japan–China collusion. To allay such fears, the government dispatched Kimura Toshio, former director-general of the Economic Planning Agency, as a special envoy to Korea, former Foreign Minister Aichi Kiichi to five countries in Southeast Asia, and Vice-Minister of Foreign Affairs Aoki Masahisa to the three countries of Indochina. It was decided that Foreign Minister Ōhira himself would visit Australia and New Zealand, and later the United States and Soviet Union.

On October 13, 1972, after the beginning of Ōhira's foreign tour, the Soviet Union sent Troyanovsky back to his posting in Tokyo, where he delivered a personal letter from General Secretary Leonid Brezhnev to Prime Minister Tanaka and again began working toward an early start of negotiations on a Japanese–Soviet peace treaty. When Ōhira arrived in Moscow from Washington, he encountered a rather chilly welcome, and the hoped-for meeting with Brezhnev did not materialize. On the morning of October 23, he had a first meeting with Foreign Minister Andrei Gromyko, explaining to him the normalization of diplomatic relations with China. Gromyko stubbornly confronted Ōhira with the "antihegemony clause"—"Neither of the two countries should seek hegemony in the Asia-Pacific region and each is opposed to efforts by any other country or group of countries to establish such hegemony"—inserted in the Japan–China joint communiqué, suggesting that it implied an offensive–defensive Japan–China alliance aimed at the Soviet Union. But during talks later that same afternoon, the two men discussed a Japanese–Soviet peace treaty and in effect began negotiations on it.

On October 24, Foreign Minister Ōhira met Premier Alexei Kosygin, and they agreed to promote further discussions at the foreign minister level on bilateral Japanese–Soviet issues, including a peace treaty. However, Ōhira judged that to eradicate the anxieties that the Soviet Union harbored with respect to the normalization of Japan–China relations, it would also be a good idea to initiate direct contact between the Japanese and Soviet heads of state. This was the underlying reason for the Tanaka–Ōhira visit to the Soviet Union in October of the following year and the resultant Japan–Soviet joint communiqué.

The Japan–China normalization had, of course, also aroused some sharp reactions at home. On seeing how Foreign Minister Ōhira, who had sometimes appeared indecisive, had switched to the resolute promotion of the agenda he had come to believe in, the pro-Taiwan Seirankai, composed mainly of junior Diet members, and party elders such as Shiina Etsusaburō grew increasingly critical and tried to warn any who would listen that "with Ōhira, we mustn't let up our guard." Even if Ōhira was determined not to be bothered by these intraparty complaints, the attempts by these dissatisfied individuals to obstruct him later contributed, in the various post-Satō political struggles, to maneuvers aimed at preventing him from gaining the party presidency.

Already in late September 1972, on his way home from Beijing, Prime Minister Tanaka had thought of requesting a renewed mandate from the people. The mood favoring a Diet dissolution was spreading rapidly, and by the time the 70th Extraordinary Diet began on October 27, all the opposition parties were also for a dissolution. On November 13, just after the Lower House passed the supplementary budget, it was dissolved, and November 20 was set as the official start of the campaign for an election on December 10.

In this thirty-third general election, the LDP hoped to capitalize on the wave of popular approval for the restoration of Japan–China diplomatic relations, and LDP Dietmen took advantage of the mood by distributing panda badges. Yet results failed to meet expectations as LDP seats fell to an all-time low of 271, compared to 288 before the dissolution. (The post-election figure later rose to 284 with the affiliation of thirteen Dietmen who had run as independents.) As had already happened in the Upper House, the difference in the comparative strengths of conservatives and progressives in the Lower House had now decreased. This was a great shock for Tanaka, who had been completely confident of a convincing LDP victory.

After this December 1972 general election, Tanaka revised his earlier strategy of appointing only mainstream LDP members to the most important posts, and adopted a system that would represent the party as a whole more equitably. Most notably, he asked his rival Fukuda Takeo to enter the cabinet as director-general of the Administrative Management Agency. Miki was retained as director-general of the Environment Agency (with the additional post of deputy prime minister), while Ōhira and Nakasone were kept as foreign minister and minister of international trade and industry, respectively. Thus, all four candidates in the last party presidential election, as well as Nakasone, were cabinet members. The Second Tanaka Cabinet was, in fact, the first and last occasion when these five influential men would share such a distinction. As for the top three party posts, Hashimoto Tomisaburō and Suzuki Zenkō stayed on as secretary-general and General Council chairman, respectively, while Kuraishi Tadao of the Fukuda faction was brought in as Policy Research Council chairman.

With the coming of the new year, 1973, both international and domestic relations seemed to be more fluid than ever. In late January, an agreement was signed between the United States and North Vietnam, promising an end to the long years of fighting. In a public address, Ōhira stated that he hoped all those engaged in the conflict would "attain lasting peace and political stability in Vietnam." Nonetheless, responding to questions from reporters, he thought for some time before saying rather glumly, "I can no longer be so optimistic about anything. You never know what may happen." On February 12 (February 13 in Japan), a 10 percent devaluation of the dollar was announced in the United States, and the relative value of the yen was increased from the rate of US$1 = ¥308 under the

Smithsonian Agreement to US$1 = ¥277. President Nixon explicitly criticized Japan: "Japan and other countries have sent large quantities of goods into the United States, which is the world's largest market, have pushed American-made goods off the store shelves, and have thrown workers out of their workplaces." Immediately afterward, he had Kissinger, who had been visiting Hanoi and Beijing, go to Japan and make strong requests for quicker capital liberalization. Japan thus continued to be greatly affected by the Nixon Administration's diplomacy.

Reflecting on the defeat in the general election, Prime Minister Tanaka began in April to show that he was intent on revising the election law with a view to establishing a "small electoral district system" in the hope of consolidating the underpinnings of a stable conservative government. Japan's electoral district system was, and still is, known as the "medium-sized district system." At present, the country is divided into 130 districts, most of which elect between three and five (now temporarily between two and six) representatives to the Lower House. Ever since the LDP was founded, there has been talk of converting this into a single-representative district system on the British–American pattern. When serving as the LDP's first president, Hatoyama Ichirō presented such a plan to the Diet, but it met fierce antagonism from the opposition parties. Tanaka's enthusiasm for a small electoral district system was truly phenomenal. He was said to collect piles of election data in his home and spend hours mapping out the contours of the small electoral districts he would like to see, memorizing the number of votes each Dietman got from such-and-such a subarea of his current middle-size electoral district.

Well aware of Prime Minister Tanaka's enthusiasm for a small electoral district system and knowing they would be greatly disadvantaged if such a system was introduced, the four opposition parties started urgent talks among the chairmen of their respective Diet Affairs committees. These talks resulted in a joint resolution of "determined opposition" and an active fight to prevent the establishment of a small electoral district system. On May 15, demonstrations sponsored by the Socialist, Communist, and Kōmeitō parties, together with the General Council of Trade Unions, were held in all of Japan's forty-seven prefectures with an estimated 320,000 people taking part. It came to be feared that if a small electoral district system was, in fact, made law, repeated demonstrations and disorder could engulf the Diet building and nearby government office buildings in central Tokyo. Even within the LDP there were not a few who had doubts about a small electoral district system, but none came out directly in opposition to the feisty prime minister, who saw this system as a grand plan for insuring a century of conservative rule. Ōhira, however, judged that to push the matter so pointedly could well endanger the life of the Tanaka Administration. He advised Tanaka: "Now we have a bridge called the LDP. But if the heavy load called the small electoral district system should try to cross it, the bridge will not hold." Finally he managed to convince Tanaka to give up the idea.

At this juncture, the Tanaka Cabinet was having to cope with several tough economic problems both at home and abroad. Most serious was the rise in prices. Wholesale prices had earlier been relatively stable in comparison to retail prices but began to rise sharply after the summer of 1972, increasing by 11 percent in the period between April 1972 and March 1973. Consumer retail prices in May 1973 were similarly 10.9 percent higher than a year before. The domestic excess fluidity of funds resulting from the trade surplus tended, in the search for investment outlets, to go into land, where prices were escalating in part as a result of Tanaka's Plan for the Remodeling of the Japanese Archipelago. From individuals to large enterprises, there was a rush to buy land. The index of land prices published by the Construction Ministry on April 2, 1973, showed that the national average of land prices had risen by 30.9 percent over the previous year, by far the largest one-year rise since the index system was established in 1970. At the same time, there were heavy investments in company stocks and speculation in commodities, and prices continued to rise rapidly, aggravated by hoarding and the resulting market scarcities. On April 11, 1973, a special committee of the Lower House summoned the presidents of six major trading companies and urged them to be mindful of their responsibilities to society.

Meanwhile, for nine days between April 28 and May 6, Foreign Minister Ōhira made a trip to Yugoslavia and to EC and OECD headquarters in Belgium and France. In Yugoslavia, he had three talks (one more than the two originally scheduled) with Foreign Minister Miloš Minić, and in France he managed to arrange, on the spur of the moment, a talk with Finance Minister Valéry Giscard d'Estaing. At the EC headquarters in Brussels, quite a sensation was caused when over a hundred reporters from various countries pressed in to scoop the news on Ōhira's talk with EC Vice-President Sir Christopher Soames. This was evidence of the fact that Ōhira's name was now known throughout the world, largely as a result of his role in restoring diplomatic relations with China. Among the many aspects of this European trip, Ōhira had pleased the Yugoslavs by saying good things about their policy of nonalignment, and in France and Belgium he pleaded for greater European understanding of Japan.

At the end of July 1973, Ōhira accompanied Prime Minister Tanaka to a summit meeting in the United States. There is no doubt that already at this time a major preoccupation of the Japanese delegation was the forthcoming summit in the Soviet Union, as indicated, for example, by Tanaka's remark during an interview at Washington's National Press Club: "There is no point in visiting the Soviet Union unless we talk about the Northern Territories."

On the afternoon of August 8, two days after Tanaka's and Ōhira's return from the United States, an unexpected headache occurred when Kim Dae Jung, former South Korean presidential candidate and a leader in the movement against President Park Chung Hee, was abducted from Tokyo's Hotel Grand Palace in the Kudan district of Chiyoda Ward by men thought to be South Koreans. On that day Ōhira was resting in Karuizawa. When he heard the first reports he intuitively felt it was a serious and complex problem going beyond a mere violation of Japan's sovereignty. In response to questions by Foreign Ministry officials, the South Korean embassy in Tokyo reported: "The Republic of Korea government has nothing to do with this incident and wants measures taken to insure Mr. Kim Dae Jung's safety." Kim's whereabouts were unknown until August 13, six days after the incident, when he turned up blindfolded in his Seoul home.

To a group of Korean and foreign reporters who rushed to the scene, Kim said: "After attending a banquet, I was surrounded in the corridor by six or seven men and made to inhale an anesthetic. Then, after being put in an elevator, I was taken by car to somewhere I supposed was Osaka, and afterward was brought to South Korea on a large ship." At a press conference in Tokyo, Ōhira said only the following: "It is irresponsible to say anything when we are still unclear about the actual facts. Our first task is to investigate the facts of the case." However, inwardly he seems to have been disturbed. To several close associates, he confided, "It is like somebody sneaking into a house that is not his own."

If the matter was handled awkwardly, it was possible that an irreparable diplomatic rift could occur between Japan and South Korea. Ōhira wanted, as far as possible, to keep the matter away from the political level and to await a thorough investigation by Japanese police, as in the case of Zhou Hongqing in 1963, and he held several consultations in strict secrecy with the director-general and others at the National Police Agency. He was greatly concerned about how the incident was to be investigated, how the evidence was to be assembled, and how the results would be made public. From this time, Ōhira's white hairs seemed suddenly to multiply.

Although South Korean authorities stuck to their original stance that their government was not involved, Prime Minister Kim Jong Pil, after a meeting with the Japanese ambassador in Seoul, sent a personal letter of apology to Prime Minister Tanaka and Foreign Minister Ōhira, stating: "I am truly sorry that this incident has caused all of you in Japan, and especially Prime Minister Tanaka and Foreign Minister Ōhira, so much trouble and put you in a politically difficult position. The facts are unclear, but it is certain that South Koreans were involved in this incident, for which I wish to apologize deeply."

In September, the special investigations headquarters of the Metropolitan Police Department ascertained that the first secretary at the South Korean embassy in Tokyo had been involved in the incident and requested, through the Japanese Foreign Ministry, that he voluntarily present himself for questioning. But at this time he was no longer in Japan. With a grave expression, Foreign Minister Ōhira commented: "Japanese–South Korean relations have a dark past [of Japanese colonial unfairness]. Thus, it cannot be said that our counseling of a fair handling of this matter might not sound somewhat hypocritical. But because we are both independent countries of equal standing and look forward to long and friendly relations in the future, we must earnestly strive to find a fair resolution. The matter is at a stage where, through Ambassador Ushiroku, we are urging the South Korean government to reconsider." Ōhira's days were thus occupied with the difficulties of negotiating, on the one hand, with foreign countries, and of attempting, on the other, to handle public opinion at home.

It was not until November 1973, approximately three months after the incident, that the Kim Dae Jung affair reached a so-called political settlement. On November 1, after Kim Dae Jung was released from the house arrest to which he had been subjected in Seoul, South Korea's Foreign Minister Kim Yong Shik announced at a press conference that the former first secretary who was involved would be removed from official duties and that Prime Minister Kim Jong Pil would make a visit to Japan. Arriving in Japan the next day, Kim spoke with Tanaka and Ōhira and handed them a personal letter of apology from President Park Chung Hee. With this the incident was considered to have reached a political resolution. Ōhira addressed the matter with these words: "It cannot be called a resolution that leaves a perfectly clean slate, but it is the result of much hard work and I hope the Japanese people will accept it." It was not clear whether Ōhira himself was satisfied.

In October 1973, before the Kim Dae Jung affair had been resolved, Prime Minister Tanaka and Foreign Minister Ōhira went to Moscow for negotiations on a Japanese–Soviet peace treaty. A year had passed since Ōhira's last visit to the Soviet Union in October 1972. To conclude a peace treaty, a solution to the Northern Territories problem would be essential.

This problem refers to the ownership of three islands and an island group—namely, Etorofu, Kunashiri, Shikotan, and the tiny Habomai Islands, all in waters northeast of Hokkaidō—currently held by the Soviet Union. These islands were occupied by the Soviet army and navy after the end of World War II, between August 23 and September 3, 1945. Japan considers Shikotan and the Habomai Islands to be part of Hokkaidō, and has consistently held that the two southernmost Kurile islands of Kunashiri and Etorofu are, historically speaking, part of "Japan's inherent territory" (*Nihon koyū no ryōdo*). This assertion is substantiated by the fact that all these islands were legally recognized as Japanese territory by the Russo–Japanese Treaty of Amity concluded in 1855 and by the Treaty of St. Petersburg of 1875, by which all of Sakhalin was recognized as Russian territory. (It had formerly been considered as belonging jointly to the two countries in exchange for Japanese possession of the middle and northern Kurile islands between Etorofu and Kamchatka Peninsula. It was taken for granted in the 1875 treaty that the islands of the Northern Territories were already, and would continue to be, Japanese.)

At the time of the signing of the San Francisco Peace Treaty in September 1951, Prime Minister Yoshida Shigeru, who had plenipotentiary powers, insisted that Japan would not give up its sovereign rights to the islands in question. During the Japanese–Soviet negotiations held during the Hatoyama Administration in 1955 and 1956, no agreement was reached between Japan, which asked for a "package return" of all the islands in question, and the Soviet Union, which considered the return of Shikotan and the Habomai Islands as the limit for possible concessions. Although in the 1956 Soviet–Japanese joint declaration it was stated that negotiations would continue for a peace treaty, and that after its conclusion the Soviet Union agreed that it would return Shikotan and the Habomai Islands to Japan, in later years the Soviet government on various occasions adopted the attitude that "the territorial issue is already resolved." This became the biggest obstacle to promoting exchanges and improving relations between the two countries.

In January 1972, toward the end of the Satō Administration, Soviet Foreign Minister Gromyko came to Japan and agreed to open negotiations on a peace treaty before the end of that year. This was clearly a way of trying to counter the possibility that Nixon's China visit might result in closer relations between Japan and China. Prime Minister Satō had showed a willingness to conclude a Soviet–Japanese peace treaty, but during his administration negotiations did not actually begin and the situation was fundamentally unchanged.

After the beginning of the Tanaka Administration, Foreign Minister

Ōhira visited the Soviet Union, as previously mentioned, in October 1972, soon after the normalization of relations with China, but he was unable to meet General Secretary Brezhnev and achieved few positive results. However, when Brezhnev indicated in December 1972 that he was willing to enter into negotiations on a peace treaty the following year, in commemoration of the fiftieth anniversary of the founding of the Union of Soviet Socialist Republics, Tanaka sent a personal letter in reply, dated March 6, 1973. In it, Tanaka did not refer directly to the territorial problem, but stated that he wished "to resolve pending issues between Japan and the Soviet Union." It was emphasized that he would "spare no effort for cooperation in the development of Siberia." Brezhnev immediately sent a reply requesting that Tanaka visit the Soviet Union for a summit meeting later in the year.

On the first leg of the 1973 trip to Moscow, Ōhira spoke before the 28th United Nations General Assembly in New York on September 23. In this speech, he expressed for the first time in an international forum his hope that Japan would become not merely a passive beneficiary of world peace but also an active creator of world peace. Then, after a stopover in Italy, he joined Prime Minister Tanaka in England, and they visited West Germany, where Tanaka and Ōhira attended a scheduled meeting of the two countries' foreign ministers, held at the State Guest House, Schloss Gymnich, in the outskirts of Bonn. Here Foreign Minister Walter Scheel, a veteran of diplomatic relations with the Soviet Union, gave this advice: "In the Soviet Union, nothing is decided in formal talks. The usual practice is that there may be something [of importance] between the scenes or just before one is about to return home. Be aware of this and stick to your principles until the end."

On October 7, 1973, Prime Minister Tanaka and Foreign Minister Ōhira arrived in Moscow. The Japanese–Soviet negotiations in the golden-domed Kremlin Great Palace took place over three days between October 8 and 10. Tanaka and Ōhira did their best to steer the talks in a direction that might offer some clues about the return of the islands, but Brezhnev stuck mainly to the topic of economic cooperation in the development of Siberia and did not refer at all to the territorial issue. Prime Minister Tanaka strongly insisted that a main purpose of his visit to the Soviet Union was to make a breakthrough on the territorial problem, and the talks came to a standstill.

However, just before dawn on the day of the scheduled departure, LDP Dietman Abe Fumio, who was part of the Japanese entourage in Moscow, telephoned Ōhira's secretary to say that Soviet Deputy Premier Kirill Mazurov had come to him to sound out his opinion about a joint declaration that included a phrase to the effect that "there exist various problems left unsettled between Japan and the Soviet Union after the war." Woken up to hear this report, Ōhira conferred with some Foreign Ministry people in the entourage and then told Abe to convey to the Soviet side that he thought "it should be possible, in principle, to accept this, provided the Soviet Union makes a definite commitment, at the same time, to continue the peace treaty negotiations in 1974." Scheel's prediction had, indeed, been accurate.

At the final meeting a few hours before the scheduled departure of the Japanese, General Secretary Brezhnev said that he wanted to revise the phrase "problem left unsettled" in the joint declaration draft presented by the Japanese side, to the plural "problems left unsettled." Prime Minister Tanaka then pressed him with the question, "Then do you definitely recognize that the four islands are included among the various problems?" Brezhnev replied, "I know." And, as if to reinforce the point, he added, "Da" (yes). Thus, the position that the Soviet Union had been insisting on, namely, that the territorial issue was already resolved, had changed.

The Ministry of Foreign Affairs considered this an epoch-making development, and aboard the special flight back to Tokyo Tanaka and Ōhira exchanged toasts and gave free rein to their imagination regarding the future of Soviet–Japanese relations. However, later developments showed their optimism to be premature as Soviet–Japanese relations, subsequently influenced by various international events, turned chilly again. The Soviet Union reverted to its former stance that the territorial issue was already resolved, and it was not until after the Gorbachev Administration began in 1985 that it started to show a more flexible posture regarding the Northern Territories.

Tanaka and Ōhira returned to Japan on October 11. A week later, on October 17, the OAPEC (Organization of Arab Petroleum Exporting Countries) conference held in Kuwait dropped the bombshell that it would restrict supplies of petroleum to all except friendly countries. The Arab countries were in difficult circumstances as a result of the Fourth Middle East War, which broke out on October 6, and this was the first instance of their use of oil as a strategic weapon in an effort to turn the war situation to their advantage. The first "oil shock" that originated from this announcement suddenly resulted in oil prices increasing by four to five times and plunging the global economy into a state of disorder. It is of interest to note that some three months before this "oil shock," Ōhira had already predicted that such a situation might arise.

On July 5, 1973, just one year after the start of the Tanaka Administration, Tanaka had opened a press conference at the Prime Minister's Official

Residence by remarking, "It's hard to realize that a whole year has passed." In the interview he refused to be bowed by the increasing difficulties of rising prices and attacks from the opposition parties, and responded with his customary pluck and optimism, "I'll do whatever needs to be done."

On the evening of the same day, Foreign Minister Ōhira also talked with reporters, but the tenor of his words was different: "This past year has been, for me, a long, long year. Situations that I had not predicted when I took office a year ago are now coming to the fore. In other words, the world has become quite fluid and unsettled.... Certainly, the world is proceeding toward a greater relaxation of tensions, but, on the other hand, the world's currency crisis is becoming more serious, and, as a result, Japan had no choice but to adopt a floating exchange rate for the yen.... We have not just a currency crisis; problems concerning resources have suddenly surfaced and Japan has felt their effects very directly. These resource issues are serious problems and mean we shall have to take a new look at what Japan has been up to the present and what Japan will be in the future. Japan has been called the world's third economic superpower, but with these resource problems coming to the surface, the outer skin of pretense is peeling off and we are revealed to be one of the world's poorest countries [in natural resources]. However, this is not to say Japan is somehow at fault. It is because the world as a whole has changed in this way."

Ōhira's awareness of the fragility of the underpinnings of economic growth had been reflected earlier in his 1971 "Commencement of a New Century" proposals, where he argued that amid the great changes in the postwar world order, the prevailing notion that economic growth should always take precedence needed to be reconsidered and that new directions needed to be taken both politically and economically. This outlook was probably further developed by his reading of the Club of Rome's *Limits to Growth*, a report published in January 1972. This made macroeconomic analyses of the current situation of mankind and, by extrapolating from current patterns, warned that by the early twenty-first century the planet could no longer support the further pursuit of material culture. It pointed out how by-products of modern life—for instance, the exhaustion of natural resources, environmental pollution, explosive population growth, and growing nuclear war potential—threatened to block further progress and could even lead to the extinction of the human race. For Japan, with meager resources, the implications of this report seemed to be especially serious. One of the Japanese members of the Club of Rome was Ōkita Saburō, a close friend of Ōhira's since they were colleagues at the Asia Development Board in the war, and through him Ōhira frequently received information on the club's concerns and activities.

Foreign Minister Ōhira gave an unusual directive to Foreign Ministry officials while attending a conference of Japanese ambassadors to Middle East countries held at the Foreign Ministry on July 9. Ōhira told them he wanted to discuss the possibility of a simultaneous occurrence of a Middle East war and an oil crisis. Various opinions were presented and the meeting ended with no clear consensus, but the ambassadors and other Foreign Ministry personnel who participated in it were greatly impressed, both then and later, by Ōhira's insight.

The October 1973 oil crisis was indeed a great challenge for Japan's economy given the fact that Japan depended on imports for almost all the petroleum it used. Prices rose rapidly, and consumers rushed to buy goods like toilet paper and detergents before supplies ran out. Public opinion moved rapidly toward stressing the need to change Japan's policy on the Middle East so Japan would be recognized by the Arab countries as a friendly nation. Yet even in the midst of these dilemmas, Ōhira showed a certain hesitancy to change Middle East policy. Although natural resources were not limitless, the present oil crisis had, after all, occurred not because oil supplies were at the time insufficient but because the OAPEC countries had taken a united action, and, Ōhira argued, although prohibiting exports for oil-exporting countries might indeed be an important weapon for the time being, a more fundamental fact was that the Arab countries would eventually have to export oil again in order to be economically viable. Thus, Ōhira did not give too much weight to arguments that Japan would have to be recognized as a friendly country in order to have the export restrictions relaxed. When voices in domestic politics began more frequently to urge a clearer pro-Arab stand, Ōhira did not budge and once asked, "Has Israel done something bad?"

Looking back on this period, Ōhira has written: "Both the government and the people were at their wit's end. It was because large cracks had occurred in the very foundations on which the economy stood, causing much unrest. It was not surprising that people wavered back and forth. To me as foreign minister, there began to be addressed strong requests that we change our diplomatic posture toward the Middle East to one favoring the Arabs. From various quarters there was also strong pressure that we devise ways of insuring oil supplies through routes other than those controlled by the major oil companies. . . . The voices asking for a change in Middle East policy became more strident each day. Although I did not necessarily agree with them, I felt that if the government was going to make a change, by all means it should first win agreement from the United States, or at least should gain the United States' understanding."

On November 14, United States Secretary of State Henry Kissinger stopped in Japan on the way back to Washington from visits to several Middle East countries. Foreign Minister Ōhira explained to him Japan's policy toward the Arab countries, but Kissinger did not indicate agreement with a change in Japan's stance. Ōhira has written: "A determination to revise its Middle East policy was gradually taking shape within the government, and I was daily being driven into an increasingly isolated position." Faced with anti-Japanese measures expected from OAPEC and the Conference of Arab Foreign Ministers, the determination to take some appropriate steps finally surfaced. Ōhira became convinced that a change was necessary and repeatedly tried, through the Japanese embassy in Washington, to gain the understanding of the United States. The U.S. State Department still indicated displeasure with such a Japanese policy change, but finally it said that although it was unable to agree with the revision in the Japanese government's Middle East policy, it was able to understand the position of the Japanese government, which had no choice but to make such a revision.

The government announced its new policy toward the Arab countries in an address by Chief Cabinet Secretary Nikaidō on November 22, which also suggested that its policy toward Israel was likely to be reconsidered. The summit meeting of Arab leaders subsequently promised to exempt Japan and the Philippines from oil supply restrictions, and Prime Minister Tanaka and Foreign Minister Ōhira decided to send Miki Takeo, then director-general of the Environment Agency, as a special envoy to the Middle East. In the course of these travels, Miki visited Saudi Arabia and seven Arab countries.

In February 1974, a conference of major oil-consuming nations was held in Washington at the invitation of the United States, with thirteen nations, including Japan, represented. The conference soon became embroiled in a dispute between U.S. Secretary of State Kissinger, who advocated Western solidarity, and France's Foreign Minister François Jobert, who emphasized dialogue with the oil-producing countries. Ōhira tried to act as a mediator between the two, and he actively searched for ways to underscore points of agreement. On the morning of the last day, Jobert said to Ōhira, "France has decided to accept the Japanese plan."

Kissinger has written the following in appreciation of Ōhira's efforts at this conference: "There was great controversy, much of it having to do with matters of prestige not relevant to the issue. Ōhira, as was his custom, said nothing but listened carefully. Finally, on the last day, he spoke for the only time at the conference. His intervention broke the deadlock; it led to the creation of the International Energy Agency, the permanent and vital organization of energy cooperation among the industrial democracies."

The last days of 1973 were truly dismal. Nobody could predict where the oil crisis might lead. Japan's foreign currency reserves had fallen sharply, and the yen, which until recently had shown admirable strength, fell in value. Both wholesale and retail prices continued to rise. Due most probably to overwork, Finance Minister Aichi Kiichi fell victim to acute pneumonia and died on November 23. It was quickly decided that Fukuda, who had been serving as director-general of the Administrative Management Agency, would replace him as finance minister. Fukuda's former position was in turn filled by Hori Shigeru, and there were two new cabinet appointments: Nakamura Umekichi as justice minister and Kuraishi Tadao as agriculture and forestry minister. Mizuta Mikio was at this time made chairman of the LDP's Policy Research Council. Most importantly, the Tanaka Administration was making full use, in a way that might not have been earlier expected, of Tanaka's three rivals in the last LDP presidential race: the economy and foreign affairs were being handled by Fukuda and Ōhira, respectively, while Miki was busily engaged as a special envoy to the Middle East.

Ōhira was showing signs of physical fatigue. At the end of the year he suffered from a bad cold in addition to his chronic ailment of kidney stones. His doctor told him he needed rest, but he refused to give up his scheduled visit to China beginning January 2, which was for the purpose of working out an agreement, in preparation for a year, on business relations. In particular, he wanted to make a breakthrough in the stalled negotiations on a Japan–China civil aviation agreement. Here the biggest problem was how to receive planes from the People's Republic of China while maintaining a Taiwanese air service with an understanding, tacit or otherwise, that Japan–Taiwan business relations could continue. On January 2, 1974, Ōhira left for China via Hong Kong. The reason for going via Hong Kong was to underscore the point that a direct Japan–China air route had yet to be established.

His partners in the negotiations were Premier Zhou Enlai and Foreign Minister Ji Pengfei, just as at the time of the negotiations on normalization. The first point that came up was the air routes between Japan and Taiwan. The Chinese insisted that they could not change the principle that "Taiwan is a part of China," as stated in the Japan–China joint communiqué. They said that continued use of the Taiwanese airline's logo would be difficult, and explained that while they would not object to leaving the Japan–Taiwan air route as a "local line," it was inappropriate for the Taiwanese company to have rights to extend its flights elsewhere from Japanese territory.

The Japanese negotiators, on the other hand, offered the following concessions: Japan would not have its flag carrier, Japan Air Lines, fly to

Taiwan; Taiwanese planes would not be allowed to land anywhere except Tokyo; until the opening of Narita airport, Chinese and Taiwanese planes would both use Haneda airport but not at the same hours; after completion of Narita airport, China's planes would land at Narita and Taiwan's planes at Haneda (which would otherwise be used only for domestic flights). A further point at issue was the Taiwanese company's use of the name China Air Lines. On this point the Chinese on several occasions told Ōhira, "We want to do something about this." At one point he retorted, in a rare burst of pique, "This is not a matter we can deal with." Back at the State Guest House, Ōhira confided his feelings to aides: "The negotiations are not progressing as hoped. However, I do not intend to back off a single step from the main points I wish to get across. Even if my assertions don't get through, even if the negotiations are not concluded, I intend to say what I have to say."

Ōhira's second talk with Premier Zhou on January 5 also ended in disagreement. That evening, Ōhira told Japanese Ambassador Ogawa Heishirō, "Tomorrow I'm going home." The next day, when Ogawa told Ji Pengfei that the Japanese negotiators were leaving, Ji detained him, saying, "I want you to wait just thirty minutes." Presently a response came from the Chinese side: "We will go along the lines proposed by Ōhira." The main points were the following: China would recognize the right of the Taiwanese airline company to fly to other countries from Tokyo; Taiwan's airline could continue using the name China Air Lines and its identifying logo; however, with respect to the airline name and logo, the Japanese government would formally announce an opinion disclaiming any interpretation of the name and logo that would go against the principles of diplomatic recognition of the People's Republic of China. During the thirty-minute interval that Foreign Minister Ji requested, it seems probable that an emergency meeting had been held at which a final agreement was reached on Zhou Enlai's decision.

On the previous day, Ōhira had talked with Mao, the second occasion for the two to meet. Just as on the first occasion, the chairman began the conversation by saying, "Have you finished your arguments? I suppose you had a good quarrel over the aviation agreement." Ōhira replied, "I'm having trouble because no matter what I say Premier Zhou doesn't understand," whereupon Zhou, who was at his side, rejoined, "It's only a small matter considering that we earlier managed to agree on Chinese–Japanese normalization." Ōhira then remarked, "Premier Zhou is always saying this, but if it is such a small matter, wouldn't it be all right not to insist so strongly concerning it?" At that point, when it appeared that the negotiations were about to recommence in front of the chairman, Mao said to Zhou, "How would it be if you conceded a little?" This was no doubt a sign that made the eventual agreement easier.

The joint communiqué and the press conferences completed, Ōhira left quickly for the airport without even having a meal. As soon as his plane took off, he spread a blanket in the aisle and lay down, saying, "Last night I didn't sleep at all." His face was pale, almost ashen.

A week after his return from China, the Ōhira home in Tokyo's Seta district was gutted by fire. Ōhira learned about the disaster when he was in Sakaide, in his native Kagawa Prefecture, to support the candidacy of a colleague running to fill a vacant Upper House seat. When asked by reporters about his feelings, he replied calmly, "This is my second fire. The first time was in May 1945, during the war. At that time I was trying to keep Tsushima Juichi away from danger, you know." He continued: "It is said that in China fires are called 'zhurong,' which means, well, something like welcoming a new departure." That night, local supporters who came to visit Ōhira in the hotel where he was staying caught a glimpse of him sitting in a darkened room, with all the lights turned off.

The problem of the Japan–China civil aviation agreement had been settled in such a way that the Japanese points, which gave due consideration to Taiwan's interests, had mostly been recognized. Ōhira had expected that "since we had gone so far to preserve Taiwan's advantages, there would no longer be any complaints from the pro-Taiwan factions." That this expectation was too sanguine became painfully evident over the next few weeks. Soon after Ōhira's return to Tokyo, the government decided on the following policy directives: (1) the Japan–Taiwan air link would be maintained; (2) Japan Air Lines would not fly to Taiwan; (3) no request would be made for China Air Lines to change its name or its symbol (that is, the Chinese Nationalist flag, depicting a white sun against a blue sky); (4) the Civil Aviation Administration of China (CAAC) would use Narita airport, while China Air Lines would use Haneda airport; (5) China Air Lines flights currently using Osaka airport would be rerouted to other airports; and (6) China Air Lines business operations in Japan would be entrusted to representative agencies or other business concerns not directly operated by Taiwan. When these directives were made known to various groups within the LDP, the pro-Taiwan Dietmen were strongly opposed, seeing the measures as "affecting the dignity and interests of the Republic of China." Diet members belonging to the pro-Taiwan Seiran-kai were especially vicious in their attacks on Ōhira, threatening to introduce a motion of no-confidence in the foreign minister unless he revised his position.

Ōhira set about explaining the course of the aviation negotiations to the party's General Council and at joint meetings held at LDP head-quarters of the party's transport and foreign relations committees, making an effort to win intraparty understanding and acceptance. However, the pro-Taiwan members continued to attack the foreign minister, coming up with one demand after another beyond what the party as a whole had decided. Many of the pro-China Dietmen tended to stay silent, unable to withstand the fury of the pro-Taiwan members. Ōhira, however, stuck to his guns, saying, "the Japan–China aviation agreement shall be signed even if I have to be drawn and quartered."

In April, as the issue was approaching its final stage, Dietman Fujio Masayuki (a member of the Seirankai) succeeded in angering Ōhira by revealing, from the text of government telegrams, some confidential details of the aviation negotiation. In the end, however, on April 20, 1974, the Japan–China Aviation Agreement was duly signed in Beijing by Ambassador Ogawa Heishirō and China's Foreign Minister Ji Pengfei. Unhappy over this development, Taiwan suspended all air travel to and from Japan. The Japanese government's expectation that Japan–Taiwan air links would be maintained was thus, for the time being, mistaken.

The agreement was submitted to the Lower House for ratification on May 10. Over eighty Dietmen stayed away to protest the voting, including Seirankai members, members of the Fukuda faction, and such party elders as Funada Naka, Kishi Nobusuke, and Nadao Hirokichi, who chaired the Japan–Taiwan Parliamentarians' Round Table Conference. The agreement was approved unanimously by all present. Although Finance Minister Fukuda was a prominent member of this conference, as a cabinet minister he voted to ratify the agreement. The suspended air link between Japan and Taiwan was reopened, as a result of later negotiations, on July 9, 1975, during the Miki Administration.

About the time the agreement was being ratified, the streets of Tokyo were enlivened not only by the new leaves of early summer but by the posters of candidates in the coming tenth election for the Upper House, scheduled for July 7, 1974. This election was carried out in an atmosphere of great partisan feeling, with the opposition parties ardently hoping for a conservative–progressive turnabout, while the LDP was intent on recouping at least some of the losses suffered in the last Lower House general election. An LDP victory in this election seemed essential to Prime Minister Tanaka, who had already served two years of his three-year term as party president, to bolster his chances for reelection to the top party post. Tanaka helped with arrangements to have well-known singers and mass-media celebrities run as national constituency candidates, and he was otherwise more active than in any previous campaign, trying to assign quotas of assured votes to certain large enterprises and using a helicopter to fly around the country. The opposition parties branded these tactics as promoting "money–power elections" (*kinken senkyo*) and "company-coopted elections" (*kigyōgurumi senkyo*), gaining the sympathy of popular and mainstream journalism.

The election results proved disappointing for Tanaka. While a conservative–progressive turnabout did not occur, LDP representation in the Upper House became (after some who had been elected as independents joined the party) eight less than before, lessening the party's margin to only seven seats more than the combined strength of the Upper House opposition members. It was, in effect, a continuation of the defeat suffered by the LDP in the last Lower House election. The apparent inability to stop the conservatives' long downward trend that had continued since the latter part of the Satō Administration was producing a sense of crisis in the LDP.

On the morning of July 12, five days after the election, Miki Takeo resigned as director-general of the Environment Agency in protest against the money–power election tactics and with the stated purpose of working for party modernization. Criticism of Prime Minister Tanaka was thus pushed even more to the forefront of public attention. Finance Minister Fukuda was sympathetic toward Miki, saying, "As for reform of the LDP, Miki's plea is something I fully understand." Chief Cabinet Secretary Hori, who was close to Fukuda and wanted to see a Fukuda administration, tried repeatedly to persuade Fukuda that now was not the time to share political activities with Miki and that he should remain duly circumspect. As Fukuda's determination gelled, Hori, disappointed that his role as a mediator between Tanaka and Fukuda had come to an end, resigned his cabinet post on July 16. On the same day, Fukuda resigned as minister of finance. Tanaka thus had to contend with powerful intraparty opposition led by both Fukuda and Miki and representing nearly half the party's strength. Suddenly the political situation had become much more tense. After Fukuda's resignation, at Tanaka's request Ōhira assumed the post of finance minister, being replaced as foreign minister by Kimura Toshio, who had once served as chief cabinet secretary.

In the two years he had served under Tanaka, Ōhira had won a commendable reputation for his tenacity in bringing Japan out of its former passive postwar diplomacy and in dealing in a multifaceted way with changing international conditions, as exemplified by the normalization of Japan–China relations and the realistic handling of energy issues. Just as during his first period as foreign minister under Ikeda, Ōhira made the keynote of his diplomacy the maintenance and strengthening of relations with the United States. To close friends he frequently lamented, "Among the

Japanese there are a lot of people who have forgotten that Japan and the United States were once engaged in a bloody war, and that Japan lost that war." He was dissatisfied that there was a tendency to regard the Pacific War as a sort of generalized war experience and to abstractly call Japan's defeat simply the "end of the war" (shūsen). Like former Prime Minister Yoshida, Ōhira felt that relations between Japan and the United States, two nations that were different historically, culturally, and in racial makeup, could not be satisfactorily maintained without constant efforts to that end. As shown by the two "Nixon shocks" of 1971 and the "oil shock" of 1973, the postwar world was in the throes of important structural changes, both politically and economically. In this situation, Ōhira hoped to keep the basis of Japan's diplomacy grounded in the Japanese–American relationship while reconstructing this relationship in keeping with the new age.

The importance he attached to relations with the United States is evident in the fact that he devoted a chapter of his 1978 autobiography to Japanese–American diplomacy, in which he emphasized the importance of mutual understanding and trust. After discussing his contacts, as minister of foreign affairs, with three American secretaries of state (Rusk, Rogers, and Kissinger), and his various talks and cooperation with them on bilateral and other issues, he states: "Whatever the issue, Japanese and American standpoints and views were not necessarily identical. But in diplomacy, even if a meeting of minds is not reached, it is indispensable for both parties to show an understanding of the other's position. Mutual understanding and trust are no less important than reaching agreements. Especially between Japan and the United States, we should say that it is absolutely essential."

On May 20, 1974, two months before he left his post as foreign minister, Ōhira and his wife traveled to the United States, where he received an honorary Doctorate of Laws from Yale University. Others who had been honored with this honorary degree from Yale had included West German chancellors Konrad Adenauer and Willy Brandt, United Nations secretaries-general Dag Hammarskjöld and U Thant, and Meiji-period Japanese statesman Itō Hirobumi. Freed for a time from the arduous schedule of his official duties in Tokyo, Ōhira enjoyed the trip and had some time before the ceremony in New Haven to savor the fresh greenery of a New England spring. On the evening before the ceremony, the university's President Kingman Brewster hosted a banquet where Ōhira was glad to see his old friend Robert S. Ingersoll (a Yale graduate), who had been American ambassador in Tokyo from 1972 to 1973. He had come with his wife all the way from Chicago. The next morning, Ōhira joined several thousand graduates for the outdoor commencement ceremony. Ōhira later wrote, "It was a moment of great emotion, just like a dream." Wearing the traditional gown and mortarboard, Ōhira advanced to the platform and received from Brewster his diploma, which read:

> In a world grown dangerously small and mutually dependent, you have had the burden of guiding the foreign policy of one of the world's most important powers. Patiently and consistently, you have worked to create an international harmony based on trust among nations. As your voice has sought calm in a world made tense by crisis, so your serenity in times of trouble has given new strength to the bonds of friendship between our two countries. Yale University is proud to confer upon you the degree of Doctor of Laws.

Chapter 23

A Scenario of Surprises

Ōhira first entered his new office at the Ministry of Finance on July 16, 1974, replacing Fukuda Takeo, who had resigned in protest over Prime Minister Tanaka's political tactics. It had been thirty-eight years since he had first worked there immediately after graduating from Tokyo University of Commerce in 1936; and twenty-two years had passed since he had left the ministry to become private secretary to Finance Minister Ikeda Hayato. On assuming his new post, he told Ministry of Finance staff, "I never dreamed that I would ever be in charge here." Among ministry staff, he was still known by his old nickname "*Otō-chan*" (Daddy).

The economic situation facing the new finance minister was, however, one of severe and pressing realities both at home and abroad. Prices were continuing to rise steeply in the wake of the previous autumn's "oil shock." Wholesale prices in February 1974 were on the average 37 percent higher than one year previously. Even though prices later became somewhat more settled, demand remained stagnant and investment in plant and equipment was slack, contributing to the poor economic climate. Imports of 300 million kiloliters of crude oil annually at high prices were proving a rapid drain on foreign currency.

Ōhira writes about this period as follows: "At the Finance Ministry, I found that the problem of settling foreign accounts was causing severe strain. As the payment deadlines for the much more expensive oil and other natural resources approached, we were kept busy day and night raising the necessary funds. Trying every scheme in the book, I attempted, in addition to raising short-term loans, to secure medium- and long-term loans. For a time we had to put up with the rather humiliating conditions of a so-called Japan rate, but by the early part of August it became clear that we would be able to manage the problems regarding foreign payments."

In a situation where there was no choice but to expect an increased government deficit due to the rapid fall in revenue, the government decided to follow a basic policy of keeping down overall demand as a measure for checking price rises, and it indicated the desirability of a transition to stable growth as a medium-term objective for the nation's economy. Soon after assuming his post as finance minister, Ōhira expressed some of his thoughts in a press interview: "Whatever the issue, the Ministry of Finance is largely engaged in applying checks and restrictions, and it is only to be expected that the minister of finance will not be very well thought of. I think that I will be able to have the prime minister and other ministers exercise adequate self-control. Friendship and government finance are two different things." This statement was widely interpreted as referring to Tanaka's expensive Plan for the Remodeling of the Japanese Archipelago, which had become a symbol of his administration. In any case, Ōhira impressed reporters with his determination to maintain fiscal responsibility. In another interview given not long after he had begun his new job, Ōhira admitted that in some respects there could be grounds for criticism of Tanaka: "I think that because the prime minister is a human being he cannot be said to be completely without the traits referred to when people ask, 'Isn't he authoritarian, or arrogant, or too self-confident?' In this respect it can be said that he has at times made utterances that have not fully respected the procedures of the government or the party." Ōhira then continued: "However, Tanaka is an unusual man, and both his thinking and his putting things into practice deserve considerable study. He is indeed a person who merits adequate study not only with respect to his outer behavior but also with respect to his inner way of thinking. As a friend, I regret that my cooperation and advice have not been adequate. But I think that I must try my best and must give him advice when it is suitable." Even if both Miki and Fukuda had left the cabinet, this statement could be taken as indicating Ōhira's willingness to continue supporting the beleaguered Tanaka Administration. The vow to help one another made between Ōhira and Tanaka in the formative stage of the administration, and the close friendship between the two, had not, after all, changed in spite of the altered circumstances.

Three of the more troublesome problems facing Ōhira and the Ministry of Finance were: (1) when to relax policies restricting overall demand; (2) to what extent charges for public services should be kept down; and (3) how to stop the vicious cycle of spiraling prices and higher salary demands. For the most part, Ōhira showed that he was willing to continue the policies laid down by Fukuda. With respect to charges for public services, he stated: "As far as possible I want to stick with keeping these down, yet by doing so to an unnatural extent problems may occur later, and we should consider how such problems could, in fact, harm the economy." As for the controversy over whether an income policy should be introduced to deal with the problem of wages and prices, he said rather bluntly, "From the point of view of maintaining a vital economy, an income policy is fundamentally undesirable." Basically, he put greatest emphasis on private-sector creativity and resourcefulness. In his basic faith that one could virtually equate the market economy with the optimum price mechanism, he differed in nuance from Fukuda's approach.

An immediate major issue was the fiscal 1974 rice prices. On July 22, 1974, only one week after Ōhira assumed his new post, it was decided that the tax-subsidized rice price paid to producers would go up by 37.4 percent. This large hike reflected the general surge in prices after the "oil shock" and the corresponding rise in wages resulting from the unions' 1974 Spring Labor Offensive. As the person responsible for fiscal policy, Ōhira was forced to choose between immediately raising the consumer rice price to come in line with the price paid to producers, or keeping the consumer price low and somehow managing to put up with a situation of growing fiscal burdens unmatched by new revenues.

Four days later, on July 26, the National Personnel Authority presented a directive calling for a 29.6 percent increase in salaries for public employees. Thus, another factor had appeared to aggravate the fiscal burden. Both public opinion and the Economic Planning Agency (which tended to be sensitive to public opinion) wanted to keep the consumer rice price as it was, but Ōhira put his weight behind a consumer price hike, and it was decided that the consumer rice price would go up by 32 percent in September.

Around this time, Ōhira confided to a friend, "Whichever I choose, there are problems. It's a matter of choosing the lesser of two evils." Apart from his dislike for increasing the fiscal burden, he seems to have held the belief that in times of government hardship individuals, too, should bear that part of the burden that might be properly expected of them. In this regard he has written: "Thus, while both central and local budgets were going deeper into the red and business profits were deteriorating, individual family budgets were being kept in balance, real incomes were being maintained, and there was no sign of a diminished propensity to save. This situation whereby family incomes were maintained at the expense of business income and government revenue could certainly not be called healthy. It later caused problems in reconstituting healthy government finances and recovering business profits."

In the summer of 1974, the domestic political situation in both the

United States and Japan tended toward instability. In the United States, the Watergate revelations had entered a critical stage, and on August 8 President Nixon resigned and Vice President Gerald Ford assumed the presidency. Throughout the world there was a growing tendency to hold political leaders strictly accountable for their conduct. Japan was no exception, and the opposition parties increased their censure of the government and the governing party. Throughout the summer and fall of 1974, criticism of Tanaka over LDP "money–power politics" (*kinken seiji*), which become a major public issue in the days leading up to the Upper House election in July, became more outspoken, demanding an end to his administration.

In the meantime, Prime Minister Tanaka left for a trip to Mexico, Brazil, and Canada on September 12. He returned looking plainly the worse for wear, and he later remarked: "That trip was a mistake. I had to fly from temperatures of more than 36 degrees Centigrade to where it was snowing. The effects of that sort of temperature change on the body are more than one can imagine." Toward the end of this trip, in Vancouver Tanaka met up with Ōhira, who had been visiting North America to attend a meeting of the International Monetary Fund (IMF). Their game of golf seems to have been Tanaka's only real diversion on the whole trip. It is not clear just what they talked about, but one version has it that Tanaka sounded out Ōhira on whether he would accept the post of party secretary-general, which Ōhira declined, saying, "Hasn't it been just two months since I accepted the post of finance minister?"

On October 9, not long after Tanaka's return to Japan, the November issue of the monthly magazine *Bungei Shunjū* carried an article, titled "Studies on Tanaka Kakuei: His Money Network and His People Network," written by a group of journalists, the most prominent of whom was the critic Tachibana Takashi. It revealed a number of shady dealings on Tanaka's road to wealth, as well as generally unknown personal associations, including some of his more intimate relations with women. For Tanaka, already physically and mentally fatigued, this was the straw that broke the camel's back. He confided to Ōhira that he was "thinking of retiring," but at the same time he seemed to vacillate, mentioning his scheduled trip to Oceania and Burma, plans for a cabinet reorganization, and President Ford's forthcoming trip to Japan. Ōhira told him in no uncertain terms: "Your trip abroad is a public duty not to be lightly abandoned. Circumstances may be dark at home and abroad, but this is no time to waver. . . . While you are abroad, you'll have to set up a radar network to pick up accurate information within both the Liberal Democratic Party and the opposition parties, to get a three-dimensional grasp of where the mountains and rivers are. How would it be if you instructed Chief Cabinet Secretary Nikaidō about this?"

At the same time, Ōhira referred to domestic political prospects and admitted that the situation was serious. With respect to Tanaka's "money connections" (*kinmyaku*), Ōhira is said to have stated: "In the first instance, it is your own doing, so you must somehow think about what measures you will take and be careful not to take the wrong path." Ōhira's approach to these "money connections" was consistently the same, and when later allegations that Tanaka had evaded taxes were taken up in the Diet, Ōhira, observing a finance minister's duty of confidentiality, said, "This is primarily Tanaka's personal problem."

A press conference with Prime Minister Tanaka at the Foreign Correspondents' Club of Japan on October 22 pursued such questions in an inquisitorial atmosphere. Before long, Tanaka's "money connections" had snowballed into an international incident, which rebounded with greater force to haunt him at home. In the Upper House Finance Committee, opposition party members began investigations not only of Tanaka's personal income but also the corporate income of enterprises with which he was associated. Within the LDP, a Dietmen's League for Party Reconstruction, formed mainly by younger members of the Miki, Fukuda, and Nakasone factions, demanded that the prime minister make a public accounting of his assets, and lobbied for the opening of an emergency party convention or an LDP Joint Plenary Meeting of Party Members of Both Houses of the Diet to clarify their stance on the prime minister's conduct.

The strong-willed prime minister was being pushed into a corner where he would have to make a serious decision on whether his administration should or should not be continued. Prior to his scheduled trip to Australia and New Zealand (due to begin October 28), Tanaka hoped to make some decision about staying on or stepping down with the help of one-to-one talks with Hori and Ōhira on October 24, with Maeo (then speaker of the Lower House) and Kōno Kenzō (then president of the Upper House) on October 25, and with Shiina (LDP vice-president) on October 26.

It is said that during his talk with Ōhira on October 24, he asked if Ōhira was willing to be the next party president. Tanaka later said, "I felt that if Ōhira was willing I would make every effort to try to realize an Ōhira Administration." However, Ōhira did not at this time clearly indicate his intentions. Basically, Ōhira felt that the Tanaka Administration, as indicated in Tanaka's call for cooperation to Kōchikai members at the administration's outset, was, in effect, already partly his own administration, and that consequently the storm of criticism against Tanaka was also directed at himself. Even if he took over from Tanaka in these circumstances, would he, in fact, be able to weather the political situation successfully? Opposition to the Tanaka Administration by Miki and Fukuda was clear, and Nakasone, too, was seen as maneuvering for his own advantage. It seemed that an Ōhira administration at this point would be likely to face public criticism as a "bad substitute for the Tanaka Administration."

Responding to reporters' questions on the "money connections" issue following this talk on October 24, Ōhira stated: "Tanaka is not thinking about his own protection. Although this is primarily his personal problem, since he is Liberal Democratic Party president it is also a problem for the party and for the cabinet. Ultimately, it is something that will have to be decided by the prime minister himself." Regarding his own thoughts on the problem, Ōhira confided: "As a friend, I am willing to share his pain. I have no conclusion as to how to deal with it. I think about it every night. When Tanaka returns from his trip, I intend to tell him some of my thoughts."

In a press interview following the Tanaka–Kōno talk of October 25, Kōno said, "Tanaka stated that he would not insist on political power." He then added his own opinion: "In any case, there are two possible ways to settle the political situation. At the end of next month there will probably be a major upheaval." The next morning all the newspapers carried such headlines as "Prime Minister Considers Retirement," thus making the matter public. Early on the morning of October 26, Tanaka had a secret talk at his home in Tokyo's Mejirodai district in Bunkyō Ward with LDP Vice-President Shiina, and he asked if Shiina would be willing to head a "transitional administration." Citing health reasons, Shiina avoided an immediate answer and promised to consult again after Tanaka's return from abroad.

As Kōno had indicated, Tanaka probably had two ways in mind. One, as evidenced by the question he put to Ōhira on October 24, was that of having Ōhira become the next party president, thus somehow smoothing over the political situation and maintaining an "Ōhira–Tanaka leadership." This would depend, of course, on Ōhira's willingness. The other way was a temporary Shiina administration, about which Shiina had already been sounded out. By this procedure a cabinet reorganization would be carried out after Tanaka returned from abroad, at which time LDP Vice-President Shiina would be brought into the cabinet as deputy prime minister; soon after, Tanaka would step down and Shiina would "receive in trust" the remainder of Tanaka's term as party president and prime minister.

It had been arranged that both Ōhira and Shiina would talk with Tanaka on his return, so a conclusion was shelved for about ten days at least. However, for Shiina the problem was rather too weighty to be dealt with alone. Mindful of his health, Shiina consulted some colleagues with whom he could talk frankly, and as a result rumors about a transitional

Shiina-led administration somehow leaked out and took on a life of their own. In the meantime, preparations for a direct path from Tanaka to Ōhira were steadily shaping up. Staff members of both the Tanaka and Ōhira factions were busy working on a scheme whereby in a cabinet reorganization the top three party posts would be given to members of both factions who would, in this scheme, support Tanaka as far as possible and, when the time came, work together to make Ōhira party president.

At the same time, to check rumors that the prime minister might be stepping down, the Tanaka faction tried to strengthen support for its leader through meetings of all three mainstream factions—that is, the Tanaka, Ōhira, and Nakasone factions—during Tanaka's overseas trip. On the day the prime minister left (October 28), Fukuda Takeo said in a press interview in Kōchi City, Shikoku, "The political situation is rapidly changing, and following the Upper House election, a situation favoring reform and a new departure for the Liberal Democratic Party, which I have long been talking about, has emerged," thus suggesting his own readiness to head a new administration.

On November 8, Prime Minister Tanaka returned to Tokyo from his trip to Australia, New Zealand, and Burma, and the next day Shiina told him that he was very much in favor of a dissolution of factions and other party reforms, but if the party setup were to continue to be dominated by representatives of the big factions he would not easily be able to manage such an administration. Shiina could, though, agree to head a temporary administration if the top three party posts went to persons whose political ideals were similar to his own. It is said that Shiina put forth specific names of persons he had in mind.

On the same day, November 9, Ōhira went to Mito at the request of LDP Secretary-General Hashimoto to give a speech. There, he learned that Tanaka had talked with Shiina, as a result of which he quickly returned to Tokyo and went directly to Tanaka's home, where the two men talked for approximately an hour and a half. Ōhira told Tanaka that Shiina's idea of excluding the large factions from party management was unrealistic and would, in his opinion, needlessly deepen the party's confusion.

Faced with these two alternatives, Prime Minister Tanaka on November 11 carried out a cabinet reorganization designed to continue the Tanaka–Ōhira leadership. As for the top three party posts, Nikaidō Susumu (Tanaka faction) and Suzuki Zenkō (Ōhira faction) remained as secretary-general and chairman of the General Council, respectively, while Yamanaka Sadanori (Nakasone faction) was made chairman of the Policy Research Council. None of the individuals proposed by Shiina had been considered.

Miki Takeo criticized this action as "seeming, in the eyes of the nation, to be a maneuver for prolonging the life of the Tanaka Cabinet," and, like Fukuda, he refused Tanaka's suggestion that he be a cabinet member. Hori Shigeru, on being asked to join the cabinet, also declined. Needless to say, Vice-President Shiina was not brought into the cabinet in the capacity of deputy prime minister, as Tanaka had once considered and as Hori and others had hoped. Ōhira, Kimura, and Nakasone remained as ministers of finance, foreign affairs, and international trade and industry, respectively. Clearly angered by this, Shiina told colleagues, "Let them do as they like," and he withdrew to his home for several days. The small middle-of-the-road factions and non-faction party veterans who had been involved in the idea of a transitional Shiina-led administration tended to harbor new antipathy toward Ōhira, seeing him as the cause of the failure.

Thus, even though there had been a reorganization, the Tanaka Administration no longer had any future. Aware of the various maneuvers within the LDP to effect a post-Tanaka regime, Ōhira counseled Tanaka following a cabinet meeting held on the morning of November 18, the day President Gerald Ford was to arrive in Japan: "Now you should put all your efforts into welcoming Ford. So long as Ford is on our territory, you should not, from the point of view of diplomatic protocol, announce your resignation." Ōhira was obviously hoping for a respite, a sort of "Ford-visit truce." However, even before the American president left Japan, political maneuvers intensified, and it was clear that the Tanaka Administration was nearing its end. Ford's official visit to Japan ended on November 20, and the following morning's newspapers all announced that Tanaka had decided to step down.

It was just the opportunity that the various factions within the party had been waiting for. An initial offensive was launched by those wishing to see an Ōhira administration. On November 21, General Council Chairman Suzuki emphasized a point of methodology, stating, "The next president should be selected by an election." If it were to be a matter of an election, the idea of a transitional administration would clearly go by the wayside, and it was widely thought that Ōhira would win. On the other hand, a talk was held on November 22 between Shiina and Hori in which the two men seemed to agree on the desirability of a transitional scheme. This did not necessarily mean one headed by Shiina, since various schemes, with different degrees of practicality, were being discussed, including even a temporary administration headed by Maeo or Hori. In any case, although Tanaka had not yet officially announced that he would step down, attention had clearly turned to the post-Tanaka era.

At a cabinet meeting on November 26, Finance Minister Ōhira reported on the supplementary budget for fiscal 1974, which was concerned largely with meeting fiscal needs for government employees' salaries and rice price supports. After the supplementary budget was given cabinet approval, Chief Cabinet Secretary Takeshita read Prime Minister Tanaka's resignation, titled *"Watakushi no ketsui"* (My Decision). Beginning with the words, "Since taking over the administration, I have for two years and four months fixed deeply in my mind the concepts of decision and execution," it ended with a certain literary flourish: "Whenever I let my thoughts ponder our nation's future course, it is with a feeling like that of staying awake all night, listening to some mighty torrent of rain over the great earth." For the party, this was the prologue to a drama of change.

Immediately after Tanaka's announcement, most party members felt there were three likely candidates to succeed him, namely, Fukuda Takeo, Ōhira Masayoshi, and Miki Takeo. The factions supporting these three immediately began to sound out one another's strategies and intentions. The Ōhira faction's basic stance was that the next party president should be chosen in an election, while the Fukuda and Miki factions were in favor of a negotiated selection. From the point of view of factional strengths within the party, it appeared to be preeminently a struggle between Fukuda, who had come in second at the time of the post-Satō election, and Ōhira, who had in that election come in third but was now sure to get the support of the Tanaka faction. Each favored the method of selecting the party president that would be to his own advantage.

LDP General Council Chairman Suzuki Zenkō, who was one of the leaders of the Ōhira faction, announced that he wished to hold a party convention for electing the next president on December 10. The reactions within the party to this initiative were various. The Fukuda and Miki factions, knowing that they stood little chance in an election, were virulently opposed and insisted on a negotiated arrangement, threatening to boycott the party convention if an election was held. Even as the rivalry intensified, secret talks, usually proposed by either Fukuda or Miki, were conducted between the contenders. The first was a talk between Fukuda and Ōhira on the morning of November 27 at the home of Japan Chamber of Commerce and Industry President Nagano Shigeo in the Matsubara district of Setagaya Ward. At this meeting, Fukuda argued for selection of the next party president through negotiations, and Nagano put in a good word by suggesting that in accordance with the principle of seniority Fukuda should be selected first. The meeting ended in disagreement after Ōhira replied: "Anyway, I want to go with an election. I think the choice will be the fairest and clearest through an election in which the candidates have made their positions clear."

Early on the morning of November 28, a meeting between Ōhira and Miki was held at the home of Miki's son-in-law near Miki's residence in the Nanpeidai district of Shibuya Ward. As in the previous meeting between Ōhira and Fukuda, those favoring negotiations and those favoring an election were diametrically opposed. Toward the end of the meeting, Ōhira was surprised when Miki hinted that he might form a new political party.

As the rift between the Ōhira faction and the Fukuda and Miki factions widened, the situation appeared hopelessly bogged down. LDP Vice-President Shiina began to act as a mediator from the afternoon of November 28, when a Party Advisers Conference (komon kaigi), with forty-nine advisers attending, was held at the behest of former Lower House Speaker Funada Naka. Although Fukunaga Kenji of the Ōhira faction and Kuno Chūji of the Tanaka faction argued for an election, the majority of advisers tended to favor a negotiated choice. Bolstered by this result, Shiina decided that consultations should first be held among five persons—Fukuda, Miki, Ōhira, Nakasone, and himself—to determine the direction to be taken.

The next day, Shiina summoned all four faction leaders to the party headquarters to consult with each individually. As before, Miki and Fukuda spoke in favor of selection by negotiations. Nakasone seemed to hint that he would consider a transitional Shiina administration when he said, "How would it be to have the selection made by the whole party, not necessarily insisting on one of these four individuals?" Of the four, only Ōhira insisted on a party election.

In the Shiina–Ōhira talk, Shiina's response to Ōhira's probing of his basic approach, was: "We are now at an important stage that we must first pass. Wouldn't it be a good thing to put together, for the time being, a transitional government until next summer, and in the meantime to put the party's affairs in order so we can later form a full-fledged administration?" Ōhira then said, "If that is the case, I suppose consideration could be given to you, given your capacity as vice-president," to which Shiina replied, "Because my health is not good, I don't have any intention of taking the initiative, but if everyone should urge me, it would probably be hard not to." He thus did not rule out the possibility of a transitional Shiina-led administration. The talk with Ōhira is said to have ended with Ōhira's statement: "Precisely because it is such an important crossroads, it would not be appropriate to set up a transitional government that would last only six months or so. I cannot agree."

During a press conference following this talk, Ōhira revealed that he had opposed the idea of a transitional administration as well as the "restless hobgoblin, going under the name of negotiations." He added, "It appears that Shiina is also willing [to be party president]." As word of this spread around Nagatachō (the district where the Diet offices are located), many began to complain that it was "like getting in the *sumō* ring and finding the referee, too, in a wrestler's loincloth." Thus, Shiina's option of staying on as mediator while keeping open the possibility of finally becoming the main actor was blocked, and he had to choose between being either a mediator or a candidate to head a transitional administration. Finally, he gave up any hope of the latter, though he couldn't conceal a certain displeasure that Ōhira, in sounding out his intentions regarding a transitional Shiina-led administration, had, in effect, quashed this possibility. Around this time he told a friend, "Ōhira seems to have intentionally laid a trap for me." In the last cabinet reorganization, Shiina had already had his plans rejected as a result of Ōhira's strategy, and now his displeasure toward Ōhira increased.

A joint meeting with Shiina and the four faction leaders began at 10 A.M. on November 30. It was first agreed that "whoever is selected as the next party president, everyone will cooperate with him in building party unity." It was further agreed that "the new party president will realize three aims: renewal of the party and the establishment of a system to insure party unity; economic stabilization and overcoming inflation; and securing social fairness." As for the first item, the following five points were proposed: (1) party and cabinet posts should be allotted to represent the whole party; in principle, the secretary-general, chairman of the LDP Finance Committee, and head of the Treasury Bureau should not come from the same faction as the party president; (2) allocation of posts should take into consideration party members' achievements, and thus be an incentive and stimulus to party members; (3) there should be a review of the current composition and activities of the General Council, with subsequent reforms; (4) there should be a strengthening of policy-related investigative and legislative functions; and (5) support for various extraparty organizations should be strengthened. At the end of the meeting, which lasted four and a half hours, Shiina stated: "Given the current situation, I'd like to ask your cooperation tomorrow, that is, Sunday."

Late that evening, amid growing rumors, it was suggested to Nakasone by someone close to Shiina that a mediated designation was likely to go to Miki. This was then relayed to Miki and Fukuda. The only thing Ōhira had word of was that Shiina might produce a specific name on December 1 and that it was possible it might be Miki's. Ōhira remarked to an acquaintance, "Even if by chance Miki's name comes up, it will not work out." At the same time, Ōhira was determined that if Shiina should nominate Fukuda, this would be completely out of the question and he would reject it straight off. He considered that if any name other than Fukuda's came up, Fukuda would withhold his approval, and, as a result of the failed attempt at mediation, an election would be necessary. Ōhira also considered the influence of Party President Tanaka to be highly consequential, and that none of the five who took part in the talk of November 30 could ignore Tanaka's views. Kōchikai members, sensing an election in the offing, busied themselves with maneuvers designed to secure the maximum number of votes for Ōhira.

At 10:30 A.M. on December 1, at the outset of the second five-man consultation, Shiina suddenly announced his nominee with this preamble: "It is regrettable that there has been no complete agreement on the method of selection, but, on reviewing the process of adjusting views up to now, I judge that the major stream of party opinion is that the new president should be smoothly chosen through negotiations." As for the persona of the new party president, Shiina stated, "He must be pure, honest, and someone who will vigorously pursue the modernization and radical reform of the party." He then continued, "At this moment I feel that Miki Takeo, an experienced politician, is the most appropriate person for the role, and I nominate him as party president."

The moment Shiina announced his arbitration, Miki exclaimed, "This is a bolt from the blue." Immediately afterward, Miki held individual talks with each of the three faction leaders. While Miki was speaking with Nakasone, Ōhira and Fukuda remained in a separate room, at which time Ōhira queried, "What does all this mean?" and Fukuda replied, "It can't be helped. Sometimes people who win the argument may still lose out. That's what's happened this time." Ōhira later admitted feeling for the first time that "after all, everything was practically settled." Ōhira's expectation that Fukuda would certainly object if Shiina came up with anyone else's name had turned out to be quite wrong.

After talking alone with Shiina, Miki read out a few words he had written down in formal acceptance of Shiina's nomination. Ōhira, still looking disappointed, said, "Let me think a little bit about this nomination. I'd like you to wait until evening." He then went to Mejirodai to talk to Tanaka about the turn of events and the best way to handle the situation. Not knowing Shiina would deliver his arbitration that day, Tanaka had gone in the morning to Saitama Prefecture to play golf; but when he learned of the situation, he quickly started for home.

While waiting for Tanaka to return, Ōhira must have pondered various things. First of all, it was natural for him to want to know the views of his close friend Tanaka, who had until then made every effort in Ōhira's favor. And it was also natural for him to have doubts about the propriety of a vice-president making an arbitration without first checking with the party president. However, the longer he waited, the calmer he became. If he rejected the arbitration, Miki might form a new party or the Ōhira faction might become more isolated; in either case it would be difficult to avoid a great deal of confusion. Besides, the end of the year was approaching and there was the supplementary budget bill and much other work the government would have to deal with. If Tanaka were to reject Shiina's arbitration, that would be one thing, but otherwise it would probably have to be accepted. Even as he waited, Ōhira was beginning to see it more objectively as "one sort of a decision." When Tanaka returned home, he told Ōhira, "I think this is something that can't be helped. Shiina played a good hand, and you lost, fifty-one to forty-nine." Ōhira then decided to accept the arbitration.

As discussed earlier, in the autumn of 1964, when Prime Minister Ikeda announced that he would step down due to illness, three faction leaders (Satō Eisaku, Kōno Ichirō, and Fujiyama Aiichirō) had announced their candidacy, and party Vice-President Kawashima had attempted to mediate. However, when none of the three candidates softened his stance, Kawashima's efforts did not bear fruit, and it was by Ikeda's choice that Satō became prime minister. When Tanaka had first announced that he would step down, Ōhira had thought that the current situation with four candidates was analogous to the situation ten years previously. As before, the vice-president was attempting to mediate, and if he failed, arbitration by the party president would probably result. Or if the choice of the new party president was not left to the current president, there would be no choice—or so Ōhira thought—but to proceed with an election in accordance with party rules. What Ōhira had overlooked was that party rules specified that "the party vice-president assists the party president, and if the president suffers an accident or is absent, he carries out his duties." In Shiina's interpretation, Tanaka had met with an "accident"; thus, Shiina felt that he was already, as vice-president, substituting for the president.

The fact that Fukuda and Nakasone rather easily accepted Shiina's arbitration, and the fact that Tanaka had also accepted it, can be seen as an indication of their acceptance of Shiina's interpretation of his duties. There remained only the question of how the Ōhira faction would react to the "postwar dispensation." First of all, the faction put before the party's General Council a resolution saying: "Today's measure was only taken as a last resort and should not set any precedent. In the future, in every case, choice of the party president should be made through election at a party convention." When Ōhira heard from Deputy Secretary-General Urano Sachio that this resolution was unanimously accepted by the General

Council, he thanked the Kōchikai Diet members for their efforts and stated, "In spite of all your concern, due to various faults I was unable to meet your expectations." Thus, although already almost within sight of heading an administration, Ōhira had no choice but to step back a while and wait.

As we have seen, the LDP was formed in 1955 as a conservative coalition of the Liberal Party and the Japan Democratic Party, both of which had roots going back before the war. Ever since, these two currents, openly or not, depending on the time and circumstances, had vied for power within the party. At times this had taken the form of fierce factional struggles, yet this rivalry had effectively promoted an intraparty alternation of power and as such had contributed to the party's vitality.

Looking back over past LDP administrations, we see that the first LDP president, Hatoyama Ichirō, was of Liberal Party origins but realized his administration with the help of Democratic Party elements. Then, after a short period under the party's second president, Ishibashi Tanzan, who came from the Liberal Party, the third party president was Kishi Nobusuke, who had been a prewar bureaucrat and a postwar secretary-general of the Democratic Party. The fourth LDP president was Ikeda Hayato, protégé of the Liberal Party's Yoshida Shigeru. Ikeda's rival, and the fifth LDP president, Satō Eisaku, had, like Ikeda, been a pupil of Yoshida, but due to the fact that he was Kishi Nobusuke's younger brother, he, in fact, represented both the Liberal Party and Democratic Party streams, which was one reason the Satō Administration lasted so long.

Within the Satō faction were both Tanaka Kakuei, who originally belonged to the Democratic Party but soon switched to the Yoshida branch of the Liberal Party, and Fukuda Takeo, with a Democratic Party background. Rivals within the Satō faction, these two men engaged in a fierce battle for the party presidency in the election held at the end of the Satō Administration. Tanaka, teaming with Ikeda Hayato's disciple Ōhira Masayoshi, became the LDP's sixth president. As a result, Fukuda became closer to Miki Takeo, who had earlier belonged to the Democratic Party, and likewise joined up with Nakasone, who had similar pre-1955 party affiliations, thus strengthening his position against Tanaka and Ōhira.

Considering this history, the emergence of the Miki Administration as a result of Shiina's arbitration can be seen as a further alternation of power, this time from the Liberal Party to the Democratic Party stream. It should, however, be remembered that Miki, who won his first Diet seat as early as 1937, had participated in the formation, after the war, of the relatively small Japan Cooperative Party and its successor (in 1947), the National

Cooperative Party, which stood to the left of the original Democratic Party, with which it merged in 1950 to form the National Democratic Party (renamed the Reform Party in 1952). Within the LDP, the Miki faction was relatively small and lacked a strong support base. In one sense this was probably one of the reasons why Shiina, who disliked having the party led by large factions, chose Miki. It was also a reason why Miki was relatively popular with the opposition parties and the mass media. Yet there was a big gap between the way Miki saw his position and the way it was perceived by the leaders of the party's main factions. While Miki saw himself as the LDP's savior, selected through Shiina's arbitration, the majority within the party regarded his administration as an interim measure. Here, indeed, was a seed of tragedy already present at the time of the formation of the Miki Cabinet.

Chapter 24

The Declaration of Fiscal Crisis

Miki Takeo as the newly named prime minister began forming his cabinet on December 9, 1974. Appointees to major cabinet posts included Fukuda Takeo as director-general of the Economic Planning Agency, with the additional rank of deputy prime minister; Inaba Osamu as justice minister; Miyazawa Kiichi as foreign minister; Abe Shintarō as agriculture and forestry minister; Kōmoto Toshio as minister of international trade and industry; Sakata Michita as director-general of the Defense Agency; and Ide Ichitarō as chief cabinet secretary. Ōhira, one of the few holdovers from the former cabinet, was kept as finance minister. Nagai Michio was brought in from outside the Diet membership—the first time in many years that such a cabinet member had been so appointed—to head the Ministry of Education, to which Miki intended to give special attention. As for party positions, Miki retained Shiina as vice-president and named Nakasone as secretary-general, Nadao Hirokichi as General Council chairman, and Matsuno Raizō as Policy Research Council chairman.

Immediately after assuming the prime ministership, Miki announced policies to promote reforms in the method of selecting the party president and in political campaigns and political funding as a way of countering dissatisfaction with the LDP's "money–power politics." A draft plan, reflecting the opinions of experts from outside the party, was made public and envisaged, in the realm of intraparty affairs, revised rules on the election of the LDP president involving the introduction of a system of preliminary elections by all party members throughout the country. In the legislative field, the plan envisaged a revision of the Law on the Control of Political Contributions, which would further restrict political funding both quantitatively and qualitatively, and the establishment of a special amendment to the Public Office Election Law, which would include limitations on publicity activities and an increase in the extent of public supervision of elections. These measures were welcomed by the general public as evidences of Miki's political posture as "Mr. Clean," although some criticisms were heard since these measures affected the party's traditional bases of support.

Another plan made public almost immediately after Miki assumed office was that of revising the Antimonopoly Law. This plan, which responded to demands for correcting company behavior in the wake of the "oil shocks," called for the breakup of enterprises holding monopoly positions, the public announcement of prime costs, an order mandating certain price cuts, limits on the holding of stock by companies and financial institutions, and stronger penalties for violators. However, a large number of LDP members could not easily accept the proposed measures.

As minister of finance, Ōhira was soon occupied with compiling the budget for fiscal 1975, for which basic policy was to continue to restrict overall demand as a means of stabilizing prices. However, in reality it was difficult to restrict government expenditure given the hikes in expenses accompanying price rises as well as other expenses incurred in the effort to cope with unruly inflationary pressures.

During this period, Finance Minister Ōhira and Economic Planning Agency Director-General Fukuda, who was popularly seen as the "economic prime minister," often clashed in their views, resulting in numerous arguments. A high official in the Ministry of Finance at the time recalls: "With the task of compiling the fiscal 1975 budget before us, an Economic Ministers Conference (keizai kakuryō kaigi) was instituted, chaired by Fukuda. Ōhira was clearly unhappy about this, as he did not think yet another sumō ring was necessary and did not welcome unnecessary interference in his work as minister of finance. . . . One of the main topics of the conference was how to go about revising public service charges. While Fukuda was on the sensitive side when it came to prices, Ōhira felt that prices should follow economic principles and that the government should not interfere unnecessarily."

In this case Fukuda's views, which were more attuned to public opinion, won out, and it was decided that public service charges, which had mostly been frozen during fiscal 1974, would again be kept low. The deficits incurred would be transferred wholly to the public purse. In a press conference on December 19, 1974, Ōhira stated: "As for so-called price policy, my concept does not, I think, depart very far from the price mechanism. We are importing precious raw materials from abroad at high prices. Thus, we should use these resources carefully, and it is not my hope that the government subsidize them or make them available free of charge. Price measures should be pursued in a reasonable manner, and I think the healthiest approach for a price policy is to be very orderly about keeping government spending strictly within limits."

In any event, the completed budget for fiscal 1975 was 14.5 percent higher than the original budget for the previous year, or 10.9 percent higher if the supplementary budget for fiscal 1974 was included. This latter rate of increase was the second lowest in ten years (next to the 10.6 percent increase for the fiscal 1967 budget). The fiscal 1975 budget was characterized by continued large increases in social welfare—up 35.8 percent over the corresponding amount in the original fiscal 1974 budget that, in turn, was 36.7 percent higher than in the fiscal 1973 budget— while expenditures for public works were only marginally more in nominal terms (2.4 percent) than the previous year. The only expected increases in revenue were from higher postage rates and higher taxes on alcohol and tobacco. When asked how he felt on completion of the budget, Ōhira replied, "As heavy as lead."

When then asked to comment on "rigidities in government finance and welfare," he replied as follows: "The biggest reason for these rigidities is personnel expenditures. Large hikes continue to be made in basic salaries, and personnel cuts are impossible. The next problem is social welfare and education. Here we are made to promise one new thing after another. A part of such expenditures are newly allocated each fiscal year and are then institutionalized in the next fiscal year. Quite literally, we are rapidly proceeding along a path to greater rigidities. Director-General Fukuda has also served as finance minister in the past, so he cannot be seen as having no responsibility. To overcome these problems we are often told to cut down existing expenditures. Anyone can agree with the general intention to overcome rigidities, but the same person will be the first to be opposed if some vested interest is affected. If we keep on this way, things will become more and more rigid and before long we'll be up to our necks in debt. There is a need to revise traditional conventions and systems, but for this purpose a revolutionary administrative reform is in order." In these thoughts we may see the beginnings of the Ōhira Administrative Reforms to come a few years later.

As shown, for example, by cuts in public works expenditures (in real terms), the fiscal 1975 budget cannot be said to have taken due account of prospects for an improved economic climate. Rather, policy seems to have been influenced by the fear that an inflationary wage–price spiral would become a built-in feature of the Japanese economy, especially if large wage hikes were carried out after the unions' 1975 Spring Labor Offensive, as had occurred in 1974. The current economic slump, Ōhira felt, was different from, and more structural than, the periodic slumps seen in previous business cycles. In a conversation with reporters on February 22, 1975, Ōhira expressed the following doubts: "So long as the present situation is called an economic slump (*fukyō*), this presupposes there is such a thing as good economic conditions (*kōkyō*). But can we really say so? Isn't it possible that the next peak will not differ much in height from where we are now?"

Ōhira's thinking along these lines was more clearly expressed in a speech titled "The Present Situation of Government Finance," which he had especially requested the opportunity to deliver before the Lower House Finance Committee of the 75th Ordinary Diet on April 15, 1975, not long after completion of the fiscal 1975 budget. This speech, which was soon to be popularly known as "The Declaration of Fiscal Crisis," indicated the problems of government finance in the period of stable growth following the oil crises, and it was the first clear exposition of the problems to be faced in restructuring fiscal policy.

In this presentation, Ōhira emphasized three points: (1) tax revenues during fiscal 1974 were expected to be approximately ¥800 billion short of the original estimate, not only because of a drop in corporate profits and a decrease in land transfers and sales but also because of structural change; the fundamental problem was that under conditions of stable growth it was difficult to put such great expectations in so-called natural increments in revenue as had been common in earlier years; (2) in fiscal 1975, it would be impossible to prevent a negative influence from the fiscal 1974 shortfall in revenue, yet this should not be rashly dealt with through increased issues of government bonds but rather by making every effort to cut back on expenditure, economize on administrative expenses, and reevaluate all current outlays; (3) since future fiscal policy would continue to be restricted due to the shortfall in revenue, there was a need to fundamentally improve government finance strategy; thus policies that required the expenditure of public monies should be very carefully selected, and new means to insure tax revenues should be studied.

Especially with respect to the third point, a number of specifics were mentioned, relating, for example, to the need to reassess the division of responsibilities for meeting social insurance needs. As for public service charges, Ōhira stated: "There is the need to reject an easy reliance on government finance and to set fees at appropriate levels in keeping with costs, based on the principle of users bearing [a good part of] the cost." As for the ¥800 billion shortfall in revenue in fiscal 1974, it was revealed that it would be somehow possible to overcome this by revising government statutes to permit a change in allocation of tax revenues, allowing some ¥400 billion in revenues collected during fiscal 1975 to be redesignated as fiscal 1974 revenue, together with policies that would put aside some ¥160 billion that need not be actually spent and would mobilize some ¥240 billion in funds other than tax revenues deposited in the Bank of Japan.

There were, of course, numerous reasons for Ōhira to make this "Declaration of Fiscal Crisis," one of the most important being that companies were now operating at a slower pace as a result of the recession following the oil crisis, which meant, in turn, that tax revenues could not be guaranteed to stay as high as before. There was also anxiety that government finances were losing their "maneuverability" due to natural increments in personnel expenses, social welfare expenses, and tax monies and subsidies transferred to local governments, a problem frequently debated since the drafting of the fiscal 1975 budget. In addition, there was a deep-rooted tendency among many government leaders to emphasize price policies, as a result of which public service charges tended to be kept unreasonably low to the detriment of fiscal considerations. In other words, Ōhira wanted to issue a warning that if things continued in that way government finances might collapse completely. And, indeed, from that time, the management of government finances became much more stringent, and criticisms of Ōhira, as the minister in charge, were at times severe.

Ōhira often talked about "taking a new and fair look at private enterprise," a view expressed in the following statement: "If we really think about it, in whatever it may be—production or distribution, software or hardware—almost everything is being done by private-sector enterprises. These are, indeed, very important to us in our daily lives. In particular, we should remember that whenever private businesses are in debt, our government finances are immediately faced with a crisis. In this sense we must take a look at private enterprise from a new angle." In 1974 and 1975, there was a general tendency to denounce private enterprises for their alleged power in various fields, as well as for the alleged size of their profits and their role in pollution. Ōhira's statement was meant to warn that such criticism could go too far and result in tendencies that could restrict in harmful ways the activities of these enterprises. At the same time, it was the beginning of the idea of introducing a general consumption tax that would stabilize goverment finances without depending only on the profits of enterprises.

Partly as a result of Ōhira's "Declaration of Fiscal Crisis," discussions of fiscal problems became more lively both inside and outside the Diet. Nevertheless, Prime Minister Miki and other LDP and government leaders tended to show more interest in realizing the promise Miki had made at the outset of his administration to revise the two laws relating to elections and the Antimonopoly Law.

Because the two election law revisions, aimed at "cleaning up" elections and clarifying sources of political contributions, intimately involved the fortunes not only of the LDP but of some opposition parties as well, Diet discussion hit a number of snags, but finally bills for revising the two laws passed the Lower House on June 24. As for revising the Antimonopoly Law, there was strong opposition from business circles and also from Vice-President Shiina and others within the LDP, with the result that the final bill was considerably less stringent than the original drafted by the Fair Trade Commission. The opposition parties, which had reacted positively to the original revisions, resorted to angry attacks on the government for removing the backbone from the law.

Discussions in the Diet became so heated that LDP Secretary-General Nakasone announced that he no longer expected the bill to pass in the current Diet session. However, Prime Minister Miki continued to push for the early adoption of this bill, which he considered his first public pledge. His maneuvers to deflate objections from both the governing and opposition parties finally succeeded, and the revised Antimonopoly Law passed the Lower House on June 24, leaving further discussion (and hopefully approval) to the Upper House. As it turned out, many Upper House LDP members showed a strong antipathy to the revised law, and, Prime Minister Miki's efforts notwithstanding, any hope of its passage virtually disappeared. Thus, the prime minister became more determined to see Upper House passage of the two bills for revising the election laws.

Caught in the fray were bills for raising taxes on alcohol and tobacco. In a situation where there was no expectation of a natural revenue increase and where public service charges were nearly all being kept low, the only way to increase government revenues was by raising taxes on liquor and tobacco, which was expected to produce some ¥200 billion. Ōhira favored this bill, which had already passed the Lower House on May 6. However, its destiny in the Upper House was uncertain amid the confusion of the various bills being discussed toward the end of the Diet session. Ōhira and his Ministry of Finance staff busied themselves with last-minute maneuvers. There were continued complications with discussion in the Upper House, and on July 4, the last day of the Diet session, Prime Minister Miki, desperate to get at least the two election laws passed, tried his best to direct affairs from the Prime Minister's Office in the Diet building, with Ōhira moving back and forth between the two houses in an all-out effort to gain support for the bill on alcohol and tobacco.

The Upper House began its final plenary session a little after 9:40 P.M., taking up first of all the bill for revising the election law. The JSP and DSP Dietmen were amenable and the bill was approved. Consideration was next given to the bill restricting political contributions. It took a long time to process the votes, but finally President Kōno Kenzō came to the microphone and announced an unexpected result: a tie, with 117 in favor and 117 opposed. Then, after citing the second paragraph of Article 56 of the Constitution specifying the president's obligation to break a tie by casting his own vote (which he ordinarily does not do), the bill passed. Ōhira went to the Prime Minister's Office in the Diet building, where Chief Cabinet Secretary Ide and Deputy Chief Cabinet Secretary Kaifu Toshiki, among others, were congratulating Miki on the passage of the two bills. However, as if to show that he considered so much merriment premature, he quickly left the room with an expression of displeasure.

After passage of the two election-related laws, the Upper House plenary session took a break. President Kōno went into his office, and it was impossible to know whether he intended to reopen the plenary session to take a vote on the alcohol and tobacco bill. Ōhira and various Upper House LDP leaders visited Kōno's office, but neither Miki nor any other government leaders seemed to show any special enthusiasm for having the law passed. LDP Vice-President Shiina and Secretary-General Nakasone entered Kōno's office a little before 11 P.M., and before long it was past midnight and a decision had, in effect, been made that the plenary session would not be reconvened. Thus, the tobacco and alcohol bill missed being passed. In view of the circumstances under which Kōno had been selected as Upper House president—with the opposition parties and the non-mainstream members of the LDP supporting his nomination—it was perhaps natural that he wanted, at the last minute, to avoid a decision on the bill, thus satisfying the opposition Dietmen.

At the general meeting of the Kōchikai held on the morning of July 5, there was a barrage of angry voices criticizing the Miki Administration's management of Diet affairs, and there were even voices saying the minister of finance should resign in protest. At this meeting, Ōhira, who had not slept the previous night, did not try to hide his disappointment when he rose to say the following: "During the last Diet session the original plan was not to introduce any heavy baggage [that is, difficult bills], in view of circumstances in the Upper House. It was wrong to have started by introducing bills like the Antimonopoly Law and the law on political contributions, yet the prime minister and persons around him did so in order to underline their political stance. Such matters do not proceed well in the absence of a consensus within the party."

Ōhira continued his sharp criticism of certain attitudes of the Miki Administration, stating: "The problem is not one that can be dismissed as a lack of skill in handling the Diet. The present condition of the Liberal

Democratic Party is quite serious. It is necessary to examine the party's health beginning with the most fundamental aspects, to take a critical look at the past and carry out discussions after returning to basic political principles." As for the suggestion that he resign in protest, Ōhira made it clear that he was not, for the time being, considering it: "Just because I might feel chagrined, it would not be right for me to abandon my job as finance minister, thinking only of my own personal advantage." He also made clear his intention to have an extraordinary Diet session opened as soon as possible to come to grips with the bill to raise taxes on alcohol and tobacco.

The newly ended Diet session had been one of great confusion—so much so that it was nicknamed the "Wandering Diet" largely because of the party leaders' ineptness in keeping it on an even course. One symptom of poor timing was that as many as six important bills (the Antimonopoly Law bill, the two election-related bills, the bill on alcohol and tobacco, plus bills for raising postage rates and for ratifying the Nuclear Nonproliferation Treaty), on each of which the ruling and opposition parties were divided, had been submitted together to the Upper House almost at the last moment. Disagreements as to the relative importance of the bills within even the government and the ruling party only added to the confusion.

Another factor was the pressures for a Diet dissolution that had begun to come from the prime minister and others near him. All the parties, with the next election in mind, were strongly aware of the interests of their supporters in deciding whether or not to agree to a piece of legislation. It was particularly in the interests of the opposition parties to work against the passage of any bills having to do with price rises. Various stalling tactics were tried, including the boycotting of Diet discussions and deliberately moving at a snail's pace when standing in line to cast votes. When the Diet session came to an end, newspaper headlines such as "Confused Diet Gives Surprise Bonus" portrayed the postponement of the alcohol and tobacco tax hikes as good news for the ordinary citizen.

In the meantime, Finance Minister Ōhira had to cope with the knotty problems of what one might call "currency diplomacy." As mentioned earlier, at the beginning of his term he was beset with the issue of how to raise enough foreign currency to settle international accounts, and now with the weakening dollar and rising oil prices, the problem was becoming more complicated daily. Ōhira has written: "With the decoupling of dollars and gold, the change to a floating system of currency exchange rates, and the ever more apparent resource crisis, it was decided that there should be frequent international conferences of finance ministers. Countries hurting in their international balance of payments were more and more often requesting assistance from friendly countries or the IMF. And it was no longer possible to ignore the problem of how to recycle the dollars that were accumulating in the OPEC countries. Given this situation, it became urgent to assist the IMF by increasing its funds. The finance ministers and heads of the central banks of five countries—the United States, West Germany, Japan, England, and France—thus met frequently for discussions and the elaboration of countermeasures. Then, to further expand these discussions, conferences of the finance ministers of ten countries were held in January and August of 1975, at both of which I served as chairman. At these meetings I was made painfully aware of my lack of linguistic fluency and lack of knowledge, but at the same time I had a new awareness of Japan's responsibilities and real potential, and also keenly felt that it was more important than ever for Japan to address international economic problems with energy and sincerity." During his tenure as finance minister, Ōhira made a total of seven trips abroad and visited eleven countries.

On July 21, 1975, not long after the end of the "Wandering Diet," the government's Financial System Advisory Council presented its Interim Report on the Management of Government Finance under Conditions of Stable Growth. This was a response to Prime Minister Miki's instructions, during a cabinet meeting of January 21, 1975, to study the question of government finance rigidities. The report, whose preparation Ōhira had entrusted to the advisory council, contained the following statement: "Until now the people's wants have been met with relatively few problems through rapid economic growth. But from now on, due to a strengthening of factors limiting growth, meeting expectations through the sort of economic growth we have had in the past will be difficult. And as people's wants diversify, the expectations placed on government finance, under the banner of improving welfare and the like, are tending to become ever greater."

Under these circumstances, what posture should government finance be expected to take? To give some numerical indications was the aim of this interim report. It did not allow for possible future changes in economic conditions, but rather made simple econometric projections for three cases, hypothesizing shortfalls in fiscal 1975 tax revenues (compared to initial estimates) of ¥1 trillion, ¥2 trillion, and ¥3 trillion, respectively. It was calculated, to everyone's surprise at the time, that in the case of a ¥3 trillion shortfall, five years later (that is, in 1980) 28.8 percent of government finance would rely on public debt.

Prime Minister Miki, who was now redirecting attention to the problems of government finance, resolved to convene, on September 11, an extraordinary Diet session to pass a supplementary budget. Already it was seen by those responsible for fiscal matters that the worsening business climate would mean an enormous shortfall in tax revenues for fiscal 1975. Ōhira urged his Ministry of Finance to hurry with new projections, but calculations on the size of the expected deficit only continued to grow, and it was not possible to finish the work of putting together a supplementary budget bill before September 11. Thus, the opening day of the 76th Extraordinary Diet was unusual for its lack of an address on fiscal matters by the minister of finance. The only major addresses were those of Foreign Minister Miyazawa on international relations and a general policy address by Prime Minister Miki.

On October 9, when the supplementary budget proposed by the Ministry of Finance was virtually at the stage of Diet passage, it was announced that the shortfall in tax revenues would be ¥3.48 trillion, which was more than the ¥3 trillion shortfall projected in the interim report's worst-case scenario. The only way to cover that amount would be to increase the issue of government bonds. Since there was room for the issuance of ¥1.19 trillion in construction bonds, the remaining ¥2.29 trillion would have to come from bond issues to cover the government deficit. The fiscal authorities attached a special provision to the Finance Law, which opened the way for the first issuance of deficit-financing government bonds in postwar government finance.

Faced with this situation, Ōhira stated: "Outright deficit-financing government bonds must be reduced. I would like to get rid of them before the end of the 1970s. Surely it must be possible to manage fiscal matters so as to get rid of the deficit during the three years between 1977 and 1979. To do so, it will be necessary to increase the tax burden by about 2 percent on the part of the central government and by about 1 percent on the part of local governments. Based on this sort of estimate one or two provisional plans are now being considered in the Diet." At the same time, Ōhira pushed plans for issuing medium-term discounted bonds, with a view to making government bonds acceptable in the market and an attractive object for investment.

Ōhira's Diet speech on government finance was delivered on October 17, after the supplementary budget had been submitted for Diet approval. Although the budget won approval on November 7, other bills submitted at the same time, namely, the government finance special provision bill to allow deficit-financing government bonds, the reintroduced bill on alcohol and tobacco revenues, and the bill for raising postal rates, ran into difficulties with the opposition parties and only became law via the extreme measure of "forced adoption" in the finance committees of both houses of the Diet.

Contrary to Ōhira's wishes, the deficit-financing government bonds he had authorized could not be eliminated during the following years (as he had hoped), and to the end of his life this problem continued to plague him. As for results, however, the timely financial measures taken in fiscal 1975 and 1976 certainly helped the business world onto the path of economic recovery. Prices and employment stabilized, and Japan was one of the first countries to get its economy in order after the "oil shocks."

At a farewell press interview on December 24, 1976, at the time of the resignation en masse of the Miki Cabinet, Ōhira was asked: "The Ōhira fiscal policy may be evaluated by later generations as having produced a lot of deficit-financing government bonds. Do you have any regrets about it?" Ōhira minced no words in replying: "I have no regrets. In this period of transition there was no other alternative."

At the same time, Diet discussions on the supplementary budget were being carried out. An important issue widely discussed throughout the country was whether the Federation of Public Corporation and Government Enterprise Workers Unions (Kōrōkyō) should have the right to call strikes by government employees. Prime Minister Miki and Labor Minister Hasegawa Takashi, referring to current troubles regarding punishments meted out for illegal behavior in connection with the 1974 Spring Labor Offensive, had said, "We would like this time to put an end to any further repetition of strikes followed by punishments such as we have seen in the past." Kōrōkyō officials had notes of this statement, and launched new demands for the right to call strikes affecting government bodies.

The presidents of three public corporations—Japanese National Railways, Nippon Telegraph and Telephone Public Corporation, and the Japan Tobacco and Salt Public Corporation—told the Lower House Budget Committee on October 21: "We believe it is desirable to recognize, with certain conditions attached, the right of the three public corporations' labor unions to strike." When the opposition parties asked Prime Minister Miki for his opinion, Miki asserted that the words of the three public corporation presidents were "official views." Within the party, however, voices were raised in opposition, especially from Dietmen who had long been uneasy about Miki's attitude. There was thus the appearance of a split in opinion between the government and the LDP. In the meantime, the Kōrōkyō passed a resolution that all nine constituent unions would strike for at least ten days beginning November 26, and postwar Japan's biggest political strike began on that day according to schedule.

Within the party, there was strong criticism of Miki, with many blaming the strike on Miki's conciliatory posture toward the opposition parties. The prime minister then gave in to LDP demands, changed his earlier stance of supporting the right to strike, and issued a sharply worded statement. The matter was resolved when the Kōrōkyō, in the face of strong criticism from the Japanese people, decided it had no choice but to call off the strike eight days after it began. The rather reckless decision to strike without the support of the people at large hastened the Kōrōkyō's later loss of influence and leadership in labor circles, and the affair was at the same time an important factor leading to the loss of support within the LDP for the Miki Administration.

Slightly before the Kōrōkyō strike, during the three-day period between November 15 and 17, Prime Minister Miki, Finance Minister Ōhira, and Foreign Minister Miyazawa took part in the first summit meeting of major industrialized democracies held at Rambouillet on the outskirts of Paris. In spite of Japan's many troubles, it was considered one of the six major countries whose economic strength could not be ignored by the rest of the world.

At home, as autumn approached, rumors of a possible cabinet dissolution, which had been rife around the time of the end of the "Wandering Diet" but had abated during the summer, began to circulate again, and by the time the extraordinary Diet session was convened, it was the general opinion in political circles that there would be a cabinet dissolution at the end of 1975 or in the spring of 1976.

Prime Minister Miki's political attitudes and policy direction had already made other party leaders uneasy and given rise to a sort of anti-Miki trend. This also provided the occasion for the forging of closer relations between Ōhira and party Vice-President Shiina, who had remained estranged ever since negotiations for the normalization of Japan–China diplomatic relations, when Ōhira, as foreign minister, had entrusted Shiina with the thankless task of visiting Taiwan. Developments were leading to a meeting of minds, which included not only Shiina and Ōhira but also Tanaka and Fukuda, regarding the desirability of Miki stepping down as soon as possible.

One morning, Ōhira visited Shiina at his residence before going to his office at the Ministry of Finance. Afterward he spoke rather nonchalantly to reporters about matters that on the surface appeared to have little relevance: "Shiina's wife is very fond of *bonsai* [miniature trees and shrubs], and in their home was a fine little *bonsai* pine tree that I was asked to take with me. I declined, saying it would be a pity if I harmed it by forgetting to water it. A collection of writings on the Middle Ages by my favorite Oxford historian, Geoffrey Barraclough, concludes with words like these: 'Roses will always someday wilt and fall to the ground. There is no rose that will proudly bloom forever. Every rose will someday fall. But, despite this, the act of daily watering the rose is history, is life.' A *bonsai* will also someday shrivel and die. But knowing that, one gives it water every day. This is history, life, something to live for. Shiina's wife said, 'My husband doesn't do anything to help.' While it is probably quite true that Shiina, who is rather slow in getting around to things, doesn't do any of the watering, all the *bonsai* looked very pretty." Whether these words were meant as a general comment on human life or as a way by which Ōhira was suggesting his own contributions to the Miki Administration, it is hard to say.

Chapter 25

Averting a Crisis

The new year, 1976, opened calmly. In his fiscal policy speech before the 77th Ordinary Diet that began on January 23, Ōhira outlined the proposed budget for the coming fiscal year. The fiscal 1976 budget was 14.1 percent larger than the original budget for the previous year, or 16.6 percent larger than the previous year's budget as later revised downward. This growth rate was kept somewhat higher than the 13 percent (nominal) economic growth forecast, in the hope it would further stimulate business activities. However, as in the previous year, a large shortfall in tax revenues was still expected, and the total issue of government bonds was expected to be ¥7.28 trillion, of which ¥3.75 trillion, or nearly half, would be deficit-financing. The overall dependence on public borrowing would be 29.9 percent, compared to 26.3 percent in fiscal 1975.

On January 29, Diet consideration of the budget got under way, more smoothly than usual. If everything continued like this, the budget could be completed by mid-March and, as the prime minister had seemed to suggest, a Diet dissolution and general election could take place between April and May. Virtually everyone in political circles entertained such ideas, but they turned out to be illusory.

The first news about the Lockheed Incident was a short item cabled from abroad and published in obscure positions in the February 5 morning papers, but before the end of the day it caused an unprecedented shock in the political world. The article reported that the Lockheed Aircraft Corporation had paid the right-wing political manipulator Kodama Yoshio US$7 million as part of its strategy for selling aircraft to Japan. The next day, Lockheed's Vice-President Archibald C. Kotchian announced that he had given US$2 million to "high officials in the Japanese government" to influence business dealings in Japan, and that one Japanese entrepreneur and two members of Japanese trading companies were also involved.

356

The Diet, which had been proceeding uneventfully, was suddenly in an uproar as speculation on the identities of the high officials in the Japanese government caused panic in the LDP. Prime Minister Miki's response was immediate. Before a Lower House Budget Committee meeting of February 6, Miki stated: "Even at the risk of dishonoring Japanese politics, it is necessary to bring this matter into the open. I will gather information wherever possible, and if a conflict with laws and regulations is found it will be strictly dealt with." Though Miki may have raised the banner of a "thorough elucidation," all the material needed to effect this was in the United States. Thus, the first discussions of the affair were based on no more than guesses. Using the initials (F and N) printed in the news story as a point of departure, the search for the individuals in question began.

The opposition parties demanded the interrogation of witnesses regarding certain individuals whose names had been suggested, and the Lower House Budget Committee was torn between interrogating these as deponents (that is, witnesses under oath), as the opposition parties insisted, or hearing them merely as "persons for reference," as the LDP wanted. Finally the LDP gave in, and from February 16 seven deponents were questioned. However, all of these denied any wrongdoing. On February 18, the government decided that it would again urge the United States to submit "all information, including that which has to do with the high government officials," and that it would send some officials to the United States to investigate the matter. Because of differing opinions over the method of shedding light on the incident in the Diet, during the period from February 18 to 25 the arguments got nowhere.

Around this time, Ōhira spoke to the press: "The stance on how to respond seems to be wavering a little. What happened? Several points have come out, but I think the picture as a whole must now be put together with a little more substance. The Liberal Democratic Party is a party that comprises a wide variety of elements. Even if such things have existed in some places in the party, it is troublesome, just because of that, to have it *categorically* [original English] decided that 'the Liberal Democratic Party is inherently such-and-such.' "

In response to a further question about whether the Diet was likely to "carry out a rigorous inquiry into the facts as is done in the U.S. Congress," Ōhira replied: "That will depend on the capabilities (*rikiryō*) of the Japanese people as a whole. . . . In the case of Greek history, too, it was ultimately the people [that counted]. . . . A solution aiming above those capabilities is difficult; however, one that aims below them will be a problem. The Japanese have considerable powers of judgment and a sense of balance, so I do not think they will reach a bad solution."

On February 23, plenary sessions of both houses of the Diet unanimously passed resolutions calling on the United States to submit information, but it was uncertain whether the Americans would agree to do so. As soon as the Upper House resolution was passed, Prime Minister Miki announced that he would be sending a personal letter to President Gerald Ford. The contents of this letter, which said in part, "To make public all relevant materials, including, if they exist, the names of persons involved, will be beneficial both for Japanese politics and for Japanese–American relations," were announced on February 25. However, because of legal reasons in the United States, it was judged that the materials in question could not be submitted once their contents were made public. Nevertheless, the materials were shown to the Japanese Public Prosecutor's Office under the provisions of the Japanese–American arrangements on mutual judicial cooperation. However, even with the accompanying restrictions on the public release of information, Miki's action came to have a determining influence on political trends and the investigation of the incident.

With respect to Miki's letter to Ford, Ōhira ruefully commented: "Why should something that could well be left to the persons directly in charge be turned into a political matter?" He no doubt felt that, just as in the case of the Zhou Hongqing Incident at the end of 1963 or the Kim Dae Jung Incident in 1973, such problems should be resolved at the level of those directly involved with the legalities and should not be brought to the political level. At the same time, Ōhira stated: "If those whose work is directly involved [with legal prosecution] investigate the truth with strict neutrality, and if the truth is made known, it will be judged according to the law. This is the best path to a solution. Politics should not step on the brake, but neither should it step on the accelerator." On this, Ōhira's thinking was rather different from Miki's.

Through March 1976, the Diet was in limbo over the question of making public the relevant materials from the United States. It became impossible to pass the fiscal 1976 budget before the late March deadline, and on March 25 the government had no choice but to submit to the Diet a temporary budget covering the period from April 1 to May 10. Although the fiscal 1976 budget was finally passed on May 8, the Diet was unable to agree on extending the session past its scheduled end on May 24. Bills for revising the Law on Special Measures for Government Finance and for raising prices of certain government-regulated commodities and public service charges remained only partially considered with no vote taken, thus curtailing government plans to stimulate the economy.

In the meantime, the Lockheed Incident continued to cause panic among LDP members of the Lower House, whose four-year terms in office, begun at the last general election in December 1972, would come to an end in November 1976. Thus, while there remained only five months at most before the next general election, the party was being given a sound public thrashing. There was also gathering dissatisfaction with the attitude of Prime Minister Miki, which seemed to many to be making the situation worse. Words attributed to LDP Vice-President Shiina, that "Miki is romping around too much," embodied this dissatisfaction and were soon being circulated.

According to one reporter close to Shiina, at the outset of the Lockheed Incident Shiina hoped Miki would: (1) apologize to the people that such an incident had occurred under an LDP cabinet and leave elucidation of the case to the Public Prosecutor's Office; (2) while waiting for a conclusion to be reached by law enforcement officers, announce and implement the much-talked-about party reforms to correct the LDP's entrenched faults and weaknesses; (3) accept in a low-key way the conclusions of the legal authorities and carry out party-directed punishment that would have the support of public opinion; and (4) once the party reforms were established, take responsibility for the matter and resign as party president.

However, Prime Minister Miki's tactics were not what Shiina had hoped. Far from sensing any personal responsibility as party president, he was trying to use the Lockheed Incident as a tool for maintaining his own administration—or so it appeared to Shiina. It was in these circumstances that in the late winter and spring of 1976 Shiina began more actively to try and pressure Miki to step down. Out of the public view, he began to muster those within the party who were critical of Miki. He held talks with Tanaka on May 7, with Ōhira on May 9, and with Fukuda on May 10, and the four reached an accord on a basic strategy of getting Miki to step down before the next general election. It is said that Shiina's advisers planned to go into action immediately after the Diet session to establish a temporary Shiina administration to pave the way for party reforms, a new type of party presidential election, and a party-unity cabinet.

However, no sooner had this plan been scooped by the *Yomiuri Shinbun* and publicized on the front page of its May 13 edition than it aroused a hornet's nest in Nagatachō. Prime Minister Miki immediately counterattacked. That very afternoon, in remarks before a regularly scheduled general meeting of the Japan Federation of Employers Organizations (*Nikkeiren*), he said, "Stirring up the political situation cannot be allowed for the sake of either the country or the people." Not only did Miki try to halt Shiina's maneuvers, but in separate talks with Fukuda and Ōhira he won promises of cooperation for the time being.

However, it had been a shock to Miki to learn that Fukuda had entered into the anti-Miki maneuvers with Ōhira and Shiina. This meant that of the four (Shiina, Miki, Fukuda, and Nakasone) factions that had been mainstream at the outset of the Miki Administration, two had become anti-mainstream, leaving the mainstream factions in an overall minority. Miki insisted that it was his cabinet's responsibility to "thoroughly elucidate" the Lockheed Incident, and his strategy was to use the support of public opinion, backed by the mass media, which criticized the Shiina-led maneuvers as an attempt at a "Lockheed cover-up," to make up for his weakness within the party. Justice Minister Inaba Osamu of the Nakasone faction lent his support, stating: "The Miki Cabinet has received a mandate from the people to elucidate the Lockheed Incident. . . . It will not do to try to frustrate the prosecuting authorities."

Before the regular general meeting of the Kōchikai on May 25, Ōhira expressed some feelings on the recent developments: "The Liberal Democratic Party is being criticized by the whole populace because of the Lockheed Incident, and it is thus facing a grave crisis. To overcome this, it is necessary to have party unity; to achieve this we will have to wash away some of the dirt that has accumulated in parts of the party in the course of its long and unbroken tenure in power. The entire party must have the intention of undergoing a *misogi* [ritual purification], must reform its body politic, must look back critically on the past, and must make a new departure. In particular, those who have come to hold important posts in the party and cabinet, myself included, should take responsibility and step down. . . . Already, paving the way for a new departure for the party as a whole, there is a great current like the Kuroshio. Even if there are small waves on the surface, the strong undertow will surely move forward. Dear colleagues, I want you to unite to address the issues at hand, and not be waylaid by the small waves on the surface." This was Ōhira's so-called *misogi* proclamation.

When the reporters asked Ōhira to clarify the meaning and the particulars of the *misogi* he had in mind, he explained: "It wouldn't do to have the '*misogi* discussion' interpreted merely in the negative light of party or government heads stepping down from power. It also has the positive aspect of coming to grips in the future with far-reaching reforms." Ōhira himself seemed to be pondering and groping his way toward the direction that should be taken in the future. No doubt, he wanted to urge party members to turn away from getting rid of Miki or investigating the facts to the wider tasks of "purifying the party," which the times required. Around this time, the Special Committee for Investigating the Lockheed Problem that had been set up in the Diet was interrogating a number of nongovernment witnesses, while within the party faction leaders and other influential people held a series of meetings to find ways to bring some order to the situation.

On June 13, Kōno Yōhei (son of Kōno Ichirō), Yamaguchi Toshio, and four other young LDP members declared that they were willing to give up their positions and work for the "regeneration of conservatism." They told the prime minister their intention to leave the party, and on June 25 formed the New Liberal Club (*Shin Jiyū Kurabu*). Public opinion, disillusioned with the opposition parties' stance of opposing anything and everything the ruling party proposed, greeted the New Liberal Club favorably, seeing it as a welcome new trend in politics.

The contention between the pro- and anti-Miki factions was by now quite irreversible, but no one could do much except wait and see what new revelations about the Lockheed Incident would emerge. A group of party elders arranged a meeting among Miki, Shiina, and Nadao on June 21, which agreed on four items, including the need to investigate the Lockheed Incident fully, and the desirability of convening, at an appropriate time, an extraordinary Diet session to pass important legislation. There appeared to be a temporary truce in intraparty infighting, but the two opposing camps did not come any closer.

Later, Miki and Ōhira left Japan to attend the second summit of major industrialized democracies in San Juan, Puerto Rico. Ōhira returned to Japan on the evening of July 3, and to reporters who came to see him that night he spoke about conversations with Miki during their trip: "Miki many times repeated, 'As for the Lockheed Incident, I have received no reports and I am not making any special effort to ask for a report.' I said, 'The problems of the party are problems that existed before Lockheed. . . . but all this is no reason to turn political power over to the opposition parties. It's a difficult situation because we have to discharge our political responsibilities while rebuilding the system.' To this Miki said, 'That's exactly right.' "

If this recollection is correct, Ōhira was not, like Shiina, trying to persuade Miki to effect a transfer of administration. He was thinking more about how to reform the party. During the San Juan Summit he was sitting next to U.S. Secretary of State Henry Kissinger at a meal when Kissinger said, "Tell me whether the general election will be held under Miki or under a new leader." Ōhira's reply was, "I don't know. When you're in the thick of things, it's hard to know what the outcome will be."

On June 22, the Lockheed Incident produced its first arrests: three members of the executive staff of All Nippon Airways and a director of the Marubeni Corporation. This was followed in the next three weeks by a series of arrests of others suspected of offering bribes, and it seemed only a matter of time before the politicians suspected of accepting bribes would be arrested, although nobody knew who they might be. Around early July, after Miki had heard a report from the justice minister, he is said to have told some of his associates: "Within the party people are saying that I should step down, but what will happen if the investigations keep going on? I wonder if those left behind will be able to find someone to replace me."

Early in the morning of July 27, Japan was shaken by news of the arrests of former Prime Minister Tanaka and his private secretary. To Ōhira, the arrest of his close friend was enormously painful, and, after hearing the first reports, he telephoned friends and political associates, saying, "Last night I didn't sleep well. I think it's a sad thing." The word *munashii* (futile, or to no purpose) kept cropping up in his speech, and he looked somewhat haggard.

With the arrest of Tanaka, Miki must have expected to be freed from the maneuvers of Tanaka and his supporters and that the political scene would take a turn for the better; public opinion had the same expectation. However, the situation in the party developed in a way that ran counter to Miki's hopes. First, the anti-mainstream forces could no longer be charged with planning a "Lockheed cover-up." Second, Miki's self-proclaimed role of uncovering the Lockheed Incident could now be said to have come to an end. The Tanaka faction, whose leader was now in legal custody, was strongly antagonistic to Miki, and, during its general meeting of August 4, passed a resolution calling for his resignation. By midsummer, political circles tended to focus on who would take over from Miki.

On August 7, on his way to make a speech in Kagawa Prefecture, Ōhira said at a press conference in Tokyo: "The public has long been aware of a slackening of the Liberal Democratic Party's discipline and a weakening in the party's numerical strength. With the painful blow dealt by the Lockheed Incident, in ordinary circumstances I think the rules of democracy and the path to party regeneration would call for ceding power to the opposition parties and putting ourselves in dock for a while to regain our strength and vigor. However, there are no voices among the people demanding a handover of power to the opposition parties, and there is no evidence that the opposition is ready to take over. If this is the case, there is no way but for the Liberal Democratic Party to try to regenerate itself. This is an extremely demanding task, and there is no time to waste." He continued: "To give substance to reforming the party we shall have to try to talk dispassionately with other members of the party who share the same concerns. I can well understand Fukuda when he talks seriously and boldly about 'reforms for a new departure.' " The more than ten members of the press corps met these remarks with a flurry of speculation that Ōhira might be willing to see Fukuda as the next prime minister.

That same day, Fukuda was in his native Gunma Prefecture to give some speeches. In the evening, after hearing of Ōhira's remarks, he gave a sort of return signal by saying, "I can well understand Finance Minister Ōhira's feelings." This was a further indication that between the two, who had long appeared to be rivals, there was an increasing movement toward cooperation. After Tanaka's arrest, Fukuda and Ōhira seemed to share the view that there was nobody besides themselves who could put things in order.

Among many junior LDP members there was a growing willingness to play some role in improving the party's situation. Members of the *Tsukinamikai* (literally, "The Ordinary Club"), an informal friendship club cutting across factional lines led by Mihara Asao of one of the middle-of-the-road factions, requested an interview with Prime Minister Miki and suggested that he step down on the occasion of the commemorative ceremonies marking fifty years of the Shōwa emperor's reign. Miki rejected the idea, and on August 9 he announced that if there was to be a Diet dissolution he would order it himself and preside over a general election. With the party thrust into disarray by the Lockheed Incident, it seemed a foregone conclusion that in a general election many candidates of factions other than Miki's would lose. Mihara and other Tsukinamikai members were angered by Miki's attitude and launched a campaign to collect anti-Miki signatures.

Ever since the surfacing of intraparty dissent, both Fukuda and Ōhira held several talks with Miki to try to bring matters to a peaceful settlement. These talks always lasted at least thirty minutes, and in some cases as long as two or three hours. However, whenever the talks touched on concrete measures for effecting a resolution, they tended to lose momentum. A talk between Miki and Ōhira on the morning of August 12 lasted two hours, and its failure to lead anywhere was discussed by Ōhira in a press conference afterward: "The prime minister showed a strong determination to overcome the difficult circumstances of the current administration. . . . For this, it will be necessary to get the cooperation and understanding of the party members and, more broadly, the understanding and trust of the nation. But the problem is whether or not he can get that support inside and outside the party. . . . We will have to think seriously about how to assemble everybody's thoughts and wishes, and at the same time keep the party together. I know it is difficult, but it is a matter that must be approached by study and agreement reached through repeated talks. . . . Concrete steps are yet to come. We are not [merely] commentators. We must *do* something, and within a limited time." To cut a long story short, no concrete agreements or steps forward were forthcoming. It would be more accurate to say that Fukuda and Ōhira exerted themselves in vain.

The anti-Miki signature campaign initiated by Mihara and his colleagues spread like a prairie fire. In just one week, 277 LDP Dietmen from the Tanaka, Ōhira, and Fukuda anti-mainstream factions, as well as from the Shiina, Mizuta, and Funada middle-of-the-road factions, endorsed the movement. The new association of Diet members brought together by this campaign was named the Liaison Council for Establishing a Party-Unity System (*Kyotōkyō* for short), and Funada Naka was made its chief manager.

The Kyotōkyō plan of action was as follows: "Recognize the Lockheed Incident as a problem affecting the whole party, have the Miki Cabinet resign en masse before the extraordinary Diet session, and hold a party convention to expedite reformation of the party. This convention will discuss specific measures for party reforms and will establish a new system of party unity to put these into practice. When the extraordinary Diet begins, accept the judgment of the people under an election system involving the entire party, thus establishing political stability."

By contrast, the Miki camp insisted that thorough elucidation of the Lockheed Incident was the responsibility of the Miki Cabinet, that the extraordinary Diet session would be held under the current administration (which it claimed had the support of the people), and that a new party system should be established after a general election. Both sides were aware that an election would be a severe trial and were equally interested in how to cope with this challenge. They differed on the question of which should come first, the general election or party reforms. The customary practice had always been to dissolve the Diet in the course of a Diet session; thus, there was much discussion of precisely when the planned extraordinary Diet session would begin and what preliminary moves there might be.

On August 19, Mihara and his colleagues presented the 277 signatures to support the demand, made to the formal party leadership, that it open an LDP Joint Plenary Meeting of Party Members of Both Houses of the Diet. When the leadership, influenced by Miki and Nakasone, refused, the Kyotōkyō asked Uehara Shōkichi, its chairman, to call a plenary meeting.

In a talk between Miki and Fukuda on August 21, Miki asked Fukuda, "After I step down, who is going to become prime minister, Ōhira or yourself?" Although there had already been agreement between Fukuda and Ōhira regarding some sort of cooperation, they had not yet fixed the fine point of who would head the next administration; Fukuda was thus at a loss for an answer and Miki felt he had won a point. Fukuda summoned a close associate who was also close to Ōhira and requested him to work this question out with Ōhira in strict secrecy.

Ōhira's feelings about the matter were not simple. If he refused to hold any talks with Fukuda and a party presidential election was held according to current party rules, the administration would almost without doubt become his. A politician's ideal is, after all, to exercise political power. Ōhira's policies had been prepared over a long period, and both his enthusiasm and stamina were second to none. Now that political power was within his grasp, would it be appropriate for him as a politician to hand this power over to somebody else? Would this count as fulfilling one's responsibilities as a statesman? On the other hand, the party had long suffered from internal struggles, now almost to the point of exhaustion. If a new struggle should occur in the course of the party presidential election, could the party, in fact, fulfill its responsibilities and continue to exist? If talks between Fukuda and Ōhira should leak even to the slightest extent, both would be subject to attack by public opinion, which would surely criticize their discussion of public affairs in private. Thus, all their talks were kept well away from the public eye.

On August 23, under the name of Kyotōkyō Chairman Uehara, notices were distributed announcing the convening of an LDP Joint Plenary Meeting of Party Members of Both Houses of the Diet, to begin the next day at 9:30 A.M. in the fifth floor hall of the Lower House. This body is the second-highest LDP decision making body after a party convention, and resolutions approved by it immediately become official party policy. To have the authority to deliberate on party matters, the joint plenary meeting must be attended by at least two-thirds of all Diet party members. The 277 members who signed the Kyotōkyō covenant would alone be sufficient, if all were present, if the meeting wanted to change party rules, disband the party, or expel party members. It could also name a new party president and vice-president. However, the question remained whether this meeting, if disapproved of by the current party leadership, could, in fact, be considered a legitimate body for decision making, and matters progressed without this point being clarified.

The August 24 Joint Plenary Meeting of Party Members of Both Houses of the Diet was attended by more than the 266 Diet members needed for a quorum. Most of those in attendance seem to have thought that this body would determine the general course of events and would at one stroke force the Miki Cabinet to step down. Matters were not to be so simple, however.

The biggest problem was that, even if the joint plenary meeting had been formally substituted for a party convention and Prime Minister Miki was forced to leave his post as party president through such methods as expulsion from the party, there was nothing the gathering could do to force him from his post of prime minister. If, after the Diet began, a motion of no-confidence was passed in an attempt to get Miki to step down, the prime minister still had the option of dissolving the Diet. If it came to this, a split in the party would be unavoidable. If a general election took place with such party infighting unchecked, it was uncertain whether the party could gain a majority, much less a victory, and this would hardly be consonant with Kyotōkyō purposes. The realization of the Kyotōkyō's basic purpose of rescuing the party's honor under a system of party unity and rebuilding it to bear the judgment of the people would necessarily mean decisions should be made through harmonious discussion. The adoption of party resolutions by a two-thirds vote of the LDP joint plenary meeting might first look like a stratagem for depriving Prime Minister Miki of his right to make decisions, but in reality it was a way of building a system that could quickly bring discussion to a conclusion. As a result, the resolution abstractly called for the "reformation of the party prior to the extraordinary Diet session."

Against the background of these trends in the party, on August 24, both Fukuda and Ōhira requested talks with Miki. At first the prime minister was reluctant, but, persuaded by Chief Cabinet Secretary Ide, the meeting was arranged for 5 P.M. in the executive room of the Prime Minister's Official Residence. This meeting lasted three hours and ended abruptly, without conclusion. Afterward, Ōhira related some of his impressions to those close to him: "The talk was mainly between Fukuda and Miki, and I was an interlocutor, shall we say, playing the role of putting the talk in context and keeping it moving forward. Fukuda tried various ways to get his point across, but whenever the talk went forward a little, Miki returned to the starting point. No matter how many times something was said, in the end we always came back to the beginning, like a broken record going around and around." A number of people from the Kyotōkyō who had enthusiastically seen Fukuda and Ōhira off to the Prime Minister's Official Residence and were eagerly waiting to hear the results could barely hide their disappointment.

A second talk among Miki, Fukuda, and Ōhira was held the next day, August 25, and delved somewhat deeper into the question of what to do about the situation. Ōhira spoke about it to reporters on August 27: "The focus of the problem was how to suggest an improvement in the political situation prior to the general election. It seemed out of the question to suggest a specific date for the prime minister to step down. If we had a relation of trust, it would have been simple, but our relations were extremely critical. I was of the opinion that a party convention should be held prior to the general election and that it should wash the dirty laundry. In our talks, Miki said, 'It would be all right to have a promise made before the party's General Council that there will be no dissolution during the extraordinary Diet session.'" Displeased over the results of the tripartite talks, the Kyotōkyō executive committee, now without any special trust in either Fukuda or Ōhira, launched a Committee for Promoting the Implementation of Party Resolutions, headed by Hori Shigeru, who was known and respected for his political acumen.

Worried over a possible intraparty clash, five party officials—Secretary-General Nakasone Yasuhiro, General Council Chairman Nadao Hirokichi, Policy Research Council Chairman Matsuno Raizō, Deputy Secretary-General Ishida Hirohide, and Chairman of the General Assembly of LDP Members of the Lower House Yasui Ken—created a compromise plan that they hoped would tidy up the situation and smooth over the differences between pro-Miki and anti-Miki sentiment. On August 30, these five party officials showed the plan, in three parts, to Prime Minister Miki to gain his approval. Miki then explained their plan to Fukuda and Ōhira, requesting their cooperation. The three main points were: (1) a change of party and cabinet personnel would take place prior to the extraordinary Diet session; (2) an extraordinary Diet session would be convened at an early date to take care of important pending legislation; (3) after the extraordinary Diet session, new party policies would be elaborated for a general election and publicized inside and outside the party. Afterward, Fukuda and Ōhira said at a press conference that they understood the purport of the plan, but the Kyotōkyō members in general were fiercely opposed, pointing out that there was no guarantee Miki would step down and that Miki's option to dissolve the Diet was not excluded. They tried to pillory Hori and took a hard line toward the party officers, insisting that any resolutions passed by the LDP joint plenary meeting should be put into effect.

Hori knew that Miki was quite prepared to exercise his authority as prime minister to convene the Diet only to have it dissolved immediately. Thus, to Hori, it was self-evident what the result would be if Miki was pressured too strongly. He must have felt frustrated to know there was nothing he could do, even though he commanded the support of two-thirds of the party. According to one reporter close to him, Hori at this point shed tears as he lamented: "There is absolutely nothing I can do. When I think about handing over the party to younger men in this ruined state, I feel miserable. For what have we practiced politics for twenty, thirty years? There is no way we can apologize to our predecessors."

On hearing this story, Ōhira must have thought that a final resolution was in the offing. That evening, in an informal chat with the night-shift reporters, he related the following parable: "There was once a young married couple who were quarreling to such an extent that they went to the Family Court to have both sides heard, with the intention of coming to a final resolution. They were told by members of the mediating committee, 'If that's the case, then decide here and now to separate.' Thinking this would be the last time they would see each other, the two went into a tea room in front of the court building. While drinking tea and reminiscing about old times, they remembered the good things about each other that they had forgotten. In a little less than an hour, they came out of the tea room smiling, having decided to start anew. Isn't it quite possible for such things to happen?"

On September 10, Miki made up his mind and summoned an extraordinary cabinet meeting, where he made the following announcement: "As for party management and organization as we approach a general election, these will be clarified inside and outside the party through an extraordinary party convention to be held in October.... Since I have decided to convene an extraordinary Diet session, hopefully on September 13, the necessary procedures will be undertaken." The first part of the announcement was what the Kyotōkyō had been calling for, while the second part was Miki's own decision. He communicated the content of the announcement to both Fukuda and Ōhira prior to the cabinet meeting.

Once the extraordinary Diet session was convened, whether or not it would be dissolved would depend entirely on Miki's intentions. Fukuda and Ōhira had requested, for the sake of "intraparty adjustment," that the cabinet meeting be postponed by one day, but the prime minister was adamant and the cabinet meeting was begun, as planned, at 5 P.M. on September 10. He did, however, concede to Fukuda's and Ōhira's wishes by postponing the opening of the Diet session until September 16.

While both the convening and dissolution of the Diet are the prime minister's prerogatives, in both cases a cabinet resolution, signed by all cabinet members, is necessary. Thus, if some cabinet members refuse to sign, a determination to force the issue will necessarily mean that the prime minister must dismiss the recalcitrant members. At the time in question, fifteen of the twenty-two members of the Miki Cabinet belonged to the Kyotōkyō. Prime Minister Miki approached the cabinet meeting with the rather high-handed attitude that anyone who objected to the convening of the extraordinary Diet should not hesitate to say so, but anyone who opposed the prime minister's wishes should be willing to resign. In response, the cabinet members who belonged to the Kyotōkyō immediately refused to sign the cabinet resolution, saying in effect: "Why must we decide today to convene an extraordinary Diet when there is such distrust of the prime minister's behavior and when we have not yet reached an intraparty consensus? We should spend a day or two making intraparty adjustments, so please postpone today's procedures."

Secretary-General Nakasone, who was one of those charged with straightening out the political situation, some years later recalled Miki's extraordinary determination at the time: "Miki was prepared to force through an extraordinary Diet session even if it meant dismissing fifteen cabinet members, and to dissolve the Diet at its outset. In this case, he was definitely willing to see a split in the party."

Contrary to the expectations of Miki and those closest to him, the cabinet meeting did not come to a quick resolution but lasted five hours, interrupted by supper and rest breaks. Finally, at the suggestion of middle-of-the-road cabinet member Sakata Michita (director-general of the Defense Agency), a crisis was averted that day, and it was decided that private deliberations among the cabinet members, to take place the following afternoon, would fix the date for convening the extraordinary Diet session.

Reaching home at 11 P.M., Ōhira faced a barrage of questions from reporters who were waiting to hear about the cabinet meeting and the political outlook. From Ōhira's remarks the reporters got the following impression: Miki's determination appeared to be quite hardened, and tomorrow he would probably ask for the resignation of fifteen cabinet members and, with the consent of the remaining cabinet members, call for the convening of the extraordinary Diet session. If that happened, the Diet would be dissolved at the outset and a party schism would be inevitable. Late that night, Ōhira said to Kōchikai Dietman Tanaka Rokusuke, who was visiting him, "At this rate a party split is unavoidable. Can't something be done?" Tanaka again came to Ōhira's home early the next morning of September 11 and proposed that Ōhira attempt to make a breakthrough by holding a confidential talk with Secretary-General Nakasone.

Beginning at 7 A.M., Ōhira and Nakasone talked for over thirty minutes at Nakasone's private office on the seventh floor of the Kitano Arms building in the Hirakawachō district near the Diet building. Nakasone later recalled: "Already there had been movements for restoring order to the situation. Various schemes for dealing with the matter had been proposed, beginning with the five party officers' plan. When I got a telephone message on the morning of the eleventh asking if I would meet and talk with Ōhira, I instinctively felt that the situation would be resolved. I think Ōhira probably felt the same."

This meeting lasted only a short time but brought positive results, underlining the urgency of the situation and also the fact that both Ōhira and Nakasone had already investigated many possibilities for effecting a compromise between the pro-Miki and anti-Miki camps. The plan for a settlement that emerged has sometimes been called the "Nakasone plan" and sometimes the "Ōhira plan," but in either case it combined the thinking of a number of people who played a role in effecting a settlement. The essential points of the plan were the following: (1) an LDP joint plenary meeting would be convened on September 14, at which the party president would directly announce his intentions to the party members; efforts would be made to hold the meeting in an atmosphere of order and moderation; (2) the party convention, earlier mentioned in the cabinet statement of the party president's intentions, would be held in October; the agenda would be decided upon by the party president and by the Party Convention Preparatory Committee; (3) during the extraordinary Diet session, all would cooperate in the passage of important legislation; consequently, a dissolution would not be considered, and the party president would declare this before the LDP joint plenary meeting; (4) a cabinet meeting would be held at 5 P.M., to decide the date for convening the extraordinary Diet session. These four items contained the essential points of the five party officers' plan, the August 10 statement of the party president's intentions, and the point of view of the Kyotōkyō members.

Secretary-General Nakasone quickly went into action, and immediately after his confidential talk with Ōhira first explained the proposal to Fukuda and Miki. Immediately, too, a conference of the five top party officers was held, at which approval was given to the Nakasone plan as an effective settlement. At 12:30 P.M., a meeting at party headquarters among Miki, Nakasone, Kyotōkyō chief manager Funada, and Chairman Hori Shigeru of the Committee for Promoting the Implementation of Party Resolutions approved the new proposal and set September 16 as the date for the extraordinary Diet session. During the morning, the Kyotōkyō convened an LDP Joint Plenary Meeting of Party Members of Both Houses of the Diet, which likewise approved the secretary-general's plan.

The settlement came about so quickly that for the majority of Diet members, who did not know all the ins and outs, it seemed, in one Dietman's words, "like some capricious typhoon that brought torrential rain but then suddenly left. We didn't know what was happening, but at least it seemed there would be no dissolution." The reaction was thus one of surprise and relief.

Ōhira had somewhat upset the early morning contingent of reporters when he eluded them and met Nakasone without their knowledge. At noon, to make up for it, he treated them to lunch and ice cream sodas in the Diet cafeteria and entertained them with informal conversation. When the news came, while they were eating, that the talk among Miki, Nakasone, Funada, and Hori had begun, Ōhira grinned as he reminded them of his previous night's parable about the young couple on the verge of divorce: "They are just entering the tea room now."

Chapter 26

Between-the-Scenes Maneuvers

The Kyotōkyō commotion, which had lasted five months, appeared to have ended harmoniously through compromise. However, this harmony only existed within the party as nothing had been resolved in the party's outside relations, and public censure of the LDP was increasing. Within two or three months, the Lower House Diet members' four-year terms would come to an end, and they would have to submit to the people's judgment in a general election. Yet because of the time wasted in intraparty strife, virtually no preparations for this general election had been made.

On September 15, the day before the opening of the extraordinary Diet, Prime Minister Miki undertook a reorganization of party and cabinet posts, which had remained unchanged for one year and nine months, ever since the Miki Administration took over. This constituted the longest period in postwar Japan without a cabinet or party reorganization. Faced with the coming Diet session and a general election, Miki wanted to make sure that his cabinet was loyal and would work in support of him. Members of the Kyotōkyō foresaw a change of administration (including the posts of party president and prime minister) as inevitable after the Diet session and general election, so they were not overly concerned by changes in cabinet personnel, which they deemed to be only of short-term importance. There was, however, much interest in who would hold the top three party posts, especially that of secretary-general.

It turned out that Miki, too, once he set to work on the reorganization at his Nanpeidai home on the morning of September 15, placed the greatest emphasis on these three party posts. Around 10 A.M., Fukuda and Ōhira received a message from Miki asking for their cooperation to make Matsuno Raizō (of the Fukuda faction) secretary-general, Sakurauchi Yoshio (of the Nakasone faction) General Council chairman, and Uchida Tsuneo (of the Ōhira faction) Policy Research Council chairman.

372

Matsuno, who came from the Yoshida Liberal Party and had been a member of the Ogata and Ishii factions before becoming a leading member of the Satō faction, had been chosen by the Fukuda faction as Policy Research Council chairman in the First Miki Cabinet. However, he later incurred that faction's displeasure by leaning too far toward Miki. Thus, many in the Fukuda faction were strongly opposed to Matsuno being secretary-general, and the Ōhira faction, too, was opposed. Those members of the General Council who belonged to the Kyotōkyō (and who constituted a majority of the council) were likewise opposed. In the party president's office at LDP headquarters, a meeting began at 1 P.M. with seven party leaders (Miki, Fukuda, Ōhira, Nakasone, Nadao, Matsuno, and Ishida), and it produced a compromise plan by which the three party appointees would remain but their posts would be switched, making Matsuno General Council chairman, Sakurauchi Policy Research Council chairman, and Uchida secretary-general. These deliberations lasted until after 3 P.M.

Like Ōhira, Uchida had begun his career in the Ministry of Finance six years before Ōhira's, and, like Ōhira, he had also embarked on his political career in 1952. Although Uchida was an expert in policy matters, he was not noted for his skill at political maneuvering, which he himself was well aware of, and as soon as he heard that he was to assume the post of secretary-general, he was both surprised and upset. Visibly shaken, he rushed into the Kōchikai meeting room where Ōhira was in the midst of an informal talk with reporters. As soon as he saw Ōhira, he proclaimed: "I will not do anything like being secretary-general. If it was Policy Research Council chairman, I might be of some use, but now I hear you're saying I'm to be secretary-general. It's not a Chinese restaurant, you know, where you can move the tables around like this. . . . A compromise is fine, but put the right man in the right place. I am not cut out to be secretary-general." Kōchikai leaders Ōhira, Suzuki, and Miyazawa together led their agitated colleague into another room and did their best to convince him, but Uchida would not budge.

A key Miki aide, Deputy Chief Cabinet Secretary Kaifu Toshiki, who was probably keeping up with developments through reporters, hurried over from the Prime Minister's Official Residence to try his hand at winning Uchida over. Prime Minister Miki had intended to finish the reorganization that day and also to conclude the *ninshōshiki* attestation ceremony in the Imperial Palace, and arrangements had already been set up with Imperial Household Agency officials. If the plan to make Uchida secretary-general should break down now, the laborious compromise would have to go back to the drawing board, and nobody knew what might result. Finally,

Uchida gave in to everyone's persuasion and, a little past 5 P.M., set out for the Prime Minister's Official Residence. The cabinet reorganization was finalized later that evening. All former cabinet members who did not belong to the Kyotōkyō remained in their posts and, with the exception of Fukuda and Ōhira, all the Kyotōkyō members were replaced. Not surprisingly, the new cabinet members were all strong Miki supporters. It was said that members of the Fukuda faction, in particular, were excluded from all preliminary consultations regarding the new appointments.

At a September 16 farewell party for the fifteen Kyotōkyō-affiliated cabinet members who had been replaced the previous day, Kanemaru Shin, former director-general of the National Land Agency, stated, "Our goals have not yet been reached. We ask Fukuda and Ōhira to talk this over later among themselves." He was referring to the so-called *ukezara* issue (that is, the question of who was to head the next administration).

During the Kyotōkyō commotion, the question had always been present, but with the latest developments its emergence at the forefront was quite unavoidable. In keeping with the formula, "Ōhira in an election, Fukuda in negotiations," which was now regarded as conventional wisdom within the LDP, those close to Fukuda who wanted a negotiated choice of leader began mobilizing various personal networks to that end. The number of maneuvers and movements behind the scenes was bewildering. One who cooperated in these was Dietman Tanaka Rokusuke, a close confidant of Ōhira who discussed the issues with Ōhira for three days in early October. On October 6, Tanaka Rokusuke received some response from Ōhira, which he later referred to in this way: "I immediately contacted Fukuda, who said he would wait for me at a restaurant in Akasaka, so I went there to see him. When I said, 'Ōhira has given his agreement,' Fukuda was very happy and said, 'One year will be fine, one and a half years will be fine.' Wanting to confirm things, I said, 'And afterward we will ask Ōhira.' Fukuda agreed and I went to the Ministry of Finance to inform Ōhira of this." This development was also communicated by Fukuda to Hori, and on October 10 Hori and Ōhira went to play golf at the Three Hundred Club in Chigasaki, Kanagawa Prefecture.

According to Hori's recollection, as he later told it to his secretary, Ōhira at that time said to him, "I am not going to insist on heading an administration." Hori responded: "Unless we decide now on what will come later, the party will lose its coordination. We have you and Fukuda [as likely candidates]. We were in a quandary but have been saved by your decision. As for what remains to be done, I'll take responsibility and put things in order in writing." Ōhira replied: "Even if I should receive some kind of guarantee in writing, I know it wouldn't really mean very much, so never mind about it." Hori's reaction was: "No, I am in the middle of things, so that won't do." Ōhira confided to persons around him: "I think Hori wanted to meet me to check out my intentions."

In Hori's subsequent efforts to firm up an agreement between Fukuda and Ōhira, he tried to persuade LDP Vice-President Shiina but found that Shiina remained firmly opposed to Fukuda serving as president and prime minister. When Shiina asked Hori: "How long would you have Fukuda serve? Two months? Three months?" Hori is said to have replied: "Certainly it couldn't be for just two or three months. It wouldn't do not to have him serve a full term. But the term should be changed from the present three years to two years."

However, Shiina's biggest dissatisfaction then was the Kyotōkyō's attitude toward Prime Minister Miki. One person familiar with the inside story recalls: "In one way or another, Shiina wanted to find a means of getting the party behind a movement to make Miki give up his posts as party president and prime minister. Thus, he constantly advocated the passage of a resolution to force Miki's resignation. Even when such efforts seemed fairly futile, Shiina still insisted that Miki step down Finally, Mihara and his friends tried to calm him down. Hori would say, 'If you did something like that, the party would split up,' but Shiina would not listen and only said, 'Get Miki to resign.' " Shiina was, of course, strongly aware of the part he had played in mediating Miki's accession to power, and now he no doubt wanted to do something that in his eyes would rectify matters and make the party's authority firmer.

The final discussions to try to find Miki's successor took place on October 20 and 27 at the Hotel Pacific Tokyo in Shinagawa among five participants: Fukuda and his faction member Sonoda, Ōhira and his faction member Suzuki, plus Hori as mediator. The main objective of the first round of talks was to ascertain Ōhira's intentions and basic approach. At the same time, the discussions dealt with how to overcome the party's current crisis, in other words, how to formulate strategy for the upcoming general election and for rebuilding a party that had become weakened over the years, and how to allocate future responsibilities and decide on the procedures for effecting political change.

The second round of talks confirmed and put into sharper focus the results of the earlier talks, and an agreement was reached on making Fukuda the next party president. When Hori suggested that "the Fukuda Cabinet should be for one term of two years," it was accepted by all present. Sonoda later wrote: "There was no doubt that the Miki Cabinet would resign en masse, and that events would naturally have led to the establishment of an Ōhira Cabinet. While that might have been all right,

Fukuda, whom I had been supporting, felt that in that case his chance to head an administration might never come, so it was at this five-man talk at the Hotel Pacific that he made this special request of Ōhira. . . . Ōhira said nothing immediately. . . . Only after the talk had progressed beyond the hypothesis that Fukuda would serve for two years did Ōhira open his mouth for the first time, in response to the question, 'What will we do after that?' to say, 'Isn't it pointless to talk about things two years from now? Shouldn't we talk about them again when two years have passed?' Less sophisticated people would have insisted, 'Put it in writing that two years from now political power is to be handed over to Ōhira.' But Ōhira did just the opposite. There was something about it that touched me deeply."

Nevertheless, a document was drawn up at this meeting, which is said to have read as follows:

—Ōhira Masayoshi will support the nomination of Fukuda Takeo as the new party president and prime minister to succeed Miki.
—Although the posts of party president and prime minister are inseparable, Fukuda Takeo will entrust most party duties to Ōhira Masayoshi.
—At the regular party convention scheduled for January 1977, party rules will be revised to make the party president's term in office two years instead of the present three years.
Fukuda and Ōhira agree to the above on the basis of mutual trust.

November 1976

FUKUDA Takeo [signature]
ŌHIRA Masayoshi [signature]
SONODA Sunao [formal seal]
SUZUKI Zenkō [signature]

Of course, the leadership of a future administration is not something that could be properly decided in such private talks, so it would be impossible to publicize any document that might be agreed upon in such talks or use it as an instrument to enforce any promises made. The fact that such a document was nonetheless drawn up was probably due to Hori's pushing for it. His aim was probably to try to insure that the agreement between Fukuda and Ōhira would be respected, not only by the two individuals in question but also by their respective factions. It was, no doubt, for this reason that Sonoda and Suzuki, as key members of their respective factions, were asked to join Fukuda and Ōhira in affixing their signatures or seals. Hori, who did not affix his own signature as mediator, is said to have later warned Ōhira "to take every precaution not to reveal this document." Ōhira himself never spoke of the document's existence.

In the 78th Extraordinary Diet of September 16, the Public Debt Special Case Bill that Finance Minister Ōhira had been pushing so hard for was finally passed (on October 15), as were bills allowing hikes in Japanese National Railways fares and telephone and telegraph charges. As a result, government finances for fiscal 1976 were at last in fairly good order. Around this time, in the process of compiling the fiscal 1977 budget, the Miki Administration passed a cabinet resolution to approve an Outline on Defense Planning (Bōei keikaku no taikō) that, partly in response to requests from the Ministry of Finance to keep defense expenditures within reasonable limits, would change the direction of defense planning from the concept of "necessary defense potential" to one of "basic defense potential." This resolution stipulated that, during the next several years, total defense-related expenditures in a given fiscal year should not exceed 1 percent of that year's GNP.

As the extraordinary Diet session neared its end, focus concentrated on the general election to take place at the end of the Lower House members' four-year term. However, the party was wholly unprepared for battle, and the campaign strength that might be expected from the factions was at a low ebb. Thus, each LDP candidate basically had to rely on his own resources, doing what he could to survive in the face of criticism from the media, the public, and the opposition parties.

The thirty-fourth Lower House general election was the first, under the provisions of the postwar Constitution, to be held after the expiration of a full four-year term. The results of the polling, which took place on December 5, 1976, were even more disastrous than anticipated, with only 249 officially endorsed LDP candidates elected, filling less than half of the total Lower House seats for the first time since the party's founding in 1955. Later, Lower House LDP membership rose to 261 with the induction and subsequent official party endorsement of 12 members who had won their seats as independents. However, this was only 5 more than the 256 needed for a majority. The people had indeed delivered a severe judgment to the LDP. Since its founding, the party had always won a stable majority in Lower House elections, guaranteeing that the administration would safely remain in LDP hands. Now the very foundations supporting any LDP administration were in real danger of crumbling.

Contrary to this, burgeoning popularity had been demonstrated by the New Liberal Club (NLC) of Kōno Yōhei and his colleagues who had left the LDP. Advances were also made by the Kōmeitō and the DSP, while the JSP and the JCP did not fare so well. In other words, the two largest parties, the LDP and the JSP, both declined, while the middle-of-the-road parties rose to greater prominence. Similar to the situation in the Upper House, where the LDP and opposition forces were almost evenly balanced, the numbers of Lower House seats held by members of the governing and opposition parties were also evening out in what appeared to be a transition from an age of a stable LDP majority to an age of progressive–conservative balance.

On December 17, Prime Minister Miki finally announced his decision to step down. LDP Secretary-General Uchida, the only anti-Miki person in a high party post, now found himself directing an election campaign where the outcome was wholly uncertain, as well as having undertaken, almost single-handedly, the difficult work of managing the ailing party's finances. He was aware that there would be changes after this election and that he would have to try to handle them smoothly. Uchida quite literally forgot about sleeping and eating as he arranged the props on the stage of political change.

Although Secretary-General Uchida had been appointed to the post as the last resort, he was a fine example of how a person, in the face of difficulties, may draw on strengths he never knew he possessed. As secretary-general, he did his best to avoid a split in the party. Soon after this work was completed, he fell ill and died, and Ōhira accorded his friend the highest praise in a funeral oration: "To do but not to be proud, to accomplish but not to be complacent—this came to him naturally. . . . His course of action, like a fine painting, was a splendid work of art."

After Miki's resignation, an LDP Joint Plenary Meeting of Party Members of Both Houses of the Diet was held in place of a party convention on December 23. Fukuda was unanimously chosen as the next party president and candidate for prime minister. Later, Ōhira justified his decision not to run at that time for party president as follows: "To overcome the economic difficulties in the wake of the oil crisis was extremely hard, as was the political situation with a balance of strength between the government and opposition forces in the Diet. Today's Liberal Democratic Party is not a big enough arena for me and Fukuda to wrestle in. We must first make the party's arena larger and stronger. First and foremost, our party must be able to respond to the people's trust as the governing party in a Diet that is almost evenly split between the Liberal Democratic Party and the other parties."

The 79th Extraordinary Diet convened on Christmas Eve, the day after Fukuda Takeo assumed his post as party president, and nominated him prime minister. There were 508 Lower House Diet members present, among whom 255—or just 1 more than half—voted for Fukuda. In the party and cabinet appointments made that evening, Ōhira became secretary-general, and a new period of what came to be known as the "Fukuda–Ōhira leadership" (*Daifuku teikei*, or *Daifuku taisei*) began.

The remaining two top party posts were given to Esaki Masumi (General Council chairman) and Kōmoto Toshio (Policy Research Council chairman). All three, together with Upper House President Yasui Ken and Chief Cabinet Secretary Sonoda Sunao, were taken into Fukuda's confidence in deliberations on the cabinet, after which the attestation ceremony at the Imperial Palace took place that very evening. The cabinet appointees included, in addition to such LDP political veterans as Suzuki Zenkō (Agriculture and Forestry), Tanaka Tatsuo (International Trade and Industry), and Ishida Hirohide (Labor), some very capable younger men, such as Hatoyama Iichirō (Foreign Affairs), Watanabe Michio (Health and Welfare), Kaifu Toshiki (Education), and Ishihara Shintarō (Environment). Hori Shigeru, who had been, so to speak, the new administration's godfather, was made speaker of the Lower House.

Just after the December 5, 1976, general election, Ōhira lost his elder brother, Kazumitsu. Kazumitsu had always been well liked by the people of Toyohama in Kagawa Prefecture, where he had served three terms as mayor before retiring. He had felt that his younger brother's showing in his tenth general election campaign would be an important step on the way to the party presidency, and he had done his utmost to see that Masayoshi would get at least 100,000 votes.

Not long after the official start of the election campaign in November, Kazumitsu felt exhausted and was persuaded to enter the hospital. Having finished a nationwide speaking tour, Ōhira visited his electoral district on December 3 and immediately went to the hospital to see his brother. As soon as he saw Masayoshi, Kazumitsu said, "How many can you win?" wanting to know the Ōhira faction's prospects. He had supposed that as soon as the general election was over there would be a contested party presidential election in which the relative strength of the Ōhira faction would be decisive. Ōhira replied: "It will be more than before."

Ahead lay a hard schedule of speeches, after which Ōhira returned to the capital. In his home district, the election was a resounding success for him as he came in top place with 98,412 votes, or 42.3 percent of the votes cast. On hearing this, Kazumitsu clapped his hands and exclaimed: "My illness is over. Let me go home quickly." But on the evening of December 7, two days after the election, he suddenly died of a cardiac infarction.

Part 6

The Stairway to the Top

Chapter 27

Preventing a Reversal

The Fukuda Administration, also popularly called the Fukuda–Ōhira leadership (*Daifuku taisei*), had come into being amidst a storm of public censure directed at the LDP. The new leadership was seen as being helped by the fact that it was descended from the two lineages that had continued within the party, the Democratic Party represented by Fukuda, and the Liberal Party represented by Ōhira. We have already seen how former Prime Minister Satō Eisaku's identification with both lineages contributed to the longevity of his regime. Although the Fukuda Administration was distinguished by a clearer division of responsibilities (with Ōhira in charge of the party and Fukuda of the cabinet), it may nevertheless be said to have shared important characteristics with the Satō Administration.

What made this possible was, above all, the sense of crisis and impending schism that had affected the entire party. However, the new regime was only realized through Ōhira allowing Fukuda to serve first as prime minister, despite Ōhira's numerical advantage among LDP Diet members. At this time, Lower House LDP members, including those who belonged to small factions or to no faction, could be classified into two groups of nearly equal size: the Liberal Party lineage (including the Ōhira and Tanaka factions) and the Democratic Party lineage (including the Fukuda, Miki, and Nakasone factions). In the Upper House, however, LDP members of Liberal Party lineage were more numerous, with the result that when members of both houses were counted together the Ōhira and Tanaka factions had an advantage. If Fukuda and Ōhira had run against each other in an election for party president by LDP members of both houses, Ōhira would have come out ahead. However, Ōhira had wanted to avoid both the continuation and widening of intraparty strife that would have accompanied such a presidential election. An important point to be considered is that both the Tanaka and Miki camps had suffered greatly from the Lockheed Incident and also from the movement to remove Miki from office. Thus, to work effectively for party unity at this time, collaboration between Ōhira and Fukuda was preferable to antagonism.

The purport of the secret agreement made earlier was that Fukuda would serve a full two-year term, after which Ōhira would replace him. It had been drawn up to give recognition to this; yet it could not be made public lest there be an uproar against the national leadership being decided by private agreement. The document in question, whose existence was kept in the strictest secrecy, did not, however, specifically state that Ōhira would be the next party president. The only guarantee to the proposal was the "mutual trust" between Fukuda and Ōhira referred to in the agreement. At the outset of the new administration, Ōhira confided to a close associate: "The key to whether this administration will function lies in whether the relationship between Fukuda and myself proceeds smoothly. The most important thing for the regeneration of the party is for me to help Fukuda without making any demands on him." To others, Ōhira explained his distinctive philosophy with respect to this relationship as follows: "Fukuda and I were born and brought up differently, and up to now our relationship has been marked more by rivalry than friendship. On various policy matters concerning foreign relations, defense, the economy, and so on, we have represented different views within the party. Now that we are going to cooperate, it will be interesting to have such two extremely different people working together."

This was almost an embodiment of the ellipse theory Ōhira had been so fond of from his youth: if the wide range of people forming the LDP could be likened to an ellipse, one of its focal points was Fukuda and the other was Ōhira. If a relationship of trust could be maintained, strength would result, but antagonism would only invite conflict and confusion. At this time, Ōhira seems to have hoped to unify the party through the tension created between these two focal points, thereby generating new vigor to cope with the difficulties of governing. Or, to use another analogy, he seems to have had the image of two trees of different species growing together and pooling their strength to support a rickety party structure.

For anyone aiming at the LDP presidency, the post of secretary-general is a vital step. With the exception of the party's first two presidents, Hatoyama and Ishibashi, the rest—Kishi, Ikeda, Satō, Tanaka, Miki, and Fukuda—had all first served as secretary-general. In Ōhira's twenty-five years in politics, he had served two years as chief cabinet secretary, a total of four years as minister of foreign affairs, one year as minister of international trade and industry, and two and a half years as minister of finance. Despite all this government experience, his only experience in one of the top party posts had been the year he served as LDP Policy Research Council chairman during the Satō Administration. Worried over this lack of background in party administration, a reporter friend had asked him, "Will you really be able to deal with all the rough jobs of a secretary-general?" After some moments of silence, Ōhira replied, "Well, it'll be something like going into a jungle." Upon assuming his post as LDP secretary-general, Ōhira broke new ground when he stressed that anyone would be welcome to walk into his office at any time. People were impressed when he said, "Let us keep this door open."

The party rules say only vaguely that the duties of the LDP secretary-general "are to assist the party president and administer party affairs." Insofar as the LDP is the governing party, its president is also prime minister, who is consequently so busy with administering the government that he has no time to look after party business. The person who actually runs party affairs is the secretary-general, and he had usually come from the party president's faction and was expected to be a representative and defender of the party president's views and intentions. The choice of Nakasone Yasuhiro as secretary-general at the outset of the Miki Administration reflected the special circumstances of the establishment of that administration, among them an agreement explicitly stating that the secretary-general should not come from the party president's faction. The division of responsibility, whereby Fukuda was in charge of the government and Ōhira in charge of the party, can be said to have followed the same pattern.

From the very outset, the Fukuda–Ōhira leadership shouldered a heavy burden. The scars of the intraparty struggle that had continued over most of 1976 were still evident, the Lockheed Incident was still unresolved, and the people's criticism of the LDP and resultant distrust of politics were still serious problems. No real start had yet been made at party reform, the December 1976 general election had brought the worst showing in the party's history, and both houses of the Diet were almost equally divided between LDP and opposition party members. In these circumstances, the party could not be managed as before with the exclusion of nonmainstream factions. If only a small number of Diet members should raise the banner of rebellion in either house, government and opposition strengths could be reversed and Diet proceedings could come to a standstill. To stabilize the situation, it was mandatory to achieve a party balance, and it was with this in mind that Kōmoto Toshio, a leader of the Miki faction, had been made chairman of the LDP Policy Research Council.

Given this background, the main tasks of the Fukuda–Ōhira leadership focused on three points: (1) to carry out the so-called new-departure party reforms (*denaoshi tōkaikaku*) that Ōhira and Fukuda had agreed on in the hope of forging a more responsible party and regaining the people's trust in politics; (2) to prevent an LDP–opposition reversal of strength in the eleventh Upper House election that would take place in six months; and (3) to assure that the Diet functions normally under conditions of approximately equal LDP and opposition strength, so as to meet the responsibilities entrusted to it by the people.

Party President Fukuda himself chaired the newly created implementation headquarters for party reform. To deal with the upcoming Upper House election, Ōhira chaired a new Election Preparatory Committee. Lower House Speaker Hori Shigeru was put in charge of managing the Diet, assisted by his close friend Kanemaru Shin of the Tanaka faction, who headed the Lower House Committee on Rules and Administration. The very important Lower House Budget Committee was to be chaired by Tsubokawa Shinzō of the Fukuda faction, and the LDP's Diet Affairs Committee was to be chaired by Abe Shintarō of the Fukuda faction, whom the mass media was calling one of the party's promising new leaders. In this way, plans were made for the Diet, the party, and the government to function effectively together.

To help with the task of preparing for the upcoming Upper House election, Ōhira appointed Takeshita Noboru of the Tanaka faction, who was familiar with election matters, as chairman of the party's National Organization Committee. As chairman of its Public Relations Committee, he appointed Kosaka Tokusaburō (with no factional affiliation), who had wide experience as a business entrepreneur. As chairman of the National Campaign Headquarters, he appointed the very able Nakagawa Ichirō (with no factional affiliation), and as head of the general affairs division of the Election Preparatory Headquarters, he appointed Okuno Seiryō (with no factional affiliation). All of these men were highly respected throughout the party. Recalling these appointments, Takeshita some years later remarked: "Secretary-General Ōhira put his faith in us younger men and entrusted us with major responsibilities, and it was because of this that we could act in such an unrestricted way. I think Ōhira put us to work quite skillfully."

Thus, in the thirty-second LDP party convention held on January 26, 1977, much attention was paid to what posture the Fukuda–Ōhira leadership would adopt toward party reform and future political management. Because it was meeting in the wake of two major blows to its prestige —the Lockheed Incident and the poor showing in the general election— the convention lacked the festive atmosphere of previous years. The Report on the Party Situation presented by Ōhira at this convention was his first such communication as secretary-general to the entire party and the people of Japan. This report, which Ōhira wrote himself, was rather severe in tone. It reviewed the intraparty strife over the past year in this way:

> Looking back, in February of last year the Lockheed Incident suddenly surfaced in the United States Senate, and throughout that year our party experienced continual jolts in an atmosphere of rising public concern. Upholding the principle of [opposing corruption] in politics, not a single person in our party was prepared to object to a thorough investigation of this incident, and, in fact, the government, with the cooperation of the United States government, assiduously pressed ahead with the investigation. For our party, the problem was not just the handling of the Lockheed Incident itself. While it was being investigated, there arose sharp opposition between those who felt the Diet should be dissolved at an early date and those who felt there was no hurry for this, believing the cabinet should first resign en masse and there should be, in full view of the people, an elucidation of the political responsibilities accompanying the incident. Of course, advocates of both courses were concerned about the party's future. Yet this difference of opinion came to have a profound influence on ways of approaching the extraordinary Diet session as well as the party's decision making on important issues. And it came to take on the aspects of severe intraparty strife.

Ōhira went on to discuss the poor showing in the last general election, the people's deep-rooted mistrust of the LDP, the advent of the Fukuda Administration, and the complex path ahead. He then emphasized the need for party reforms:

> The relaxing of party discipline and our shortcomings in responding to the times have become evident during the long reign of the Liberal Democratic Party and, unfortunately, have meant that the party cannot meet the expectations of many thoughtful Japanese. The new administration, whatever it does, must make an all-out effort to stem such mistrust and respond to the expectations of the people, who are asking for a restructuring of our party. . . .
>
> Ever since the party's founding, popular support for it has gradually declined, leading to the disastrous showing in last year's general election. I do not believe that this indicates a rejection of the party's basic stance, which is to preserve a free society, but I think the people have shown great dissatisfaction

with our party's political posture and health, and with its activities. From another perspective, this dissatisfaction is manifest in the fact that the proportion of people with no party preferences has swelled, almost before we knew it, to nearly half the total voters. This must surely be evidence that our party, as the leading party, has not been able to respond adequately to the aspirations and needs of the majority of the people.

To remedy this situation, Ōhira proposed the urgent "regeneration of a party with an organization and a vitality in keeping with present conditions." His proposal focused on five points: (1) expanding the party's organization and number of supporters; (2) stabilizing the party's finances; (3) expanding and improving public relations; (4) improving party management, including the problem of factions; and (5) revising the rules on party presidential elections and other party matters. This last item had been suggested earlier in the proposals for party reforms made by former Party President Miki Takeo on his resignation. In outline, the Miki proposal called for "a two-step scheme, consisting of nominating elections (preliminary elections) in local areas followed by a runoff election (main election) between the two leading candidates carried out by LDP members of both houses." Among the proposed revisions of party rules was also the change, as stated in the secret agreement between Ōhira and Fukuda, in the term of the party presidency from three years to two.

This party convention further decided that an extraordinary party convention would be held in April, and that before that time some conclusions would be reached on the most urgent questions of party reform. It was agreed that prior to the start of the Upper House election campaign in June, the reforms deemed absolutely necessary would be accomplished so the party could begin the campaign with a new face.

January 31, 1977, saw the opening of the first Diet since the LDP's founding in which the LDP and opposition strengths in both houses were almost even. The main focus of this 80th Ordinary Diet was, as with other ordinary Diet sessions, the Budget Committee of the Lower House. What was different this time was that the Budget Committee had an equal number of members from the government and opposition parties, and if the non-voting chairman of the committee was selected from the governing party, the opposition parties would have a voting majority. Therefore, if all the opposition party members joined against a government-backed position, the governing-party position would be defeated. Of course, even if a bill was rejected in the committee, the original bill could still be passed in a Lower House plenary session. However, given the principles of Diet management that gave central importance to committees, to resurrect a bill that had already been defeated in the committee was not easy. Also, to do so was not necessarily a wise tactic, since if in a plenary session the governing party should force the passage of a bill in this way, this was likely to arouse organized cooperation among the opposition parties that might make the passage of other important bills virtually impossible. In any case, the situation was now such that, prior to taking a vote on any government-presented budget bill, the opposition parties could present a resolution for a reformulation of the bill and see it passed by a majority of the Budget Committee members.

In the case of a mere revision of the budget, there was no problem so long as the government accepted the revision. However, a resolution for a budget reformulation was, in effect, equivalent to a Diet rejection of the government bill in question. In this case, for the government to reformulate the bill, it would have to submit an entirely new budget request. This would require a great amount of time and effort and would delay passage of the budget, causing great inconvenience to the country's economy and to the nation. Given these circumstances, a major aim of the opposition parties during this Diet session was to see how much the government and the LDP would concede. For the opposition parties, the handling of proceedings on the front stage of the Budget Committee could be said to be a tool for bringing the governing party to backstage political negotiations. The government and LDP were well aware of this from the start; nevertheless, the stress felt by those party executives who had overall responsibility for the handling of Diet affairs was immense.

Political negotiations involving the Budget Committee could be broadly divided into two levels. At the first level, there was the question of whether the five opposition parties (the JSP, Kōmeitō, DSP, JCP, and NLC) could transcend their differences in character and viewpoint to present a unified demand for a budget revision. For the opposition parties, the near-parity in Diet strength meant that, unlike the earlier situation where the LDP held a safe majority, if they played their cards carefully, they might push the governing party into revising the budget, thus realizing their own plans. In this sense, such negotiations provided an assessment of the true capabilities of the opposition parties. At the second level, if the five nongoverning parties presented a united front, and if the objectives of the first level had been accomplished, the opposition could then see to what extent the LDP would accept their demands.

In the days following the presentation of the budget to the Diet on February 3, 1977, there were intense backstage negotiations between the governing and opposition parties and among the latter parties themselves. Unless the budget was passed by the end of March, or the beginning of April at the latest, a provisional budget for the new fiscal year would have to be compiled. To avoid this, it would be necessary to get the budget approved by the Lower House (which takes precedence over the Upper House in budgetary matters) no later than early March. If this was done, even if the budget should not be approved by the Upper House, it would nevertheless become law thirty days after passage in the Lower House. Keeping in mind the early March deadline, interparty negotiations in the Lower House Budget Committee gradually grew more tense. The nongoverning parties, which were at first split in their views, moved toward a compromise, and on March 5 reached agreement on a budget revision that would increase expenditures for social welfare and would reduce taxes by a total of ¥1 trillion against the government plan for reducing taxes by ¥353 billion.

In talks among the chairmen of the Diet Affairs committees of the LDP and opposition parties on March 7, the five opposition parties demanded of the LDP, "Are you willing to come to terms with a budget revision or not? First make this clear." In response, the LDP side jabbed the opposition's weak point by saying, "If you are going to ask for a revision, indicate its content and purpose." The next day, the LDP General Council decided to urge party members to exert themselves to pass the budget and other budget-related legislation as soon as possible, and entrusted the three top party officers, including Ōhira, with specific implementation. On this day, LDP Diet Affairs Committee Chairman Abe suggested a meeting of the parties' secretaries-general on March 9. However, by then, the time limit for the automatic establishment of the fiscal 1977 budget, that is, before the end of the 1976 fiscal year, would have already passed.

Prime Minister Fukuda and Secretary-General Ōhira had prepared to make available ¥350 billion in government resources to cope with a possible budget revision. This amount proved insufficient, however, in the face of opposition demands for considerable new social welfare expenditures and a ¥1 trillion tax reduction. Through informal contacts, the information was relayed from opposition party heads that there would be agreement as long as the tax reduction was over ¥500 billion; but the gap between the LDP and opposition positions was still large.

The three top LDP officers charged with handling negotiations on the budget met on March 9 in the office of the LDP president on the third floor of the Diet building. Ōhira looked around at the tense faces of the party leaders and asked, "Well, the time has finally come, so do you have anything to lay on the table?" Policy Research Council Chairman Kōmoto, somewhat uncharacteristically, told Ōhira: "As you probably know, in such cases it will not do to give an answer in bits and pieces. I'd like to ask that we proceed with the intention of reaching a conclusion by the day's end." Ōhira nodded and, seeing there were no other comments, said, "I'll leave you now. Let's talk again when the negotiations are finished." With his usual unhurried movements, he got up and left. Regardless of the uncertainty over whether he would be successful, his expression was no different than if he was going to chat with friends over tea. The faces of the other party leaders watching him leave the room showed intense anxiety.

The budget talks, which were attended by JSP General Secretary Ishibashi Masashi, Kōmeitō Secretary-General Yano Jun'ya, DSP Secretary-General Tsukamoto Saburō, JCP General Secretary Fuwa Tetsuzō, NLC Secretary-General Nishioka Takeo, and Ōhira, began at 11 A.M.. The format was primarily one where the opposition side discussed the proposals put forward by Ōhira. In the third session at around 5 P.M., after an afternoon break, Ōhira underlined the essence of what he intended to accomplish: "The proposal I'm about to present contains figures that are literally not exaggerated. Be aware as you hear it that I cannot give a single penny more if I am asked." With this preface, Ōhira began to explain the proposal. His attitude and voice clearly showed his determination. When he came to the end, he pressed, "Just answer yes or no." After a break of about fifteen minutes, the fourth session began around 8 P.M., at which the various party representatives' reply was, "We are not satisfied, but it can't be helped." With that, they acceded to the Ōhira plan, and the tax reduction agreed upon was ¥715.8 billion (¥362.8 billion more than the original government plan).

A look of relief returned to the faces of LDP staff members anxiously awaiting the outcome of the negotiations. Ōhira was greeted with shouts of "Thank you" and "Well done." It had been uncertain what complications might arise and how many days might be involved, but the negotiations had wound up in a single day and the current Diet session had thus passed its greatest hurdle. Ōhira smiled from time to time as he made his report to Prime Minister Fukuda and other party leaders. The following day's newspapers carried what they called a "rare photo" of a smiling Ōhira shaking hands with JCP General Secretary Fuwa, while the top negotiators from the other four parties looked on.

In this ordinary Diet session during the spring of 1977, of the seventy-six bills introduced by the government, sixty-five were passed. Compared to other ordinary Diet sessions (the period of the Miki Cabinet being an exception), this number was not especially large, but the "batting average" of 85.5 percent—helped, it must be admitted, by the fact that none of these bills was terribly controversial—was even greater than the usual 80 percent in times when the LDP had a stable majority of Diet seats.

Some people saw this as a sign of the maturing of democratic politics in Japan and the good sense of the governing and opposition parties, while others attributed it to the personality and capabilities of the LDP's secretary-general. In any case, it may be said that given the reality of an evenly matched Diet, the center of politics had very perceptibly moved from the government to the Diet. Ōhira later commented: "Each party in its own way brings together and represents the people's will. In democratic politics it is desirable to reflect the will of as many people as possible. It is because of this that in our democracy it is considered such a good thing if there can be unanimous agreement, so the process by which the various parties talk with one another and make joint efforts is very important." This sort of thinking developed into the Ōhira strategy that came to be known as "partial coalition" (*pāsharu rengōron*).

Once passage of the budget bill was assured, the interest of the political world came to focus on the eleventh Upper House election to take place in three months. The Upper House has 252 members, 100 of whom are elected by the country at large and 152 by prefectural constituencies, with 1 to 4 members from each of Japan's forty-seven prefectures. (Through an August 1982 change in the election law, effective from June 1983, proportional party representation was adopted for determining winners in the national constituency category. Each voter indicates one or another party list in which candidates are ranked in a predetermined order.) The term in office is six years. Unlike the Lower House, the Upper House is not subject to dissolution, and half of its members are elected every three years.

Prior to the 1977 election, the LDP held 127 Upper House seats, just 1 more than half. What was now particularly troublesome for the party was the fact that 65 of its seats were up for reelection compared to just 58 of the opposition parties' seats. Unless the LDP maintained at least its current number of seats, a reversal in strength between the government and the opposition was inevitable. Judging from the party's past performance, this would not be easy, and there was a deep-seated distrust of the LDP caused by the previous year's intraparty fighting and the still unresolved Lockheed Incident. In addition, the party's election preparations were slow to take shape. Unlike Lower House elections, which might occur any time after a Lower House dissolution, the Upper House elections took place only once every three years, and so it was not uncommon for candidates to be provisionally selected and election preparations begun about a year in advance. This time, however, due to the long intraparty turmoil, the LDP was behind in its recruitment of candidates and in the work of

matching candidates and electoral constituencies. Furthermore, in the atmosphere of the times, when the LDP was often looked on as "the bad
guys," there were few people who would agree lightly to the suggestion
that they become LDP candidates. During March and April, Secretary-
General Ōhira put a great deal of effort into searching for candidates to
stand for election by the nation at large, in which category the dearth of
promising candidates was most severe.

In the meantime, the opposition parties launched, with much fanfare, a
number of plans for a coalition government. Several new political associations (for example, the *Shakai Shimin Rengō* [Socialist Citizens' League]
and the *Kakushin Jiyū Rengō* [Reform Liberal League]) were born, with the
aim of absorbing part of the no-party-preference segment of the population that had helped the NLC's popularity. The Upper House election campaign promised to be much livelier than in previous years, and the media,
which considered a government reversal in the Upper House to be a
foregone conclusion, was fond of discussing the coming "coalition era."

Faced with this situation, Ōhira roughly calculated that a strategy that
brought to the Upper House at least eighteen LDP candidates elected by
the nation at large, coupled with the election of, on average, one LDP candidate from each prefecture, would add up to the sixty-five candidates
needed to prevent a reversal. There only remained the question of how to
make this possible. First, in the case of candidates elected by the nation at
large, the key was to accurately estimate the party's ability to attract votes,
followed by a decision on how many candidates to put up and what sort of
vote distribution to aim for among them. In the tenth Upper House election in 1974, the LDP had run an inefficient campaign in the national constituency, so that prominent candidates had received especially large
numbers of votes that cut into those won by borderline candidates, with
the result that many of the latter were defeated.

In the case of the prefectural constituencies, the biggest question was
why, in many prefectures where LDP candidates from the Lower House
districts managed to win half or more of the Lower House seats, Upper
House candidates risked losing. An often-recalled example was the ninth
Upper House election of 1971, in which LDP candidates lost in eight of the
twenty-six prefectures electing just one Upper House member. In the 1974
election, with the exception of Okinawa Prefecture, every prefecture
elected at least one LDP Upper House member, but in 1977, depending on
what progress had been made in a shared strategy among the opposition
parties, it seemed possible that the 1971 pattern could be repeated. Faced
with this possibility, Ōhira instructed his colleagues to make careful
analyses and plans.

With the approach of the Upper House election, Ōhira became busy attending "political and economic culture parties" (*seikei bunka pātī*), which had first been organized two years previously under the Miki Administration. The first such gathering in 1977 was held on January 29 in Osaka, followed by a spate of similar events in other prefectures throughout the country. Prime Minister Fukuda or Secretary-General Ōhira, or both, would always be present, and on these occasions they deepened their friendships with local persons of prominence who supported the LDP. Prior to the June 1977 Upper House election, 63,000 people in thirty prefectures had participated in these gatherings. Ōhira's schedule became impossibly busy, with sometimes four or five different groups of visitors waiting to see him at the same time. Although he might run back and forth from group to group, with often only time to talk with them standing up, he seemed to enjoy these contacts. He often accepted interviews with foreign journalists, and his visitors included numerous important personages and personal friends from other countries. On April 13, he met with the British Conservative Party leader Margaret Thatcher, and later that month talked with the American singer Pat Boone.

On April 25, 1977, an LDP extraordinary party convention began in the Bunkyō Public Hall under the rather awkward name of Comprehensive Rally for LDP Reform and Rapid Advance. This gathering intended to act as a springboard for party reform, which it hoped would help lead to success in the Upper House election. One of the items discussed at this convention was the five-point plan for party reform already proposed by Ōhira in January. Approval was given to the introduction of a system of preliminary elections as part of the process of choosing the party president, in which all party members (*tōin*) and so-called fraternity members (*tōyū*, or party supporters who made financial contributions that were somewhat larger than the very modest party membership fees) would have the right to vote. It was decided that the first such preliminary election would take place on December 1, 1978, just two years after Fukuda had become LDP president. At the same time, resolutions were passed to clarify the qualifications for party membership, to increase the numbers of party and fraternity members, and to set up a Liberal National Congress of fraternity members. At Fukuda's insistence, all party factions had been formally dissolved prior to this extraordinary party convention.

Ōhira felt that human beings were at a very fundamental level group-oriented animals, and he once expressed himself on the subject as follows: "It is natural for groups to form as the result of human relations and of shared predilections and tastes. It is the same with political associations. The factions have their own roles with respect to matters that cannot be handled only at the party level, such as friendship and mutual cooperation among faction members, the search for men of ability, the education of their members, and the transmission of information. It is too extreme to label them categorically as bad." Ōhira did not approve of becoming removed from reality or talking about impossibilities as if they were possible. He could not, however, ignore the reality of the current Fukuda–Ōhira leadership or the fact that voters calling for the dissolution of factions were gaining in influence.

In his Report on the Party Situation at the January party convention, Ōhira had stated: "Although I am not one to deny that the factions have functioned as systems for information and education or as forces preventing party dictatorship, it is not impossible for the pride and exclusivism of the factions to interfere with the party's integrity. Thus, it has recently been decided to dissolve the existing factions." On the same occasion, he also pointed out: "The roles that factions of LDP Diet members have carried out in the past—that is, the search for new men of talent, the education of party members, and the exchange of information—must in some form or other be continued by the party. We must be careful that after the dissolution of the factions people do not start talking about a decline in the party's vitality." Both statements give an indication of the complexity of Ōhira's thoughts with regard to this dissolution of the factions.

After May, with the approach of the Upper House election, none of the parties was in a mood for dispassionate discussions in the Diet. On days when the Diet did not meet, Ōhira was busy attending political and economic culture parties sponsored by LDP prefectural federations or meetings in various prefectures to launch the campaigns of Upper House candidates. For example, he traveled to Akita and Miyagi prefectures on May 1, Hyōgo Prefecture on May 16, Niigata Prefecture on May 18, Saitama Prefecture on the May 19, Kagawa Prefecture on May 21, and Hiroshima Prefecture on May 22. In between, his time in Tokyo was filled with Diet proceedings, consultations on the election, and meetings with various organizations, including those set up in support of Upper House candidates seeking election by the nation at large. As polling day drew closer, his schedule became even busier: on May 29 he was in Okayama, on May 30 in Tottori, on May 31 in Miyagi, on June 1 in Niigata, on June 3 back in Tokyo, on June 4 in Aomori, and on June 5 in Fukui. He did not allow himself a single day of rest.

By the beginning of June, the LDP Upper House candidates had been selected and the party's local organizations were in fairly good order. Addressing staff members, who were often undecided whether to be optimistic or pessimistic over the fluctuating election forecasts, Ōhira counseled: "In elections there are no methods or guides for working miracles. I think all we can do is to carry out as far as possible what we can think of, and then quietly accept the voters' response." Ōhira seemed personally full of confidence that he had carefully considered everything as far as possible, that he had made credible preparations, and that he had taken the measures that were most necessary.

A series of public opinion polls revealed that while support for the Fukuda Cabinet remained stagnant, support for the LDP was on the upturn (although only slightly) for the first time in a decade. Ōhira voiced broad optimism: "When the immediate contest comes, there is no reason for us to lose. Things will surely work out if everyone is involved." Nevertheless, he was keeping in mind some fairly precise personal calculations based on statistics, analyses of local conditions, and responses to campaign efforts. Replying to a question following a speech at the Japan National Press Club on June 1, Ōhira gave a fairly precise prognosis: "I think we can win forty-five seats in the local [prefectural] constituencies. As for those elected by the nation at large, I expect us to divide the vote skillfully and win all sixty-five of the LDP seats up for reelection. So I don't contemplate losing our majority." The media saw this merely as an expression of hope by the LDP secretary-general and gave it virtually no news coverage. What the media were mainly interested in was Ōhira's suggestion that "on various issues that may arise, it will be realistic to put together a 'partial coalition' around an LDP axis." Every newspaper carried stories with such headlines as "LDP Responds to Coalition Era." The dominant media view was that the majority would change, ushering in a new age of coalition.

Around this time, Ōhira was beginning to receive results from public opinion surveys showing the LDP's standing to be rapidly improving, even in prefectures where the party had been said to be at a disadvantage, and suggesting that if such trends continued more LDP candidates should be able to win than had been previously supposed. The problem was whether or not these hopes could be realized in the little more than one month that remained before the election.

On June 17, the eleventh Upper House election campaign formally began, with the voting date set for July 10. After initial expressions of support at party headquarters, Ōhira encouraged the LDP candidates running for election in the nationwide constituency by attending kickoff ceremonies at their various campaign headquarters. He then made a fast four-day, three-night trip to the crucial prefectures of Aomori, Akita, Yamagata, and Miyagi at the end of June. During a visit to Kaminoyama Hot Spring in Yonezawa, Yamagata Prefecture, for talks with local LDP leaders, he took part in preparing *karami-mochi* dumplings and pounding glutinous rice. Jokes were made around the Japanese adage about "being skilled with the old pestle" (meaning to utilize to advantage one's experience of former days).

After the beginning of July, various newspapers featured interviews with Ōhira and reported his remarks concerning the election. One reporter asked, "With the LDP facing its biggest crisis since its founding, how do you feel about this?" to which Ōhira replied, "Well, it's rather like being on a raft. Even if you don't like the current, there's nothing you can do about it except glide with the stream, at the same time trying to avoid running into a cliff or getting caught in rapids." Another reporter asked, "Many in the LDP are asking what you have in mind these days," to which his reply was: "Both yesterday or today, I've been thinking and acting at the same pace. Nothing has changed particularly. It's not in my nature to say things just for the sake of alleviating people's anxieties. In any case, I think the Japanese people are more prudent than some might suspect, and they have a sense of balance. In both domestic politics and diplomacy, there will be some dissonant notes; yet the balance will not be upset, so I think there is no need to make frenzied pronouncements about a sense of crisis."

At that time, what Ōhira continued to ponder was how to approach that segment of the people without any party preference, which had grown so noticeably in recent years. The proportion of the population replying to pollsters that they had "no party preference" or "don't know" had grown to at least 24.5 percent, and in some surveys it was as large as 40 percent. Thus, out of a total voting population of approximately 78 million, between 20 milion and 30 million had no established party preferences and would make their final decisions just before casting their ballots. It would be disastrous if the majority of them should vote for the opposition parties at the last moment. What should be done to prevent these floating voters from turning against the LDP? Ōhira felt that it would be best not to propose policies too glibly. At a time of widespread distrust of the LDP, to present too many nice-sounding policies could have the reverse of the intended effect. The opposition parties were thus likely to put forth sweeter words and figures, even though they had no experience with bringing policies to fruition. Since the media were statutorily obliged to treat all parties equally during election campaigns, the LDP got only one-sixth to one-seventh of media attention, which was by no means advantageous to a party fighting to keep its majority.

Ōhira's course was set: in the campaign it would be acceptable not to highlight points of contention. His plan was to refrain from presenting any new policies, to refrain from contending with the opposition, and to rely mainly on the LDP's internal sense of crisis. However, this was necessarily risky because should the opposition parties see through this and attack the LDP, the latter would be at a loss to respond.

Three or four days before the polling date, the JSP's Policy Board Chairman Tagaya Shinnen and the DSP's Secretary-General Tsukamoto Saburō expressed dissatisfaction with the LDP's strategy, saying, "The Liberal Democratic Party is being too crafty. It has not put forth any policies." This statement found its way into a small newspaper article, but it was already too late to do much damage. The LDP headquarters had already issued its final "assault orders," which said, in effect, "Get the entire camp into line and fight as one until the last moment to win a sure victory." Ōhira now awaited the day of the election with the hope that everyone would continue working as before for three more days. On July 7, the day of the traditional Tanabata Festival, Ōhira taunted those reporters who foresaw a loss of the LDP majority by asking them a question: "Is this any different from an ordinary election?" The reporters were somewhat taken aback by his good spirits. When they asked, "Has the mist cleared?" Ōhira looked up at the cloudy sky and replied, "If these dark clouds go away. It will be good if the weather is fine on the tenth." He continued looking up at the sky for some time, as if offering a prayer.

On election day, the weather, which had been a matter of concern until the last, was good throughout the country. Voter turnout was high, and there was nothing to do but wait for the results. That evening, the party leaders returned one after another to headquarters in Hirakawachō. They gathered in the fourth-floor lounge to await the verdict. Secretary-General Ōhira and General Council Chairman Esaki came at 9 P.M., and Prime Minister Fukuda appeared a half hour later.

The opening of the ballots had begun on schedule at 7:30 P.M. It soon became apparent that the LDP candidates representing the northeastern prefectures of Aomori, Akita, and Yamagata, which had been considered especially difficult, were sure of victory, and the pink rosettes placed over a map of Japan to indicate "certain victory" gradually increased. A little past 10 P.M., when the number of rosettes totaled over twenty, Prime Minister Fukuda suddenly looked more relaxed. Ōhira, however, who was carefully watching the incoming results at his side, continued to look tense.

The vote count was completed in the early evening of the twelfth. The LDP won forty-five prefectural seats and eighteen nationwide seats, totaling sixty-three. This soon became sixty-six, with the official acceptance into the LDP fold of one who had run under the name of his own group of supporters and two who had run as independents. This made one more than before the election. Seven months after the start of the Fukuda–Ōhira leadership, the predictions of a reversal in the Upper House election had been proved wrong. Now that this immediate hurdle had been overcome, party members who had entertained fears about their fate could breathe more easily. The sense of failure on the part of the opposition parties was great, especially in the JSP, whose Chairman Narita Tomomi and General Secretary Ishibashi Masashi took responsibility for losing five seats and resigned.

Not long after this election, the first LDP National Summer Study Meeting was held. This was planned as a sort of substitute for the various study meetings formerly organized by the now-dissolved factions. In a speech before this gathering titled "Guidelines for Political Management in a Period of Change," Ōhira referred to lessons from the recent Upper House election as follows:

> Many asked how the election results should be interpreted. First of all, it would seem that the voters do not want big changes in the political situation, are not overly dissatisfied with the status quo, and have, so to speak, a point of view that affirms the status quo.
>
> Moreover, we can see these results as indicating a cool reaction to the idealistic proposals of the opposition parties for an opposition coalition government. In every election there has always been, among the opposition parties, one or more arguing for forming an anti-LDP league of opposition parties to replace an LDP administration. This time was no exception. In the discussions about forming an opposition coalition, it has not been decided, nor does it seem likely to be decided soon, whether it would be based on the Japan Socialist Party and the Japan Communist Party, or on the Japan Socialist Party, the Kōmeitō, and the Democratic Socialist Party. It would, no doubt, involve even more difficult talks to effect such a coalition in a form that would include all the opposition parties at once. But whenever there is an election, whatever the situation, this old refrain is always naively sung. The majority of voters have not on any occasion lent their ears to such old tunes, and we may say that this was also the case in the most recent election. . . . However, there is one thing we must pay attention to now. According to recent public opinion polls, the proportion of voters with no party preference has grown rapidly from 20 percent to 40 percent. This rapid expansion of the so-called no-party stratum is, I think, a trend we must pay a great deal of attention to.

According to scholars, in the last Upper House election, as well as in last year's Lower House election, there was no winning party, and this has only caused the no-party stratum to expand. Yet at the same time we may say that voter awareness is on the whole healthy and, with a sense of balance that is both striking and admirable, has passed a solid judgment that, on the one hand, has warned politicians not to indulge in self-complacency or arrogance, and, on the other hand, has prevented serious instability in the political situation. The voters have said to the party, "Liberal Democratic Party, don't be arrogant." But I think they have also given both a reminder and an encouragement that "the Liberal Democratic Party bears a heavy responsibility."

Ōhira further expressed his basic approach to the LDP:

The Liberal Democratic Party . . . may be said to have been, so to speak, the "party with the most human smell." In a modern sense, it can by no means be said to be a party with a handsome appearance. It cannot be said to be a clean or good-looking party. Thus, I don't think, in spite of our own biases, that it is a truly popular party among the people. Nevertheless, our nation's postwar management has been accomplished with this party at the helm, and it is a fact that it has achieved uncommon successes. This postwar management has had to face great trials, worldwide in scope, and while there are many countries that have fallen behind in postwar management, ours has succeeded in achieving economic balance and self-reliance. This, in other words, shows the strength of the Liberal Democratic Party's capacities for adaptation. It may not have the graceful carriage of a thoroughbred, but it has the performance of a sturdy, ordinary work cow. In that sense, the Liberal Democratic Party is our country's chief public asset. If one set out from scratch with the express purpose of creating such a party, it could not be accomplished easily.

Ōhira's speech and the attitude he displayed at this meeting caused the media to comment on "his confidence being very much in evidence."

Chapter 28

Springlike Days

It is strange how happy events often occur together, just as bad luck may run in streaks. This was how it was for Ōhira after he assumed the post of LDP secretary-general in the Fukuda Administration, when a series of happy occasions touched his personal life. Of particular importance was the completion of his new residence at the end of 1976. After his house burned down in January 1974, he had rented a house in the same Seta district of Setagaya Ward while his new home was under construction. The Ōhiras had moved several times in the past and had owned many houses, but these had all been designed and built by others. Even if Ōhira never had any particularly strong desire for material possessions, he did show avid interest in the plans for his new home. Although he once said, "The children will all be living on their own, so this is just a place for us two old-timers," the plan gradually grew until the new house was almost as large as the previous one. One part of the garden was sectioned off for a house for the Ōhiras' second son, Hiroshi, and his wife, Kimiko. Just behind the Ōhiras' property stood the residence of their daughter, Yoshiko, and son-in-law, Morita Hajime. Their youngest son, Akira, was the only one still living at home. In May 1977, Akira became engaged to Uehara Yoshiko, granddaughter of Upper House Dietman Uehara Shōkichi, and the wedding was fixed for the autumn.

The 81st Extraordinary Diet, following the Upper House election in which the LDP managed to retain its majority, was convened on July 27, 1977. During this session, Ōhira, together with nine Lower House colleagues, received a certificate of commendation to commemorate twenty-five years of service in the Diet. Most of the recipients of this award, including Prime Minister Fukuda, had first won their Diet seats in the twenty-fifth general election of October 1, 1952, the first held after Japan regained independence. Together they had experienced a quarter-cen-

401

tury of change and reconstruction. Following the presentation ceremony during a plenary session of the Lower House, photographs were taken in the lounge outside Speaker Hori Shigeru's office as the recipients were congratulated by him. One happy picture shows Hori together with Ōhira, Fukuda, and their wives.

Around this time, Ōhira was generally regarded as the next prime minister and LDP president, and his words and actions were reported daily in the press. His life was full of bright rays of sunshine, with few clouds of anxiety in view. In early August, he went to his native Kagawa Prefecture to give some lectures commemorating his twenty-five years in the Lower House and to congratulate his former secretary Manabe Kenji, who in the last Upper House election had won one of the two seats for Kagawa Prefecture. Despite the blistering August heat, Ōhira was welcomed by an enthusiastic turnout of local people. Returning to speak before many of the same supporters who, twenty-five years before, had spearheaded the campaign of a little-known new candidate, Ōhira Masayoshi was now a statesman of stature, and his supporters were understandably proud and felt their efforts had been justified. Indeed, their dream, already some ten years old, of seeing the first prime minister from Kagawa Prefecture seemed about to become a reality. Ōhira's speeches discussed with concrete figures the social changes and improvements in standards of living that had taken place over the past quarter-century and spoke of the future path Japan should follow as one of the world's major democracies.

After this trip to Shikoku, Ōhira finally allowed himself some time off, free from the stress and hard work he had known since becoming chairman of the Kōchikai, foreign minister, finance minister, and now LDP secretary-general. He secluded himself in Hakone with the idea of compiling a book of speeches, proposals, and essays he had delivered or written subsequent to his last publication, *Tanbo kaikō* (Random Thoughts, Morning and Evening), which had appeared in 1970. This publication would commemorate his quarter-century as a member of the Lower House, and serve as a milestone in his career and a means of putting his personal life into perspective. Ōhira did not keep a diary, but he liked to write and often put down his impressions and feelings on *shikishi*, white cardboard squares on which poems or maxims were written. He knew by heart well over a hundred of the set phrases in the Chinese classics, and for those who asked for samples of his calligraphy he added words appropriate to the position and personality of the recipient. He was constantly increasing his fund of apt sayings, and, in the course of his reading, whenever he came across phrases that especially appealed to him, he would carefully jot them down in a notebook. The phrases that he wrote on *shikishi* can be said to reflect his feelings at the time. It is said that he was taught his style of calligraphy by his mentor Tsushima Juichi, who was known as an able calligrapher. Ōhira's brushstrokes, executed in what seemed a free and easy manner, in fact reflected considerable skill. In contrast to his solid physique and what at first sight might seem an impassive countenance, his brushstrokes were unusually delicate and had a particular flavor that some compared to the characters on *mokkan* (wooden strips used for writing) in the Nara period (710–94). The following are a sampling of phrases he dedicated to friends around this time.

> Above the mountains are more mountains, many layers of mountains.

> Between waves are paths leading in many directions.

> Good food tastes plain, great men appear ordinary.

> Do not complain about days past, complain only about days lost.

Drawn to religion in his youth, Ōhira surely retained in his heart a attraction to the lofty ideals of a boundless God and a love of humanity. Indeed, a dual motif throughout his life was his yearning for perfection together with, and for that very reason, his striving to understand and empathize with imperfect human beings.

Ensconced in the Hakone Kankō Hotel, Ōhira enjoyed several days completely removed from politics. He played golf with old friends in the mornings, took afternoon naps (an unusual luxury), and worked on manuscripts he had brought along. The time he allowed himself for rest was short, but it was sufficient to recharge his batteries. Letting his thoughts turn to the past as well as the future, he savored the solitude of this brief period. After Hakone, Ōhira spent the latter half of his summer vacation resting in Karuizawa, and then returned to Hakone on August 30 to address the LDP's first National Summer Study Meeting, mentioned in the previous chapter.

While Ōhira continued to work on the book to commemorate his twenty-five years in the Diet, it was decided that it would be published at the end of the year under the title *Fūjin zasso* (Wind-Scattered Writings). In November, Ōhira's youngest son, Akira, was married to Uehara Yoshiko, and Ōhira personally selected the gifts for guests at the wedding: an atlas of the world and a map of Japan. Around the same time, he agreed to write a series of autobiographical articles for the *Nihon Keizai Shinbun* column called "*Watakushi no rirekisho*" (My Curriculum Vitae), which carried first-person accounts of the lives of well-known people in various walks of life, usually in thirty to forty installments. He was persuaded to do so in part at the encouragement of a journalist friend, but another reason was no doubt that at this time—a year before he was likely to be selected as the next LDP president—he felt the need to look back over his life, an opportunity that this project provided. His manuscripts were published in thirty installments from New Year's Day, 1978.

Around the time of the LDP's first National Summer Study Meeting held in Hakone at the end of August, Ōhira had said to one of his secretaries: "While I am still able to see where I'm heading, I'm going to make a clean break from politics and follow a road I like." By "a road I like," he meant sponsoring a research organization that would bring together like-minded scholars and journalists. He thus intended to lead a scholarly life, where he would devote himself to his favorite pursuits of philosophy and the study of social problems, diplomacy, and history. He confided: "If I should give up my job as a Diet member, it would be boring to stay at home, but if I set up a research institute, I could give useful advice to younger people if they came to consult me." To another of his secretaries he said: "I have for a long time benefited from things done for me by everyone back home. I want to leave behind something for them to remember me by. My benefactor Katō Tōtarō left the Katō Scholarship Foundation. One idea would be to expand the present Ōhira library, but I'd like you to come up with some ideas." His secretary said, "You still have great work ahead of you as a statesman, so can't it wait until after that?" However, Ōhira did not seem satisfied with this reply and sought further advice on the matter. The idea later took concrete form in the Masayoshi Ōhira Memorial Foundation, established after his death, and the Masayoshi Ōhira Memorial Hall.

From Akira's wedding day the Ohira residence became home only to Ōhira and his wife. However, the Ōhiras had little time to themselves since they were regularly visited by journalists assigned to cover the secretary-general. Unless there was some unusual event, the journalists would begin arriving before 7 A.M., and those who came in the evening would usually stay until after 11 P.M., chatting, exchanging information, and generally acting almost as if the Ōhiras' new residence was their own. When a reporter once asked what his bedroom looked like, Ōhira, with a little humor, refused to show it, saying, "You fellows and I may be on friendly terms, but that's the one room I won't show you. It's my wife's and my sacred citadel, you know."

Ōhira once told reporters, "Regardless of how busy I am, I try at least once a month to make time to dine out alone with my wife." Ōhira expressed his affection for his wife in a short essay he was asked to contribute to a newspaper under the title *"Boku no madonna"* (My Madonna). This essay, which gives us valuable insights into Ōhira's perceptions of his family and private life, as well as human life in general, reads in part as follows: "My wife and I have lived together for over forty years since our marriage. Our life together has been a peaceful one. She is an ordinary woman and I an ordinary man. But . . . I must state that I feel my wife has several womanly virtues. They may be quite ordinary; yet for me they are precious and irreplaceable.

"First, I appreciate the earnest dedication that she has all along shown me and our children. This has never changed; neither have the marriage vows we made to remain faithful in sickness and in health, in fortune and in misfortune. Dedication means regarding certain other people as more important than oneself, and giving those persons not a part of oneself but one's all, and in this we see not a jot of self-interest, not a trace of vanity. . . .

"To have children is a big burden for a woman, but it is at the same time something to be proud of. To give birth to a child is what gives a woman an immediate purpose to life and is a role she can rightly be proud of. My wife was fortunately blessed with four children. Even though she is not particularly strong, she did very well in bearing them. The children get along very well with their mother and often, like friends, share in her activities. It is a beautiful thing to see. The children now all have their own families, and only the two aging parents remain at home; yet there are still many occasions when my wife and the children come together as a family. And it is always my wife who sits in the middle. For her, these times have always been the ones she likes best.

"Arranging get-togethers with relatives and friends has in most cases always meant work for my wife, but such occasions are oases in one's life. At these times, respect and appreciation for others are, of course, important, but even more so is service and a spirit of kindness. We must take good care of human relationships—the small ones as well as the larger ones—with which we are blessed during our short lives. This is precisely what life is about; we can say that life is lived according to the importance we give these relationships.

"My wife's role is to carefully nurture the various ties that hold these relationships together and to continue to water and fertilize them. My wife does all these things without appearing to consider them a burden. She treats everyone equally, regardless of social position or wealth. I definitely think an important role that Heaven expects a woman to fulfill is to bring nourishment to a hungry world, tranquillity amidst turbulence, and calm amidst harshness."

Chapter 29

Splitting Up

The trend toward party unity under the Fukuda–Ōhira leadership, together with the voters' growing desire for stability, demonstrated some definite merits not only in the Upper House election but in other elections, too. In 1977, there were two by-elections to replace vacant Upper House seats and seven elections of prefectural governors. In all these, LDP candidates were victorious. And in the Tokyo Metropolitan Assembly elections held on the same day as the Upper House election, the LDP and NLC together won fifteen additional seats to gain a majority, while the JSP (to which Tokyo Governor Minobe belonged) and JCP together lost fifteen seats and fell to minority status. In elections for city mayors, there was a noticeable trend for progressives to lose to conservatives. Thus, both Fukuda, as LDP president and prime minister, and Ōhira, as LDP secretary-general and likely candidate in the next presidential election, were continuing to establish their credentials with the public. Nevertheless, just at this period some ambiguous changes were taking place that touched the very core of the Fukuda–Ōhira collaboration.

First, there was talk of a Diet dissolution. Immediately after the LDP victory in the Upper House election, Prime Minister Fukuda had remarked, as if in jest, how nice it would be if there could later be "a general election directed by Fukuda." Then, in early August 1977, before his official visit to Southeast Asian countries, Fukuda asked Ōhira, "Won't you let me carry out a Diet dissolution?" The gist of Fukuda's reasoning went probably like this: even if the favorable results in the Upper House election had prevented a reversal and there were continuing LDP victories in local elections, the precarious balance in the more important Lower House remained. However, if a general election was carried out that took advantage of the swing toward the conservatives and the intraparty unity that had been fostered by the Fukuda–Ōhira cooperation, the LDP might expect to increase its Lower House strength by at least ten seats and, if things went really well, perhaps as many as fifteen seats, thus stabilizing the political landscape.

However, Ōhira indicated that he did not favor the prime minister's stance on a Diet dissolution. Just because the Lower House Budget Committee had an opposition party majority, it would not be proper to resort to the ultimate measure of a Diet dissolution at the mere pleasure of the LDP or in the absence of some popular new LDP policy initiative. In the eyes of the nation, a dissolution without a clear reason could hardly expect to receive widespread support. Besides, the LDP had scant funds for a new election campaign, having exhausted its resources in the recent Upper House election. The Lower House Diet members had been in office less than a year, following the hard-fought December 1976 general election at the end of a full four-year term, and Ōhira considered a dissolution under these circumstances too inconsiderate.

Ultimately, due to Ōhira's negative reaction, Fukuda's hopes for a dissolution never reached the stage of serious discussion. It may be surmised that Fukuda's interest in a dissolution was backed by a hope that, with a strong LDP victory in a general election, the Fukuda Administration would gain greater acceptance among the public and consequently the secret agreement with Ōhira for a change of administration after Fukuda had served two years would be weakened. Whatever Fukuda's own feelings, persons close to him generally took it for granted that he would serve two terms (that is, four years) or longer. It seems likely that Fukuda never communicated the purport of the secret agreement to his close associates. One of them later recalled: "I knew absolutely nothing about the secret pact. I subscribed to the theory that Fukuda would hand over the administration to Ōhira one year after reelection to the party presidency, and Ōhira would continue as prime minister for three years. But even this view was seen as heretical by most of those around him."

From around this time, public attention began to focus on the scheme—one of the main features of the so-called new-departure party reforms—for a preliminary election, by all party members and fraternity members of two top candidates for the LDP presidency. At the end of October 1977, LDP Election Committee Chairman Fukunaga Kenji announced details of the plan. Unless the selection of the party president was settled through negotiations, ballots for the preliminary election would be mailed to eligible voters one year later, on November 1, 1978, and votes would be opened and counted on November 27. This preliminary election would select two candidates for the party presidency, who would contest a final vote by Upper and Lower House LDP Diet members. However, at this point, nobody had a clear idea whether Fukuda and Ōhira would both enter the preliminary contest, or what the future of the Fukuda–Ōhira arrangement might be.

On almost every occasion, Fukuda spoke positively about the close Fukuda–Ōhira relationship, using phrases like "Fukuda–Ōhira unity" and "the Fukuda–Ōhira relationship is watertight." Ōhira, for his part, adopted the same tone and continued to deny the possibility of any power contest between the two. In a typical statement on the matter he said, "Ōhira and Fukuda will not contest power. In today's LDP there is no room for such a contest."

In mid-November, as the extraordinary Diet was nearing its final days and a full year had passed since the Fukuda Cabinet was formed, there suddenly arose the issue of cabinet and party personnel changes. The media watched carefully for hints regarding what the Fukuda–Ōhira relationship might be a year later. The main focus of the personnel reorganization was the post of chief cabinet secretary and the factional balance among the top three party posts next to the president. Ōhira had felt a personal closeness to the other top two party officers, namely, General Council Chairman Esaki Masumi and Policy Research Council Chairman Kōmoto Toshio, and was not enthusiastic about any change that would affect the good teamwork among them. Nevertheless, persons close to Prime Minister Fukuda had begun expressing a wish to see Nakasone serve in one of the posts. Ōhira felt that so long as Fukuda was going to serve a two-year term, this reorganization would be the last to be carried out during the Fukuda Administration, and so out of consideration for the Fukuda–Ōhira cooperation he was willing to respect Fukuda's wishes as far as possible. Thus, immediately after the end of the extraordinary Diet session, Fukuda and Ōhira reached agreement that a reorganization would, in fact, take place, and discussions were begun on the particulars.

From 10 A.M. on November 27, Ōhira and Fukuda met alone for four and a half hours at Fukuda's residence in the Nozawa district of Setagaya Ward to discuss personnel matters. Preliminary agreement was reached on making Nakasone LDP General Council chairman and shifting Esaki to chairman of the Policy Research Council, as well as on various cabinet changes. The new cabinet was announced without delay the next day, with no changes from what had been tentatively agreed on. Abe Shintarō was made chief cabinet secretary, a post in which he had indicated strong interest, and Sonoda Sunao was transferred from being chief cabinet secretary to the post of foreign minister. Murayama Tatsuo of the Ōhira faction became finance minister, and Kōmoto, who had been Policy Research Council chairman, became minister of international trade and industry. Miyazawa Kiichi was made director-general of the Economic Planning Agency. It was agreed at the same time that Funada Naka was the leadership's choice for party vice-president, to be confirmed at the party convention scheduled for January 1978.

The mass media failed to understand Ōhira's true thinking and tried to interpret the personnel changes only within the scheme of a supposed Fukuda–Ōhira rivalry, hypothesizing which points had been scored by Fukuda and what sorts of objections had been made by Ōhira. Nakasone's selection as General Council chairman was interpreted as a wedge driven by Fukuda into Ōhira's dominance over party affairs. Ōhira lamented: "Once something gets reported in the media, it takes on a life of its own as fact, even if it is not true. In this sense, historical facts are created by a mixture of reality and the way things get reported." As for the overall significance of these personnel changes: "Their major premise was a recognition of the Fukuda–Ōhira cooperation. The media has forgotten this point." The various factions were influenced by the media's conjectures of Fukuda–Ōhira rivalry, and competitive feelings began to increase. In the circumstances, it was perhaps only natural that the Fukuda faction should aim at reelecting Fukuda as party president and that the Ōhira faction should, in keeping with its long-held aspirations, hope for an early Ōhira-led government.

Politics tended to be divided into two streams, one that flowed on the surface and another underneath. The surface stream naturally focused on the election of the party president expected to take place in the autumn of 1978. The hidden one was the relationship between Fukuda and Ōhira, especially as it concerned their secret agreement. It may well be imagined that Fukuda, encouraged by friends and associates and by the sense of mission that people in power almost inevitably feel, was gradually coming to hope more strongly that he would be reelected; yet in so far as he was restricted by the secret agreement with Ōhira he could not publicly speak about a reelection or otherwise extend the period of his administration without Ōhira's consent. After all, Ōhira was carrying out his side of the gentlemen's agreement, and had respected Fukuda's wishes in the recent government reorganization, so Fukuda had no excuse to discard the agreement. Even if he should do so, and oppose Ōhira in an election, it seemed unlikely that he could win, given his disadvantage in faction size within the party. Thus, if Fukuda was to have another term as party president, he would have to approach Ōhira and gain his consent to altering their agreement, or else he could call a general election in the hope that he could increase the numbers of his faction, thereby strengthening his position and weakening the raison d'être of the secret agreement. The political situation was extremely complex, with the surface currents suggesting rivalry and hidden currents suggesting negotiations. These currents sometimes merged and sometimes kept strictly separate, but they never failed to influence each other.

The preliminary election for party president slated for the autumn of 1978 was to be such that voting rights would be given to all party members who had paid the nominal membership fees for at least fiscal 1977 and 1978, and to fraternity members who had paid their slightly higher dues for fiscal 1978. The deadline for completing the procedures for party membership for fiscal 1977 was set for January 31, 1978. At one time, many party members had doubted that the preliminary election for party president would actually take place, but when plans for the election were formally announced, the various factions began to think seriously about how they could gain adherents among new party members. At this time, a rather unsettled atmosphere prevailed as each of the factions eyed rival factions' activities with disfavor.

Meanwhile, the LDP's National Organization Committee, headed by Takeshita Noboru, went into action with the catch phrase, "You, too, can elect the party president," and the goal of achieving a party membership of 1 million. Because the LDP had previously had only about 400,000 members, this would mean an increase of two and a half times. Most people within the party looked on this campaign as being too ambitious and would have been satisfied if party membership rose to 500,000 or 600,000. Yet around the end of the year, all factions joined with renewed zeal in the membership campaign.

In the Ōhira faction, the management of intrafaction affairs had come to be the special domain of Suzuki Zenkō. He was an experienced politician who had on numerous occasions been behind the scenes in political infighting, and as one of the cosignatories of the secret agreement was well acquainted with its particulars. He was the perfect person to complement Ōhira's idealistic tendencies, and the fact that he was put in charge of coordinating the faction's affairs was indeed a big plus in preparing for an election to choose the next party president.

Almost every day, newspapers carried stories about political plans accompanying the new preliminary election campaign. The media were intrigued by emerging signs that General Council Chairman Nakasone and International Trade and Industry Minister Kōmoto would enter the race, and this eventuality seemed daily more probable to party members. Given the increasing interest in gaining new party members, the deadline for party enrollment was extended until the end of February. By January 14, 1978, party membership stood at 479,079, and according to National

Organization Committee Chairman Takeshita, it was "no dream to eventually have 1 million members."

In late January and in February, party headquarters received from the LDP prefectural federations 20,000 to 30,000 applications for membership daily, and by the end of February there were 1,331,000 party members and 181,000 fraternity members. Together with the 4,800 members of the National Political Association, who also enjoyed the right to vote in the preliminary election, this made a total of approximately 1,517,000 who could cast votes. Nearly 1 million new party members had enrolled in a period of a little over a month. Under these circumstances, nobody could know precisely how many of these votes were committed to a given faction and how many were "floating." It was therefore not possible to predict the outcome only on the basis of the numbers of party and fraternity members whose allegiances were definitely known.

On February 18, Secretary-General Ōhira went to his home town to attend a special convention of the LDP's Kagawa Prefectural Federation, which greeted him enthusiastically and passed a unanimous resolution "to make an Ōhira presidency a reality." The Kagawa Prefectural Federation's party membership campaign enrolled 37,000 new members, considerably more than its goal. Ōhira spoke before this gathering as follows: "The election of the party president is a great undertaking involving the destiny of the party. . . . More important than who becomes party president is the fact that the election is carried out fairly. As secretary-general, I am making every effort to this end." As for his own intentions, he stated: "I should like to decide my course of action when the time is ripe, judging what is best for the party and for society in general, and as a result of asking Heaven's guidance." Some newspapers greeted this with headlines such as "Ōhira Indicates Zeal [to be party president]," although the majority of headlines were more like "Ōhira Appears Troubled." This ambivalent impression surely mirrored Ōhira's own dilemma arising from his position of having to deal with some matters that could be publicly revealed and some that could not.

It was around this time that certain policy differences between Ōhira and Fukuda began to surface. The Fukuda Cabinet, in order to try to overcome the stagnation in the world economy, had proclaimed at the March 1977 U.S.–Japan talks (between Fukuda and newly elected President Carter) that Japan would maintain a growth rate of 7 percent so as to fulfill its responsibilities as one of three driving forces of the world economy. But in early 1978, the Japanese economy was still growing less vigorously than most would have liked, and the 7 percent figure naturally became an issue in compiling the fiscal 1978 budget. The question of whether or not it could be achieved was being debated within the government. Prime Minister Fukuda considered "the 7 percent figure as only an indication of a goal to strive for." Ōhira, however, in a speech before the Nikkeiren at a hotel in Tokyo on January 18, emphasized: "The U.S.–Japan negotiations came to a successful conclusion due to the fact that the government explicitly stated that it would achieve a 7 percent growth, and therefore we will have to honor our promise." The newspapers immediately took this up with reports that Ōhira "appears to have referred indirectly to the responsibility that would be borne by the government and by Prime Minister Fukuda if the 7 percent goal is not achieved." It is true that Ōhira's pursuit of this goal was more insistent and uncompromising than was usual for him, which the Fukuda camp interpreted as an Ōhira maneuver to weaken the administration. Thus, the gap between Ōhira and Fukuda widened.

The drama of budget revision in the 84th Ordinary Diet abetted this view. The opposition parties, emboldened by their achievement in obtaining a revision of over ¥700 billion in the last budget, were fierce. On February 17, a conference among those in charge of policy issues in the five opposition parties presented a unified demand for budget revision totaling ¥1.24 trillion. At a national conference of LDP youth and women's sections held at LDP headquarters on February 19, 1978, Ōhira suggested a flexible attitude on budget revision, saying: "So long as the opposition parties' demands, including those for a reduction in income taxes, are rational, we will deal with them in a realistic manner." But many in the government strongly opposed this stance, and those around the prime minister also began to show opposition to any budget revision. The main stage for intraparty opposition to revising the budget was the General Council, chaired by Nakasone. Those council members belonging to the Fukuda and Nakasone factions took the lead by unanimously attacking Secretary-General Ōhira and his associates who favored compromise. Fifty-six first- or second-term LDP Diet members signed a document opposing revision. Chief Cabinet Secretary Abe, representing the prime minister, let it be known that if the budget were revised there would be a Diet dissolution.

On February 22, the LDP Diet members rejected the opposition parties' unified demands for revision. As a result, between February 23 and 26, the Lower House Budget Committee was in limbo due to a boycott by opposition parties. The reason why Ōhira and his aides dared to adopt the attitude they did was seen as both a test of the degree of unity among the five opposition parties and an attempt to prevent LDP hard-liners from paralyzing Diet proceedings in their zeal to oppose a budget revision. From 7:20 P.M. on February 24, a meeting was held of LDP and opposition party secretaries-general. Matters were now critical. Ōhira explained the LDP's thinking, prefacing his remarks as follows: "I am going to explain in precise Japanese, so listen carefully."

In summary, his proposals were: (1) the government budget draft would be revised by only ¥340 billion, that is, an amount covering items on which the LDP and the opposition parties could agree, with this revision not to require a reformulation of the budget; and (2) the tax reduction and welfare increases demanded by the opposition would be finalized through negotiations within the relevant Diet committees. The results would be realized during consideration of a supplementary budget in an extraordinary Diet session in the autumn. Ōhira is said to have explained to the opposition: "You are saying, 'Go to the second floor,' but we cannot do so at this time. Once your [further] demands have been passed in the committees they can be realized later, so it's not a matter of not being able to go up. Therefore, strictly speaking, we are neither on the first floor nor on the second, but on the mezzanine floor." Among opposition party members there were many who appreciated the pains Ōhira had taken. Although his plan was opposed (on the surface, at least) by the JSP, Kōmeitō, DSP, and JCP, it was openly supported by the NLC.

The special session of the LDP General Council held the next day, the twenty-fifth, resolved that "the top three party officers shall support the basic original budget draft and attempt to see that revisions are made without departing from the main points emphasized in the budget draft." Under this rather vague framework, which gave the party leaders responsibility for overseeing the budget revision, the crisis had for all practical purposes been overcome. As a result, the budget for fiscal 1978 passed the Lower House on March 7, within the time limit for establishing the new budget before the March 31 end of the current fiscal year. It was evident that the difficulties encountered in this budget revision reflected a reoccurrence of factional infighting in the LDP.

The China–Japan Peace and Friendship Treaty, which had been pending ever since the normalization of diplomatic relations, similarly highlighted policy differences between Ōhira and Fukuda. It had been ascertained that the Chinese side was ready and the time was ripe, yet Fukuda took a cautious stance and aroused dissatisfaction among those in the party who wanted to expedite such a treaty. Thus, Japan–China relations were again a cause of intraparty dissension. As if to prod Prime Minister Fukuda over his slowness in moving ahead, on April 13 a fleet of over a hundred Chinese fishing boats suddenly entered Japanese waters near the Senkaku Islands in western Okinawa Prefecture. On April 21, China explained this as a chance occurrence during routine fishing operations in order that it should not interfere with the signing of the treaty. The incident nevertheless aroused public opinion in Japan, and within the LDP there was growing antagonism between the doves, who felt the situation had been invited by Fukuda's lack of leadership, and the hawks, who decried China's incursion into Japan's waters. At meetings of the LDP's General Council, Dietmen belonging to the Seirankai attacked Ōhira, who had been foreign minister at the time diplomatic relations were restored. Throughout these attacks, Fukuda took a passive stance. Later it was said that the infringement of territorial waters near the Senkaku Islands was instigated by factions within China opposed to a China–Japan treaty.

Another confrontation between the hawks and the doves in the LDP General Council was provided by the forced entry into the control tower at Narita Airport on March 26 by persons implacably opposed to appropriating more land for airport expansion. The doves favored a resolution through negotiations, and the hawks used the incident to clamor for a special law on public security.

Meanwhile, in preparing for an election in Kyoto to replace JSP Governor Ninagawa Torazō, who was retiring after twenty-eight years, the LDP proposed Hayashida Yukio, an Upper House Dietman from the Ōhira faction, as its candidate to capture the governorship from the opposition. At first, Ohira was unhappy at the prospect of losing Hayashida's seat in the Upper House, where the LDP barely held a majority, but Hayashida's candidacy was nevertheless finalized, helped by the support of Maeo Shigesaburō, who was from Kyoto. With the support of both Ōhira and Maeo, Hayashida won the April 9 election, compounding the loss of opposition control of local governments that had started the previous year.

These trends only bolstered Fukuda's desire to dissolve the Diet, but should he go ahead with a dissolution at the likely expense of an open break with Ōhira, or should he bank on negotiations adhering to the spirit of the secret Ōhira–Fukuda agreement? It was when he was at this political crossroads that Fukuda departed for a visit to the United States on April 30. Stopping over in Honolulu on his way home on May 5, he spoke to accompanying reporters about the political situation, and his words had considerable repercussions within the party, especially for the Ōhira camp.

The prime minister stated: "The Ōhira–Fukuda system is airtight. Both the secretary-general and I are agreed that the most important aspect of Japanese politics is to avoid a confrontation between us. It will be best to wait until the autumn to decide how we will approach the choice of the next party president. When that time comes, Ōhira and I will probably handle the matter after consultations." While this statement seemed to support a meeting of minds, the fact that Fukuda subsequently seemed to go out of his way to state that there was likely to be an extraordinary Diet session "after August" was interpreted as showing an intention to dissolve the Diet before autumn.

As a result of Fukuda's remarks, Ōhira supporters openly adopted a dual strategy of keeping up hope for a negotiated transfer of power while raising the prospect of an Ōhira candidacy in a party election. On May 10, the Ōhira faction leaders held a joint meeting with the *Suiyōkai* (Wednesday Club), a study group composed of younger members of the faction. This meeting both opposed a Diet dissolution and passed a resolution to support Ōhira in a party election.

On May 25, Ōhira delivered a lecture at Tokyo's Imperial Hotel, which was reported as his announcement of running in the presidential election. Fukuda talked things over with Ōhira, and two days later in Nagoya, where both had gone for the same speaking engagement, he announced that as a result of their talk "the question of a party election is being frozen until the autumn, and for the time being we must put all our efforts into managing the current political situation." Ōhira then publicly expressed his "same feeling," and thus a sort of political truce was effected.

However, with the ordinary Diet session coming to an end, the factions began to maneuver more actively, and rumors of a Diet dissolution were increasingly heard from the Fukuda camp. In early June, several exasperated LDP Diet members launched a campaign to collect signatures opposing a dissolution without a just cause. This movement spread quickly to the so-called middle-of-the-road factions, and eventually it collected the signatures of 70 percent to 80 percent of Lower House LDP Diet members. Fukuda and his faction were, of course, greatly concerned lest the signature campaign against dissolution turn into an anti-Fukuda movement. If the majority within the party should turn against Fukuda, hope would diminish not only for a dissolution but for a continuation of the Fukuda Administration. It was no longer possible to talk about a dissolution except with the utmost caution.

On June 16, the 84th Ordinary Diet ended its extended 180-day session. At noon that day, Ōhira addressed a meeting of LDP legislators in the Diet: "The prime minister, who has the power to dissolve the Diet, has clearly stated that he does not at present intend to do so and that he does not have the latitude to do so. It is the duty of the party to trust this statement, to work together with the cabinet to stabilize the political situation, and to concern itself with furthering policy objectives." He went on: "The party must adopt thorough and decisive measures to assist the government with economic recovery and the handling of diplomatic matters. At the same time it must, in the basic spirit of the party reforms, creditably carry out the election for party president scheduled for the autumn. I hope that it will work with diligence, self-confidence, and a sense of normalcy to expand the party's strength and to redefine policy."

Ōhira's choice of the word "normalcy" (heijōshin) was meant to clearly guarantee to LDP Lower House members that there would be no dissolution, and many of the latter were quick to voice feelings of relief. Afterward, when Ōhira paid a courtesy call, customary at the end of a Diet session, on Lower House Speaker Hori at his Official Residence, Hori is said to have remarked: "As secretary-general you have left absolutely no stone unturned in assisting the prime minister. I have been greatly impressed."

The next day, June 17, talks were held between Fukuda and Ōhira, and it was formally agreed that the two would impose a freeze on any incipient movements aimed at promoting either of their candidacies in the presidential election. From then until October, over ten formal and informal talks were held between them. Those who were unaware of the secret agreement felt it strange that there were such frequent meetings between the LDP president and secretary-general. The distance between the surface and the hidden currents was growing.

During the political truce, Ōhira had regarded the autumn party presidential election with the assumption that Fukuda would honor his pledge and withdraw from the race. As for Fukuda, his state of mind seemed to vacillate between running and not running in the election. In his talks with Ōhira during this period, Fukuda made some remarks that would suggest he intended to let Ōhira become party president at the end of his two-year term. For instance, he once stated, "I'll leave you to take care of the summit next year," and at another point, "I'll be one of those endorsing you for the presidential election." However, later he began to hint that he wanted to have his period in office extended somewhat, with remarks such as, "I wonder if there isn't some other way. Can't you think about it?" On repeated occasions he said, "I want to preside over a general election, and hand the administration over to you after the political situation has stabilized."

The political truce had always been rather vague, and it seemed to come to an end on July 19, when Prime Minister Fukuda stated in Brussels, on his way home from the Bonn Summit, "At next year's Tokyo Summit, I hope to perform the duties of the host nation." This was interpreted as a declaration of intent to run in the presidential election, and it generated a new wave of excitement in Japan's political arena. As if in response to Fukuda's remarks in Brussels, Ōhira on July 22 began an address before the LDP's Kagawa Prefectural Federation as follows: "When the time comes I will announce my decision to be a candidate, and I should like to consult all of you. . . . I was born in Sanuki [the pre-Meiji name for Kagawa], grew up in Sanuki, and feel I must die in Sanuki. I like to think that whatever my success, it is due to all of you here in Sanuki." On July 23, LDP General Council Chairman Nakasone indicated his intention of running in the presidential election, and on July 30 Kōmoto Toshio, minister of international trade and industry, announced that he, too, would be a candidate. Thus, by the end of July, the public assumed that it would be a four-way race including Fukuda. The factions, which were supposed to have been dissolved the previous year, had publicly resumed their activities, and on the surface, at least, the political truce had ended.

In the meantime, Prime Minister Fukuda, in response to requests by Zhang Xiangshan, vice secretary-general of the China–Japan Friendship Association, agreed on August 6 that Foreign Minister Sonoda would go to China to conclude a China–Japan Peace and Friendship Treaty, and this was signed soon after in Beijing on August 12. That evening, as he watched the television news in the first-floor smoking room of the Prime Minister's Official Residence, Prime Minister Fukuda looked happy. Ōhira, who had been asked to join him, sat in silence, his gaze as much on the prime minister as on the television screen. The signing of the China–Japan Peace and Friendship Treaty was welcomed by all the parties and positively received by most of the nation. The media announced that "the prime minister is confident of reelection," and members of the Fukuda faction were encouraged by the favorable nationwide response. Fukuda had not necessarily been an enthusiastic promoter of the treaty, so it was ironic that its signing during his term in office seems to have added to his popularity. In a public opinion poll conducted by the *Yomiuri Shinbun*, the approval rate of the Fukuda Cabinet, which had only been 20 percent in the spring of 1978, rose to 27 percent in September.

The truce between Ōhira and Fukuda had brought an unexpected political result. As a positive evaluation of what appeared to be a stable Fukuda–Ōhira leadership mounted within the party, more and more party members came to feel that there was no need to change the setup and to hope that the next presidency might be arranged by negotiations between the two men. Moreover, the economic doldrums following the oil crisis had bottomed out and some bright signs were appearing. Compared to the time the political truce was begun at the end of May, the situation was starting to develop in a way that seemed advantageous to Fukuda's reelection. On August 22, the LDP's second National Summer Study Meeting was opened at Hakone. Noting the trend toward more lively discussions on national defense, Ōhira emphasized to the participants the need for a "politics that does not lose its balance." General Council Chairman Nakasone adopted a somewhat adversarial position, calling for "the establishment of the nation's authority." Fukuda, in his remarks before the group, noted that "the fate of the party depends on the party presidential election," which was interpreted as showing he intended to continue to head the administration.

Tanaka Kakuei, who had retreated into the political background following the Lockheed Incident, understood Ōhira's state of mind from their long association, and in August requested a secret meeting with Ōhira. At Ōhira's request, this meeting was held at the Shinanomachi residence of the late Ikeda Hayato, who could be called both men's political mentor. Ōhira told Tanaka about his conversations with Fukuda, and Tanaka exclaimed, "You've been putting too much faith in a check that can never be cashed." Tanaka had decided that Fukuda was absolutely certain to run in an election, and he showed Ōhira the results of his own calculations for the most likely vote-counts in both a preliminary and a final election. According to Tanaka's estimates, Ōhira could not come out in first place in a preliminary election, but in a final election he could win a majority of the votes cast by the 380 LDP Diet members of both houses. This analysis tallied with Ōhira's own estimates.

Tanaka reiterated his belief that if in the preliminary election Ōhira fell behind Fukuda by only a small margin, he would definitely win the final election. He is said to have encouraged Ōhira to begin preparations for a serious election campaign by October 10 at the latest, taking into consideration the fact that the preliminary election campaign was to begin officially on November 1. On returning from the Ikeda residence, Ōhira confided to associates, "Today I was scolded by Kakuei." Around the time of his talk with Tanaka, he also talked with Lower House Speaker Hori, who was deeply concerned about the situation within the party.

The deadline for paying party membership dues for fiscal 1978 was the end of August, by which time it was clear that there would be a combined total of over 1.5 million party members and fraternity members eligible to vote in an election. When Ōhira had agreed to let Fukuda hold the presidency first, he had said, "Shouldn't we talk about [things] again when two years have passed?" That time was now only a couple of months away. When registration of eligible voters was completed at the end of August, the mass media tried various ways of gauging the choices of the 1.5 million voters. A number of public opinion polls were carried out, and these all indicated that Fukuda, whose cabinet was receiving higher public ratings than a few months previously, held the advantage. Given these circumstances, Fukuda's attitude in his talks with Ōhira also began to change in subtle ways.

Several staff members at Kōchikai headquarters began pushing for preparations for an election, but Ōhira admonished them, saying, "Don't exert yourselves so." He thus put a damper on any moves by his own faction to take sudden initiatives that could stimulate Fukuda supporters, but he stated, "When November comes, the situation may change." Even at this point, Ōhira still had hopes that the secret agreement between Fukuda and himself would be upheld. However, after the beginning of September, most of the views Ōhira heard from those around him cautioned, "It's naive to think the presidency will come about through negotiations," or, "It won't do to be deceived by the other side." Ōhira obstinately refuted such views and at times even showed a trace of anger. To get the other party to respect the gentlemen's agreement entered into two years before, there was no choice but to honor its spirit and to do one's best to live up to it. However, such an approach now seemed to strengthen the other side's resolve to ignore the agreement. Ordinarily easygoing and ready to respond to taunts or criticism with a laugh or a smile, Ōhira must surely have had a lot on his mind to betray this sort of irritation.

The words that he confided to an old schoolmate who visited him around this time give an insight into his frame of mind: "I, too, entered an unexpected walk of life, and fortunately have been given the chance to do various things. I think that in the future there is only one other job I should do. It is not necessarily something that I am myself seeking; it is something I will do because I am asked by everyone to do it. If they tell me, 'Don't do it,' I'll give up. But if I should do it, I don't want to expose ugly and doddering aspects like some older colleagues. If I am asked to do it, I want to summon all my stamina and courage and go all-out to achieve something worthwhile, regardless of my own interests and without having to be bothered by vested party interests. If I cannot be given that opportunity, I would prefer to resign from public office. Luckily the children have all grown up, and my wife and I are in such a position that we will not starve in our old age. I am thinking about retiring because there is still another road I'd like to take. The decision about which road to take will come, I think, around the end of this year. Therefore, this is the most decisive year in my life." Around this time, Ōhira told several persons, "There have been people like Komura Jutarō, Mutsu Munemitsu, and Saigō Takamori, who did excellent work and made their mark on history even though they did not become prime ministers. For a statesman, it is not so much a matter of what one becomes but what one achieves."

Shintai wa ten ni toi, eijoku wa mei ni shitagau (Consult Heaven on advancing or retreating, follow fate on success or failure): these were words that Ōhira always recalled whenever he stood at a crossroads. He had voiced them when he entered his first party presidential race in 1972, and he had recently done so again before his supporters back home in Kagawa Prefecture. The words surely expressed some innermost feelings as he approached what would be a momentous decision toward the end of 1978.

The 85th Extraordinary Diet was convened on September 18, 1978. The biggest item pending was the supplementary budget, which would have to take account of those matters agreed upon among the political parties at the time of the spring budget revision the previous March. Until this time, in an environment that public opinion polls showed was turning in Fukuda's favor, Fukuda had stopped indicating that he might force a Diet dissolution, but it is said that those around him, expecting that the extraordinary Diet would have rough going on the supplementary budget issue, were making provisional plans for a dissolution at the start of the Diet session. While aware of this danger, Ōhira tried to have the agreements he had reached with the opposition parties in formulating the original budget reflected in the supplementary budget.

At the beginning of the extraordinary Diet session, the JSP, Kōmeitō, and DSP placed their demand for a ¥1 trillion tax reduction, revealing that they were going to submit to the Lower House Budget Committee a motion to reformulate the supplementary budget. However, in the NLC, there was a positive evaluation of the Ōhira-led negotiations, and the inclination to take the realistic position that more could be done to promote its interests by extracting concessions through negotiations with the LDP than by a confrontational stance in cooperation with the opposition parties. In talks with the NLC's Secretary-General Nishioka, Ōhira sought ways toward a compromise. Given this situation, the aim of the JSP, Kōmeitō, and DSP was more to deflect the negotiations between the LDP and NLC in directions that would be advantageous to themselves than to pass a motion to reformulate the supplementary budget bill. They, of course, realized that in the unlikely event such a motion was passed it would only give the Fukuda Cabinet an excuse for dissolving the Diet.

As part of its strategy to extract the maximum concessions from the LDP, the NLC had hinted at a strong policy whereby, "If the LDP does not accede to our demands, we will have no choice but to agree to a JSP-Kōmeitō-DSP motion for reformulation." But in the end, the NLC drew a line between itself and the three opposition parties, definitely opposing any such motion, and the government's supplementary budget bill was passed with the approval of the LDP and the NLC. A tense situation had been overcome thanks to Secretary-General Ōhira's skillful maneuvers, and the possibility of a dissolution was almost completely eliminated.

From the end of September to the first days of October, around a month before the official start of the party presidential campaign on November 1, the Kōchikai's secretarial staff and Diet members made every effort to analyze available information, although unaware of much of Ōhira's own thinking or the progress of his talks with Fukuda.

The preliminary election, which was to select two candidates for final election by LDP Diet members, was to be carried out under an untried points system. Each prefecture was assigned a certain number of "points" (*mochiten*), one point per thousand eligible voters, or a fraction thereof. Hokkaidō, for example, with 59,664 eligible voters, was assigned 60 points. The total points for each prefecture were to be distributed between the two top vote-winners in the ratio of these candidates' relative strength. In a given prefecture, candidates ranking third or below were to be disregarded in the point allocation. The total number of prefectural points would determine the top two candidates nationwide.

Before the election, Tanaka said: "If in the preliminary election Ōhira can keep within 100 points of Fukuda, I'm sure he can make a turnaround in the final election. But such a turnaround will be difficult if the margin is over 100." Around this time, most of the mass media tended to interpret the results of various surveys as indicating that, of the 1,525 points nationwide, Fukuda would win 700 to 800, Ōhira 400 to 500, Nakasone 200 to 300, and Kōmoto under 100. Moreover, media opinion held that Fukuda's votes were on the rise while Ōhira's were falling, in part because of stiff competition from a rapidly advancing Nakasone.

For the Ōhira camp, the biggest issue was still why, with over twice the number of Diet members supporting Ōhira, Fukuda was expected to win by such a large margin in the preliminary election. In analyzing the surveys, the Ōhira camp concluded that in Tokyo and almost all other prefectures, most eligible voters recognized the positive results of the Fukuda–Ōhira leadership and that this generally translated into support for Fukuda as the incumbent party president. Thus, so long as voters continued to support this arrangement, Ōhira could not expect to win in the preliminary election. Ōhira's supporters nonetheless urged him to press ahead with election preparations as soon as possible if both he and Fukuda were going to run.

Although Fukuda was said to enjoy an overwhelming advantage, his supporters were irritated that, despite the closeness of the start of the campaign period, Fukuda had still not issued any campaign directions for the preliminary election. He had, in fact, perhaps not yet reached a final decision to scrap his secret agreement with Ōhira. His close advisers interpreted this delay as meaning there would "probably be, before the preliminary election, negotiations to unify party support behind Fukuda."

In the preliminary election, eligible voters were to mark a circle above the name of the candidate of their choice and dispatch their ballots by mail. The blank ballots would be mailed from LDP headquarters to the LDP prefectural federations, which, in turn, would mail them to all eligible voters. Considering that the mailing of the ballots to individual voters would begin on November 1, the official start of the campaign, they might not all reach the voters' hands until November 5 or 6. The voting period, specified as twenty days, would begin on November 7, and all ballots reaching the prefectural federations by November 26 (the day before returned ballots were to be opened) would be valid. In the twenty-day period during which ballots could be returned, each candidate would be allowed up to fifteen speeches in any prefecture. Thus, it was an unusual system in which voting and campaigning would proceed concurrently. The fact that Tanaka had told Ōhira he should go into action by October 10 at the latest had taken into consideration his estimate that the peak of the balloting would be around November 10, and that a month of intense effort would be needed to insure that his campaign reached party and fraternity members throughout the country.

The October 10 issue of the *Yomiuri Shinbun* announced estimates, based on a survey of 15,000 party members, that Fukuda would win 900 points, Ōhira 370, Nakasone 229, and Kōmoto 29. Analyzing these estimates, the Ōhira camp concluded that if 90 percent of Ōhira-faction party members and 80 percent of Tanaka-faction members could consolidate behind Ōhira, Ōhira could compete in a meaningful way with Fukuda. On October 12, Suzuki Zenkō, Saitō Kunikichi, and Sasaki Yoshitake, all Kōchikai staff members, consulted with Ōhira at his home to confirm campaign plans. It was decided that Kōchikai members should return to their home electoral districts to work in the preliminary presidential campaign. However, Ōhira still did not announce his candidacy in the election.

On October 13, Ōhira asked some of his associates, "What do you think about the phrase, 'An end of the Fukuda–Ōhira leadership and a consolidation of new political forces'?" At first glance this seemed rather bold, but because it did not completely negate the Ōhira–Fukuda relationship, many of Ōhira's associates thought it too moderate. For the time being, however, they set to work on composing a declaration for the end to the current setup along lines advocated by Ōhira. This declaration was to be made public on October 14 at a press conference after a political and economic culture party in Tokushima, Shikoku.

On the night of October 13, LDP General Council Chairman Nakasone, who was being watched as a likely runner in the presidential election, requested a secret meeting with Ōhira, which took place for about an hour and twenty minutes from 8 P.M. in a room in the Hotel Ōkura. After this conversation, Ōhira told friends: "Nakasone said he wanted me to tell him whether there was a secret agreement between me and Fukuda. I told him that no such agreement existed and that once the election was over, I hoped, given the lack of talented members in the party, he and I could cooperate in holding appropriate posts." Afterward, Nakasone remarked of this conversation: "Ōhira explained in sequence the content of his conversations with Fukuda since around July, and said that he had become upset over the way Fukuda's tone had gradually changed." It may be surmised that Nakasone wanted some assurance from Ōhira because he feared that if there was a secret agreement between Ōhira and Fukuda, his announcing his candidacy would be meaningless.

In his Tokushima press conference of October 14, Ōhira first of all emphasized: "Under the Fukuda–Ōhira leadership, we have fought successfully in the Upper House election and promoted party reform. We have dealt reliably with pending issues of domestic politics and foreign relations and have fulfilled our responsibilities." However, he went on: "With the emergence of a new political setup in the coming election, the Fukuda–Ōhira collaboration will have been brought to a fine conclusion." At the same time, he expressed his view that the political truce would end its role with the closing of the extraordinary Diet session.

On October 20, the last day of the extraordinary Diet, Ōhira visited Prime Minister Fukuda at his Nozawa residence around 8 P.M.. During talks lasting an hour and twenty minutes, Ōhira stated his position as having no choice but to run as a candidate. He then asked Fukuda to understand that he wanted to attend the general meetings of both the Kōchikai and the Tanaka faction, which were to be held the next morning, and to say a few words of greeting at each. Even at this late date, Ōhira seems to have expected that he would hear Fukuda say that he would not run. However, Fukuda pointed out that for the sake of LDP stability a relationship of trust between the two was still necessary, and though he accepted Ōhira's declaration to run in the coming election he said nothing about whether he would do the same.

Fukuda did state that he wanted Ōhira to trust him, and then added two requests. The first had to do with guidelines on expressing policy views. Both men agreed that "if [policy views] become too specific, a situation may arise whereby one becomes trapped in them; thus, policy views and arguments should be restricted to a level that will give voters some idea of a candidate's personality and thinking, while specific judgments on such matters will be left to the Party Headquarters of the Presidential Election Control Committee." The other request was that Ōhira refrain from appearing at the general meeting of the Tanaka faction. On this point, too, Ōhira gave his consent, although is not clear what the nuances of the exchange were. Yet, in spite of these conditions, which were definitely disadvantageous to Ōhira's election campaign, the fact that Ōhira accepted them leads us to surmise that there may have been some specific statement from Fukuda that sufficed to raise Ōhira's expectations.

After a press conference at the headquarters of the Hirakawa Club (the press club of reporters exclusively covering the LDP) on the evening of October 20, Ōhira told Suzuki Zenkō, who was waiting alone in Kōchikai headquarters to hear the outcome of the talks with Fukuda, that he wanted Suzuki to appear in his stead at the next day's general meeting of the Tanaka faction. Ordinarily gracious and easygoing, on this occasion Suzuki firmly declined with the words: "Are you still saying such things? It won't be any good unless you appear at the Tanaka faction's general meeting." Ōhira had no choice but to go along. Late that night he telephoned Fukuda's private residence and asked for the latter's understanding.

As for his other promise to Fukuda concerning public statements on policy, Ōhira himself wrote and showed Kōchikai members a draft on policy statements that was wholly in accord with his agreement with Fukuda. If it was not a statement of policy, neither was it an appeal aiming at the posts of party president and prime minister. It was nothing more than a general statement of his thinking and the fact that he had no choice but to run in the election. On seeing it, Ogawa Heiji and others on the Kōchikai Policy Committee were upset, wondering if Ōhira was really ready to put up a fight.

Briefly stated, although both the Ōhira and Fukuda camps had set off on the road to a face-off in the presidential election, neither appeared to have really left the stage of initial hesitancy. After accepting a resolution for his nomination at the Kōchikai general meeting held on the morning of October 21 at the Hotel Ōkura, Ōhira responded to questions from the press in ways that seemed purposely designed to ward off overzealousness.

"What are your hopes as you approach this election?"

"This election represents the first step in regenerating the party, and through it we will establish an authoritative leadership. To do this, an appropriate election strategy must be displayed. However, because it is something within the party, I recognize that there are limitations. I intend to maintain party unity and basic mutual trust, and I intend to ask for the voters' understanding within [general] policy framework, while indicating to the maximum extent my own policies."

"Will this election become a contest between yourself and Fukuda?"

"I don't especially like the nuance of the word 'contest,' but there is only one leader, and not more than one. Who to select is up to the voters. Won't it be all right to simply leave it to their judgment? Rather than a contest, isn't it a matter of vying for the voters' approval? It has nothing to do with mutual trust, and it mustn't have."

"How about the differences between yourself and Fukuda?"

"It is not Fukuda I am challenging but the LDP leadership. The [party president's] term is over, so all candidates are standing at the same starting line. I don't consider this to be challenging Fukuda. Our personalities are different. It is not easy to be asked just how they differ. All of you are well aware of this. If Fukuda is a candidate, we will engage in a fair competition, and it is only proper that we should reveal our personalities clearly. We will have the voters make a fair judgment." These statements were, of course, only too faithful to Fukuda's request of the previous day.

In the meanwhile, Fukuda, now fully aware of Ōhira's intention to run in the election, seems to have been uncertain how to cope with it. On the day after his talk with Ōhira, Fukuda invited his close friend Shiokawa Masujurō to his Nozawa home, saying: "Since Ōhira came, there will have to be an election. He is taking quite a definite position. I'm really at a loss." Nevertheless, Fukuda did not give Shiokawa any instructions regarding the upcoming campaign.

Three days later, on the morning of October 24, there was a phone call at Ōhira's residence. A maid answered it and learned that it was Prime Minister Fukuda on the line. Ōhira, who had been chatting with reporters, changed his expression a bit as he went to the phone. The conversation lasted less than a minute, but by the time Ōhira returned to his seat his face was pale. When the reporters asked who had called, Ōhira declined to answer, but after some time said: "Although I have a certain weakness that comes from a shyness I can't seem to get rid of, I am attracted by Yoshida's strength in not compromising." After leaving the reporters with these enigmatic words, he briskly got up and went into another room. From that day until the end of the election, Ōhira's living room displayed a *shikishi* with these characters written by Yoshida Shigeru: *Zensha wa fuben, bensha wa fuzen* (The virtuous speak little; those who speak much lack virtue).

With the establishment of the Fukuda–Ōhira leadership, Fukuda had undoubtedly become gradually more interested in the idea of a second term; yet he was always aware that the secret agreement with Ōhira restricted his freedom in this regard. As to why he ultimately broke the agreement, it may be easy to point to problems of trust, but we may propose three more fundamental reasons. The first has to do with the character of the secret agreement itself. As already mentioned, the agreement promising the transfer of the party presidency to Ōhira after Fukuda had served a single two-year term constituted an essentially private arrangement about the dispensation of political power. This part of the agreement was oral, and as such nobody could publicly object if it was not upheld. Ōhira was well aware of this from the outset. In Japan's postwar political history, there had indeed been well-known examples of promises (even in writing) concerning the transfer of political power that were later worth nothing. Although Ōhira might have hoped that the agreement would be honored so long as he did his best to merit Fukuda's trust, the fact that this crucial part was not put in writing can be seen as gradually strengthening Fukuda's interpretation of the agreement in ways that would favor his hope for reelection.

Second, virtually none of Fukuda's close associates knew about the secret agreement. On the other hand, Ōhira, who had "yielded" the party presidency to Fukuda, had needed to let his faction members know, in some way of other, about the gist of the agreement to gain their acceptance. Fukuda, though, had no comparable need to do so, and this accounts for the fact that, from the early days of the Fukuda–Ōhira leadership Fukuda supporters expected him to serve two full two-year terms or at least three years, before letting Ōhira have the presidency. It also accounted for the appearance of movements within the Fukuda faction that wanted to try to solidify Fukuda's chances of reelection through a Diet dissolution and general election. If Fukuda had been determined to adhere strictly to the spirit of the agreement, he would have tried to stop such movements; yet his wish for reelection only propelled him to welcome them. However, Fukuda could not choose the path of reelection without the consent of Ōhira, who was the other pillar in the Fukuda–Ōhira system. This consideration was part of the reason behind the more than ten talks between Fukuda and Ōhira following their political truce.

The third reason concerns the specifics of what was discussed at these meetings. The specifics are only suppositions, but no doubt both men shared an awareness that a break between them would give rise to a serious situation for the party and for the government of the nation. Fukuda had often said, "It would be terrible if Fukuda and Ōhira fought." This was no doubt not only what he honestly felt but also what Ōhira felt. However, this shared awareness may, in fact, have impeded frank communication between the two. In such cases where communication is faulty, the political world often makes use of a mediator. Between Fukuda and Ōhira, such a mediator indeed existed. However, it seems clear that the reason even this mediator did not succeed was due to the fact that both Ōhira and Fukuda misunderstood the other's ultimate intentions until just before the election was to be officially announced.

Two days after Ōhira received the telephone call from Fukuda, Fukuda entrusted his closest colleague to request a meeting with Ōhira and to relay to one of Ōhira's secretaries a note reading, "I was very impolite to Ōhira. By all means I want to meet with him and talk." However, Ōhira rejected the proposal, saying, "At this point is there any more need for me to meet with Fukuda?" Having rejected further talks, Ōhira no longer had any of the hesitancy he had shown earlier. The answer that he had gotten from "consulting Heaven" was to fight with all his strength. In this way, the last slender bond tying Ōhira to Fukuda was removed.

Chapter 30

The Decisive Battle

With Prime Minister Fukuda's entry into the race for the party presidency, the election became a four-way affair among Fukuda, Ōhira, Nakasone, and Kōmoto. Suzuki Zenkō and his group in charge of campaign strategy for the Ōhira faction immediately sent appeals for help to Diet members and members of local governments who belonged to the faction. They also mobilized their secretaries and the staff of their own support groups in seeking the help of party and fraternity members who had pledged allegiance to the Ōhira faction to persuade still-uncommitted voters to vote for Ōhira.

Those faction leaders in charge of policy matters publicized some specific basic policies that Ōhira had until the last not elaborated out of deference to Prime Minister Fukuda. These policies can be summarized around three main points. The first was a Comprehensive Security Strategy (*Sōgō anzen hoshō senryaku*), which incorporated much of the thinking Ōhira had propounded over the years on the maintenance of peace. The second was the Garden-City Concept (*Den'en toshi kensetsu no keikaku*, literally, "Plan for Building Garden-Cities"), which he had first proposed in the LDP presidential election in 1972, when he had referred to "a nation of garden-cities" (*den'en toshi kokka*). The third was the Concept of Strengthening the Family Base (*Katei kiban jūjitsu*), aimed at building a society with an enhanced purpose in life. All that remained was the timing of the announcement. In Kyoto, on October 26, on his way to give a speech in support of the LDP candidate for governor of Hyōgo Prefecture, Ōhira explained his Garden-City Concept, and two days later, in a speech before the Japan National Press Club, he announced the Strengthening the Family Base Concept.

Asked in an NTV (Nihon Television) interview on October 30 about rumors of a secret agreement with Fukuda, Ōhira replied: "The conferring or receiving of political power is not something that should be done by

428

private arrangement. Both Fukuda and I like to think that our cooperation was unconditional, and, therefore, I think there is no value in pursuing such a rumor. Even if such an agreement did exist but was not upheld, it would not pose any problem." His attitude was thus one of not being bound by events that had already passed.

November 1 was the day set for the official start of the preliminary election campaign for LDP president. At a press conference following his submission of documents for filing his candidacy, Ōhira stated: "It is a great honor for me to run in this election, which will have much to do with the rebirth of the Liberal Democratic Party, the planning and preparation of which I myself am responsible. It is an extremely emotional honor. . . . I presume it will be a fair fight and hope it will open the road to party regeneration." After this interview, he went to Aoyama Cemetery to pay his respects at the graves of former prime ministers Ikeda and Yoshida.

At 1 P.M. on November 1, a rally was held in the Hotel New Ōtani to support Ōhira's candidacy for party president, planned by the Ōhira and Tanaka factions. In front of the hotel his supporters carried banners that read, "Let's realize the wish of the people of Kagawa Prefecture: An Ōhira Cabinet." The hall where the event took place was crammed with over 7,000 participants. After initial greetings by Suzuki Zenkō on behalf of the Nomination Headquarters for the Candidacy of Ōhira Masayoshi for Party President, Nishimura Eiichi, a veteran of the Tanaka faction, expressed his faction's support, saying, "We are determined to fight as if you were one of our own." Nikkeiren Chairman Sakurada Takeshi offered these words of encouragement, "In another 3,000 or 4,000 days I will depart for the other world. Please let me be able to say to Ikeda when I meet him that 'Ōhira was even greater than you.' " Ōhira responded, "I am grateful to be so honored by this opportunity. I will make every effort to fight to the last." It was evident to all that Ōhira had discarded all his former hesitancy and was now eager for the fray. After the rally, Ōhira paid a courtesy call on Lower House Speaker Hori, whom Fukuda had visited that same morning. Hori was critical of Fukuda when he told Ōhira, "I feel responsible for what happened two years ago. These ears have not forgotten what they heard."

The deadline for filing candidacies was November 4, and on that day it was decided after drawing lots that subsequent mention of the candidates would be in the following order: Fukuda Takeo, Nakasone Yasuhiro, Kōmoto Toshio, Ōhira Masayoshi. The atmosphere at this drawing was somewhat tense, as the order of names was believed to subtly affect a candidate's fortunes. On the same afternoon, in a press conference given by the four candidates, both Nakasone and Fukuda argued for establishing a law on emergency national defense contingencies (yūji rippō), but they were countered by Ōhira who argued for his Comprehensive Security Strategy, saying, "I don't think Japan's security can be upheld unless we adopt this soon." As for revising the Constitution, he stated his opposition, saying, "The people are not ready for it." After several days of media interviews, Ōhira finally set off on a nationwide speaking tour.

The scheduling of this tour was not easy and taxed the skills of the campaign staffs. As explained in the previous chapter, in the preliminary election the electoral points in each prefecture were to be distributed only between the first two vote-winners, with candidates in third or fourth place disregarded. Campaign strategy, therefore, needed to distinguish between prefectures with large numbers of eligible voters, where it was absolutely essential to come at least second, and other prefectures where points could be sacrificed if necessary. The Ōhira camp set up a speaking schedule in accordance with strategies worked out some time in advance, in which the first speech would be given in the city of Kōfu in Yamanashi Prefecture. It was especially important to keep a tight grip on this, the home prefecture of Kanemaru Shin, who was a member of the Tanaka faction but was close to Prime Minister Fukuda.

In his Kōfu speech, Ōhira referred to some of his basic beliefs, stating: "We have come to a stage where politics cannot be conducted merely by always telling people they must move forward. We must plan a bold transition from an era of quantitative expansion with high economic growth, such as we have had up to now, to an era of qualitative improvements." He continued, "I am no genius, and neither am I a 'go-getter' type of politician, but I believe in sticking to the road of honesty and working hard at it." Beginning with this speech in Kōfu, Ōhira traveled a total of 18,000 kilometers during the election period and addressed over 50,000 voters.

In the early days of the preliminary election campaign, the media and public opinion polls predicted that Ōhira would trail Fukuda by a large margin. However, as LDP Diet members returned to their constituencies and came into direct contact with local party and fraternity members, they found that most of them were maintaining a cautious attitude, waiting until they had taken a good look at the personalities and policies of the various candidates. It was estimated that voters in this category constituted almost half the total, which was more than expected. This was very encouraging to the Ōhira camp. Meanwhile, the Fukuda camp, relying on earlier estimates of an overwhelming victory, adopted the attitude that Fukuda was already home and dry. It was fully confident of victory, and its tactics amounted to little more than taking advantage of this mood, which was reflected in such slogans as "The World's Fukuda" and "From Every Corner of the Nation, Voices Are Saying Fukuda Must Make His Stand."

After some days, the steadfast efforts of the Ōhira camp were being widely commented upon, but still there was no indication that Fukuda was in any danger of losing his lead. Throughout the middle and last stages of the campaign, virtually all the mass media stuck to their prediction of a victory for Fukuda. The Fukuda camp judged that if Fukuda won either a majority of the 1,525 points or came out ahead of the second contender by more than 100 points, the contender would yield and victory would be declared without going through a final vote. Mobilizing the combined authority of the incumbent party president and prime minister, the Fukuda faction used LDP prefectural governors and prefectural federation leaders in an intense campaign to influence LDP members "from above." The goal for the Fukuda camp was over 800 points.

By contrast, the Ōhira camp, which started out with the low goal of 400 points, adopted the tactics of working "from below" through Kōchikai Dietmen, their secretaries, and the staff of Ōhira's local support groups in Kagawa Prefecture, who traveled throughout the country to make personal visits to eligible voters. All sorts of organizations that had hitherto shown support for Ōhira were mobilized. These canvassers were people who brought their own box lunches, and who literally got blisters on their feet and wore out several pairs of shoes. It was in this way that Ōhira's policies and personal qualities reached the voters. The results of this grass-roots activity were shown in the enthusiastic welcome and encouragement given to Ōhira during his nationwide speaking tour. As those who made door-to-door visits to as many eligible voters as they could find sensed the rewards of this, they became all the more energetic.

In Ōhira's Kagawa Prefecture, the activities of his supporters, including relatives and old friends, reached "Sanuki fever" pitch. Irrespective of their present addresses, large numbers of people born or brought up in Kagawa Prefecture volunteered to help in the campaign, and the results of their efforts were soon evident, especially in the large vote reservoirs of Tokyo and Osaka, where support for Ōhira had been relatively weak. The staff of Diet members who supported Ōhira walked the streets in search of party members about whom they knew nothing except their names and addresses. Even for staff members who had worked in previous election campaigns, seeking out voters in Tokyo, with its haphazard system of addresses, was no easy task. These campaigners, who toiled from early morning until late evening, were occasionally scolded when they knocked on doors that belonged to LDP campaign workers supporting other candidates, but in most cases they were met with good will and offered tea. The preliminary election was so set up that it would be evident to all Diet members working in the campaign what percentage of votes from their own electoral districts (as prefectural subunits) went to each of the candidates. In this way it would be possible for Dietmen to judge the degree of loyalty to their own faction; thus, many felt constrained to put as much energy into this presidential election as into their own campaigns in a general election.

On November 8, Fukuda said, "If a clear conclusion is reached in the preliminary election, it should be respected in the final election." This meant that if he came in first and Ōhira second, Ōhira should give up running against him in an election by LDP Diet members. Ōhira retorted, "Unless one of the two candidates retires from the race, the matter should not be decided through talks, without a final election. Things should be done in an impartial way according to the rules."

Ōhira's election headquarters carefully studied the progress of the campaign in each prefecture and continued to revise its overall estimates. The initial prediction of 400 points grew to 500 points, and midway through the election it approached 600. Ōhira's staff became confident that even if Ōhira could not take the top position, he would come within 100 points of Fukuda. By the time such projections were being made, Ōhira, when confronted by reporters who continued to predict a Fukuda victory, began to make bullish statements like, "Do you fellows really think Ōhira is going to lose?" By now, the Ōhira camp was even making careful preparations for the final election, searching out sympathizers among LDP Diet members. These activities were carried out parallel with the preliminary election campaign, and the camp gradually came to expect victory should the matter be brought to a final election.

Voters' ballots had to be mailed by November 26 at the latest, and it had originally been expected that the mailing would peak around November 12 or 13. However, according to surveys by the Ōhira camp, it was found that only 57 to 58 percent of ballots had, in fact, been mailed by then. This was happy news for the Ōhira camp, which wanted more time to penetrate the grass-roots level. The supposition was that most of the people who had not yet cast their ballots did not support any particular candidate. To win their votes, campaign activities could not slow down. Thus, the original strategy—which aimed to end campaigning by November 17 and have all Dietmen supporting Ōhira return to the capital by November 20 to prepare for the final election—was abruptly altered and instructions were issued to Diet members to continue campaigning in their home areas for another week. Tanaka Kakuei advised, "Even as late as November 20, there will still be 10 percent of the ballots to be sent in, so don't let up until the very end." He also provided detailed data that he had compiled, analyzing the four candidates' expected showings in each prefecture.

After November 20, there still remained a few prefectures (such as Hokkaidō, Saitama, Mie, and Nagasaki) where it was difficult to predict results, but the Ōhira camp felt it could by this time be confident of gaining around 700 points, which, while not a clear-cut victory, would mean a close contest. Even in Tokyo, where Ōhira had been thought to be at a disadvantage, good results were expected from the sort of mass-penetration tactics that had been carried out by the staffs of Dietmen in the Ōhira and Tanaka factions.

Feeling a sense of crisis over the unexpected showing of strength by the Ōhira camp, Fukuda addressed Diet members of his faction at a gathering in a Tokyo hotel on November 22 and complained, "Despite our original intentions, we have seen incidents of 'tactics of using overwhelming resources' (butsuryō sakusen) and the emergence of bad aspects such as the spread of factions in local areas." Although no names were mentioned, this was taken as criticism of the Ōhira and Tanaka factions. At this, Ōhira promptly put up a strong defense: "Fukuda says he is worried about a dirty election, but there should be no problems so long as the candidates (that is to say, Fukuda and myself) carry out a fair and clean election. It is not anyone's problem but our own. I don't think that my camp has carried out any particularly dramatic 'tactics of using overwhelming resources.'" Reflecting the Fukuda camp's frustration and its feeling that a final election would be unavoidable, the November 23 issue of the Yomiuri Shinbun carried an article about moves toward a Miki–Fukuda–Nakasone coalition in preparation for a final face-off.

November 27, the day for opening the votes, finally arrived. That morning, Ōhira rose at 6 A.M., a little earlier than usual, and read a favorite book until the newspapers were delivered. When asked how he felt by reporters on the early morning shift, he replied nonchalantly, "My frame of mind is the same as usual, I guess maybe because I'm thick-skinned. . . . It's important to remember that this is just the preliminary examination." When asked about the likely results, he replied easily, "The interesting thing is that nobody knows. There's some fun to be had from groping in the dark. I guess maybe that's part of God's wisdom."

After around 10 A.M., when the first ballots began to be opened in the prefectures, it became evident that Ōhira was doing better than expected. Counting took place simultaneously in LDP prefectural federation headquarters throughout the country, and, as in ordinary elections, the numbers of votes for each individual candidate were relayed by telephone to the Kōchikai's election headquarters in its Tokyo office. The focus of interest was, of course, on the ratios of votes won by Ōhira and Fukuda in each prefecture. During the campaign, the Kōchikai's election headquarters had already produced their own estimates of points expected to be won in each prefecture, and with the opening of the ballots everyone there became absorbed in comparing these with the actual results. The latest predictions had held that Ōhira would gain between 680 and 710 points, while Fukuda would gain around 700, or almost the same number. At the very worst, Ōhira was expected to trail by no more than 50 points.

As the first counts were reported from Aomori, Fukushima, and Osaka, the ratio of votes was seen to be more in Ōhira's favor than predicted. Happy exclamations could be heard from the ten or so staff members gathered in the Kōchikai chairman's office. None of the counts being relayed from the election headquarters gave Ōhira a worse showing than the latest predictions. By the time around 100 points for Ōhira had been confirmed, many Kōchikai staff already felt sure of victory, and their voices betrayed their optimism. This trend did not change as the hours passed. At around 11:30 A.M., results came from the first prefectures to complete their count. In many cases Ōhira had gained one or two more points than predicted, and in the worst prefectures his points were exactly as had been forecast. In the big vote-reservoirs of Tokyo, Saitama, and Hokkaidō, about which there had always been some anxiety, it became clear that he would come in second after Fukuda.

At around noon, those in charge of analyzing the votes announced they were sure Ōhira win. By this time the office was packed not only with members but also with journalists and TV crews. Each time a prefecture's point distribution was announced, a cheer would go up. A number of Kōchikai members, who had been following the election results elsewhere on TV, decided to join in the excitement at Kōchikai headquarters after they had seen that Ōhira had done better than expected in their home prefectures. Many looked relieved as they said, "I couldn't show my face at the Kōchikai until the results were in." Congratulations were pouring in by telephone from Diet members of the Tanaka faction. Reporters who came a little before 1 P.M. to get the latest news for the evening editions were told that "Ōhira is ahead and certain to come in first." By this time, there were even some who thought Ōhira could gain a majority of the total points. By around 4 P.M., all ballots had been opened and reported. The final results gave Ōhira Masayoshi an overwhelming victory with 748 points (about 550,000 votes), Fukuda Takeo 638 points (about 470,000 votes), Nakasone Yasuhiro 93 points (about 198,000 votes), and Kōmoto Toshio 46 points (about 89,000 votes). A flood of newspaper extras ran the headline "Ōhira in First Place."

Diet members of the Ōhira faction were greatly satisfied with the victory, and toward evening they met for a party with Ōhira at the Hotel

Ōkura. However, the election process had not yet come to an end. Although a major step had been accomplished, it was still uncertain what attitude Fukuda would take toward a runoff election by LDP Diet members. Ōhira himself kept a serious countenance and restricted his comments to, "I feel the weight of the voters' expectations." He left for home at 6:40 P.M.

The Fukuda camp was in a state of confusion over what the prime minister would do. After 4 P.M., when the results of the preliminary election were clear, several of the staff and junior members of Fukuda's faction came to see him in the Prime Minister's Official Residence. A hard-line group represented by Nakagawa Ichirō urged him to proceed with the runoff election at all costs, but others like Shiokawa Masajūrō counseled against it. There followed over three hours of heated debate. Fukuda made up his mind at 7:30 P.M. and left for LDP headquarters to give a press conference: "Seeing those results I was frankly surprised. I have always said that I would respect the results of the preliminary election. In other words, I have decided not to run in the final election. . . . Well, I think it sometimes happens that Heaven's voice is a strange one. Today a vanquished general should not talk of battles."

This was Prime Minister Fukuda's declaration of his withdrawal from the race, and it was at this moment that Ōhira Masayoshi became, in effect, president of the LDP. Ordinarily, this would be an occasion for shouts of victory, but not one of Ōhira's colleagues watching the press conference on TV at Kōchikai headquarters reacted in that way because the prime minister's expression was simply too stiff. In spite of the victory, an oppressive silence fell over the room.

At the request of the press corps, the new party president was asked to return quickly to Kōchikai headquarters. In the crowded conference room, lit by arc lights for television, Ōhira said: "A few moments ago I listened to Prime Minister Fukuda's press conference and I greatly respect him for his decision. The fact that the prime minister has carried out what he promised during the preliminary election campaign—even though he has sufficient strength to continue the contest—reflects a spirit of love for the party and the desire not to encourage unnecessary confusion, and for this I owe him my deep respect. In the future management of party affairs, I intend to keep this spirit alive." After this statement, Ōhira responded to a question as follows: "[The basis of the Ōhira Administration] must be to give precedence to harmony within the party. It is a critical time domestically and internationally, and so it is necessary for the party to address issues with unity and solidarity. I think I must lead these efforts. I haven't yet gotten around to thinking about the specifics of putting together a new political setup, but I think that, in order to have talented people work to the best advantage, we must refrain from having any narrow or biased party management. To put together a fresh, strong administration is my appointed duty." He continued: "There are times when a single moment is significant, and there are times when ten or twenty years pass by without bearing fruit. History is strange, indeed." As he spoke, Ōhira's face was the epitome of solemnity. It was a victory interview in which each word seemed to be carefully pondered and selected.

The fact that Ōhira had come out on top by a wide margin in the preliminary election ran counter to most media forecasts, and they later tried to attribute this result to the "tactics of using overwhelming resources" of the Tanaka faction. It was true that the Tanaka faction had fought for Ōhira as if he was its own candidate; otherwise, such a victory would probably not have been possible. Credit must also be given, of course, to the correctness of the campaign strategy that Tanaka had suggested. Tanaka had felt sorry that when he stepped down from the party presidency, the Miki Administration came into being through LDP Vice-President Shiina's arbitration, rather than an administration headed by his close friend Ōhira. He had, no doubt, felt that if this chance for becoming party president by an election was missed, an Ōhira administration might never be realized. Thus, he had thrown himself wholeheartedly into this campaign, staking both his friendship and his own abilities as a politician. Indeed, the greatest single reason for the victory was the immense energy of Ōhira's supporters (including those in the Tanaka faction) during the campaign. Tanaka Kakuei later recalled, "During our long friendship, this was the only occasion that Ōhira showed no trace of perplexity or hesitation."

This contest in which Ōhira had staked his political life had surely achieved a great victory; yet Ōhira's wish that his agreement with Fukuda would retain some moral force and that he might attain the premiership with the blessing of the whole party, with no danger to party unity, was not granted. After Ōhira's first press conference as party president, colleagues came in small groups to his home, but there was no festive atmosphere and hardly any smiles or expressions of joy. It seemed as if the long-cherished, hard-won victory had also brought a sort of emptiness. On November 29, two days after the preliminary election results were counted, Ōhira entered LDP headquarters for the first time in eight days, and the room he entered was not that of the secretary-general but that of the party president. A full schedule awaited him, including media interviews and the drafting of his speech as party president before the upcoming extraordinary party convention.

On December 1, 1978, the thirty-fifth party convention was held at

Hibiya Public Hall. LDP Presidential Election Control Committee Chairman Fukuda Hajime made the following announcement: "The opening of the preliminary election ballots made Ōhira Masayoshi and Fukuda Takeo candidates for party president. We have received a written communication from Fukuda saying, 'I withdraw my candidacy in the final election for president.' The control committee has accepted this, and consequently there is only one candidate, Ōhira Masayoshi, for the new party president." Convention Chairman Nemoto Ryūtarō asked all those present for a decision on the nomination, and it was approved unanimously.

In his opening remarks as the new party president, Ōhira said:

> At this moment, in the name of this convention, I have been selected as president of the Liberal Democratic Party. It is truly an extraordinary and most moving honor for me. First, I wish to express my heartfelt gratitude for the way former Party President Fukuda has, in that capacity, contributed tirelessly, day and night, to the party's reconstruction. Moreover, I must express my profound respect for his courageous decision, in the interests of party harmony and unity, to withdraw his candidacy in the election process.
>
> For our party, the most important task at present is to promote harmony and solidarity. If there were disharmony, dissonance, and impediments in the past, the party must sweep these aside and strive to come together to expand party strength on the basis of mutual trust. I am determined to take an all-party position, to work for a fair and open party administration, and at the same time to push forward party reforms I have already been involved with, and I look forward to an honest and vigorous party regeneration. I ask for the further support and encouragement of you all.

Both Fukuda and Ōhira had said that "it would be terrible" for the party if they ever competed in an election for the presidency. Now that such a contest had taken place, the most pressing matter was to restore party harmony. Yet from the very start of the Ōhira Administration, the emotional entanglements that had come with this election continued to make themselves felt.

The date of his designation as prime minister was set for December 6, and Ōhira set to work on organizing his cabinet. His plan was to give particular importance to the selection of the top three party officers and to lend a fresh cast to the cabinet by selecting a number of first-time members. He was, first of all, determined to appoint as secretary-general

Suzuki Zenkō, who as one of the leaders of the Kōchikai had long shown his skills as Ōhira's right-hand man and had always assisted him with party liaison when Ōhira had held important cabinet posts in the past, However, the Fukuda, Miki, and Nakasone factions—that is, the groupings around the candidates who had come second, third, and fourth in the preliminary election—opposed this because it would go against the agreement reached at the outset of the Miki Administration that the secretary-general and the party president should not come from the same faction. Prior to this, on November 28 and December 5, Ōhira had visited Fukuda twice for talks on important preliminary arrangements for the coming administration, and agreement was reached on party solidarity and a smooth management. Ōhira was, therefore, unprepared for the criticism from the Fukuda faction about making Suzuki secretary-general. He had firmly believed that Fukuda would cooperate; after all, Ōhira had put forth no conditions at the outset of the Fukuda Administration. Thus, he now saw Fukuda's attitude as contributing to disarray within the party. On the other hand, Fukuda no doubt held the view that, in the face of their continued cooperation, his opinions on party management should be respected.

Many in the Fukuda faction went so far as to take the uncompromising position that they would cast blank ballots in the Diet vote for prime minister if an LDP secretary-general were appointed from the Ōhira faction. Certain junior members of the Fukuda faction intent on preventing Suzuki Zenkō from becoming secretary-general made this pronouncement: "We will be the battle contingent for party reform, and will show our intentions in the nomination of the prime minister." On the evening of December 5, Ōhira, having decided that to avoid political disruption by forgoing certain things, invited Suzuki to his residence to talk about ways of coping with the situation. Suddenly he put forth the plan of appointing, in Suzuki's stead, Saitō Kunikichi, also a member of the Kōchikai. Saitō was a good-natured man and well thought of by many members of other factions. There was, in fact, nobody else within the Kōchikai more likely to win approval for this post. Suzuki understood Ōhira's feelings and consented to the proposal, and Ōhira telephoned Fukuda to report this change in plan.

Although Fukuda personally approved the change, most of the Fukuda and Nakasone faction members were still threatening to boycott the Lower House plenary session unless Ōhira withdrew the idea of appointing a secretary-general from the Kōchikai, that is, the Ōhira faction. The confusion continued and the Lower House plenary session originally scheduled for December 6 to designate the prime minister was unprecedentedly postponed. On the evening of December 6, Tokai Motosaburō and Katō Mutsuki of the Fukuda faction visited Ōhira's home to ask if it would not be possible to make Saitō secretary-general only for a temporary period, or else to appoint him to one of the two other top appointive party posts. Ōhira refused, saying, "That sort of thing I can't do."

At 8 A.M. on December 7, Ōhira told reporters who had come to see him, "I'm going to Nozawa [Fukuda's residence]. I'll be back." When he returned, he reported, "Fukuda said he would cooperate. He has agreed to talk with the Nakasone faction." His face showed that a great weight had finally been lifted. The two had agreed that "to appoint the secretary-general from the president's faction will be a temporary measure limited only to this time." With the more recalcitrant members of the Fukuda faction persuaded to put away their knives, Ōhira was finally designated prime minister on the evening of December 7. It was a hard start after an equally hard-won victory.

Part 7

Trust and Consensus

Chapter 31

Beyond Modernization

At 5:05 P.M. on December 7, 1978, the 86th Extraordinary Diet, which had started the previous day, convened a plenary session of the Lower House to appoint the prime minister. All LDP members and independent conservative members cast their votes for Ōhira, while those belonging to the opposition parties voted for their respective party heads. At 5:42 P.M., it was announced that of the total 491 Lower House votes cast, Ōhira had won 254, a majority. In the Upper House, too, Ōhira was given majority approval, with 126 out of the total 224 votes cast. On that day, despite his poor health, Lower House Speaker Hori Shigeru, who had mediated the Fukuda–Ōhira meeting two years before that had produced the secret agreement and had ever since looked forward to an Ōhira Administration, was present to make the official announcement naming Ōhira prime minister. Thus, on December 7, 1978, Ōhira Masayoshi became Japan's forty-third prime minister (heading the sixty-ninth cabinet) since the establishment of a parliamentary cabinet system under Prime Minister Itō Hirobumi in 1885, and he was the ninth prime minister to head an LDP administration.

At the announcement by the speaker, Ōhira, who was sitting toward the back of the chamber, briskly stood up and gave a deep bow toward the government party and the opposition party members. His expression still betrayed signs of tension: he had been named prime minister only after many difficulties and a day later than scheduled, and, given the almost equal numbers of LDP and opposition seats, the Lower House had approved his nomination by a majority of only eight votes.

He wore a smile, though, as he made the rounds of Diet building rooms to deliver greetings to the parties, the speaker and vice-speaker of the Lower House, and the president and vice-president of the Upper House. Yet when he left the building through the main entrance hall adjoining the

Lower House chamber and got into the prime minister's official car—the applause and congratulations now behind him—the smile disappeared. To receive him on his arrival at the front entrance of the Prime Minister's Official Residence were several guards and some of the employees. After the bright lights of the Diet building, the residence looked dark and deserted. Straight ahead of the entrance hall was a gently rising staircase covered with a red carpet. Ōhira climbed this and turned left to enter his new office on the right. Its main furnishings were a desk, a cabinet with a photograph of the emperor and empress and a Japanese flag on it, a globe, and a sofa set. Prime Minister Ōhira gave a look around and then stood for a while as if lost in thought.

Not too long afterward, the four men who were to assist him in putting together the new cabinet began to arrive: first of all, Policy Research Council Chairman Kōmoto Toshio, then Secretary-General Saitō Kunikichi, General Council Chairman Kuraishi Tadao, and finally Chief Cabinet Secretary Tanaka Rokusuke. It was first decided that Nishimura Eiichi would be made party vice-president at the next LDP convention in January. The selection of new cabinet members proceeded quickly: the first appointees were contacted by phone before 9 P.M., and the new cabinet was finalized just after 10 P.M. New members were Furui Yoshimi (Justice), Sonoda Sunao (Foreign Affairs), Kaneko Ippei (Finance), Naitō Takasaburō (Education), Hashimoto Ryūtarō (Health and Welfare), Watanabe Michio (Agriculture, Forestry and Fisheries), Esaki Masumi (International Trade and Industry), and Moriyama Kinji (Transport). Surrounded by reporters on his way from the residence to the Imperial Palace, Ōhira gave a concise answer when asked about the character of the new cabinet: "It is one that will pay the greatest attention to practical matters. And it will be served by many first-time members." The ceremony of imperial investiture (*shinninshiki*) for the prime minister and the ceremony of imperial attestation (*ninshōshiki*) for the other ministers, both presided over by the emperor, took place after 11 P.M. in the Imperial Palace. By the time the first meeting of his cabinet was adjourned at the Prime Minister's Official Residence, it was after 1 A.M.

At this first cabinet meeting, Ōhira made the following remarks:

> On this occasion I have come to shoulder the responsibilities of prime minister. I intend to carry out, sincerely and unpretentiously, the responsibilities that history has entrusted to me. The fact that our country has, over the past thirty-three years, been able to rise from the ashes of defeat to enjoy the freedom and prosperity of today is very definitely due to the efforts of

our predecessors. In particular, former Prime Minister Fukuda showed excellent leadership in resolving various domestic and international issues. I intend to take over where my predecessors left off and spare no effort in building a stable Japan. Our nation's environment, both at home and abroad, is a harsh one in many ways, and does not permit irresponsible illusions or wishful thinking. I intend to let the people know frankly what can and cannot be done by politics, what ought and ought not be done by politics, and to approach this important period of transition into the twenty-first century respecting, as much as possible, the creativity and vitality of the people. I sincerely hope for the understanding and cooperation of every one of Japan's citizens.

It had been approximately eight years since Ōhira had become chairman of the Kōchikai. The 1970s were almost over, and times had greatly changed. The postwar international economic order had altered considerably, and the family of nations was searching for new ways of doing things. Values centering on economic growth had become a thing of the past, and improving the quality of life was now more important than mere material wealth for true comfort, satisfaction, and a sense of stability. Reflecting this awareness, political conditions, too, had changed. The ideological confrontation between conservatives and progressives was receding, and there were no longer such large gaps in the positions taken by the various parties. In other words, the times were following a path similar to what Ōhira had suggested earlier. Nevertheless, as the twenty-first century approached, people's conceptions of the future were by no means well defined. In his declaration of candidacy prior to the party presidential election, Ōhira had said: "The times are rapidly changing. After long and difficult trials, a brighter prospect is finally before us. Even if the surroundings are still dark, if we raise our heads and look ahead, we can see a ray of light in the future. Rather than stand still and look back to the past, shouldn't we go forward and welcome this light?" To explain the nature of this light and to indicate ways in which the nation could advance was the mission that Ōhira would have to pursue as prime minister.

His long-term task was to clear away the vestiges of a cloudy era, to shed light on what society should look like in the future, and to construct specific methods by which Japan might attain these goals. For the middle term, he would need to give directions as to how Japan, now a prominent member of the free world, could make global contributions commensurate with its strength and international position. Tasks of immediate urgency included overcoming such problems as the fiscal crisis and the issues of energy, resources, and the environment. Such an achievement would require skillful economic management and a readiness to take a new look at systems and organizations; yet the most urgent task of all was to bring an end to the infighting within the LDP, to achieve party unity, and to work for political stability in a situation where the government and opposition camps had nearly equal numbers of Diet seats.

Entrusted with this mission, the Ōhira Cabinet adopted the slogan "Trust and Consensus" (*Shinrai to gōi*) to express its political philosophy. The practice by which each new administration encapsulated its underlying philosophy in a short slogan began with the Ikeda Cabinet, when then Chief Cabinet Secretary Ōhira coined the phrase "Tolerance and Patience." Afterward, the Satō Cabinet, with the Osaka Expo '70 in mind, came up with the slogan "Progress and Harmony." The Tanaka Cabinet's slogan was "Decision and Execution," referring both to the Plan for the Remodeling of the Japanese Archipelago and the restoration of China–Japan diplomatic relations. The Miki Cabinet used "Dialogue and Cooperation," and the Fukuda Cabinet, in reference to the need to overcome the intraparty turmoil of the Miki period, chose the phrase "Cooperation and Solidarity." Leaving aside the question of the degree to which the various administrations adhered to their slogans, each of these reflected something of the mood of the times as well as the hopes and concerns of each head of state.

It is thought that Ōhira first used the phrase "trust and consensus" during a press conference on December 1, 1978, just after being elected the LDP's new president. At that time he said, "Trust and consensus . . . means to trust one another and to agree on things. It is the same as tolerance and patience." In his first press conference as prime minister on December 8, he amplified on this: "First, I want to close the gap between politics and the people as much as possible. I want the two to come together. Politics must not depend too easily on authority. I want politics to be at one with the people and to reflect their sorrows and joys. Second, politics must refrain from scattering unrealistic illusions before the people. At the same time, people should not have exaggerated expectations of politics. I want a politics in which there is understanding on both these points and from which there will come effective results. Third, the times have changed dramatically as we advanced from postwar poverty to reconstruction and prosperity. Democratic politics has taken root, and the notion of free economic activity has attained nationwide approval without significant dissent. The framework for national security is also developing in the direction of nationwide approval. If these trends are respected and we have a politics that faithfully reflect them, we can avoid the sorts of confrontations where there is no compromise. The nation, too, has matured politically. Politics must not lag behind when it comes to this sort of maturity."

In other words, Ōhira's slogan "Trust and Consensus" was meant to encompass the notion that a basic national consensus was already taking shape with respect to parliamentary democracy, the free market economy, and the security treaty defense system. Postwar conservative forces had focused on the establishment and maintenance of these three systems, and gradually, with most of the opposition parties coming to support them, a national consensus was indeed in the process of maturing. Ōhira's slogan can thus be said to express his determination to continue what he had inherited from his predecessors and to proceed from there to establish his own brand of politics.

From the early morning of December 8, 1978, his first full day as prime minister, visitors arrived at his private residence. When asked by reporters around 8:30 A.M. for some comments on the new situation, he ventured: "It's still, should I say, something like burned-out Tokyo at the end of the war, with no time yet for things to settle down. Rather than being in a position to see the results of the new cabinet objectively, I'm just at the point of looking back over the process of its creation. There hasn't been time to think about how it will turn out."

He entered the Prime Minister's Official Residence at 9:35 A.M., and not long afterward received a congratulatory phone call from President Carter. At first an interpreter was used, but Ōhira then decided to carry out most of the conversation in English. A cabinet meeting began at 10 A.M. For lunch, Ōhira had curry and rice, which he had often eaten with Prime Minister Ikeda when he was chief cabinet secretary. Following a 3 P.M. press interview, he paid several courtesy calls and then went to Aoyama Cemetery to report on his new administration to the spirits of former prime ministers Yoshida and Ikeda. That evening he dined with members of the Ōhirakai (Ōhira Club), a group of bankers and businessmen, and returned home at 8:20 P.M.

Two days later, on December 10, an election was held for the governorship of Okinawa Prefecture, and Nishime Junji, a former LDP member of the Lower House, won by a wide margin over the opposition parties' candidate, ending the long period of opposition dominance in Okinawa politics. On December 11, the Asahi Shinbun reported that in a public opinion poll the Ōhira Cabinet had the support of 42 percent of the people and was "getting off to good start." Asked on the same day about his feelings at the outset of the new administration, Ōhira replied, "It's like walking on thin ice." He was no doubt acutely aware of the trying times lying ahead.

Soon the end of the year arrived with little time for rest. After the New Year festivities in Tokyo, Ōhira paid his respects at Ise Shrine in Mie Prefecture, south of Nagoya, on January 4. The next day, the Ministry of Finance's draft budget for fiscal 1979 was presented for cabinet consideration and was finally approved at a cabinet meeting on January 11.

The policy speech to be given by the prime minister at the opening of the Diet session to be convened in late January was the object of much interest and speculation, as Ōhira had let it be known that he intended to confer with the nation as a whole regarding his ideas on policy. Ōhira prepared this speech with great care, and in the initial stages asked his secretaries to comment on the following memo, which dealt with "awareness of the times" (*jidai ninshiki*):

1. How to see the present age, how to determine the role of politics in this age. In this context, develop policies on economics, culture, education.
   (a) Transcending economics or finding a way out of an economy-oriented society (*datsu keizai*); not the same thing as underrating the importance of economics (*keizai keishi*).
   (b) An age without definite beliefs; the importance of vision, creativity.
   (c) Emphasis on culture; a feeling of purpose in living (*ikigai*), fulfillment in life.
   (d) Transcending ideology; liberating politics from existing stereotypes.
2. How to see today's international situation. In present circumstances, what should Japan do and not do? In this context, develop security policy, economic and regional diplomacy.
   (a) Multipolarization, decentralization; how to pursue stability amid instability.
   (b) U.S.–Soviet "planetization" (*wakuseika*). [This rather enigmatic term presumably suggests a continuing U.S.–Soviet interest in being at the center of systems with political "satellites."]
   (c) Widening of North–South gap.
   (d) National tensions concerning resources.
   (e) Protectionism and regionalism.

The central point in the first part of Ōhira's memo was no doubt "transcending economics" (*datsu keizai*). Rather than use the phrase "post-industrial society" (*datsu kōgyōka shakai*), which was already popular among journalists, he seems to have chosen this expression to convey something of the nuance of an English phrase (perhaps suggested by William Wordsworth or the educator and statesman Nitobe Inazō) he had been fond of since his youth, "Simple life and high thinking," implying that high thinking is facilitated by a simple life rather than by a life of material excess. His approach to the direction of the times was premised on the notion that, as civilization reached a stage of maturity, people's aspirations would naturally turn more to spiritual and cultural concerns. He recognized that Japan's postwar years had been a period in which material things had been highly valued, and he felt that as these needs were met, spiritual values would have to take priority.

The second item on Ōhira's memo had to do with awareness of international affairs. For postwar Japan, international relations had been regulated by the United States and other major foreign countries. They were something bestowed on Japan, and Japan had tended to keep rather aloof. However, in the 1980s, not only in the field of economics but also in politics and culture, the nations of the world would come to expect a larger role and responsibility from Japan. Besides, some of the pillars that had supported the postwar world were weak and crumbling. The question of how to deal with these changes was of great concern to Ōhira.

Given this political situation and awareness of the times, the Ōhira Cabinet began an unprecedented experiment in regard to the way its policies were to be formulated. This involved the activities of the Policy Study Association (*Seisaku Kenkyūkai*), made up largely of persons in academia and business. Ōhira had always been dissatisfied when policy making was monopolized by the bureaucracy, believing that a nation's policies should evolve from the ideas of politicians and should only later be worked out in detail by bureaucrats. Thus, to give optimum content to his own ideas as prime minister, he resolved to refine these concepts with the help of ideas and suggestions from people in all walks of life.

Three persons, chosen from among the section chiefs of the Ministry of Finance, Ministry of Foreign Affairs, and Ministry of International Trade and Industry, supervised the establishment of various study groups that were to act as advisory bodies for the prime minister. Some of the more active members of these groups were Asari Keita (stage director and producer), Iida Tsuneo (professor at Nagoya University), Ishii Takemochi (professor at Tokyo University), Kumon Shunpei (professor at Tokyo University), Kōsaka Masataka (professor at Kyoto University), Kōyama Ken'-ichi (professor at Gakushūin University), Satō Seizaburō (professor at

Tokyo University), and Yamazaki Masakazu (professor at Osaka University). On January 17, nine study groups were established as follows (in the order of the actual start of their activities):

(1) Study Group on the Garden-City Concept, chaired by Umesao Tadao, director of the National Museum of Ethnology.

(2) Study Group on Economic Policy Toward Foreign Countries, chaired by Uchida Tadao, professor at Tokyo University.

(3) Study Group on Life Values in a Multifarious Society, chaired by Hayashi Chikio, director-general of the Institute of Statistical Mathematics.

(4) Study Group on Pacific Basin Cooperation, chaired by Ōkita Saburō, chairman of the Japan Center for Economic Research.

(5) Study Group on Strengthening the Family Base, chaired by Itō Zen'ichi, professor at Tokyo Woman's Christian University.

(6) Study Group on Comprehensive Security Strategy, chaired by Inoki Masamichi, president of the Research Institute for Peace and Security.

(7) Study Group on the Age of Culture, chaired by Yamamoto Shichihei, owner of Yamamoto Bookstore.

(8) Study Group on Economic Performance in the Age of Culture, chaired by Tachi Ryūichirō, professor at Tokyo University.

(9) Study Group on the Historical Evolution of Science and Technology, chaired by Sassa Manabu, director of the National Institute for Environmental Studies.

Each of these groups brought together fairly young persons who were expected to become leaders in their various academic, cultural, and economic fields, and they also included capable civil servants from those ministries and government agencies that were major formulators and administrators of policy. The groups were chaired by scholars with wide experience in their fields, and the total number of members in the nine groups was 176. Thus, a broad-based policy research system came into being, whose members included both government and private-sector employees, cutting across academic specialties and bureaucratic boundaries. The fact that such cooperation could come about between government and academic circles, which traditionally tended to be jealously protective of their respective fields, was due largely to their high regard for Ōhira's personality, his understanding of people, and his respect for learning.

Ōhira attached no difficult conditions to the management of these study groups. His only requirement was that this experiment take a long-range, comprehensive viewpoint focused on the twenty-first century, rather than on the Ōhira Cabinet or on the prime minister himself, and that it debate freely and present recommendations on what would be necessary for Japan in the future, even if these conflicted with current government views. Ōhira actively sought the advice of these groups on many matters beyond politics and economics. On occasion he would invite group members to his home, where the conversation was likely to touch on such broad questions as the meaning of civilization.

On January 24, 1979, at the LDP convention held in Hibiya Public Hall, Ōhira stressed "Trust and Consensus" and pointed out that "to fulfill our duties, we must first correct our own attitudes and take the lead in thorough self-reform." The following day, he made his first important policy speech before the Diet as prime minister. It began by voicing his concept of the times as follows:

> For the more than thirty years since the end of the war, we have striven single-mindedly with remarkable success in pursuit of economic affluence. This was the culmination of the more than a hundred years of modernization patterned after Western models since the Meiji Restoration. The freedom, equality, progress, and prosperity that we enjoy today are indeed the fruits of the untiring efforts of our people.
>
> However, it is difficult to claim that we have always given due consideration to harmony between man and nature, the balance between liberty and responsibility, the spiritual meaning of being, and the quality of life. Today, there is increasing concern for these values. This concern ought not to be seen as a simple questioning of our past rapid economic growth. Rather, it symbolizes our having reached the limits to modern rationalistic urbanization and materialistic civilization. We are, if you will, on the threshold of a new age transcending the age of modernization; we have moved from an age centering on economics to a new age with an emphasis on culture.

Thus, in our "new age transcending the age of modernization," the way for Japan to exist with honor was neither to go back to a premodern period nor to stress Japan's uniqueness. Rather it was to harmonize and bring into flower the special character of Japanese culture on the foundations of the achievements of modernization. With this perspective as its base, the speech went on to describe the sort of society that Japan should try to achieve:

> The new society that is our goal is one in which distrust and confrontation are overcome, and understanding and trust are cultivated in pursuit of a truly worthwhile life in all its aspects, touching the home, the community, the state, and the global society. It is a society in which the individual's creativity is welcomed and his labor is justly rewarded, in which there is respect for law and order, in which each is true to his own responsibilities and restraints and there is ample understanding and consideration for others.
>
> Accordingly, I intend to make respect for culture and the revival of human qualities the basic philosophy behind all my policies, and to work for the creation of a just and proper Japanese welfare society through such means as Strengthening the Family Base and promoting the Garden-City Concept.

Thus, the Garden-City Concept and the Concept of Strengthening the Family Base, both of which had long been close to Ōhira's heart, were now given due recognition in the discussions of policies actually being worked out. As for international affairs, Ōhira focused on "the age of a global society" and expressed himself on the subject as follows:

> Our earth is today an increasingly interdependent community interreacting ever more sensitively to events. Whatever incidents or problems occur anywhere on the face of the globe have instant ramifications elsewhere, and it is impossible to formulate effective responses unless we consider the global society in its entirety. The very survival of mankind will be imperiled unless we abstain from confrontation and conflict and, instead, seek mutual understanding and cooperation.
>
> However, the world today is witnessing an increasing tendency toward political multipolarization and an increase of factors encouraging instability. The GATT–IMF system, which supported the international economic order for a quarter of a century after the war, has recently been shaken by major upheavals, and the world is groping for new responses. There has also been a heightening of tensions arising from resource issues and nationalism, and the disparity between North and South is growing larger.

The global reality is thus extremely severe. We can no longer indulge in optimistic dreams or policies of wishful thinking. We must view the world as a single community, realize our role and responsibilities in the world, and resolutely develop suitable policies both at home and abroad.

What then, in this global society, should be done to guarantee Japan's security?

It is the prime duty of the government to insure Japan's own peace and security, and to that end we must firmly maintain our present security arrangements based upon a prudent self-defense capability supplemented by the U.S.–Japan Security Treaty. However, defense capability alone is not sufficient to insure genuine security. It goes without saying that we must, based upon a stark awareness of global realities, seek to develop vigorously comprehensive and orderly domestic policies and make positive diplomatic efforts to create an international climate of peace. . . .

In this way, a conceptual backing was given to the Comprehensive Security Strategy that had been one of the basic policy points Ōhira had put forward during the election campaign for party president.

The "new age transcending the age of modernization" mentioned in Ōhira's first policy speech before the Diet sought depth in "an age of culture" and breadth in "the age of a global society." Although Ōhira was not a "radical progressive" in the scheme of Japanese politics, he knew that to cope with the difficult times ahead it was essential to be farsighted. In the mass media, this speech was criticized by some as being overly idealistic and even too similar in style to the sort of things journalists and editorial writers were likely to come up with. Although, in its entirety, it may not have met unconditional praise, it was almost everywhere characterized as unusual and noteworthy for its forthright exposition of Ōhira's philosophy.

On the evening of January 30, following two days of questions in the Diet, Lower House Speaker Hori Shigeru, gratified that he had been able to preside over the Diet proceedings at the opening of the Ōhira Administration, submitted his resignation for health reasons. He was replaced by former Minister of Health and Welfare Nadao Hirokichi. About a month later Hori died, and at his funeral Ōhira eulogized him as "the guardian deity of the conservative party." He commented further: "The refined and mature way he used the reins of authority as speaker had much in common with the consummate skills of an accomplished stage performer."

Chapter 32

The Ōhira Administration

T he new administration was initially praised by the mass media as "getting off to a good start." But very soon thereafter a number of incidents occurred that warned of difficult times ahead. On December 15, 1978, just after the start of the Ōhira Administration, the evening papers announced that the United States Securities and Exchange Commission (SEC) had taken the McDonnell Douglas aircraft manufacturing company to court on charges of illegal payment of over US$8 million to highly placed foreign officials. According to the next morning's papers, these officials were said to include persons connected with the Japanese government. This, together with a similar incident exposed later involving the Grumman Corporation (another American aircraft manufacturer), saddled the new administration with a taxing issue.

On December 17, an OPEC meeting held in Abu Dhabi in response to changes in the oil supply situation brought about by the revolution in Iran, announced its decision to hike oil prices by 14.5 percent in four stages, the first being a hike of 5 percent, with the average rise over the next twelve-month period expected to be 10 percent. This second "oil shock" was expected to have an immense impact on the world economy, which still had not completely recovered from the first "oil shock" of 1973.

After Ōhira's policy speech and the questions from the various parties, the next item on the Diet agenda was the budget. However, since the opposition parties continued to put questions concerning the McDonnell Douglas and Grumman incidents, discussion of the budget was often brought to a standstill.

After the beginning of February, preparations for the ninth unified local elections, scheduled for April 1979—the first nationwide elections under the new administration—were getting into full swing. At the January 1979 LDP convention, Secretary-General Saitō Kunikichi, encouraged by the results of recent local by-elections, announced his hope of seeing "the trend toward a conservative recovery continued" in the upcoming polling. Ever since the Upper House election of July 1977, which Ōhira as secretary-general had done much to orchestrate, a certain conservative upswing had indeed become evident. There were no doubt many reasons for this, but a major one was that despite the voters' wish for stability under the harsher international environment that had followed the first oil crisis, the opposition parties could not come up with superior responses. According to a public opinion poll by the *Asahi Shinbun* made public on October 13, 1978, 46 percent of industrial workers supported the LDP and only 24 percent supported the JSP. This could only be called a complete reversal from the situation in the latter half of the 1950s, when only 25 percent of industrial workers backed the LDP and 50 percent supported the JSP.

Encouraged by this surge in conservative strength, the LDP's greatest hope was to win back the governorships of Tokyo and Osaka, two of the last major progressive strongholds. However, this was difficult for the LDP to accomplish on its own, so a coalition method was envisaged, which had been tried when Ōhira was secretary-general. The LDP mapped out a complex strategy, showing it was ready to cooperate on occasion with the Kōmeitō and the DSP, both of which, as a reflection of subtle changes in public opinion, showed a willingness to carry out policy changes in a practical, realistic direction. With one eye trained on the rivalry between the JSP and the JCP, the LDP at times had found itself cooperating with the JSP. It was against this background that Diet consideration of the budget was proceeding.

The compilation of the fiscal 1979 budget was somewhat delayed due to the recent change of administration, and it was finally given cabinet approval on January 11, 1979. The proposed general account government budget for fiscal 1979 was ¥38.6 trillion, which was only 12.6 percent more than the year before, or the lowest rate of increase in fourteen years. The rate of dependence on government bonds for financing was planned at 39.6 percent, never exceeded throughout the postwar period.

In his January 25 policy speech before the Diet, Ōhira had addressed these fiscal realities as follows:

> The reordering of our finances has become urgent.... The present financial situation is such that we must rely upon the issue of public bonds to a far greater extent than last year, and it is clear from prospects for the future that fiscal reordering is a national task demanding, now more than ever, our serious attention. This government is resolved to give positive study to

this problem, including both revenues and disbursements, at the national and local levels. We must rid ourselves of the dream dating to the rapid economic growth era that public finances can somehow satisfy every demand. Accordingly, I sincerely hope that there will be full discussion in the Diet and elsewhere on the question of tax burdens, including the possible adoption of a general consumption tax.

The concept of introducing a new tax had long been discussed by financial authorities as one way to get rid of the deficit, and was recommended under the name of a "general consumption tax" (*ippan shōhizei*) in the Interim Tax System Report prepared by the government's Tax System Council in October 1977. The LDP's Outline for Reforming the Tax System (issued every year before the compilation of the budget), which in 1977 referred primarily to the financial policy for fiscal 1978, likewise recommended serious consideration of the merits of such a tax. Afterward, the political decision to put it into effect was postponed due to a cooling of the business climate resulting from the rising value of the yen and other factors. Then, in December 1978, both the LDP and the government proposed a plan for putting a general consumption tax into effect in April 1980. Ōhira had been receptive to the idea and stated, during his January 4, 1979, trip to Ise Shrine, "I hope to find an occasion to introduce it as early as possible in 1980."

However, during the consideration of the budget in the Diet in early 1979, this issue was not yet taken up in its entirety, and discussion focused rather on tax reductions. On February 14, the JSP announced a plan for a revision that would raise old-age pensions and increase the budget by ¥1.14 trillion. The JCP, on the other hand, proposed cutting residence and income taxes, while the NLC proposed lower taxes on educational bodies, the further elimination of certain tax breaks for doctors, and cutting certain government subsidies to allow for a reduction of deficit-financing government bonds. The Kōmeitō and DSP jointly presented a budget revision plan that called for reducing income tax, increased old-age pensions, and more effective measures to encourage full employment. Those who promoted this plan called for an increase of ¥155.5 billion in the general account budget and ¥45.5 billion in special accounts, insisting on a so-called formal revision to this effect.

Such a revision would involve not merely substantial changes through the manipulation of reserve funds but also changes in budget allocation for various items, thus necessitating a complete reformulation and reprinting of the draft. This kind of change in the budget, which lay at the center of policy, would mean completely revising policy itself, not something the government could easily tolerate. However, because the Lower House Budget Committee had a majority of members from the opposition parties due to the poor LDP showing in the last general election during the Miki Administration, if the LDP should bluntly refuse the opposition parties' call for a formal revision, it was feared this could invite the situation (which had never come about since the LDP's founding) of a budget being rejected in the Budget Committee.

Prime Minister Ōhira both pushed for refining the contents of the proposed revision through negotiations by top party officers, including the chairman of the LDP Policy Research Council, and on February 28 held talks with the heads of the JSP and JCP, and on March 1 with the heads of the Kōmeitō, DSP, and NLC. Takeiri Yoshikatsu of the Kōmeitō and Sasaki Ryōsaku of the DSP indicated that they would approve the draft budget if it underwent a formal revision. One reason for this relatively flexible attitude was that both parties, which had made big gains in the last general election, could not only demonstrate their position as middle-of-the-road but also, if things went well, might eventually share political power. At first the LDP was opposed, but the particulars of the proposed revision continued to be worked out in negotiations with the opposition parties, and the Kōmeitō and DSP finally went so far as to say that if a formal revision was accepted they would approve not only the budget but all the other bills put forward by the government. Many of those in the LDP entrusted with the difficult tasks of dealing with Diet matters in conditions of nearly equal government–opposition strengths inclined toward accepting this proposal.

On the evening of March 1, following his talks with the heads of the Kōmeitō and DSP, Ōhira held a meeting of LDP officers. Among those present, Vice-President Nishimura and some others expressed caution, but most were of the opinion that a formal revision would have to be tolerated. A conclusion was postponed until the following day after the prime minister said, "Let's rest overnight and think about it again when we're fresher." Most of the top party officers felt that the prime minister had just about decided to go ahead with the formal revision. The next morning's newspapers boldly reported that a formal revision was a near-certainty. LDP Deputy Secretary-General Sasaki Yoshitake called on Ōhira just as the prime minister was reading these headlines, and Ōhira bluntly told him, "I've decided to put a stop to formal revision." Sasaki replied with surprise, "But sentiment within the party has already gone forward." Ōhira, however, remained firm.

At that morning's cabinet meeting it was resolved to leave the issue of budget revision up to the prime minister. A conference of party officers then started at 10 A.M. in the LDP president's office in the Diet building. Without the slightest hesitation, Ōhira began the meeting by stating his views approximately as follows: "The DSP, Kōmeitō, and NLC have on occasion taken a common stand on certain policies, but because the budget is something that defines the entirety of government policy over a whole year, I think we must handle it with caution. In making revisions, if the LDP, Kōmeitō, and DSP all take the same stand, it means they have agreed on policy matters in their entirety and entered into a pact to see them carried out in a certain way. If we do it this year, we'll be faced with the same situation next year, and it will develop into our doing everything together, from the compilation stage on. This greatly oversteps the boundaries of a partial coalition and becomes more of a full-fledged coalition government. If we go along with this proposal, we will cause the DSP and Kōmeitō to have exaggerated expectations of the LDP. There is no consensus now in the LDP on sharing cabinet posts with the Kōmeitō and DSP; and neither have relations between the Kōmeitō and DSP matured to the point where this would be possible. I think it is necessary to have a little more communication, and on that basis decide whether or not to deepen our relationship. I have heard the wishes of the DSP and Kōmeitō party leaders and know that, even without a formal revision, it is not impossible for us to satisfy those wishes. In any case, I myself have never once promised a formal revision. I think that if we show our sincerity on substantial points we can get them to agree. Because the Budget Committee has a majority of opposition party members, the draft budget will probably be rejected there, but it can be approved by a majority vote in the plenary session. This being the case, there should be no real necessity to accept the proposed budget revision." To the surprise and doubts of all those present who had made up their minds to accept a formal revision, Prime Minister Ōhira continued to explain his thinking. In the course of this meeting, which lasted one hour and ten minutes, he spoke fourteen times.

There was great anger and discouragement in the Kōmeitō and DSP when their proposal was rejected. No doubt they felt that they had been betrayed by Ōhira in spite of the fact that talks had seemed successful at the level of the respective party officers in charge of Diet strategy. No doubt they were disappointed in their hopes of advancing one step closer to political power. That evening, Ōhira was asked by reporters about what they called his "bold decision," and he replied, "No, it was very *orthodox* [original English]. We always approach things on the basis of hard realities." He then added, "This decision was just the lesser of two evils."

In response to Ōhira's decision to reject a formal revision, the government and the LDP approached the four largest opposition parties and sought their cooperation in a plan to effectively revise the budget upward by ¥110 billion, with such provisions as an increase in old-age pensions. However, the opposition parties refused to cooperate. Ultimately, on March 7, the fiscal 1979 budget was rejected in the Lower House Budget Committee but nevertheless gained Lower House approval through a plenary session vote the same day. It was the first time since 1948 (during the Ashida Administration) that a plenary session passed a budget rejected by the Budget Committee. Takeshita Noboru, who was Lower House Budget Committee chairman, recollects, "In the decision at that time one sensed how politics often goes to the very limits of what's possible. We had a bitter experience, but the decision was wise."

Simultaneous with this drama were negotiations among the various parties concerning the upcoming unified local elections. Of special importance was the campaign for the Tokyo governorship, which was seen by the Kōmeitō and DSP, both of which were looking for new opportunities to increase their influence, as a chance to advance closer to political power.

Tokyo's Governor Minobe Ryōkichi, who, with the backing of the JSP, Kōmeitō, and DSP, had served three consecutive four-year terms since 1967, had announced his intention to retire from the coming race, and attention focused on whether the progressives could again win political control in the nation's capital. The various parties began the selection of their candidates, yet the JSP, one of the coalition of three governing parties in the Tokyo Metropolitan Assembly, let the days slip by without making any definite commitment on a candidate. On the other hand, the Kōmeitō and DSP, likewise coalition governing parties in the local assembly, this time rejected the strategy of forming a unified front with the JSP and early on placed their support behind Suzuki Shun'ichi, who had formerly served as deputy governor of Tokyo. The LDP, which was the "opposition party" in the Tokyo Metropolitan Assembly, planned to regain political power by backing a candidate with one or more of the middle-of-the-road parties (Kōmeitō, DSP, or NLC). Besides Suzuki, the names of several other candidates were mentioned. Some in the LDP sympathized with backing a certain candidate being proposed by the NLC, but Prime Minister Ōhira took a cautious attitude, knowing that if the conservative and middle-of-the-road forces put forth more than one jointly backed candidate they risked losing the election. The potential choice of candidates was whittled down, and the LDP was essentially faced with the choice between backing Suzuki or putting forth a candidate of its own.

In late January, Ōhira held a confidential talk with DSP Secretary-General Sasaki and Kōmeitō Secretary-General Takeiri, during which they provisionally chose Suzuki Shun'ichi as their joint candidate. At the same time, progress was made among the three parties in adjusting policies on Tokyo's administration. This cooperative stance was part of the background to the forthright assertions by the Kōmeitō and DSP that they would agree to all the legislative bills presented by the government if the LDP consented to a formal revision of the budget.

Plans for conservative and middle-of-the-road cooperation in a number of local election campaigns proceeded steadily, but popular interest was focused on Tokyo and the question of whether Suzuki, backed by the LDP, Kōmeitō, and DSP, could defeat Ōta Kaoru, the JSP and JCP candidate, and Asō Yoshikata, the man put forth by the small United Social Democratic Party (*Shaminren*), which was formed in March 1978 by Dietmen who had left the JSP. In Osaka Prefecture, it appeared that there would be a close contest between the incumbent governor, Kuroda Ryōichi, backed by the JCP, and Kishi Sakae, jointly put forth by the LDP, JSP, Kōmeitō, and DSP, with additional support from the NLC. Gubernatorial campaigns in fifteen prefectures, including Tokyo and Osaka, officially began on March 14. Prime Minister Ōhira stood together with Kōmeitō Secretary-General Takeiri and DSP Secretary-General Sasaki at the Sukiyabashi crossing in Tokyo's Ginza district and appealed to passers-by to revitalize a city that had shown many signs of decay in the years of the Minobe regime: "No city in the world has more vitality than Tokyo. It is a city that brings together the best of a heritage of three centuries as Edo [the former name of Tokyo until 1868] and the one century that has passed since the Meiji Restoration. Tokyo is in the forefront of the Japanese people's affections and is the center of the nation's life. However, Tokyo is beset with problems and finds itself in an unhealthy state. . . . Although the Kōmeitō, DSP, and LDP each have differing approaches and policies, when it comes to giving Tokyo new life they are in complete agreement. . . . For the sake of the citizens, and for the sake of rescuing Tokyo from the sickbed, we must win this fight."

The voting for prefectural governors on April 8 resulted in every case in victory for candidates either directly sponsored or otherwise backed by the LDP. In the elections for city mayors held a few days later, among candidates supported by the LDP alone there were nineteen victories and three defeats; among those supported by the LDP together with the Kōmeitō and DSP there were twelve victories and three defeats, and among those supported by conservative–progressive coalitions there were ten victories and only one defeat. The newspapers carried such headlines as: "Local Governments Move Toward Conservative–Moderate Era." In the elections for prefectural assembly members, which traditionally reflected trends in party strength, it was seen that in comparison with the last such elections four years previously, a brake had been applied to the downward trend in LDP strength, while the decline of the JSP continued, the Kōmeitō and DSP stayed on an even keel, and the JCP registered an upswing.

Questioned on overall results by reporters on April 24 (the day the ballots cast in the mayoral elections were opened), Prime Minister Ōhira replied, "I am happy that the elections were carried out in a peaceful and orderly fashion." He went on to state calmly, "The people's approach to local autonomy and local politics was cool-headed and realistic. It is said that the conservative and middle-of-the-road forces have expanded and to some extent this may be true. We feel we have been partly responsible."

Both before and after the unified local elections, what attracted the most discussion in the Diet were the issues of an "era name law" (gengōhō) and the continuing rumors of illegal dealings in connection with the McDonnell Douglas and Grumman aircraft sales. The issue of establishing an era name law concerned the proposal to give a legal basis to the traditional system of assigning an era name—such as Meiji, Taishō, Shōwa—to each future emperor's reign. This proposal had for some time been pushed by a number of people within the LDP and in other circles. After the beginning of 1978, during the Fukuda Administration, this proposal was bolstered by a resolution adopted by the NLC and DSP. The parliamentary movement grew as the Kōmeitō expressed its approval. As a party, the LDP had generally adopted a cautious attitude, but it, too, became caught up in the momentum and passed a party resolution supporting the legislation. As a result, in the autumn of 1978, the Fukuda Cabinet passed a resolution to the effect that era names should be continued on a legislated basis rather than the previous system of depending on cabinet notification. Ōhira, who at that time was LDP secretary-general, gave his approval to this resolution and agreed that a relevant bill should be submitted to the next regular Diet session.

This bill was submitted on February 2, 1979, and explanations of its purpose were given before a Lower House plenary session on March 16. Both the JSP and JCP held that to legislate an era name law would go against the spirit of the Constitution and urged the government to withdraw the bill. However, Prime Minister Ōhira rejected the request by saying, "Era names are a cultural inheritance from our forbears and the people hope the era names will be continued." Starting on April 10, special hearings on an era name law were held in Tokyo and other cities at which various persons were invited to state their views. The bill was approved in the Lower House on April 24 and in the Upper House on June 6, near the end of the

Diet term. Thus, era names became formalized in law, to be instituted by government ordinance. It was in accordance with the provisions of this law that the era name Heisei was immediately and without objection instituted with the change of reigns when the Shōwa emperor died on January 7, 1989.

Already before the unified local elections, the focus of attention in the McDonnell Douglas and Grumman affairs had switched to the question of whether former Prime Minister Kishi and former Defense Agency Director-General Matsuno Raizō, both of whom were suspected of having received bribes, would be called as witnesses in a Diet inquiry. The LDP was opposed on the grounds that investigations were still under way and claimed that Diet members should not be made to testify in the absence of a law explicitly dealing with Diet testimonies regarding criminal cases. On this issue the LDP continued to be at loggerheads with the opposition parties. Nevertheless, the investigation continued, and in early April there was a series of arrests of managers of the Nisshō Iwai trading company, and the ultimate focus of the investigations turned to high government officials suspected of taking bribes.

Following a brief letup at the time of the unified local elections, the opposition parties began even more strident demands that Kishi and Matsuno be summoned to testify before the Diet, and public criticism of the LDP, which continued to reject these demands, became daily more intense. Even after it was learned in early May that the Tokyo District Public Prosecutor's Office had heard particulars of the case directly from Matsuno, the LDP was unable to accede to demands that Kishi and Matsuno testify before the Diet, given their high positions within the party. Consequently, the opposition parties began tactics of holding up consideration of Diet bills. Beginning on May 10, Diet proceedings were at a standstill, and rising criticism was directed at LDP leaders. On May 15, the criminal investigation, which had lasted five months, came to an end with the indictment of a Nisshō Iwai vice-president and another company employee. Before a Lower House Special Investigative Committee on Aircraft Imports, the results of the criminal investigation were reported by the Ministry of Justice's Criminal Affairs Bureau Director-General (later prosecutor-general of the Supreme Public Prosecutor's Office) Itō Shigeki as follows: (1) it had not been possible to accept the whole SEC report on the McDonnell Douglas and Grumman companies as containing grounds for suspicion of illegal acts; and (2) Nisshō Iwai had between 1967 and 1971 paid ¥500 million to a certain unspecified politician in connection with the sale of F4E Phantom military jet fighters, but it was impossible to prosecute him because of jurisdictional restrictions of the prosecutor's office and the considerable time that had elapsed since the alleged bribery.

Following this, former Defense Agency Director-General Matsuno Raizō decided to testify before the Diet, where he was questioned, amid much public interest, by the above-mentioned Lower House Special Investigative Committee on Aircraft Imports on May 24, and by a similar special committee in the Upper House on May 28. He testified that the ¥500 million had been a "political contribution" to him personally, an explanation that was greatly at odds with that of authorities in the Public Prosecutor's Office, who considered the payment to have been in the nature of a reward for services rendered. The opposition parties reacted by forcing Diet discussion to a standstill on June 6. With the situation still unresolved, the 87th Ordinary Diet came to an end on June 14, leaving a number of important bills null and void for lack of formal debate.

During these events, Ōhira adopted the stance that "since these are issues that relate to trust in politics, they must be clarified until no doubts remain." He often repeated statements like the following: "Trusting in the investigating authorities and respecting their investigations, the government is doing its best. Insofar as possible, the government will not shrink from cooperation in the exercise of the Diet's authority to investigate matters of national administration." In other words, he was trying to follow the principle of a separation and balance of powers among the executive, legislative, and judicial branches. In Ōhira's opinion, "If the executive branch should on its own make public personal secrets ... when the executive is linked to certain political forces, this can affect the continuation in power of a given administration, and there would thus be the danger of adding autocratic elements to a democratic system." This was said to have been completely contrary to Miki's stance at the time when the Lockheed Incident was revealed.

However, Ōhira tried hard to prevent the recurrence of similar headaches. As the result of a cabinet resolution of May 22, it was decided to study effective measures from a new perspective and to strengthen government ethics. The government also established the Council on Measures to Prevent Aircraft Scandals as an advisory body to the prime minister, made up of a number of capable and knowledgeable persons. The first meeting of this body was held on May 31, and after subsequent meetings and discussions its conclusions were reported to the prime minister on September 5 in the form of recommendations under four headings: (1) measures for "purifying" politics; (2) measures for preserving enterprise ethics; (3) measures for preserving fairness in public administration; and (4) the improvement and strengthening of penal regulations.

Chapter 33

The Tokyo Summit

The biggest event on the diplomatic agenda, for which the Ōhira Cabinet had to prepare from its very inception, was the summit meeting in Tokyo of the heads of state of the seven major industrialized democracies on June 28 and 29, 1979. Whether this would be a success had great significance for international politics, and the diplomatic skills of the host country would be tested before the world. As the international community was becoming more pluralistic and interdependent, it was not always easy to agree on how world order should best be maintained. Subtle changes were seen in the U.S.–Soviet balance, and tensions were growing in several regions, making for global instability. As for trends in the world economy, the influence of the second oil crisis stemming from the revolution in Iran was becoming more pronounced, most countries were suffering from inflation and unemployment, and there was growing worldwide concern over economic friction.

Given the fact that economic frictions between Japan and the United States had been increasing since the Fukuda Administration, it was no surprise that the first overseas visit that Ōhira made as prime minister was to the United States. Japan's large current account surplus invited criticism from the United States and Europe, and Ōhira's statement at a press conference soon after assuming office that it would be difficult for Japan to achieve an economic growth rate of 7 percent, as previously hoped, seemed to add fuel to the controversy. Irritated by this statement, President Carter sent Ōhira a letter chastising Japan for giving up the 7 percent growth target. In an interview published on New Year's Day, Prime Minister Ōhira explained as follows: "I have never abandoned the 7 percent growth rate. But even during the previous administration I judged that rate to be difficult to achieve in current circumstances. In this administration, too, I feel that it will be hard to achieve it during the current year. However, I'd like you not to use the words 'give up,' as they cause misunderstanding. The problem is to aim for as high a growth rate as possible, to try and increase domestic demand, and to decrease the current account surplus."

However, at the start of 1979, U.S.-Japan economic relations were becoming even more strained. There were signs of distrust in the United States, as if Japan was suspected of not doing enough. Problems surfaced in regard to frustrated American hopes for greater Japanese imports of cars, leather, and other products, as well as American demands for more open procurement of equipment by the Nippon Telegraph and Telephone Public Corporation (NTT), discussed at the Tokyo Round of GATT talks. It was even feared that U.S.-Japan economic frictions could escalate to affect questions of national defense, and the prime minister was repeatedly urged to visit the United States to improve relations. Then, when President Carter somewhat indirectly suggested that he would welcome a visit to the United States by Prime Minister Ōhira prior to the Tokyo Summit, Ōhira was convinced he should make the trip as soon as possible. In a speech before the Foreign Correspondents' Club in Tokyo on February 22, Ōhira stated, "This matter goes beyond economics, and we must by all means prevent [economic frictions] from developing into large political problems." He went on to say, "To work for an early resolution of these problems at the top level, I hope to visit the United States at a time convenient for both countries." On March 23, Prime Minister Ōhira conferred at the Prime Minister's Official Residence with Special Envoy Henry Owen, and it was decided that Ōhira would visit Washington on May 2.

In late March, Ōhira—in the hope of resolving the immediate frictions caused by the NTT procurement issue prior to his talks with President Carter—dispatched Ushiba Nobuhiko, who had earlier held a cabinet portfolio for foreign economic relations, to Washington. However, Ushiba's negotiations in Washington turned out to be more difficult than anticipated. The American stance was firm, and this particular problem was seen as a serious one, which might not be cleared up before the prime minister's visit.

Ōhira and his entourage left Haneda airport for Washington at 3 P.M. on April 30, 1979, amid light rain. The next day, Ōhira attended a breakfast meeting sponsored by Katharine Graham, owner of the influential *Washington Post*, and chatted to newspaper staff. Even before his arrival, *The Washington Post* had featured articles on his personality and policies, one result of the public relations efforts of Ōhira's staff, who had sent to the United States, for advance distribution, pamphlets introducing the prime minister and copies of a translation of his autobiographical

Watakushi no rirekisho, titled in English, *Brush Strokes: Moments from My Life.*

May 2, the day scheduled for the meeting with President Carter, was a cloudless spring day, and a little before 10 A.M. Prime Minister Ōhira and his wife arrived at the South Lawn of the White House and exchanged greetings with President and Mrs. Carter. On meeting Ōhira, President Carter's first remark was, "The first time I saw you in Japan, I said, 'Next time let's meet at the White House,' but I didn't get around to saying, 'I'll meet you as prime minister.' Well, I'm very happy that we are able to meet here." As President Carter mentioned, the two had previously met in 1975 in Ōhira's office when he was minister of finance in the Miki Cabinet. At that time, Carter had just resigned as governor of Georgia to prepare for the presidential election the following year, and he was still virtually unknown in Japan. Ōhira was in conference before their meeting, and it turned out that he kept Carter waiting for forty-five minutes. Ōhira had not forgotten this, and as soon as he heard President Carter's humorous remark he made a wry face, which caused a laugh.

Before the official talks, President Carter hosted a welcoming ceremony, at which he communicated the importance of Japan by stating, "We consider the relationship with Japan to be the cornerstone of the implementation of American policy throughout Asia." In reply, Ōhira said, "I am convinced that Japan and the United States can overcome a variety of challenges to fulfill their constructive roles. I believe this because we have among us the spiritual resources as well as abundant material and technical resources to see these tasks through to a successful conclusion. Japan . . . is fully cognizant of its responsibilities in all these areas. In close and productive partnership with the United States, our irreplaceable friend and ally, we have great tasks to perform. That is why I have come."

Insofar as Japan and the United States were linked by their security treaty, it was a well-known fact that they were allies; yet until this time the Japanese government had never formally employed the word "alliance" (*dōmei*) or "ally" (*dōmeikoku*), presumably to avoid provoking political forces in Japan that were opposed to the U.S.–Japanese military cooperation that formed the basis of the security treaty. Ōhira's deliberate use of the word "ally" was no doubt meant to remind his listeners of the crises faced by the liberal democracies and the responsibilities of the United States that affect their destinies, as well as to express his view that Japan would give unstinting support to the United States in its efforts to promote the ideals of liberal democracy. Ōhira stated: "I even feel that if the United States did not fulfill its worldwide responsibilities as the leader of democracy and freedom, the world would not be worth living in," and in general he encouraged President Carter to continue to address his presidential responsibilities with courage and self-confidence.

The talks in Washington between the two leaders covered China, Vietnam, relations with the ASEAN countries, Indochinese refugees, issues relating to Middle East problems, negotiations on strategic arms limitation and other defense issues, U.S.-Japan economic issues, and the upcoming Tokyo Summit. The second conversation, held in the afternoon, concerned the president's visit to Japan and preparations for the Tokyo Summit. The end of the talks was marked by a joint communiqué, which included agreement on setting up an Advisory Group on U.S.-Japan Relations, which came to be popularly known as the "Wise Men's Group." (This was formally set up on November 16 with four Japanese members—Foreign Ministry Adviser Ushiba Nobuhiko, Nomura Research Institute President Saeki Kiichi, Daiichi Kangyō Bank President Muramoto Shūzō, and Sony Chairman Morita Akio—and four American members, including former Ambassador to Japan [1972–73] Robert S. Ingersoll. The group's first meeting was held in Washington on December 14 and 15.)

Ōhira had often said: "Summits are meaningful because they offer a chance to meet and talk together. In some cases, a single handshake may be all that's really needed because, to insure success, both parties entrusted with handling matters at the working level do their very best to see that all problems are solved." As these words might indicate, in talks with President Carter defense issues were not discussed at any length, and others had been delegated to work on resolving economic frictions. As for the NTT procurement issue, which was expected to be the most difficult, there was agreement on the basic approach of seeking solutions in keeping with mutually acceptable principles. Following their talks, both Prime Minister Ōhira and President Carter seemed satisfied and in good spirits. That same evening, at a banquet hosted by President Carter, the president asked Ōhira about the meaning of a quote from the Mongolian Ogadai Khan's prime minister, the Kitan Prince Yelü Chucai (1190–1244), which he had included in his autobiographical *Brush Strokes*: "Better to eliminate one wrong than to initiate one right." The president's intention was no doubt in part to show that he had actually read Ōhira's book, and in his reply Ōhira was able to show that his thinking had some nuances that differed from Western political philosophy. This had the effect of deepening his personal rapport with President Carter. The next day, most American newspapers carried positive reports on the Carter-Ōhira talks. *The Washington Post* and *The New York Times* carried this meeting on the front page, together with large photographs of the two leaders. For both publications this was unusual treatment of a visit by a Japanese prime minister and contrasted with their previous practice of carrying such news (even when there was a meeting with a U.S. president) on inside pages devoted to the economy or international affairs.

Ōhira attended a luncheon at the National Press Club on May 3, where he confirmed five objectives Japan should give the highest priority to in external politics: (1) to reduce Japan's world trade surplus; (2) to strive for a more open and freer world trading system; (3) to further liberalize foreign exchange controls; (4) to provide foreign producers with easier access to Japanese markets; and (5) to bring the domestic economy in tune with the world economy, utilizing the dynamism of the private sector. Then, referring to the problems of developing countries, he stated: "I believe we should move beyond the traditional forms of economic exchange, centered on the flow of capital and goods, and should speed the transfer of know-how and technology to those developing countries that have the capacity and the will to utilize this knowledge in their modernization. . . . Japan is committed to a vigorous role in our common efforts to build a broader-based and more open international economic system in the 1980s. . . . In particular, as an Asian nation, we wish to fulfill our role and responsibilities by supporting those trends toward stability in Asia, while discouraging tendencies toward instability." Before closing, he said: "Even as we share a fundamental commitment to democracy and the freedom and dignity of the individual, we have very different cultural heritages and perspectives. Just as it is the American tradition to build *e pluribus unum*, so must it be our aim to build unity out of the diversity of the Japan–America relationship. We still have much to learn from each other." When he came to the Latin phrase chosen two centuries ago for the credo on the U.S. seal, he stumbled over its pronunciation and twice tried to get it correct, but with less than complete success, making everyone laugh. Afterward, an American journalist consoled him by saying, "There's nothing wrong about your stumbling over the pronunciation. President Carter has trouble with the same words." That day, Ōhira also visited both houses of the U.S. Congress and exchanged views with congressional leaders. As an elected politician, he was able to empathize with them while underlining Japan's policy of cooperation with the United States.

After the agenda in Washington, Ōhira and his party left for New York a little after 10 A.M. on May 4, where he immediately attended a luncheon hosted by David Rockefeller, chairman of the Chase Manhattan Bank. Approximately forty influential members of the banking community were present. Among them Ōhira noticed former Treasury Secretary Douglas Dillon, with whom, as foreign minister, he had negotiated on the American interest equalization tax issue over ten years before. In his speech he thanked Dillon for the consideration shown for the Japanese position at that time. He then reminisced about what a great psychological support it had been to hear the encouraging words of those in New York's investment and securities circles who had said that they were always ready to make necessary funds available to Japan. After this luncheon, Ōhira suddenly changed his schedule and dropped by the Doubleday Bookstore on Manhattan's Third Street. It was for only six or seven minutes, but he obviously enjoyed looking over the bookshelves and savoring the store's quiet atmosphere. After a packed schedule in New York, Ōhira and his party proceeded to their last American destination, Los Angeles, where Ōhira enjoyed a game of golf with former U.S. Ambassador to Japan (1974–77) James D. Hodgson and took the chance to relax. His first exercise in diplomacy as prime minister had been a success.

Only two days after he returned to Japan on May 7, Ōhira left again, this time for the Philippines to attend the 5th Session of the United Nations Conference on Trade and Development (UNCTAD) in Manila. At this conference, held six weeks before the Tokyo Summit, Ōhira wanted to show that Japan placed importance on North–South problems and on Asian diplomacy, and that he intended to communicate the views of the developing countries, especially those of Southeast Asia, to the representatives of the developed nations. Among the 4,000 persons from approximately 150 countries who attended this conference, Ōhira was the only leader who would attend the Tokyo Summit in June.

At 4:30 P.M. on May 10, the fourth day of the conference, Ōhira gave a thirty-minute speech in English, encouraging the developing countries in their efforts toward self-reliance:

> The international community must respond positively to the legitimate desire of the developing countries to attain economic independence. It is, therefore, essential to assist the self-reliant efforts of the developing countries by such measures as the transfer of resources and technology from developed countries. At the same time, however, the North–South problem cannot be solved unless the developing countries themselves are prepared to devote the requisite will and effort to their own development. . . . It is my belief that effective coordination and cooperation in our interdependent world can be attained only on a foundation of positive individual action by every country of the world community. Every country should strive, in accordance with its stage of development, to increase its capability by mobilizing its human and natural resources

within the framework of a long-term vision of economic and social development.

Afterward, Philippine Foreign Minister Carlos Romulo, who was conference chairman, praised this speech highly, and many people came up to shake Ōhira's hand. At a press conference later the same day, Ōhira announced that, as part of Japan's cooperation with ASEAN programs for education and training, students and trainees from those countries coming to Japan would be assisted with scholarships totaling U.S.$1 million per year over the next ten years.

Meanwhile, the second oil crisis—which began around the same time as the Ōhira Cabinet—was causing worldwide economic havoc with inflation, larger disparities in the international balance of payments, and unfavorable business conditions. Spot prices for crude oil began to rise precipitously, from US$12.50 per barrel in December 1978 to over US$30 per barrel in February 1979, and there were fears that the era of US$40 per barrel was at hand. The oil-consuming nations were naturally concerned about this situation, and on March 1 and 2, 1979, there was a meeting of the governing board of the OECD-affiliated International Energy Agency (IEA) in Paris, where it was agreed to take concerted action to cut oil demand by 5 percent. For Japan, which had experienced hoarding and frenzied price rises during the first oil crisis of 1973, it was essential to avoid the same mistakes and to chart a careful course of economic management. Japan was being squeezed on two fronts: to reduce its balance of payments surplus by stimulating domestic demand (requested by other nations), and to stabilize prices in a way that could absorb the rising price of oil. Wasting no time, on March 15 Ōhira approved a specific plan for a 5 percent cut in oil utilization put forward the same day by a government-sponsored Conference on the Promotion of Energy and Resource Conservation. He subsequently encouraged all government ministries and agencies to adhere to the plan. As for economic management, it was decided to reduce the trade surplus "in a way that will be eloquently told in figures" by thoroughly expanding domestic demand, helped by fiscal and investment policies. On the other hand, the official rate was raised (for the first time in five years) by 0.75 of a percentage point to 4.25 percent. In such ways, efforts were made to change the direction of economic management from a one-sided emphasis on the business climate to a stance that paid equal attention to business climate and prices.

The OPEC member countries announced that a general meeting would be held in Geneva on June 26, to begin just before the Tokyo Summit, and hoped in this way to check the moves of the oil-consuming countries. This gave the world all the more reason to place hopes on energy-related deliberations at the Tokyo Summit. For Japan, the summit was to be the first experience of having seven heads of state gathered in its capital at one time, and the Prime Minister's Official Residence, the Foreign Ministry, and the police units assigned to security prepared intensively. During his visit to the United States in May, Ōhira, the Tokyo Summit's host and chairman, had formed a close relationship with President Carter that was expected to help mutual understanding, but for both Japan and the United States the Tokyo Summit would be a meeting where West European countries sitting around the same table were expected to present some different and challenging positions. What the outcome might be was hard to guess. Careful preparations were made in Japan as information on trends and opinions in each country was collected through official and nonofficial channels. Ōhira himself attended five study sessions with members of the Foreign Ministry and other concerned ministries, and to familiarize himself with past economic summits he talked with Fukuda on July 18 and Miki on June 19. On June 22, he conferred over lunch with heads of the opposition parties and that afternoon heard the views of Japanese representatives of international labor organizations who would attend a "labor summit" to be held in Tokyo. The Japanese ministries and agencies, lacking a firm grasp of the likely approaches of the summit participants, were rather worried, but as the summit approached Prime Minister Ōhira voiced a more sanguine attitude when he said, "It is already 80 percent successful just by having the heads of state of seven countries sitting around the same table."

Just before the Tokyo Summit, from June 24 to 26, President Carter was to visit Japan as a state guest, and since it was planned that U.S.-Japan summit talks would continue from those held in Washington at the beginning of May, the newspapers dubbed the entire week "summit week." When President Carter arrived at Haneda airport, he became the second U.S. president to visit Japan while in office, following President Ford's visit of November 1974. On the morning of June 25, U.S.-Japan summit talks, attended also by some cabinet members from both countries, took place at the Prime Minister's Official Residence. Chief Cabinet Secretary Tanaka Rokusuke later commented, "The atmosphere was relaxed, and one had to marvel at the great camaraderie that had developed in the two months [since Ōhira's visit to America]."

Between the two leaders, much time was devoted to an exchange of views on the energy problem. Because it had become clear that energy would be the main topic at the Tokyo Summit, the focus of attention was expected to be how oil-consuming countries could reduce consumption, and how oil imports could be cut. Ōhira stressed the need, in enforcing import restrictions, to take into account the circumstances of each country and sought understanding of Japan's special dependence on imported oil.

A noon luncheon on June 25 was hosted by Prime Minister Ōhira and his wife, followed by an evening banquet in President Carter's honor at the Imperial Palace. The following day's session of the U.S.–Japan summit talks was held, not in Tokyo, but, with a view to making it more memorable for both sides, at the residence of the late Prime Minister Yoshida in Ōiso, Kanagawa Prefecture. At the conclusion of these talks, President Carter flew by helicopter on June 27 to Shimoda at the southern tip of the Izu Peninsula, where the original Treaty of Peace and Amity between the United States and Japan had been signed in 1854. There he partook in a meeting with local residents, exchanging ideas and adding a new page to over twelve decades of friendship.

On June 26 and 27, Canada's Prime Minister Joseph Clark, West Germany's Chancellor Helmut Schmidt, EC Commission President Roy Jenkins, Italy's Prime Minister Giulio Andreotti, France's President Valéry Giscard d'Estaing, and Britain's Prime Minister Margaret Thatcher arrived, in this order, for the Tokyo Summit. Ōhira held talks with each of the leaders to get a feel of their personalities and viewpoints and to confer on procedural matters. It had been established that the summit meetings would be attended by the head of state and two cabinet members of each country. By precedent, the two cabinet members had always been the ministers of finance and foreign affairs, but because energy was to be a focus of discussion it had been decided that, according to the issue under discussion, cabinet members entrusted with energy-related matters might replace foreign and/or finance ministers. In Japan's case, besides Foreign Minister Sonoda Sunao and Finance Minister Kaneko Ippei, International Trade and Industry Minister Esaki Masumi also took part, substituting at some of the sessions for the finance minister. These three cabinet members tried hard to make contacts with their counterparts before the start of the formal meetings. The fact that no conclusions were reached prior to the summit meetings themselves was only natural, since the summit was first and foremost an opportunity for the heads of state to exchange views in their search for viable conclusions.

June 28 saw the opening of the fifth major industrialized democracies' summit since the inaugural meeting held at Rambouillet in France in November 1975. From 7:45 A.M., the various heads of state began arriving at the Prime Minister's Official Residence, and the official ceremonies began with a breakfast meeting, at which the agenda was confirmed. Following this, the first plenary session began at 9:45 A.M. in the Hagoromo room of the Akasaka Palace State Guest House. It was agreed that the summit would cover general economic matters (growth, employment, inflation, and so on) and four other major topics: energy, North–South problems, trade, and currency. The morning of the first day was devoted to general economic issues, while the afternoon concentrated on energy issues, including energy conservation. As conference chairman, Ōhira began on a humorous note by saying: "I extend my welcome to all the heads of state and members of your respective cabinets. I particularly wish to express my happiness at welcoming our new members, Prime Minister Clark and Prime Minister Thatcher, and in the same sense I, also a first-time participant, hope to receive the blessing of all of you." He then continued, "At this meeting of heads of state. . . . I would like us to take off our jackets and talk freely with one another in the same spirit as is expressed by the Japanese phrase 'to open one's collar,' which means to talk frankly."

At the OPEC conference in Geneva, it was decided on June 28 that oil prices would be raised by more than 20 percent. Thus, in his or her opening comments, each of the seven heads of state at the Tokyo Summit stressed that discussion of economic questions would be difficult without taking up the energy issue. After this, Ōhira said that he would like to take the floor not as the chairman but as the representative of Japan. He gave a summary of trends over the year since the previous Bonn Summit, pointing out that there had been much unwarranted optimism about political developments in the Middle East and that not enough effort had gone into devising long-term energy measures. He also expanded the scope of the discussion by saying that more efforts should be addressed to structural problems, for which countermeasures were still inadequate. He explained that mere controls on demand would be insufficient.

At a 1 P.M. luncheon meeting, discussion of the morning's session developed at the table reserved for heads of state, and the various leaders held forth for over three hours in a sometimes heated debate on how to set standards for restricting oil imports. Midway, Ōhira suggested that the discussion be moved to the plenary session, but the others wanted to continue the discussion then and there. Consequently, the afternoon plenary session began an hour later than scheduled. Following this second plenary session on June 28, Ōhira told reporters: "After we reconvened at 4:10 P.M., energy issues were taken up. Energy conservation, import restrictions, and methods for achieving them, such as selection of a standard year and time period, were discussed. Various ideas were brought up, and right now they are being worked on in meetings among the deputies. They are not yet at a stage that I can report on." With the discussions on energy still far from ended, an evening banquet was held at 7 P.M. in the Hōmeiden hall of the

Imperial Palace. This was the first time in its long history that so many heads of state had assembled there at one time. That evening, the staff from the seven countries were busy working on the contents of what would become the Tokyo Declaration.

It is said that the original plan proposed by the United States was that oil-consuming countries should, through a unified formula, restrict imports during 1979 and 1980 to levels that would reflect the 5 percent conservation goal of the IEA resolution, and then, each year through 1985, hold yearly consultations that would strive to keep imports as close as possible to the 1977 level. On the other hand, the European Community had issued a statement following the EC Summit of June 22 expressing "its resolve to continue and step up [the] effort to limit oil consumption and, through energy saving, the development of indigenous production and the progressive use of alternate energy, to maintain Community imports between 1980 and 1985 at an annual level no higher than that for 1978." Given this declaration, the EC leaders hoped to convince the other participants at the Tokyo Summit to set similar long-range import figures, even if the formulas were different for each country.

Japan, while basically in agreement with the idea of oil-consuming countries jointly taking measures to restrict oil imports to effect the 5 percent economy in consumption agreed upon by the IEA, was in favor of limiting the period for these restrictions to 1979 and 1980. The reason was that Japan's conditions were different from those in the United States and Canada, which had oil resources within their borders, or from the EC, which had access to North Sea oil. Taking into account previous consultations with the Americans, Japan expected the United States to be opposed to the EC proposal of setting long-term import ceilings for each country. It also expected that, even within the EC, West Germany would come out against such long-term import ceilings, placing emphasis instead on market forces. Discussion of the draft of the Tokyo Declaration continued among summit staff members until almost dawn on the twenty-ninth, but no consensus was reached on recognizing Japan's position on oil imports, so it was decided to leave this matter to the second day's plenary sessions.

However, in multilateral negotiations at the deputy head of state level, it was reported that both the United States and West Germany had come to agree with the idea of long-term import ceilings for each country until 1985, which was strongly insisted on by France. The Japanese thought that if this was so and if oil imports were indeed to be kept down to the 1978 level, Japan's economy, which was highly dependent on oil and was thought to have little latitude for further conservation since it had already taken drastic measures in that direction, would inevitably experience inconvenience. The Seven-Year Plan for a New Economy and Society being drawn up by the Economic Council (*Keizai Shingikai*), an advisory body to the Prime Minister's Office, estimated that oil import needs for 1985 would be between 7 and 7.5 million barrels per day. It seemed clear that if imports were frozen at the 1978 level of 5.23 million barrels per day, this plan would be quite impossible. When the above intelligence was secretly relayed to Ōhira by one of his secretaries early in the morning of June 29, the Prime Minister looked annoyed and said, "That shouldn't be. I haven't heard anything like that. We are supposed to have been negotiating in order to prevent that from happening." However, from 8 A.M., the heads of state of the United States, Britain, France, and West Germany met, without advising Japan beforehand, at the residence of the French ambassador, and on the basis of a consensus reached there proceeded to the day's plenary session. Japan found itself "outside the mosquito net," as the Japanese expression has it.

The third plenary session began at 9:50 A.M. on June 29, and from its outset Ōhira felt "something strange in the air." As if in confirmation of this, Giscard d'Estaing proposed that each nation set a ceiling for 1985 oil imports that would not exceed the figure of a recent period, and this was agreed to by the United States, West Germany, and Britain. Ōhira valiantly appealed once more for understanding of Japan's special energy situation, while insisting that Japan could not accept this. Because Canada and Italy also agreed to the French plan, Ōhira was isolated. With further consideration of the problem entrusted to a conference of cabinet ministers dealing with energy problems, Ōhira told the Japanese representatives, "I am going to keep at this, so you, too, negotiate with conviction." Thus, the cabinet ministers directly concerned with energy issues and their deputies worked until the last minute to further elucidate the issue.

Meanwhile, the heads of state attended a midday banquet hosted by Ōhira at the Yūshintei dining room of the Akasaka Palace. As they looked out over a garden that was all the more verdant in the falling rain, the leaders seemed to enjoy the Japanese-style dishes that had been painstakingly prepared at the high-class Kitchō restaurant in Tokyo's Tsukiji district. However, Prime Minister Ōhira, still troubled over the issue of oil import restrictions, hardly touched his food. When asked what was the matter, Ōhira shrugged and said, "However hearty an eater I may ordinarily be, when I start to think about oil, all this nice food just doesn't go down." At this, the room filled with laughter and the atmosphere became more relaxed.

The United States took the initiative in sounding out Japan on how it might be "to let Japan's quota for 1985 be a minimum of 6.3 million barrels [per day] and a maximum of 6.9 million barrels," and after this had been accepted by Ōhira the Americans began to try to get acceptance of this from the other heads of state prior to the opening of the fourth and final plenary session at 3 P.M. At the start of this session, Ōhira stated: "On 1985 import restrictions, I will go along with what has been suggested by the United States." This was accepted by the others, although Giscard d'Estaing hoped Japan would "try to keep as close as possible to the lower limit."

Just before its close, the meeting adopted the Tokyo Declaration, which addressed the energy issue as follows: "The European Community has decided to restrict 1979 oil consumption to 500 million tons (10 million barrels a day) and to maintain Community oil imports between 1980 and 1985 at an annual level not higher than 1978. . . . Canada, Japan, and the United States will each achieve the adjusted import levels to which they are pledged in IEA for 1979, will maintain their imports in 1980 at a level not higher than these 1979 levels, and will be monitoring this." It was further stated that the United States goal for 1985 import levels was "not to exceed the levels either of 1977 or the adjusted target for 1979, i.e., 8.5 million barrels a day, while the four European countries would strive for a ceiling on 1985 oil imports equal to the 1978 figure." It also said that "Japan adopts as a 1985 target a level not to exceed the range between 6.3 and 6.9 million barrels a day. Japan will review this target periodically, making it more precise in the light of current development and growth projections, and do their utmost to reduce oil imports through conservation, rationalization of use and intensive development of alternative energy sources in order to move toward lower figures."

The Tokyo Declaration also mentioned other aspects of the energy issue, such as oil market transactions, oil stockpiling, developing and increasing use of coal, and expanding nuclear power capacities. The document called for boosting productivity and continuing the tasks agreed upon at the Bonn Summit in the area of general economic matters; in the trade area it called for the steady implementation of the Tokyo Round agreements and the upholding of the free trade system; and in currency issues it called for strengthening the IMF's supervisory role in policing currency exchange markets. In regard to North–South problems, mention was made of the need to give special consideration to the non-oil-producing developing countries faced with rising oil prices. The inclusion of this point was strongly supported by Prime Minister Ōhira, who had announced at the 5th UNCTAD meeting in May that he wanted "to be better able to convey to the heads of government attending the Tokyo conference in June what the developing countries feel about the North–South problem." In addition to this declaration, the summit participants also adopted a Special Statement on Indochinese Refugees and a Press Release on Airline Hijacking. The proceedings ended at 4:45 P.M. with Italian Prime Minister Andreotti's proposal that the next summit be held in Venice and its unanimous adoption.

From a little after 5:30 P.M., the heads of state gave a joint press conference, during which Ōhira said: "As Japan's prime minister, it took considerable courage to set forth specific figures for long-term restrictions through 1985. However, it was a decision made on the basis of the need to build a stable base for our country's economy while responding effectively to the global problem of oil insecurity. In fields other than oil, and especially in regard to inflation and employment problems, the strong concern shown by all the countries for basic, long-range measures to support the industrialized democracies was completely heartening. I was also heartened that the industrialized nations, in spite of the fact that they are themselves in a difficult period economically, expressed great interest in their relations with the developing countries. The world economy is indeed a single unit. It is through sharing a new sense of responsibility between North and South and through sharing a new *partnership* [original English] that I hope to see constructive and cooperative relationships moved forward." The other heads of state expressed their own viewpoints, at the same time emphasizing the advanced industrial nations' unity and their shared hardships and their responsibilities.

On the evening of June 29, President Carter left Haneda airport after telling Prime Minister Ōhira that he felt the Tokyo Summit had been most successful. The Italian, British, and West German heads of state, as well as the EC Commission president, also left the same evening, and the French president and the Canadian prime minister departed around noon the next day. As Prime Minister Ōhira watched the airplane from Canada, the last to leave, disappear into the clouds, he looked relieved and was heard to say to himself, "It's over."

Subsequent world trends in oil supply and demand followed quite a different course from that forecast at the time by most informed persons, including the statesmen who attended the Tokyo Summit. The major reason was the decline in oil consumption caused in part by the overall slump in the world economy, but important contributing factors included spectacular advances subsequently made in the fields of alternate energy sources and energy-saving technologies. The effects were most noticeable in Japan, the country with the least energy resources. Thus, while the Tokyo Summit conference forecast that Japan could be importing close to 7 million barrels of oil per day in 1985, when that date arrived six years later, actual imports were only 4.52 million barrels per day, considerably less than the 5.23 million barrels per day imported in 1978 or the 5.67 million barrels per day imported in 1979.

However, the sense of crisis was far stronger in 1979 than can now be imagined, with many economists predicting oil prices of US$100 per barrel by the end of the 1990s. Given this, Ōhira's efforts to keep oil imports at what seemed a realistic level was natural enough from the perspective of national interest. At the same time, it was precisely because of this sense of crisis that private enterprises made such efforts to develop alternative energy sources and energy-saving technologies, which played such an essential role in preventing an actual crisis.

Chapter 34

A Sense of Mission

Despite the many difficulties it faced, to most people the first six months of the Ōhira Administration had appeared fairly smooth. On the domestic front, despite the deepening sense of LDP unease engendered by the problems of budget revision and fiscal reconstruction, in the unified local elections of April 1979 in all the fifteen electoral districts where prefectural governors were to be chosen, including Tokyo and Osaka, victory had gone to candidates who were either exclusively nominated by the LDP or otherwise had LDP support, thus ending the so-called era of *kakushin* (non-LDP) local governments that characterized the decade between 1965 and 1975. According to *Asahi Shinbun* polls, popular support for the LDP had sunk to an all-time low of 37 percent in February 1977, but rose to 50 percent in October 1978. This percentage fell somewhat after the beginning of 1979, due partly to the aircraft purchase scandals, but the general recovery seemed firm. In foreign affairs, the administration had developed a deeper sense of responsibility as a member of the Western alliance, which was helped by Ōhira's trip to the United States, and at the Tokyo Summit the issue of oil imports was resolved satisfactorily after mounting tensions. Both these developments helped raise the popular estimation of Prime Minister Ōhira at home and abroad.

However, Ōhira was still plagued by the close numerical strengths of government and opposition party members in the Diet, and it was particularly difficult for him to tolerate a situation where a major fiscal restructuring was seen as necessary, but the opposition parties' clamor to keep taxes down gave the government little choice but to compromise. After six months, Ōhira was filled with a strong sense of mission. This reflected both a sense of responsibility and a sense of crisis, as well as the confidence that he had so far dealt with matters satisfactorily. He began to think seriously of trying to stabilize the political situation through a Diet dissolution and a general election, measures that had never been far from his thoughts since the start of his term. His dissatisfaction with the current Diet makeup only increased when a large number of bills were aborted during the 87th Ordinary Diet because of the opposition parties' strength.

At issue was the timing for a dissolution. The full four-year term for Lower House Diet members chosen in the previous general election would not be up until December 1980, and if an earlier dissolution were to take place, the choice seemed to be either the autumn of 1979 or the summer of 1980, which would allow a general election to be held simultaneously with the Upper House election scheduled for July 1980. Ōhira preferred to break free of the situation of Lower House near-parity in LDP and opposition strengths prior to compiling the fiscal 1980 budget. Moreover, the longer a dissolution was postponed, the more uncertainty there seemed to be. Among the most worrisome factors were trends among the non-mainstream factions within the party; for example, there were rumors originating with persons close to Fukuda that the ex-prime minister was saying he would somehow prevent Ōhira from exercising his right to dissolve the Lower House. Yet one factor that seemed to encourage an early dissolution was the prospect of steep price rises (and thus consumer dissatisfaction) in 1980 caused by the second oil crisis. When he had been LDP secretary-general during the previous Fukuda Administration, Ōhira had done his best to prevent an early dissolution, but now he was becoming set on taking this course, and close associates began to make discreet preparations for it.

The first public indication of developments to come was chosen to coincide with a trip to his home prefecture of Kagawa—the first since taking office—on July 7 and 8, one week after the Tokyo Summit. Already on July 3 he had conferred at his Seta residence with LDP Secretary-General Saitō Kunikichi and Chief Cabinet Secretary Tanaka Rokusuke about the political agenda, reaching the decision to convene an extraordinary Diet session in September. Although this July 3 decision was supposed to be confidential for the time being, nearly all the next morning's papers carried such headlines as "Dissolution Seen at Beginning of Extraordinary Diet Session." Ōhira hoped that his Kagawa trip could be "as quiet and unobtrusive as possible," but he was met by enthusiastic crowds of well-wishers everywhere. In the two days between his arrival at and departure from Takamatsu airport, he covered 228 kilometers, the roads lined in many places by people holding Japanese flags, and gave eight speeches at sites decorated with huge welcoming arches, and in some cases enlivened by blimps in the sky. In Kan'onji, where he lodged and had his local headquarters, there were festive firework and drumming displays in his honor.

He visited the house where he was born, spoke with his sisters and other relatives, accepted the warm sentiments of local friends and supporters, and knelt before the graves of his ancestors. In Toyohama, he enjoyed a drum performance at a local Shintō shrine festival, where he had an emotional reunion with elementary school classmates of sixty years before.

On July 7, at the beginning of his Kagawa trip, amid cheers and applause, he held a press conference in Takamatsu and spoke of the political situation: "I recognize that there is discussion of an early dissolution; there are, in fact, opinions advising me to go ahead with this, and there are also opinions advising caution. At issue, I think, is one's understanding of the situation. This is now quite serious, and we must be well prepared in our approaches to both domestic politics and foreign relations. Thus, one can understand the arguments for going ahead with a dissolution and dealing with matters once the political setup has been renovated. On the other hand, one cannot fail to understand the thinking that says because we are in this sort of situation we should not waste our energy. There's no need to tell you that July and August are very hot months. Yet I'd like to have you expect that [the convening of an extraordinary Diet session] will take place as soon as possible." It was a careful turn of phrase, but it was enough for the reporters. The next morning's papers, on July 8, displayed headlines like "Prime Minister Decides on Early Dissolution," and the currents favoring a Diet dissolution seemed definitely stronger.

In the meantime, the non-mainstream LDP factions showed their strong disfavor for the prime minister's mood for dissolution. Throughout their terms, former prime ministers Miki and Fukuda had kept carefully sheathed the potential weapon of Diet dissolution, a symbol of authority and a threat of the last resort, though not one ultimately carried out. As discussed earlier, to avoid intraparty strife and for other practical considerations, Ōhira himself had been one of the main opponents of Diet dissolutions; yet within only six months of assuming the prime ministership he was encouraging a mood favoring an early dissolution. It was no surprise that non-mainstream LDP members had mixed feelings, and there were moves to bolster cooperation among the non-mainstream Miki, Fukuda, and Nakasone factions, which called for party reforms prior to any dissolution.

To get the party ready for a general election, it would be necessary to disperse this opposition and form a consensus. With such thoughts in mind, Ōhira held talks on July 20 with Miki and Fukuda. On this occasion, Miki was critical of giving in to the mood favoring dissolution, asking, "Unless the government first indicates measures on important issues and only then asks the people for their cooperation, aren't things the wrong way around?" Fukuda, too, tried to hold Ōhira back, saying, "It is a serious matter, in such a critical situation, to cause a political standstill for two months." Yet both the Miki and Fukuda camps had already begun preparations for an election and were drawing up speaking schedules. It seemed that in both the mainstream and non-mainstream factions, there was a widespread, albeit poorly defined, feeling of optimism that if an election was held it would be to the LDP's advantage. Although thoughtful and intelligent sources tried to suggest to Ōhira that it was too early for a general election, the situation and the prime minister's feelings had already gone beyond the point where this advice could be heeded. Through consultations among the government, the LDP, and the opposition parties, agreement took shape on the following order of events: the convening of an extraordinary Diet on August 30, the prime minister's policy speech, with interpellations by opposition parties a few days later, the passage of legislation on vital issues affecting people's daily lives, and a Lower House dissolution on September 7. It was to be, in effect, a dissolution by consensus.

Meanwhile, it was coming to be seen that the coming general election would focus on a general consumption tax to be applied to all goods and services, with the exception of certain food items and other specified categories. On goods, the proposed tax would be applied to the margin between the end distributor's price and the retail price. In that sense it would still take the form of an indirect tax borne by the consumer. In the advanced countries of Europe and in the United States, one form or another of such a general consumption tax was already in place. The new tax would aim at stabilizing and guaranteeing revenues in spite of the business slump. The specifics had already been carefully studied in negotiations between the Ministry of Finance and the LDP's Research Commission on the Tax System (*Zeisei Chōsakai*).

As mentioned before, Ōhira considered a general consumption tax to be the key to regenerating government finances. As to when it should be introduced, he seems to have become convinced that now, when popular support for the LDP seemed to have been restored, was the appropriate time to appeal to the people on this issue. His sense of mission about fiscal reconstruction was no doubt nurtured by past experience and by the fact that he had been responsible, as finance minister in the Miki Administration, for what was at the time the unusual decision to issue ¥3.75 trillion worth of government bonds, which he had judged were needed to keep the government afloat and to protect the nation's economy and the people's welfare from the worldwide economic recession.

On July 31, at a press conference in Nagoya (where he had gone to attend an "Art Exhibition by Children of the World and Children of Japan")

Ōhira mentioned his desire to convene an extraordinary Diet session at an early date and his commitment to fiscal reconstruction. A few days later at a press conference following an LDP political and economic culture party in Fukuoka, he referred to fiscal reconstruction and the need for increased tax revenues, but only on condition that the government carry out "administrative reforms that will cut out the fat and get down to the bone." Although Ōhira did not directly mention introducing a consumption tax at these press conferences, the mass media nevertheless carried stories saying the prime minister had "decided on a general consumption tax" and had "suggested increasing income taxes."

A universal and timeless axiom for persons engaged in politics is that to increase or talk about increasing taxes will work to one's disadvantage in an election. The LDP was now gearing up for one, and within the party there was strong disapproval of certain words and actions of Ōhira prominently reported in the media that led people to expect a tax increase. A large number of party members formed a Parliamentarians' Conference on Fiscal Reconstruction (*Zaisei Saiken Giin Kondankai*) opposed to a consumption tax. It soon included 214 members from both houses, or a majority of all LDP Diet members. Reflecting this trend, LDP Policy Research Council Chairman Kōmoto met with Ōhira at the Prime Minister's Official Residence on August 2 for a conversation to clarify what new policies, if any, the party should adopt. Prime Minister Ōhira stated, "I haven't the slightest intention of increasing taxes for the middle-income bracket or for farm households." On the general issue of tax increases, he said, "I'll first look at the future pace of the economy and make a decision at the end of the year, when the budget is compiled." This position is said to have accorded with that of Kōmoto. Thus, the issue of a tax increase was postponed by mutual consent for the time being, yet there remained differences in outlook: Kōmoto felt that if the economy was properly managed, by the end of the year enough natural tax revenue increase would be generated to allow a cut-back in the issue of government bonds, but Ōhira doubted that the natural increase would be large enough to enable a reduction in government debt and that the issue of increasing taxes could ultimately be avoided.

On August 22, at the LDP's National Summer Study Meeting in Hakone, Ōhira clearly suggested a tax increase in the form of a general consumption tax. He stated that to restore fiscal health, the streamlining of administration alone would not suffice, and that "in the case that there is still a deficit, there is no other way than to win the people's understanding and ask for their consent, explaining to them that . . . 'I'd like to have all of you lend your strength and cooperate in rebuilding government finances.'"

Just before the Diet dissolution, Ōhira told close associates: "There are times when [we politicians] have to do certain things that the nation's people may not find pleasant. That's part of politics." One could virtually sense within him the notion, almost an article of faith, that "if you appeal to reason and use persuasion, the people will understand." Ōhira undoubtedly felt that to avoid mentioning the problem during the election campaign and then to ask the people to bear new tax burdens after the election would be to betray the bond of trust that should exist between the government and the people. On August 30, the day the 88th Extraordinary Diet was convened, the only thing he said was, "There is nothing special [to say today]. I'll do my best to pitch with all my strength."

The policies that Ōhira intended to appeal for in the general election campaign found a concise format in the prime minister's policy speech presented before the Diet on September 3. In this, the immediate issues were: (1) coping with the energy problem; (2) restoring fiscal policy flexibility; and (3) strengthening political morality. He explained that the policy base for the first and second areas of concern was to be the Seven-Year Plan for a New Economy and Society, which was submitted on August 3 by the Economic Council and which posited a yearly growth rate of 5.7 percent. Ōhira's speech defined the central task of the energy problem as "overcoming constraints." At the same time, it plainly stated that, in accordance with agreements on oil import ceilings reached by the advanced countries at the Tokyo Summit, Japan would over the short term carry out a 5 percent cut in oil consumption. For the medium and long term, Ōhira favored the development of and transition to new energy sources so that the current 75 percent rate of dependence on oil for Japan's energy needs would drop to 65 percent by the mid-1980s and, ten years afterward, to the 50 percent level already seen in West European countries.

The second task of restoring fiscal policy flexibility concerned those policies issues that Ōhira felt most needed to be explained to the nation. He said:

> The oil crisis of 1973 marked the start of a global recession, and Japan was also visited by severe recession, which resulted in massive deficits in our finances. Despite these financially harsh circumstances, the government embarked upon positive fiscal management including the massive issue of public bonds to overcome the harsh recession and to stabilize employment through business recovery, while maintaining former high levels of administration. These policies have been visibly successful. As a result, however, fiscal disbursements have become

bloated and revenues have been unable to keep pace, with the result that we had to rely heavily upon national bond issues, which have been increasing annually. We can no longer continue this fiscal management in which debts produce still greater debts. To push onto future generations a greater debt than we already have is intolerable. If we leave things as they are, the fiscal situation will only lead to inflation, which will throw people's lives into confusion and will disrupt social justice. We must promptly rectify the structure of fiscal policy and seek to restore its flexibility in the future. In this sense, the restructuring of finance is an urgent concern, and there is no way a responsible government can avoid facing up to this issue.

Ōhira's declaration went on to clarify his intention of freeing the government from further special-case bond issues by fiscal 1984, while sharply cutting back on administrative costs and simplifying the administrative apparatus. To accomplish this he proposed three measures:

First, in the budget of the coming fiscal year, we will lower the absolute volume of public bond issues and will allocate the natural increment in tax revenues with a priority on reducing national bond issues. Second, we will conduct a review of the special taxation measures and will promote a more equitable distribution of the tax burden. Third, although we will do our utmost to reduce expenditures, we will have no choice but to ask public understanding and to seek additional public responsibility if financial resources prove insufficient for the necessary increments in expenditure.

The "additional public responsibility" in the third item meant a general consumption tax.

The *Asahi Shinbun* morning edition of September 3, the day of the prime minister's speech, announced that while a growing proportion of people disapproved of the Ōhira Cabinet in nationwide public opinion polls, the rate of popular support for the LDP as a whole had increased to 52 percent, equal to the previous high reached toward the end of the Ikeda Administration. The LDP's recovery now seemed undeniable. On September 7, while the Upper House was in the process of finalizing the passage of several bills relating to issues of immediate concern in people's daily lives, JSP, Kōmeitō, and DSP Diet members jointly submitted a motion of no-confidence in the Ōhira Cabinet before the Lower House. Then, just as the JSP general secretary was getting ready to explain the motion, the Diet was dissolved. Immediately afterward, an extraordinary cabinet meeting set September 17 for the formal opening of the thirty-fifth general election campaign, with voting to take place on October 7.

The LDP fielded a total of 322 candidates, hoping to win the stable majority it desired. The opposition parties made the consumption tax the principal issue, and the mass media rather uncritically followed suit. The prime minister's fiscal restructuring proposals were attacked from all sides as small businesses, agricultural organizations, and consumer groups opposed any new taxes. As luck would have it, the day after the Diet dissolution, the media reported that the Japan Railway Construction Public Corporation had routinely allocated money for fictitious business trips and used these funds, amounting to an enormous sum, for cash payments to high-ranking employees. This misuse of public funds brought immediate public censure and further fueled public feeling against the proposed tax increases.

Even within the LDP, the overwhelmingly dominant feeling was that "we can't go into an election proposing a tax increase." As if responding to this trend, LDP Policy Research Council Chairman Kōmoto declared before an LDP National Conference of Prefectural Federation Secretaries-General on September 12 that "if we do not err in our economic management over the coming six months, ¥5 trillion in natural revenue growth should be possible." This prospect of fiscal reconstruction without increased taxes found widespread sympathy, and on September 13 former Prime Minister Miki declared, "A dictatorial pushing through of a tax increase will not do."

From around this time, Prime Minister Ōhira became more cautious in what he said. Nevertheless, he still did not believe it would be possible to achieve the goal of eliminating deficit-financing government bonds by fiscal 1984 without a large-scale tax increase. He was aware of the difficulties involved in carrying out administrative reforms and the limits imposed by the budget, but his thinking remained, "Keep cutting unnecessary expenditures, but when funds are still short there is no choice but to ask the nation to assume additional responsibility." Still, in the people's eyes, the controversy seemed to stem from LDP mismanagement. It was widely argued that deficit-financing bonds and the fiscal crisis were the result of mistakes in government fiscal policies. By this time, many LDP candidates were publicly saying that they would oppose tax increases and a general consumption tax.

Not long before the official start of the election campaign, the prime minister sourly asked some fellow Dietmen, "Isn't it the duty of LDP candidates to explain to the people the necessity of fiscal reconstruction?" However, he finally came to feel the futility of too forceful an approach, and in his first campaign speech at Tokyo's Ueno Station on September 17 to kick off a nationwide speaking tour he asserted that he would not necessarily insist on a general consumption tax. In Sapporo, on September 18 he said, "I will present you a conclusion you can be comfortable with before compiling the budget. I ask you to give me your trust."

Meanwhile, new incidents of the waste of public funds were revealed almost daily in the newspapers. Investigations by the Board of Audit revealed fictitious business-trip expenses in the Environment Agency and other wasteful expenditures by the Ministry of Posts and Telecommunications, the Prime Minister's Office, and the Ministry of Finance. As for fiscal restructuring, it was widely voiced that the government should give precedence to learning from past errors and restoring its own unsteady ethics; and the public was becoming ever more averse to tax increases. It should not be forgotten, of course, that certain segments of the media went so far as to give an admixture of exaggerated or even false stories to bolster the anti–consumption tax mood.

On September 24, in a speech in Tokyo to support LDP candidates, Ōhira finally announced his abandonment of a general consumption tax for the time being, stating: "It is true that I had been considering a general consumption tax as a means for restructuring government finances. However, I am well aware that there are not only structural and organizational problems but also severe objections to the adoption of such a tax from the viewpoints of prices and overall economic policy. I can understand a situation in which economic circumstances make it impossible to proceed with such a tax. All over the country, waves of opposition are coming thick and fast. In a situation like this, without winning the people's understanding and cooperation, even if such a tax was introduced there is no reason to expect it to succeed. Neither the government nor the LDP has ever once said it would introduce a general consumption tax. I am doing my best to think of ways of accomplishing a fiscal reconstruction without a tax increase, and in particular without a general consumption tax. Without the people's understanding and cooperation, I will not lightly introduce new taxes or rashly insist on a tax increase." This was the prime minister's personal decision. In later campaign speeches and press interviews he reiterated the abandoning of the tax increase. All the opposition parties, however, criticized this as a way of concealing the intent to raise taxes later.

Within the LDP, which had been successful across the board in the last round of local elections, there was no sense of crisis even if the public temper had developed as it had. This optimism was undoubtedly encouraged by the mass media's continued reports of superior LDP strength. All factions within the party looked forward to victory. During the short twenty-day period officially allotted for campaign speeches, Prime Minister Ōhira traveled throughout the country, visiting thirty-seven electoral districts. He delivered his last campaign speeches in Tokyo's suburban Tama region on a rainy October 6, the day before the election. It was a little past 7 P.M. by the time he entered the gate of his private residence in Setagaya Ward. He looked fatigued from five hours of non-stop speeches as he confessed, "I've done all I could. I have no regrets. It is a feeling akin to praying." The 9 P.M. meteorological forecast reported that Typhoon 18, traveling along a low-pressure zone, was fast approaching the Japanese archipelago from the south.

Chapter 35

A Sea of Malice

On election day, October 7, the rain that had started in Tokyo the night before showed no sign of letting up and only became heavier, with the wind blowing the rain aslant. Because of the typhoon, all of Japan except Shikoku, Kyūshū, and the westernmost part of Honshū was covered by dense cloud with many places experiencing gale-force winds. It was a little after 9 A.M. when Prime Minister Ōhira and his wife, Shigeko, cast their ballots at Seta Elementary School, the polling place nearest their home. Asked by reporters about the possible effects of the weather, Ōhira stared at the falling rain beseechingly as he replied, "I hope it will clear up quickly. It's better to have a high voter turnout." He knew that in recent elections a high voter turnout had tended to help the LDP at the expense of the opposition parties. However, the rain only became heavier, and many voters preferred to stay indoors. In the electoral districts of Tokyo and the Tōkai region, along the southern coast between Tokyo and Nagoya, voter turnout was a consistent 10 percent below that of the last general election. After the polls closed, it was reported that the turnout was only 68 percent, the second-lowest rate for a general election since the end of the war.

At 9 P.M., Prime Minister Ōhira showed up at the center for monitoring election results set up in the fourth floor lobby of LDP headquarters. As votes were tallied in electoral districts whose ballots were scheduled to be opened on the day of the election, it was soon evident that certain LDP candidates with strong support in their local districts were decisively ahead of their rivals. After 10:30 P.M., however, the tally of new LDP victories suddenly came to a halt. LDP candidates who had in the first hours of vote-counting been neck and neck with opposition candidates lost one after another. Even some well-known LDP Dietmen who had been thought sure to win were defeated. The situation for the LDP was especially bad in the prefectures around Tokyo, the Tōkai region, and the region around Kyoto, Osaka, and Kōbe. The earlier excitement at the monitoring center dwindled, and people began to leave dejectedly, party officers included. Districts where ballots were to be counted the following day tended to be those where the opposition parties had been relatively strong in past elections and where prospects of LDP victories were not therefore especially bright.

Ōhira returned home late that night only to stare for hours on end at the list of his party's candidates. He was completely unable to sleep. The next morning's newspapers ran headlines announcing an LDP defeat. As he left for LDP headquarters, the prime minister acknowledged the LDP's poor showing to reporters, and commented: "My intention was to do the best we could and be judged accordingly, and so I have no regrets. In any case, I'm taking these results seriously." Ōhira seemed downcast as he entered party headquarters a little before 10 A.M. After 10:30, for some twenty minutes, he visited campaign headquarters but seemed unable to bear the spectacle of continuing LDP defeats in public, so he withdrew to the secretary-general's office, where he watched the results on television. In the larger cities and their environs, LDP Diet veterans and party leaders were defeated in rapid succession. By noon, only two or three electoral districts had yet to produce a final count. By that time everyone saw it would be difficult for the LDP to hold the same number of seats as before, and it seemed uncertain whether it would manage a bare majority even after the formal acceptance into the party of conservative candidates who had run as independents.

When the time approached for Ōhira to leave for an informal meeting with members of the Hirakawa Club (the club of reporters covering the LDP), he stayed glued to the TV screen and, unlike his usual punctual self, arrived five minutes late. In his comments, he again acknowledged the party's poor showing, saying, "The situation is now critical. As to how we should cope with it, as one entrusted with political responsibility, I cannot easily say. I want to think about it seriously and earnestly." From the nuances of this statement, many perceived that the prime minister might be wondering if he would have no choice but to resign. This was the impression he conveyed to the media, and it was reported nationwide. Prime Minister Ōhira returned to LDP headquarters at 3 P.M. and this time sequestered himself in the party president's office. Surprised at media reports that Ōhira might be intending to resign, close colleagues like Itō Masayoshi, Tanaka Rokusuke, and Sasaki Yoshitake, now back in Tokyo from their electoral districts, telephoned him to give words of advice and encouragement. The final Diet tally had been officially determined at a little after 2 P.M. on October 8. Broken down by party, the results of this and the previous general election were as follows:

	This time (1979)	Last time (1976)
LDP	248	249
JSP	107	123
Kōmeitō	57	55
JCP	39	17
DSP	35	29
NLC	4	17
Shaminren	2	0
Independents	19	21

The number of Lower House members elected on the LDP ticket was one less than in the previous general election of 1976, held after the expiration of a four-year term of office during the Miki Administration. However, immediately after the election, ten conservative independents joined the party, giving it a bare majority.

Ōhira continued his lonely contemplation in the party president's office. An important decision was approaching: should he take responsibility and resign, or should he stay and carry on with his duties? Thinking over his personal feelings and his share of responsibility for the situation, Ōhira made up his mind, just before a 4 P.M. appearance at the Hirakawa Club, that the only way to fulfill the responsibilities entrusted to him as party president elected by all party and fraternity members would be to continue to shoulder the burdens of a difficult political situation. This appearance at the Hirakawa Club was the first occasion after the final tally for Ōhira to express his views in public. Reflecting on the seriousness of the situation, a larger than usual crowd of reporters was present, most of them rather solemn. Ōhira stated: "Frankly, we were handed a more severe judgment than expected. I humbly acknowledge this and hope to make it a lesson for the future management of the party and of policy." In regard to the question of responsibility for the election results, he said: "Politics is in a difficult situation, and I acknowledge this more keenly than anyone. Considering this outcome, I intend to increase my understanding of the will of the people and to put this understanding to practical use in the government from now on." This statement was meant to express his intention of continuing to head the government. The prime minister mentioned, as a specific means to this end, "dealing with politics through a unified party setup," and "talking with influential party members." Furthermore, he called for "giving importance to a conciliatory stance through talking more with the opposition parties than has been done in the past."

On the same day, Miki Takeo lost no time in laying the blame for the poor election results on Ōhira, complaining, "A politician ought to face his responsibility squarely." Fukuda seemed to take a broader view when he said, "Before saying anything about Ōhira's responsibility, the LDP should in all humility take a hard look at its past." Former LDP Secretary-General Nakasone revealed no clear-cut stance. The attitude of most of the party's officers was to first consider carefully how the LDP would cope with the situation, chosen by the voters, of near-parity between the governing and opposition parties. Public opinion—in its judgment of Ōhira's and other top LDP officers' reasons for dissolving the Lower House and calling an election—had been critical and had dealt the LDP a great defeat; yet it had not gone so far as to insist that Ōhira step down to make way for a change of administration. Most of the LDP Dietmen were still in their electoral districts as they watched the situation unfold.

A careful scrutiny of the election results showed that while the LDP had done extremely poorly in comparison with preelection expectations and surveys, the election could hardly be termed a victory for the progressives since the JSP had lost sixteen seats and the NLC had lost thirteen seats. However, the JCP and the centrist Kōmeitō and DSP each came out with increased Diet representations. It seemed clear that the adverse weather had worked to the advantage of those parties whose adherents had the strongest loyalty. It was also evident that the low 68 percent turnout reflected the fact that the turnout was even lower in those areas hit by the heaviest rains. The votes lost thereby were votes that would otherwise have gone to the LDP; hence, low voter turnout was the primary reason for the LDP's poor showing. Of course, there were other contributing factors: the talk of tax increases that antagonized public opinion, complacency among certain LDP factions that allowed themselves to be put off guard by the election mood, and the reports of the misuse of public funds by the Japan Railway Construction Public Corporation and other government agencies. These undoubtedly did much to weaken LDP support during the last week of the campaign.

The mass media outside Japan seemed less perturbed over the election results. For example, a correspondent for *The Christian Science Monitor* wrote that Prime Minister Ōhira had gained victory in the election because the LDP had retained its majority. According to the principles of parliamentary democracy, this had indeed been the case. In this election the percentage of votes going to LDP candidates was, at 44.6 percent, in fact 2.8 percentage points higher than in the previous general election. However, the crux of the matter was whether there had been victory or defeat in terms of Japanese political opinion, hence the focus on the prime

minister's responsibility. In these circumstances, LDP Vice-President
Nishimura began on October 11 to work for a meeting of minds within the
party. On October 15, talks were to be held between Ōhira and Nishimura
and between Ōhira and Miki; on October 16, between Ōhira and
Nakasone; and on October 17, between Ōhira and Fukuda.

After the Ōhira–Miki meeting in the LDP president's office at party
headquarters, Miki again spoke about Ōhira's responsibility for the poor
showing in the election, insisting on "clarifying things in a way the people
can be comfortable with." He was referring here, albeit indirectly, to the
issue of whether or not the prime minister should step down. Following his
talk with Ōhira on October 16, LDP Secretary-General Nakasone stated:
"Party President Ōhira formally expressed his feeling of regret to all party
members for the defeat in the general election and is giving urgent consideration to ways of building party unity. One specific means would be to
set up a moderating body made up of a small number of influential party
members and to entrust the question of retirement or continuation in
office to this body. If Ōhira was again selected as party president, that
should be enough to end the controversy." Still scheduled was a talk with
former Prime Minister Fukuda, but Fukuda had up to then been the most
restrained in his remarks, so Ōhira expected there might be room for a constructive exchange of views. When Ōhira left home the following morning,
reporters asked, "Do you think you have crossed the mountain [that is, the
most difficult point]?" Ōhira revealed his state of mind by quoting from a
favorite Chinese poem: "Above the mountain are more mountains." He
added, "There is more than one mountain, you know."

The meeting with Fukuda was to begin at 2 P.M. in the party president's
office at LDP headquarters. Ōhira waited a while in the secretary-general's
office on the same floor, where shortly before the appointed hour he received the information that Fukuda had left his office, saying, "Today I'm
in no mood to care what happens to me. I'm going prepared for a duel to
the death." Ōhira and Fukuda walked alone into the president's office. A
tense exchange began as soon as the door was closed. What was said is not
known in detail, but part of the conversation is said to have been approximately as follows:

> **Fukuda:** The party is in confusion over how to interpret the
> political situation. The equation is simple. The reason for the
> confusion is that people are mixing up the question of respon-
> sibility and that of straightening things out. The two should be
> thought about separately. The first discussion about respon-
> sibility is also simple. Given the results of the general election, I

suggest some way of dealing with the matter that will reflect the seriousness of the people's judgment and be easy for the people to understand.

Ōhira: Does that mean you are telling me to resign?

Fukuda: I am afraid that is the case.

Ōhira: Looking at the results of the general election, I don't think that we have been handed down such a bad judgment that I should take responsibility and resign over it.... There are a lot of difficult problems ahead and the way for me to exercise my responsibilities is to do my best to try and resolve them. So long as a party organ does not tell me to quit, I am unable to quit. I would like to transfer the matter to the party machinery for any decision.

Fukuda: What do you mean by that? Isn't this something you should decide yourself and not something to be handled by the party machinery?

As the exchange continued, Ōhira is said to have pushed for having the matter discussed in an LDP Joint Plenary Meeting of Party Members of Both Houses of the Diet, designated by party rules as an official organ for party decision making. Fukuda, on the other hand, is said to have argued that post-election designation of the prime minister by the Lower House should come first, and that any such discussion should be carried out by a General Assembly of LDP Members of the Lower House. For Ōhira, Fukuda's attitude, which seemed to be that preliminary discussions were useless and that he should simply accept responsibility and resign, was unacceptable as a means of settling the situation. And for Fukuda, Ōhira's idea concerning the Joint Plenary Meeting of Party Members of Both Houses of the Diet no doubt seemed like a ploy for shelving his responsibility and forcibly arranging to stay in power by strength of numbers. The reason why Fukuda and Ōhira held different opinions was that there was no clear-cut stipulation in the party rules as to how the party's candidate for prime minister was to be elected in the Diet, since in the LDP it had always been assumed that the party president would automatically be nominated.

As already discussed in chapters 27–30, there was a gap between Ōhira's and Fukuda's perceptions of the political situation. From Ōhira's standpoint, Fukuda had unilaterally broken a secret agreement to effect a change of administration after two years, as a result of which he became party president only after running against Fukuda in an election by all party and fraternity members. In Fukuda's thinking, he had not gone 100 percent against the secret agreement because he had honored the results of the preliminary election and did not oppose Ōhira in a runoff election, so by his logic Ōhira ought to respect Fukuda's wishes on party management. Yet Ōhira had gone ahead with the Diet dissolution and general election without Fukuda's agreement, and this, from Fukuda's point of view, could be nothing less than a posture of willful disdain. The unfavorable election results no doubt sparked Fukuda's dissatisfaction, leading to his emotional outburst. In any case, once the two men's feelings of distrust had been detonated, however one might try to rephrase things, it was difficult to return to a harmonious dialogue. From this day, October 17, the Fukuda faction suddenly hardened its attitude, approaching the hard-line stance of the Miki faction. There began to be fewer formalistic arguments about responsibility and more talk about changing the administration and competition for power. And the political map again took on the character of the former rivalry between those factions descended from the Democratic Party and those from the Liberal Party.

The Constitution states that a Diet session must be convened within thirty days of a general election, and that upon its first convocation the cabinet shall resign en masse, after which "the Prime Minister shall be designated from among the members of the Diet by a resolution of the Diet." Over ten days had already passed. Ōhira and his supporters were faced with having to restore harmony to the party through talks and negotiations. They thus decided to ask LDP Vice-President Nishimura to arrange another series of face-to-face talks. In a conversation between Nishimura and Fukuda that took place on October 20, Fukuda said it would be futile to talk with Ōhira unless it was agreed beforehand that Nishimura would be entrusted with making a decision on whether or not Ōhira was to remain party president. The party rules mentioned entrusting such a question to the vice-president only if the president had met with an "accident," in which case the vice-president would temporarily carry out the president's duties, as had been the case at the end of the Tanaka Administration.

Ōhira accepted the formality of delegating matters of party coordination to Nishimura, but there ensued ten days of intraparty argument over whether this delegation of authority included the power to decide on whether Ōhira would stay in office. The public was beginning to complain about how this seemingly interminable intraparty strife ignored the people's interests, and the impression gained ground that the turmoil stemmed from little more than ugly personal feuds. To pass each day in this situation, which had developed quite differently than anticipated, was for Ōhira like being made to sit on a pincushion. He had always said, "I at least want to have the circumstances of my eventual departure from politics clear-cut." He probably would have wanted to resign as soon as possible if it had been a matter that involved only himself, but to resign without finding specific ways of straightening out the resultant political situation would simply be too irresponsible for a party president elected by the party members. Whether he eventually resigned or not, the matter would have to be subjected to formal party procedures. From his critics' viewpoint, however, this attitude was construed as being an overfondness of power.

Thanks to Vice-President Nishimura's efforts, a parley between Ōhira and Fukuda was finally arranged for October 24. During this three-hour talk, Fukuda did not retreat a single step from his view that Ōhira should resign. Ōhira said after the talk: "Our paths were not wholly non-intersecting and neither did they cross."

On October 25, talks were held between Ōhira and Miki and between Ōhira and Nakasone. The non-mainstream factions led by Miki and Nakasone seemed to be leaning toward Fukuda's hard-line anti-Ōhira arguments; thus, for Ōhira, the talks with these two faction leaders were more difficult than the previous time. From that evening, a second turning point was seen in the party's temper when discussions began among the Miki, Fukuda, and Nakasone factions regarding the issue of a successor government. For the non-mainstream factions to make the unequivocable attempt to overthrow Ōhira, they would have to decide on his successor and what character the new government would have. Toward the end of the movement to unseat Miki, Miki had confounded Fukuda and Ōhira with a similar problem, as a result of which the Fukuda–Ōhira secret agreement had emerged. Now that the discussion of a successor to Ōhira had begun, LDP former Secretary-General Nakasone, who had previously restrained the anti-Ōhira members of his faction and assumed a more or less neutral position, subtly changed his attitude, encouraging more active cooperation among the Miki, Fukuda, and Nakasone factions.

When the second round of talks among faction leaders ended inconclusively, there was hardly any hope left that the political situation could be settled through negotiations. The Miki, Fukuda, and Nakasone non-mainstream factions had, in fact, become "anti-mainstream" factions sharply opposed to the "mainstream" Ōhira and Tanaka factions. Certain party officers belonging to small middle-of-the-road factions tried to work toward a resolution by proposing a plan that would separate the offices of party president and prime minister, but Prime Minister Ōhira considered that such a separation would only exacerbate rivalries and refused to accept it. Over twenty days had now passed since the general election and less than ten days were left before the deadline for convening a special Diet session.

On October 29, a final Ōhira plan was submitted to the party's council of officers (*yakuinkai*), reading as follows: "I will delegate to Vice-President Nishimura the conclusive handling (*torimatome*) of the responsibility issue, including the question of my remaining in office. I will respect the results of such jurisdiction." Based on this, Vice-President Nishimura in turn put a request to Miki, Fukuda, and Nakasone as follows: "President Ōhira has delegated this matter to me and I should like, in turn, to delegate the three of you to make needed adjustments." However, the three faction leaders declined to be so delegated, and on October 31 Vice-President Nishimura gave up his negotiating efforts, which had continued for over twenty days. Now there seemed to be little choice but for the two rival camps to proceed along separate paths.

Each camp set up its own strategy and began consolidating in preparation for a standoff. The Ōhira supporters resolved to convene an LDP Joint Plenary Meeting of Party Members of Both Houses of the Diet, whose functions as an organ for party decision making were contained in the party rules. This joint plenary meeting would hopefully pass a party resolution nominating Ōhira as LDP candidate for prime minister. In the meantime, the three anti-mainstream factions had used the occasion of tripartite talks among Miki, Fukuda, and Nakasone on the evening of October 29 to bring into the open the coalition-oriented maneuvers that had earlier been pursued behind the scenes, and were beginning a process of agreeing on a candidate to challenge Ōhira for the post of prime minister.

Before either camp had come to any final decision, the 89th Special Diet session convened on October 30, and the next day an Association for Improving the LDP (*Jimintō o Yokusuru Kai*) was formed, consisting mainly of members of the three anti-mainstream factions. Helped by this new initiative for joint action, a further meeting among Miki, Fukuda, and Nakasone on November 1 approved a plan for making Fukuda the three factions' candidate for prime minister. As a means to achieve their goal, they hoped to get a formal nomination by a majority of the General Assembly of LDP Members of the Lower House, where the non-mainstream factions felt they could garner the necessary majority support. The focus of attention was on how many Diet members could be mobilized for the Ōhira-support camp in an LDP Joint Plenary Meeting of Party Members of Both Houses of the Diet, and for the Fukuda-support camp in a convocation of Lower House party members in line with the two camps' respective strategies. The breakdown of LDP factions in the two houses of the Diet was as follows:

Factions	Lower House	Upper House	Total
Ōhira	51	23	74
Tanaka	48	34	82
Fukuda	50	29	79
Nakasone	40	8	48
Miki	30	11	41
Middle-of-the-road	22	19	57
Unaffiliated	17	0	17
Total	258	124	382

As these figures show, in any General Assembly of LDP Members of the Lower House, no more than 99 members (in the Ōhira and Tanaka factions) could definitely be counted on to support Ōhira, or about 20 fewer than the 120 members of the three Fukuda-support factions. Theoretically, the decisive votes were held by the 39 members belonging to the middle-of-the-road factions or unaffiliated members, but it seemed fairly clear that the anti-Ōhira forces were in a superior position. On the other hand, if one looked at the LDP members in both houses, those who definitely supported Ōhira numbered 156, which was not so far from the combined total of 168 in the three Fukuda-support factions. There was relatively strong support for Ōhira among those belonging to middle-of-the-road factions and unaffiliated members, and the general expectation was that, in an LDP Joint Plenary Meeting of Party Members of Both Houses of the Diet, the Ōhira camp had an advantage. In this way, then, both the Ōhira and Fukuda camps chose arenas that would be advantageous to themselves.

Meanwhile, South Korea's President Park Chung Hee was assassinated on October 26 Ōhira had intended to attend his funeral, but because of the deepening turmoil former Prime Minister Kishi was delegated to go in Ōhira's stead. On October 30, the special Diet to name the Prime Minister was convened, with the session fixed to end on November 16. But as neither the Ōhira nor the anti-Ōhira camps changed their stands, the election of the prime minister was postponed. On the morning of November 2 the two camps vied with each at their chosen convocations. The three anti-mainstream factions opened a General Assembly of LDP Members of the Lower House in the Diet building at 11:00 A.M., attended by 155 members, and voted for Fukuda's nomination as candidate for prime minister. At 11:30 A.M. in the ninth-floor conference hall at LDP headquarters, the two mainstream factions held their Joint Plenary Meeting of Party Members of Both Houses of the Diet. A little after 11:15 A.M., five dissident members of the Nakasone faction came in, to everyone's applause, and members of the middle-of-the-road factions showed up according to plan. The meeting then selected Ōhira as its candidate for prime minister. There were in attendance 125 Diet members from the Lower House and 75 from the Upper House, or 200 in all. Since everyone attending voted for Ōhira, these votes represented a clear majority of the 382 LDP Diet members.

For the LDP to have presented two different candidates for prime minister was unprecedented. On the whole, Ōhira appeared to hold the advantage, but it was a touch-and-go situation in which the final outcome was expected to be decided by some 15 LDP Lower House members who were ill (and might or might not be present to cast their ballots) or whose positions were still unclear, and it seemed certain that maneuvers would be carried out by both camps to try to change or maintain the allegiances of dissident anti-mainstream, non-faction, and neutral faction members who had attended the joint plenary meeting of party members.

On the evening of November 2, Lower House Speaker Nadao was visibly displeased as he stood before a Lower House plenary session to complain: "It is not desirable to have two candidates for prime minister from the same party. It is a problem when the Liberal Democratic Party's disharmony is brought into the Diet." Vice-President Nishimura, Diet Affairs Committee Chairman Kanemaru, and former Chief Cabinet Secretary Abe submitted a plan that included reselecting the party president by the LDP convention scheduled for the next January, and otherwise worked for a last-minute reconciliation between Ōhira and Fukuda. However, the anti-mainstream factions were dominated by a hard-line stance that they should aim for a standoff even if it meant a party split. The situation could hardly be more tense.

At a meeting of the Board of Directors of the Lower House Standing Committee on Rules and Administration earlier the same day, a member of one of the anti-mainstream factions is reported to have said to one of the opposition party members that "a new grouping is in preparation." This rumor of an LDP breakaway group sent shock waves through the Diet. In any case, the anti-mainstream factions' tactics of delaying Diet proceedings on November 2 succeeded in postponing a standoff until Monday, November 5, following a two-day break that included Culture Day, a national holiday, on November 3.

The opposition parties' ultimate responses to these movements within the LDP were hard to guess. The JSP was calling for unity among the opposition parties so as to replace the LDP in power; the DSP's attitude was one of watching and waiting, believing that in the case of an LDP split it might be possible to take part in a coalition cabinet. No easy predictions could be made about the response of the Kōmeitō or the NLC. At this point, with the internal rivalries of the LDP affecting the opposition parties, the political world seemed on the brink of a major upheaval. What was at stake in the upcoming Lower House election of the prime minister was the question of whether the reign of the LDP, in power now for twenty-five years, was coming to an end. For individual Diet members, who according to the Diet rules had to clearly affix their names to their ballots, it was to be both a choice of the direction politics should take and a test of their own political loyalties. To Ōhira's mind, the only way of avoiding a split in the party was for him to win. It was rumored that the non-mainstream factions were thinking of a coalition with opposition parties and were actively approaching both the DSP and the NLC. To block this, Ōhira had to triumph over Fukuda, which would close off any such path. Parallel with the negotiations and maneuvers to gain majority support, behind-the-scene approaches were also being made to the opposition parties by both camps.

The Diet vote to name the prime minister had been set for Monday, November 5, and over the weekend it was decided to hold one last talk, beginning on the morning of November 5, between Ōhira and Fukuda. When the appointed time came, the two men began to discuss a plan put forth by LDP members in the Upper House (who had to ready themselves for a scheduled Upper House election the next summer and were greatly alarmed by the prospect of a party split) to "entrust the LDP convention in January of the next year with the selection of any new party president." This was the same plan that had been proposed by Nishimura, Kanemaru, and Abe. At first, it appeared that both Ōhira and Fukuda might be willing to compromise on the basis of this plan, but because of Fukuda's insistence, spurred on by hard-liners in the anti-mainstream factions, Ōhira would then have to promise not to run in the January selection process, Ōhira refused, saying, "It is not reasonable for the party president to declare when he will quit." The conversation ended in disagreement.

To accommodate these last-minute Ōhira–Fukuda talks, the session for naming the prime minister was postponed yet another day and rescheduled for 1 P.M. on November 6. In the meantime, both the Kōmeitō and the DSP decided that they would, as had always been the case, nominate their own party heads to run in the plenary election for prime minister. It was now clear that the JSP and JCP would also put up their own candidates and try to avoid being caught up in LDP maneuvering. Only the intentions of the NLC remained unclear. Since the end of October, Chief Cabinet Secretary Tanaka Rokusuke and Deputy Secretary-General Sasaki Yoshitake, both of the Ōhira faction, had been making overtures to it, and finally, on the night of the fifth, an agreement on cooperation was reached between Prime Minister Ōhira and NLC Dietman Kōno Yōhei. On

November 6, Prime Minister Ōhira arose before 6 A.M. to check final assessments. It appeared that on the first ballot, even without the promised votes from the four NLC Diet members, Ōhira would win by a margin of around five votes with LDP votes alone.

At 1 P.M., the plenary session to choose the prime minister was finally convened. Because the voting was so close and three or four votes could change the results, both camps were tense as they waited to vote. As neither camp could expect an absolute majority on the first ballot, it was virtually certain there would be a runoff vote, in which most of the opposition party members were expected to abstain. In the initial balloting, Ōhira Masayoshi won 135 votes, Fukuda Takeo 125. They were followed by Asukata Ichio (JSP) with 107, Takeiri Yoshikatsu (Kōmeitō) with 68, Miyamoto Kenji (JCP) with 41, Sasaki Ryōsaku (DSP) with 36, and Den Hideo (Shaminren) with 2. Seven ballots were invalid.

Although Ōhira came first, the votes he received were far from an absolute majority. Before the runoff vote between Ōhira and Fukuda, the Lower House plenary session took a thirty-minute break. It was a tense thirty minutes, during which it still seemed uncertain whether Fukuda would ultimately decline the challenge and allow Ōhira to remain as the party's single candidate, or whether he would fight to the finish. No one could tell what the attitude of the opposition parties would be in the runoff. After the break, it was clear that Fukuda would remain in the runoff vote scheduled for 2:20 P.M. The results were:

Ōhira Masayoshi	138
Fukuda Takeo	121
Abstentions	251
Blank votes	1

In the plenary session of the Upper House, held to confirm by ballot the Lower House designation, Ōhira won 97 votes against runner-up Asukata Ichio with 52 votes. There was 1 invalid vote, and 87 blank votes were cast. Thus, Ōhira was again designated the nation's prime minister.

This sort of balloting, in which each Diet member was obliged to affix his or her name to the ballot, highlighted personal ties and loyalties. While there was not a single case of disloyalty among members of the Ōhira and Tanaka factions, in each of the Fukuda, Miki, and Nakasone factions there were several individuals who either voted for Ōhira or abstained, refusing to adhere to the policies of their factions.

After being named prime minister, Ōhira paid several courtesy calls within the Diet building and then left for the Prime Minister's Official Residence where, in a press conference, he confessed, "I feel as though

I've finally come out after soaking for a long time in very hot water. But from now on I expect to be in even hotter water, so I think it's going to be tough." At 4:30 P.M., he conferred with the top five party officers at the residence and then, before the day was over, had to drag his tired body to pay courtesy calls at the private residences of former prime ministers Fukuda and Miki as custom dictated. The next day, November 7, the anti-mainstream factions held a meeting of their own and agreed to face the future "in an unbiased manner."

Ōhira's first difficulty would be naming the top three party officers. He promised to "carry out personnel matters fairly and not have a secretary-general from the party president's faction." However, the anti-mainstream factions fixed on a scheme whereby they would insist that the ultimate choice of secretary-general should be left to Miki, Fukuda, and Nakasone. Thus, the appointment of the top three party posts was delayed as personnel procedures became bogged down in intraparty struggles to impose conditions.

On November 8, Ōhira decided to postpone the party appointments and go ahead with organizing his cabinet. By 8:40 P.M., the Second Ōhira Cabinet was ready to be announced. Ōhira's close friend Itō Masayoshi was made chief cabinet secretary. The new cabinet was characterized by the appointment of many who had not previously served in top government positions. Ōkita Saburō, an economist of international stature, was brought in from the private sector as minister of foreign affairs. Other important cabinet appointments were the following: Kuraishi Tadao (Justice), Takeshita Noboru (Finance), Noro Kyōichi (Health and Welfare), Mutō Kabun (Agriculture, Forestry and Fisheries), Sasaki Yoshitake (International Trade and Industry), and Gotōda Masaharu (Home Affairs). Ōhira originally also held the minister of education portfolio, which he offered to give to NLC Dietman Tagawa Seiichi some days later if the NLC would accept this appointment of a single cabinet post. However, the NLC refused, incensed that it was not given more posts, and Tanigaki Sen'ichi of the Ōhira faction was ultimately made minister of education.

Party appointments were finally settled on November 16, a week after the announcement of the new cabinet. The key post of LDP secretary-general was given to Sakurauchi Yoshio of the Nakasone faction, whose honesty and sincerity were viewed as especially suited for restoring harmony to a party still fatigued and in disarray. Suzuki Zenkō, whom Ōhira had unsuccessfully tried to make secretary-general in the last cabinet, became General Council chairman (a post in which he had served many times previously), while the relatively youthful Abe Shintarō, from the Fukuda faction, who was widely expected to become Fukuda's successor, was chosen as Policy Research Council chairman, a post in which it was hoped he would gain experience valuable to his future career. Ōhira's appointments were thus complete, and for the time being an end had been put to the post–general election intraparty battles that had lasted some forty days since early October.

Toward the end of this stressful period, Ōhira remarked to a certain Dietman who had tried to adjust views between Ōhira and Fukuda in the hope of avoiding a party split: "My good name has already been tarnished about as far it possibly could. If I get a bit more dirt thrown at me, there is really nothing to lose. The other party [Fukuda] can get some satisfaction from it and I'll manage to put up with it." Ōhira may have triumphed numerically, but Ōhira had also been hurt most. Taking a vote may have been one way of deciding the matter at hand, but it did not resolve the fundamental problems and may, in fact, have even preserved antagonisms within the party, where they might flare up again in the future. Not unexpectedly, the morning papers on November 7 reported the Ōhira Administration's new start as one badly scarred.

During this "forty-day struggle," the flames of the revolution in Iran that began in February 1979 were spreading, and on November 4 the United States ambassador in Teheran was taken hostage by extremist students. Hearing that the ex-Shah Reza Pahlevi had moved from Panama to New York to undergo medical treatment, many Iranians carried out anti-American demonstrations demanding that he be returned to Iran to be punished for past deeds. Hearing the news of the abduction of the U.S. ambassador, which came just as he was getting ready for the decisive vote in the Lower House, Ōhira was heard to lament, "Something really worrisome has happened. Disorder is hardly the word for it." Still, at that point there was nobody who understood the exact significance this incident was to have for Japan.

Part 8

The Road to the Future

Chapter 36

A Second Start

At the first meeting of the Second Ōhira Cabinet on November 9, 1979, the prime minister stated: "It is indeed regrettable that the designation of the prime minister by the Special Diet and the formation of the cabinet were delayed, causing political and administrative holdups. I apologize sincerely to each one of you. I humbly accept the judgment given by the people in the last general election. I intend do my utmost in administering the country, and I hope to gain the nation's understanding and cooperation."

Due to a combination of miscalculation and bad luck, Ōhira had failed to achieve his objectives in the general election, and in order to resolve difficult issues at home and abroad he needed to restore public trust in the LDP, as well as to stabilize the political situation to insure an LDP victory in the Upper House election scheduled for the summer of 1980. However, within the party the embers of the recent struggle were still smoldering, ready to flare up. The opposition parties saw the LDP defeat in the general election as a sign of a new era of coalition, either among themselves or between the conservatives and progressives, and were eager to win a place in the government in the future. The Ōhira Administration had been expected to be a long one, but commentators and the mass media were beginning to doubt if his administration could last beyond the LDP convention scheduled for January, if the budget bill could be passed, and if the LDP could win the 1980 Upper House election. In any event, the general media consensus was that the Ōhira Cabinet would be short-lived.

Ōhira viewed the situation seriously and, in making a new start, centered his policy on the strict enforcement of party discipline and political morality, combined with reforms in politics and government. He was determined to see political principles more firmly established and instructed all cabinet members to draw up plans for reforms in their ad-

507

ministrative spheres. As for the enforcement of discipline, Ōhira insisted on: (1) the thorough investigation of all misuse of funds in government-related organizations or breaches of ethics by government employees, with strict punishments meted out where appropriate; (2) an end to exchanges of gifts and to dining and entertaining between government agencies or government-affiliated organizations; and (3) the elimination of all fictitious travel expenses and other improper uses of budgeted funds.

With respect to other government reforms, he emphasized the following three points: (1) drawing up, before the end of the year, plans to reorganize and streamline the special public corporations (*tokushu hōjin*) and all other organizations subordinate to government ministries and agencies, including all local branches; (2) drawing up, before the end of the year, plans to simplify administrative procedures and subsidies; and (3) self-restraint by cabinet members, who were asked to refrain from demanding any salary hikes. Well aware of the prime minister's enthusiasm for administrative reforms, all the cabinet members cooperated in working out the necessary plans. A cabinet meeting on December 18 approved guidelines for reducing the number of employees in special public corporations and having more than 50 percent of them be from the private sector rather than government personnel. Because this issue directly touched on personnel matters within the ministries, opposition was strong, but the new chief cabinet secretary, Itō Masayoshi, maintained a determined attitude throughout. A further step was taken on December 29, when cabinet approval was given to the Interim Administrative Reform Plan (*Chūki gyōsei kaikaku keikaku*), which among other things envisioned a substantial reduction in the number of special public corporations by 1986. Later, in March of the next year, 1980, specific plans were approved to reorganize and simplify procedures in local branches of ministries and agencies. At the same time, the need for government licenses or permissions was eliminated for 1,200 items, and the submission of written reports was either eliminated or simplified for 1,500 items. Thus, within two or three months of the Second Ōhira Cabinet, a number of administrative reforms were sketched out, some of which had been expected to be extremely difficult. A corpus of administrative reforms for fiscal 1980—popularly called the Ōhira Administrative Reforms (*Ōhira gyōkaku*)—was ready for implementation at the beginning of the new fiscal year on April 1. These were the first of a series of administrative reforms that continued over the next decade.

The 89th Special Diet that had appointed the prime minister ended on November 16, 1979, after naming the chairmen of the various standing and special committees but without a policy speech by the prime minister.

This speech was instead given on November 27 before the 90th Extraordinary Diet convened on November 26. In keeping with the policy lines enunciated at his first cabinet meeting after the election, Ōhira emphasized: (1) the enforcement of discipline in the administration and firm guidelines for political morality; (2) reforms to streamline and simplify administration; (3) recovery by government finance of its potential; and (4) energy and economic management policies. The speech showed that the prime minister was determined to complete the budget compilation for fiscal 1980 (which was considerably delayed) by the end of the 1979 calendar year, and for quick results he sought the cooperation of all government offices concerned. A cabinet meeting on November 30 decided to reduce government bond issues during fiscal 1980 by ¥1 trillion compared with the current fiscal year. Taken together, these initiatives signaled a change from previous budgetary trends whereby shortfalls in revenues resulted in greater national debt, and, moreover, demonstrated the earnest endeavor of the prime minister and finance authorities to restructure the financial situation without resorting to increased taxes. Simultaneous with these domestic developments, there were signs of deepening crisis on the international scene.

First, there was the continuing turmoil in Iran. When the the United States embassy in Teheran was occupied in November 1979, there were fears that this could unfavorably affect oil supplies to Japan, but the tendency was still to look on it as somebody else's problem. However, when the situation took a turn for the worse and months passed by without the release of the U.S. ambassador and other hostages, it became clear that Japan was certainly going to be affected. Iran's revolutionary leader, the Ayatollah Khomeini, not only supported the extremist students and refused to negotiate with the United States but also rejected offers of mediation from the Palestine Liberation Organization (PLO) and appeals for the release of the hostages from Pope John Paul II and the United Nations Security Council. The Americans had immediately retaliated by placing an embargo on imports of Iranian crude oil, and Iran had responded with the expropriation and nationalization of American-owned assets on its territory, virtually the equivalent of a break in diplomatic relations. The United States then began to show irritation with other Western countries that were still buying Iranian crude oil.

Not long after the occupation of the United States embassy, Ōhira was told by one of his secretaries that the United States was considering asking other major free-world countries to stop imports of Iranian oil. Ōhira looked uneasy as he commented, "That will be troublesome for us. The United States is no doubt annoyed, but this will throw our domestic economic situation into complete disorder." Although Japan's oil imports from Iran had declined due to the revolution there, they still accounted for 13 percent of its total oil imports, and to stop these abruptly would damage Japan's economy considerably. Caught between cooperation with the United States and maintaining friendly relations with Iran, Ōhira racked his brains over how he should refer to this problem in his policy speech before the 90th Extraordinary Diet. At first, he thought of making a strongly worded statement that, while Japan wished to maintain friendship with Iran, the hostile occupation of the American embassy constituted a violation of international law. However, he could not overlook the fact that the Iranian-Japanese Petrochemical Complex (IJPC), which was receiving help from the Japanese government, was under construction at Bandar Shahpur (later renamed Bandar Khomeini), and the cancellation of the project would cause both Japan and Iran political and economic losses. The Ministry of Foreign Affairs had no definite position but considered it unwise to anger Iran unnecessarily and recommended that a humanitarian appeal would be the most appropriate. Thus, in his policy speech, Ōhira's phrasing was: "Our country is carefully watching, with deep concern, the relations between the United States and Iran, which have rapidly grown more strained, and strongly hopes that the situation will see a harmonious resolution from a humanitarian point of view at the earliest possible date."

Between December 5 and December 9, Ōhira took five days from his busy schedule in Tokyo to make a trip to China that he had long been planning, which is discussed in the next chapter. During this time the United States was showing greater dissatisfaction over Japan's continued oil purchases from Iran. When Foreign Minister Ōkita Saburō attended a meeting of cabinet ministers sponsored by the IEA in Paris on December 10, he was admonished by American Secretary of State Cyrus Vance: "It is insensitive of Japan to buy large quantities of Iranian crude oil at a high price when the hostage incident in Iran is still unresolved." On December 11, Republican Party members of the United States Senate submitted a resolution criticizing Japan.

On the same day, Prime Minister Ōhira, now back from China, told reporters, "In this [Iranian] affair, politics and economics are superimposed. If the situation should get worse, future restrictions on imports are possible." This statement was meant to show some readiness to respond to American requests. At the same time, Ōhira sought to allay American criticisms through meetings with U.S. Ambassador Mike Mansfield on December 15 and with U.S. Deputy Secretary of the Treasury Robert Carswell on December 17. Thanks to such statements and the talks with American officials, American criticism of Japan's oil imports subsided for a while; on the other hand, Iran reacted against what seemed to be Japan's growing pro-American attitude, and several times issued warnings that oil supplies could not be guaranteed under these circumstances.

By the end of December, mediation efforts by United Nations Secretary-General Kurt Waldheim had failed, and the hostage problem in Teheran showed no signs of ending. The United States took further retaliatory measures and again demanded the cooperation of other major free-world countries. At this juncture, the Soviet army invaded Afghanistan on December 27, as if to take advantage of the fact that the world's attention was fixed on Iran. The next day President Carter denounced this, calling it "the third time in the postwar period when the Soviet Union has taken military action to control a neighboring country." After consulting with Foreign Minister Ōkita, Prime Minister Ōhira announced his basic stance and communicated it to the Soviet ambassador in Tokyo: "The Japanese government hopes that the Soviet government will immediately halt its military intervention in Afghanistan and will act on a basis of respecting that country's independence and sovereignty." As the end of the year approached, President Carter on December 29 used the "hot line" to the Kremlin to ask General Secretary Brezhnev to withdraw Soviet troops, warning: "If this is not accepted it will have serious repercussions on relations between the United States and the Soviet Union." Soon afterward, he asked the United States Congress to suspend deliberations on the ratification of the SALT II treaty to limit nuclear armaments. On January 4, President Carter announced further retaliatory measures against the Soviet Union and asked other Western nations to cooperate. As the new decade of the 1980s began, the international arena looked gloomy.

After paying the customary New Year visit to Ise Shrine, Ōhira held a press conference on January 4 in which he referred to the Soviet army's entry into Afghanistan and the United States' retaliatory measures, saying: "As this is a problem affecting the larger framework of [relationships between] the two great powers, the United States and the Soviet Union, I am extremely worried. . . . I would like to ask the Japanese government to support the idea of having the matter discussed in the United Nations Security Council, to search for peace." At a cabinet meeting on January 8, he said: "I will take careful measures on the basis of cooperation with the United States, at the same time giving adequate consideration to relations with the Soviet Union."

At the United Nations, a meeting of the Security Council began on January 7, at which a resolution was presented demanding the immediate and unconditional withdrawal of all foreign troops from Afghanistan. However, the Soviet Union exercised its veto, and the resolution was defeated. An emergency session of the United Nations General Assembly was held from January 10 to 14, at which a resolution was adopted by an overwhelming majority calling for the immediate withdrawal of foreign troops from Afghanistan and the provision of aid for refugees. While taking the basic stand that the problem should be resolved peacefully, Prime Minister Ōhira agreed to cooperate in the sanctions imposed on the Soviet Union by the United States. One of the first measures intended to express Ōhira's displeasure at the Soviet Union's military intervention was the postponement of negotiations on a Soviet–Japanese cultural agreement. He also postponed a meeting of top LDP officials with the Soviet ambassador and a planned visit to Japan by members of the Soviet Presidium.

With respect to both the Iranian and the Afghanistan problems, what most troubled Ōhira was how to convince the United States that while Japan would adhere to the policy of cooperating with the United States, it had its own interests and could not adopt the same policies as its trans-Pacific neighbor in every case. In a speech at the Japan National Press Club on the afternoon of January 22, Ōhira took up the Iranian and Afghanistan problems, emphasizing that "there must not merely be words and written statements but also action." Yet at the same time he mentioned some of the difficulties involved when he said, "Such measures will be strictly decided and carried out from Japan's standpoint, and I cannot be absolutely certain they will be fully satisfactory to the United States." In the same speech he gave his view of the Soviet Union: "The Soviet Union is a gigantic country that cannot be easily understood. It is a country that is *defensive* [original English], very cautious, and very experienced at diplomacy; thus, even now, I still do not think it is a country that will do something rash." This statement had repercussions both in Japan and abroad, and many criticized the prime minister's image of the Soviet Union as too easygoing. Yet Ōhira did not change his opinion and said, "I think the Soviet Union takes the approach that it cannot be at ease unless it has the assurance of 200 percent security." Not long before, the prime minister had made a trip to Oceania between January 15 and 20, where he spoke about his Pacific Basin Cooperation Concept, which will be discussed in the next chapter.

The year 1980 marked the twenty-fifth anniversary of the founding of the LDP. At the thirty-seventh party convention held on January 23, Prime Minister Ōhira told members: "Reflecting the ways in which people have come to pursue a variety of values, new political forces continue to appear, and there is an ever-larger group of people with no party affiliation; thus, the so-called system of 1955, built around opposition between two large parties, is crumbling and we are entering an era of party multipolarization (*tatōka no jidai*)." He continued: "We must arrange for a broader system that can accommodate the demands of these groups of people with a more flexible posture not bound by the inertia of the past."

On January 25, Ōhira gave his policy speech before the 91st Ordinary Diet. In contrast to his first such speech a year earlier at the beginning of his administration, which had focused on the character of the times and on attitudes toward politics, this one tended to be more specific, dealing with such immediate concerns as the hostage incident in Iran, Soviet military action in Afghanistan, and other events of international importance. Lasting thirty-five minutes, it was his longest Diet speech. He began as follows:

> We are finally into the 1980s.... The problem confronting mankind today is that of how to sustain modernization's successes achieved thus far and how to further develop them in the twenty-first century. I cannot but believe that our success or failure in this task of securing a vigorous existence in the twenty-first century will hinge upon the wisdom and efforts we demonstrate in this decade of the 1980s.

In the same speech, he explained four "signposts" of "innovations and responses" to help in getting through the present age and entering the next:

> We must first, in order to maintain the basic international order beset with serious trials, positively fulfill our roles and responsibilities commensurate with Japan's international position. Accordingly, the pressing issue to that end is that of developing our policies at home and abroad in an integrated fashion and to shift from a passive to an active response to international problems.
>
> Second, we must mount a determined technological revolution and move boldly toward a new lifestyle and industrial structure befitting the new environment. It is urgent that we thus seek to escape from our oil-dependent structure.
>
> Third, with the benefits of modernization to date, we must build a Japanese-style welfare society that takes full advantage of our people's traditions and culture. For that purpose, it is necessary to work to harmonize the man-made and the natural to create spiritual wealth and caring human relations.
>
> Fourth, as a fundamental condition for overcoming these severe trials, politics and administration must be just and open, and must respond to the trust of the people. To this end, efforts

to raise political ethics, to rectify administrative morality, and to demonstrate an appropriate perspective on the changing times and the people's demands are indispensable.

Next, the prime minister addressed the core issues of the foreign policy that Japan should carry out in the current age, asserting his intention to strengthen relationships of joint responsibility with the countries of the free world, and on that basis to expand circles of friendship and cooperation throughout the world. After this declaration of Japan's standpoint as a member of the Western camp, he made a strong appeal for a peaceful solution to the Afghanistan problem:

> To contribute to the resolution of this grave situation, the government will continue to make efforts befitting our nation, on the basis of our solidarity with the United States and in cooperation with other friendly countries in Europe and in other parts of the world. . . . I believe that we must not shun these measures even if they may involve sacrifices on our part. I also wish to make it clear that Japan has no intention to engage in any activities that may undermine the measures taken by other friendly countries or lessen their effects.

This declaration, which may seem quite natural from today's perspective, took great courage at the time, when feeling ran strong that it was all right for Japan to think only of its own interests and minimize its involvement elsewhere in the world.

Ōhira had by no means given up his ideas for improving Japan at home in preparation for the next century. In his policy speech, he referred to three aspects of his Garden-City Concept, namely, his intention to push for its realization through (1) harmony between man and nature, (2) the development of regional cultural activities, and (3) the promotion of industries and employment opportunities in all regions of the country. As for Strengthening the Family Base, he announced his intention to build policies grounded in the fundamental concepts that "children are our ambassadors to the future, the carriers of our culture." He closed his speech by reiterating some of his hopes and expectations for Japan in the 1980s:

> It is precisely the superior character and dedicated efforts of the Japanese people that are our strengths for the future. Now, more than ever, is it my hope that we can build a future of certainty and contribute to the culture of all humanity by nurturing and sustaining these qualities in our society.

This was the last speech Ōhira would give in the Diet. After this, the

Lower House began to consider the government's draft of the fiscal 1980 budget. Controversy immediately began over budget revisions proposed by the opposition parties, something that had come to be expected as a sort of annual ritual in the early part of each year ever since the LDP and opposition parties had entered a period of near-parity in Diet numbers. During the tenure of the Second Ōhira Cabinet, the government and the LDP made administrative reforms and economies in public expenditure a prime focus of the budget. The total size of the general account budget was set, by a December 29 cabinet resolution, at approximately ¥42.59 trillion, or a 10.3 percent increase over the budget for fiscal 1979. Since the government and the LDP had promised to cut the issue of government bonds by ¥1 trillion and make fiscal 1980 the first year of a fiscal reconstruction, they had to see the budget pass without any basic changes. The problem was how the opposition parties would behave.

Three of the opposition parties—the JSP, Kōmeitō, and DSP—had for some time been eyeing the possibility that a campaign coalition among the opposition parties might help defeat the LDP in the next summer's Upper House election, and had been pursuing talks with this and related matters in mind. The more they talked of mutual cooperation, the larger became their demands for budget revision, until finally, on February 20, a draft outline was approved by the three parties for revising the budget upward by the enormous sum of ¥1.26 trillion, incorporating all the demands originally made separately by each party. The JCP presented its own demands for budget revision. The LDP rejected all of these proposed revisions, and as a result the JSP, Kōmeitō, and DSP refused to discuss the budget in the Lower House Budget Committee. The JCP followed suit, and Diet proceedings came to a standstill.

Complex negotiations, both open and secret, continued at several levels. Ōhira held to the basic stance of wanting to avoid any formal revision. Finally, by allowing for some additional expenditures on welfare and in support of price policies, agreement was reached behind the scenes with the LDP, JSP, Kōmeitō, and DSP for what was in effect an upward revision of ¥140 billion. The budget was rejected in the Lower House Budget Committee on March 8, and it was subsequently passed in the Diet plenary session as in the previous year. Thus, the annual drama of the budget came to a close.

No sooner had the budget passed the Lower House than the attention of the political world focused on the Upper House election set for July. Because of the LDP's unexpected failure in the last general election to break free from the situation of near-parity in LDP and opposition strengths in the Diet, there was for the time being no choice but to acknowledge that this parity played a key role in the nation's political setup. The Upper House election would help predict whether there would be a move toward an eventual coalition government or toward an LDP comeback and the rebuilding of a stable conservative government. In that sense, the election was expected to be a key indicator of Japan's political path in the 1980s. For the Ōhira Cabinet, winning this election was now a central goal.

For the opposition parties, and especially for the JSP, Kōmeitō, and DSP, which hoped for a coalition government, to reverse the strengths of the conservatives and progressives in the Upper House would be an important steppingstone and essential means to that end. Therefore, at the outset of the Second Ōhira Cabinet, these three parties worked actively to overcome earlier differences in standpoint to promote a cooperative relationship. Taking the lead in these efforts, in December 1979 the Kōmeitō reconfirmed a partnership with the DSP, and in January 1980 came to an agreement with the JSP on the concept of a coalition government. The result was the formation of a "joint-struggle bridge," with the Kōmeitō as the central support. The cooperation among the three parties during the budget revision drama could be called a sort of preliminary skirmish against the LDP in preparation for the Upper House election.

The response of the prime minister, now released from the shackles of the budget, was a search for opportunities to change from a defensive to an offensive stance and to regain political leadership. Ōhira was thoroughly familiar with how to fight an Upper House election, since in the 1977 campaign, as LDP secretary-general and as head of the party's ad hoc campaign headquarters, he had prevented a turnaround in the numbers of LDP and opposition seats. The problem now was how best to guide the situation to the LDP's advantage before the 1980 Upper House election. First and foremost, it would be necessary to continue restoring party foundations, which had been badly shaken in the recent "forty-day struggle," and to bring the party together in the campaign. Particularly in the case of Upper House elections, where the number of Diet members elected was smaller and each electoral district was larger than in the case of general elections for the Lower House, LDP members were more likely to find themselves campaigning for candidates who belonged to factions other than their own; party unity was thus all the more necessary and also seemed to be an important way to regain the people's trust in the party.

Another important issue was how effective LDP and government policies and measures would be in the face of the many changes taking place at home and abroad. There were problems, for example, of how to deal with escalating prices following the second oil crisis, mounting global tensions caused by the situation in Afghanistan and Iran, and the related energy insecurity. Seen as requiring the most urgent measures was the problem of prices, which, of course, had a direct bearing on people's daily lives. Following the Teheran hostage incident and the subsequent deterioration in U.S.–Iran relations, oil prices continued to climb, and the spot price at the end of 1979 reached US$43 per barrel, or nearly three times that of a year earlier. In reflection of this, Japanese wholesale prices rose an average of 1.8 percent in December 1979, compared with the previous month, and another 2.1 percent in January 1980. At this rate, the yearly rise would exceed 20 percent. Compared to wholesale prices, consumer prices were relatively stable, but by February 1980 even these had increased by 8 percent over the levels of a year earlier, the steepest hikes in two years.

In the face of these consumer price hikes, the opposition parties began to demand direct government intervention. Prime Minister Ōhira replied, "The basis for price stability will be to increase supply and stabilize demand." At almost every meeting he underlined his view that "in June prices will be out of the patch of air turbulence and on a stable flight pattern." The Ōhira Cabinet's response was to avoid government-dictated price intervention and to work to maximize energy savings and to assure stable oil supplies, allowing the economy to adapt itself to the new situation through market forces. This was in contrast to the policies adopted by Finance Minister Fukuda Takeo in the Tanaka Administration during the first oil crisis, in which public service charges were frozen and, through administrative guidance, efforts were made to freeze prices of oil-related products.

In his January 1980 policy speech, Ōhira had stated: "The rise in the price of oil means, in the last analysis, a transfer of income from our country to the oil-producing countries, and the increased burdens must be appropriately shared by various sectors of the economy." He felt a certain degree of readjustment in electricity and gas charges and some rise in the prices of products using oil in their manufacturing process would be unavoidable.

Ōhira was, of course, critical of the idea that a material civilization of mass production and mass consumption could or should expand ad infinitum. Always an active proponent of energy conservation, during the oil crisis the previous summer he had supported a campaign to cut back on electricity consumption for air conditioning by sporting special short-sleeved suits (dubbed the "energy-saving look") in his office, where he kept the air conditioning turned off. At the end of 1979, he had issued a directive that all government offices, and if possible the whole country, should throughout fiscal 1980 try to beat other countries to the goal of achieving a 7 percent savings on energy.

To wage an all-out war for price stability, Ōhira mobilized a variety of economic and financial means, including the credit mechanism, as he tried to keep public expenditures to a minimum and supported hikes in the official rate aimed at curbing inflation. During the 1979 calendar year, the official rate had gone up in three stages from 3.5 percent to 6.25 percent, but when price increases continued unabated after the new year, the Bank of Japan on February 28 again raised the rate by one percentage point, to 7.25 percent. This broke the taboo that the official rate should never be juggled either up or down while the budget was still under consideration in the Diet; yet it caused no noticeable disturbance.

As prices continued upward, on March 18 the official rate was again raised, this time to 9 percent, on a par with the highest rate ever. The next day, a comprehensive package of price countermeasures was decided upon in a cabinet meeting, and among these Ōhira insisted most strongly on those aimed at strengthening productivity. Average wholesale prices in April 1980 were 24 percent above what they had been a year before, but then fell in May to somewhat below the April level. The exchange rate of the yen against the U.S. dollar had been falling since the autumn of 1979, but after bottoming out at ¥260.70 to the dollar on April 8, the yen began to rise in value. The general outlook was that prices were now almost certain to follow a more stable course. We must also credit the efforts of private enterprises to increase productivity and save energy, which began to bear fruit, due in large measure to policies that Prime Minister Ōhira had instigated.

Chapter 37

Pacific Basin Cooperation

Shortly after the Second Ōhira Cabinet was formed, Ōhira made two overseas trips, the first in December 1979 to China, where he had been repeatedly invited since taking office, and the second in January 1980 to Oceania. The China trip was his third since the end of the war. Compared to the first and second trips, which entailed difficult negotiations, this one was a leisurely visit and a welcome respite from the mental anguish of the recent political strife within the LDP. In China, the "Gang of Four" had been purged and Deng Xiaoping and other party cadres had made a comeback as their pragmatic policies were beginning to bear fruit.

The special Japan Air Lines plane with the prime minister and his wife, Foreign Minister Ōkita, and a medium-sized entourage landed at Beijing airport on the afternoon of December 5, 1979. Smiling broadly, China's Premier Hua Guofeng approached the airplane and shook Ōhira's hand firmly, appearing delighted to be greeting the first Japanese prime minister to visit China since the normalization of relations between the two countries. Ōhira's main purpose in going to China was to meet, for the first time, Hua, who had replaced both the late Chairman Mao Zedong and the late Premier Zhou Enlai in China's top political positions.

The official schedule began with a visit to the Great Hall of the People for a friendly exchange of courtesies with Premier Hua, who presented Ōhira with a catalogue about the giant panda Huan-Huan, to be given by the Chinese government to Tokyo's Ueno Zoo to replace the panda that had died. Formal talks between the two heads of state began that afternoon at 5 P.M. and lasted approximately two hours; a second session, also about two hours long, was held from 3 P.M the next day.

The first session was on international affairs: problems on the Korean Peninsula, the situation in Indochina, the Iranian problem, and relations with the Soviet Union. The second round of talks dealt mainly with economic cooperation between Japan and China. Premier Hua underscored the significance of the recently launched Four Modernizations campaign, and Prime Minister Ōhira stated the three principles Japan intended to follow in its economic cooperation with China: (1) not to carry out military cooperation with any country; (2) not to pursue economic cooperation with China at the expense of any already existing cooperative relationships with ASEAN and other developing countries; and (3) not to seek exclusive types of arrangements aimed at monopolizing the Chinese market. He also announced that Japan would make available a ¥50 billion loan to help finance the first year's work on six large projects, including improvements in the railroad system and the construction of harbors and hydroelectric power stations, which together were expected to cost US$1.5 billion and for which China had requested Japanese assistance. This was the first Japanese loan made to China since the restoration of diplomatic relations, and it was highly appreciated as an indication of a favorable attitude toward China's development plans. During the same meeting on the afternoon of December 6, Ōhira invited Premier Hua to visit Japan, paving the way for what was to become another historic first in the relations between the two countries.

Between these meetings, a morning meeting was held between Ōhira and Vice-Premier Deng Xiaoping, who remarked frankly, "There are some differences between the standpoints of Japan and China, but they are not such as to influence the overall situation." Ōhira was perhaps most concerned over the question of Japan's relations with Taiwan, and when he explained to Deng that these relations were being taken care of within the framework of Japan–China normalization, the vice-premier immediately replied, "I well understand," thus putting Ōhira at ease.

On the morning of December 7, his third day in Beijing, Ōhira addressed some 1,100 people at the Hall of the Chinese People's Political Consultative Conference in a speech titled "Japan–China Relations for a New Century: Making Them Deep and Broad." It was broadcast throughout China on television and radio, another historic first. After acknowledging the achievements of the late Chairman Mao Zedong and Premier Zhou Enlai and praising China's modernization policies, Ōhira emphasized the significance of Japan–China relations and characterized them as contributing to peace and stability in Asia and the world. In regard to China's efforts at modernization, he promised, "Our country will certainly lend active cooperation." He then explained the three basic principles for economic cooperation with China that he had broached in his conversations with Premier Hua. He ended his speech with this appeal:

In the coming era, as we enter the twenty-first century, we will probably encounter many rough waters. Moreover, in these difficult times there may be situations where Japan and China sometimes have differing opinions and interests. However, if we continue our efforts, while remembering our history of cultural exchange and friendly intercourse over the past two thousand years and not losing the feelings of mutual trust that we now have, our descendants can surely take pride in the long-lasting peaceful and friendly relations between our two countries. I hope from my heart for such long-lasting relations of peace and friendship, and in intercourse between the two countries I would like to seek, together with all of you, ever greater depth and breadth.

The tremendous welcome given to Ōhira was perhaps natural enough considering the respect in which he was held for having worked so hard in the past to restore diplomatic relations; nevertheless, it continued to astound him and all who accompanied him from Japan. Over Chang'an Boulevard, Beijing's major east–west thoroughfare, hung row after row of colorful banners proclaiming, in large characters, "A Warm Welcome to the Prime Minister and His Wife." Wherever Ōhira's motorcade passed, people smiled or waved spontaneously. Taking time from his official schedule, Ōhira paid his respects on December 6 at the Mao Zedong Memorial Hall, visited the Museum of History, and talked with a number of Japanese working in Beijing. That evening, Culture Minister Huang Zhen took him to see a performance of Beijing Opera. On the afternoon of December 7, after the end of his official schedule, he dropped by the Wangfujing district (Beijing's Ginza), where he first of all visited the East Wind Market. He stopped by some bookstores and confectionery shops and entered a nearby restaurant where he chatted with a Chinese family. He finished off a plate of Chinese dumplings, then signed and handed to the little boy sitting next to him a sheet of Japanese commemorative stamps. He was visibly pleased with this chance to mix with the people.

After his schedule in Beijing, following arrangements made by his Chinese hosts, Ōhira left at midday on December 8 for Xi'an, a city he had long wished to visit. Located some 1,200 kilometers to the west of Beijing, Xi'an—once known as Chang'an—and its environs had been the site of several dynastic capitals, from the Zhou Dynasty in the eleventh century B.C. and including the Qin, Han, and Tang dynasties. Over some two centuries beginning in A.D. 630, several thousand Japanese, including diplomatic envoys to the Tang Court, monks, and students, had visited this city and played a central role in transmitting Chinese culture to Japan. The famous Japanese Buddhist monk and educator Kōbō Daishi (Kūkai), who came from the same Kagawa Prefecture as Ōhira, had come there in A.D. 804, having traveled to China on the same ship as a diplomatic mission. Xi'an was thus of central importance in the history of cultural exchange between China and Japan.

On arriving at the airport a little before 2 P.M., Ōhira and his entourage left immediately for the museum housing the famous clay figurines of horses and soldiers unearthed near the underground mausoleum of the first Qin emperor to the east of the city. Along the thirty-seven-kilometer route from the airport to the museum complex, it seemed as though the whole population had turned out to greet the Japanese visitors; the several kilometers through the city center were awash with people lining both sides of the motorcade route. Ōhira waved to the applauding citizenry. When accompanying Japanese journalists teased, "In Japan you are criticized all the time, but in China you get all this incredible affection," Ōhira joked, "It's a surprise anyway. With all this popularity maybe I'd better move my electoral district to Xi'an."

On his second day in Xi'an, Ōhira toured a number of historical places linked to the height of the Tang Dynasty. He visited the Shaanxi Provincial Museum, Xingqing Park and the memorial tablet erected in memory of Abe no Nakamaro (698–770), an official in the Tang government who came to China from Japan as a young student, and the Ci'en Temple, whose treasures include sutras copied by Xuan Zang (602–64), the Chinese monk renowned for his accounts of his travels in western China and India. Fascinated by the sight of these places brimming with Chinese history and culture, Ōhira came to the end of his pleasant and refreshing two days in Xi'an.

Ōhira's next overseas trip, to Australia, New Zealand, and Papua New Guinea covered the six days between January 15 and 20, 1980. There were two basic reasons why he wanted to visit Oceania. One was that the region's largest country, Australia, had in recent years been changing its image from that of being a member of the British Commonwealth to that of being a member of the Asia–Pacific Region. Australia and Japan, with very different land areas and population sizes, and situated in different hemispheres, had seen their annual trade increase by more than twenty times over the past twenty years and had developed strong bonds in the process. Ōhira hoped to personally reconfirm this relationship and further their friendship and cooperation. The second reason was that he wanted to sound out Australian leaders on his long-held Pacific Basin Cooperation Concept and thus gain a better grasp of its practical possibilities.

In his youth, Ōhira had felt that because Japan was a maritime country, if at some future time it should have to choose between close relations with countries oriented to great continental land masses and countries with a strong Pacific Ocean identity, Japan should pick the latter. It is said that his Pacific Basin Cooperation Concept was bolstered when, serving his first term as minister of foreign affairs, he was shown by Edwin O. Reischauer, then United States ambassador to Japan, a world map redrawn to show countries in terms of "economic sizes and distances," on which the vast Pacific Ocean appeared greatly shrunken in size like an inland sea. The following remarks were written by Ōhira in 1972: "What, after all, is the basic starting point for Japan's diplomacy? What is it that makes possible Japan's existence and good reputation? Japan is needless to say a maritime country situated in Asia. . . . Japan's existence and prosperity, and its security and reputation, depend on the security, so to speak, of the seas surrounding it. Of course, this has been a constant characteristic throughout our history, but with the growth of Japan's economy its importance can absolutely not be overlooked."

When Ōhira later served as LDP secretary-general he expressed the same idea more concretely: "Just as the United States gives special consideration to the countries of Central and South America, and West Germany gives special consideration to the countries of the EC, and the EC gives special consideration to the countries of Africa, it is natural that Japan should give special consideration to the countries of the Pacific region. It is also a role that the international community expects from Japan, which, together with West Germany, has come to have the greatest economic strength next to the United States of America. This is because the development of the Pacific region is an integral part of world development. . . . In the Pacific region . . . development levels are quite disparate, with some countries industrially advanced and others at the developing stage; some have rich resources and others have already achieved a considerable degree of industrialization. Because of this, it is not practical to think in terms of an EC-like regional cooperation. The approach and the way of promoting cooperative policies must give careful consideration to each country's situation, making for a flexible cooperation."

Among the prime minister's advisory bodies, the Study Group on Pacific Basin Cooperation was continuing its work and had already in November 1979 submitted an Interim Report, which Ōhira ordered to be translated into English and sent to interested persons abroad prior to his Oceania trip. Prime Minister and Mrs. Ōhira, Foreign Minister Ōkita, and their entourage arrived in Canberra on January 15, 1980, at 8:30 P.M., local time. Because it was summer and the country was on daylight-saving time, the peaks of the nearby hills were still brilliantly lit by the rays of the setting sun.

Talks between Prime Minister John M. Fraser and Ōhira were held in two sessions, one in the morning and one in the afternoon of January 16. In these, the two countries' basic stance of support for the United States was confirmed with respect to the Iran and Afghanistan issues. The Pacific Basin Cooperation Concept was taken up in the afternoon session as the focal point for discussion of Asia and the Pacific. Ōhira explained that this concept was "to be considered an open and flexible cooperation centered on working together in economic and cultural areas, without intruding into political or military matters." This was the first time a postwar Japanese prime minister had announced such a far-ranging concept. Prime Minister Fraser expressed his agreement with the idea and stated that, as a way for Australia to help its realization, he was ready to hold a nongovernmental seminar to discuss it at the Australian National University in Canberra in the autumn of 1980.

There was mutual recognition that in the fields of resources and energy Japan and Australia had a complementary relationship, and when Ōhira expressed his hope that such energy resources as coal, uranium, and natural gas would continue to be supplied, Fraser promised that Australia would cooperate to the greatest possible extent as a reliable supplier nation. Both men considered that their talks had significant success in firming up a new "basis for creative relationships" in the Pacific era. The results of the Fraser–Ōhira talks were summed up in a thirty-page joint communiqué that covered twenty-six items, which was released on the evening of January 16.

The next morning Ōhira and his party left Canberra for Australia's former capital, Melbourne. At a little past noon, in the auditorium of Melbourne's National Gallery, Ōhira began a speech titled "Creative Partnership for the Pacific Age." In it he stated:

> There has recently been conspicuous progress made in the relations of friendship and cooperation among the Pacific basin countries . . . The vast and broad Pacific basin region has come to meet the prerequisites or making possible the creation of a regional community. . . . Most forms of regional cooperation to date have been founded upon common languages, common cultures, or common traditions, and have strengthened their bonds through homogeneity. Therefore, it may well be asked whether it is possible to create a new cooperative relationship, and hence to create a new culture among these Pacific countries with their different cultural and historical backgrounds and their different stages of economic development. Yet I

believe we can overcome these difficulties if we create regional cooperation recognizing and respecting each country's cultural independence and political self-determination. It is an open regional cooperation befitting the age of the global community. In this sense, the community of the Pacific basin countries is not intended to form an exclusionist bloc. Indeed, this concept is intended ultimately to generate welfare and prosperity not only for the peoples of the Pacific basin countries but for all peoples everywhere.

On the afternoon of January 17, Ōhira left Melbourne for New Zealand, the second country on his itinerary, arriving in Auckland that evening. The next day, he held two sessions of talks, one in the morning and the other in the afternoon, with New Zealand's Prime Minister Robert D. Muldoon, who showed a keen interest in the Pacific Basin Cooperation Concept and stated his intention of promoting it. The following morning, Ōhira and his entourage flew back to Australia, this time to Sydney, where they enjoyed a leisurely afternoon cruise around Sydney Harbor, which helped them to recover from their fatigue. On January 20, they left Sydney, stopping at Port Moresby, the capital of Papua New Guinea, on the way back to Japan. It was the first time a Japanese prime minister had visited that country. Prime Minister Michael T. Somare came out to greet Ōhira at the airport and the two men talked at a nearby guest house, where they exchanged ideas on Pacific cooperation. When Ōhira reboarded his plane, his thoughts turned to problems that were likely to be awaiting him in Tokyo, where he touched down at 8:21 P.M.

Later developments in the Asia-Pacific region were indeed remarkable. The growing prominence of the so-called newly industrializing economies (that is, South Korea, Taiwan, Hong Kong, and Singapore) and the continuing economic progress made by the Asian developing countries have clearly shown that the diversity that was once thought to doom Asian countries to backwardness, in fact, contains enormous creative potential. The fact that, since the mid-1980s, the volume of trade to and from the United States across the Pacific overtook the volume of trans-Atlantic trade is a reflection of these developments. In a 1984 speech on foreign policy, President Reagan called the United States "a Pacific country," and the Soviet Union's General Secretary Gorbachev, when visiting Vladivostok in 1986, called his country a "member of the Asia–Pacific Region."

Today Pacific cooperation is no longer a dream or a slogan but, confirming Ōhira's insight, has become a motivating guide for our progress into the twenty-first century. The fact that, in contrast to apprehensions about what sometimes appear to be "bloc-like" trends in the U.S.–Canada free trade zone and in the efforts toward greater EC unity, one does not sense similar tendencies in the Asia–Pacific region, and this surely owes much to the prudent and farsighted way in which Ōhira presented his concept of an Asia–Pacific community.

Chapter 38

The Last Overseas Trip

In the last days of 1979 and the first days of 1980, the Ōhira Cabinet was swamped with the work involved in the many domestic and international problems that had emerged, although during the same period the situation within the LDP seemed relatively calm. Both the mainstream Ōhira and Tanaka factions and the anti-mainstream Miki, Fukuda, and Nakasone factions had all but exhausted their energies in the "forty-day struggle" of the previous autumn. Public opinion had been extremely critical of this type of party infighting that seemed to ignore the welfare of the people and nation, and the general mood was not one that would allow another struggle of this kind. Most LDP Diet members returned to their home districts for the New Year holidays, probably after two or more months' absence, and they felt uncomfortable at not being able to offer any satisfactory justification for the LDP infighting, even to their closest supporters.

Nonetheless, it should not be forgotten that both Fukuda, who had lost out in the Diet vote for prime minister, and Miki, who had supported him, were still nursing psychological wounds, which were all the more difficult to heal because the means they had resorted to in trying to wrest the prime ministership from Ōhira were not ordinarily thought allowable for party members. Neither should it be forgotten that both Fukuda and Miki felt that each had been forced to vacate the seat of power through the machinations of Tanaka Kakuei and that each had not committed any important mistakes to justify such action. This feeling, combined with Fukuda's injured pride because of his failed second bid for the premiership, aggravated the dissatisfaction. It is said that Fukuda, Miki, and many of their supporters were disgruntled by the fact that their year-end and New Year callers were far fewer than usual. It can well be imagined that they found it hard to control their anger over these and other perceived slights. At the same time, Ōhira, the victor in the recent Diet election, still found it difficult to bear the lingering public perception of him as one in blind pursuit of power, quite the contrary of his own sense of trying calmly to follow "Heaven's will" without becoming a prisoner to power.

After the first half of January, this half-hidden rivalry began to crop up again when some of Ōhira's close associates received a warning from a political commentator close to Fukuda that "Fukuda is thinking things over very seriously. This is not something that can be dismissed lightly." Then, toward the end of January, Ōhira began to receive such reports as: "Fukuda is waiting for the time when the opposition parties present a motion of no-confidence during budget discussion in the Lower House to overthrow the cabinet." Another report was: "Fukuda is saying he'll corner Ōhira before the end of the ordinary Diet session."

Thus, at the beginning of February, Ōhira and a small number of others held confidential meetings to prepare contingency plans. The most important aim was to try to keep the anti-mainstream factions from sympathizing with any motion of no-confidence put forward by the opposition parties, and to prevent these factions from boycotting the Diet during a vote on any such motion. It was agreed, however, that in the event such a motion was passed, there would not be a resignation en masse but rather a dissolution of the Lower House and another general election. According to the Constitution, "If the House of Representatives [Lower House] passes a non-confidence resolution, or rejects a confidence resolution, the Cabinet shall resign en masse, unless the House of Representatives is dissolved within ten days." There seemed to be adequate grounds to suppose that if it came to a dissolution and another general election, the LDP might split up between the mainstream and anti-mainstream factions. Even so, the conclusion of the confidential discussions in which Ōhira took part was that, given the circumstances, this could not be helped and that if such a time came the matter should be put squarely before the people. Even when traveling overseas, Ōhira had always to be wary lest some ominous movement should surface from the dissatisfied anti-mainstream factions.

What finally lit the fuse of rebellion was the news of the Las Vegas Incident involving LDP Lower House mainstream Dietman Hamada Kōichi, which first hit the headlines on March 6. It was alleged that Hamada had been given money to pay off part of his gambling debts to a Las Vegas casino by a certain wealthy businessman who had been accused of giving false testimony before the Diet in connection with the Lockheed scandal. Anti-mainstream activists seized on this as the perfect opportunity to attack the mainstream factions. An organization called the LDP Reform League (abbreviated to *Sasshinren* in Japanese) was formed on April 2 and included leading staff and junior members of the three anti-mainstream factions and a group around Nakagawa Ichirō, with party veteran Akagi Munenori as its chief representative. Hamada resigned his Diet seat on April 11, but the Reform League nevertheless demanded that he be called to testify in the Diet. It likewise badgered the government to clear up the recently exposed allegations of bribery of government officials and other misdeeds by employees of the government-regulated KDD (Japan's former international telecommunications monopoly). Needless to say, the true aim of the Reform League was to use these incidents to bring Fukuda, Miki, Nakasone, Nakagawa, and their followers even closer together in order to overthrow Ōhira. The political scene suddenly changed from superficial calm to mobilization for battle.

In the meantime, preparations were continuing for the upcoming Upper House election. From the end of the previous year, Ōhira's close associates had already been instructed to formulate strategy for setting the election date and presenting policy issues during the campaign. After hearing the results of their deliberations, Ōhira approved a plan to use the slogans "A Single Promise" (Hitotsu no chikai), which aimed to revitalize the party, and "Three Securities" (Mittsu no anzen), referring to security of the country, defense of the people's livelihood, and guarantees for the future. Like the strategy adopted for the Upper House election three years before, these slogans in a sense said everything, yet nothing very specific, since a part of the intention was to deny giving the opposition parties an easy handle for engaging in policy debates.

On March 23, Prime Minister Ōhira kicked off a nationwide speaking tour by appearing at an LDP-sponsored political and economic culture party in Tochigi Prefecture. At a press conference in Utsunomiya held in conjunction with this event, he noted: "We have to win at least 63 of the seats up for reelection to get a majority. We must meet LDP responsibilities by doing our utmost to win this majority." In this way he announced his own criterion for victory or defeat. To maintain an overall majority of the 252 Upper House seats, strictly speaking it would be necessary to win only 61 seats to combine with the 66 seats won by the LDP in the election three years earlier that were not up for reelection. Even so, the situation did not allow for undue optimism. In the case of candidates running for election by the nation as a whole and in relatively populous prefectural constituencies, which were to elect two or more Upper House members, there was not much worry. The problem lay in the number of LDP seats that could be won against opposition party coalitions in the twenty-six prefectures that were to elect just one Upper House member. Some feared that, taken together, only 60 seats might be won in all, in which case the LDP would lose its overall majority. It was for this reason that in Japan's political circles 61 seats was the most generally accepted dividing line between LDP victory and defeat. In these circumstances, for the prime minister to put forth the goal of "at least 63 seats" could only be called bold, especially at a time when the anti-mainstream factions were looking for a chance to topple his cabinet.

From the end of March, Ōhira made a point of speaking in support of LDP candidates in crucial prefectures where close contests were expected. He began to devote his weekends to this endeavor, and his packed schedule included speeches in Ishikawa Prefecture on March 30, in Miyagi and Akita prefectures on April 6, in Hokkaidō on April 12, in Gifu Prefecture on April 13, in Ōita Prefecture on April 19, in Toyama Prefecture on April 20, in Fukui Prefecture on April 26, and in Hiroshima and Aichi prefectures on April 27. Although his image had been somewhat damaged in the "forty-day struggle" of the previous autumn, he was well received everywhere he went. Visibly pleased, he was cheerful as he held forth on such topics as price policy, the international situation, and energy problems. Because he seemed to be all the more stimulated by direct contact with the people, there were few who noticed that his physical and mental stamina were being drained by these speaking engagements. According to a public opinion poll reported around this time in the *Asahi Shinbun*, popular support for the Ōhira Cabinet remained stagnant at around 27 percent, while that for the LDP had leveled out at 46 percent, down from earlier levels but showing no sign of further decrease. The Upper House election would be sharply contested, but there was now a possibility that, with continued effort, Ōhira's hope of winning sixty-three LDP seats might be realized.

Extreme care was paid to fixing the date of the election, especially in view of the LDP's bitter experience with the general election of October 1979, which was jinxed by heavy rain. With a view to maximizing the prospect for good weather and capitalizing on the results of the upcoming Venice Summit, the most desirable date was first thought to be either July 6 or July 13. Almost immediately after the Lower House passed the budget on April 4, candidates from the LDP and the opposition parties began to maneuver in earnest, and soon it seemed as if the campaign had in effect entered its final stages, even though it had not yet officially started. Because in Upper House elections some candidates were chosen by the nation as a whole and others by prefectural constituencies, campaigning usually meant traveling and appealing to people over a wide geographical area. After the end of the ordinary Diet session on May 18, 1980, the still unofficial campaign entered a new period of frenzy, bringing greater pressure on the candidates. Candidates who had already served one or more terms in the Upper House hoped that the rest of the campaign would be as short as possible. Already by mid-April, plans to move the election date forward a little were being presented by the LDP, the earliest date proposed being June 22. Finally, the party's top three officers decided on June 29.

At the same time as Japan was concentrating on the Upper House election campaign on its home front, internationally the country was being pressed to make some difficult decisions arising from the hostage incident in Iran and the Soviet military presence in Afghanistan. Among possible measures being discussed in response to the Soviet presence in Afghanistan, the question of participation in the Moscow Olympics was especially troubling. Prime Minister Ōhira remarked, "Problems involving either sports or religion must be handled with special care. If not, the results can be pretty bad." This reflected, among other things, his and others' concern about possible effects on the Upper House election should there be a decision to boycott the Olympic Games.

In late January, President Carter had already announced that the United States would boycott the Moscow Olympics, and had called for holding the games elsewhere, a stand supported by Great Britain, Canada, Australia, and other Western countries. The Japanese government then requested the Japan Olympic Committee to make an appropriate response, and communicated the government's view that "serious attention must be paid to international public opinion toward the Soviet invasion of Afghanistan." To associates who were apprehensive that this announcement could affect the Upper House election results, Prime Minister Ōhira emphasized that Japan should make clear its support for the United States. He told them, "If we compare the Olympics and oil, oil is the more important, and if we compare oil and the United States, the United States is the more important." In a February 9 meeting of the International Olympic Committee, the motion put forward by the United States Olympic Committee opposing holding the games in Moscow was rejected; thus, the ultimate response of the Japan Olympic Committee was still undecided.

In the meantime, to help prevent unrest spreading beyond the borders of Afghanistan, Japan extended economic assistance to Pakistan and other neighboring countries. During February and March, former Foreign Minister Sonoda Sunao, as the prime minister's special envoy, visited seven countries in the Middle East and South Asia, including Pakistan and India. During these travels he explained Japan's views in regard to various situations affecting the still unstable Middle East and neighboring areas, while listening carefully to the opinions of his hosts. On this occasion he announced an offer of ¥32 billion in economic assistance to Pakistan, which was two and a half times the amount of the previous year. During this trip, the government also promised US$100 million in economic assistance to Turkey and ¥57 billion to Thailand, which was having to shoulder heavy economic burdens due to the influx of refugees from Kampuchea. These were all actions to demonstrate, in concrete ways, Japan's role-sharing and cooperation with the Western countries, and as first examples of so-called strategic assistance from Japan, they were highly valued by the Western world.

Since the beginning of April, some changes were apparent in the Iranian situation, especially when Iran's President Abolhassan Bani-Sadr announced that he would transfer the hostages from the control of the students to the supervision of the Revolutionary Council. The United States acknowledged this hopeful step by communicating its intention to postpone further economic sanctions. Its hopes were disappointed, however, when on April 7 the Ayatollah Khomeini rejected the transfer of authority over the hostages. On the same day, the United States government broke off all diplomatic relations with Iran and imposed harsher sanctions, prohibiting the export to Iran of everything except food and medical supplies. Japan was requested by U.S. Secretary of State Cyrus Vance to join with other Western countries in these economic sanctions, and Ōhira took the view that while Japan should try to restrain the United States from resorting to military action, Japan had no choice but to keep in step with other Western countries. After discussing possible measures at a special conference of cabinet members and heads of agencies concerned with the Iran issue, he made an official request to President Bani-Sadr to release the hostages.

The issue of oil imports from Iran entered a critical stage around this time. In consideration of the American standpoint, imports had not been raised above the level that existed at the time the hostage incident began. At the end of March 1980, the Iranian government announced that after April Japanese buyers would have to pay US$35 per barrel for DD-grade crude, instead of US$32.50 per barrel as stipulated in long-term contracts. Most people in the Japanese oil industry responsible for assuring stable supplies tended to feel that this demand would have to be complied with, but the government, which had pledged itself internationally and at the strong request of the United States to refrain from oil purchases at high prices, was unable to give its approval. Minister of International Trade and Industry Sasaki Yoshitake issued administrative guidance to the oil industry that this demand from Iran should be refused and reported this to Ōhira, who grumbled, "It's a pity," yet indicated his acceptance of this position.

On April 19, Iran sent a message saying that if Japan did not accept

US$35 per barrel retroactive to April 1, it would halt all supplies of crude oil to Japan from April 21. The oil industry, following the instructions of the Ministry of International Trade and Industry, rejected this, and as a result shipments of crude oil from Iran were stopped on the twenty-first. As reflected, for example, in a *New York Times* editorial of April 22 titled "Thanks, and Oil, to Japan," the Americans highly praised this decision. Around this time a meeting of EC foreign ministers was held in Luxembourg to discuss the problem of sanctions against Iran. Ōhira had decided on a policy of cooperation with the EC in this regard and arranged for Foreign Minister Ōkita to visit Europe at the time of this meeting to adjust views with his EC counterparts.

Meanwhile, Ōhira continued to finalize plans to take advantage of the "Golden Week" series of national holidays at the beginning of May for another trip abroad. Two possible journeys were in the air, one to Mexico and America, and the other to the much nearer ASEAN countries. Ōhira personally inclined toward a visit to Mexico and other countries of Latin America, such as Brazil and Argentina, which he had never visited. Japan's ambassador in Mexico, Matsunaga Nobuo, and several Foreign Ministry officials also recommended a visit to Mexico to help in negotiating for larger purchases of Mexican oil and thus further Japan's policy of diversifying its oil supply.

On the other hand, Chief Cabinet Secretary Itō, concerned that Ōhira should not overtire himself when the crucial period of the Upper House election campaign was drawing near, recommended a visit to Southeast Asia, which could be done in a shorter time. Ultimately, on Ōhira's own decision, a schedule was set up that would take him first to Mexico, then to Canada—a country with which Japan's economic relations, especially in the area of resources, were rapidly becoming closer—and then to the United States. Former Prime Minister Tanaka was quick to advise, "When I went to Mexico, I got sick. You must be careful about your health." Finally, the route was adjusted for the convenience of the host countries to take Ōhira first to the United States, then to Mexico, and lastly to Canada. The trip to the United States was to be an unofficial one, at the private invitation of President Carter, while those to Mexico and Canada were to be official state visits.

As for the Moscow Olympics, Chief Cabinet Secretary Itō was in charge of deliberations on whether Japan would participate or not. There was strong feeling in favor of participation among the Japan Olympic Committee and the sports teams, and the government needed to try to win them around to its point of view. Ōhira said he would respect the conclusions of those cabinet members whose areas of concern were most relevant to the problem. This resulted in a government declaration of April 25 advising "self-restraint" (in effect, nonparticipation). This statement read in part as follows: "Under these circumstances, the government has concluded that it is not desirable to participate in the Moscow Games. It fully understands the feelings of the many athletes who have been training single-mindedly, dedicating all their youthful energy for the games. Nevertheless, from the standpoint of our country, which makes peace a national policy, there is no other choice."

That same afternoon, a study meeting was being held in the small dining room in the Prime Minister's Official Residence, attended by top members of ministries and agencies with a special interest in Ōhira's American trip planned for May. There, at around 4 P.M., the news reached Ōhira that a U.S. Special Forces paramilitary action to rescue the hostages in Iran had failed. Ōhira, who had asked the United States to refrain from using force, was visibly surprised and was heard to complain, "What can the United States be thinking of?" In retaliation, Iran immediately ordered the hostages to be dispersed and hardened its attitude toward the United States while preparing for renewed American attempts to free the hostages by military means. Within the United States, there was much support for the surprise raid, but the Soviet Union sharply denounced it, and among the EC countries there seemed to be a widening distrust of American intentions and capabilities. Such criticisms of the United States could hardly be expected to improve matters. At a press conference held in conjunction with a political and economic culture party that Ōhira attended in Fukui on April 26, the prime minister stated: "It is not impossible, in terms of feeling, to understand how the United States, which has endured [this problem] for so long, might have resorted to such an action." Then, to reporters on April 28, Ōhira said, "In regard to the United States' rescue attempt there are various opinions, but I do not think that because of it our country should change its attitude toward the United States."

In keeping with the agreement reached by the EC foreign ministers in Luxembourg, the EC jointly demanded the quick release of the hostages, but when no progress was seen, a second meeting of EC foreign ministers was held in Naples on May 17, which put into effect a second round of economic sanctions against Iran. In content, it was quite similar to the proposal for sanctions that the United States had submitted to the United Nations Security Council in January 1980, namely, a comprehensive ban until the hostages were released on all exports to Iran contracted since the beginning of the hostage incident, with the exception of food and medical supplies. Ōhira was determined, in keeping with policy already developed, to cooperate with the EC in every way possible; thus, on May 22 he convened a meeting of cabinet ministers concerned with the Iranian situation, at which the decision was made to adopt sanctions similar to those of the EC. Certain later events—notably the death in Cairo of the former shah—gave some hope of change, but the situation continued unaltered, and its resolution would have to wait until January 1981, immediately before Carter ended his single term in office after failing to be reelected.

Even though the Japanese government had announced its decision regarding participation in the Moscow Olympics on April 25, the Japan Olympic Committee overrode it by passing a resolution the next day saying it would participate in the games. However, on May 24, after most Western countries had officially withdrawn and after Prime Minister Ōhira had returned from abroad, the same Japan Olympic Committee reversed its stand and decided on nonparticipation. When Ōhira learned of this development from Chief Cabinet Secretary Itō, he said with some feeling, "Is that so? They did a good job of thinking it over. It's too bad for the team members, though."

Ōhira left for the United States, Mexico, and Canada on April 30, 1980, accompanied by his wife and Foreign Minister Ōkita. The night before, Ōhira told Chief Cabinet Secretary Itō: "When I go to the United States, just like last year, I plan to *encourage* [original English] President Carter. Almost every day Carter receives world leaders who come to Washington only to complain or ask for loans. He must surely have had his fill of this. I plan to tell him that Japan will do a good job with what it ought to do, so please have confidence and teach us how to help with the world's problems." Itō then suggested: "If President Tito should die during your trip, I think it would be a good idea for you to make a side trip to Yugoslavia. And if you go to Yugoslavia, wouldn't it be a good idea to meet Chancellor Schmidt, with the summit coming up?" Itō felt that to prevent Japan from becoming isolated again from the Western European countries at the upcoming Venice Summit, as had happened at the Tokyo Summit, it would be desirable for Ōhira to hold a meeting beforehand with the head of state of West Germany, a country with a number of conditions similar to Japan's.

The talks between Ōhira and Carter would be the third occasion for the two men to meet as heads of state, following Ōhira's visit to the United States in May 1979 and the Tokyo Summit. Despite the fact that their third meeting would be unofficial, it involved some serious requests made to Japan in relation to the Iran and Afghanistan problems and concerning the bolstering of Japan's defense capacities and its policy toward the Soviet Union; indeed, circumstances had made the importance of these talks between the Japanese and American leaders even greater than on the previous two occasions.

Ōhira arrived in Washington on the afternoon of April 30. From noon the next day, he talked with Carter in the Cabinet Room for over two hours, interrupted only by a lunch break. The two men first exchanged views on the problems of Iran and Afghanistan. In the course of the conversation, Ōhira declared that Japan fully recognized the difficult situation the United States was in, and, as one of the major advanced countries, looked on matters with an attitude of "shared living and shared suffering." These remarks were no doubt meant to convey a sense that Japan was in the same boat as the United States. As if reflecting the same feeling, when the conversation got around to strengthening Japan's defense capacities, Carter stated: "I understand that Japan has domestic constraints, but in order to cope with the new situation, wouldn't it be possible to have the plan within the Japanese government realized as early as possible? If that could be done it would surely be beneficial to peace in Asia." Ōhira's reply was: "We understand that it is becoming necessary to improve our defense capabilities, and we have so far made great efforts. I appreciate your understanding that Japan has various constraints affecting its improvements in these capabilities. We will continue to strive to think seriously about how we should behave as an ally."

The "plan within the Japanese government" that Carter spoke of referred to the Interim Operations Forecast, a five-year plan beginning from fiscal 1980 that the Defense Agency had drawn up aiming at improvements in the major types of defense facilities and armaments. It was still considered an internal document of the Defense Agency, and not having been submitted to the six-member National Defense Council (changed to the Security Council of Japan in 1986), chaired by the prime minister, it could not yet be called a government plan. In spite of the fact that Japan had made no specific promises, when some Americans began saying that agreement had been reached on "steadily and clearly" increasing defense expenditures, some of the Japanese media took this as proving that Japan had promised to push forward with the Interim Operations Forecast and severely criticized Ōhira.

At the time, the United States had moved all the aircraft carriers of its Seventh Fleet to the Indian Ocean in response to the situation in Iran, leaving none in waters near Japan. Prime Minister Ōhira's statement on defense efforts no doubt stemmed from wanting to relieve, as much as possible, America anxieties and wanting to respond to President Carter's goodwill within the maximum limits allowable. With a view to maintaining an effective defense and security partnership with the United States, Japan in subsequent years steadily increased defense expenditures in spite of stringent budgetary constraints.

Following their conversation in the Cabinet Room, Ōhira and Carter went to the South Lawn of the White House, known as the "Rose Garden," where each read a short declaration. Ōhira read his competently in English, ending as follows:

> As true friends should, we will each air what is on our mind without fear of breaking the unique bond that exists between us. For in times of need, in times of crisis, we will not fail to extend the help needed by the other. We, the Japanese, may not be the most eloquent, but we remain a determined and a most dependable friend of your country. We know you are there in the same way for us.

Afterward, Ōhira remarked to Deputy Chief Cabinet Secretary Katō Kōichi, who had accompanied him, "You fellows probably want to make all kinds of complaints to the United States. However, the United States is patiently performing its job as leader of the free world. If the United States should not be around to do so, someone else would have to do it. None of you understands how difficult a job it is."

After the visit to Washington, Ōhira and his party left for Mexico, the second country on the itinerary, on the evening of May 1. In his initial talks with Mexican President José López Portillo the following day, Ōhira explained Japan's thinking on North–South problems and on the Iran and Afghanistan issues. He also requested a change in Mexican government policy to allow for an increase in Japanese imports of Mexican oil from the current 100,000 barrels per day to, if possible, 300,000 barrels per day over the next few years. According to information gathered from various sources prior to his trip, Ōhira was led to believe that if he were to visit Mexico, an increase up to 300,000 barrels was virtually certain, and it was hoped that such a promise would be a highlight of the trans-Pacific journey. However, President López Portillo's reaction was cool, and he was worried that increasing oil exports to this extent to Japan would mean diminishing the shares traditionally accorded other countries. That afternoon, Foreign Minister Ōkita also tried his best in oil discussions with representatives of the Mexican government, but to little avail. The Japanese felt all the more perplexed when it became clear that a yen loan requested by Mexico to finance a steel mill project was far larger than had been stipulated in the Japanese proposal. After a welcome banquet hosted by the Mexicans that evening, a long and busy day should have come to an end, but on returning to his hotel Ōhira still had other problems to attend to. As to how economic assistance from Japan and increases in Mexican oil exports should be linked, the advice of the Foreign Ministry was squarely contrary to that of the Economic Planning Agency, the Ministry of Finance, and the Ministry of International Trade and Industry, and even after one o'clock in the morning no conclusion was in sight.

At 10 A.M. on May 3, a second round of talks was held between the two heads of state, but ultimately no firm promises were elicited from the Mexicans and similarly no specific conclusions were reached in regard to the steel project. In the final joint communiqué, both issues were phrased in rather vague terms. Ōhira spoke no words of dissatisfaction—in fact about the only thing he said was, "so I guess this is about the way things are"— but his face could not hide his disappointment. It seemed that the two days of hard work had taken their toll when Ōhira remarked on the evening of May 3, "I don't think it's altitude sickness, but for a while I was short of breath and I wondered what might happen." The next day Ōhira and his party left Mexico for the third and last country on their itinerary, Canada. As their specially chartered Japan Air Lines plane flew over New York, a news bulletin announced the death of Yugoslavia's President Josip Broz Tito. Before his departure from Tokyo, Ōhira had tentatively planned to ask either Fukuda Takeo or Foreign Minister Ōkita Saburō to attend the funeral in his place. Now on the plane with him, Ōkita suggested that he would go to the funeral if Ōhira was tired, to which Ōhira replied, "Yes, if you could, I would be grateful."

After reaching Ottawa, Ōhira was still not keen about attending the funeral, and was heard to remark: "I must go back to Japan quickly and get on with preparations for the Upper House election. . . . I don't think it's good to be away from Japan for too long." When Deputy Chief Cabinet Secretary Katō telephoned Chief Cabinet Secretary Itō for an opinion, Itō replied: "If the prime minister doesn't want to, it can't be helped, but since there's nothing for him to worry about at home, it would be good if he went." When this was relayed to Ōhira, he changed his mind and said simply, "Then I'll go." Itō no doubt felt it was important for Japan not to lag behind other countries that would send heads of state to Tito's funeral.

In the summit talks between Ōhira and Prime Minister Pierre Trudeau on May 5 in Ottawa, the fast-changing international situation formed the core of the discussion. They agreed that to prevent the United States from taking unilateral action on the Iranian problem, the free-world countries should band together to offer the United States their support. On the afternoon of May 5, Ōhira visited Canada's Parliament, where he delivered a speech in English titled "Neighbors Across the Pacific." It drew special attention as the first speech any head of state from outside the Commonwealth had ever delivered before the Canadian Parliament, and in this way, too, symbolized the importance of Japanese–Canadian relations.

The following afternoon, Ōhira and his party flew from Ottawa to Vancouver, as did Trudeau, who flew there in a separate plane, and later the two heads of state held a second summit conference. Ōhira's plane left Vancouver at 8 A.M. the next day, May 7, via Anchorage, Alaska, for Cologne airport, from where, after about an hour's stop to refuel in the early morning of May 8, it proceeded to Belgrade, Yugoslavia. It had not been easy to sleep on the plane two nights in a row; the next chance for a proper rest in bed would be thirty-four hours after getting up in Vancouver.

On landing in Belgrade at 8:20 A.M. on May 8, Ōhira encountered bright, almost mid-summer, sunlight, and the temperature was warmer than expected. He first went to the federal government office complex, where he conveyed his condolences to Yugoslavia's top leaders; then he went to the Federal Assembly building to lay flowers on Tito's casket. After resting for a while at the home of the Japanese ambassador, at around 11:30 A.M. he again went to the Federal Assembly building, in front of which was a square where the casket had been placed. The attendance by numerous heads of state made it an occasion for a sort of summit diplomacy, and Prime Minister Ōhira exchanged greetings with the representatives of many nations. China's Premier Hua Guofeng came up to shake hands and told Ōhira he looked forward to meeting with him later in the afternoon. Panama's President Arístides Royo Sánchez, who had recently visited Japan, inquired with great interest if anything had been discussed between Ōhira and President Carter in Washington in regard to the possibility of constructing a second Panama Canal. Ōhira also spoke with United Nations Secretary-General Kurt Waldheim and with President Ziaur Rahman of Bangladesh. Although he shook hands with the Palestine Liberation Organization's Yasir Arafat, whose presence was drawing much attention, the two did not enter into conversation.

After watching the casket leave the square for burial, Prime Minister Ōhira talked for some time with India's Prime Minister Indira Gandhi, then went to the garden outside what had been President Tito's Official Residence for the burial ceremony. Before it began, as Ōhira passed in front of the Soviet delegation who were taking their seats in the front row, he was offered a handshake by the Soviet Foreign Minister Andrei Gromyko and then shook hands with the Soviet Communist Party General Secretary Leonid Brezhnev. After the burial, Ōhira returned to the Japanese ambassador's residence, where he talked for forty-five minutes with China's Premier Hua Guofeng. As soon as this was over, he went to the airport and left for West Germany, arriving at Cologne airport a little after 10 P.M. and then proceeding to nearby Bonn. A long, long day had finally ended.

Travel fatigue notwithstanding, on the morning of the following day, May 9, Ōhira talked for some forty minutes at his hotel with West Germany's Economic Minister Otto Graf von Lambsdorff. Then, a little after noon, he visited the Office of the Federal Chancellor (Bundeskanzleramt), and after a welcoming ceremony spent two hours and forty minutes talking, in part over lunch, with Chancellor Helmut Schmidt in his office.

With respect to the hostage issue in Iran, the two agreed it was in the interests of Japan and the EC to cooperate in supporting the United States for a peaceful resolution. Regarding Afghanistan, Ōhira noted that "as long as there is no clear movement toward a withdrawal of Soviet troops from Afghanistan, participation in the Moscow Olympics is not desirable," and Chancellor Schmidt replied, "I am of the same opinion." They agreed on these and numerous other points. During a part of their discussion in which the two leaders talked alone except for the interpreters, Chancellor Schmidt is said to have given some candid evaluations of American policies toward the Soviet Union and toward the Middle East as well as his views regarding the state of East–West relations and his personal readings of the character, competence, and skills of other heads of state. Ōhira spoke positively about the role Japan should play among the free-world nations. He was in a good mood following these talks as he commented: "Chancellor Schmidt gave me his frank and clear opinions. With this, my thinking has been put into better order."

The official functions of this grand tour, which had spanned a large part of the globe, were now almost at their end. As if enlivened by a certain feeling of relief, Ōhira suddenly suggested a game of golf, which he had not played in a long time—nine holes right away and a full round the next day. He quickly changed clothes and headed for the Refrath Golf Course near Cologne. Perhaps because this half round was only begun around 5 P.M. and was so hastily played, Ōhira's score was not to his liking. Joking, "Let's keep today's score a secret," he took part that evening in a wind-up party at the Japanese ambassador's residence, together with accompanying journalists and aides. There he was heard to give this overview of the long trip: "I keenly feel Japan has at last reached a position where it can conduct diplomacy that is really diplomacy."

The last day of the journey was Saturday, May 10. Beginning at 7:30 A.M., Ōhira talked for more than an hour at the hotel with Foreign Minister Hans-Dietrich Genscher, and then left for the Mettmann Golf Club in the suburbs of Düsseldorf. On its well-tended greens, he finally played a full round. It was the last game of golf he would ever play. Ōhira and his party left West Germany for Japan at 4 P.M. that afternoon.

Chapter 39

Decision

When Ōhira got home from Haneda airport on May 11, 1980, after his long trip, his face betrayed signs of fatigue. From mid-March, he had had a completely full schedule. He had had to handle an extremely difficult Diet session and had spent his weekends attending political and economic culture parties in different parts of the country. The arduous twelve-day trip of over 50,000 kilometers that had just ended had not been easy on his seventy-year-old body.

However, there was still no time for rest. The evening he returned, he was visited at his Seta residence by LDP Secretary-General Sakurauchi Yoshio, Chief Cabinet Secretary Itō Masayoshi, and Deputy Secretary-General Tanaka Rokusuke to discuss the handling of important bills in the Diet, which was to end in just another week. During Ōhira's absence, a conference of the chairmen of the Diet Affairs committees of the LDP, JSP, Kōmeitō, and DSP had agreed on May 8 that "any bills that the four parties cannot agree on will not be passed." Because of this, a whole series of bills of importance to the Second Ōhira Cabinet were pending, including a revised Political Funding Control Law, a revision of the Public Office Election Law, and a proposed law on reorganizing local branches of government offices. Even if the conciliatory LDP Diet strategy adopted on May 8 might have its defenders, given the dual handicaps of near-parity in governing and opposition party numbers and the lack of cooperation with the cabinet by the anti-mainstream LDP factions, Ōhira was greatly dissatisfied over the way those entrusted with handling Diet strategy had been treating the bills in question. He felt it a pity to see lack of action, because of such compromises, on important pieces of legislation on which so much effort and work had been expended. He thus urged renewed efforts to see this legislation pass.

In any case, only a week remained until the close of the Diet session on

May 18, and it seemed certain that before this date the opposition parties would at least present (even if no vote was taken) a motion of no-confidence, thinking this would at least help rally public support in preparation for the Upper House election. With this pressure from the opposition, it was extremely difficult to get through the Diet any important bill on which there were strongly conflicting positions between the LDP and opposition parties. Nevertheless, on the basis of the above-mentioned consultation at Ōhira's Seta residence on the evening of May 11, the government held a conference with top LDP leaders at noon the next day, asking for their cooperation in getting these important bills passed. However, the attention of most of the party representatives was fixed on the Upper House election campaign, and they failed to show much interest. Then a Lower House plenary session on the afternoon of May 13 approved a motion to extend the Diet session by nine days until May 27. In this way, the Diet would remain in session until just before the official start of the Upper House election campaign on May 30. All the parties were, in fact, busy with this election, though it was still very uncertain what success each might attain.

As election day approached, the opposition parties, hoping to muster strength and improve morale, continued their puzzling maneuvers of threatening a no-confidence motion against the Ōhira Cabinet. The JSP favored a joint presentation of any such motion with the cooperation of as many of the opposition parties as possible; ·the Kōmeitō and the DSP, however, were hesitant about such a plan, with the DSP fearing that if a no-confidence motion was passed with the help of a boycott by the anti-mainstream LDP factions, it could bring a dissolution of the Lower House. Finally, the JSP decided on May 13 that it would, even if independently, present a motion of no-confidence within a week.

A conference of JSP, Kōmeitō, and DSP party heads the next day revealed that while the Kōmeitō favored the idea of presenting a no-confidence motion, it would keep in abeyance its attitude on whether it would be a formal cosponsor. The DSP indicated a rather negative attitude toward the whole idea and decided to hold another meeting of its Central Executive Committee to discuss means of coping with the situation. By this time, the maneuvers of the LDP Reform League, spearheading the anti-Ōhira movement within the LDP, were becoming more impatient. Seeing that this league was tending to sympathize with the JSP's plans for a motion of no-confidence, LDP officials tried their best to apply restraint, but with no discernible results. In the meantime, the JSP decided on May 16 as the date for presenting its motion.

At 10 A.M. on May 16, the LDP opened a Joint Plenary Meeting of Party

Members of Both Houses of the Diet in the auditorium at party headquarters. This body was expected to approve a long-considered plan for a
charter on ethics and a plan for setting up a committee for revising party
rules, which would facilitate a reorganization of the Party Discipline Committee. However, when the appointed hour had passed, attendance of anti-
mainstream Diet members was poor and there was no quorum to allow the
joint plenary meeting to function as an official policy-making body in place
of a party convention. Finally, the gathering was opened as an "ordinary"
joint plenary meeting without official policy-making status. To those attending, Prime Minister Ōhira used the occasion to underscore the urgency of
establishing firm ethical principles in the party. The plan for a Party Ethics
Charter was unanimously accepted. Next, a motion was passed that the
LDP should unite and go into the Upper House election campaign having
defeated the opposition's motion of no-confidence. The virtual boycott of
this meeting by anti-mainstream Diet members was, however, a portent of
things to come.

At 10:39 the same morning, the JSP completed the procedures for
entering on the agenda its motion of no-confidence in the cabinet, citing as
reasons allegations that the Ōhira Cabinet had: (1) neglected domestic
policy and turned its back on welfare, prices, and other issues affecting
people's daily lives; (2) tried to hide cases of corruption like the Las Vegas
Incident involving Dietman Hamada Kōichi; and (3) kowtowed to the
United States and failed to promote "peaceful diplomacy." This motion
was to be allowed so-called emergency presentation on the agenda of the
Lower House plenary session that afternoon, when a vote would be taken.
The LDP members in the Reform League who supported the hard-line motion of no-confidence had been rapidly decreasing in number. Some of
such remaining members, wanting to emphasize their loyalties to one or
another anti-mainstream faction leader, had even asserted that they would
"take action, resigned to the fact that this could split the party"; yet it did
not appear that practical preparations had, in fact, gone that far. Persons
on the LDP Diet Affairs Committee estimated that the motion of no-confidence would be rejected by a majority of over ten votes.

After being updated on these trends, Ōhira returned from the LDP
joint plenary meeting to the Prime Minister's Official Residence. By this
time the JSP had already completed procedures to enter the motion of no-
confidence on the agenda, and the DSP had decided in favor of solid support for the motion together with all the opposition parties. Questioned by
reporters, Ōhira replied that he was confident the motion would be rejected, saying: "The [party's] executive staff is being active in various ways,
so it seems we should be able to crush the motion." Evening newspapers

reported the prospects as "No anti-mainstream move to join opposition: motion to be rejected by evening."

However, no sooner had the emergency presentation before the Diet plenary session been actually decided upon than the LDP's anti-mainstream factions again began hasty maneuvers. At noon staff members of the Fukuda faction held a meeting that adopted a resolution to "entrust decisions to former Prime Minister Fukuda." The Miki faction similarly held an emergency general meeting at noon, which resolved to defer a stance until later. On the other hand, the Nakasone faction held an emergency meeting at 2:45 P.M., at which former LDP Secretary-General Nakasone decisively supported the stance of rejecting the motion of no-confidence, stressing that his faction should "unite, with no stray threads, in this contest with the opposition parties."

At 1 P.M., the Lower House's Standing Committee on Rules and Administration decided to convene the plenary session at 3:30. In the meantime, the Reform League, which had tried since the previous evening to set up a meeting with the prime minister, had again in the morning requested such a meeting through the party's executive staff. Secretary-General Sakurauchi judged that "to meet him at this juncture would serve no purpose," and Deputy Secretary-General Tanaka Rokusuke announced, after checking with Ōhira, that the prime minister would not be forthcoming about a meeting. When the Reform League begged him to reconsider, some of Ōhira's close associates understood this to be "an offer to sheathe their swords if the prime minister should reply with sincerity." Lower House Standing Committee on Rules and Administration Chairman Kameoka Takao and Chief Cabinet Secretary Itō Masayoshi also counseled that "perhaps a meeting would clear things up and be worthwhile." As a result, talks were scheduled for later that afternoon.

Beginning at 2:50 P.M., Ōhira met with the Reform League representatives in the Cabinet Reception Room of the Diet building. The visitors made three demands: (1) Hamada Kōichi should be summoned to testify before the Diet; (2) an official disciplinary committee should be established in the Diet to clarify the KDD problem; and (3) Senior Deputy Secretary-General Tanaka Rokusuke should retract a statement he had made in a TV broadcast on May 13 to the effect that the Reform League was a sort of publicity stunt for certain people to gain recognition among the public. The prime minister was requested to make a quick response. While the discussion proceeded, the scheduled 3:30 P.M. opening of the plenary session was fast approaching.

A message was sent to Ōhira by the LDP's Diet Affairs Committee Deputy Chairman Tazawa Kichirō and Lower House Standing Committee on Rules and Administration Director Ishii Hajime reporting, "The opposition parties say they can't wait more than an hour." The Reform League visitors also applied pressure by saying, "If you want to be present at the Diet plenary session we won't keep you. However, we will not go in to vote." Having stayed calm throughout the meeting, Ōhira finally said, "I'll consult with the party's executive staff and give you an answer." The Reform League representatives asked only that the answer be given quickly and left. Summoned immediately for consultation with the prime minister (and with Secretary-General Sakurauchi and Deputy Secretary-General Tanaka, who were also present) were LDP Vice-President Nishimura, General Council Chairman Suzuki, Policy Research Council Chairman Abe, and Diet Affairs Committee Chairman Kanemaru. When news came that the opposition parties were making 4:30 the time limit for opening the plenary session, Sakurauchi requested that it be delayed a further thirty minutes.

An answer to the Reform League's demand was soon produced, in Ōhira's own handwriting. Like the three demands, it also had three parts: "(1) with respect to the summoning of Hamada, the party president will bear in mind the Diet's authority to investigate matters having to do with administration and will instruct the party's executive staff to have the Lower House Special Investigative Committee on Aircraft Imports produce a conclusion in keeping with the Diet's authority; (2) the party president will instruct the party's executive staff to study the matter of establishing an official Diet Committee on Discipline; and (3) as for the words of LDP Senior Deputy Secretary-General Tanaka Rokusuke, the party president will endeavor to have Tanaka retract them if on examination there is truth to the allegations."

Secretary-General Sakurauchi communicated this answer by reading the memo out loud over the phone from the Cabinet Reception Room to the Reform League's head liaison officer Nakao Eiichi. During the few remaining minutes he stayed in the Cabinet Reception Room before the opening of the plenary session, Ōhira was heard to mutter twice, to nobody in particular: "It is because of my shortcomings that I am causing you all such a lot of trouble."

After nearly thirty minutes, it was learned that the Reform League was complaining that it had not yet received the prime minister's answer. Obviously, the answer that should have been communicated had been deliberately prevented from reaching the parties concerned. Sakurauchi and the others then repeated the message by phone to Reform League leaders. As they were doing so, it became known that the anti-mainstream LDP Diet members were staying away from the plenary Lower House session and were gathering in a conference room of the No. 1 Diet Members' Office Building and other nearby locations. At 4:20 P.M. a talk was held by Fukuda, Miki, Nakasone, and Nakagawa, attended also by some of the Reform League members.

The minutes were ticking by, and still there was no authoritative word from the Reform League. As the deadline approached, Ōhira stopped by the room in the Diet building where a General Assembly of LDP Members of the Lower House was being held (this time attended mainly by anti-mainstream members) and then went to the Lower House plenary session. The bell announcing the session's opening was rung a little before 5 P.M. Just a few minutes earlier, Secretary-General Sakurauchi had informed the Reform League that the plenary session would begin at 5 P.M., and the latter had then checked to confirm that this was indeed the case.

The plenary session opened on schedule, but the seats of the anti-mainstream LDP members remained mostly empty. The order of business was, first, an explanation by JSP Chairman Asukata of the motion of no-confidence, followed by a refutation of these arguments by LDP member Ōno Akira, and then by arguments in favor of the motion from each opposition party. As soon as this debate ended, the chamber would be barred, but as long as Diet members entered the chamber during this period of debate, they would still be in time to cast their votes. Ōhira and his associates were still of the opinion that most LDP members would show up in time.

Before long, however, former Secretary-General Nakasone personally telephoned Secretary-General Sakurauchi from the Reform League's office, saying, "It will still take some time to persuade Miki and Fukuda, so can't we break for a while?" When LDP Diet Affairs Committee Chairman Kanemaru was told this by Sakurauchi, he sounded out Speaker Nadao on the possibility of calling a recess in Diet proceedings. According to Kanemaru, Nadao said, "Plenary sessions, which the nation watches closely, are not something that can be recessed at will or extended at the LDP's convenience."

Immediately afterward, Sakurauchi left the plenary session to see Fukuda and Miki, who were still in conference with Nakasone, but his efforts to persuade them were to no avail. By this time, the plenary session was a scene of noisy disorder, and if things continued the motion of no-confidence seemed sure to pass. In that case, either a dissolution or a cabinet resignation en masse was imminent. In the Lower House, little attention was paid to the arguments being expounded from the rostrum as leading members of the various parties milled about the floor, conferring in groups of three or four. At 5:52 P.M., Deputy Chief Cabinet Secretary Katō delivered from the floor a memo to Chief Cabinet Secretary Itō, who was then in the ministers' gallery, asking, "At this rate should the plenary session be continued or not?" Itō handed the memo, in turn, to Prime Minister Ōhira, who replied: " We'll proceed according to the plan." This reply referred to the fact, mentioned earlier, that ever since early February Ōhira had confided to a few very close associates his resolve to opt for a dissolution if this sort of situation should ever materialize.

Meanwhile, at 6:10 P.M., Secretary-General Sakurauchi again tried to persuade the Reform League, but to no avail. Sakurauchi finally said, "What comes afterward is your decision," and, abandoning any further attempts at persuasion, returned to the Diet building to enter the Lower House chamber. Just four minutes before entry to the chamber was barred, Nakasone arrived with several Diet members who held leading positions in his faction. At the same moment there was a move in the opposite direction, when Policy Research Council Chairman Abe was almost literally carried out of the chamber by members of his faction. At 6:35 P.M., the Lower House chamber was closed off, and the motion of no-confidence against the Ōhira Cabinet passed with 243 votes in favor and 187 against. It was the third time since the war that a motion of no-confidence had passed, the first one being in 1948, which gave rise to the "dissolution by agreement," and the second one being in 1953, causing the "*bakayarō* dissolution" by Prime Minister Yoshida Shigeru.

The prime minister's face bore all the sternness of one determined to take the responsibility for making a decision of grave importance. Even after leaving the chamber and entering the Prime Minister's Office in the Diet building, Ōhira did not say a word but only stared at the corner of the room. At that juncture, one of his secretaries came to inform him that cabinet members had gathered in the Cabinet Meeting Room next door. The secretary said: "We would like to request a cabinet meeting, sir."

"Oh," replied Ōhira, as if only then noticing somebody else was present. He then asked, "What about preparations?"

"They are all gathered next door waiting."

"Really? In that case then . . ." So saying, Ōhira rose from his chair, seeming to have come back from another world.

The initiative for holding this extraordinary cabinet meeting came from plans made in the plenary session by Chief Cabinet Secretary Itō and Finance Minister Takeshita, who had managed to communicate to all cabinet members that they should assemble in the Cabinet Meeting Room in the Diet building immediately after the plenary session.

The cabinet meeting began at 7:06 P.M., and Prime Minister Ōhira made this pronouncement: "You have done your very best working for the administration of the country, so it is a pity this sort of thing has come to pass. According to the Constitution there are only two ways left, either a dissolution or a resignation en masse. As to which choice would be better, you may leave it up to me or you may decide on the matter right now."

For some time there was silence, until the oldest cabinet member, Justice Minister Kuraishi, said, "I leave it up to the prime minister." Finance Minister Takeshita and all the other cabinet members agreed. Home Affairs Minister Gotōda then added the phrase, "I leave it up to the prime minister on the assumption that there will be a dissolution." The others indicated that they felt likewise, in effect recommending a Lower House dissolution. The cabinet meeting took a break to allow preparation of a statement and consultations with LDP Secretary-General Sakurauchi and other members of the LDP executive staff. When Prime Minister Ōhira said calmly, "I will carry out a dissolution," a cabinet resolution to this effect was unanimously approved. After the wording of the government statement was decided upon and approved, the meeting ended at 8:07 P.M. It was decided to move forward, by a week, the Upper House election that had been scheduled for June 29 and to hold it simultaneously with the upcoming general election on June 22. It was the first time in the history of Japan's parliamentary democracy that Upper and Lower House elections were to be held on the same day.

On May 17, the day following the vote of no-confidence and the government statement, the newspapers all reported that the LDP would go into the forthcoming elections divided into two groups. It was no exaggeration to say that the questions of how the anti-mainstream factions that had boycotted the Lower House plenary session would behave and how the party's executive staff would react were to deeply influence the path the political system would follow in the 1980s.

On leaving his home that morning, Ōhira had told reporters: "It will probably mean causing the nation a lot of trouble, but it is no good to leave things half-done with a lot of problems still remaining. I want to face the political situation with a sharp and clear posture, to get to work on promoting policies, and to have my attitude understood. . . .As to the rebels within the party, somehow or other the impossible has happened, but I want to make my reasons very clear. Because they are persons who were once colleagues, I think this problem must be handled with care and sincerity, and it must be done in a reasonable way as befits a political party."

When Ōhira arrived at LDP headquarters, he was awaited there by Policy Research Council Chairman Abe Shintarō. Abe offered his resignation, but Ōhira refused to accept it, saying, "Political stability is the priority. Because you are a person able to see the overall picture in perspective, I think you will be able to understand my decision." During that day, some unsettling trends continued, such as the decision taken by the anti-mainstream factions to inaugurate a "liaison association" to prepare for their own separate election campaign.

Just after 1:00 P.M. on May 19, Speaker Nadao read the *pro forma* imperial edict declaring the Lower House dissolved, whether those who had just lost their positions as Dietmen agreed or not. All would have to return to their electoral districts and fight to be reelected. In a press conference afterward, Ōhira explained his choice: "There are two paths, dissolution and resignation en masse. I saw no reason for a resignation en masse because I cannot agree with the three reasons put forward by the JSP, so I chose dissolution. I thought that to cope with this sort of event the most logical way in a constitutional government would be to return to the basic point of departure for the government and Diet and seek the judgment of the people. If there was a resignation en masse, naturally the government would be entrusted to the largest of the opposition parties, which would form a caretaker cabinet to oversee the next election. To go through that procedure would only double the confusion in the political situation. Such a path should not be taken. Without any hesitation I chose the path of dissolution. . . . There have been struggles within the party for a long time, and the fact that they have not been wholly resolved is one of the main factors linked to this Diet dissolution. This is an intraparty problem. The question of whether or not to call a dissolution is a problem of the government and the Diet. To borrow the Diet as a place for airing intraparty problems is something that, while having precedents, should not be repeated. It is regrettable that the party did not stick together as a single, solid entity, but this is what happens when not enough attention is paid to intraparty harmony. Although I have tried to give rather careful consideration to such matters in managing the party, I must bear some of the responsibility for [problems in] management."

In the meantime, the anti-mainstream factions inaugurated the Party Regeneration Council (*Tōsaisei Kyōgikai*) on May 20, with Abe Shintarō and Kōmoto Toshio as its representative managers (*daihyō sewanin*). This group could not help but note, in its members' electoral districts, the strong criticism of the boycott of the recent Diet session, so their zeal for rebellion had considerably cooled, especially in light of the coming general election. Economic circles, too, worked for LDP unity, and the rivalries within the party began to appear less acute. Ultimately, the party's executive staff prevailed on those who had boycotted the plenary session to write a document promising to maintain party unity, and then allowed them to stand for election on the LDP ticket. On the evening of May

22, LDP Vice-President Nishimura, Secretary-General Sakurauchi, and General Council Chairman Suzuki conferred with Abe and Kōmoto of the Party Regeneration Council, together with Nakagawa Ichirō and other anti-mainstream Diet members, and this established a new harmony for building a system of party unity in preparation for the elections. It included a promise that, for the time being at least, the activities of the Party Regeneration Council would cease.

On the morning of May 23, Ōhira met with Abe and Kōmoto to personally confirm this agreement. Several days later, at the National Conference of LDP Prefectural Federation Secretaries-General, Ōhira stated his determination to carry out overall party renewal and maintain a non-coalition LDP government. Ōhira's speech before this gathering won enthusiastic applause, especially when he said, "I want you to fight the campaign by bringing together both the care it takes to cook a small fish and the boldness it takes to move mountains." The LDP then followed procedures to recognize the party membership of all but the few who chose to retire from the political arena.

Even before the official start of the election campaign, Ōhira found no time to rest. On the twenty-fourth, he attended a political and economic culture party in Shiga Prefecture, and a similar party in Wakayama Prefecture the next day. From May 27, a series of functions was held to welcome Premier Hua Guofeng, the first Chinese head of state to visit Japan. The results of the two talks between the Japanese and Chinese leaders were announced on the afternoon of May 29 in a joint press release. While recognizing certain differences in standpoint, Ōhira and Hua stressed their intention to make the cooperation between Japan and China a steadily advancing reality. It was shown that relations between the two countries had entered a practical working phase.

Around this time reports from the various policy study groups in which Ōhira was placing much hope were beginning to appear. On May 19, a report by the Study Group on the Pacific Basin Cooperation Concept was presented by Professor Iida Tsuneo of Nagoya University. On May 29 came a report from the Study Group on Strengthening the Family Base. Celebrating its completion—and as befitting its recommendations for enhancing the importance of the family—an informal party for project members and their families was held at the Prime Minister's Official Residence, which Ōhira attended in the company of his wife. Small but animated circles of people surrounded the prime minister, moving slowly about the room with him. Their conversation ranged from evaluations of people and of human life in general to discussions of books and opinions on the family. In spite of repeated urging by his secretaries, the prime minister was having such a good time that he found it hard to leave and would gladly have stayed longer. It was the last meeting he ever attended at the Prime Minister's Official Residence. In order to attend a banquet hosted by Hua Guofeng that same evening, Ōhira left the residence just as the sun was about to set. It was 6:24 P.M. on the day before the official opening of the Diet election campaign.

Chapter 40

The Call of Destiny

The campaign leading to the critical double election (the thirty-sixth general election and twelfth Upper House election) of June 22, 1980, entered its crucial stage on May 30, officially the first day of the Upper House campaign. The weather was clear at dawn, with a high-pressure area centered on the Pacific Ocean and extending over Japan, but once the sun was up, a summer atmospheric pressure pattern prevailed, bringing a humid heat.

At 9 A.M., Prime Minister Ōhira attended a farewell ceremony at the State Guest House for visiting Chinese Premier Hua Guofeng. After this, he changed into a gray suit and burgundy necktie and arrived at LDP head-quarters at 10:15 A.M. for the ceremony marking the official start of the campaign. After delivering an impassioned statement with many spirited gestures, he left for Shinjuku to speak in support of LDP candidates. From the top of a campaign truck equipped with loudspeakers, he addressed a throng of about 3,000 people: "The election campaign for the Upper House is now under way. We will soon have to ask for your cooperation in the general election for the Lower House as well. . . . I wish to remind you all that in any group of people you will find dissension and conflicting opinions. In the home, at the workplace, in any kind of group, to have differing views and from there go on to create something worthwhile is, I think, the way our lives develop and the way of democratic government. Ever since its founding, the LDP has seen arguments and disputes; nonetheless, there has been not the slightest deviation in its main purpose of protecting the security of the people, defending the people's livelihoods, and taking responsibility for the country's future."

As he spoke, the prime minister gradually increased his intensity, his white-gloved hands grasping the railing around the roof of the campaign truck, causing it to shake. He spoke in a passionate tone without any

552

pauses or rephrasings, as if he wanted to make the whole country hear. He first launched an appeal as follows: "Our party has the solemn responsibility of guaranteeing peace and protecting security. . . . If, as the JSP and JCP assert, we rejected the security treaty with the United States . . . and found we had to protect ourselves with only our own military strength, we would have to sacrifice our present-day prosperity and standard of living." He next promised to defend this standard of living and asked for the people's appreciation of the fact that Japan had overcome two "oil shocks," was in favorable economic circumstances in comparison with the United States and Europe, and had carried out economic policies that had averted an oil shortage. He asserted: "This is proof that a free economic system, which puts to use the vitality of the market, and in which the people do their best, with the government offering appropriate guidance, is not a mistake." Then he spoke of security for the future: "We must plan for a secure future for all our children . . . and a second, purposeful life for our elderly. It is again clear that, when speaking of a secure future amid all our many difficulties . . . the political party that can facilitate this is the LDP." This was a high-keyed presentation, rather unlike the prime minister's ordinary style. Those who had assembled listened attentively, and large numbers of passers-by also stopped to hear him. Some commented, "It's a little different from his usual speech."

Suddenly, Ōhira's voice became a bit hoarse and he lost some of his spirit. Without losing track of his arguments, however, he went on to deliver some sharp attacks on the opposition parties: "Both communist and socialist political systems adopt the attitude that the people 'should be kept dependent and not informed' (yorashimu beshi, shirashimu bekarazu) [a phrase used by certain pre-Meiji Tokugawa ideologues]. Having a system in which the people know nothing at all about what those in power are doing or thinking or how they live, how can one have political morality or establish law and order in administration? Our Liberal Democratic Party responds to the right to know of each person in the nation. Those of our colleagues who have been under suspicion of wrongdoing are being thoroughly investigated by the legal authorities. Can the nation really trust persons who sidestep their lack of ability to make adequate political responses and do not even question this lack, yet receive salaries for doing nothing morning to night but probe into the mistakes of others?"

After this speech, which lasted some thirty minutes, the prime minister looked unusually tired. In the car that took him from Shinjuku to LDP headquarters in Hirakawachō, where he planned to rest, he remarked to a companion, "It's hot, and I'm not feeling too good. There's a pain at the back of my throat." Then, wiping the sweat from his face, he eagerly asked of his speech, "How was it?" When he arrived at LDP headquarters, his head was tilted back and his face was white. Because his undershirt was completely soaked in sweat, he used several towels to try to wipe himself dry, but the sweating did not stop. Although he lay down on a sofa, his color did not immediately improve. However, after an hour, his coloring gradually began to get better. He hardly touched a bowl of noodles that was brought to him and ate only a bite or two of a muskmelon, one of his favorite fruits. Cancelling the speeches scheduled for the afternoon was considered, but it was the first day of a campaign that would decide the fate of Japan's politics, and the effect of having the prime minister, who was supposed to be at the fore of the campaign, call off his speeches because of health reasons seemed to be so negative that his advisers did not urge him to do so.

Ōhira finally got up and complained in a low voice, "It's no good to be so tired on the first day." He then left for Yokohama, where he was to speak at four places. Taking into consideration advice to limit his speeches to about five minutes, he resolved to make them as short as possible and to rest as much as he could in the car. In Yokohama, when he first stood up to speak on the roof of a campaign truck, his face at times betrayed physical pain. Toward the end of the afternoon, however, he appeared to have recovered, and his speeches, interspersed with vigorous gestures, lasted up to twenty minutes. Judging from this, those accompanying him tried to banish their worries and convince themselves that nothing was seriously wrong, although, in fact, the prime minister was using up the last of his strength.

Having spoken at five different places in the course of the day, Ōhira returned to his Seta residence at 6:30 P.M. and almost immediately lay down on bedding that had been prepared for him in a Japanese-style room at the back of the house. There, he had a cardiogram taken by his family doctor, who had been waiting for some time. As the machine traced the prime minister's heart function, the doctor's expression clouded, and he told Shigeko: "I am afraid these could be the symptoms of a heart attack, or myocardial infarction. He has really done well to hold out the way he has." Three heart specialists were called in, and their unanimous recommendation was complete rest and immediate hospitalization. All those waiting felt a shock run up their spines. Around 9 P.M., Chief Cabinet Secretary Itō, who had earlier been tied up in a meeting, arrived to help in whatever way he could.

The doctors made arrangements for Ōhira to enter Toranomon Hospital, and they discussed matters with Shigeko, Chief Cabinet Secretary Itō, and Ōhira's secretaries. The first matter was what to call the prime minister's illness. There was disagreement between the doctors

—who were quite certain that there was a restriction in the blood supply to the heart and did not want to announce anything too far from the truth—and the secretaries, who were concerned about the political effects of the announcement. Ultimately, the statement read: "Due to fatigue, the prime minister's pulse is temporarily irregular. Because this will require a few days' rest, it is advisable for him to enter the hospital." Later the same evening, Deputy Secretary-General Tanaka Rokusuke, who had been with Ōhira during the day, hurried to Ōhira's residence without informing anyone else. Only a very small number of party officers knew the true circumstances of the hospitalization.

It was 11:20 P.M. when newspaper reporters outside the Ōhira home left the scene. Afterward, a car specially equipped with a bed arrived and the prime minister was carried into it on a stretcher, his eyes closed and the palms of his hands placed together on his chest. He was fully conscious and assured his family and others present, "It's nothing serious." On arriving at the hospital, the prime minister was immediately taken to the sixth-floor Cardiac Intensive Care Room. Monitors were attached to his chest to facilitate constant observation, and he was given intravenous nutrition and medication. Helped by tranquilizers, he soon feel asleep. After his admittance to the hospital had been confirmed, at around 2 A.M. on May 31 party members at LDP headquarters relayed the message to those concerned that Ōhira's speeches scheduled that day for Kumamoto in Kyūshū would have to be cancelled. Because this change of plan was so sudden, the media were in great confusion. In the hospital, Ōhira spent most of the time asleep or dozing, no doubt a reaction to the tranquilizers, but from time to time he would seem to gesture or say something or other in a low voice. Noticing this during a visit, his grandchildren remarked, "Grandpa is on an election campaign."

Throughout June 1, a large number of telegrams arrived from abroad, wishing Prime Minister Ōhira a fast recovery. A bouquet of flowers was sent by an anonymous woman. On June 2, it seemed that the prime minister had regained his spirits and was no longer in pain. From time to time he asked his doctors about his condition, and at times he cracked jokes or asked his secretaries about the campaign. Get-well cards came from members of the party and government, from friends and members of the business world, and also from the opposition parties. This day was the official opening of the Lower House election campaign, which Ōhira had intended to kick off with a speech in Osaka to discuss the country's future prospects and his policy convictions. Instead, he sent from his hospital bed a written message to "each of the Japanese people," urging understanding and support for the LDP.

The group of physicians, wanting to be as meticulous as possible in their diagnosis, held a press conference at 11 A.M. that morning, at which Dr. Mimura Nobuhide, representing the group, read out the following memo: "The name of the malady is 'stricture of the heart,' or 'angina pectoris,' presumably brought on by overwork. . . . However, the patient has been doing well up to now, and there is little likelihood that the condition will worsen. As for how much longer he will need to be hospitalized, without further observation of his condition it is difficult to judge, but at present we feel that it will be necessary to have him remain in the hospital for at least another week of careful observation." From the reporters came a barrage of questions about whether Ōhira could campaign, whether he could attend the Venice Summit due to begin on June 22, and whether there was the possibility of a myocardial infarction. Trying their best to allay the reporters' fears, the doctors replied in a matter-of-fact way that speechmaking would be difficult, but that Ōhira should be able to attend the summit; a week's bed rest, they said, was necessary to prevent a myocardial infarction from developing. However, the physicians had, in fact, agreed among themselves that it would be necessary for Ōhira to remain hospitalized for a month and a half, to be followed by a month and a half of medical treatment at home.

On June 3, the prime minister seemed much better. He asked about the yen–dollar exchange rate, and worried over the election campaign. When LDP Secretary-General Sakurauchi came to visit him, Ōhira raised the head section of his hospital bed to receive him. Sakurauchi recollected that, "When I said, 'How are you feeling?' he extended his hand. And when I said, 'The campaign is going well, there is no need to worry,' he offered words of encouragement, saying, 'I am causing you a lot of trouble, but I leave matters in your hands. In any case, we're going to win.' He then gave some specific instructions for taking thorough precautions. His voice was weak, but I did my best not to miss a single word. The fact that the party president was worrying over so many aspects deeply impressed me." On this day, too, a message came from President Carter, saying, "I am looking forward to seeing you in Venice." Other telegrams of encouragement continued to arrive from abroad.

To those around him, the prime minister's condition seemed to improve daily. For members of his family who stayed at his bedside, and for Chief Cabinet Secretary Itō and others who visited every morning and evening, this was a great relief. On June 4, a TV set was brought into his room, and he was allowed to watch videotapes of golf tournaments and rakugo comedy for thirty minutes a day. When LDP General Council Chairman Suzuki visited him that day, the prime minister offered his own assessment of his health: "The doctors are being very careful, but I am completely OK." He continued to make progress the next day, by which time he was getting bored. In the afternoon of June 6, cabinet ministers came in turn to Ōhira's hospital room, and he sat up in bed to sign necessary documents. At 9:30 A.M. on June 7, LDP Vice-President Nishimura came to pay his respects, at which time Ōhira made this request: "In party matters, you please take the lead."

Chief Cabinet Secretary Itō and other members of the secretarial staff for the Venice Summit consulted on several occasions with the group of doctors, who sympathized with the wish that the prime minister should attend it if possible, yet did not go so far as to give their permission. There were some rather heated exchanges between LDP Deputy Secretary-General Tanaka Rokusuke, who was convinced that the prime minister should go to the summit, and the cautious doctors. About a week after Ōhira's admission to the hospital, newspapers ran headlines such as "Hospital Stay Prolonged," "Summit Participation Doubtful," or "Possible Proxy Attendance." Through such reports there was increasing talk about the political situation being at a critical juncture.

The mass media came up with all sorts of speculations on the prime minister's physical condition, and rumors were rife. With a view to squashing needless conjecture on the part of reporters who stationed themselves in the Toranomon Hospital's Conference Room, Prime Minister Ōhira personally suggested an appearance before newsmen from the major papers, if only for a very short time. His doctors acquiesced on the condition that they also be in the room, that the duration be short, and the number of visitors small. The prime minister agreed and invited three journalists from the Cabinet Reporters' Club for a two-minute interview, beginning at 9:24 A.M. on June 8. Replying to short questions, the prime minister said that his primary concern was "getting out of bed as soon as possible, that's all." He showed that he was also much concerned about the upcoming elections, which he regretted had not been adequately prepared for, but which he felt confident that "the Japanese people will, in their own way, carry through knowledgeably and competently." At the very end of the allotted time, one of the reporters commented, "There is interest in your being able to go to the summit, if possible, when you are well." Ōhira replied simply, "I know. Thank you."

An interview with Ōhira's doctors was scheduled for June 9, but before it took place, Ōhira issued his own statement: "Today I heard the doctors' report on my progress since entering the hospital and their plans for further treatment. According to them, I have been progressing well and may soon be in a state of health that will not interfere with my political activities. I received a strict warning, however, that to this end the initial treatment following the illness is extremely important. Giving due consideration to this advice, I should like, for the time being, to refrain from making campaign speeches. As for participation in the summit, apart from whatever might be the case a week before the summit is held, I was told that as far as can be judged at present, there is a certain degree of danger involved and I should thus consider carefully. Because of the significance of the summit and the role that Japan should play, I am certainly still hoping to take part. I am asking the doctors to continue to do their best, and I intend, by the seventeenth, to decide myself whether or not I will participate."

During a press conference with the doctors, which began at 5:45 P.M., Dr. Yamaguchi Hiroshi stated, "Hospitalization will be necessary for at least two more weeks." This caused the next morning's papers to carry headlines such as: "Summit Participation Hopeless," or "Prime Minister's Stepping Down Inevitable?" Yet, in spite of these headlines, Ōhira seemed to be recovering well. He joked with doctors and nurses and composed this Chinese-style poem for an old friend who came to see him: "One knows the kindness of old friends even more when one is ill; and in daylight one often thinks of the long night's solitude." Officially and unofficially, there were various views on Ōhira's course after the election. Some asserted the need for a generational change; others declared they would ask the prime minister to make a decision only after considering the overall situation. It is thought that Prime Minister Ōhira himself had decided to resign.

At the end of the Ikeda Administration, when Prime Minister Ikeda was struck down by illness, Ōhira had been deeply concerned and immediately involved with how to help the administration to its end and create a new one. Now, too, he was surely greatly concerned over the question of how to avoid unnecessary political confusion. With Chief Cabinet Secretary Itō and other close associates, he exchanged candid views on the character and personal qualities of a number of political figures, no doubt an indication of his interest in who might best succeed him. He was eager to know in detail about the election campaigns, the results of which would be of key importance to the future political scene. However, for his state of health, which most of all required rest for body and mind, all these ruminations and the resultant nervous tension could hardly have been a good thing.

On June 10, Ōhira issued a message to all LDP members urging victory in the upcoming elections. It included a phrase, inspired by the writings of the early American statesman, William Penn, "No victory without hardships, no glory without agony." As for taking part in the summit, Ōhira was in two minds. From his statements and even from his expression, one knew that he basically felt that, while he should not attempt the impossible, he would like to attend if possible. To the extent, too, that participation in the summit could affect the question of Ōhira's continuing as prime minister or stepping down, it was positively recommended by Cabinet Chief Secretary Itō and LDP Deputy Secretary-General Tanaka Rokusuke. Indeed, the pace of Ōhira's recovery seemed to indicate that his participation would be possible. Nevertheless, Ōhira told a friend who came to visit him on the evening of June 11, "The summit is a small matter; the political situation is more crucial." Perhaps he had concluded that attending the summit could claim his life. And if that should happen, what of the political situation afterward? The party was virtually in a state of schism, and the results of the elections were wholly unpredictable. For a smooth political transition his presence was very much needed, and in this sense he ought not to force himself against reason to attend the summit. That was probably Ōhira's conclusion, and it may be surmised that he already had in mind the person to whom he felt future affairs should be entrusted.

That same evening, Ōhira's secretaries tried to ascertain the prime minister's most likely itinerary in Europe and set up specific arrangements for medical and nursing care if he made the trip, such as the installation of a bed on the plane, the designation of doctors and nurses to accompany him, the type of medical equipment to take along, and arrangements for taking necessary rests during the Venice Summit deliberations. It was decided to send a secretary from the Foreign Ministry to Venice to get information before the seventeenth, when the prime minister was to announce his decision. These plans were immediately approved by Chief Cabinet Secretary Itō and reported to Ōhira, who only replied, "Is that so? I understand." At 9 P.M., a nurse gave him the day's last round of medication.

He woke up in the middle of the night and asked, "What time is it?" When a night nurse replied, "Around twelve o'clock," he said, "I see," and went back to sleep. The turn for the worse occurred suddenly in the predawn hours. At 2:25 A.M., Ōhira's son-in-law and private secretary, Morita Hajime, who was sleeping in an adjacent room, was woken by the night nurse saying, "Get up quickly." When he entered Ōhira's room, he saw the nurse, who had a little earlier discovered something amiss, pounding Ōhira's chest with her fists. On being told of the crisis, Ōhira's wife, Shigeko, their second son Hiroshi's wife, Kimiko, their third son, Akira, and his wife, Chief Cabinet Secretary Itō, and several secretaries arrived as quickly as they could. LDP Deputy Secretary-General Tanaka Rokusuke was also called. Ōhira made several low sounds, and Shigeko and Kimiko recall that he made small motions with both hands, as though trying to deliver a campaign speech. Heart massage and electric shock treatments were continued, but without effect. Between 5 and 5:30 A.M., when there seemed to be no hope of recovery, messages saying Ōhira was in a critical condition were communicated to former Prime Minister Tanaka, LDP General Council Chairman Suzuki, Secretary-General Sakurauchi, and other party and government leaders with whom Ōhira had been especially close. A "sudden change in the prime minister's condition" was announced to the press.

It was 5:54 A.M. when the doctors informed Shigeko of her husband's death. Ōhira Masayoshi's seventy years and three months on earth had come to an end.

Chapter 41

The Eternal Now

"PRIME MINISTER OHIRA DIES." This tragic news was carried on wires and airwaves around the world, and all those who had hoped for and believed in his recovery were stunned. From early morning a stream of people began arriving at the hospital to offer condolences, finding it difficult to believe that he had passed away so suddenly. Among them were General Council Chairman Suzuki, former Prime Minister Tanaka, LDP Vice-President Nishimura, Secretary-General Sakurauchi, former prime ministers Fukuda and Miki, those members of the cabinet and other LDP Diet members who were in Tokyo, the heads of the opposition parties, and leaders in the economic community such as Sakurada Takeshi and Nagano Shigeo. Transcending differences in political position and viewpoint, all who stood before Ōhira's body shared a sense of sorrow and deep loss and answered sparingly to reporters' questions.

The morning summer sun was already high in the sky at 7:30 A.M., when Chief Cabinet Secretary Itō held a press conference, which he began: "When I went to the hospital upon hearing at 2:30 A.M. of the sudden change in the prime minister's condition, he had already lost consciousness." Then, in accordance with what Ōhira had instructed beforehand, he explained that he was now serving as acting prime minister as a temporary measure. At 8:40 A.M., the doctors who had attended the prime minister made this announcement: "At 2:25 A.M., a sudden cardiac arrhythmia caused a condition of cardiac shock. There was no positive response to any treatment that was tried, and death occurred at 5:45." An autopsy was performed and the prime minister's body was then taken temporarily to a room in the hospital's first-level basement. The physician who performed the autopsy stated: "The coronary arteries were as young as in a person in his fifties or early sixties. He must have been under unimaginable mental stress, because of which spasms and constriction occurred in one of the coronary arteries, resulting in a stoppage of blood flow." All who heard this candid pronouncement were silent as they thought of the burdens the prime minister had had to cope with.

The last family members to arrive were Ōhira's second son, Hiroshi, and his eldest daughter, Morita Yoshiko, both of whom had recently been in Kagawa Prefecture helping in their father's election campaign. To give solace to the family members assembled before Ōhira's body, a prayer was offered by Sawa Kunisuke, a Christian pastor: "Lord, we ask that the soul of this believer who has left this world may rest in peace."

Before long, Ōhira's body was placed in a casket, which was then draped with a black cloth bearing an embroidered white cross and carried by near relatives to the hearse. Preceded by two police motorcycles, the hearse left the hospital at 11:09 A.M. to circle the Prime Minister's Official Residence and the Diet building, both of which displayed flags at half-mast and both of whose employees stood outside to bid farewell. It then headed toward Ōhira's home along the freeway he had used to commute to work. At his home, the hearse was met by neighborhood residents, and family members carried the casket into the house. The sight of Ōhira's grand-children, looking intently with reddened eyes at the coffin bearing their *Ojii-chan* (Grandpa), who would never speak to them again, brought tears to the eyes of a good many of those present. Visitors offering condolences came to both the Ōhiras' Seta residence and the Prime Minister's Official Residence throughout the day and into the evening. At 3 P.M., an envoy from the Imperial Household Agency came to offer the condolences of the emperor and empress to Ōhira's family. That night there was a preliminary wake just for family members. A temporary altar had been set up in the living room facing the garden, which had always been one of Ōhira's favorite rooms and where he had received guests. White flowers nearly covered the body in the casket. On the night of June 13, there was a formal wake held for persons outside the family. Then, from 1 P.M. on June 14, an informal funeral ceremony was held at the Seta residence. A volunteer choir sang Christian hymns as some 4,000 people filed past to offer white flowers to Ōhira's spirit.

In preparing for Ōhira's formal funeral, Itō Masayoshi, the acting prime minister, served as head of the funeral committee. To give what was considered appropriate recognition to Ōhira's sense of modesty, it was de-cided that this would not be a state funeral but a joint cabinet and LDP ceremony. On the day of the ceremony, July 9, rain poured down from early morning. The chief mourner, Ōhira Hiroshi, who carried the urn con-taining his father's ashes, arrived together with his mother at the Nihon Budōkan hall, where some six thousand persons were waiting inside. To signal the ceremony's start, solemn music was complemented by a salvo of nineteen cannonades echoing through the overcast skies as a salute in Ōhira's honor.

Ōhira's ashes were placed on the central ceremonial platform decorated with red and white carnations in the form of the Japanese national flag, with white chrysanthemums and green cedar branches along the sides. After one minute of silence and a short recording of Ōhira's voice, the memorial addresses began. The first to speak was Itō Masayoshi, head of the funeral committee, who started his oration as follows:

"Prime Minister Ōhira: You were a person who was always zealous to keep faith, who valued friendships, who was farsighted and prudent, and who, once a decision was taken, did not waver in carrying it out; one whose life was dedicated, quite literally, to the nation and to the people. Your seventy years of life were brought to an end by death from an unexpected illness in the midst of a political campaign. At this moment of eternal parting, and treasuring the memory of your kindly face, words cannot express the myriad feelings that well up in my heart."

Time stood still, as if frozen. Those who filled the arena sat motionless as Itō, in a voice filled with sorrow, recounted the late prime minister's upbringing and achievements. These recollections from various periods mingled as in a kaleidoscope and touched the hearts of all present. A large photograph of the late prime minister smiled gently down from its place on the central platform. Itō continued: "Then, too, with rich insight, you always showed superb statesmanship. Your concept of a nation of garden-cities, which foretold the coming of an age of local regions and an age of culture, is . . . another result of your ideals."

On the day after Ōhira's death, Acting Prime Minister Itō had asked the various policy study groups to complete, as "a last gift from Prime Minister Ōhira to the nation," several still incomplete reports to submit to the Ōhira Cabinet before it finished its duties. Within one month, the drafting committees of these study groups produced nine proposals, often by working until late at night or even till dawn. Contained in a box made of the white wood of a three-hundred-year-old Kiso cypress, the completed reports had been placed on the funeral altar as a way of praying for the repose of the late prime minister's soul and honoring his legacy to the future.

Itō continued: "Prime Minister Ōhira: Amidst a tense international situation, you promoted summit diplomacy and contributed to elevating our country's international standing. You deepened friendly relations with many foreign nations and made every effort toward preserving and developing world order and peace."

Telegrams received from overseas on the day of Ōhira's death had expressed the profound sense of loss on the part of other government leaders around the world. This feeling was especially strong in the United States and China, each of which Prime Minister Ōhira had visited several times. Present at the funeral ceremony were representatives from 108 countries and two international organizations, including those from 48 countries who had come to Japan especially to attend the ceremony. The latter included President Jimmy Carter from the United States, Premier Hua Guofeng from China, Prime Minister Malcolm Fraser from Australia, Governor General Edward Schreyer from Canada, Prime Minister Prem Tinsulanonda from Thailand, President Ziaur Rahman from Bangladesh, Acting Prime Minister Park Choong Hoon from the Republic of Korea, First Lady of the Philippines Mrs. Imelda Marcos, First State Commissioner Bo-Boliko Lokonga from Zaire, Prime Minister Daniel M. Lisulo from Zambia, and Deputy Head of State Tupua Tamasese Lealofi from Western Samoa. Among the black funeral apparel of those present, the bright ethnic clothing worn by some of the representatives of Asian and African countries added touches of color to the gathering. Following the ceremony, President Carter, Premier Hua, and Mrs. Marcos visited the Ōhira home, where they again expressed their sorrow.

The late prime minister had felt that politics' greatest mission was to plan for world peace and prosperity, and he had spared no effort in helping deepen understanding and trust among nations. His last overseas trip to the United States, Mexico, Canada, Yugoslavia, and West Germany, covering 50,000 kilometers in twelve days, surely contributed to that goal, although it also increased the fatigue that seemed to have led to his untimely death.

As Itō said in his oration: "In response to our suggestion that you take a little rest, you did not agree, saying, 'In politics one stops only after one is dead.'. . . Then, as if lying in wait for you on your return from that long journey on which you bore the country's destinies and fulfilled an important mission, a motion of no-confidence in the cabinet was presented and, due to unexpected circumstances, was passed. . . .

"And then upon you, who with your gentle heart deeply loved people and did not like disputes, who sought quiet meditation and used to say, 'I value the sensibility of the person who will water a flower that is going to die the next day,' the times forced ever more cruel stress and self-denial." Itō's voice wavered, and outside the rain seemed to fall more heavily.

"No sooner had the news come that the prime minister had become incapacitated by illness than the voices of the nation's people, praying for your recovery, filled every street and byway, and a great number of heartfelt wishes for a speedy recovery arrived from overseas. Helped by the dedicated care of the doctors and nurses, it appeared that your condition was daily improving. We then felt relief, and you, pushing yourself despite your ailing body, quickened your resolve to attend the Venice Summit and gave instructions on various preparations for it."

Even though Ōhira was not ultimately able to participate in the Venice Summit in late June he had so wished to attend, his photograph graced the summit table and watched over the progress of the conference. With the agreement of the other participating heads of state, Japan sent Foreign Minister Ōkita as its chief representative, together with Finance Minister Takeshita and International Trade and Industry Minister Sasaki. Faithful to instructions left by Ōhira in case he might not be able to attend, the Japanese participants promised Japan's continuing solidarity with the West.

"Prime Minister Ōhira: Even in your sickbed, you continued to think of how to bring more stability to politics. The elections have ended well and with excellent results. Yet, however much I want to report them to you, your kindly face is there no longer. When one speaks of a broken heart, this is precisely what is meant."

Ōhira's dramatic death had stirred many LDP members to fight all the harder in the simultaneous Upper and Lower House election campaigns and helped dissipate the earlier ill will stemming from intraparty rivalries. Most of the party candidates hung black-ribboned photographs of the late prime minister in their offices and wore black armbands while delivering their campaign speeches.

The simultaneous Upper and Lower House Diet elections took place on June 22, 1980, the same day as the opening of the Venice Summit. Voter interest had been rapidly rising, and the turnout for the Upper House election was the highest in postwar history, while that for the Lower House election was the fourth-highest during the same period. This June 1980 election gave the LDP 284 seats in the Lower House, an increase of 36 seats from the 248 won in the previous election. With the adherence of three who ran as independents, the party's Lower House seats later totaled 287. In the Upper House, the LDP won 70 seats (69 for candidates "officially endorsed" and 1 for an "officially recommended" candidate), bringing the total to 135 seats, including those not currently up for reelection. Thus, the six-year-long near-parity in LDP and opposition party numbers was ended, and the more stable political situation that Ōhira had hoped for was assured. On June 24, the day the final election results were announced, Acting Prime Minister Itō, LDP Vice-President Nishimura, and Secretary-General Sakurauchi all visited Ōhira's home to report before his altar the party's victory in the double election.

"Prime Minister Ōhira: When the times were at a critical turning point, God chose you as our country's leader and entrusted you with its destiny. Through your profound thinking and tireless efforts you have well fulfilled that mission. However poor our abilities, by inheriting your aims, we pledge to restore faith in politics and open a new era. . . . You were a person who tirelessly strove for your ideals, even while enduring many hardships. Now I can only say these words of eternal parting, while praying for the peaceful repose of your soul."

Outside the Nihon Budōkan, several thousand people waited patiently in the rain. Some were housewives carrying shopping bags, others were old people with canes or students on their way home from school. Not a few had come from places far from Tokyo.

When the memorial addresses and the offering of flowers by those inside the hall were over, still more flowers were offered by those who had been standing outside. Many gave deep bows as they passed the central platform and a good many, looking up at Ōhira's photograph, would say something in a low voice. To a background of music, the long line filed past for about two hours, in the course of which the rain finally stopped.

The question of the degree to which Ōhira, as a politician, fulfilled the mission accorded him had best be left to future historians. However, in looking back over his life, one can surely say that Ōhira Masayoshi adequately fulfilled the aim he had set for himself when he said, "Before being a politician, I want to live as a real human being."

Stone memorials erected in Ōhira Masayoshi's memory are found in two cemeteries, one in the Tama region of Tokyo's western suburbs and one in his native Toyohama. On the back of them are engraved these words, selected by his close friend Itō Masayoshi:

> You live in the eternal now
> Even if you died while in office.
> You do not tire of seeking your ideals
> And even in death have not ceased.

Epilogue

Already ten years have passed since Ōhira Masayoshi left this world in June 1980, and since then, with the many changes within Japan and throughout the world, there has been a renewed appreciation of Ōhira's foresight and leadership as a politician, his unpretentious philosophy, and his warm, modest personality. With the passage of time, it is becoming clear how deep was his imprint on the 1980s, how accurately he pointed out the path for Japan to pursue in the world, and how worthy were his qualities both as a person and as a statesman.

In retrospect, the 1980s were for Japan a decade of reforms, including fiscal reconstruction, administrative reorganization, educational reform, market opening measures, industrial restructuring, and various economic and tax reforms. Many of these were begun soon after the Ōhira Administration started in December 1978, and were carried forward and developed by successive administrations.

Although Ōhira was prime minister for only one year and seven months, his basic directions for reform and his indications of the path for a Japan in transition served as signposts for the changes of the 1980s and suggested the road to be followed by Japan and the world as we continue into the 1990s and the next century. The tax reform that the Ōhira Cabinet tried so hard to institute finally came about, however faultily, ten years later, and the political reforms that Ōhira so strongly hoped for are once again becoming an acute national concern. In both cases we are reminded of Ōhira's unusual insight into the future.

Ōhira Masayoshi was born at the end of the Meiji era (1868–1912) that had seen Japan's rapid modernization, and received his primary and the first part of his secondary education during the Taishō era (1912–26), which was characterized by a strengthening of democratic ideals. When the Shōwa era (1926–89) began, he was in his third year of middle school.

567

During the New Year holidays of 1928, the year Ōhira entered the Takamatsu Higher School of Commerce, the young Shōwa emperor presided over the first poetry-reading ceremony (*utakaihajime no gi*) of his reign, held at the Imperial Palace, at which he read the following poem he had composed: *Yamayama no iro wa arata ni miyuredomo / Waga matsurigoto ikani ka aruran*, which might be translated as "The colors of the mountains look fresh again / Yet how will our administration fare?" The era soon witnessed drastic change and the increasing unease of which the emperor, even at the start of his reign, seems to have had some presentiment.

The Shōwa era, which was the longest reign period in Japanese history, may be divided roughly into the two decades up to the end of World War II and the subsequent four and a half decades. The latter period can be further classified into (1) the 1945–55 period of postwar reconstruction; (2) the 1955–70 period of rapid economic growth; and (3) the post-1970 period of transition. This last period can again be subdivided into the 1970s—which future historians may deem a decade of haphazard groping toward reforms and toward a framework for defining its own character—and the 1980s, when the nature of the period and the reforms were better defined and were being put into practice. The decade of reforms that began with the Ōhira Administration in late 1978 corresponds to the latter subdivision, that is, the 1980s.

Indeed, the capacity for insight that Ōhira's developed over his lifetime can be symbolized by this decade, which provided abundant evidence to show that among Japanese politicians he was one of the first to perceive the true nature of the times and the need for various political, economic, and social changes.

An Awareness of the Nature of the Times

Let us first consider how Ōhira forecast the future at the start of the 1970s. In a magazine article in January 1970, he wrote: "As we are about to enter the 1970s, if we turn our thoughts to our nation's past and its future, we sense that we are in a period of transition, about to step onto a new stage. Since the Meiji Restoration of 1868, our nation's goal had been, in short, to catch up with, or even surpass, the advanced nations of Europe and America. . . . But as we stand at the threshold of the 1970s, Japan is finally about to end the stage of catching up. . . . We should look on the era of emulative development—which depended on importing knowledge and technology from advanced countries—as having ended. In other words, I think we are about to change to an era of 'creative development,' when we will discover new fields by our own endeavors, and by our own efforts walk a self-reliant path."

This sort of awareness of the times was expressed even more clearly in his September 1971 proposals, made in his position as Kōchikai chairman, titled, "Let Us Turn the Tide: Commencement of a New Century." In a preface to these proposals, he stated:

> Our country is just now at a turning point that might be called the end of the postwar era. Until now we have worked intently in the quest for more material wealth, but we have not necessarily been able to find true happiness or purpose of life in the wealth we have attained. We have run full speed ahead, without pause, along the path of economic growth, but because of the very speed with which this growth has taken place we now have no choice but to aim again at stability. With considerable nonchalance we have attempted economic advances abroad, but because of the intensity of these advances we have sometimes become the object of jealousy and resistance in other countries. Our keynote has been cooperation with the United States and we have avoided [full] participation in international politics, but certainly with the present weakening of the dollar system we must embark on the difficult path of a self-reliant diplomacy. Our nation has concentrated on economic reconstruction, but precisely because of the scale of our economic growth, as "global insiders" we now have no choice but to support an internationalization of the economy.

He went on to assert, "This must surely be called an important turning point," and appealed for "bold revisions in policy approaches."

With the advent of the 1970s there was much discussion in Japan and elsewhere about this "time of transition." While Ōhira was thus by no means alone in his use of the phrase, his policy proposals of September 1971, made just after the two "Nixon shocks," were especially worthy of note for their thorough analysis.

In an August 1973 speech titled "Signposts to a New Order," Ōhira indicated his feeling that the world environment had become much more complex and serious than he had envisioned two years previously, stating, "This tectonic shift is of a scale that will affect the history of the human race. It appears to shake the very foundations of civilization and, naturally enough, the ensuing confusion causes not only changes in various relationships within the country but is itself developing into an international problem." The timing of this statement seems all the more appropriate when we remember that immediately afterward came the first oil crisis that affected the entire world.

After he became prime minister, Ōhira's first policy speech given in the Diet in January 1979 elaborated on his view of the 1980s. Here his emphasis was that Japan has "reached the limits to modern rationalistic urbanization and material civilization. We are, if you will, on the threshold of a new age transcending the age of modernization; we have moved from an age centering on economics to a new age with an emphasis on culture."

We may say that this understanding of the times was characterized by his assertion of a change of truly historic proportions involving the simultaneous coming together of three processes of transition: (1) structural changes in the postwar world brought about in large part by a relative rise of other countries' international positions vis-à-vis the United States; (2) the end of the catching-up type of modernization that had continued since the Meiji Restoration; and (3) the emergence of a postmodern information civilization.

Simple, Efficient, and Small Government

What did Ōhira believe the role of government should be in this sort of time of change? An indication is given in words he liked to quote from Ogadai Khan's Prime Minister Yelü Chucai (1190–1244): "Better to eliminate one wrong than to initiate one right." He meant that if politicians promise too much and become the objects of unrealistic expectations from the people, the results are sure to be disappointing. It is rather more important that politics should have the less pretentious aim of eliminating, one by one, the larger and smaller evils that afflict the people. It is said that when Ōhira visited the United States as prime minister and was asked by President Carter about the significance of the above quotation, he replied, "It is the voice of lamentation of any politician aspiring toward an ideal society." In any case, at the root of his thinking was what might truly be called a conservative philosophy, which while pursuing ideals, advocated not the hurried pursuit of unsubstantiated argument and ideology but step-by-step progress, always keeping an eye on actual specific conditions in society. His political philosophy seems also to have been influenced by a story about the legendary Emperor Yao, who is said to have been an ideal ruler in ancient China. In the story, all is peaceful with the world, so Yao disguises himself and goes to a busy crossroad to observe conditions among the people. A certain old man, oblivious of any need to express gratitude for the emperor's good government, drummed his stomach and tapped the earth as he sang: "The sun comes up and we work, the sun goes down and we rest, we dig wells and drink, we cultivate the fields and eat. What is the power of the emperor? Does it have anything to do with us?" (Vol. 1 of *Shiba shiliao*)

Within this story is the notion that for the people the ideal government is one that is so natural, reserved, and modest that its authority and even its benefits are hardly noticeable. From time to time, Ōhira confided to friends that he was more fond of the Chinese sages Laozi (Lao-tze) and Zhuangzi (Chuang-tze), who espoused a minimalist type of government, than of Kongzi (Confucius), who was more a stickler for forms and conventions, and from this we can perceive Ōhira's basic stance toward politics. It is of interest to look at Ōhira's speeches and interviews during the 1978 campaign for the LDP presidency for clues to his thinking on politics and administration at a time when he could already foresee the administration he would lead. Some relevant quotes follow:

> The government is too indulgent toward the people, while the people are too indulgent toward the government. This results in excessive expectations of politics, and intervention that is beyond the capacity of politics. I think this is the reason the administrative apparatus has become so heavy and fiscal management has gotten into such straits. Toward this sort of indulgence, both the people and the government must give some serious thought.

> We must avoid any sort of excessive political intrusion into every aspect of people's lives. On the other hand, the people should, as much as possible, refrain from too many expectations (or, alternatively, too much criticism) that everything is the government's responsibility.

> It is going too far to think that government is something given to us, or that it is natural to place such great expectations in government and politics. The nation should agree to be satisfied with the limited power that the government actually possesses.

At least three basic ideas went into this concept of simple government. The first of these, centered on liberal market economics and private enterprise, held that when government intervenes too much in economic activities (as in the case of "controlled" or "planned" economies), there are only disadvantages without any compensating advantages.

This respect for liberal economic principles was very well demonstrated when Prime Minister Ōhira opted, at the time of the second oil crisis, not for direct government intervention but for letting the economy adjust to the new environment through the market mechanism. A similar attitude could be seen in the doubts he held, when serving as head of the Indirect

Taxation Department of the Sendai Tax Supervision Bureau in 1938, about meting out punishments for the home brewing of alcoholic beverages (in violation of a government monopoly), or in the scheme he elaborated, as head of Tokyo Local Finance Bureau's Indirect Taxation Department during the war, for the sale to consumers (via People's Taverns) of alcoholic beverages that would otherwise have been unavailable to them under the strictly supervised wartime procurement and distribution system.

Immediately after the end of the war, in 1946, Ōhira, then thirty-six years old and working in the Budget Bureau of the Ministry of Finance, expressed similar thinking in the policy proposals he presented under the title "The Problem of Disposing of Government Enterprises." One interesting point was his suggestion that if government enterprises "could be released from existing accounting regulations and restrictions ... and made into places for engaging the spirit of private enterprise, these undertakings will be able to develop fresh and vigorous activities." Elsewhere in the same proposals he stated: "It should be sufficient for the government to retain and give superior treatment to only a small number of especially capable administrative officers and otherwise to carry out a thorough revision of personnel regulations. It is not logical that it should have to retain an overwhelmingly large number of industrial officials."

The second element was an extension of the first, and envisioned a "Japanese-style welfare system" that would keep down any enormous growth in the government budget through efforts at self-help and a "strengthening of the family base." Proposals along this line included "the establishment of an equitable and effective Japanese-type welfare state that fully preserves the Japanese people's spirit of self-reliance and self-help, their close-knit interpersonal relations, and their methods of maintaining order in society, while adding public welfare provisions where appropriate" and "planning, as we encounter a society with a growing proportion of older people, for a type of living that is characterized by self-composure, kindness, and time to spare." These and similar pronouncements were made on the basis of a keen realization that welfare states built with too much administrative complexity and a hypertrophy of government expenditures could, in fact, sap the vitality of a society, giving rise to "advanced nation diseases" and self-defeating mechanisms leading to fiscal bankruptcy.

Third, there was the concept of administrative and fiscal reforms aiming at simple, efficient, and cheap government and a fundamental interest in restructuring government finance and restoring its flexibility and capacity to respond to actual needs. Time and again he made assertions like: "We must eliminate the inefficiencies resulting from too much hierarchy in administration and must foster a cheap and efficient government"; "We must severely criticize inflexible government attitudes rooted in authoritarian tendencies, and in order to realize a cheap and efficient government that rejects excessive intervention we must resolutely simplify procedures in the granting of licenses and subsidies"; "Some of the government bodies created during the period of rapid economic growth have ended their usefulness or have become something of a nuisance, and from these the government should withdraw."

The basic outlines of the fiscal reconstruction and administrative and fiscal reforms begun during the Ōhira Administration were taken over and developed by the succeeding administrations. If these basic outlines for simple, efficient, and small government had not been established during the Ōhira Administration, the succeeding administrations might have had much more difficulty in taking the steps they did, and the progress of Japan's economy during the 1980s might have been greatly impeded.

From Quantitative Wealth to Qualitative Wealth

At the root of Ōhira's assertion of the need for a simple, small government and a temperate politics was the notion of the need for important cultural changes in the way people regard the concept of "abundance," involving a shift from a quantitative to a qualitative perspective. The basic idea in the "Commencement of a New Century" speech referred to earlier was that it was time to break away from the thought patterns dominating the era of rapid economic growth from around 1955 to 1970. This was indeed a proposal, persuasively made, for major policy changes, coming from the same man who had been Prime Minister Ikeda's chief cabinet secretary and had done much to help carry out Ikeda's National Income-Doubling Plan.

Reflecting later on the Ikeda Administration's Income-Doubling Plan, Ōhira once stated: "Because Japan's is not a planned economy, it is erroneous to have a government 'plan' for doubling incomes. It would be sufficient to have the figures in any such plan held up as a sort of mirror in carrying out government policies so that their relative success or failure could be judged by looking in this mirror." Also of great interest is his penetrating awareness of the problems involved with any policy concentrating on quantitative expansion and the accurate way with which he saw the limitations and constraints of the times. To break away from material poverty, quantitative growth through policies to facilitate rapid economic growth was necessary. But quantitative growth was only a process on the way to true abundance. Ōhira felt that this process was likely to bring various strains and negative influences on the people and their ways of living that could hinder the attainment of what was truly valuable. This idea is expressed in his "Commencement of a New Century" speech as follows:

> The Japanese people now want, more than the boundless pursuit of material wealth, a stable life with ample room for the spirit. . . . To respond to these hopes, we must build on our four islands a human society in harmonious balance with nature.

Put forward in this regard were the concept of a nation of garden-cities, the concept of strengthening the family base, and the concept of an age of culture. At the root of these concepts, the motifs were the transition from material to spiritual abundance, from quantitative to qualitative abundance, from abundance of material goods to abundance of cultural stock, from wealth in hardware to wealth in software, from abundance in possessions to abundance in human relations.

The abundance of postwar Japan's period of rapid economic growth had been primarily one that could be measured by material, quantitative indices. It had been ultimately an abundance that could be measured in terms of GNP or per capita GNP. In the "catching up" era of modernization and industrialization, abundance had been understood in these terms, and the policies promoting rapid economic growth had been chosen precisely because they still corresponded to this stage of development. But now that per capita GNP had reached the levels of other advanced countries, Japan as a major power was having to grapple head-on—as was indeed the case for industrial civilization as a whole—with the problem of what true abundance for human beings is. Ōhira was fond of saying, "In a time of abundance the problems are different from the problems of poverty." He also often said, "We must build a civilization that can cope lastingly with peace and abundance." When he talked of "going beyond the modern," he had in mind the efforts that would have to be associated with this task.

To transcend the limitations of the modern and gradually change the nature of abundance, Ōhira had in mind at least three main policy tasks. The first of these came from apprehension lest the traditional type of modernity so biased in favor of material, quantitative abundance result in a retrogression of culture, in other words a culture crisis that would lower the meaning of abundance; it thus envisaged that in an era transcending the modern it would be essential to give much greater importance to culture so as to overcome these threats to cultural degradation. During the campaign leading to the 1978 LDP presidential election, he stated: "I think the age has changed from one with the focus on 'economics' to an 'age of culture.'. . . It is an age when the people's interests are shifting to culture, from the material to the spiritual." This sort of approach was later developed in the work of the study groups under the Policy Study Association he set up as prime minister, namely, those concerned with the "age of culture" and "economic performance in the age of culture."

The second main policy task Ōhira had in mind centered around the Concept of Strengthening the Family Base, which had as its motif the achievement of more satisfying human relationships. There was here an awareness of the importance of family-type human relations that the rationalistic world view associated with European–American modernization had tended to overlook. Of course, Ōhira tried to adhere closely to the important principle that politics must definitely refrain from intruding into the home and the family. He preferred not to use the term "family policy," and when using the phrase "strengthening the family base," deliberately tried to set limits to the role he perceived for government policy. In this area we see how he consistently tried to keep to a political philosophy that held that politics should never overly interfere in the family, as families were seen to be the inner sanctums for the free and pluralistic manifestation of people's values, spirit, and ways of living. We may say that it was with this approach that Ōhira searched for a clearer vision of a Japanese welfare society that would transcend the limitations of the welfare state models of Europe and America.

In 1978 he made the following statement: "Our nation's families, reflecting the longer life-spans and the continuing effects of the rapid changes that followed the war, have shown certain weaknesses. We must hasten to strengthen the family's material and spiritual base and improve the quality of its members' lives so as to see families emerge with greater calm, greater kindness, greater latitude, and more distinguished characters. At the same time, we should build families able to adequately compensate for the deficiencies of our economic and social systems. To be more specific, we should draft a comprehensive scheme to facilitate the strengthening of the family base and should carry out appropriate measures with respect to employment, aging, health, housing, leisure, culture, education, and so on, paying due attention to ways of adequately encouraging Japanese-type flexibility and the capacity to undertake multiple tasks."

A third political task Ōhira set for transforming the nature of abundance had the motif of how to respond to the gaps, and sometimes antagonisms, that had arisen between urban and rural areas in the modernization process. As a way of overcoming these gaps, there was his Garden-City Concept, which could, to a great extent, bridge some of the traditional differences between the cities and the rural areas. Ōhira described the merits of this plan as follows: "It would mean joining, on a higher plane, nature's abundance in the countryside with the high productivity of the cities, and it would mean the building of a network of healthful, tranquil garden-cities and the development of local units of community life throughout the nation. Therefore, we would promote the balanced development of our nation's territory, would give Tokyo and other local governments functions concerning revenue sources, employment opportunities, education, and culture, and would entrust to local governments the functions of welfare administration. We would encourage each of these local areas to display a high degree of self-government, to promote various local industries, and to see the flowering of distinctive local cultures." This new formulation brought some qualitative changes to earlier expositions of his concept of "a nation of garden-cities" (den'en toshi kokka), and was meant, at the same time, to go beyond Tanaka Kakuei's Plan for the Remodeling of the Japanese Archipelago, which was heavily weighted toward economic and GNP-centered considerations.

This concept of Ōhira's was generally welcomed by the people, and during the first half of the 1980s come to be referred to in the term chihō no jidai, which might be translated as "local age" or "age of local initiatives." Throughout Japan, village and town improvement movements spread, helped by the birth of new industries resulting from scientific and technological innovations. For a while, the future of the "local age" looked bright, but, in the latter half of the 1980s, there was a renewed concentration of population and activities in the largest cities, especially around Tokyo. Among the direct causes were changes in the industrial structure, accelerated by the rising value of the yen (allowing overseas factories, in some cases helped or underwritten by Japanese investments, to compete successfully with factories in Japan), as well as the rising importance of Tokyo as an information center of global importance. However, we may say that a more fundamental reason obstructing the realization of local potentials was a deficiency in the political will to make it absolutely clear that the possibilities of the "local age" would be integrated with sufficient care into the nation's economic and political framework. In that sense, Ōhira's Garden-City Concept may yet find a new departure.

A Creative Strategy for Peace

In his generation, Ōhira was one of few Japanese politicians who always tried to think about politics from an international viewpoint. This stance was grounded in an awareness of the world that had two balanced focal points, as in an ellipse: one was his deep appreciation of Western culture and history, no doubt encouraged through his encounter with Christianity in his youth; and the other was his deep understanding of East Asian

culture and history, nurtured in part by his experience of living in China as
a young bureaucrat.

Given his global awareness, Ōhira had a thorough dislike for politicians
who made no effort to see the world or Japan except through the window
of a narrow, self-complacent nationalism and old stereotypes. Ōhira was a
statesman who, having seen at close range some of the less fortunate relations between Japan and the world before, during, and after World War II,
felt deeply the importance of peaceful international relations. He was thoroughly aware that to have lasting world peace it was necessary to have a
creative peace strategy backed by firm, yet flexible and realistic thinking,
and that persistence would be needed to build new types of international
relations on this foundation. Essential parts of Ōhira's political thinking
found expression in his Comprehensive Security Strategy (*Sōgō anzen
hoshō senryaku*) and his Pacific Basin Cooperation Concept (*Kantaiheiyō
rentai kōsō*), which together may be said to be the first future-oriented,
creative peace strategies elaborated by Japan as a nonmilitary, economic
power that had learned some important lessons from the prewar, wartime,
and postwar periods.

This sort of international awareness is shown in the following passage
from the speech delivered by Ōhira, as foreign minister, before the 18th
United Nations General Assembly in 1963, the year after the Cuban
missile crisis:

> This crisis, which occurred in one corner of the globe, immedi-
> ately had a direct bearing on the very survival of the world and
> of all mankind. All of us today indeed share a common fate.
> Such a situation has never before existed in the history of our
> world and is one of the foremost characteristics of our times.
>
> But it is not only in such a negative sense that we share this
> common fate. Developments in science and technology have so
> dramatically increased intercourse in all aspects in human life
> that the people of one nation are now closely linked with the
> people of all other nations politically, economically, culturally.
> As no individual can live in isolation in his own country, no na-
> tion can exist in isolation from the rest of the world. In life, and
> indeed in death too, mankind is linked together by a fate that is
> one and inseparable.

In this speech Ōhira went on to state that the peace we seek cannot be
a mere tactical slogan but must be a concrete peace, accompanied by
freedom and backed by respect for human rights. Disharmony and opposition, hatred and distrust among nations were, he asserted, resolvable

through persistent efforts, and through proofs of trust in dealing with various specific matters one at a time.

Ōhira's fundamental stance with respect to the international community remained always the same. In his first policy speech as prime minister, he stated: "Our earth is today an increasingly interdependent community interreacting more sensitively to events. Whatever incidents or problems occur anywhere on the face of the globe have instant ramifications elsewhere, and it is impossible to formulate effective responses unless we consider the global society in its entirety. The very survival of mankind will be imperiled unless we abstain from confrontation and conflict, and, instead, seek mutual understanding and cooperation."

How, then, should we cope with an international society which continues with its antagonisms and strife? When we survey postwar Japan, the problem of how security should be arranged has seen the most sharply divided public opinion. This was true in 1951, with respect to whether there should be a single peace treaty with all belligerents in World War II or first a treaty with only a majority of the parties involved; it was true with respect to the 1960 unrest over revision of the U.S.-Japan Security Treaty, and it was similarly so with respect to the conditions for the reversion of Okinawa.

Much of the thinking that Ōhira put into his Comprehensive Security Strategy was being developed and refined many years before he became prime minister. For example, in a speech he gave at the LDP's Central Academy of Politics in 1967, when he was serving as deputy chairman of the party's Research Commission on Foreign Affairs, he stated: "In countries where an orderly domestic administration is carried out, where there is a well-developed economy, and where the flowers of a refined and distinctive culture are in bloom, other countries are unable to interfere even if they might wish to do so.... The first necessity for preserving peace is to have an orderly domestic administration, to have a consensus on self-defense, and to be faithful to agreements with other countries." Later in the same speech he asserted: "If a nation's people do not put faith in its politics and are not inclined to love their country, there is no reason for it to be trusted by other countries."

When Ōhira ran in the 1978 LDP presidential election, he further refined such thinking and announced that as party president and prime minister he would establish a Comprehensive Security Strategy. Its contents could be summarized, with some paraphrasing, in the following way:

1. Japan clearly states its national will never to arm itself with nuclear weapons, even if this might be technologically,

economically, or politically possible. As a peaceful nation, Japan will strive to continue to take moral and political initiatives aimed at eliminating all nuclear weapons, wherever they might be located.

2. Japan clearly establishes its national will to live as a peace-loving nation that upholds its Constitution, advocates "defensive defense," does not export weapons, and whose moderate defensive expenditures represent no more than about 1 percent of the gross national product.

3. However, so long as international tensions exist, Japan will complement its "defensive defense" posture with defense cooperation with advanced Western democracies that share its values of freedom and democracy and with a collective security system centered on the U.S.–Japan Security Treaty. Responding to a situation of increasing military might deployed by the Soviet Union, Japan will, within limits, actively bear an appropriate share of the responsibilities and expenses associated with this collective security.

4. Nevertheless, the main fields in which Japan, as a non-military, economic power, can make international contributions should be the following: (1) economic and technological cooperation; and (2) cooperation in educational and cultural pursuits. Military cooperation should be tightly restricted.

The second pillar of Ōhira's creative strategy for peace was the Pacific Basin Cooperation Concept. Postwar Japanese diplomacy, learning from earlier mistakes, had always adhered to three standpoints: (1) Japan as one of the industrially advanced democracies; (2) Japan as a part of Asia; and (3) Japan as a member of the United Nations. The Pacific Basin Cooperation Concept was a framework for international cooperation that effectively brought these three standpoints together on a higher plane. It was meant to be a long-term, comprehensive, and balanced diplomatic initiative elaborated with due regard to the failures of past concepts that had been too one-sided, like prewar ultranationalism, the 1940 Tripartite Pact with Germany and Italy, or the prewar debate about whether Japan should distance itself from Asia and emulate European thinking or reject Europe to befriend Asia.

The Pacific Basin Cooperation Study Group, which was part of the Ōhira Cabinet's advisory Policy Study Association, elaborated on Ōhira's ideas to produce a new vision of Asia–Pacific cooperation into the twenty-first century in the following way:

1. This must not be an exclusive regionalism closed to cooperation with countries outside the region. All Pacific Ocean countries should utilize part of their dynamism to take an active part in global activities.
2. Within the region the aim should always be to form free and open relationships of interdependence. Cultural plurality should be fully respected and every effort should be made to promote free trade and capital transfers. Through economic and technological cooperation, market opening measures (first initiated by industrially advanced countries), and steady efforts at self-help on the part of the developing countries, this region should be a new model for resolving North–South problems.
3. Pacific cooperation will not conflict in any way with any existing bilateral or multilateral cooperative relationships. Rather it will build mutually beneficial relationships from the positive results already achieved.

Learning from its past, this was the first clear, geopolitical concept put forward by Japan for the promotion of peace and prosperity. It is notable, too, for an outlook grounded in cultural history that foresaw both the expansion of common aspects in material ways of life and the simultaneous growth of variety, or pluralism, in the spiritual aspects of people's lives.

At the time they were first presented, it could not necessarily be said that either the Comprehensive Security Strategy or the Pacific Basin Cooperation Concept won sufficient understanding, either in Japan or abroad. Yet the subsequent decade has shown that Ōhira's thinking and observations were a good barometer of the times. For example, both the United States and the Soviet Union, which had made such a trememdous issue of a "balance of terror" as a tool in their quest for security, are finding military preparations too much of a burden on domestic policies and are disbanding the cold war stance maintained since 1945. Contacts and exchanges in every field among the Pacific Rim countries are developing more rapidly and on a greater scale than most people imagined, and are expected to be an enormous motivating force for the world in the twenty-first century.

As the situation that has prevailed in the world since the end of World War II continues to change and as international society searches for ways toward greater stability and prosperity, Ōhira's ideas will surely continue to be important signposts.

Placing Faith in the People

A special characteristic of Ōhira's approach to politics was the fact that he always tried to look clearly at politics from the standpoint of ordinary people. He once said: "There is a saying: There will be good politics where there are good newspapers. However, if you ask me, I think the saying should go: There will be good politics where there are good people.... I think that all people are at present taking part in politics. Each family or each business, in its own way, determines whether a nation's politics is good or bad. Unless they are of excellent quality, Japan and Japan's politics will not be of excellent quality. Politics is, in a way, like a vast orchestra in which all the nation's people participate. If, when each musical instrument becomes part of the whole, there is harmony, rhythm, and a sense of proportion, there will automatically be politics of good quality.... Politics is, you know, something for grown-ups."

This concept that everyone takes part in politics was a sign of the great faith that Ōhira placed in the people. Following the Upper House election of June 1971, when a large number of registered voters failed to vote and the LDP's showing was unexpectedly poor, Ōhira commented: "We shouldn't see this as a lack of interest in politics. I say this because citizens' movements (*shimin undō*) are becoming ever more active and are seeking a more direct political participation that would avoid having us as intermediaries."

Following the Lockheed Incident during the Miki Administration, when a split in the LDP was narrowly averted, and a near-parity in governing and opposition parties seats came about in the Diet, he commented: "The people have shown an uncanny sense of balance, and even though they are asking the LDP to undergo some hard self-reflection, still they did not give a majority to the opposition parties." He was often heard to speak of "the people's uncanny sense of balance."

Given such thinking, Ōhira placed great importance on contacts between politicians and ordinary people and on ordinary people's understanding of politics. An example is seen in the way Ōhira urged Ikeda, at the beginning of the Ikeda Administration, to refrain from engaging in extravagant pastimes that would distance him from the ordinary populace. In a similar vein, Ōhira once expressed himself as follows: "Politics is something that should be developed with policy as its main axis. Policy is said to be the life-force of politics. I do not deny this. But in actual politics, the present situation asks that we devote a great deal of attention to reappraising the behavior of those individuals entrusted with drafting and executing policy and to setting up the conditions and environment in which policies can be effectively operative. I think these efforts are even more important than the relative merits of the policies themselves. Otherwise policies will end up as mere scraps of paper and not bear fruit." During the

LDP presidential campaign that led to the Ōhira Administration, he repeatedly commented on how politicians ought to behave and orient themselves. The following are excerpts from interviews carried in newspapers during October, 1978:

> Politicians must carry out what they promise, no matter how difficult this may be.

> What has been said should be carried out. Surface explanations and true intentions must be brought together. . . . It is easy to say things and difficult to do them, so we must try all the harder.

> We must guard against inflexible attitudes rooted in authoritarian tendencies. . . . Politics must be always modest, must not neglect self-reform, and must show an attitude of being ready to respond effectively to the times.

> Confrontations and antagonisms that are too rigid are unwise. Master swordsmen say a sword should be grasped "like an unboiled egg." Otherwise one cannot cope with unexpected events. I intend to use methods that are firm, yet flexible.

> Agreements are reached through patient persuasion and understanding.

> It is not easy to bring into focus matters in which there are complex interests. However, a politician should, by continuous self-reflection, strive very hard, if necessary, to explain his points of view and seek agreement. It is a dishonest politics that too readily relies on established authority.

Prior to the Diet dissolution and general election in the autumn of 1979, Prime Minister Ōhira, referring to his plan for fiscal reconstruction and the introduction of a general consumption tax, confided to persons around him, "There are times when the people will have to do certain things even if these are unpleasant. This is part of what politics is about." At the root of this statement was his faith in the people's good sense and conscience. He believed it would not be right to wait until after the election to inform people of an increased tax burden, discussion of which had been avoided during the campaign. He felt that if LDP politicians made earnest efforts to convince people of the need for the new tax, the people would surely understand and give their consent. Looking back, we see that the tasks Ōhira entrusted himself with had to do with resolving the problems that Japan was encountering as it was trying to turn an important corner of the era.

Ōhira not only placed great faith in the Japanese people but also had faith in Japanese traditions. "Japan's culture has a tradition of paying careful attention to balanced harmonies between such mutually contrasting things as man and nature, spirit and material, freedom and responsibility," he said. On another occasion he stated, "I hope to place a high value on Japanese ways of resolving problems, characterized by the Japanese people's spirit of self-reliance and self-help, and human relationships that emphasize kindness, consideration for others, and mutual assistance." We here have a suggestion of what might be called a Japanese-type democracy growing from Japanese group-oriented traditions and differing somewhat in nuance from Western European democracy based on the separate identity of the individual.

Dealing with Political Reform

As the long Satō Administration neared its end, the LDP began to face a period that could be called the most confused since the party's founding. At that time, Ōhira, as one of the party's most influential members, had to plunge into this confusion, whether he liked it or not. The theme of dissolving political distrust, which he placed at the head of his policy proposals of the time (presented under the title "Commencement of a New Century"), has continued, with changes in emphasis and intensity, to be a major issue for the LDP to this day.

When Ōhira spoke out for political change, he was naturally aware of the need for political reforms in several areas, including the Diet, the political parties, and elections. However, at the same time, he knew that such reforms could not be accomplished as easily as they were talked about. Thus, he was unable to fully agree with the simplistic calls for party modernization espoused by Miki Takeo or with the rather heavy-handed and authoritarian party regeneration proposed by Fukuda Takeo. It was a historical irony that Ōhira, while serving as LDP secretary-general during the Fukuda Administration, was in charge of putting into effect the new election process for party president (with the participation by all rank-and-file party members) that Miki Takeo had advocated, and then as a result of the first election held under this new system was chosen as party president and prime minister. (The intraparty rancor amidst which he died had unfortunately not abated as a result of this election and may even have worsened because of it.)

Whenever party reform is discussed, the biggest issue is invariably the intraparty factions (*habatsu*), and in dealing with the issue Ōhira refused to be carried away by pretty-sounding generalities. Rather, he keenly perceived that there were both weak and strong points in party organizations, which he saw as a natural manifestation of human groupings, as well as in Japan's overall culture, with its emphasis on human relations. When questioned about the factions, Ōhira was almost sure to reply, "It is said of human beings that if three people get together, two of them are sure to form a faction." What he had in mind were gradual reforms that would recognize such realities. The following comments give testimony to his thinking on party matters:

> Water as it exists is not H_2O.... Neither does a society of human beings have the purity of distilled water. I think what we call "faction" activities can be admitted and accommodated if they are influenced to move in the right direction. Should such activities veer toward egoism with respect to the allocation of party and cabinet posts or in other ways, such tendencies must be corrected.... Isn't this what historical realities are all about?

> Political parties mean "harmonized disunities" that ultimately must become united. The LDP has a self-regulating capacity for adjustment.

In the 1980s the LDP factions experienced considerable change, and, most importantly, they began to take on aspects that have made them resemble joint-stock companies. Previously, with the exception of the Kōchikai, they had been formed around a leading individual, and if that person should for some reason lose his influence, the usual practice had been for the faction members to form a new faction or join other factions under other leaders. In the 1980s, however, factions were motivated not so much by leaders as by intrafactional organizations, and not so much by political ideals or policies as by the personal interests of faction members. This has meant that factions have changed from being the means to help a faction leader attain the prime ministership to being interest groups for their members. During the Satō Administration, it had become an unwritten rule that the assignment of party and cabinet posts would be considerably influenced by the numerical strengths of the factions, and this trend has become stronger since then. Within the factions there even exists a sort of "seniority system" reminiscent of large enterprises.

These trends, together with the LDP's long hold on power, have contributed to stabilizing the factions and their respective "shares," and have brought on the phenomenon of all factions being almost equally "mainstream," with a resultant avoidance of interfactional rivalries. This has lessened their former vitality, as a result of which the vitality of the party, which had come in no small part from these interfactional rivalries, has also been diminished. The issue of factions in the LDP must thus be seen from a somewhat different angle than was the case during Ōhira's lifetime.

A further change in the political world, especially toward the end of the 1980s, has been the loss of respect by the people for the LDP as a governing party. In the joint Lower and Upper House elections of June 1980, immediately after Ōhira's death, the LDP won 284 seats in the Lower House, where it had held a bare majority of the 511 seats, increasing its representation by 28 seats. However, in the thirty-seventh general election held during the Nakasone Administration in December 1983, the LDP's Lower House representation dropped to only 250 seats. Then, in the joint thirty-eighth Lower and fourteenth Upper House elections of June 1986, also during the Nakasone Administration, the LDP more than recouped this loss, winning 300 out of the 512 Lower House seats. The Takeshita Cabinet, which succeeded the Nakasone Cabinet, took up the issue of tax reform and in December 1988 introduced a general consumption tax with the support of the majority of LDP legislators. Around the same time political scandals also shook the people's confidence, leading to Takeshita's resignation. Then, in the July 1989 Upper House election, the LDP suffered a great defeat, its representation there dropping below a majority for the first time in the party's history. In the meantime, it was revealed that several influential opposition-party Diet members had also been involved in incidents of alleged bribery and other scandals.

The thirty-ninth Lower House election took place in February 1990 under the Kaifu Administration, which had succeeded the short-lived Uno Administration established after Takeshita Noboru resigned, and certain changes in the political situation resulted from this election. The LDP, despite prior predictions that it might lose its majority also in the Lower House, won a considerable majority, even if the victory was not as overwhelming as in the 1986 general election. The reasons for this success are conjectured to be the poor policies of the opposition parties and their lack of unity. Thus, Prime Minister Kaifu was able continue his administration, and the LDP is certain to remain in power for some time at least. However, the LDP's numerical inferiority in the Upper House will continue to affect not only Diet management but also the routine processes of Japanese politics. Thus, political reforms are once again becoming urgent. It is of interest to note that in September 1978, at a time of approximately equal Diet representations of the governing and opposition parties, Ōhira answered to a question about the future of conservative rule: "In discussing political administrations, we can either talk about composition, that is, which parties make up an administration, or talk about function, that is, what functions an administration carries out. I feel that even if it is not an independent administration, even if it is, for example, a conservative–progressive coalition government, if an administration can function smoothly, it will be a desirable thing. . . .

"In the management of the Diet, too, I would, in the case of a partial coalition, have the LDP present a certain stance and then see whether the other parties are in agreement or not, testing their reactions to find out, for example, if a certain party might be opposed while another party might go along if slight changes were made. I don't think there is any other realistic method except to finalize each legislative issue through such partial alliances. . . .

"Japan's political map is not of the Northern European type, and neither is it of the Southern European type. I think it has a more stable structure of authority. In Northern Europe, the conservative and social democratic forces are polarized; in Southern Europe, the conservative and leftist forces are polarized. In Japan's case, the conservative forces are stronger than in Northern or Southern Europe, and there is the additional weight of a large middle-of-the-road force. So I think the structure of Japan's political forces is . . . of a Japanese type and is relatively stable."

Simple Living and High Thinking

Ōhira's political philosophy and political behavior no doubt derive from his character and personality, which were, in turn, influenced by his abilities and his growth and development. His personality is clearly mirrored in his outlooks on life and in the following quotes from statements he made during the 1978 LDP presidential campaign:

> Human beings are weak creatures, and there is no point in overstraining ourselves. It is all right to do things on an even keel, with a feeling of everyday normality.
>
> Human beings are not strong, and are even at times rather stupid. This is my sort of resigned view. However, that does not mean that we should come to a stop. Every day we water the morning glories that will one day wither and die. This is the attitude I want to keep.

Ōhira often spoke about self-discipline in terms such as these words written in 1968: "We may be so much in a hurry, searching for immediate better conditions, that when they are not attainable we become irritated, angry, or even depressed. . . . Even if we are dissatisfied with the present we should remember that things might be worse. Any measure always has its positive and its negative aspects; there is no such thing as a measure that is completely positive. . . . Whatever we may be engaged in, before criticizing others it is important to think more of one's family, friends, local community, and the nation than of oneself, and to act accordingly. True enjoyment comes not from criticizing others but from what we do to serve others."

On his sixtieth birthday in 1970, Ōhira wrote: "I must, first of all, guard against pride and neglect and find new ways of living for others. In other words, I must treat people with generosity and sincerity, regardless of relative social position and of whether or not I may feel attracted to them. . . . It may be 'learning at sixty' [as spoken of in a Japanese saying], but I must put greater effort into continuous study. I believe the question of whether one advances or retreats must depend on Heaven, and being praised or censured must follow the dictates of destiny. From now on this will be my signpost for self-instruction."

As these excerpts show, Ōhira's tolerance and self-control made him a somewhat unusual man in Japan's political world, with its large proportion of combative, self-important individuals. Clues to his philosophy of moderation may be glimpsed in some of the terse, classical Chinese-style aphorisms he was often asked by friends to write with a brush on cardboard squares as souvenirs. The following are among those he often used:

Advancing one step at a time, one covers a thousand miles.

A hundred tactics cannot compare with purity of heart.

Ridding oneself of illusion, one attains truth.

Treat resentment and criticism as if they applied to oneself.

The wise shopkeeper keeps his best goods out of sight so that
the store appears only modestly stocked.

In the course of his efforts at self-improvement, Ōhira paid particular attention to refining his capacities for perseverance and creative thinking. The self-control that he had shown as a boy developed into a remarkable capacity for patience and endurance. It was probably no accident that as chief cabinet secretary in the Ikeda Administration, Ōhira devised the slogan "Tolerance and Patience" (Kan'yō to nintai). Around the same time, he did his best to exert some restraining influence on Ikeda—who at times tended to gallop like an unbridled horse—and steer the administration's policies onto a steady course of execution. At the time it was Ōhira's patience and endurance that the public desired. His endurance was again demonstrated in the midst of the intraparty strife following the LDP's poor showing in the 1979 general election held during his administration.

He had an extraordinary ability to endure physical discomfort, and whether running a high fever or nearly exhausted by overwork, he never complained of pain or allowed discomfort to stop him. He paid no attention to those close to him who advised him to rest more, an attitude that no doubt hastened his death. His almost superhuman endurance was undoubtedly conditioned by his strong sense of mission. However, Ōhira had not intended to devote his entire life to political activities, for he was looking forward, after the end of his political career, to spending more time on hobbies and other enjoyments.

One of these was reading, a hobby that began in his youth and showed no signs of decline as the years passed. Reading surely helped nurture his capacity for creative thinking, which, in turn, helped him in his political concepts and his awareness of the times. In his busy schedule Ōhira devoted almost all his spare moments to reading. He had a special interest in history and philosophy, and enjoyed looking through new English-language publications in these fields. Sometimes, when translators presented him with copies of their books in translation, they were surprised to learn that he had already read them in the original English.

Given his great love of reading, it is quite natural that he also paid much attention to writing. Unlike many politicians whose speeches were drafted by advisers or government officials (to which they might add some revisions), Ōhira wrote all his own speeches, unless he was pressured for time. In cases when he did not have the time to write his own, he heavily revised the drafts until he was completely satisfied. Many of his former assistants recall being asked to produce clean copies of drafts that had become almost illegible with corrections.

We might say that Ōhira found positive enjoyment in putting his thoughts on paper. If that had not been the case, it seems unlikely that he would have published seven volumes of collected writings in his lifetime. His approach to writing was not to be too choosy or particular about words and expressions. Certainly, in the process of drafting and polishing he felt it was to some extent important to select his words with care and make his meaning precise. Yet his style was not that of *belles-lettres*; rather it was a style quite his own and one that should be seen as the fruit of considerable effort and of his own distinctive thinking. After his death, there were some who considered Ōhira a great thinker and others who saw him as a lofty idealist. Yet he can perhaps be best characterized as a person who, with considerable effort and thought, was always seeking after deeper ideas and higher ideals. In any case, a large part of his charm rested in the fact that he was an unpretentious man.

Some have felt Ōhira lacked decisiveness because of the way he sometimes hesitated and postponed decisions. Some have taken his habit of pausing between words as another indication of such an alleged shortcoming. However, during what might seem to be moments of hesitation, the thoughts he was turning over in his mind could be complex, and he can no doubt be defended as having wanted to make the most of the pauses between his words to ponder how best to express his thoughts.

While he, of course, thought a great deal about what ought to be done, he also thought always about what ought not to be done. He felt that no matter how many good deeds one might do, one's overall accomplishments could be negated by a single bad error. However, once he had come to a decision, his actions were resolute and firm. This was seen, for example, in his handling of relations with China during his second period as foreign minister, and in his decision to dissolve the Diet following its passage of a motion of no-confidence. At such times, whatever the obstacles, he would launch himself squarely into dealing with the matter at hand, and there would always be many who would see in Ōhira a different person. After Ōhira's death, President Carter said, "He was an inspiration to me personally." Perhaps we may be permitted to comment, cum Thomas Edison, that while he was indeed a man of inspiration, much of what he accomplished came from perspiration as well.

Ōhira's daily life was very simple. This was not merely because of his knowledge that when politicians lived in a style too removed from the ordinary there was the risk that politics itself would become estranged from the people, but also because of his love of simple and non-artificial things. He retained throughout his life a fondness for such ordinary foods as steamed sweet potatoes, glutinous rice cakes, and the thick Sanuki noodles he had enjoyed as a child.

The following words are from a short essay he penned in August 1966: "*Simple living and high thinking* [original English]: This means that high thinking is rather to be found in conjunction with simple living. A comfortable living environment is in itself a good thing; however, it is only a means and never a goal. Our goal is to pursue high thinking, and to strive earnestly to refine our character. Only this makes for true joy in life."

Bonshin tsukushite, tenchi hiraku
By making the most of oneself, even the ordinary person can open new worlds.

ŌHIRA MASAYOSHI, PRIME MINISTER

Postscript

Ōhira Masayoshi kaisōroku (A Memoir of Ōhira Masayoshi), consisting of three volumes—a biography, reminiscences, and reference materials— was published in 1982, two years after Ōhira's death. This is a translation of the biographical volume. Prior to translating it, the original text was much revised in consideration of foreign readers. Although I am not so well acquainted with foreign-language publications, I believe that, with the exception of Yoshida Shigeru, no full biography of a contemporary Japanese statesman has been published in a foreign language.

Today, in keeping with Japan's increasing international influence and role, Japanese politics is drawing the attention of the nations of the world as never before. However, it can be said that foreign people's understanding of Japanese politics is still insufficient, and one sees many incidents of misunderstandings and unbalanced viewpoints leading to friction between Japan and other countries. Politics is a matter of real people handling real issues, but unless we know the processes by which people who part take in politics try to realize their political ideals, it is difficult to understand what politics really is. In this sense, it is truly gratifying that this publication provides an opportunity for Japan's politics to be better understood.

The present volume has received the cooperation of a large number of persons. While I will not here name each one, I wish to offer very special thanks to Professor Edwin O. Reischauer, who has always striven to make Japan known more accurately to the world. Eight years ago he contributed a splendid manuscript to the *Ōhira Masayoshi kaisōroku* volume of reminiscences. Now he has taken time from his busy schedule to read over this present volume and write for it a perceptive Introduction. For this I am deeply grateful.

I was for many years a friend of the late Prime Minister Ōhira, and for a short time served as his chief cabinet secretary, between November 9, 1979, and the day he died, June 12, 1980, when I was at his bedside. The period he served as prime minister was short but was marked by rapid developments that caught the world's attention, such as the occupation of the United States embassy in Teheran, the Soviet invasion of Afghanistan, and the West's boycott of the Moscow Olympics. Prime Minister Ōhira made clear Japan's position as one of the world's democracies and always maintained an attitude of cooperation in assisting the West's leading member, the United States.

The ten years since the late Prime Minister Ōhira's passing have indeed gone by in a flash. Prime Minister Ōhira always had a great interest in both domestic politics and international issues; just now both are in what is perhaps the most important period of change in the postwar era. At such a time I—as one of the representatives of those who worked to publish the original version eight years ago—am especially moved to think that this can help people around the world gain an accurate understanding of the statesman Masayoshi Ōhira, and of how he pursued his ideals throughout his eventful life.

ITŌ MASAYOSHI

Acknowledgments

The late Prime Minister Ōhira Masayoshi took his first step as a politician by winning a seat in the House of Representatives (Lower House) in 1952 as a member of the Liberal Party led by then Prime Minister Yoshida Shigeru. However, since 1949, he had participated in the inner workings of Japanese politics by serving as special assistant to Finance Minister Ikeda Hayato, who became prime minister in 1960. During the period between 1960, when he became chief cabinet secretary in the Ikeda Cabinet, and 1980, when he died while in office as prime minister, he played a central role in Japanese politics. The period during which he was active as a politician spanned the years between recovery from the ravages of World War II and Japan's regaining of independence in 1952 to its development into one of the world's leading economic powers. In this way, Ōhira Masayoshi's political career was inseparably linked to Japan's postwar politics. However, what set him apart from the majority of the politicians of his time was, more than anything else, his vision of the future, which was backed by his deep understanding of history, his earnest, unflagging attitude in pursuing his ideals, however difficult this was, and his warm personality and intellectual integrity, which placed great store in the trust that must exist between individuals.

Not long after Ōhira's death in the midst of the electoral campaigns for the same-day Lower and Upper House elections of June 1980, a committee was formed (headed by former Foreign Minister Itō Masayoshi and former Governor of the Bank of Japan Morinaga Teiichirō) to expedite the publication of materials to give, insofar as possible, an accurate record of Ōhira's life, accomplishments, and personality. A "Reminiscences" volume (*tsui-sōhen*), an anthology of recollections and essays by persons who knew him well, was first published in 1981, followed the next year by a "Biography" volume (*denkihen*), which traces the events of his life, and a

"Materials" volume (*shiryōhen*), which contains the texts of many of his writings and speeches, chronological tables, photographs, and so on. The three of us entrusted with the editorial supervision of the biographical volume were able to gather a great amount of material, thanks to a large number of persons, including many who had been intimately acquainted with the late prime minister and gave valuable oral recollections. We again wish to offer our profound thanks to the many people who gave us their cooperation at that time. Fortunately, this biographical volume attracted the interest of a considerable number of non-specialist readers and was republished in 1983 by Kajima Shuppankai, together with certain reference materials. No revisions were made at that time to the original volume except to correct a few factual errors and misprints.

As one way of commemorating the tenth anniversary of Ōhira's death, and with the assistance of the Masayoshi Ōhira Memorial Foundation, the biographical volume has been substantially revised, incorporating materials that were not earlier available. Because this revised version is to be published in both Japanese and English, we have tried not only to insure the accuracy of the contents but also to make revisions that readers in other countries would find helpful.

As in the case of the original biographical volume, we have received the cooperation of a great many persons. We especially extend our heartfelt thanks to: Fukukawa Shinji and Yasuda Masaharu, who undertook part of the writing, read the entire manuscript, and offered many valuable suggestions; Abe Atsushi, who also made helpful suggestions; Fukushima Masamitsu, who undertook a major part of the writing and edited the manuscript; William Carter, who did the English translation; Jules and Erika Young, who edited the English version; Suzuki Chikara, who checked the translation; Ichiba Shinji of Kōdansha International, who coordinated the English publication; and Saitō Hideo, Hanaoka Hiroshi, Nohara Hiroshi, and Ōhira Takeshi of the Masayoshi Ōhira Memorial Foundation. Without the dedicated efforts of all these people it would not have been possible to complete this book for the occasion of the tenth anniversary of Ōhira's death.

In respectful memory of the late Ōhira Masayoshi,

SATŌ SEIZABURŌ
KŌYAMA KEN'ICHI
KUMON SHUNPEI

April 1990

Chronology

EVENTS IN GENERAL

1853

July 8 — Commodore Matthew Perry of the American East Indian Fleet arrives in Uraga.

1854

March 31 — Treaty of Peace and Amity between the United States and the Empire of Japan.

1858

July 29 — U.S.–Japan Treaty of Amity and Commerce.

1868

Jan. 3 — Restoration of political power to the emperor.

Oct. 23 — Era name changes from Keiō to Meiji.

1881

Oct. 29 — *Jiyūtō* (Liberal Party) established.

1882

April 16 — *Rikken Kaishintō* (Constitutional Reform Party) established.

1885

Dec. 12 — Cabinet system promulgated; First Itō Cabinet.

1889

Feb. 11 — Constitution of the Empire of Japan (Meiji Constitution); House of Representatives Members Election Law promulgated.

1890

July 1 — 1st general election (300 seats).

Nov. 29 — 1st Ordinary Diet convened.

1894

Aug. 1 — Sino-Japanese War begins.

1900

Sept. 15 — *Rikken Seiyūkai* (Friends of Constitutional Government Party), descended from Liberal Party, established.

1904

Feb. 10 — Russo-Japanese War begins.

1910

Aug. 22 — Annexation of Korea.

1911

Feb. 21 — U.S.–Japan Treaty of Commerce and Navigation establishing complete tariff autonomy.

1912

Feb. 12 — Fall of Qing Dynasty in China.

July 30 — Era name changes from Meiji to Taishō.

EVENTS IN ŌHIRA'S LIFE

1910
March 12   Ōhira Masayoshi born the third son to father, Rikichi, and mother, Saku, in Wada Village, Mitoyo District, Kagawa Prefecture.

1914

July 28   World War I begins; Japan becomes a belligerent on Aug. 23.

1917

Nov. 7   Soviet government established in Russia (October Revolution).

1918

Aug. 2   Japanese troops sent to Russian Far East.

Aug. 3   Rice riots erupt in Toyama Prefecture.

Sept. 29   Hara Cabinet (first party cabinet).

1919

June 28   Versailles Peace Treaty.

1920

Jan. 10   League of Nations established.

1921

Nov. 4   Prime Minister Hara assassinated.

Nov. 12   Washington Conference on naval arms limitation and Pacific and East Asian affairs begins.

1923

Sept. 1   Great Kantō Earthquake.

1925

March 2   Universal Manhood Suffrage Law.

March 7   Peace Preservation Law (*Chian Ijihō*).

1926

Dec. 25   Era name changes from Taishō to Shōwa.

1927

March 15   Financial crisis of 1927.

June 1   *Rikken Minseitō* (Constitutional Democratic Party), descended from Constitutional Reform Party, established.

1928

Feb. 20   16th general election (first under universal manhood suffrage).

1929

Oct. 24   New York stock market crash, leading to the Great Depression.

1930

Jan. 21   London Naval Conference.

1916

April   Enters Taishō Public Elementary School (now Toyohama Elementary School) in Wada Village.

1923

April   Enters Mitoyo Prefectural Middle School (now Kan'onji No. 1 High School).

1927

Aug. 29   Father Rikichi dies aged 56.

1928

April   Enters Takamatsu Higher School of Commerce (now Economics Department of Kagawa University).

April   Joins *Iesu no Shimobekai* (Servants of Jesus Society) headed by Dr. Satō Sadakichi.

1929

Dec. 27   Baptized by Rev. Buchanan at Kan'onji Church.

1931	
Sept. 18	Manchurian Incident.

1932	
March 1	Manchukuo government established.
May 15	Prime Minister Inukai assassinated (May 15th Incident).

1933	
March 27	Japan leaves League of Nations.

1936	
Feb. 26	Coup d'état attempted by Japanese army faction (February 26th Incident).

1937	
July 7	Marco Polo Bridge Incident (start of Sino-Japanese War).

1938	
April 1	National Mobilization Law.

1939	
Sept. 1	Germany invades Poland; World War II begins.

1940	
Sept. 23	Japanese army invades northern Indochina.
Sept. 27	Signing of Tripartite Pact among Japan, Germany, and Italy.
Oct. 12	*Taisei Yokusankai* (Imperial Rule Assistance Association) established; all parties dissolved.

1941	
April 13	Soviet-Japanese Neutrality Pact signed.
Dec. 8	Pacific War begins with Japanese attack on Hawaii and Singapore.

1942	
June 5	Japanese defeat in naval Battle of Midway.

1943	
Feb. 1	Japanese retreat from Guadalcanal, Solomon Islands.
Sept. 8	Italy surrenders unconditionally.
Dec. 1	Cairo Declaration announced.

1932

March	Graduates from Takamatsu Higher School of Commerce.
April	In Osaka, works at Momotani Juntenkan pharmaceutical company.

1933

April	Enters Tokyo University of Commerce (now Hitotsubashi University).

1935

Oct.	Passes Higher Civil Service Examination in Administrative Division.

1936

March	Graduates from Tokyo University of Commerce.
April 10	Enters Ministry of Finance, works in the Deposit Department of the Banking Bureau.

1937

April 15	Marriage to Suzuki Shigeko.
July 1	Begins work as director of Yokohama Tax Office.

1938

Feb. 6	First son, Masaki, born.
June 25	Appointed to head Indirect Taxation Department of Sendai Tax Supervision Bureau.

1939

May 31	Appointed to head Economic Section of Mongolian Border Region Liaison Department of Asia Development Board (*Kōain*); arrives at post in Zhangjiakou, China, June 20.
Oct. 17	Second son, Hiroshi, born.

1940

Oct. 15	Appointed head of Second Section of Economic Department at Asia Development Board headquarters in Tokyo; returns to Japan end of the month.

1941

Dec. 8	Appointed Asia Development Board *chōsakan* (research officer), making occasional visits to China.
Dec. 30	Eldest daughter, Yoshiko, born.

1942

July 30	Begins work in Budget Bureau of Ministry of Finance; helps establish government-financed Japan Scholarship Foundation.

1943

Nov. 5	Appointed to head Indirect Taxation Department of Tokyo Local Finance Bureau.

1944

June 6	Allied forces land at Normandy, France
June 19	Japanese defeat in Battle of the Marianas.
July 18	Tōjō Cabinet resigns en masse; followed by Koiso Cabinet.

1945

April 5	Suzuki (Kantarō) Cabinet.
May 7	Germany surrenders unconditionally.
July 26	Potsdam Declaration announced.
Aug. 6	Hiroshima destroyed by atomic bomb; Nagasaki A-bombed Aug. 9.
Aug. 15	Japan surrenders unconditionally.
Aug. 17	Higashikuni Cabinet.
Aug. 28	GHQ set up; directives to demilitarize and democratize Japan.
Oct. 9	Shidehara Cabinet.
Nov. 2	Nihon Shakaitō (Japan Socialist Party) established.
Nov. 9	Nihon Jiyūtō (Japan Liberal Party) established.
Nov. 16	Nihon Shinpotō (Japan Progressive Party) established.
Dec. 1	Japan Communist Party's 4th Congress.
Dec. 18	Nihon Kyōdōtō (Japan Cooperative Party) established.

1946

April 10	22nd (first postwar) general election for House of Representatives (Lower House).
May 22	First Yoshida Cabinet.
Nov. 3	New Constitution promulgated by Emperor Hirohito.

1947

Jan. 31	MacArthur calls off general strike set for Feb. 1.
March 8	Kokumin Kyōdōtō (National Cooperative Party) established, descended from Japan Cooperative Party.
March 31	Minshutō (Democratic Party), descended from Japan Progressive Party, established.
April 20	1st House of Councillors (Upper House) election.
April 25	23rd general election.
May 3	New Constitution comes into effect.
June 1	Katayama Cabinet.

1948

March 10	Ashida Cabinet.
March 15	Minshu Jiyūtō (Democratic Liberal Party), descended from Japan Liberal Party, established.
Aug. 13	Republic of Korea established; Democratic People's Republic of Korea established in North Korea Sept. 9.
Oct. 19	Second Yoshida Cabinet.
Nov. 12	International Military Tribunal for the Far East ends.

1944

May 5	Establishes so-called People's Taverns in metropolitan Tokyo.

1945

March 19	Appointed secretary to Finance Minister Tsushima Juichi.
April 5	With retirement of Tsushima returns to Budget Bureau.
May 25	Home in Ushigome Ward burned down in air raid.
Aug. 17	Again becomes Tsushima's secretary when he is made finance minister in Higashikuni Cabinet.
Aug. 28	Mother Saku dies aged 72.
Oct. 13	Returns to Budget Bureau.

1946

June 25	Appointed head of the Third Section of the Finance Ministry's Compensation Bureau.
Sept. 9	Third son, Akira, born.

1947

April 1	Establishes Government Employees' Mutual Benefit Societies Federation; becomes its managing director.

1948

July 10	Sent on loan to Economic Stabilization Board to head Public Works Section of the board's Construction Bureau.

1949

Jan. 23	24th general election.
Feb. 16	Third Yoshida Cabinet; Ikeda Hayato becomes minister of finance.
March 7	Dodge Line on fiscal austerity announced.
May 6	Federal Republic of Germany established; German Democratic Republic established in East Germany Oct. 7.
Oct. 1	People's Republic of China established.

1950

March 1	*Jiyūtō* (Liberal Party), descended from Democratic Liberal Party, established.
April 28	*Kokumin Minshutō* (National Democratic Party), descended from Democratic Party, established.
June 4	2nd Upper House election.
June 25	Outbreak of Korean War.
Aug. 10	National Police Reserve established.

1951

April 11	General MacArthur dismissed; replaced by General Ridgway.
July 10	Korean armistice talks.
Sept. 4	San Francisco Peace Conference.
Sept. 8	San Francisco Peace Treaty and U.S.–Japan Security Treaty.
Oct. 24	Japan Socialist Party splits into Right-wing Socialist Party and Left-wing Socialist Party.

1952

Feb. 8	*Kaishintō* (Reform Party), descended from National Democratic Party, established.
April 28	San Francisco Peace Treaty and U.S.–Japan Security Treaty enter into effect.
May 1	Violent May Day demonstrations.
Oct. 1	25th general election.
Oct. 30	Fourth Yoshida Cabinet.
Nov. 29	Ikeda resigns as minister of international trade and industry.

1953

March 5	Stalin dies.
March 14	"*Bakayarō* dissolution" of Lower House.
April 19	26th general election.
April 24	3rd Upper House election.
May 21	Fifth Yoshida Cabinet.
July 24	Korean Armistice Agreement signed.

1954

Feb. 8	Shipbuilding Scandal revealed.
July 9	Self Defense Forces (*Jieitai*) established.
Nov. 24	*Nihon Minshutō* (Japan Democratic Party), descended from Reform Party, established.

1949

June 1   Becomes secretary to Finance Minister Ikeda Hayato.

1950

May 9   Sent on loan to the Indirect Taxation Department of the National Tax Administration, while serving concurrently as secretary to the minister of finance.

1951

Aug. 13   Leaves for U.S. under the auspices of U.S. government's National Leaders Program; returns to Japan Oct. 21.

1952

Sept. 5   Leaves Ministry of Finance.

Oct. 1   Elected for first time from Kagawa Second Electoral District on Liberal Party ticket.

1953

April 19   Elected second time.

Nov. 28	Yoshida resigns as president of Liberal Party.
Dec. 10	First Hatoyama Cabinet.

1955

Feb. 27	27th general election.
March 19	Second Hatoyama Cabinet.
May 14	Warsaw Treaty Organization established.
Sept. 10	Japan joins General Agreement on Tariffs and Trade (GATT).
Oct. 13	Japan Socialist Party reunified.
Nov. 15	*Jiyū Minshutō* (Liberal Democratic Party) formed through conservative coalition.
Nov. 22	Third Hatoyama Cabinet.

1956

July 8	4th Upper House election.
Oct. 19	Joint Soviet–Japanese Declaration reestablishing diplomatic relations.
Oct. 23	Hungarian uprising.
Dec. 18	Japan joins the United Nations.
Dec. 23	Ishibashi Cabinet.

1957

Feb. 25	First Kishi Cabinet.
June	Kōchikai established.
Oct. 4	U.S.S.R. launches first Sputnik satellite.

1958

May 22	28th general election.
June 12	Second Kishi Cabinet.

1959

Jan. 1	Cuban Revolution.
June 2	5th Upper House election.
Aug. 29	Miike Coal Mines dispute.

1960

Jan. 19	U.S.–Japan Treaty of Mutual Cooperation and Security signed, replacing 1951 security treaty.
Jan. 24	*Minshu Shakaitō* (Democratic Socialist Party) established.
June 16	President Eisenhower's trip to Japan postponed due to turmoil surrounding ratification of security treaty.
July 19	First Ikeda Cabinet.
Oct. 12	Japan Socialist Party Chairman Asanuma assassinated.
Nov. 20	29th general election.
Dec. 8	Second Ikeda Cabinet.
Dec. 29	National Income-Doubling Plan adopted.

1961

April 12	U.S.S.R. launches first manned space flight (Vostok 1).
May 5	U.S. launches its first manned space flight.
June 12	Agriculture Basic Law promulgated.
July 18	Reorganization of Second Ikeda Cabinet.

1955
Feb. 27	Elected third time; becomes deputy chairman of Finance Division of Liberal Party's Policy Research Council.
Nov. 15	Becomes member of new LDP.
Dec. 3	Appointed head of the Prime Minister's Office Division of LDP's Policy Research Council.

1956
May 18	Appointed member of the Investigative Commission on Problems of Overseas Property, under Prime Minister's Office.

1957
Aug. 7	Appointed deputy chairman of Finance Division of LDP's Policy Research Council.
Nov. 6	Becomes member of LDP's General Council, with responsibilities for Chūgoku and Shikoku regions.

1958
May 22	Elected fourth time.
June 22	Appointed vice chairman of LDP's Policy Research Council.

1959
June 30	Appointed chairman of Lower House Education Committee.
—	During this year, works to establish the Assistance Society for Frequent School Non-attenders.

1960
July 9	For announcement of Ikeda's candidacy for party president, coins slogan "Tolerance and Patience."
July 19	Appointed chief cabinet secretary.
Nov. 20	Elected fifth time.
Dec. 8	Reappointed chief cabinet secretary.

1961
July 18	Reappointed chief cabinet secretary.
Oct. 30	Marriage of daughter Yoshiko to Morita Hajime.

1962

July 1	6th Upper House election.
July 18	Second reorganization of Second Ikeda Cabinet.
Oct. 24	Cuban crisis (U.S. naval blockade).

1963

Nov. 21	30th general election.
Nov. 22	President Kennedy assassinated; Johnson becomes U.S. president.
Dec. 9	Third Ikeda Cabinet.

1964

July 18	Reorganization of Third Ikeda Cabinet.
Aug. 2	Tonkin Gulf Incident.
Oct. 1	Tōkaidō Shinkansen "bullet trains" begin service.
Oct. 10	Tokyo Olympic Games begin.
Nov. 9	First Satō Cabinet.
Nov. 17	Kōmeitō (Clean Government Party) established.

1965

Feb. 7	U.S. bombs North Vietnam.
June 22	Treaty on Basic Relations Between Japan and the Republic of Korea.
July 4	7th Upper House election.
Aug. 13	Prime Minister Ikeda dies at age 65.

1966

May 16	The Cultural Revolution begins in China.

1967

Jan. 29	31st general election.
Feb. 17	Second Satō Cabinet.
Nov. 25	Reorganization of Second Satō Cabinet.

1968

Jan. 27	Satō reconfirms Japan's Three Non-nuclear Principles in Diet policy speech.
Jan. 29	"Student struggles" at Tokyo University begin.
July 7	8th Upper House election.
Aug. 20	Soviet tanks enter Prague, Czechoslovakia.
Nov. 30	Second reorganization of Second Satō Cabinet.

1962

July 18	Becomes minister of foreign affairs.
Sept. 15	Addresses 17th UN General Assembly; returns September 21.
Sept. 25	Visits England, France, West Germany, Italy, the Vatican, Belgium, and the Netherlands to prepare for Ikeda's European trip; returns Oct. 5.
Nov. 12	Talks with Kim Jong Pil, head of Korean Central Intelligence Agency.
Nov. 30	Goes to U.S. to attend 2nd U.S–Japan Joint Committee of Trade and Economic Affairs; returns Dec. 8.

1963

July 31	Goes to U.S. to discuss interest equalization tax.
Aug. 25	Visits three Scandinavian countries, England, France, and Iran; returns Sept. 10.
Sept. 15	Addresses 18th UN General Assembly in New York; returns Sept. 22.
Nov. 21	Elected sixth time.
Nov. 26	Attends funeral of President Kennedy with Prime Minister Ikeda; returns Nov. 28.
Dec. 9	Reappointed minister of foreign affairs.

1964

May 28	Attends funeral of Prime Minister Nehru in New Delhi; returns May 31.
July 3	Goes to Taiwan to talk with Chiang Kai-shek.
July 18	Resigns as foreign minister.
July 21	Appointed LDP senior deputy secretary-general.
Aug. 6	Eldest son, Masaki, dies aged 26.

1965

Feb. 2	Appointed deputy chairman of the Research Commission on Foreign Policy of LDP's Policy Research Council.

1966

Oct. 14	Marriage of second son, Hiroshi, to Endō Kimiko.

1967

Jan. 29	Elected seventh time.
Nov. 25	Appointed chairman of LDP's Policy Research Council.

1968

Nov. 30	Appointed minister of international trade and industry.

1969

July 20	Apollo 11 mission lands on the moon.
Nov. 21	Satō–Nixon joint communiqué on return of Okinawa in 1972.
Dec. 27	32nd general election.

1970

Jan. 14	Third Satō Cabinet.
March 14	Osaka Expo '70 opens.

1971

June 17	Agreement on reversion of Okinawa signed.
June 27	9th Upper House election.
July 16	Nixon announces visit to China by May 1972 (first "Nixon shock").
Aug. 15	Nixon announces measures to defend US dollar (second "Nixon shock").
Oct. 25	People's Republic of China admitted to UN; Nationalist Taiwan government expelled.

1972

Feb. 21	Nixon visits China.
May 15	Reversion of Okinawa.
June 17	Satō announces resignation.
July 5	LDP presidential election; Tanaka Kakuei becomes LDP president.
July 7	First Tanaka Cabinet.
Aug. 31	Tanaka–Nixon talks in Hawaii.
Sept. 25	Tanaka visits China; joint communiqué on normalization of diplomatic relations signed on Sept. 29.
Dec. 10	33rd general election.
Dec. 22	Second Tanaka Cabinet.

1973

Jan. 27	Vietnam peace agreement signed.
May 17	Watergate Incident hearings begin in U.S. Senate.
July 29	Tanaka visits U.S.; U.S.–Japan summit talks held.
Aug. 8	Kim Dae Jung abduction incident.
Sept. 26	Tanaka visits Europe; U.S.S.R.–Japan summit talks.
Oct. 6	Fourth Middle East War erupts.
Oct. 17	OAPEC decides to cut oil exports to countries friendly to Israel (first "oil shock").
Nov. 25	Reorganization of Second Tanaka Cabinet.

1969

May 12	Talks with U.S. Secretary of Commerce Maurice Stans on textile exports and capital liberalization.
Oct. 17	Makes friendship visits to nine European countries; returns Nov. 3.
Dec. 27	Elected eighth time.

1970

Jan. 14	Resigns as minister of international trade and industry.
Nov. 18	Kōchikai five-man leadership group (Ōhira, Suzuki, Kodaira, Ogawa, Shiomi) established.

1971

April 17	Becomes third Kōchikai chairman.
Sept. 1	Presents proposals under title, *Let Us Turn the Tide: Commencement of a New Century* at study meeting of Kōchikai Diet members.

1972

June 17	Announces candidacy for LDP presidency.
July 5	Wins 101 votes in presidential election, comes in third place.
July 7	Becomes minister of foreign affairs.
Aug. 31	Accompanies Prime Minister Tanaka to Hawaii for U.S.–Japan summit talks; returns Sept. 3.
Sept. 25	Accompanies Prime Minister Tanaka to China; talks with Chairman Mao, Premier Zhou, and Foreign Minister Ji; on Sept. 27 states that Japan-Taiwan peace treaty ended; returns Sept. 30.
Oct. 10	Visits Australia, New Zealand, the U.S., and the U.S.S.R. to explain normalization of relations with China; returns Oct. 25.
Dec. 10	Elected ninth time.
Dec. 22	Reappointed minister of foreign affairs.

1973

April 28	Visits Yugoslavia, France, and Belgium; returns May 6.
July 29	Accompanies Prime Minister Tanaka to U.S. for summit talks; returns Aug. 6.
Sept. 23	Attends 28th UN General Assembly in New York; then visits Italy, U.K., West Germany, and U.S.S.R.; returns Oct. 11.
Nov. 25	Reappointed minister of foreign affairs.

1974

April 20	China–Japan Air Transport Agreement signed.
July 7	10th Upper House election.
Aug. 9	Nixon resigns; Ford becomes U.S. president.
Nov. 11	Second reorganization of Second Tanaka Cabinet.
Nov. 18	Ford visits Japan.
Nov. 26	Tanaka Kakuei resigns.
Dec. 4	Miki Takeo becomes LDP president through arbitration by party vice-president Shiina.
Dec. 9	First Miki Cabinet.

1975

April 30	Fall of Saigon; end of Vietnam War.
Nov. 15	First summit of major industrialized democracies held in Rambouillet near Paris.
Nov. 26	Strike for "right to strike" by government employees.

1976

Feb. 4	Lockheed Incident revealed.
Feb. 16	First Lockheed Incident witnesses heard before Lower House Budget Committee.
June 25	*Shin Jiyū Kurabu* (New Liberal Club) established.
July 27	Tanaka arrested in connection with Lockheed Incident.
Aug. 19	Liaison Council for Establishing a Party-Unity System (*Kyotōkyō*) formed.
Sept. 9	Mao Zedong dies.
Sept. 15	Reorganization of Miki Cabinet.
Dec. 5	34th general election.
Dec. 24	First Fukuda Cabinet.

1977

July 10	11th Upper House election.
Nov. 28	Reorganization of Fukuda Cabinet.

1974

Jan. 2	Visits China to conclude China–Japan Air Transport Agreement and other agreements; returns Jan. 6.
Feb. 8	Attends conference of Energy Coordination Group of major oil-consuming countries in U.S.; returns Feb. 15.
May 18	Gives speech at New York's Japan Society; receives honorary Doctorate of Laws from Yale University on May 20; returns May 23.
July 12	Resigns position as foreign minister to replace Fukuda as finance minister.
Sept. 25	Attends meetings of International Monetary Fund (IMF) and World Bank in U.S.; returns Oct. 8.
Nov. 11	Reappointed minister of finance.
Dec. 9	Reappointed minister of finance.

1975

Jan. 12	Attends meetings of IMF and World Bank in U.S.; returns Jan. 19.
April 7	Attends meeting of Organization for Economic Cooperation and Development (OECD) in France; returns April 12.
April 15	Gives speech "The Present Financial Situation," often called "The Declaration of Fiscal Crisis" in Lower House Finance Committee.
Aug. 28	Chairs conference of finance ministers of ten IMF member countries in U.S.; returns Sept. 4.
Oct. 15	Decides to issue deficit-financing government bonds.
Nov. 13	Attends 1st summit of major industrialized democracies at Rambouillet, France.

1976

Jan. 4	Attends conference of finance ministers of ten IMF countries in U.S.; returns Jan. 13.
June 25	Attends 2nd summit of major industrialized democracies in Puerto Rico; then visits Belgium; returns July 3.
Sept. 15	Reappointed minister of finance.
Oct. 20	First Ōhira–Fukuda talks.
Oct. 27	Second Ōhira–Fukuda talks (secret agreement).
Dec. 5	Elected tenth time.
Dec. 7	Elder brother, Kazumitsu, dies aged 68.
Dec. 24	Appointed LDP secretary-general.

1977

April 25	Advocates renewal of LDP at Comprehensive Rally for LDP Reform and Rapid Advance.
July 27	Receives commendation certificate for 25 years in Lower House.
Nov. 4	Marriage of third son, Akira, to Uehara Yoshiko.
Nov. 28	Reappointed LDP secretary-general.

1978

March 26	*Shakai Minshu Rengō* (United Social Democratic Party) established.
May 20	Narita airport opens.
Aug. 12	China–Japan Peace and Friendship Treaty signed.
Sept. 8	Iranian revolution begins.
Dec. 1	Ōhira chosen 9th LDP president in first election by all party members.
Dec. 6	86th Extraordinary Diet.
Dec. 7	First Ōhira Cabinet.
Dec. 22	87th Ordinary Diet.

1979

Jan. 4	Further aircraft marketing scandals revealed.
April 8	Suzuki Shun'ichi elected governor of Tokyo.
April 24	Era Name Law passed.
June 18	SALT II Treaty signed.
June 24	President Carter visits Japan.
June 28	Tokyo Summit (5th meeting of major industrialized democracies) begins; agreement reached on question of oil import ceilings.
Aug. 30	88th Extraordinary Diet.
Oct. 7	35th general election (LDP nearly defeated); "forty-day struggle" begins.
Oct. 26	South Korea's Park Chung Hee assassinated.
Oct. 30	89th Special Diet.
Nov. 4	U.S. ambassador and others taken hostage in Teheran.
Nov. 6	Diet elections for prime minister.
Nov. 9	Second Ōhira Cabinet.
Nov. 26	90th Extraordinary Diet.
Dec. 21	91st Ordinary Diet.
Dec. 27	U.S.S.R. sends troops into Afghanistan.

1978

Oct. 21	Announces candidacy for LDP presidency.
Oct. 26	Announces Garden-City Concept at Kyoto press conference.
Oct. 28	Announces Concept for Strengthening the Family Base at Japan National Press Club.
Nov. 1	Submits official papers for candidacy in LDP presidential election.
Nov. 27	Wins first place in LDP presidential election with 748 "points" (550,889 votes).
Dec. 1	Announces political slogan "Trust and Consensus" in interview on assuming post as LDP president.
Dec. 7	Becomes prime minister by Lower House plenary session; forms cabinet.

1979

Jan. 4	States plan to introduce general consumption tax "as soon as possible" during fiscal 1980.
Jan. 25	Policy speech before both houses of the Diet.
April 30	Goes to U.S. for talks with President Carter; addresses National Press Club in Washington on May 3; returns May 6.
May 9	Attends 5th Session of the United Nations Conference on Trade and Development (UNCTAD) in the Philippines; returns May 11.
May 22	Cabinet meeting decides to establish Council on Measures to Prevent Aircraft Scandals.
June 25–26	Talks with President Carter in Tokyo and Ōiso.
June 28–29	Hosts Tokyo Summit at Akasaka Palace State Guest House.
July 7	First trip to native Kagawa Prefecture since becoming prime minister; returns to Tokyo July 8.
Aug. 10	Cabinet meeting approves New Economic and Social Seven-Year Plan.
Sept. 3	Policy speech before both houses of the Diet.
Oct. 7	Elected eleventh time.
Oct. 8	Talks with LDP leaders about poor showing in general election.
Nov. 6	In Lower House plenary session, both Ōhira and Fukuda are put forward as candidates for prime minister from LDP, reflecting party disunity; Ōhira reelected prime minister.
Nov. 27	Policy speech before both houses of the Diet; emphasizes the enforcement of official discipline and the streamlining of administration.
Dec. 5	Travels to China for talks with Premier Hua Guofeng and Vice Premier Deng Xiaoping; signs China–Japan agreement on cultural exchange; visits ancient capital of Xi'an; returns Dec. 9.

1980

Jan. 14	Demand for withdrawal of foreign troops from Afghanistan adopted by emergency meeting of UN General Assembly.
April 24	U.S. attempts surprise raid to rescue hostages in Iran.
May 16	Lower House passes opposition parties' motion of no-confidence; extraordinary cabinet meeting decides on Lower House dissolution.
May 19	Lower House dissolved.
May 22	Cabinet members concerned with Iran recommends sanctions in the form of restricted exports.
May 24	Japan Olympic Committee decides not to participate in Moscow Olympics.
June 12	Ōhira dies.
June 22	36th general election and 12th Upper House election.
July 17	Suzuki (Zenkō) Cabinet.

1980

Jan. 15	Leaves for Australia and New Zealand; talks with prime ministers Fraser and Muldoon; agreement on promotion of Pacific Basin Cooperation Concept; talks with President Somare in Papua New Guinea; returns Jan. 20.
Jan. 25	Policy speech before both houses of the Diet; criticizes Soviet armed intervention in Afghanistan, advocating restrictions on exports to U.S.S.R. and moving away from overdependence on oil.
Feb. 1	States government view concerning participation in the Moscow Olympic Games that "serious attention must be paid to international public opinion toward the Soviet invasion of Aghanistan."
March 24	Talks with Panama's President Royo Sánchez.
April 14	Welcomes Sweden's King Carl XVI Gustav to Japan.
April 22	Talks with the Netherlands' Prime Minister van Agt.
April 30	Goes to U.S., Mexico, and Canada for talks with President Carter, President López Portillo, and Prime Minister Trudeau; on May 8 attends funeral of Yugoslav President Tito; talks with Chancellor Schmidt in West Germany; returns May 11.
May 14	Talks with Fiji Prime Minister Kamisese Mara.
May 27	Talks with Chinese Premier Hua Guofeng.
May 30	During Upper House election campaign speech in Tokyo, has temporary trouble speaking and complains of pain in throat; following medical examination at home that evening, undergoes further tests by heart specialists.
May 31	Enters Toranomon Hospital 12:35 A.M.
June 2	At official start of campaign for 36th general election, sends a message from hospital bed to "each of the nation's people" urging support for LDP candidates.
June 10	Sends message to party members: "No victory without hardship, no glory without agony," expressing hope that the election campaign would be vigorously pursued.
June 12	Condition suddenly worsens at 2:25 A.M.; dies from stricture of heart at 5:54, at age of 70; receives posthumous "Second Grade, Senior of the Court Rank" and "Grand Cordon of the Supreme Order of the Chrysanthemum," both granted by the emperor and Imperial Household Agency.
July 9	Joint cabinet–LDP funeral ceremony held at Nihon Budōkan, with Itō Masayoshi as funeral committee chairman.

Bibliography

Books by Ōhira Masayoshi

Zaisei tsurezuregusa (Random Notes on Financial Administration). Josui Shobō, 1953.

Sugao no daigishi (A Dietman as He Really Is). Nijusseikisha, 1956.

Shunpū shūu (Spring Wind and Autumn Rain). Kajima Kenkyūjo Shuppankai, 1966.

Tanbo kaikō (Random Thoughts, Morning and Evening). Kajima Kenkyūjo Shuppankai, 1970.

Fūjin zasso (Wind-Scattered Writings). Kajima Shuppankai, 1977.

Watakushi no rirekisho: Ōhira Masayoshi (My Curriculum Vitae: Ōhira Masayoshi). Nihon Keizai Shinbunsha, 1978.

Fukugōryoku no jidai (An Age of Combined Strengths), coauthored with Tanaka Yōnosuke. Raifusha, 1978.

Eien no ima (The Eternal Now). Kajima Shuppankai, 1980.

Brush Strokes: Moments from My Life (English edition of *Watakushi no rirekisho*, translated by Simul International). Japan Foreign Press Center, 1980.

The bulletin *Kenteki*, published by Ōhira's office, contains a number of speeches and writings by Ōhira: No. 1 and 2 (1967); No. 3 and 4 (1969); No. 5 (1971); and No. 6 (special issue commemorating his serving twenty years in the Diet; 1972).

Other References

Tsushima Juichi, *Hōtō zuisō* (Hōtō [Tsushima's posthumous name] Miscellaneous Writings), Vols. 6 and 18. Hōtō Kankōkai, 1960 and 1979.

Kaya Okinori, *Watakushi no rirekisho* (Vol. 19 of "My Curriculum Vitae" series). Nihon Keizai Shinbunsha, 1963.

Nihon Ikueikai, ed., *Nihon Ikueikai nijūnen kinenshi* (Twenty-year History of the Japan Scholarship Foundation), 1964.

Itō Masaya, *Ikeda Hayato: sono sei to shi* (Ikeda Hayato: His Life and Death). Shiseidō, 1966.

Matsuura Shūtarō and Shiga Kenjirō, ed., *Ikeda Hayato sensei o shinobu* (Remembering Ikeda Hayato *sensei*), 1967.

Haji Fumio, *Ningen Ikeda Hayato* (Ikeda Hayato the Man). Kōdansha, 1967.

Hayashi Fusao, *Zuihitsu: Ikeda Hayato, haisen to fukkō no gendaishi* (Ikeda Hayato—a Modern History of Defeat in the War and Reconstruction). Sankei Shinbunsha, 1968.

Shōwa Ōkurashō Gaishi Kankōkai, ed., *Shōwa Ōkurashō gaishi* (An Unofficial History of the Shōwa Ministry of Finance), Vols. 2 and 3. Zaikei Shōhōsha, 1968–69.

Ōkurashō Hyakunenshi Henshūshitsu, ed., *Ōkurashō hyakunenshi* (One Hundred Years of the Ministry of Finance), Vols. 1, 2, and Supplement. Ōkura Zaimu Kyōkai, 1969.

Uchida Kenzō, *Sengo Nihon no hoshu seiji* (Postwar Japan's Conservative Politics). Iwanami Shoten, 1969.

Satō Sensei o Shinobu Kai, ed., *Satō Sadakichi sensei tsuisōroku* (Reminiscences of Satō Sadakichi *sensei*), 1970.

Hōtō Kankōkai, ed., *Tsushima Juichi tsuisōroku* (Reminiscences of Tsushima Juichi), 1972.

Mitoyo-gun Yakusho, ed., *Kagawa-ken Mitoyo-gun-shi* (History of Mitoyo District, Kagawa Prefecture). Meicho Shuppan, 1973.

Tagawa Seiichi, *Nitchū kōshō hiroku: Tagawa nikki—jūyonen no shōgen* (A Personal Account of Japanese-Chinese Negotiations: The Tagawa Diaries—A Testimony of Fourteen Years). Mainichi Shinbunsha, 1973.

Toyohamachō-shi Henshū Iinkai, ed., *Toyohamachō-shi* (History of Toyohama). Toyohamachō Yakuba, 1974.

Shioguchi Kiotsu, *Kikigaki: Ikeda Hayato* (A Record of Things Heard: Ikeda Hayato). Asahi Shinbunsha, 1975.

Kokka Kōmuin Kyōsai Kumiai Rengōkai (Federation of National Public Employees Mutual Benefit Societies), ed., *Nijūgonenshi* (History of Twenty-five Years), 1976.

Fujiyama Aiichirō, *Seiji, waga michi: Fujiyama Aiichirō kaisōroku* (Politics, My Course: Memoirs of Fujiyama Aiichirō). Asahi Shinbunsha, 1976.

Ōkurashō Zaiseishi-shitsu, ed., *Shōwa zaiseishi* (A History of Shōwa Government Finance), Vols. 4 and 10. Tōyō Keizai Shinpōsha, 1977 and 1980.

Kōno Kenzō, *Gichō ichidai: Kōno Kenzō kaisōki* (My Time as President of the House of Councillors: Memoirs of Kōno Kenzō). Asahi Shinbunsha, 1978.

Jiyū Minshutō, ed., *Tō kaikaku no shinro o hiraku: dai ikkai Jiyū Minshutō Kaki Zenkoku Kenshūkai kōen kiroku* (Opening the Path for Party Reforms: Record of Speeches Given at the First Liberal Democratic Party National Summer Study Meeting), 1978.

Yoshida Shigeru, *Gekidō no hyakunenshi: waga ketsudan to kiseki no tenkan* (History of a Hundred Years of Rapid Change: My Decisions and Miraculous Changes). Shirakawa Shoin, 1978.

"*Ōhira Masayoshi seisaku yōkō shiryō*" (Materials on Ōhira Masayoshi's Policy Platform). Unpublished bulletin, December 1978.

Shioguchi Kiotsu et al., ed., *Asahi Shinbun kisha no shōgen 1: seiji e no gyōshi* (The Testimony of an Asahi Newspaper Reporter, Vol. 1: Focus on Politics). Asahi Sonorama, 1980.

Jiyū Minshutō Kōhō Iinkai Shuppankyoku, *Ōhira sōri no Seisaku Kenkyūkai hōkokusho* (The Reports of Prime Minister Ōhira's Policy Study Association), August 1980.

Nakamura Keiichirō, *Miki seiken: 747 nichi* (The Miki Administration: 747 Days). Gyōsei Mondai Kenkyūjo, 1981.

Watanabe Ryōjirō, *Sonoda Sunao: zenjinzō* (Sonoda Sunao: Portrait of the Whole Man). Gyōsei Mondai Kenkyūjo, 1981.

Naikaku Sōridaijin Kanbō (Secretariat of the Prime Minister's Office), ed., *Ko Ōhira Masayoshi Naikaku–Jiyū Minshutō gōdō sōgi kiroku* (Record of the Cabinet-Liberal Democratic Party Joint Funeral for the Late Ōhira Masayoshi), 1981.

Morita Hajime, *Saigo no tabi: nokosareta yuitsu no Ōhira saishō nikki* (The Last Journey: The Only Diary Left by Prime Minister Ōhira). Gyōsei Mondai Kenkyūjo, 1981.

Arai Shunzō and Morita Hajime, *Bunjin saishō Ōhira Masayoshi* (The Man-of-Letters Prime Minister Ōhira Masayoshi). Shunjūsha, 1982.

Kawauchi Issei, *Ōhira seiken: 554 nichi* (The Ōhira Administration: 554 Days). Gyōsei Mondai Kenkyūjo, 1982.

Ōhira Masayoshi Kaisōroku Kankōkai, ed., *Ōhira Masayoshi kaisōroku* (A Memoir of Ōhira Masayoshi) in 3 vols.: *tsuisōhen* (Reminiscences), 1981; *denkihen* (Biography), 1982, reissued by Kajima Shuppankai 1983; *shiryōhen* (Materials), 1982.

Tanaka Kunio, *Issun saki no yami: Sankaku-daifukuchū no jūnen* (The Darkness an Inch Ahead: Ten Years of Tanaka, Miki, Fukuda, Ōhira and Nakasone). Kyōdō Tsūshinsha, 1983.

Okina Kyūjirō, *Omoide no hitobito* (People I Remember). Chūō Hōki Shuppan, 1983.

Nagatomi Yūichirō, ed., *Kindai o koete; ko Ōhira sōri no nokoshita mono* (Beyond Modernization: The Late Prime Minister Ōhira's Legacy) in 2 vols. Ōkura Zaimu Kyōkai, 1983.

Yanagisawa Hakuo, *Akaji zaisei no jūnen to yonin no sōritachi: zaiseika taibōron* (Ten Years of Deficit Government Finance and Four Prime Ministers: In Search of Statesmen in Finance). Nihon Seisansei Honbu (Japan Productivity Center), 1985.

Jiyū Minshutō, ed., *Jiyū Minshutō tōshi* (A History of the Liberal Democratic Party), 1986.

Yoshida Masanobu, *Ōhira Masayoshi no seijiteki jinkaku* (Ōhira Masayoshi's Political Character). Tōkai University Press, 1986.

Ishii Kōnosuke, *Faindā no kochiragawa: hōdō kameraman ga mita Shōwa-shi* (This Side of the View-finder: Shōwa History as Seen by a News Cameraman). Bungei Shunjūsha, 1987.

Kishimoto Kōichi, *Politics in Modern Japan: Development and Organization*, 3rd ed. Japan Echo Inc., 1988.

Nagatomi Yūichirō, ed., *Masayoshi Ōhira's Proposal to Evolve the Global Society* [in English]. Foundation for Advanced Information and Research (FAIR), 1988.

Uchihashi Katsuto, *Shirizokigiwa no kenkyū* (Studies on Approaching Retirement). Nihon Keizai Shinbunsha, 1989.

Satō Seizaburō, Kumon Shunpei, and Kōyama Ken'ichi, ed., *Ōhira Masayoshi: hito to shisō* (Ōhira Masayoshi: The Man and His Thought). The Masayoshi

Ōhira Memorial Foundation, 1990. [This is the Japanese biography on which the present English translation is based.]

Copies of the Japanese edition of this book and other information regarding Ōhira's life and legacy may be obtained from the Masayoshi Ōhira Memorial Foundation, Suite 915, Sannō Grand Building, 14-2 Nagatachō 2-chōme, Chiyoda-ku, Tokyo 100. Tel. (03) 580-3294.

Index

622